THE UN CONVENTION ON CONTRACTS FOR THE INTERNATIONAL SALE OF GOODS

Updated and expanded for the second edition, this volume provides attorneys, academics, and students with a detailed yet accessible overview of the United Nations Convention on Contracts for the International Sale of Goods (CISG). Adopted by more than eighty nations and governing a significant portion of international sales, the CISG regulates contract formation, performance, risk of loss, conformity to contractual requirements, and remedies for breach. This volume explains the CISG doctrines and their ambiguities, and appraises the extent to which the doctrines reduce transaction costs for commercial actors. Its topic-based approach will be ideal for those pursuing academic analysis or subject-specific research.

CLAYTON P. GILLETTE is the Max E. Greenberg Professor of Contract Law at New York University School of Law. He is the author of numerous articles on commercial law and coauthor, with Steven D. Walt, of *Sales Law: Domestic and International* (3rd Edition, 2016).

STEVEN D. WALT is the Percy Brown, Jr., Professor of Law at the University of Virginia School of Law and a widely published author in the areas of commercial law and jurisprudence.

The UN Convention on Contracts for the International Sale of Goods: Theory and Practice

Second Edition

CLAYTON P. GILLETTE
New York University School of Law

STEVEN D. WALT
University of Virginia School of Law

CAMBRIDGE
UNIVERSITY PRESS

CAMBRIDGE
UNIVERSITY PRESS

32 Avenue of the Americas, New York NY 10013–2473, USA

Cambridge University Press is part of the University of Cambridge.

It furthers the University's mission by disseminating knowledge in the pursuit of education, learning, and research at the highest international levels of excellence.

www.cambridge.org
Information on this title: www.cambridge.org/9781316604168

© Clayton P. Gillette and Steven D. Walt 2016

First published 2016

Printed in the United States of America by Sheridan Books, Inc.

A catalog record/or this publication is available/rom the British Library.

Library of Congress Cataloging in Publication Data
Gillette, Clayton P., author. | Walt, Steven D., author.
The UN Convention on Contracts for the International Sale of Goods : practice and theory / Clayton P. Gillette, Steven D. Walt.
Second edition. | New York NY : Cambridge University Press, 2016. |
Includes bibliographical references and index.
LCCN 2015042656| ISBN 9781107149625 (Hardback : alk. paper) |
ISBN 9781316604168 (Pbk. : alk. paper)
LCSH: United Nations Convention on Contracts for the International
Sale of Goods (1980 April 11) | Export sales contracts.
LCC K1028.3198 .G55 2016 | DDC 343.08/78–dc23 LC record
available at http://lccn.loc.gov/2015042656

ISBN 978-1-107-14962-5 Hardback
ISBN 978-1-316-60416-8 Paperback

Contents

Preface

In this volume, we explain and comment on the United Nations Convention on Contracts for the International Sale of Goods (CISG), a treaty that regulates the sale of goods among businesses located in different nations. While our focus is on the CISG generally, we are writing in part for an audience that is familiar with different national sales laws. The text at points compares and contrasts the CISG with a sample of these laws, including the Uniform Commercial Code. The purpose of the exercise is to avoid the inference, made by many, that national and international regulatory regimes incorporate identical rules and risk allocations in sales transactions. Our objectives are both to provide information and commentary for commercial law practitioners, and to present a methodological lens, informed by academic literature, for the analysis of commercial law generally.

At the same time, we take an informal theoretical approach to the CISG's provisions that we believe helps illuminate its provisions and assists in their application. This lens suggests that the function of commercial law is to provide default rules that reflect bargains parties would otherwise have reached on their own. In this way, commercial law reduces the costs that attorneys and parties must incur to reach agreement. Analysis of the CISG leads us to be critical of provisions that we find inconsistent with the preferences of commercial parties.

We are indebted to students who performed diligent and thorough research in the preparation of this work. These include Elena Hadjimichael, NYU Law School Class of 2017; Rena Kelley, University of Virginia Law School Class of 2012; Elana Lobo, NYU Law School Class of 2014; Vanessa Richardson, NYU Law School Class of 2013; and Matthew Simon, NYU Law School Class of 2014. Andrew Walker, NYU Law School Class of 2015, reviewed the entire manuscript. Kent Olson of the UVA Law Library was invaluable in discovering source materials. We benefited from numerous substantive conversations with Stefan Kröll and Joseph Lookofsky. Our greatest intellectual debt is owed to Franco Ferrari, who both encouraged the project and meticulously read and commented on the manuscript. In the process he saved us from numerous errors. Those that remain are attributable only to us. Even more valuable is the constant friendship he provides to both of us. Finally, we thank our respective deans, Trevor Morrison and Paul Mahoney, for the time and resources necessary to complete this project. Clayton Gillette especially wishes to thank the Filomen D'Agostino and Max E. Greenberg Research Fund for financial support.

1

The CISG:

history, methodology, and construction

I. THE CISG AS A SET OF COMMERCIAL DEFAULT RULES

The United Nations Convention on Contracts for the International Sale of Goods ("the CISG") is one of the most successful international commercial law treaties ever devised. It has been ratified by most of the world's important trading countries and become a template for the manner in which commercial law treaties are drafted. As of this writing, the CISG has been adopted by eighty-three countries. These nations are referred to as "Contracting States." Every major trading nation except India, South Africa, and the United Kingdom has ratified the CISG. Cases interpreting it currently number in the low thousands, and more than 135 United States cases have referred to the CISG. With unreported arbitration awards added, this number must be considerably higher. The effect of the CISG within a Contracting State may vary with domestic law. For example, within the United States, which ratified the CISG in 1986 and where it entered into force in 1988, the CISG is considered a self-executing treaty. The CISG therefore creates a private right of action in federal court under federal law.[1] The CISG provides the default set of rules that govern contracts for the sale of goods between parties located in different Contracting States,[2] and, in some cases, where only one of the parties is located in a Contracting State. Where applicable the CISG preempts contrary provisions of domestic sales law, such as Article 2 of the Uniform Commercial Code ("UCC") and other state contract law in the United States, and conflicting provisions of the German Civil Code ("BGB") or the French Civil Code.

---

[1] See *Saint Tropez Inc. v. Ningbo Maywood Industry and Trade Co., Ltd.*, 2014 U.S. Dist. LEXIS 96840 (S.D.N.Y. July 16, 2014); *Weihai Textile Group Import & Export Co., Ltd. v. Level 8 Apparel, LLC*, 2014 U.S. Dist. LEXIS (S.D.N.Y. March 28, 2014); *Hanwha Corp. v. Cedar Petrochemicals, Inc.*, 760 F. Supp. 2d 426 (S.D.N.Y. 2011).

[2] See *Microgem Corp. v. Homecast Co., Ltd.*, 2012 U.S. Dist. LEXIS 65166 (S.D.N.Y. April 26, 2012).

The CISG is relatively well known and researched in Europe. The academic literature on uniform sales law is dominated by European scholars, and some of the methodological developments in legal analysis that have prevailed in the United States have been applied only sparingly to CISG scholarship.[3] As a result, at least in the United States, the CISG remains an understudied, largely misunderstood, and somewhat esoteric body of law, unfamiliar to many American commercial lawyers. Many of its provisions are reminiscent of the Uniform Commercial Code, and many American attorneys and courts improperly infer that those similarities mean that the UCC and the CISG have identical scope and meaning. Other provisions of the CISG are largely foreign to common law academics and lawyers. These gaps frequently lead attorneys who are involved in the planning of transactions for the international sale of goods to opt out of the CISG without sufficient consideration of whether a client's interests would be better served by its incorporation.[4]

Our objective in this text is to address these issues by providing material, directed at both American and foreign commercial lawyers, that explains and evaluates the CISG, and to do so through a particular lens. Because most of the cases and commentary on the CISG derive from European or Asian sources that follow civil law traditions and rely on modes of analysis that differ from those in common law traditions, we attempt to introduce civil law concepts to a common law audience and to introduce civil lawyers to comparable provisions within common law nations.

We also bring a particular perspective to our study that is not adequately represented in the doctrinal or theoretical literature on the CISG. Many students of international commercial law celebrate the benefits of uniform law in reducing transaction costs by avoiding the need for each party to understand the law of a counterparty's jurisdiction. We acknowledge that the reduction of transaction costs is a vital objective of commercial law. In addition, we acknowledge that, in theory, a

---

[3] Major European treatises appearing in an English language version include UN Convention on Contracts for the International Sale of Goods (CISG): Commentary (Stefan Kröll, Loukas Mistelis & Pilar Perales Viscasillas eds. 2011) [hereinafter "Kröll et al."]; Joseph Lookofsky, Understanding the CISG (4th (Worldwide) ed. 2012); Schlechtriem & Schwenzer, Commentary on the Convention on the International Sale of Goods (CISG) (Ingeborg Schwenzer ed., 3d ed. 2010). The primary reference work by American scholars has been John O. Honnold, Uniform Law for International Sales Under the 1980 United Nations Convention 190 (Harry M. Flechtner ed., 4th ed. 2009) [hereinafter "Honnold/Flechtner"].

[4] There is debate over the extent to which opting out occurs. Some efforts to measure the phenomenon conclude that opting out is occurring at rates that are decreasing or that are lower than predicted. The unscientific nature of these studies, however, raises issues about their accuracy. There is a risk that surveys sent to practitioners concerning their knowledge and use of the CISG will have a higher response rate from those who utilize it. These factors, however, tend not to be considered in the empirical evaluations. For unrigorous efforts to measure opting out, see, e.g., Ingeborg Schwenzer & Christopher Kee, *International Sales Law – The Actual Practice*, 29 Penn. St. Int'l L. Rev. 425 (2011); Ulrich G. Schroeter, *To Exclude, to Ignore, or to Use? Empirical Evidence on Courts', Parties' and Counsels' Approach to the CISG (With Some Remarks on Professional Liability)*, in The Global Challenge of International Sales Law 649 (Larry DiMatteo ed., 2014).

uniform law can have that effect. Uniformity itself, however, does not perform that function. Whether or not a particular body of uniform law reduces transaction costs depends on whether the default rules it creates reflect the risk allocations to which the parties otherwise would have bargained. If they do not, then the parties will have to invest additional transaction costs in negotiating around the defaults. Thus, it is untenable to maintain the claim that uniform international law, simply by virtue of avoiding the need for one party to learn another party's law, necessarily reduces transaction costs.[5] To take an extreme case, a uniform law that said "all disputes will be resolved by a coin flip" would avoid the need to learn national law, but it is doubtful that most commercial actors would want to adopt it. Uniformity also prevents a countervailing benefit that arises when legal systems compete with one another. As with competition for goods themselves, competition for law is likely to lead to improvements in legal rules that benefit all parties. Uniform law can become difficult to amend, especially – as with the CISG – when legal change is needed and there is no permanent regulatory or legislative body that has jurisdiction over its provisions. The CISG, promulgated some thirty-five years ago, already suffers some of the effects of its immutability. There is, for instance, substantial debate about its applicability to contracts for software, especially software that is downloaded through electronic means unforeseen at the time of the CISG's drafting. Perhaps more problematically, many of the CISG's provisions reflect compromises among social, economic, and political cultures that have subsequently converged. It is by no means clear that compromises that were necessary to bring both capitalist and socialist nations into the fold in the 1970s would be struck today, or that they reflect the preferences of the commercial actors whose contracts are governed by the CISG.

Throughout this text, we attempt both to explain and to analyze the provisions of the CISG. Our evaluation is measured against the goal of reducing transaction costs and providing default rules that do reflect the preferences of most commercial actors. As with most sales law, the CISG consists almost entirely of default rules: terms that apply unless the parties' agreement provides otherwise. Default rules that consist of terms that most contracting parties prefer to have govern their contracts ("majoritarian" default rules) save the parties the cost of supplying them. Only the minority of parties who prefer different terms must incur the cost of negotiating the terms that suit their contract. If the cost of supplying terms is the same for all contracting parties, a default rule that reflects the preferences of most parties reduces the total cost (the cost of incorporating both default rules and individually negotiated terms) of providing contracting parties with the terms they prefer. Even when contracting costs differ between parties, a majoritarian default rule reduces total contracting costs if the aggregate contracting costs to the majority of parties are

---

[5] See Ingeborg Schwenzer & Pascal Hachem, *The CISG—Successes and Pitfalls*, 57 Am. J. Comp. L. 457 (2009). For a general critique of the assumption that the CISG reduces transaction costs, see Clayton P. Gillette & Robert E. Scott, *The Political Economy of International Sales*, 25 Int'l. Rev. L. & Econ. 446 (2005).

greater than the aggregate contracting costs to the minority. Concerns that might justify other standards of evaluation, such as paternalistic or other non-economic standards, are rarely implicated in the range of transactions – transactions between commercial actors – to which the CISG applies. We therefore evaluate many of the CISG's rules we discuss through the lens of optimal default rules: rules that minimize the costs of entering into, negotiating, and enforcing contracts for most contracting parties.

Judged by this standard, we question whether many of the CISG's rules are majoritarian default rules. They sometimes encourage strategic behavior in the performance and enforcement of the contract, forcing parties to incur the cost of preventing the behavior or risk its presence. At the same time, the CISG's rules are often (but not always) malleable enough to allow tribunals to construe them to minimize contracting costs for most parties. Where that is the case, we argue that tribunals often but not always use their interpretive authority to reach results consistent with cost-minimization. The fact that tribunals frequently do so does not cure the inefficiency of many of the CISG's default rules. For one thing, the reported cases may or may not be representative interpretations of relevant provisions. This is because arbitral tribunals likely are the bulk of fora interpreting the CISG,[6] and most arbitral awards are unreported. In addition, even the parties and sales transactions in the reported cases may not be representative of parties who choose not to litigate or arbitrate their sales contracts. For both reasons, a tribunal's construction of the CISG's malleable provisions in a contract cost-minimizing fashion in a particular case does not assure that the provisions are construed in a way most contracting parties prefer.

II. THE HISTORY AND STRUCTURE OF THE CISG

The inefficiency of many of the CISG's rules is due in part to the process by which they were produced. The CISG was promulgated by the United Nations Commission on International Trade Law (UNCITRAL). UNCITRAL is an arm of the United Nations that drafts model commercial laws for enactment as national law and conventions to be ratified as treaties. It organized the effort to create the CISG in response to the failure of prior efforts to create widely acceptable uniform sales law.[7] The International Institute for the Unification of Private Law, or UNIDROIT, had

---

[6] See Loukas Mistelis, *CISG and Arbitration*, in CISG Methodology 375, 388 (Andre Janssen & Olaf Meyer eds., 2009) (speculating that more than 70 percent of cases relating to the CISG through 2009 have been arbitrations); Andre Jansen & Matthias Spilker, *The Application of the CISG in the World of International Commercial Arbitration*, 77 Rabelszeitschrift 131, 133 (2013) (through 2012, 33 percent of cases were arbitrations).

[7] The following history is based largely on material in Michael Bonell, *Introduction to the Convention*, in Commentary on the International Sales Law 2–16 (Cesare M. Bianca & Michael J. Bonell eds., 1987) [hereinafter "Bianca & Bonell"]; Honnold/Flechtner, supra note 3; and The UNCITRAL Guide: Basic Facts About the United Nations Commission on International Trade Law (2007) [hereinafter "UNCITRAL Guide"].

previously undertaken a three-decade effort that resulted in the 1964 promulgation of two treaties, the Uniform Law for International Sales (ULIS) and the Uniform Law on the Formation of Contracts for International Sales (ULF). Neither attracted adoption by more than nine nations, in part because the result was considered to have been dominated by European legal concepts that were not recognized elsewhere.[8] UNCITRAL believed that it could increase adoptions by revising the prior treaties to reflect a more international flavor. UNCITRAL's membership was organized to ensure broad representation in drafting projects. Membership currently is limited to delegations from sixty states selected by the United Nations General Assembly, and is allocated along geographic lines. (UNCITRAL had thirty-four member states at the time of the CISG's drafting.) States from Africa, Asia, Eastern Europe, Latin America, and "Western Europe and Others" all have membership assured under the UNCITRAL charter.[9] Thus, the project of reforming the ULIS and ULF necessarily involved representation from affluent and developing countries, common law and civil law systems, and market-based and socialist economies (recall that the project pre-dated democratic movements in Eastern Europe).[10]

UNCITRAL traditionally employs Working Groups to create initial drafts before submitting a proposed treaty to a conference of delegates from a broader range of states. The Working Group for a project consists of representatives from a diverse set of political and economic systems. Working Groups meet for one or two one-week sessions annually and work primarily from preparatory materials provided by the Secretariat of UNCITRAL, a full-time body composed largely of international lawyers.[11] The materials prepared by the Secretariat include draft statutory texts with alternatives that are intended "to facilitate debate and decision with a minimum of confusion or misunderstanding."[12] UNCITRAL and its working groups operate by consensus and almost never take a formal vote on their substantive proposals.[13] Indeed, proceeding outside of a formal majority or unanimity rule appears to be a matter of pride for some involved in the process.[14]

---

[8] See Honnold/Flechtner, supra note 3, at 5–9; Michael P. Van Alstine, *Dynamic Treaty Interpretation*, 146 U. Pa. L. Rev. 687, 725–26 (1998); Gyula Eörsi, *A Propos the 1980 Vienna Convention on Contracts for the International Sale of Goods*, 31 Am. J. Comp. L. 333, 335 (1983).

[9] See John O. Honnold, *The United Nations Commission on International Trade Law: Mission and Methods*, 27 Am. J. Comp. L. 201, 207 (1979) [hereinafter *Mission and Methods*].

[10] See The UNCITRAL Guide, supra note 7, at 6–7.

[11] See UNCITRAL Rules of Procedure and Methods of Work, Practice and the Implementation of the Applicable Rules of Procedure, A/CN 9/638 paras. 22 & 24 (2007) [hereinafter UNCITRAL Rules of Procedure].

[12] Honnold, *Mission and Methods*, supra note 9, at 209; see The UNCITRAL Guide, supra note 7, at 7.

[13] See UNCITRAL Rules of Procedure, supra note 11, at Add. 4 paras. 11 & 12. The decision not to reconsider the decision to relocate the Secretariat from New York to Vienna in 1979 was taken by vote.

[14] See Honnold/Flechtner, supra note 3, at 8.

In the case of the CISG effort, UNCITRAL created an initial Working Group that comprised representatives from a broad geographic, political, and cultural range of states.[15] UNICITRAL charged the Working Group with the development of legislation that would be acceptable "by countries of different legal, social, and economic systems."[16] The Working Group met in nine sessions from 1970 through 1977. While the Working Group initially proposed revisions to the ULIS and the ULF, UNCITRAL ultimately decided to consolidate the two treaties into a single document. UNCITRAL thus established a Drafting Committee for this purpose composed of representatives from Chile, Egypt, France, Hungary, India, Japan, Mexico, Nigeria, the USSR, and the United Kingdom.[17] That Committee completed its work in 1978. UNCITRAL approved the draft that resulted and requested the United Nations to convene a Diplomatic Conference to consider it. The Conference was held at Vienna during a five-week period in 1980. Representatives of sixty-two states attended.[18] Representatives from a variety of non-governmental and intergovernmental agencies interested in international trade attended as observers.[19] Two committees performed most of the work for what became known as the Vienna Conference. One committee prepared the substantive provisions of the CISG, while

---

[15] The original representatives were from Brazil, France, Ghana, Hungary, India, Iran, Japan, Kenya, Mexico, Norway, Tunisia, USSR, the United Kingdom, and the United States. Representatives from Austria, Czechoslovakia, the Philippines, and Sierra Leone were added later. See Bianca & Bonell, supra note 7, at 6.

[16] See Documentary History of the Uniform Law of Sales 3 (John O. Honnold ed., 1989) [hereinafter, Documentary History].

[17] See Bianca & Bonell, supra note 7, at 6.

[18] Argentina, Australia, Austria, Belgium, Bolivia, Brazil, Bulgaria, Burma, Byelorussian Soviet Socialist Republic, Canada, Chile, China, Colombia, Costa Rica, Cyprus, Czechoslovakia, Denmark, Ecuador, Egypt, Finland, France, German Democratic Republic, Federal Republic of Germany, Ghana, Greece, Hungary, India, Iran, Iraq, Ireland, Israel, Italy, Japan, Kenya, Libyan Arab Jamahiriya, Luxembourg, Mexico, Netherlands, Nigeria, Norway, Pakistan, Panama, Peru, Philippines, Poland, Portugal, Republic of Korea, Romania, Singapore, Spain, Sweden, Switzerland, Thailand, Tunisia, Turkey, Ukrainian Soviet Socialist Republic, Union of Soviet Socialist Republics, United Kingdom of Great Britain and Northern Ireland, United States of America, Uruguay, Yugoslavia, and Zaire. Venezuela sent an observer. See 19 I.L.M. 668 (1980). Some commentators characterize the participants by reference to their political cultures. Thus, Alejandro Garro notes that "[s]ixty-two nations were represented at the Vienna Conference. Roughly speaking, twenty-two from the 'Western developed' part of the world, eleven from 'socialist regimes,' and twenty-nine from 'Third World' countries." Alejandro M. Garro, *Reconciliation of Legal Traditions in the U.N. Convention on Contracts for the International Sale of Goods*, 23 Int'l Law. 443 (1989).

[19] These included the World Bank, the Bank for International Settlements, the Central Office for International Railway Transport, the Council of Europe, the European Economic Community, the Hague Conference on Private International Law, the International Institute for the Unification of Private Law, and the International Chamber of Commerce. Pre-Conference proposals for the convention were circulated to these observers, and they made comments on various provisions. See Documentary History, supra note 16, at 392. For instance, the ICC recommended the deletion of an article, similar to present Article 8, concerning a general rule on interpretation. See id. at 394. For the role of participation of observers in UNCITRAL projects, see UNCITRAL Rules of Procedure, supra note 11, at Add. 5 para. 6 (2007).

the other prepared the "final clauses," which dealt with such issues as reservations, declarations, and ratification by Contracting States.[20] Members of the Conference debated the text of each article, but ultimately approved the CISG unanimously. The CISG was then submitted to states for their approval according to domestic processes for adopting international treaties. According to its terms, the CISG was to become effective among signatories, denominated "Contracting States," approximately one year after the tenth state deposited with the United Nations an instrument indicating its acceptance of the treaty.[21] China, Italy, and the United States became the ninth, tenth, and eleventh Contracting States in December 1986. As a result, the CISG became effective among then-Contracting States as of January 1, 1988.

The participants who drafted the CISG tended to come from either universities or ministries in their home state.[22] They were appointed by the governments of their various states, rather than by the United Nations. Appointing authority varies among the states. In some instances (for instance, Italy), the office of the Secretary of State made the appointment; in other instances (for example, Germany and Switzerland), the appointment was made by the Ministry of Justice. There was apparently no minimum credentialing required for appointment. Some commentators suggest that the representatives were experts in their field. Honnold reports that representatives to UNCITRAL projects tend to be academics who work in commercial or comparative law, practicing attorneys, and members of government ministries with significant experience in international lawmaking. This may be a bit of an overstatement. While most states do send experts, much of the expertise has been gained from academic study rather than participation in international business, and some states simply appoint members of the state's Permanent Mission to the United Nations.[23] Of the thirteen representatives from nations involved in the first Working Group that led to the CISG, nine were legal academics, three were bureaucrats, and one was a member of the country's Permanent Mission to the United Nations. Participants continued to hold their academic or ministerial positions while serving in the process of drafting the uniform law.

The predominantly academic affiliation of the participants and UNCITRAL's voting rule together help explain the character of many of the CISG's provisions. A substantial number of these provisions we discuss in detail in the following chapters are vague. They lack a precise standard for their application or, in some cases, any standard at all. The interests of academic participants do not necessarily coincide with those of businesses whose contracts will be governed by the CISG. Businesses prefer their contracts to be governed by rules that maximize the contract surplus: the difference between the value of performance and its cost (including negotiation and enforcement costs). They therefore desire that legal rules minimize

[20] See Bianca & Bonell, supra note 7, at 6.   [21] See Article 99.
[22] See Honnold, *Mission and Methods*, supra note 9, at 209.
[23] See Documentary History, supra note 16, at 187–88.

transaction costs directed at the negotiation and enforcement of contract terms. By contrast, an academic's principal interest in uniform law may be in having UNCITRAL's membership approve the proposed convention and having states widely enact it. Participation in an approved and widely adopted convention is a signal of expertise and enhances the academic's reputation. This interest is served even by a uniform law that does not maximize the contract surplus for contracting parties. Put crudely, adoption, not efficiency, is the UNCITRAL participant's primary goal. At the same time, UNCITRAL's voting rule, which requires consensus, effectively gives participants a veto over proposals for a uniform law. This makes achieving a consensus costly with respect to majoritarian default rules among participants from very different legal systems, and risks failure of the underlying project.[24] On the other hand, vague rules with few reservations serve the participants' interests: Vague rules make consensus easier to achieve, because they do not contain contestable terms that are inconsistent with domestic law and thus potentially objectionable to some participants.[25]

Consider, for example, a rule that requires "reasonable" conduct but that does not specify the criteria of reasonableness. Omitting criteria of reasonableness attracts support from participants who might object to specified criteria that are inconsistent with their domestic law. At the same time, no participant is likely to believe that its domestic law is "unreasonable." Thus, no participant is likely to face domestic resistance to a proposed uniform law on the grounds that its vague provisions are inconsistent with domestic law. The dominance of vague rules in the CISG therefore is unsurprising. This is not to say that ambiguity is necessarily a hallmark of interests other than those of commercial parties. A treaty such as the CISG that is intended to cover a broad array of transactions will necessarily include vague terms, because different goods require different treatment with respect to issues such as delivery, payment, or quality. It is only to say that the incentives of the participants likely generated more than an optimal degree of vagueness from the perspective of those whose transactions are subject to the CISG.

Given the objective of creating uniform international sales law, the CISG is notable both for what it contains and for what it omits. The first Part, containing thirteen Articles, deals with the Convention's sphere of application. Article 1(1) recites that the CISG applies to "contracts of sale of goods between parties whose places of business are in different States."[26] Nevertheless, neither the term "sale" nor the term "goods" is defined within the CISG, except for exclusions of particular transactions,[27] and the definition of "place of business" leaves significant ambiguity

---

[24] The classic discussion of the decision costs of an unanimity rule among multiple parties is James M. Buchanan & Gordon Tullock, The Calculus of Consent 84–96 (1962).

[25] See Gillette & Scott, supra note 5.

[26] All references within this text to a specific "Article" (e.g., "Article 1(1)(a)") are to Articles of the CISG unless otherwise indicated.

[27] See Article 2 (excluding certain transactions from the scope of "sale"), Article 3 (excluding certain transactions in which the buyer supplies materials for goods or in which the "seller" primarily provides labor or services).

about what law governs where a party has multiple places of business. Part II concerns the formation of contracts. Part III covers the obligations of each party, such as the obligations of buyers and sellers, remedies for breach, passage of risk, anticipatory breach, and damages. The final Part concerns procedural issues for the CISG, such as the capacity of Contracting States to make declarations with respect to specific Articles, and the terms under which the CISG becomes effective among Contracting States. The CISG explicitly excludes certain aspects of sales law, however. Article 4 recites that matters of contract validity and the effect of a contract on property rights in the goods sold are beyond the CISG's jurisdiction. Thus, nothing in the CISG addresses issues such as unconscionability, capacity defenses, or the rights of a bona fide purchaser to goods that turn out to have been stolen.

Even with respect to issues that are covered, the CISG provides only a set of default rules, subject to variation by the parties. This concept of "party autonomy" is illustrated most vividly by Article 6, which provides that the parties to a contract otherwise governed by the CISG "may exclude the application of this Convention or, subject to Article 12, derogate from or vary the effect of any of its provisions."[28] This provision permits parties to opt out of the CISG as a whole or any part of it. The process of opting out, however, may be more demanding than Article 6 suggests. As we discuss in Chapter 2, most courts have required a very specific statement of intent to avoid application of the CISG. Selection of the law of a Contracting State, standing alone, typically will not suffice, because the CISG itself will constitute a part of that jurisdiction's law. Opting out of a particular article of the CISG, on the other hand, may be implied merely by the inclusion in the contract of a clause that conflicts with an article of the CISG. For instance, a contractual limitation of warranty to a twelve-month period was interpreted by an arbitral panel as derogating from the two-year statute of repose under Article 39.[29] In addition, contractual clauses may clarify vague standards within the CISG. Article 39 prevents a buyer from relying on a lack of conformity of the goods unless the buyer has given the seller appropriate notice within a "reasonable time." A contractual clause that required the buyer to report any complaint within five days of delivery was an effective specification of what would constitute a reasonable time.[30]

---

[28] Article 12 makes certain parts of the CISG that eliminate writing requirements inapplicable where any party has its place of business in a Contracting State that has made a declaration under Article 96, and prohibits derogations or variations from Article 12. Certainly it would be incongruous to allow parties to circumvent a Contracting State's determination to require writing requirements by opting out of a provision intended to permit the Contracting State to retain the same requirements. We discuss Article 12 in Chapter 3.I. Similarly, courts have concluded that parties may not opt out of those provisions of the CISG that are directed to matters of public international law rather than to the substantive terms of the contract. See District Court Padova (Italy), 11 January 2005, available at http://cisgw3.law.pace.edu/cases/050111i3.html.

[29] See ICC Arbitration Case No. 11333 of 2002, available at http://cisgw3.law.pace.edu/cases/021333i1.html.

[30] See District Court Arnhem (Netherlands), 11 February 2009, available at http://cisgw3.law.pace.edu/cases/090211n1.html.

III. CISG METHODOLOGY AND THE LIMITS OF INTERNATIONALITY

One of the enduring difficulties related to the CISG involves the appropriate methodology by which its provisions are to be interpreted. Even assuming that uniformity in international commercial law is desirable, the means by which the CISG attempts to implement that goal imposes substantial limitations. Some of these limitations are the necessary consequence of the political environment in which the CISG was promulgated and adopted. Others result from the inherent variations in judicial and arbitral processes involved in the interpretation of a convention intended to have international application. Still others are a consequence of the CISG's own requirements for its interpretation.

The sources of difficulty begin with the text itself. UNCITRAL promulgated the CISG in six languages: Arabic, Chinese, English, French, Russian, and Spanish. In theory, each of these versions is intended to be equally authoritative.[31] The desire for equality among these versions, however, necessarily interferes with uniformity. Translation from one language to another is imperfect, especially when what must be translated is a legal concept that is unfamiliar in the language to which it is being translated.[32] In addition, other jurisdictions have translated the CISG into other languages. Some courts have attempted to deal with the principle of equality by deviating from it. The Swiss Federal Court had to determine whether a buyer that had complained of an unusable machine without specifying individual defects had given sufficient notice to the seller.[33] That determination hinged on the degree of specificity implied by the notice requirement in Article 39. But that implication varied with the different translations of the CISG:

> According to the German translation of Art. 39(1) CISG, the buyer must precisely specify the nature of the lack of conformity in the notice to the seller. The English and French texts of the Convention talk about "specifying the nature of the lack of conformity" and *"en précisant la nature de ce défaut,"* respectively. Thereby, the notice must specify the nature, type or character of the lack of conformity (*cf.* Merriam-Webmaster [sic] Dictionary, which defines "nature," being a synonym for "essence," as "the inherent character or basic constitution of a person or thing," *cf.* also Le Grand Robert de la langue française, which equates "nature" with "essence"). What must be considered is that the verbs "specify" and *"préciser"* cannot only be translated as *"genau bezeichnen"* (precisely describe), but also with *"bezeichnen"* (describe) or with *"angeben"* (indicate). Consequently, the original

---

[31] The Witness Clause included at the end of the CISG recites that it was "done at Vienna . . . in a single original, of which the Arabic, Chinese, English, French, Russian and Spanish texts are equally authentic."

[32] See Royston M. Goode, *Reflections on the Harmonization of Commercial Law*, 1 Unif. L. Rev. 71 (1991).

[33] See Federal Supreme Court (Switzerland), 13 November 2003, available at http://cisgw3.law .pace.edu/cases/031113s1.html.

versions do not require the description to be as precise as could be expected according to the German translation.

Indeed, the court accepted a hierarchy of authority even within the "official" languages, as proposed by numerous continental commentators. It concluded that "[i]n the case of ambiguity in the wording, reference is to be made to the original versions, whereby the English version, and, secondarily, the French version are given a higher significance as English and French were the official languages of the Conference and the negotiations were predominantly conducted in English."

The second limitation on uniformity arises from the fact that the CISG does not provide a unitary mechanism for resolving disputes that might arise with respect to its own meaning. The CISG is domestic law, interpreted by domestic courts. Article 7(1) instructs courts and other tribunals interpreting the CISG to have "regard" to "its international character" and to the "need to promote uniformity" in its application. Perhaps the ideal way to achieve uniformity would be to have an international commercial court hear cases under the CISG, or at least serve as a court of last resort to resolve conflicts among domestic courts. But the CISG creates no such apparatus. The reason, apparently, has less to do with the merits of uniform interpretation than with practical politics. As Bonell concludes, "[t]o expect that all adhering States, notwithstanding their different social, political and legal structure, could even agree on conferring to an international tribunal the exclusive competence to resolve divergences between the national jurisdictions in the interpretation of the uniform rules, would be entirely unrealistic."[34]

Some efforts have been made to compensate for the absence of an official arbiter of conflicting opinions. An unofficial "CISG Advisory Council" consisting of reputable law professors has issued a variety of opinions concerning issues as to which divergent interpretations have arisen.[35] But the Advisory Council is self-appointed and its opinions do not have the imprimatur of any national or international organization. While many courts have cited to these opinions, they have no more authority than a well-reasoned commentary. Where foreign tribunals have interpreted a provision of the CISG, uniformity in application almost inevitably requires a domestic tribunal to consider foreign case law. Courts and arbitrators typically do so, to a greater or lesser extent. The difficult question is the precise legal authority of foreign case law under the CISG. Clearly this case law is not binding legal authority for domestic courts. The CISG is enforced in national courts and arbitral tribunals, and these fora lack judicial power over foreign courts. Even in the United States, except for the Supreme Court's construction of the CISG, a federal court's construction of the CISG is not binding on state courts. On the other hand, Article 7(1)'s demand for uniformity in interpretation makes the constructions of foreign tribunals more than mere information about how they interpret the same

---

[34] Michael Bonell, *Interpretation of Convention*, in Bianca & Bonell, supra note 7, at 89.
[35] The opinions are available at www.cisgac.com/.

treaty provision. Foreign case law therefore has legal relevance that is more than mere information but less than binding authority.

It is difficult to determine between these extremes the required deference to foreign case law interpreting treaties. The Supreme Court's statements on the matter are at points guarded and inconclusive. The Court has repeatedly said that foreign law interpreting a treaty is entitled to considerable weight.[36] However, it is unclear about the sort of deference required. Deference to the decisions of foreign courts can mean different things. Foreign case law can be used to confirm conclusions a domestic court reaches independently. Alternatively, foreign case law interpreting a treaty can have considerable weight only when the interpretations are those of a country's highest court.[37] Finally, the decisions of both inferior and superior foreign courts can have sufficient weight to override an interpretation the court would adopt otherwise. The Supreme Court appears to give "considerable weight" to the decisions of superior foreign courts to corroborate interpretations it reaches on independent grounds. The interpretations of inferior foreign courts do not merit reliance even for purposes of corroboration.[38]

In *Abbott v. Abbott*[39] the Court had to interpret the term "right of custody" under the Hague Convention on the Civil Aspects of International Child Abduction to which the United States is a party. In implementing the Convention, Congress directed that it be given a "uniform international interpretation."[40] Based on this directive, the Court used case law of superior foreign courts to "further inform"[41] its own conclusion as to the construction of the "right of custody" under the Convention. It found that the case law "confirms" this conclusion. The Court in *Abbott* defers to foreign law only to corroborate its own interpretation of the Convention; it does not rely on that law as an independent basis for its interpretation.[42] Article 7(1) of the CISG takes no position on the required deference to foreign case law. It merely requires that in interpreting the CISG "regard" be had to the need to promote uniformity in its application.

The prevailing position among commentators is that courts of one nation will treat opinions on provisions of the CISG from courts of other nations as at least

---

[36] See *Abbott v. Abbott*, 560 U.S. 1 (2010); *El Al Israel Airlines v. Tseng*, 525 U.S. 155, 176 (1999); *Air France v. Saks*, 470 U.S. 392, 404 (1985).

[37] For case studies in the treatment of precedent in different national legal systems, see Interpreting Precedents (D. Neil MacCormick & Robert S. Summers eds., 1997); for the different ways in which precedent cases may bind, see Aleksander Peczenik, *The Binding Force of Precedent*, in id., at 461.

[38] See *Olympic Airlines v. Husain*, 540 U.S. 644, 655, n.9 (2004); but cf. id. at 660–61 (Scalia, J., dissenting) ("Finally, even if we disagree, we surely owe the conclusions reached by appellate courts of other signatories the courtesy of respectful consideration").

[39] 560 U.S. 1 (2010).   [40] See 42 U.S.C. § 11601(b)(3)(B).   [41] See *Abbott*, 560 U.S. at 25.

[42] Cf. *El Al Israel Airlines v. Tseng*, 525 U.S. 154, 176 (1999); *Abbot*, 560 U.S. at 74 ("Indeed, the interest in having our courts correctly interpret the Convention may outweigh the interest in having the *ne exeat* clause resolved in the same way that it is resolved in other countries") (Stevens, J., dissenting).

probative of the correct interpretation of that provision, even if the foreign opinion is neither authoritative nor binding precedent. At most, foreign opinions have persuasive, but non-binding effect, which suggests that the reasoning of the opinions may have more import than their holdings.[43] Even the fact that a majority of foreign courts has decided an issue in a particular way does not bind other courts. That is not simply because there is no supranational CISG court of last resort. It is also a function of the fact that the authority of courts that decide an issue is likely to vary dramatically within their own national systems. How many decisions by trial courts in different nations would be necessary to offset a contrary decision of the German Federal Supreme Court on the same issue? What weight should be given to arbitral tribunal decisions compared to those of courts?

Issues like these render impractical any effort to create a hierarchy of international decision makers, which would be necessary to construct a meaningful rule of international or supranational "precedent." Increasingly, and consistent with the admonition in much of the commentary about the need for interpretations of the CISG to be determined autonomously rather than as variations on any domestic law, courts have explicitly recognized the mandate to interpret the CISG with regard to its international character. This recognition typically takes the form of citing opinions from other jurisdictions to support interpretations of the CISG.[44]

American courts have frequently been chastised in European commentary for lack of fidelity to the objective of international interpretation.[45] Indeed, some American courts have demonstrated inattention to relevant opinions from other jurisdictions,[46] and have appealed to the UCC to interpret CISG provisions.[47] This trend has changed. More recent American opinions have indicated a willingness to consider foreign opinions. For instance, in *Chicago Prime Packers, Inc. v. Northam Food*

---

[43] See Franco Ferrari, *Interpretation of the Convention and Gap-Filling: Article 7*, in The Draft UNCITRAL Digest and Beyond: Cases, Analysis and Unresolved Issue in the U.N. Sales Convention 138, 150 (Franco Ferrari, Harry Flechtner & Ronald A. Brand eds., 2004) [hereinafter "Ferrari, Flechtner & Brand"]; Joseph Lookofsky, *CISG Foreign Case Law: How Much Regard Should We Have?*, in id. at 216, 218; Schwenzer & Hachem, supra note 5, at 468.

[44] See District Court Rimini (Italy), 26 November 2002, available at www.cisg.law.pace.edu/cisg/wais/db/cases2/021126i3.html; District Court Vigevano (Italy), 12 July 2000, available at http://cisgw3.law.pace.edu/cases/000712i3.html; Foreign Trade Court of Arbitration attached to the Serbian Chamber of Commerce (Serbia), 28 January 2009, available at http://cisgw3.law.pace.edu/cases/090128sb.html.

[45] See Pilar Perales Viscasillas, *Article 7*, in Kröll et al., supra note 3, at 117 n.30; Franco Ferrari, *The CISG's Interpretative Goals, Interpretative Method and General Principles in Case Law (Part I)*, 13 Internationales Handelsrecht 137 (May 2013).

[46] See *Zapata Hermanos Sucesores, S.A. v. Hearthside Baking Co.*, 313 F.3d 385 (7th Cir. 2002), which rejected an award of attorney's fees under Article 74. While the result may have been correct, the opinion ignores alternative holdings from other jurisdictions. For a more recent American case addressing the same issue that takes into account foreign case law, see *Stemcor USA, Inc. v. Miracero, S.A. de C.V.*, 66 F. Supp. 3d 394 (S.D.N.Y. 2014). The issue is discussed in more detail in Chapter 9.I.A.7.

[47] See, e.g., *Schmitz-Werke Gmbh v. Rockland Industries, Inc.*, 2002 U.S. App. LEXIS 12336 (4th Cir. June 21, 2002); *Delchi Carrier SpA v. Rotorex Corp.*, 71 F.3d 1024, 1027–28 (2d Cir. 1995).

Trading Co.,[48] the district court construed Article 39(1) to determine whether the
buyer gave timely notice that the goods did not conform. It relied on a German
lower court case to place on the buyer the burden of showing that its notice was
timely and on an Italian lower court's decision to find that the length of the notice
period depends on the nature of the nonconformity. In *Medical Marketing Inter-*
national Inc. v. *Internazionale Medico Scientifica. S.r.l,*.[49] the seller argued that an
arbitral award could not be confirmed because it was in manifest disregard of law.
The arbitrators had found, based on a German Federal Supreme Court decision,
that the seller must deliver goods that conform to the regulatory requirements of
the buyer's place of business when it knew or ought to have known of these
requirements. Noting that the arbitrators had considered the decision carefully,
the court concluded that the award did not show a "manifest disregard of international sales law." The Third Circuit has explicitly acknowledged the directive to
courts to be mindful of the CISG's "international character and ... the need to
promote uniformity in its application and the observance of good faith in international trade."[50]

Foreign case law shows the same increasing regard for foreign decisions interpreting the CISG.[51] Nevertheless, many American courts still seem to have difficulty
discovering CISG cases from outside the United States.[52] We do not want to
exaggerate the reliance on foreign case law interpreting the CISG. Because Article
7(1) requires only "regard" to uniformity in interpretation, a court can comply with
the mandate while giving no consideration to foreign case law it believes mistaken.[53]
In doing so it still gives "regard" to the mistaken decision by refusing to follow it.
Foreign case law also may be ignored when it is divided fairly evenly on an issue,
since a regard for uniformity does not help resolve the issue. Finally, citations of
foreign decisions might overestimate the reliance on them, as a court might have
other grounds for reaching the same conclusion. On the other hand, citation
numbers might underestimate reliance in jurisdictions where judicial style of
opinion writing does not favor case citations generally.[54] Even with these provisos,

---

[48]   320 F. Supp. 2d 702 (N.D. Ill. 2004).

[49]   1999 U.S. Dist. LEXIS 7380 (E.D. La. May 17, 1999).

[50]   See *Forestal Guarani S.A.* v. *Daros International, Inc.*, 613 F.3d 395, 398 (3d Cir. 2010). See also
       Amco Ukrservice & Prompriladamco v. *American Meter Company*, 312 F. Supp. 2d 681 (E.D.
       Pa. 2004).

[51]   See, e.g., District Court Forli (Italy), 16 February 2009, available at http://cisgw3.law.pace.edu/
       cases/090216i3.html.

[52]   See, e.g., *Urica, Inc.* v. *Pharmaplast S.A.E.*, 2014 U.S. Dist. LEXIS 110015 (C.D. Cal. August 8,
       2014); *Allied Dynamics Corp.* v. *Kennametal, Inc.*, 2014 U.S. Dist. LEXIS 107920 (E.D.N.Y.
       August 5, 2014).

[53]   For appropriately cautionary remarks about the impact of access to international case law on
       uniform interpretation, see Joseph Lookofsky, *CISG Foreign Case Law: How Much Regard*
       Should We Have?, in Ferrari, Flechtner & Brand, supra note 43, at 216–20.

[54]   For the case of French law, see Mitchel de S.O.-l'E. Lasser, *Judicial Self-Portrait: Judicial*
       Discourse in the French Legal System, 104 Yale L. J. 1323, 1355–69 (1995).

the increased citation of foreign cases in interpreting the CISG's provisions is consistent with reliance.

A third limit on uniform international commercial law involves the need for an "autonomous" interpretation that also applies to interpretive methods.[55] The substantial number of ambiguous standards in the CISG renders their interpretation both important and subject to substantial variation based on different interpretive styles in different jurisdictions. Domestic standards of interpretation, such as a plain meaning rule, do not directly apply to CISG cases. Instead, the appropriate interpretive methodology must be derived from the CISG itself. We are, however, not aware of any case that dictates a particular interpretive methodology. Several cases indicate that the CISG's drafting history, or *travaux préparatoires*, are appropriate sources for interpretation.[56] The Vienna Convention on the Law of Treaties confirms this view. Article 32 of that Convention provides that "[r]ecourse may be had to supplementary means of interpretation, including the preparatory work of the treaty and the circumstances of its conclusion" to confirm the meaning that would be derived from other principles of interpretation.[57] In the case of the CISG, the *travaux préparatoires* include the Secretariat Commentary, UNCITRAL Committee Reports, Diplomatic Conference Proceedings, and Working Papers submitted by many of the Working Groups. These materials are readily available on websites.[58] Scholarly writing is also acceptable as a source of interpretation. Indeed, and somewhat surprising to the common law commercial lawyer, in civil law jurisdictions absence of a principle of *stare decisis* tends often to elevate scholarly writing over case law interpretations.

One key example of how different interpretations can affect uniformity involves Article 7(1). That Article requires that interpretations of the CISG have regard for "the observance of good faith in international trade." We deal with the concept of good faith in Chapter 4. It is noteworthy, however, that the concept does more work in civil law countries than in common law countries. This friction was revealed during the drafting of the CISG. Representatives of civil law jurisdictions favored inclusion of a good faith obligation during the formation stage of the contract, while representatives of common law jurisdictions expressed concerns about the vagueness inherent in any good faith obligation. Article 7(1)'s mandate to interpret CISG provisions in a manner that promotes "the observance of good faith in international

---

[55] See, e.g., Franco Ferrari, Contracts for the International Sale of Goods: Applicability and Application of the 1980 United Nations Sales Convention 12-13 (2012); Decision 4505/2009 of the Multi-Member Court of First Instance of Athens (Greece), available at http://cisgw3.law .pace.edu/cases/094505gr.html#ii2.

[56] See, e.g., Netherlands Arbitration Institute, Case No. 2319 (Netherlands), 15 October 2002, available at http://cisgw3.law.pace.edu/cases/021015n1.html; District Court Aachen (Germany), 20 July 1995, available at http://cisgw3.law.pace.edu/cases/950720g1.html.

[57] See Vienna Convention on the Law of Treaties, 1155 U.N. Treaty Series 331 (1969).

[58] See www.uncitral.org/uncitral/en/commission/working_groups/2Sale_of_Good.html; www.cisg .law.pace.edu/cisg/conference.html.

trade" leaves much open. The phrase is not even accompanied by a definition as indefinite as the "observance of reasonable commercial standards of fair dealing," the definition of good faith within the Uniform Commercial Code. Taken literally, the requirement of Article 7(1) applies only to interpretation of the CISG itself, not to the interpretation of contracts governed by it. Thus, Article 7(1) arguably imposes no independent obligation of good faith on parties; rather it imposes an obligation on those interpreting the CISG to read its provisions in a manner consistent with good faith performance.

As we discuss at greater length in Chapter 4, however, courts and commentators have often taken a broader view. They have read Article 7(1) to confer substantial authority on courts and arbitral panels with respect to the obligations of the parties to the contract. One author concludes that the "good faith" principle in interpretation "ought to be considered a moral or ethical standard to be followed by businesspersons, projecting fundamental ethical values in international sale contracts," apparently including the right to find a fundamental breach of contract where goods are produced under circumstances that violate human rights.[59] Taken to an extreme, interpretation to vindicate good faith may conflict with explicit provisions of the CISG. In one case, a German appellate court declared that a buyer could recover damages under Article 76, even though the buyer had failed to avoid the contract as expressly required by that Article.[60] The court concluded that because the seller "seriously and conclusively refused to perform its contractual obligations by disputing the existence of a binding contract," a declaration of avoidance was no longer required. One might reach such a conclusion on a waiver principle. But the court appealed to the obligation to interpret the CISG to promote the observance of good faith; it held that Article 7(1) "pave[s] the way for the consideration of established and fixed principles of the national legal systems of the Contracting States." The court included the maxim *venire contra factum proprium*, or "no one may set himself in contradiction to his own previous conduct," within those principles that could be incorporated through the good faith provision. That maxim, in turn, could be used in interpreting the CISG and applied to preclude a party who refuses to perform from complaining about the counterparty's failure to avoid the contract. We are unclear on how this kind of ad hoc analysis adds to the uniformity that the CISG is supposed to attain. We might feel more comfortable with an open-ended "good faith" tool if we were convinced that courts and arbitral panels could readily identify and distinguish opportunistic behavior that should be constrained from more acceptable self-interested conduct. At this point, however, we note only that the debate over the role of good faith as an interpretive principle continues.

Finally, the prospect of uniform international commercial law is constrained by the provisions of the CISG itself. The need to obtain political compromises

---

[59] See Viscasillas, *Article 7*, in Kröll et al., supra note 3, at 120.
[60] See Court of Appeals Munich (Germany), 15 September 2004, available at http://cisgw3.law .pace.edu/cases/040915g2.html.

required allowing Contracting States to deviate from the rules set forth in the CISG, so that different Contracting States will have different versions. As we will see, Contracting States have adopted varying provisions involving issues such as the scope of the CISG and the need for formal writing requirements. In addition, while the CISG allows parties a broad remedy of specific performance when the other party defaults, Article 28 makes that right dependent on the law of the forum in which the dispute is heard. The CISG's limited scope means that some issues relating to the sale of goods will continue to be governed by the application of domestic law. Each of these provisions may have been necessary in order to achieve the broad adoption of the CISG, but their effect is to dilute the uniformity of uniform international law.

IV. THE HOMEWARD TREND IN INTERPRETATION

The absence of a court of last resort not only means that domestic courts may vary in their interpretations of the CISG, but also that those interpretations may be affected by similar, but not identical, legal concepts in domestic law.[61] This tendency, frequently referred to as the "homeward trend," does not necessarily reveal an antipathy to international commercial law. Instead, it may simply reflect that judges who are familiar with a legal concept from domestic law assume that similar concepts share similar meanings in other cultures. An American judge trained in common law conceptions of "foreseeability" is likely to draw on that experience in applying the same term in the CISG rather than to reason from first principles. There is nothing invidious or necessarily jingoistic in this practice. It simply reflects the tendency of judges with limited time to assume that their understanding of terms and concepts is similar to that of other judges faced with the same expression.

In theory, however, the meanings of terms used in the CISG should be derived "autonomously" from the legislative process and purposes of the CISG. The CISG is not an embodiment of any nation's domestic law. It is an independent body of law with its own meanings and principles. That does not mean that domestic concepts are irrelevant. It does mean that courts should not incorporate domestic law wholesale into interpretations of the CISG simply because a similar term or concept appears in both. Early interpretations of the CISG appeared to suffer from the homeward trend in ways that generated substantial criticism. A series of decisions from Germany, Austria, and Switzerland originally interpreted the timing requirements of Articles 38 and 39 for a buyer to give notice of nonconformities to the seller by referring to domestic statutory law that very precisely fixed

---

[61] See, e.g., Franco Ferrari, *Homeward Trend and Lex Forism Despite Uniform Sales Law*, 13 Vindobona J. Int'l Comm. L. & Arb. 15 (2009).

the time for giving notice or that set an exact period for giving notice regardless of the nature of the goods.[62]

As noted previously, American courts have often been too quick to interpret CISG provisions by reference to UCC sections that contained similar language. The Seventh Circuit's opinion in *Chicago Prime Packers, Inc. v. Northam Food Trading Co.*,[63] as opposed to the District Court opinion mentioned before, may be a prime offender. In that case, the court determined that the conformity requirements of Article 35(2) mirrored the structure and content of UCC § 2–314. The court then made the unfortunate leap that similarity in content required that the burden of proof on the issue of conformity also be allocated similarly. Courts that apply domestic law in such a wooden fashion ignore the obligation to interpret the CISG "autonomously," that is, as an independent body of law in which the meaning of words must be derived from the drafting history and the international commercial context in which they are used.[64] As one court has defined autonomous interpretation, "the Convention must be applied and interpreted exclusively on its own terms, having regard to the principles of the Convention and Convention-related decisions in overseas jurisdictions. Recourse to domestic case law is to be avoided."[65]

This is not to say that drawing analogies from domestic law is inappropriate. Unless one is completely cynical about the law-making process, the fact that one or more jurisdictions embrace the same default rules serves as some evidence that the common rule reflects party preferences. And if that is the case, then using domestic interpretations of a term common to both domestic law and the CISG might at least be evidence of what the term means in the latter. It does not, for example, offend the notions of autonomous meaning or internationality to interpret the CISG's use of the term "sale" by inquiring into how the same term is defined under the UCC. The issue is one of degree. One cannot conclude that the UCC meaning has been incorporated wholesale into the CISG simply because the same term has been employed. Perhaps the most precise one can get about the proper relationship between domestic law and the CISG is the verbal formulation used by several courts: "Caselaw interpreting analogous provisions of Article 2 of the Uniform Commercial Code (UCC) [domestic law] may

---

[62] See, e.g., CISG Advisory Council Opinion No. 2, ¶¶ 5.1–5.15, available at www.cisg.law.pace .edu/cisg/CISG-AC-op2.html; Court of Appeals Düsseldorf (Germany), 8 January 1993, available at http://cisgw3.law.pace.edu/cases/930108g1.html; Ingeborg Schwenzer, *The Application of the CISG in Light of National Law*, 10 Internationales Handelsrecht 45, 50 (April 2010).

[63] 408 F.3d 894 (7th Cir. 2005).

[64] See, e.g., Franco Ferrari, *Applying the CISG in a Truly Uniform Manner: Tribunale di Vigevano (Italy)*, 12 Unif. L. Rev. 203 (2000).

[65] See High Court of New Zealand (New Zealand) (*RJ & AM Smallmon v. Transport Sales Limited and Grant Alan Miller*), 30 July 2010, available at http://cisgw3.law.pace.edu/cases/ 100730n6.html. See also Multi-Member Court of First Instance of Athens (Greece), 2009, available at http://cisgw3.law.pace.edu/cases/094505gr.html.

also inform a court where the language of the relevant CISG provisions tracks that of the UCC [domestic law]. However, UCC [domestic] case law 'is not *per se* applicable.'"[66]

Unfortunately, once courts find analogies to domestic law, they sometimes turn those analogies into authoritative statements of what the CISG means. The court in *Raw Materials Inc. v. Manfred Forberich GmbH & Co.*[67] purported to employ UCC § 2–615 on excuse as a "guide" to interpret the corresponding exemption provisions of CISG Article 79. The court was careful to note that the UCC could "inform" a court's analysis of the latter.[68] But the court's subsequent analysis used § 2–615 as a template for the CISG, and applied the tripartite test of that provision as if it was embedded in Article 79.

The ability to use foreign decisions as authority and thus generate uniform interpretation is, of course, conditional on the accessibility of opinions from multiple jurisdictions. To date, the most substantial source of opinions in English has been the website maintained by Pace Law School at http://cisgw3.law.pace.edu/#treaty. For many years, that website has collected CISG decisions from around the world. It also has arranged to have a substantial number of decisions in other languages translated into English. The quality of those translations varies substantially. In addition, the number of new translations has declined in recent years. Throughout this text, we use the Pace website as the primary reference for non-U.S. opinions. Universities and organizations in other jurisdictions maintain CISG websites, but the cases collected on those websites typically are only those from the particular jurisdiction and in the original language. A list of websites can be found through www.cisg.law.pace.edu/network.html. UNCITRAL maintains a database, CLOUT, that collects abstracts of CISG cases from around the world. It is available at www.uncitral.org/uncitral/en/case_law/abstracts.html and is searchable through www.uncitral.org/clout/showSearchDocument.do?lf=898&lng=en. The CLOUT abstracts, however, are just that – abstracts. They do not contain the full opinion of the court or arbitral tribunal and thus may omit some of the nuances and distinctions that determine the degree to which a holding is relevant to other cases. UNCITRAL also has published Digests of CISG opinions, most recently in 2012, and made them publicly available.[69]

Finally, practical politics likely impose some constraints on deference to foreign opinions and exacerbate the homeward trend. We are dubious that relatively high courts in many nations will make the effort to search for or concede much ground to what are viewed as lower courts in many other jurisdictions.

---

[66] See *Delchi Carrier SpA v. Rotorex Corp.*, 71 F.3d 1024, 1028 (2d Cir. 1995).

[67] 2004 U.S. Dist. LEXIS 12510 (N.D. Ill. July 6, 2004).

[68] Id. at *13 (quoting *Delchi Carrier SpA v. Rotorex*, 71 F.3d at 1028).

[69] See UNCITRAL Digest of Case Law on the United Nations Convention on Contracts for the International Sale of Goods, 2012 Edition, available at www.uncitral.org/pdf/english/clout/CISG-digest-2012-e.pdf.

V. GAP FILLING

While the CISG purports to regulate various aspects of international sales, and explicitly excludes others, some issues may fall between those two categories. The extent to which the CISG applies to the gap is dictated by Article 7(2). That provision requires that matters governed by the CISG that are not expressly settled in it are to be resolved in accordance with the "general principles" on which it is based. In the absence of such principles, questions are to be resolved in conformity with the law applicable by virtue of the rules of private international law. The reference to "private international law" in the latter clause means that choice of law rules will dictate which jurisdiction's law govern the situation. To the extent that general principles drawn from the CISG can be enlisted to fill gaps in explicit terms, there will presumably be less appeal to domestic law. The underlying general principles become relevant under Article 7(2) only once it is necessary to resolve an issue that is "governed" by the CISG but that is not "expressly settled" by it. There can be substantial debate about whether an issue falls within that range, depending on how narrowly or broadly one defines the issue. Take, for instance, the issue of how to treat the availability of an exemption from performance due to financial hardship. As we discuss in Chapter 8, there is a wide range of opinion on the issue. Does the fact that the CISG deals with "exemptions" mean the issue is governed by the CISG? Does the fact that the CISG does not explicitly provide for an exemption for economic hardship mean that resolution of the issue is not "expressly settled" by the CISG? Or does the failure to mention economic hardship negatively imply that the issue is "expressly settled" against allowing exemption for economic hardship? Similarly, at least one court has maintained that set-off rights are governed, though not settled, by the CISG and thus are subject to resolution through its general principles.[70] Multiple other cases, however, have excluded setoff from the matters governed by the CISG.[71]

Once the CISG is determined to govern an issue, but not expressly settle it, its resolution depends on the underlying principles. Commentators have proposed a variety of principles that they find embedded in the CISG. Professor Magnus finds twenty-six of them.[72] Nevertheless, one searches in vain for an explicit recitation of such principles within the CISG, with the possible exception of the requirement of good faith interpretation in Article 7(1). Indeed, as we discuss at length in Chapter 4, for some courts and commentators, the principle of good faith incorporated into Article 7(1) for purposes of interpreting the CISG does not exhaust the role of that

---

[70] See Court of Appeals Hamburg (Germany), 26 November 1999, available at http://cisgw3.law .pace.edu/cases/991126g1.html.

[71] See, e.g., Supreme Court (Switzerland), 7 July 2004, available at http://cisgw3.law.pace.edu/ cases/040707s1.html.

[72] See Ulrich Magnus, General Principles of UN-Sales Law, available at www.cisg.law.pace.edu/ cisg/biblio/magnus.html.

concept. Instead, many suggest that either Article 7(1), or Article 7(2), or both embody a general principle of good faith that imposes substantive responsibilities on the parties as well.[73] For instance, the principle of good faith may be used to require a party to provide copies of standard terms and conditions that it desires to incorporate into a contract, rather than to require the counterparty to request them.[74]

Courts and commentators have struggled mightily to discern the relevant general principles with which to fill gaps in the CISG.[75] They have seized on principles of "good faith," mitigation of harm, informality of requirements, estoppel, and cooperation.[76] Some of these "principles," however, are explicitly recited in Articles of the CISG, while others are derived from principles of law that the CISG does not purport to displace and therefore would apply even without the invocation of the CISG's underpinnings. Several writers and courts attempt to discern general principles from specific Articles in the CISG. For instance, Schwenzer and Hachem derive a principle that parties may not disclaim liability for their own intentional or grossly negligent conduct from provisions that preclude a party from relying on certain facts the falsity of which it knew, or of which it could not have been unaware.[77] They discern that principle from provisions such as Article 40, which prevents a seller from relying on late notice concerning nonconformities of which the seller was aware. Certainly a principle that a party cannot disclaim liability for intentional or grossly negligent conduct seems plausible, but one might wonder why Article 40 was necessary at all if the principle was ingrained in the CISG under Article 7(2). The fact that knowledge constitutes an effective estoppel against a claim of delayed notice does not readily transfer into that same knowledge serving as a bar to a contractual clause limiting the seller's liability. There may be alternative grounds on which to attack such a disclaimer, as we discuss in Chapter 6.

It might be asking too much to find within specific CISG Articles principles that are sufficiently generalizable to fill as many gaps as some commentators and courts suggest. Article 40, for instance, has been invoked to support propositions as broad as

---

[73] See Michael Bonell, *Interpretation of Convention*, in Bianca & Bonell, supra note 7; Phanesh Koneru, *The International Interpretation of the UN Convention on Contracts for the International Sale of Goods: An Approach Based on General Principles*, 6 Minn. J. Glob. Trade 105, 138 (1997).

[74] See Court of Appeals Celle (Germany), 24 July 2009, available at http://cisgw3.law.pace.edu/cases/090724g1.html.

[75] For an excellent summary and bibliography, see Franco Ferrari, *The CISG's Interpretative Goals, Its Interpretative Method and Its General Principles in Case Law (Part II)*, 13 Internationales Handelsrecht 181 (October 2013).

[76] Id. at 190–95.

[77] See Schwenzer & Hachem, supra note 5, at 473–74; accord John Felemegas, *The United Nations Convention on Contracts for the International Sale of Goods: Article 7 and Uniform Interpretation*, Review of the Convention on Contracts for the International Sale of Goods (CISG) 115, 288 (2000-2001).

"a principle of fair trading,"[78] and a more specific principle that a negligent buyer deserves more protection than a fraudulent seller.[79] Ferrari suggests that principles of estoppel can be derived from Articles 16(2) and 29(2).[80] A somewhat less creative United States District Court simply used Article 7(2) to infer from Article 46, which addresses substitute goods, a "general principle" concerning a seller's substitute performance.[81] Numerous commentators have inferred that "reasonableness" is an underlying general principle of the CISG, given its frequent invocation in specific Articles,[82] and courts have frequently, if not controversially, considered the reasonableness of a party's behavior, even without an explicit citation to Article 7(2).[83]

In the absence of even a general principle on which the CISG is based, matters governed by it, but not settled in it, are to be decided under the law applicable by virtue of the rules of private international law. Essentially that requires the forum to apply choice-of-law rules to determine which jurisdiction's law would govern the issue and then to apply that law. A Russian tribunal looked to Russian law to determine the enforceability of a penalty clause in a contract once it determined that the issue could not be resolved by reference to the general principles on which the CISG is based.[84] Domestic law, therefore, is viewed as a "last resort" for the resolution of issues that are within the domain of commercial sales, but not addressed directly or indirectly by the CISG.[85] In *Zapata Hermanos Sucesores, S.A. v. Hearthside Baking Co.*,[86] a federal appellate court in the United States concluded that the issue of awards for attorneys' fees was neither expressly settled in nor mentioned in the CISG, nor resolvable by reference to a general principle.

---

[78] See Stockholm Chamber of Commerce (Sweden), 5 June 1998, available at http://cisgw3.law .pace.edu/cases/980605s5.html.

[79] See Court of Appeals Köln (Germany), 21 May 1996, available at http://cisgw3.law.pace.edu/ cases/960521g1.html.

[80] See Ferrari, supra note 75, at 191; Urich Magnus, *The Remedy of Avoidance of Contract Under CISG—General Remarks and Special Cases*, 25 J. L. & Comm. 423, 429 (2006); accord Lookofsky, supra note 3, at 35, 35 n.182 (reporting similar reasoning in cases and commentary); Cf. Ferrari, *Scope of Application: Articles 4-5*, in Ferrari, Flechtner & Brand, supra note 43, at 108-09 (principle of estoppel is a general principle underlying the CISG); Ferrari, *Interpretation of the Convention and Gap-Filling: Article 7*, in id., at 163. Ferrari suggests that general principles include mitigation of damages and the binding effect of recognized usages, though these "principles" are explicitly incorporated into specific CISG provisions, Articles 77 and 9(2) respectively, and thus present no gap that needs to be filled by reference to Article 7(2). See id., at 166-67; Ferrari, supra note 76, at 192.

[81] See *Hilaturas Miel, S.L. v. Republic of Iraq*, 573 F. Supp. 2d 781 (S.D.N.Y. 2008).

[82] See, e.g., Joseph Lookofsky, *Walking the Article 7(2) Tightrope Between CISG and Domestic Law*, J. L. & Comm. 87, 89 (2006); Koneru, supra note 73, at 139.

[83] See, e.g., Court of Appeals Frankfurt (Germany), 31 March 1995, available at http://cisgw3.law .pace.edu/cases/950331g1.html.

[84] See Tribunal of International Commercial Arbitration at the Russian Chamber of Commerce and Industry (Russia), 11 April 2006, available at http://cisgw3.law.pace.edu/cases/060413r1.html.

[85] See American Arbitration Association, International Centre for Dispute Resolution (United States) (*Macromex Srl. v. Globex International Inc.*), 23 October 2007, available at http://cisgw3 .law.pace.edu/cases/071023a5.html.

[86] 313 F.3d 385 (7th Cir. 2002), *cert. denied* 540 U.S. 1068 (2003).

Thus, the issue was left to domestic law, and the American rule, which provides that each party bears its own legal costs, applied. Similarly, most tribunals that award interest under Article 78 note that the CISG does not stipulate an interest rate and no general principle specifies one. Thus, domestic law must be used to resolve the issue.[87] An Argentine court concluded that, while the CISG established liability for delivery of nonconforming goods, it did not establish a procedure, or even a general principle, for determining whether goods were conforming.[88] Thus, it applied domestic law concerning the proof of defects, which implicated the need for an expert opinion.

---

[87] See Bulgarian Chamber of Commerce and Industry Arbitration Case 33/98 (Bulgaria), 12 March 2001, available at http://cisgw3.law.pace.edu/cases/010312bu.html.

[88] See Court of Appeals (Argentina) (*Mayer Alejandro v. Onda Hofferle*), 24 April 2000, available at http://cisgw3.law.pace.edu/cases/000424a1.html.

2

The scope of the CISG

I. INTRODUCTION

The globalization of trade in goods creates a problem for parties to an international sales contract. Aspects of the contract potentially are subject to the law of more than one jurisdiction, and different applicable laws can give the parties different rights under the contract. Parties typically prefer to know in advance which jurisdiction's law governs. Although they might provide in their contract for the applicable law, doing so sometimes is not cost-effective. For one thing, the benefit of selecting law depends on the law that is applicable in the absence of a contractual choice. Selecting law also can involve costly negotiations. Even if cost-effective, the parties have no assurance that their choice of law will be honored should a dispute over the contract later arise. For all these reasons, contracting parties usually like to know the law applicable to the contract when the contract does not select it.

The conflict of laws rules adopted by most jurisdictions provide contracting parties only limited help. Because these rules are vague, contracting parties cannot predict with confidence the results of their application. This is true both of American and European conflicts rules, as well as the rules in force elsewhere. More important, conflicts rules are rules of the forum (whether judicial or arbitral) and therefore can vary among fora. The majority of United States jurisdictions adopt the rule of Section 188 of the Restatement (Second) of Conflict of Laws. Under that Section, the law applicable to a contract is the law of the jurisdiction that has the "most significant relationship" to the transaction and the parties. The contacts that the paragraph identifies as relevant to determine that relationship include the place of contracting, negotiation and performance, as well as the place of residence of the parties. These non-exhaustive contacts, which can identify different jurisdictions, make it difficult to predict in advance the law applicable to the issue. The conflicts rule of the Uniform Commercial Code ("UCC") is similarly vague. Section 1–301(b) makes the UCC as adopted by the forum state applicable to a transaction when it bears an "appropriate relation" to the forum state.

European conflicts rules are not much better. Under Article 4(1)(a) of the 2008 EU Regulation on the Law Applicable to Contractual Obligations,[1] the law of the seller's habitual residence governs contracts for the sale of goods. However, this rule applies unless it is "clear" that the contract is "manifestly more closely connected" with another country. In that case the law of that country governs the contract.[2] The closeness of a contract's "connections" to a country remains difficult to determine. As a result, the need to decide whether there exist sufficient connections with a jurisdiction other than the seller's leads to uncertainty.[3] For its part, Article 9 of the Inter-American Convention on the Law Applicable to International Contracts[4] selects as applicable the law of the country having "the closest ties" to the contract. This conflicts rule is as vague as the Restatement's rule. Finally, Article 21 (1) of the International Chamber of Commerce's International Arbitration Rules requires arbitral tribunals to select applicable law according to the conflict of laws rule it considers "appropriate."[5] All of the conflicts rules mentioned, in different ways, retain a measure of uncertainty in their application.

II. THE CISG'S APPLICATION UNDER ARTICLE 1(1)(a)

The CISG only partly avoids the uncertainty in applicable law created by conflicts rules. This is because it does not entirely displace them. Instead, the CISG limits the circumstances in which general conflicts rules operate. The CISG applies in either of two circumstances. First, according to Article 1(1)(a), the CISG applies to a contract for the sale of goods when the contracting parties have their places of business in different countries, each of which has ratified or acceded to the CISG ("Contracting States"). In this case Article 1(1)(a) displaces the forum's conflicts rules that would otherwise select applicable law. Article 1(1)(a) of course is itself a conflicts rule. The rule directs that the CISG governs the sales contract when the parties have their places of business in different Contracting States. Article 1(1)(a), not the

---

[1] Regulation (EC), No.593/2008 ("Rome I").   [2] Id. at Article 4(3).

[3] Recital 20 to the Regulation is of limited assistance in this regard: "In order to determine [the country manifestly more connected to the contract,] account should be taken, *inter alia*, of whether the contract in question has a very close relationship with another contract or contracts." Where the sales contract is independent of other contracts, as in an ordinary sales contract, the factor mentioned by the Recital cannot be taken into account to determine the place most closely connected to the contract. The exception to the "seller's habitual residence" rule inevitably leaves "a certain discretion" to the court, as Magnus delicately puts it; see Ulrich Magnus, *Article 4 Rome I Regulation: The Applicable Law in the Absence of Choice*, in Rome I Regulation 27, 49 (Stefan Leible ed., 2009).

[4] Available at www.oas.org/juridico/english/treaties/b-56.html.

[5] ICC Arbitration and ADR Rules, Article 17(1) (2012); cf. European Convention on International Commercial Arbitration, Article VII(1) (1961) (failing selection of applicable law by parties, arbitrators shall apply law under conflicts rules that they deem applicable).

forum's conflicts rule that applies to other contracts, selects applicable law when the contract is governed by the CISG. Second, under Article 1(1)(b), the CISG applies when the forum's conflicts rules ("principles of private international law") select the law of a Contracting State. Here, rather than displacing the forum's general conflicts rules, the CISG's application depends on their use.

To say that Article 1(1)(a) or 1(1)(b) applies means that the courts of a Contracting State must apply the CISG. It does not mean that arbitral tribunals in the Contracting State must apply the Convention. As a treaty, the CISG binds only Contracting States and their organs, including courts. Because arbitral tribunals are not courts, absent arbitral legislation they are not obligated to apply the CISG even when the transaction satisfies the criteria of Article 1(1)(a) or 1(1)(b). Thus, an arbitral tribunal in a Contracting State could conclude that different default rules govern the sales contract.[6] The tribunal properly could conclude that rules other than the CISG control. For example, assume that the contracting parties have their respective places of business in States A and B, which are both Contracting States. Assume also that, aside from the parties' places of business, all of the relevant connections with the sales contract are to State C, which is not a Contracting State. For instance, assume that the contract was negotiated and performed entirely in State C. Finally, assume that the parties' contract calls for arbitration in State A but is silent about the substantive law governing the contract. On these facts the CISG applies under Article 1(1)(a). Nonetheless, in an arbitration in State A the arbitrator might permissibly rely on a conflicts rule that selects State C's law, not the CISG, as governing the contract. This is because the conflicts rules of the seat of the arbitration (State A) do not generally bind the arbitrator.[7] As a result, the arbitrator might determine that State C's law is applicable or appropriate to the contract.[8]

A. *The requirement of internationality*

Article 1(1)(a) and Article 1(1)(b) share some requirements. First, each applies only if the transaction is a contract for the sale of goods. Second, the places of business of the contracting parties must be in different countries ("States"). We treat the issue of whether a transaction is a contract for the sale of goods later in this chapter. The requirement that the contracting parties have places of business in different States means that the sales contract must be international in character. Thus, if the parties' places of business are in the same State, the sale is domestic, not international, and

---

[6]   Cf. infra 2.II.C.

[7]   See Gary B. Born, 2 International Commercial Arbitration 2620 (2d ed. 2014); Ole Lando, *The Law Applicable to the Merits of the Dispute*, 2 Arb. Int'l. 104 (1986).

[8]   See, e.g., ICC Case No. 4237, X Y.B. Comm. Arb. 52 (1986); UNCITRAL Model Law on International Commercial Arbitration, Article 28(2) (where contract is silent about applicable law, arbitrator is to select the rule of law "applicable" to the contract); Nouveau code de procedure civile (N.C.P.C.), art. 1511 (Fr.) (in selecting law arbitral tribunal shall take trade usage into account)

the CISG does not apply under Article 1(1). Note that what matters is the location of the parties' place of business. The nationality of the contracting parties is irrelevant to Article 1's application, as Article 1(3) makes clear. The place of a party's incorporation is similarly irrelevant. Because the internationality of a sale is determined only by the places of business of the contracting parties, the international performance of the contract also is irrelevant to the CISG's application. For example, a sales contract between a United States–based seller and a France-based buyer is international for purposes of Article 1(1). This is because the parties have their places of business in different States. The sales contract is international in the required sense even if it calls for the United States seller to produce the goods in the United States and deliver them to the French buyer at a construction site in New York. On the other hand, a contract that requires a New York seller to ship goods to France for the benefit of a New Jersey buyer is not an international sale for purposes of the CISG.

1. Contracting parties and their places of business

For the CISG to apply under Article 1(1)(a), a third requirement also must be met: the parties' places of business must be in different Contracting States. In the preceding example, because the United States and France have both ratified the CISG, they are Contracting States and the requirement is met. If the contract were between a business in the United States and a business located in the United Kingdom, which is a non-Contracting State, the CISG would not apply under Article 1(1)(a), even though the contract involved was between parties located in different States, because the businesses were not in different Contracting States.

The CISG does not define the "parties" to the sales contract or contain rules for identifying them.[9] Usually this does not create a problem because the identity of the contracting parties is apparent from the contract or circumstantial evidence. Their places of business then must be determined. However, sometimes identifying the contracting parties is difficult. One sort of difficult case involves a sale through an intermediary. Assume that S, located in the United Kingdom, has I, located in Germany, arrange for a sale to Buyer, located in France. I and Buyer conclude the sales contract. If I is the party to the contract, the CISG applies under Article 1(1)(a). The United Kingdom is not a Contracting State. Thus, if the party to the contract is S, the CISG is inapplicable under Article 1(1)(a). Controlling rules of agency law, which fall outside of the CISG's scope, identify the contracting parties.[10]

---

[9] Article 4 provides that the CISG governs "only ... the rights and obligations of the seller and the buyer ..." Thus, the rights of remote purchasers or purported third-party beneficiaries are not governed by the CISG. See *Beth Schiffer Fine Photographic Arts, Inc. v. Colex Imaging*, 2012 U.S. Dist. LEXIS 36695 (D.N.J. March 19, 2012).

[10] See, e.g., District Court Vigevano (Italy), 12 July 2000, available at http://cisgw3.law.pace.edu/cases/000712i3.html; Court of Appeals Lugano (Switzerland), 12 February 1996, available at http://cisgw3.law.pace.edu/cases/960212s1.html; District Court Kassel (Germany), available at http://cisgw3.law.pace.edu/cases/950622g1.html.

For instance, if applicable agency law considers S to be an undisclosed principal and I its agent, S is the party to the contract.[11]

Another difficult type of case arises when several entities located in different States communicate with the buyer or seller before the contract is concluded. One of these entities subsequently executes the contract. As before, the CISG's applicability to the contract turns on which of the entities is a party to the sales contract. To determine the places of business of the contracting parties, the parties to the contract first must be determined. *McDowell Valley Vineyards, Inc. v. Sabaté USA Inc.*,[12] although arguably reaching the right result, reverses the order of analysis. There the California buyer purchased wine corks from three parties: one party located in California (Sabaté USA) and the other two parties located in France. In concluding that the CISG did not apply under Article 1(1)(a), the court found that the representations concerning the corks came from Sabaté USA. The sales invoice was under Sabaté USA's letterhead, advertising literature for the corks named Sabaté USA, and the corks were sent by the French firms to Sabaté USA for delivery to the buyer. Based on these representations, the court located the parties' place of business in California. Although the court's conclusion is reasonable, its reasoning misses a step. Article 1(1)(a) requires determining the place of business of the "parties" to the sales contract. Thus, the court needed to determine first the "parties" to the contract. Once the parties to the contract are identified, their places of business must be determined. The representations of Sabaté USA arguably made it the "party" to the sales contract with the California buyer. The French concerns were not parties to the contract. Because both Sabaté USA and the buyer's place of business were in the United States, the CISG was inapplicable under Article 1(1)(a).[13]

"Place of business" is a personal criterion. It ties the contracting party to a country for purposes of the CISG's application. The criterion of place of business makes irrelevant to the CISG's application facts that might otherwise appear important. Some examples illustrate the point. Assume that a French seller located in Paris is owned by citizens of the United States. A concern located in New York purchases goods from the seller. Under Article 1(1)(a), the CISG's application turns on the place of business of the French concern, not on the citizenship or location of those who own it. Assume that the seller, although located in Paris, is a Delaware

---

[11] See, e.g., Restatement (Third) of Agency § 2.06 (2006).

[12] 2004 U.S. Dist. LEXIS 15797 (N.D. Cal. November 2, 2004).

[13] Alternatively, the facts supported a finding that one of the three sellers (Sabaté USA) had its place of business in California. Because in multi-party sales contracts Article 1(1)(a) requires that the seller and buyer parties have their places of business in different Contracting States, the CISG is inapplicable under the Article. Cf. Zurich Chamber of Commerce (Switzerland), 31 May 1996, available at: http://cisg3.pace.law.edu/cases/960531s1.html. For an analysis of Article 1(1)(a)'s application focusing on the identity of the "party" to the sales contract, see *Visions Sys., Inc. v. EMC Corp.*, 2005 Mass. Super. LEXIS 67 (Mass Super. Ct. February 28, 2005); cf. *2P Commercial Agency v. Familant*, 2013 U.S. Dist. LEXIS 9186 at *8 (M.D. Fla. January 23, 2013) finding that supplier was seller does not preclude a finding that guarantor also was seller.

corporation. Again, Article 1(1)(a)'s application turns on the place of business of the contracting parties, not the place of their organization or incorporation. Finally, assume that the French seller is a wholly owned subsidiary of a New York corporation located in New York. Although the New York parent controls the French seller, the seller's place of business is in France. As long as the French seller is the party to the sales contract, its place of business determines Article 1(1)(a)'s application. The fact that the seller is controlled by a corporation located in New York is by itself irrelevant.

As with "party," the CISG does not define "place of business." In typical cases the undefined term causes no problems because its application is uncontroversial. Nonetheless, a party's place of business will sometimes be difficult to determine. For example, assume that a New York corporation is formed to sell widgets. As part of its business plan, the firm rents offices in an international trade exhibit in Germany. The first day the German office is open the firm makes a sale to a German firm. A short time later, after deciding that its business plan was a poor one, the firm closes the office, stops selling widgets and dissolves. If the seller's place of business is in Germany, the CISG does not apply to the sale under Article 1(1)(a). If the firm's place of business is in the United States, Article 1(1)(a) makes the CISG applicable.[14] Several courts have interpreted "place of business" to be a location that is permanent, stable, and at which sales decisions can be made independently.[15] The seller's German location is temporary and apparently not stable. Thus, it does not count as the seller's place of business, even if the seller's sales decision was made independently at that location. At the same time, although incorporated in New York, the seller might have a physical presence only at its German office. In this case, it is unclear where the "permanent, stable, and independent" test locates the seller's place of business. If the seller's place of business is not in Germany, where is it?

2. Multiple places of business

Other difficult cases occur when a contracting party has places of business in multiple countries. Article 10(a) provides that if a party has more than one place of business, the relevant place of business is that which has "the closest connection to the contract and its performance." In determining this place, regard must be had for circumstances known by the parties at the conclusion of the contract. Article 10 (a) applies only when the party is located at more than one place of business, for

---

[14] Assuming that Article 1(2)'s requirement of apparent internationality, discussed below, is satisfied.

[15] See, e.g., Court of Appeals Stuttgart (Germany), 28 February 2000, available at http://cisgw3 .law.pace.edu/cases000228g1.html; District Court Rimini (Italy), 26 November 2002, available at http://cisgw3.law.pace.edu/cases021126ie.html; cf. Paris Court of Appeals (France), 22 April 1992, available at http://cisgw3.law.pace.edu/cases920422f1.html (liaison office not a place of business).

purposes of the CISG. Thus, according to several courts, it applies only when the party has a permanent, stable, and independent presence in more than one country.[16] Branch offices or information centers that do not make independent sales decisions, for instance, do not count as places of business. Where the locations make independent decisions, they all are among the party's places of business.

Article 10(a)'s standard for selecting the place of business is vague. Even slightly complicated sales contracts can be negotiated, concluded, and call for performance in different countries. For example, assume that the seller has fully functioning offices that operate autonomously in States A, B, and C. Its negotiations with the buyer occur at each of these offices and involve personnel from the respective offices. Although the contract is eventually signed at the seller's office in State C, most of the negotiations occurred in the offices in States A and B. The buyer's place of business is in State A. Thus, if the seller is deemed to be located in State A, the CISG will not apply; but if the seller is located in State B or C, it applies. A simpler but still difficult variant is one in which the seller has fully autonomous offices in States A and C. The sales contract, which is negotiated and signed at the seller's office in State C, calls for delivery at the seller's office in State A. As before, the buyer's place of business is in State A. In both examples the buyer knows all of these facts at the time it concludes its contract with the seller.

The seller's place of business is difficult to determine in both examples. The first example is difficult under Article 10(a) because the Article gives no guidance concerning which of the seller's offices has the "closest relationship" to the conclusion of the contract. Article 10(a) selects the place of business as the place having the closest relationship to "the contract and its performance." Accordingly, the second example is difficult because the Article is silent about which of the seller's offices is the relevant "place of business" when the contract is concluded at one office (in State C) while performance is due at another office (in State A). The few cases that have interpreted Article 10(a) have found the place of business with the "closest relationship" to the contract to be the place of the business that made the relevant representations regarding the goods or from which communications that form the basis of the dispute were sent.[17] This does not help in the first example presented, where the seller might well have made representations in the course of negotiations in its different offices. But at least courts might make the effort to determine which jurisdiction has the relevant relationship. In *VLM Food Trading International, Inc. v. Illinois Trading Co.*,[18] the district court proceeded in a less flexible fashion.

---

[16] See, e.g., Court of Appeals Hamm (Germany), 2 April 2009, available at http://cisgw3.law
     .pace.edu/cases/090402g1; District Court Padova (Italy), 25 February 2004, available at
     http://cisgw3.law.pace.edu/cases/040225i3.html.
[17] See *Visions Systems, Inc.* v. *EMC Corp.*, 2005 Mass. Super. LEXIS 67 (Mass Super. Ct.
     February 28, 2005); *Asante Technologies Inc.* v. *PMC-Sierra, Inc.*, 164 F. Supp.2d 1142 (N.D.
     Cal. 2001).
[18] 2013 U.S. Dist. LEXIS 29791 (N.D. Ill. March 5, 2013).

A Canadian seller of commodities contended that the CISG applied because relevant communications and invoices were sent to an Illinois buyer from Montreal. The court, however, found it conclusive that the seller's license under the Perishable Agricultural Commodities Act that permitted it to enter into the disputed sales indicated that it had a business office in New Jersey. The appellate court, in reversing the district court, took a more flexible approach to the inquiry. Noting that most of the seller's business was conducted from Montreal and that its New Jersey office bore no relationship to the contract's performance, the court concluded that the seller's place of business "clearly" was in Canada.[19]

The diplomatic history of Article 10 is sparse. There is a suggestion that the information available to the parties at the time the contract is concluded determines the party's place of business.[20] However, the suggestion does not make Article 10(a)'s application any easier in the examples provided here, where the buyer knows that the seller maintains multiple places of business.

3. The limitation of apparent internationality

Article 1(2) limits the application of Article 1(1)'s requirement of internationality. Article 1(1)'s requirement is met when the parties have their places of business in different States. Their nationality or the commercial character of their sales contract does not affect the CISG's application, according to Article 1(3). However, Article 1 (2) makes the international character of the transaction inoperative ("is to be disregarded") when the fact that the parties have their places of business in different States is not apparent at or before the contract's conclusion. This fact is not apparent if it is not evident from the contract, the parties' dealings, or from information disclosed by the parties. If the internationality of the sales contract is not apparent, the CISG is inapplicable to it under Article 1.

By making the CISG inoperative, Article 1(2)'s limitation in effect makes domestic law applicable when the sales contract appears to the parties to involve a domestic transaction. Although the court in the *McDowell Valley Vineyards* case discussed earlier did not explicitly advert to the limitation, its reasoning is based on it. In finding that the defendants'-sellers' place of business was in California, the court relied on the circumstances known to or contemplated by the parties.[21] Because all

---

[19] See *VLM Food Trading International, Inc. v. Illinois Trading Co.*, 748 F.3d 780, 787 (7th Cir. 2014).

[20] See *Documentary History of the Uniform Law for International Sales* 409 (para. 7) (John O. Honnold ed., 1989) [hereinafter Documentary History].

[21] Article 1(2)'s limitation applies only where the parties' places of business in different States are not apparent at the contract's conclusion. The States do not have to be Contracting States. For a case in which the court applies Article 1(2)'s limitation even when it was apparent that a party's place of business was in a non-Contracting State, see *Impuls I.D. Int'l S.L. v. Psion-Teklogix Inc.*, 234 F. Supp. 2d 1267 (S.D. Fla. 2002) (Canadian defendant acquired by United Kingdom concern after contracting with plaintiffs; defendant's place of business in a Contracting State disregarded under Article 1(2)).

of the sellers' representations came from the California concern, the court located the sellers' places of business in California. The buyer apparently had no reason to know that the sellers had places of business in France.

The CISG does not expressly assign the burden of proving that the internationality of the contract was not apparent to the parties. Some cases and commentary maintain that the party relying on a provision has the burden of proving its application.[22] Accordingly, in their view the party claiming that a party's place of business was not apparent at the conclusion of the contract must prove this fact. Whether the CISG regulates burden of proof is controversial, and a respectable case can be made that it does not deal with the matter. Article 4 limits the CISG's scope to the rights and obligations of the parties "arising from" the sales contract. A burden of proof does not define an entitlement; it instead allocates the responsibility for proving it. Article 4 therefore excludes burden of proof assignments about the applicability of the CISG from the CISG's scope. Because the CISG's Article 1 (2)'s limitation of apparent internationality determines the CISG's application, not the rights and obligations arising under the CISG, the CISG does not allocate the burden of proving apparent internationality. In addition, in the single case where the CISG allocates burden of proof in Article 79(1), it does so expressly. A reasonable inference from the CISG's silence in other instances is that it leaves the matter to applicable domestic law. Burden of proof is discussed further in Chapters 6.XI and 9.I.A.4.

B. *Territorial limitations on Article 1(1)(a)'s scope: Article 93's reservation*

Article 93 entitles a Contracting State under prescribed conditions to make the CISG inapplicable to some of its territorial units. According to Article 93(1), a Contracting State consisting of more than one territorial unit may "declare that the CISG is to extend to all its territorial units or only to one or more of them ..." The declaration is available only to States whose territorial units enjoy a certain degree of independence from the State.[23] In addition, Article 93(1) allows a declaration only for States whose constitutions allow their territorial units to have different systems of law applicable to matters covered by the CISG. To have a different system of law, the territorial units must have the power to enact their own sales law. Article 93's purpose is to enable a Contracting State to become a party to the CISG even if it

---

[22] See, e.g., Federal Supreme Court (Germany), 9 January 2002, available at http://cisgw3.law .pace.edu/cases/020109g1.html; District Court Vigevano (Italy), 12 July 2000, CISG-Pace; Peter Huber & Alastair Mullis, The CISG 36 (2007); Franco Ferrari, *Burden of Proof Under the CISG*, Review of the Convention on Contracts for the International Sale of Goods (CISG) 1 (2000); for the opposing view, see ICC International Court of Arbitration, Case 6653, 26 March 1993, available at http://cisgw3.law.pace.edu/cases/936653i1.html; Warren Khoo, *Exclusions from the Convention*, in Commentary on the International Sales Law 34, 39 (Cesare M. Bianca & Michael J. Bonell eds., 1987) [hereinafter "Bianca & Bonell"].

[23] See Malcolm Evans, *Federal States*, in Bianca & Bonell, supra note 22, at 645–48 (para. 2.1).

lacks the power to make the CISG applicable in these territorial units.[24] States within the United States do not qualify as territorial units under Article 93, because exclusive federal treaty-making power enables the CISG to displace state sales law.

Article 93(1)'s phrasing is a bit misleading. By allowing a Contracting State to "declare" that the CISG is to extend to some or all of its territorial units, it suggests that the CISG extends to a territorial unit only if the Contracting State makes a declaration to this effect. However, Article 93(4) provides that if a Contracting State makes no declaration under subsection (1), the CISG extends to all of the State's territorial units. Given this default rule, the CISG applies to all territorial units within the State unless the State declares that it does not apply to one or more selected territorial units. Thus, to make the CISG inapplicable to a territorial unit, the State must make a declaration to this effect. Otherwise, the CISG applies to the territorial unit. To date Australia, Denmark, and New Zealand have made reservations under Article 93. Canada, which originally made the reservation, subsequently declared that the CISG applies to all of its provinces.

Article 93(2) requires the reserving State to deposit its reservation in writing.[25] (Article 89 requires deposit with the Secretary General of the United Nations.) The notice of declaration must state expressly the territorial units to which the CISG extends. Article 93(3) describes the effects of the declaration of the reservation. Essentially the subsection considers that a territorial unit to which the CISG does not extend is not a Contracting State, and a place of business in that territorial unit is a place of business in a non-Contracting State. Thus, the CISG does not apply under Article 1(1)(a) when one of the parties to the contract has a place of business in a territorial unit to which the CISG does not extend as a result of an Article 93 reservation (and the party does not have a place of business in a Contracting State with a closer connection to the contract or its performance). For example, assume that Contracting State S has two territorial units, A and B, both of which enjoy the political independence required by Article 93(1). Contracting State S makes a proper Article 93 declaration to the effect that the CISG does not extend to B. Finally, assume that Seller is located in A and Buyer in B. Because Seller's place of business is in a Contracting State and Buyer's place of business is in a non-Contracting State, the CISG is inapplicable to their sales contract under Article 1(1)(a). It applies to the contract under Article 1(1)(b) only if the forum's choice of law rules select the law of a Contracting State. Of course, the same result holds if Seller's place of business is in Contracting State X which has not made an Article 93 reservation. Given Contracting State S's Article 93 reservation, Buyer's place of business is in a non-Contracting State.

---

[24] See Rolf Herber, *Article 93*, in Commentary on the UN Convention on the International Sale of Goods (CISG) 694, 695 (Peter Schlechtriem ed., 2d ed. 1998); cf. Michael Bridge, The International Sale of Goods: Law and Practice 542 n.207 (2d ed. 2007) ("real utility" of Article 93 is to allow a federal State to adopt the CISG incrementally through each adoption by each of its territorial units).

[25] See Article 97(2).

Thus, as before, the CISG applies to their sales contract under Article 1(1)(b) only if the forum's choice of law rules select the law of territorial unit A.

The applicability of Article 93 has proven controversial in the cases of Hong Kong and Macao. Both of these areas constitute Special Administrative Regions of China. Hong Kong was returned to China by the United Kingdom in 1997, and Macao was returned by Portugal in 1999. Neither the United Kingdom nor Portugal was a Contracting State at the time of the respective returns. Thus, neither area was governed by the CISG at the time of its return to China. In 1997, China deposited with the Secretary-General of the United States a list of treaties to which China was a party and that China would consider applicable to Hong Kong.[26] The CISG was not included on the list. Subsequently, China submitted a diplomatic note with a similar list with respect to treaties that would apply to Macao. Again, the CISG was not on the list. Nevertheless, China did not jump through the explicit hoop of Article 93, which recites that a Contracting State may declare that its territories that have different systems of commercial law are subject to the CISG. Recall that the default rule of Article 93(4) provides that failure to make a declaration means that the CISG applies to all of a Contracting State's territorial units. So does China's failure to make an explicit declaration with respect to Hong Kong or Macao mean that they are subject to the CISG? Or is the negative implication from the list that China did deposit with the United Nations sufficient to exclude those territories?

Courts and commentators have divided on the question.[27] In a case involving a party with a place of business in Hong Kong, the French Supreme Court inferred that China's clear intent was to exclude that territory from the CISG's coverage.[28] The court relied on a note submitted by the French Minister of Foreign and European Affairs, "who questioned the Chinese authorities on this point." The court concluded that China's submission to the Secretary-General of a list of treaties that did not include the CISG constituted "a formality equivalent to what is provided for in Art. 93," and equivalence was sufficient to satisfy the requirement.

The first United States District Court opinion to address the issue disagreed with the French decision. In *CNA International Inc.* v. *Guangdon Kelon Electronical Holdings*,[29] a federal district court in Illinois concluded that, although China had

---

[26] See *Letter of Notification of Treaties Applicable to Hong Kong after July 1, 1997 (June 20, 1997)*, 36 I.L.M. 1675, 1676 (1997).

[27] For commentary on the issue, see, e.g., Fan Yang, *A Uniform Sales Law for the Mainland China, Hong Kong SAR, Macao SAR and Taiwan—The CISG*, 15 Vindabona J. Int'l Comm. L. & Arb. 345 (2011) (uncertainty prevails); Ulrich G. Schroeter, *The Status of Hong Kong and Macao Under the United Nations Convention on Contracts for the International Sale of Goods*, 16 Pace Int'l L. Rev. 307 (2004) (parties from Hong Kong and Macao have their places of business in a Contracting State).

[28] See Supreme Court (France) (*Societe L.* v. *CM Ltd.*), 2 April 2008, available at http://cisgw3 .law.pace.edu/cases/080402f1.html.

[29] 2008 U.S. Dist. LEXIS 113433 (N.D. Ill. September 3, 2008).

submitted a declaration to the Secretary-General, that document failed to satisfy the Article 93 requirement of expressly identifying the territorial units to which the CISG extends. Thus, the default rule of Article 93(4) applied, and the CISG was applicable to Hong Kong. The policy of removing barriers to international trade, which the court assumed would be affected by application of the CISG to Hong Kong, supported the court's interpretation. Another federal court in the same district subsequently affirmed that view.[30] A week later, a Georgia federal district court – apparently unaware of the Illinois district court decisions – sided with the French Supreme Court on the grounds that the evidence revealed that China did not intend to extend the CISG to Hong Kong.[31] An Australian court in an unpublished opinion also found that China's failure to make a declaration of notice under Article 93(2) makes the CISG inapplicable to Hong Kong.[32] Relying in part on the French Supreme Court's opinion, the court noted that "China has apparently not taken the necessary steps to have the CISG apply to Hong Kong."

The cases that find China has not made an effective declaration that the CISG is inapplicable to Hong Kong have the better argument. In order for a declaration to make the CISG inapplicable to selected territorial units under Article 93(1), the declaring State must give a notice of declaration that meets Article 93(2)'s requirements. Article 93(2) in turn requires the notice to state expressly the territorial units to which the CISG extends. The Article therefore does not allow a "formality equivalent" to the required notice of the sort allowed by the French supreme court, that is, one in which the CISG is not even mentioned. A declaration that does not refer to the CISG or to the territorial units to which the CISG extends is not an express statement required by Article 93(2). This requirement also makes irrelevant China's intent in failing to list the CISG among the treaties that extend to Hong Kong. China's intent, however clear, simply was not accompanied by a notice of declaration in accordance with Article 93(2).

Article 93(2)'s requirement that the notice of declaration expressly state the territorial units to which the CISG extends is a formality that has a lot going for it. An implicit declaration of the type approved in the French and *Innotex Precision* decisions prevents the CISG's extension to a territorial unit under Article 93(4) when the notice of declaration fails to expressly state units to which the CISG

---

[30] See *Electrocraft Arkansas, Inc.* v. *Electric Motors, Ltd.*, 2009 U.S. Dist. LEXIS 120183 (N.D. Ill. December 23, 2009).

[31] See *Innotex Precision Limited* v. *Horei, Inc.*, 679 F. Supp. 2d 1356, 1359 (N.D. Ga. 2009) ("no American court has addressed whether Hong Kong is a Contracting State").

[32] See Federal Court (Australia) (*Hannaford* v. *Australian Farmlink Pty Ltd.*), 24 October 2008, available at www.austlii.edu.au/au/cases/cth/FCA/2008/1591.html; cf. Hubei High People's Court (China) (*Wuhan Yinfeng Data Network Co. Ltd.*), 19 March 2003, available at http://cisgw3.law.pace.edu/cases/030319c1.html (". . . Hong Kong is a Special Administrative Zone of China with a different legal system. Hong Kong is not a Contracting State of CISG. Therefore, the CISG is not applicable."); Michael Bridge, *A Law for International Sales*, 37 Hong Kong L. J. 17, 18 (2007) (Hong Kong has not "joined the ranks of Contracting States").

applies. This diminishes the certainty provided by Article 93(2)'s notice requirement. The better inference is that a declaration under Article 93(1) must be express: It must refer to the CISG and select the territorial units to which the CISG extends. Even considered apart from Article 93(2), implicit declarations are suspect. Declarations of notice that do not even list the CISG send a noisy signal to contracting parties. They can have a difficult time knowing whether the CISG extends to select territorial units of the declaring State. To resolve doubt, parties will have to draft a governing law clause calling for the CISG[33] or a forum selection clause that assures the forum selected will apply the CISG. These measures needlessly increase transaction costs. For both reasons, we do not think that Article 93(1) allows for implicit declarations, and would conclude that China has not made a declaration under Article 93(1). Thus, under Article 93(4), the CISG extends to all of its territorial units, including Hong Kong and Macao.

C. *The CISG's application under Article 1(1)(b)*

Article 1(1)(a) makes clear that the CISG applies to contracts for the international sale of goods between parties located in different Contracting States. Under Article 1 (1)(b), the CISG also applies if the parties have their places of business in different States and the "rules of private international law" select the law of a Contracting State. "Rules of private international law" in this context mean the conflict of laws rules of the forum in which the dispute is heard. Where parties have included a governing law clause in their contract, most but not all conflicts rules give effect to the law chosen by the parties. The European Union Regulation governing the choice of law in contracts also makes applicable the law selected by the parties, as does the 1955 Hague Convention on the Law Applicable to the International Sale of Goods.[34] Finally, the conflicts rules of arbitral institutions give effect to the parties' choice of law.[35] The Restatement (Second) of Conflict of Laws, relied on by a number of American courts, is more restrictive. It applies the law of a jurisdiction chosen by the parties only if the law of the chosen jurisdiction has a substantial relationship to the parties or transaction, or the parties' choice has another reasonable basis.[36] Because the CISG is part of the law of Contracting States, it applies under Article 1(1)(b) when the parties' contract selects the law of a Contracting State and the forum's conflicts rules honor the parties' selection of law.

---

[33] Cf. Fan Yang, *CISG in China and Beyond*, 40 Unif. Comm. Code L. J. 373 (2008) (describing cases in which Chinese courts and arbitrators have applied the CISG based on express or implicit agreement). For the possibility of opting into the CISG, see infra 2.III.B.

[34] See Regulation (EC) on the Law Applicable to Contractual Obligations 593/2008, Art. 3(1); 1955 Hague Convention on Law Applicable to the International Sale of Goods, Art. 2.

[35] See, e.g., ICC Arbitration Rules § 21(1); cf. UNCITRAL Model Law on International Commercial Arbitration, Article 28(1).

[36] See, e.g., Restatement (Second) of Conflicts of Law (1969) § 187(1), (2)(a).

The CISG also applies under Article 1(1)(b) when the parties do not select the law of a Contracting State, if the forum's conflict of laws rules lead to the application of the law of a Contracting State. Where the parties have not included a governing law clause in their contract, the particular criteria identified by the forum's conflicts rules select the State whose law controls. The criteria vary depending on the conflicts rules used by the forum. Some conflicts rules use vague criteria to select law, as noted previously. Under Article 4(1)(a) of the European Union Regulation on applicable law, the law of the seller's habitual residence governs the sales contract. However, according to Article 4(3), the law of the country controls when it is "manifestly more connected" to the contract. For their part, American courts following the Restatement (Second) of Conflicts of Law must determine the State which, with respect to the specific issue, has the "most significant relationship" to the transaction and parties. To determine this, the courts must in turn take into account a non-exhaustive list of contacts provided by the Restatement.[37]

Bear in mind, however, that there are two questions that the forum must answer, and that Article 1(1)(b) is only implicated in the second of these. The first question that the forum must ask is what rules select the law governing the sales contract. For a judicial forum in a Contracting State, Article 1 of the CISG states the rules that it must apply to select that law. The court in a Contracting State, therefore, does not begin the analysis by resorting to the conflict of laws rules of the forum. The fact that the forum has adopted the CISG, including Article 1, means that the choice of law rules within it prevail over the jurisdiction's general conflicts principles. As a more limited set of conflicts rules that apply only to transactions governed by the CISG, Article 1 displaces within its scope more general conflicts rules that would otherwise apply.[38] Once the forum determines that Article 1(1)(b) applies, the second question it must ask is whether that Article requires the application of the CISG to the contract. To answer this question, the forum must rely on its general conflicts rules. Assume, for instance, that a case arises before a French court and that the case involves a party from France (a Contracting State) and a party from the United Kingdom (a non-Contracting State). Assume also that the only potentially applicable law is French law or the law of the United Kingdom. Because France is a Contracting State, Article 1(1)(b) obligates the French court to apply the substantive rules of the CISG if the court's conflicts rules select French law as governing the contract. Thus, the court, applying Article 1(1)(b), would have to determine whether its conflicts rules pointed to French law or to United Kingdom law. If the former, the substantive provisions of the CISG would apply. If the latter, the CISG would not. That is, if the French court determined that its conflicts rules pointed to United

---

[37] See id. § 188(2).
[38] See, e.g., District Court of Forli (Italy), 16 February 2012, available at www.globalsaleslaw.org/content/api/cisg/urteile/2336.pdf.

Kingdom law, then the forum would apply the substantive provisions of United Kingdom domestic law under Article 1(1)(b).

Article 1(1)(b) potentially will be most frequently at issue in international sales contracts containing arbitration clauses. This is because the pattern of litigation under the CISG to date suggests that a very significant number of sales contracts governed by the CISG contain arbitration clauses.[39] Statistics released by the International Chamber of Commerce indicate that in some years about a fifth of contracts arbitrated under its rules have not selected applicable law.[40] Because they are not judicial bodies, arbitral tribunals are not obligated to apply the rules of private international law binding on courts in the place of the arbitration. Instead, the UNCITRAL Model Law on International Commercial Arbitration and national legislation that adopt it direct arbitrators to apply the private international rules they consider "applicable."[41] The standard of "applicability" is unstated and obviously vague. Rather than avoiding conflicts rules to determine the CISG's application, Article 1(1)(b) relies on them.

D. *Article 95 reservation: a problem of interpretation*

Note from the preceding example concerning a contract between a party located in France and a party located in the United Kingdom that Article 1(1)(b) has an asymmetrical effect on the domestic law of the parties to a contract. If the case were brought in France and French law applied, the French courts would look to Article 1 (1)(b) of the CISG, which would tell them to apply the substantive provisions of the CISG, and thus to subordinate their domestic law to the international convention. If United Kingdom law applied, however, United Kingdom domestic law would not be subordinated to the CISG because the United Kingdom is not a Contracting State.

During the drafting of the CISG, this asymmetry posed a problem for some States. States that contemplated adoption of the CISG might have been willing to

---

[39] Cf. Loukas Mistelis, *CISG and Arbitration*, in CISG Methodology 375, 388 (Andre Janssen & Olaf Meyer eds., 2009) (speculating that more than 70 percent of cases relating to the CISG through 2009 have been arbitrations) [hereinafter "Janssen & Meyer"]; Andre Jansen & Matthias Spilker, *The Application of the CISG in the World of International Commercial Arbitration*, 77 Rabelszeitschrift 131, 133 (2013) (through 2012, 33 percent of cases have been arbitrations). Both studies rely on the Pace database, which does not contain all reported cases in which CISG is applied.

[40] About 14 percent of contracts arbitrated in 2008, 12 percent of the contracts arbitrated in 2009, and 1 percent of those arbitrated in 2010 had no applicable law clause. See ICC Annual Statistical Report, 22 ICC Int'l Ct. Arb. Bull. 5, 14 (2011).

[41] See UNCITRAL Model Law on International Commercial Arbitration, Article 28(2); Rev. Stat. Ontario I.9, Sch., Article 28(2); cf. UK Arbitration Act 1996 § 46(3) (absent party designation of law arbitral tribunal to designate law according to conflicts rules it finds "appropriate"); Swiss Code on Private International Law Article 187(1) (absent choice of law by parties, arbitral tribunal is to decide the case according to the law with which the case has the closest connection).

subordinate their domestic law to a uniform international convention when their resident businesses were dealing with businesses of other countries that had similarly agreed to subordinate their domestic law. But some States were unwilling to subordinate their domestic law to an international convention when their resident businesses were dealing with businesses in States that had refused to adopt the same international convention. They noted that, in such a situation, Article 1(1)(b) meant that disputes involving a business located in a Contracting State and a business located elsewhere would be settled by an international convention if the Contracting State's law applied, but by domestic law if the non-Contracting State's law applied. For some States, including the United States, this asymmetry was unacceptable. For other States, the vagueness of Article 1(1)(b) was more troublesome than the relatively clear and verifiable rule of Article 1(1)(a). Other States found the asymmetry less problematic. The compromise (and the CISG is full of compromises) was that Contracting States were allowed to ratify the CISG, subject to a reservation, permitted by Article 95, that they would not be bound by Article 1(1)(b). The United States position has been that a Contracting State that takes such a reservation declares that, under its law, the CISG applies only when the criteria of Article 1(1)(a) are satisfied, that is, when each of the parties to the contract has its relevant place of business in a Contracting State. The United States has taken such a reservation. The effect is that United States law does not include Article 1(1)(b), and the CISG does not apply when the conditions of Article 1(1)(b) alone are satisfied. In short, the United States has indicated that the CISG is inapplicable when there is a contract between a party that has a place of business in the United States and a party that has its place of business in a non-Contracting State, but the rules of private international law select United States law. To date, five other Contracting States have also made Article 95 reservations: China, the Czech Republic, Saint Vincent and the Grenadines, Singapore, and Slovakia.

Article 95's application is uncertain because its interpretation is unclear. The Article provides that a Contracting State may declare that "it will not be bound by subparagraph 1(b) of article 1 of the Convention." The State to which "it" refers is ambiguous. The pronoun might refer to the Contracting State in which the forum is located. In that case, a court in a State that has made an Article 95 reservation ("it") is not bound by Article 1(1)(b). Accordingly, the CISG does not apply even if the forum's conflict of laws rules make the law of a Contracting State applicable to the sales contract. The CISG applies only if Article 1(1)(a)'s criteria are met.

Alternatively, the pronoun "it" might refer to the Contracting State whose law is selected by the forum's conflict of laws rules. In that case Article 1(1)(b) is inapplicable only if the Contracting State whose law is selected has made an Article 95 reservation declaring that it will not be bound by Article 1(1)(b). Otherwise, the CISG applies under Article 1(1)(b). For ease of reference, call the view that interprets the Article 95 reservation to refer to the reservation by the forum State the "forum reservation view," and the view that interprets the Article 95 reservation to refer to the Contracting State's law selected by the forum's conflicts rules the "selected State reservation view."

The competing interpretations of Article 95 will give the same result when the forum State and the State whose law is selected by the forum's conflicts rules are Contracting States and (1) both have made an Article 95 reservation, or (2) neither has made one. For instance, assume that the seller's place of business is in the United States (an Article 95 reservation State) and the buyer's place of business is in the United Kingdom (a non-Contracting State). Assume also that the forum is a court in China, an Article 95 reservation State. Finally, assume that the forum's conflict of law rules select United States law as applicable to the sales contract. Because the United Kingdom is not a Contracting State, the CISG does not apply to the contract under Article 1(1)(a). It applies, if at all, only under Article 1(1)(b). However, both the United States and China have made Article 95 reservations. Thus, according to both the forum reservation view and selected State reservation view of Article 95, the CISG is inapplicable. The forum reservation view makes it inapplicable because China, as a reserving State, declares that it is not bound by Article 1(1)(b). The selected State reservation view also makes the CISG inapplicable, because United States law, which is selected by the forum's conflicts rules, has made an Article 95 reservation. As such the United States in effect has declared that Article 1(1)(b) is not part of its law. We recognize, however, that some commentators and courts disagree. They would say that when the Chinese forum looks to United States law, it applies the CISG without regard to the United States reservation, because the CISG is part of United States law.[42] The reservation, on this view, only binds United States courts.

In other cases, different results follow according to how Article 95 is interpreted. Consider two variants of the example just given: Cases 1 and 2. In Case 1, assume again that the dispute is between a United States seller and a United Kingdom buyer, and the forum is a French court. France is a Contracting State that has not made an Article 95 reservation. Assume that the French court's conflict of law rules lead to the application of the law of the United States. According to the forum reservation view, France is bound by Article 1(1)(b) because it has not made the Article 95 reservation, and the French court therefore must apply Article 1(1)(b). Since the United States is a Contracting State, the French court must apply the CISG. For the forum reservation view, it is irrelevant that the United States has made an Article 95 reservation declaring that it will not be bound by Article 1(1)(b). The result is different under the selected State reservation view. Because the French forum's conflicts rules have selected United States law and the United States has made an Article 95 reservation declaring that it will not be bound by Article 1(1)(b), the CISG is inapplicable under Article 1(1)(b).[43]

---

[42] See Franco Ferrari, Contracts for the International Sale of Goods: Applicability and Applications of the 1980 United Nations Sales Convention 88–9 (2012).

[43] The selected State reservation view would have the same result in Case 2 if the forum were a non-Contracting State. In that case the forum's conflicts rules, as before, lead to the application of the law of the United States. Part of United States law is the CISG, and the United States has

In Case 2, assume that the seller is located in France, the buyer is located in the United Kingdom, and the forum is a court in the United States. Assume also that the court finds the law of France applicable to the dispute. Recall that the United States has made an Article 95 reservation, so that the court does not make the choice of law determination under Article 1(1)(b). Instead, the court would make that determination under its general conflict of laws rules. Even though the court finds the law of France, a Contracting State, applicable, the forum reservation view makes the CISG inapplicable to the transaction. On the other hand, the selected State reservation view makes the CISG applicable under Article 1(1)(b). Because France has not made an Article 95 reservation, the American court remains bound by Article 1(1)(b) when its conflicts rules lead to the application of French law. The fact that the United States has made the reservation is irrelevant.

Although the forum reservation view is better supported by the CISG's language, the selected State reservation view seems truer to the sparse diplomatic history. When read together with Article 1(1)(b), Article 95's wording appears to refer to a reservation made by the forum State. Article 1(1)(b) makes the CISG applicable when the forum's conflict of laws rules lead to the application of the law of a "Contracting State." A Contracting State that has made an Article 95 reservation remains a Contracting State. Thus, Article 95 is plausibly understood not to obligate the forum to apply Article 1(1)(b) when its conflicts rules lead to the application of that State's law. This requires the forum State to make the Article 95 reservation. If the CISG's drafters wanted to make Article 1(1)(b) inapplicable when the State whose law is selected makes an Article 95 reservation, they knew how to do so. Article 92 allows a reservation opting out of Parts II or III of the CISG's provisions. It also states the effect of doing so: A State making the reservation is not considered a "Contracting State" with respect to issues governed by those Parts. The absence of a similar provision in Article 95 suggests that the reservation must be one made by the forum State. On the other hand, the diplomatic history supports the selected State reservation view. The delegates that lobbied for Article 95, skeptical about the vagueness of conflicts rules or jealous of their domestic jurisdiction, did not want conflicts rules to have any role in the CISG's applicability.[44] These delegates apparently could not convince others to eliminate Article 1(1)(b). The concession these delegates wanted would make the CISG inapplicable when conflicts rules led to the application of their law. The forum reservation view fails to give effect to their desires.

---

made an Article 95 reservation. The forum would give effect to the United States' reservation. Because the forum is a non-Contracting State, it has not made an Article 95 reservation and according to the forum reservation view will apply the CISG when the forum's conflicts rules select United States law.

[44] See Legal Analysis of the United Nations Convention on Contracts for the International Sale of Goods (1980), Message from the President of the United States, Treaty Doc. No. 9, 98th Cong., 1st Sess. at 21–22 (Appendix B) (1983); Peter Winship, *Private International Law and the U.N. Sales Convention*, 21 Cornell Int'l L. J. 487, 507–08 (1988).

European commentators were the first to notice the ambiguity in Article 95's interpretation.[45] The trend among commentary seems to favor the selected State reservation view.[46] The German government apparently is convinced of the superiority of the selected State reservation view too. Although Germany has not made an Article 95 reservation, it deposited with the United Nations the following statement of understanding:

> The Government of the Federal Republic of Germany holds the view that parties to the Convention that have made a declaration under Article 95 of the Convention are not considered Contracting States within the meaning of subparagraph (b) of Article 1 of the Convention. Accordingly, there is no obligation to apply—and the Federal Republic of Germany assumes no obligation to apply—this provision when the rules of private international law lead to the application of the law of a Party that has made a declaration to the effect that it will not be bound by subparagraph (b) of Article 1 of the Convention.[47]

Germany's understanding makes the selected State reservation view easy to apply. If the forum's conflicts rules lead to the application of the law of a Contracting State that has made an Article 95 reservation, that State is not considered a Contracting State for purposes of Article 1(1)(b). Thus, the CISG applies only if Article 1(1)(a)'s criterion is met. Although workable, Germany's understanding has the slight disadvantage that it is at odds with Article 1(1)(b)'s language. Germany considers Contracting States that have made an Article 95 reservation not to be Contracting States even though they are Contracting States under Article 1(1)(b). The German government's view about the proper interpretation of Article 95 is codified by statute and therefore binds German courts.[48] Its view, of course, is not authoritative for other national courts and may or may not persuade them.

American courts have not discussed the ambiguity in Article 95's interpretation. Nonetheless, they have applied Article 95 in a manner consistent with the forum reservation view. A representative case is *Prime Start Ltd.* v. *Maher Forest Products Ltd.*[49] There, a buyer with its place of business in the Virgin Islands sued sellers with places of business in Washington state in federal court. The Virgin Islands is not a

---

[45] See Franco Ferrari, *Specific Topics of the CISG in the Light of Judicial Application and Scholarly Writing*, 15 J. L. & Comm. 1, 45–48 (1995); Peter Schlechtriem, Ingeborg Schwenzer, & Pascal Hachem, *Article 95*, in Schlechtriem & Schwenzer; Commentary on the Convention on the International Sale of Goods (CISG), 1190, 1190–91 (Ingeborg Schwenzer ed., 3d ed. 2010) [hereinafter "Schlechtriem & Schwenzer"]; Peter Huber & Alastair Mullis, supra note 22, at 52–57.

[46] See Schlechtriem, Schwenzer, & Hachem, supra note 45. For American authority see John O. Honnold, Uniform Law for International Sales under the 1980 United Nations Convention 38 (Harry M. Flechtner ed., 4th ed. 2009) [hereinafter "Honnold/Flechtner"]. For a description of the selected State reservation view, see Franco Ferrari, *CISG and Private International Law*, in The 1980 Uniform Sales Law 31–32 (Franco Ferrari ed., 2003).

[47] UN Depository Notification C.N. 365.1989.

[48] See Bundesgesetzblatt II 586 (1989) (Article 2).   [49] 442 F. Supp.2d 1113 (W.D. Wash. 2006).

signatory to the CISG. Because the parties did not have places of business in different Contracting States, the CISG was inapplicable under Article 1(1)(a). The buyer nonetheless argued that the CISG was applicable under Article 1(1)(b), if the forum's conflicts rules selected the law of a Contracting State, such as Canada or Russia. The court rejected the argument, finding that the United States' reservation under Article 95 made the CISG applicable only under Article 1(1)(a): "the CISG cannot apply to the dispute, even if traditional choice-of-law analysis leads to the application of the law of the United States (or one of its states) or any other signatory state."[50] Canada and Russia are signatory States that have not made Article 95 reservations. Accordingly, under the court's reasoning, the CISG does not apply even though conflicts rules select their law, because the forum's Article 95 reservation eliminates the applicability of the CISG under Article 1(1)(b). Thus, the *Prime Start* court implicitly assumes that the forum reservation view of Article 95 is correct. Other American courts agree.[51]

III. OTHER SCOPE ISSUES

A. *What is a sale of goods?*

Article 1(1) makes explicit that the CISG extends to international contracts for the sale of goods. The CISG contains no definition of "sale." Nevertheless, other Articles imply a meaning. Article 30 requires the seller to deliver goods and transfer the property in the goods, and Article 53 requires the buyer to pay the price and take delivery. Thus, the concept of sale at least minimally appears to entail a transfer of title and possession for a price. Other Articles restrict the CISG's scope. Articles 2 and 3 delineate the transactions to which the CISG does not apply, and Articles 4 and 5 limit the issues addressed by the CISG arising from a sales contract to which the CISG does apply. Accordingly, a contract can be outside the CISG's scope because the transaction it governs is not a sale. The CISG also can be inapplicable because the subject matter of the sales transaction is not goods. In addition, it does not govern certain sale of goods contracts. Finally, specific issues arising from the sales contracts governed by the CISG can be outside of the CISG because the CISG does not address them.

Unlike many domestic laws, the CISG does not define "goods."[52] The obligations created by the CISG, however, provide some basis for inferring that "goods," as in the

---

[50] Id. at 1118.

[51] See *Princesse D'Isenbourg Et Cie Ltd.* v. *Kinder Caviar, Inc.*, 2011 U.S. Dist. LEXIS 17281 (E.D. Ky. February 22, 2011); *Impuls I.D. Int'l S.I.* v. *Psion-Teklogix Inc.*, 234 F. Supp.2d 1267 (S.D. Fla. 2002). For early European cases adopting the selected State reservation view, see District Court Hamburg (Germany), 26 September 1990, available at http://cisgw3.law.pace.edu/cases/ 900926g1.html; Court of Appeals Frankfurt (Germany), 13 June 1991, available at http://cisgw3 .law.pace.edu/cases/910613g1.html.

[52] See, e.g., U.C.C. § 2-105(1) ("goods" are movable things at time of identification to the contract); English Sale of Goods Act § 61 ("goods" includes all personal chattels).

case of the UCC, are restricted to movables. For instance, Articles 31 through 33 impose delivery obligations that imply movability. Perhaps they also imply that the goods be tangible, though (as we discuss later) the ability to "deliver" items such as software without any tangible manifestation of it creates some ambiguity. Article 2 (a)–(f) provides a list of items that appear to qualify as goods, but sale of which is not covered by the CISG. The items listed are a disparate lot. Some of the exclusions turn on the type of good sold. For instance, Article 2(a) excludes sales of consumer goods (at least unless the seller neither knew nor ought to have known that the goods were bought for any such use), and Article 2(e) excludes sales of ships, vessels, hovercraft, and aircraft. Transfers of ownership of vessels, hovercraft, and aircraft are subject to a variety of domestic statutes that could have impeded harmonization efforts. Other goods are excluded based on how they are sold. Article 2(b) excludes sales by auction, and Article 2(c) excludes execution sales or other sales by operation of law. Finally, Article 2 excludes some sales based on disagreement in domestic law about their character as goods. Semi-intangible assets might be in this category. Article 2(d) makes the CISG inapplicable to the sale of negotiable instruments or investment property such as stock, and Article 2(f) makes it inapplicable to the sale of electricity.[53]

Sales of consumer goods generally are not governed by the CISG. The exclusion reflects the diversity among national laws concerning the proper regulation of consumer sales. Article 2(a)'s exclusion employs a specific notion of a consumer sales transaction. Subsection (a) applies to "goods bought for personal, family or household use." Thus, the buyer's purpose in purchasing controls. Whether the good purchased is normally used for a consumption purpose is irrelevant to the transaction's character as a consumer sale.[54] So too is the use to which the buyer puts the good (except as an evidentiary matter bearing on purchasing purpose). For example, a household freezer bought for home use but later installed in the buyer's business remains a sale covered by Article 2(a). Because the subsection supposes that the buyer's purchase is either for a consumer or commercial purpose ("bought for personal, family or household use"), dual purposes in purchasing cause trouble. A buyer who purchases a car to use half the week at his home and the other half of the week at his business seemingly buys the car for both consumption and commercial purposes. Nothing in Article 2(a)'s language requires that the purpose in buying the good be solely a consumer purpose. While comparable domestic law definitions of consumer goods focus on the buyer's

---

[53] For disagreement over the character of electricity as a good under Article 2 of the Uniform Commercial Code, compare *Enron Power Marketing* v. *Nevada Power*, 55 UCC Rep. Serv.2d 51 (S.D.N.Y. 2004) (electricity a good) with *In re Samaritan Alliance, LLC*, 2008 Bankr. LEXIS 1830 (Bankr. E.D.Ky. June 20, 2008) (electricity not a good).

[54] Contrast Magnuson-Moss Warranty Act, 15 U.S.C. § 2301(1) ("consumer product" is one "normally used" for personal, family, or household purposes)

primary or predominant purpose in purchasing the good, Article 2(a) does not.[55] Article 2(a)'s unqualified language can make the characterization of some sales transactions difficult.

Article 2(a) contains a limitation that restricts the consumer goods transactions excluded from the CISG. The exclusion applies "unless the seller, at any time before or at the conclusion of the contract, neither knew nor ought to have known that the goods were bought for any such use." The limitation makes sense. Article 2 (a)'s limitation responds to a problem of asymmetric information sometimes present between sellers and buyers. In a consumer goods transaction the buyer knows the use to which it intends to put the goods while the seller is ignorant of the buyer's intended use. When the seller learns of the buyer's intended use, the asymmetry in information is eliminated and the parties can select the law or particular contract provisions appropriate for the transaction. The seller might learn of the buyer's intended use of the goods from the buyer herself. Alternatively, it might reasonably infer an intended use from the character of the goods or the purpose to which they usually are put. A buyer is very unlikely to purchase a jumbo jet for consumer purposes. The trouble cases are those in which the buyer purchases for consumer purposes a good that usually is put to commercial purposes or the buyer presents itself as acting in a commercial capacity, notwithstanding its intent to use the good for personal purposes. Here the information about intended use is asymmetrical and the seller is in a comparatively poor position to discover the buyer's intended use. By comparison, the buyer can eliminate the asymmetry by disclosing its intended use to the seller. For example, in a German case, the court concluded that a seller of an automobile was entitled to assume that the buyer was purchasing for a business purpose because "it was obvious" that the buyer was acting as a company, even though it intended to purchase the automobile for the private use of an employee.[56]

Article 2(a)'s limitation induces the consumer buyer who wishes to avoid application of the CISG to disclose his or her intended use to the seller, and thus to get the benefit of non-CISG consumer protections under domestic law, when the seller is in a comparatively poor position to discover this fact. If the good typically is not purchased for consumer purposes, the seller can be justifiably ignorant of the buyer's purpose to put them to a consumer use. Article 2(a) does not exclude the sales transaction from the CISG's scope in such a case unless the buyer discloses to the seller her consumer purpose in purchasing the goods. Of course, this assumes, rather heroically, that the consumer buyer is aware of the CISG's default application, and of the consumer's understanding that disclosure is necessary to avoid it. If the consumer discloses to the seller the information about his or her intended purpose

---

[55] See, e.g., U.C.C. § 9-109(a)(23) ("consumer goods" are used or bought "primarily" for personal, family, or household purposes), (26) ("consumer transaction" a transaction in which the individual incurs an obligation "primarily" for personal, family, or household purposes).

[56] See Court of Appeals Stuttgart (Germany), 31 March 2008, available at http://cisgw3.law.pace .edu/cases/080331g1.html.

for the goods, the seller learns of the intended purpose and Article 2(a) makes the CISG inapplicable to the sales contract. At that point the parties can contract for the law they prefer to govern their transaction, where permitted by conflict of laws rules. Alternatively, once the CISG is rendered inapplicable, the applicable consumer protection law could control without further bargaining. As a result, Article 2(a)'s limitation in effect forces the buyer to disclose information the seller does not have in order to avoid making the CISG applicable to their contract. Sometimes nondisclosure benefits the buyer. In one case, a Danish owner of a yacht on which he stayed during the summer purchased a generator from a German seller to operate the yacht's cooling system.[57] The power ratings for the cooling system the buyer gave the seller required a commercial generator. In his suit against the seller, the buyer argued that the CISG applied to the sale. The buyer got the law he wanted applied to his lawsuit. The power ratings the buyer provided to the seller apparently gave it no reason to know that the buyer was using the generator for a consumer purpose. Article 2(a)'s limitation therefore did not operate to exclude the consumer sales transaction from the CISG's scope.

1. Bailment for services and Article 3(1)

Assume that the seller contracts with a buyer to manufacture goods for the buyer. Also assume that the seller can obtain some of the materials needed to manufacture the goods from the buyer. There are two ways that the seller can do so. One is for the seller to purchase the needed materials under a separate sales contract. Once purchased the seller owns all the materials needed to manufacture the final product for sale before it contracts to sell the product to the buyer. The other way to get needed materials is for the buyer to allow the seller to use them, along with materials the seller owns, to manufacture the product. In both arrangements the buyer supplies the seller with needed materials. However, in the first arrangement the seller purchases the materials from the buyer, so that it owns them at the time it agrees to manufacture the product it will sell to the buyer. In the second arrangement the sales contract requires the buyer to supply some of the materials it continues to own that are needed to produce the product for sale. The seller never owns the needed materials supplied by the buyer.

The second arrangement is a bailment for services. The buyer supplies materials it continues to own, allowing the seller to use them to produce a product the buyer will purchase. The seller is a bailee who has agreed to fashion the buyer's materials into a product it will make available to the buyer and the buyer is the bailor. Distinguishing the first arrangement (a sale) from the second arrangement (a bailment for services) requires determining whether the buyer retains ownership of the materials it supplies

---

[57] See District Court Düsseldorf (Germany), 11 October 1995, available at http://cisgw3.law.pace
.edu/cases/951011g1.html.

to the seller.[58] Article 4(b) does not deal with the effect of the sales contract on title ("property") in the goods sold. The CISG therefore does not use the buyer's retention of ownership in the materials it supplies to determine the character of the transaction. A bailment requires determining ownership of property, and Article 4 is clear that the CISG deals only with contractual rights and obligations. Instead, the CISG in effect considers some, but not all bailments for services to be a sale.

Article 3(1) provides that, even if goods are being sold, there is no sale within the CISG's scope if ("unless") the goods are to be manufactured by the seller and the buyer ("the party who orders the goods") supplies a substantial part of the materials needed to manufacture or produce them. The obvious problem is to determine when materials supplied constitute a "substantial part" of the materials needed to produce the good. The language of Article 3(1) helps somewhat. The proportionate value of the materials supplied by the buyer does not necessarily determine "substantiality." Article 3(1) speaks of a substantial part "of the materials," not "of the value." This has not prevented a tribunal from gauging the "substantiality" of the materials supplied by the buyer quantitatively, by their value.[59] At the same time, it is hard to see what other unit of measure can be used. Weight or volume are eccentric quantitative standards for measuring the substantial character of materials supplied by the buyer. Perhaps the proportionate value of materials supplied is the only plausible quantitative standard, whatever Article 3(1) says.

If value is the standard of "substantiality," what percentage of value makes materials that the buyer supplies a "substantial part" for purposes of Article 3(1)? A "substantial part" does not require a majority of the value of the finished product. One can reach this conclusion because Article 3(2) refers to a "preponderant part" of the obligations of the party providing the goods in the context of determining whether the CISG applies to a hybrid contract that involves both goods and services.[60] "Preponderant part" means "majority," according to ordinary understanding and courts interpreting the phrase.[61] By using different terms in different subsections of the same Article, the CISG's drafters likely intended "preponderant" to refer to a different quantitative measure than "substantial." Thus, a "substantial part" can refer to less than a majority but more than merely some of the parts.[62] Even

---

[58] See, e.g., *In re Sitkin Smelting & Refining, Inc.*, 648 F.2d 252 (5th Cir. 1981); *In re Medomak Canning Co.*, 588 F.2d 818 (1st Cir. 1988).

[59] See, e.g., Arbitration Court of Budapest (Hungary), 5 December 1995, available at http://cisgw3 .law.pace.edu/cases/951205h1.html (value of goods supplied to price of final product); accord CISG Advisory Council Opinion No. 4, Contracts for the Sale of Good to be Manufactured or Produced and Mixed Contracts (Article 3 CISG) ¶ 2.6 (2004), available at: www.cisg.law.pace .edu/cisg/CISG-AC-op4.html.

[60] See infra III.A.3.,4.

[61] See, e.g., District Court Forlì, (Italy), 16 February 2009, available at http://cisgw3.law.pace.edu/ cases/090216i3.html.

[62] Some courts and commentators disagree with our conclusion. Cases and case law give different percentages required for "substantiality," ranging from 15 percent to more than 50 percent; the differences are documented in http://cisgw3.law.pace.edu.cases95120h1.html (value of goods

using a quantitative standard of "substantiality," some decisions applying Article 3(1) seem questionable at best. A French court considered instructions and specifications concerning manufacture to be relevant to Article 3(1)'s application.[63] Article 3(1) excludes sales contracts requiring manufacture only when the buyer supplies a substantial part of the materials. Instructions or specifications are not materials. The court's application threatens to make the CISG's scope dependent on whether the buyer's order calls for specially manufactured goods. Indeed, Article 65 appears to exclude specifications from the criteria for goods. That Article allows the seller to provide specifications for goods where the buyer was obligated, but failed to do so. Article 65 would make little sense if the provision of specifications for the manufacture of goods counted against the classification of the contract as one for goods.

The qualitative aspect of substantiality is evident in a French decision, *Societe A.M.D. Electronique v. Rosenberger SIAM S.p.A.*[64] An Italian producer of electronic components ordered adapters from a French seller. The contract required the adapters to be produced according to the buyer's specification and checked in accordance with quality-control standards dictated by the buyer. The contract also prohibited the seller from making any use of the adapters other than selling them to the buyer. The court held that these restrictions placed the transaction within the Article 3(1) exclusion, although it did not define what percentage of the materials constituted a substantial part. The decision seems questionable at best, insofar as the buyer provided no raw materials or goods to the seller. Rather, the contractual restrictions only limited what the seller could do with its own goods. Those restrictions do not appear to affect the role of the seller as a manufacturer of goods, and thus the facts seem to fit the scenario of a sale that the CISG was intended to cover.

A Hungarian arbitral tribunal found that Article 3(1) did not take a contract for the sale of garbage containers and bins out of the CISG.[65] It reasoned that the value of the buyer's supplied materials was a small proportion of the price of the containers. Although the tribunal's conclusion might be correct, the tribunal relied on the wrong ratio. The price of containers reflects costs other than the costs of materials contributed by both the seller and buyer. Accordingly, the tribunal should have considered the value that the buyer's materials bore to the value of the seller's materials in the containers.

supplied to price of final product); accord CISG Advisory Council Opinion No. 4, Contracts for the Sale of Good to be Manufactured or Produced and Mixed Contracts (Article 3 CISG) ¶ 2.8 (2004), available at http://cisgw.law.pace.edu. CISG-AC-op4.html.

[63] See Court of Appeals Chambery (France), 25 May 1993, available at www.cisg.law.pace.edu/cases/930525fi.html. For contrary authority, see Commercial Court Zurich (Switzerland), 10 February 1999, available at http://cisgw3.law.pace.edu/cases/990210s1.html.

[64] Court of Appeals Chambery (France), 25 May 1993, available at http://cisgw3.law.pace.edu/cases/930525fi.html.

[65] See, e.g., Arbitration Court of Budapest (Hungary), 5 December 1995, available at http://cisgw3.law.pace.edu.cases95120h1.html

The standard of "substantiality" also illustrates the problem of translation that can undermine the objective of uniform application of the CISG. As discussed in Chapter 1, the CISG does not have a single canonical translation; instead, there are six equally authoritative language versions of its provisions. The French version of the relevant phrase in Article 3(1) is "une part essentielle," or an "essential" part of the materials necessary for manufacture or production of the goods. The phrase suggests a qualitative standard of "substantially." According to this standard, materials supplied are essential if they are necessary for manufacture or operation of the final product. The proportionate value of the materials does not determine their character as essential. A computer chip may be essential to the operation of the computer, even if it constitutes a small percentage of the computer's value. Thus, materials supplied by the buyer can be essential and therefore substantial parts even if they constitute a low proportion of the total materials, if they are also necessary to the performance of the good.[66]

Taken together, the difficulties in interpreting Article 3(1)'s exclusion are serious. Parties can avoid them by writing a more specific contract. At a minimum, parties do well to specify which language version of the CISG is applicable to their agreement. This avoids some of the uncertainty associated with the operative standard of "substantiality." A more significant way is to contract to avoid all of the uncertainties in Article 3(1). Article 6 of the CISG permits the parties to exclude the application of the CISG entirely or particular provisions, or to alter their effect. Accordingly, parties who are engaged in a transaction that involves the supply of materials by the buyer and who desire to clarify the application of the CISG to their transaction can exclude Article 3(1)'s application to their contract by appropriate drafting.

2. Information technology and "goods"

The application of the CISG to the sale of information technology, such as computer software, is unclear and controversial. The CISG governs contracts for the sale of goods that meet Article 1's criteria. Computer software and other information are stored in an electronic form. Thus, a software or internet transaction is not governed by the CISG if the transaction either is not a sale or does not involve goods. Even if the transaction in software is a sale of goods, the CISG does not apply under Article 3(2) when the services provided by the seller constitute a predominant part of its obligations. Accordingly, for the CISG to govern a software transaction, it must be a contract for the sale of goods in which the seller's service obligations do not predominate. Courts and commentators disagree about whether or when a software transaction satisfies these requirements.

---

[66] For cases that relies on a qualitative standard based on the French language version of the relevant language, see Court of Appeals Munich (Germany), 3 December 1999, available at http://cisgw3.law.pace.edu/cases/991203g1.html; Court of Appeals Grenoble (France), 21 October 1999, available at http://cisgw3.law.pace.edu/cases 991021f1.html.

The dispute matters because, if the software transaction is subject to the CISG, its default rules define many of the obligations of the parties in ways that might vary from the understanding of the parties. For instance, unless the contract provides otherwise, Article 30 requires the seller to deliver the goods and title to them to the buyer, and Article 31(c)'s residual provision requires the seller to make the goods available at its place of business. Article 35(2) defines several criteria of conformity that a seller must satisfy with respect to the goods. And Article 74 allows the aggrieved buyer to recover consequential damages resulting from the seller's breach. The rules may or may not be optimal for transactions in software or other information technology. As information, software has no physical form that can be delivered, and the purposes for which the software is used may be sufficiently unpredictable to make it inefficient for the seller to bear the risk of nonconformity. In addition, the use to which software is put might be so varied and dependent on the particular circumstances that the software provider cannot easily predict the consequences of a breach. Finally, software sellers might need to prevent the buyer from continuing to use software after any sort of breach. For these reasons, the CISG's default rules might be inappropriate for software transactions. This possibility does not mean that these transactions are not governed by the CISG. However, it does underline what is at stake: the application of the CISG's default rules to software transactions.

The sale of a patent, copyright, or trade secret does not implicate the CISG. These sales are governed by patent, copyright, and general contract law, respectively. No one thinks the CISG applies to their sale. The controversial cases involve the sale, license, or right to copy copyrighted works such as software. Some courts find that the CISG applies to the sale of software.[67] However, they have not been careful to identify the transactions to which it applies or the issues it governs.

To determine the CISG's application to software, three different sorts of software transactions need to be distinguished. (1) *Sale of a physical copy*. Here the seller sells a computer disc, thumb drive, or computer hardware in which copyrighted software is recorded. The device on which the software is delivered is a tangible asset. It is uncontroversially a "good," and the buyer becomes the owner of the device. If Article 1(1)'s other requirements are met, the CISG governs the sale of the disc, thumb drive, or hardware. Copyright law restricts the right of the buyer to use and transfer the software. According to its "first sale" doctrine in effect in some jurisdictions, the sale of the disc containing software eliminates the copyright owner's right

---

[67] See, e.g., District Court Arnhem (Netherlands), 28 June 2006, available at http://cisg3.pace.law
.edu.cases/060628n1.html; Supreme Court (Austria), 21 June 2005, available at http://cisg3.pace
.law.edu.cases/050621a3.html; Federal Supreme Court (Germany), 4 December 1996, available
at http://cisg3.pace.law.edu.cases/061204g1.html; Court of Appeals Munich (Germany), 8 February 1995, available at http://cisgw3.law.pace.edu/cases/950208g1.html; *American Mint LLC* v.
GOSoftware, Inc., 2006 U.S. Dist. LEXIS 1569 (M.D.Pa. January 6, 2006) (assuming that CISG
applies to a software sale if sales contract proven).

to distribute the copy of the software on the disc.[68] The buyer therefore can sell or otherwise dispose of the disc, thumb drive, or hardware purchased in which the software is embedded. The buyer and transferees, however, cannot copy the software. They can copy the software only if they also acquire the copyright to it.

The sale of hardware in which software is embedded is an example. In *American Mint LLC* v. *GOSoftware, Inc.*,[69] an American defendant shipped software for facilitating credit card billing to a German plaintiff. After the software was installed and produced billing errors, the plaintiff sued the defendant under the CISG. In finding that the German plaintiff failed to prove that it was a party to the sales contract with the defendant, the court assumed that the CISG applies to the sale of the software as well. It did not distinguish between the tangible medium in which the software was shipped and the software itself. Nor did it hold that the CISG applies generally to software sales. Importantly, the case did not involve a dispute concerning whether the sale transferred ownership of the software to the German plaintiff. Had that issue been in dispute, applicable copyright law would control, not the CISG. The case arguably stands for the narrow proposition that the CISG applies to a software sale when it is part of a sale of a tangible medium in which the software is recorded.[70]

(2) *Online transactions for software.* Increasingly, "virtual goods" such as software or video games are sold online over the internet. "Virtual goods" consist of electronic codes stored in a database. They are not embedded in physical objects and have no physical location, and are not delivered through a physical copy such as a disc or other tangible medium. For the CISG to govern an online sale of software, the transaction must be a sale of goods. Online software transactions typically are not sales and arguably do not involve goods. In the typical online transaction information is copied for a price. The software is not transferred in a manner that makes the purchaser the owner of the software or of any tangible asset.[71] Because the online transaction does not involve transfer of title, it is not a sale. Even if the online transaction is a sale of software, the software sold is not a good. The CISG does not define "good" (or "sale"). Nonetheless, its provisions clearly suggest that a "good" is a moveable tangible asset. Article 30, for instance, requires the seller to deliver the goods as required by the contract and the CISG. Article 67(1) passes risk of loss to the buyer when the seller hands the goods over to the carrier. Both Articles contemplate

---

[68] See 17 U.S.C. § 109(a) (2010).

[69] 2006 U.S. Dist. LEXIS 1569 (M.D. Pa. January 6, 2006).

[70] For cases to this effect, see Commercial Court Zürich (Switzerland), 17 February 2000, available at http://cisgw3.law.pace.edu/cases/000217s1.html; Federal Supreme Court (Germany), 4 December 1996, available at http://cisgw3.law.pace.edu/cases/961204g1.html. Lookofsky suggests that *American Mint* supports the broad proposition that the international sale of computer software should be governed by the CISG. See Joseph Lookofsky, Understanding the CISG 19 (4th (Worldwide) ed. 2008).

[71] See Hiroo Sono, The Applicability and Non-Applicability of the CISG to Software Transactions, available at http://cisg.law.pace.edu/cisg/biblio/sono6.html.

a physical asset that can be moved from one location to another.[72] A software program is information in an encoded form, and information is intangible. It cannot therefore be a good.[73]

To be sure, as an undefined term, "good" might be interpreted to apply to intangible assets such as software. However, there are strong reasons against the interpretation. Article 7(1) directs that the CISG be interpreted to take into account its international character and the need for uniformity in its application. And Article 7(2) provides that questions governed by the CISG but not expressly settled by it be settled in accord with its underlying principles or, when they do not apply, in accord with applicable domestic law. Neither subsection supports categorizing software as goods. Uniformity in the CISG's application is achieved when its provisions are interpreted in a consistent manner across national courts. The desire for uniformity alone does not favor deeming software to be "goods" or "not goods." More important, the domestic sales laws of almost all common law countries construe "goods" to refer to moveable physical objects – "corporeal movables," as civil law describes them.[74] They do not consider information by itself to be corporeal or moveable and therefore not "goods." Thus, even if domestic law definitions inform the CISG's notion of a good, software is not a good and software sales therefore are not governed by the CISG.

Courts have not squarely addressed whether the CISG governs online software sales, and commentators are divided on the question. Lookofsky and Diedrich both conclude that the CISG does not limit the category of goods to tangible assets.[75] In Green and Saidov's view, software is tangible and in moveable form when it is stored electronically.[76] Both positions make the CISG applicable to software sold online. Schlechtriem believes that the CISG should apply to online software sales, for

---

[72] Accord District Court Forli (Italy), 11 December 2008, available at http://cisgw3.law.pace.edu/cases/081211i3.html.; District Court Padova (Italy), 11 January 2005, available at http://cisgw3.law.pace.edu/cases/050111i3.html.

[73] Accord District Court Forli (Italy), 16 February 2009, available at http://cisgw3.law.pace.edu/cases/090216i3.html; District Court Padova (Italy), 25 February 2004, available at http://cisgw3.law.pace.edu/cases/040225i3.html; Court of Appeals Köln (Germany), 26 August 1994, available at http://cisgw3.law.pace.edu/cases/940826g1.html (only moveable things are "goods"). United States courts are divided on the issue; compare *Rottner* v. *AVG Technologies USA, Inc.*, 80 UCC Rep. Serv.2d 730, 737 (D. Mass. 2013) (software comparable to a sale of tangible good) with *Specht* v. *Netscape Commn'ns. Corp.*, 306 F.3d 17, 29 n.13 (2d Cir. 2002) (Article 2 of the UCC does not obviously apply to downloaded software).

[74] See, e.g., U.C.C. § 2-105(1); Sale of Goods Act § 61(b) (United Kingdom) ("goods" includes all personal property); cf. Principles of European Law on Sales Article 1:104(a) (2004). For the different position of some civil law countries, see Ingeborg Schwenzer, Pascal Hachem & Christopher Kee, Global Sales and Contract Law 106 (2011). Schwenzer et al. concede that the predominant understanding of the notion of a good in the CISG is that of the common law.

[75] See Lookofsky, supra note 70, at 19–20; Frank Dietrich, *The CISG and Computer Software Revisited*, 6 Vindobona J. Int'l Comm. L. & Arb. 6 (2000).

[76] See Sarah Green & Djakhongir Saidov, *Software as Goods*, J. Bus. L. 161, 165–66 (2007).

reasons of uniformity and ease of application.[77] We believe that the stronger case is against the CISG's application to online software sales. The notion of a "good" connotes a tangible and moveable asset; the CISG therefore does not have to limit the category of goods to such assets because the notion itself does so. Fakes and Mowbray separately agree with this conclusion.[78] The idea that software becomes tangible when stored in a tangible medium seems to us to confuse the medium in which computer information is stored and the information itself. Storing information in a tangible medium does not make the information tangible; it merely makes the information retrievable from that medium.

Finally, we do not find that uniformity and ease of application favor application of the CISG. As noted, uniformity in the CISG's interpretation merely requires consistency in application among national courts. By itself it is not an independent reason for extending the CISG's scope to include online software sales. Some of the CISG's default rules, such as rules concerning delivery and risk of loss, apply only to tangible assets. Even its default rules that could apply to intangible assets, such as rules creating warranties and supplying remedies for breach, might be inefficient when applied to online software sales. The comparative precaution-taking abilities of parties and features of software might justify different risk allocations than those allocated by the CISG's defaults. Even commentators who judge that the CISG applies to online software sales concede that its provisions must be modified when applied to them.[79] The concession acknowledges that some of the CISG's defaults are not optimal for online software sales.

(3) *License of software.* Software can be licensed, whether delivered by disc or made available online. A license gives a limited right of use for a term; it does not transfer title to the software to the licensee. The transaction therefore is not a sale. Because the "first sale" doctrine applies only when the copyright owner sells a copy of the copyrighted work, a license allows the licensor to limit the licensee's right to

---

[77] See Rolf Herber, *Article 2*, in Commentary on the UN Convention on the International Sale of Goods (CISG) 30 (Peter Schlechtriem & Ingeborg Schwenzer eds., 2d (English) ed. 2005). The third edition of the book simply asserts that the CISG applies to online software sales; see Ingeborg Schwenzer & Pascal Hachem, *Article 1*, in Schlechtriem & Schwenzer, supra note 45, at 35-36. See also Loukas Mistelis & Anjanette Raymond, *Article 3*, in UN Convention on Contracts for the International Sales of Goods (CISG): Commentary 60 (Stefan Kröll, Loukas Mistelis & Pilar Parelas Viscasillas eds., 2011) (recommending that the distinction between software and goods be "minimized" for purposes of the CISG's application) [hereinafter "Kröll et al."].

[78] See Jacqueline Mowbray, *The Application of the United Nations Convention on Contracts for the International Sale of Goods to E-Commerce Transactions: The Implications for Asia*, 7 Vindobona J. Int'l Comm. L. & Arb. 121 (2003); Arthur Fakes, *The Application of the United Nations Convention on Contracts for the International Sales of Goods to Computer Software and Database Transactions*, 3 Software L. J. 584 (1990).

[79] For a view that a license of software can fall within the CISG, see Lookofsky, supra note 70, at 20. See also Peter Schlechtriem & Petra Butler, International Sales Law: The UN Convention on the International Sale of Goods 30 (2009).

transfer even the licensed copy of software.[80] The CISG governs international sales of goods and therefore does not apply to licensing agreements.

Distinguishing a sale from a license is easy in most cases. A license clearly is created if the licensor expressly reserves title in the copyrighted software and grants a license to it, limits the licensee's use of the software during the term of the license, and requires the licensee to return the medium on which the software is stored at the end of the term.[81] At the other extreme, a sale clearly is indicated if title to the copy of the software is expressly transferred, no restrictions are placed on the transferee's use or transfer, and the transferee has no obligation to return the copy. A German case deciding that a contract for a market analysis is not governed by the CISG falls on the license side of the spectrum.[82] The contract apparently called for the analysis to be delivered in paper form. Although paper is a good, the court concluded that the contract's purpose was the market analysis; the tangible medium in which it was delivered was unimportant. Finding that the contract granted the right to use the ideas in the analysis, the court concluded that the contract was not for a sale of goods. The court's sensible conclusion relies on two different considerations. One is that the subject matter of the contract was intangible property (the marketing analysis), not a good. The other consideration is that the firm that produced the market analysis apparently licensed the use of the ideas in the analysis. The contract therefore did not involve a sale.

Harder cases are those that fall within the spectrum between a license and a sale. For instance, a transfer of a software copy might be labeled a license, expressly reserving title in the transferor. The "license" is perpetual and does not require the transferee to return the copy of the software or destroy it. Finally, the transfer requires the "licensee" to make a single lump-sum payment called a "licensing fee." The difficulty here is that the transaction has characteristics of both a license and a sale. The transferor's reservation of title indicates a license, not a sale, as does the label of the transaction. On the other hand, the perpetual term of the "license" gives the transferee all of the economic benefits and risks around the software copy's value. The "licensee" therefore owns the software copy in everything but name. Further, single payment is consistent with both a sale (price) and a license (licensing fee). Taken together, these characteristics could indicate either a sale or a license. Use restrictions also do not favor a license characterization, because the software copy can be sold subject to them as well. The difficulty in distinguishing between a license and a sale in some cases is general and not peculiar to transactions potentially governed by the CISG.

Some courts and commentators maintain that the CISG's application turns on whether the software is standard or made to suit the particular needs of the purchaser. The CISG governs a contract for the sale of standard software; it does not govern the

---

[80] See 17 U.S.C. § 109(d) (2010).
[81] See, e.g., *Vernor v. Autodisk, Inc.*, 621 F.3d 1102 (9th Cir. 2010).
[82] See Court of Appeals Köln (Germany), 26 August 1994, available at http://cisgw3.law.pace.edu/cases/940826g1.html.

sale of custom-made software.[83] The distinction by itself seems to us and others[84] irrelevant to the CISG's application. An international sale of a copy of software in a tangible medium is a sale of a good, whether the software is standard or custom-made. At the same time, the online international sale of software, whether standard or custom-made, is not a sale of a good. Article 1 makes the CISG applicable to the former sale and inapplicable to the latter sale. The character of the software as standard or custom-made is irrelevant to its application. On the other hand, the terms of a contract for the sale of custom-made software can take the sale outside of the CISG. In particular, the sale of the software might call for the seller to supply services too, such as writing, installing, and maintaining the software. Article 3(2) makes the CISG inapplicable to contracts in which the preponderant part of the seller's obligation consists in providing labor or other services. Thus, if the seller's labor or service obligations constitute the preponderant part of its obligations, the CISG does not govern the sale of custom-made software.[85] In this case the "services" aspect of the contract makes the contract essentially a services contract, not a sale of goods. This has nothing to do with the custom-made character of the software. The CISG is made inapplicable by Article 3(2) simply because the contract is predominantly one for services, not goods. Again, the custom-made character of the software is irrelevant.

3. Barter and other countertrade transactions

Barter involves the simultaneous exchange of goods without the use of currency or other recognized medium of exchange. Other forms of countertrade, such as buybacks and offsets, are contracts in which the exchange of goods occurs at different times. Common to these countertrade transactions is that the price is paid in goods, not currency. The CISG does not explicitly address the issue of whether a countertrade transaction, such as barter, is considered a "sale" subject to its provisions, and both case law and commentary are mixed on the issue, sometimes in cases decided within the same Contracting State. Ukrainian cases have denominated barter transactions as sales and thus applied the CISG.[86] A Russian arbitral tribunal applied

---

[83] See id.; Court of Appeals Köln (Germany), 16 October 1992, available at http://cisgw3.law.pace .edu/cases/921016g1.html; Trevor Cox, *Chaos Versus Uniformity — The Divergent Views of Software in the International Community*, 4 Vindobona J. Int'l Comm. L. & Arb. 3, 5 (2000) (documenting position).

[84] For criticism of the position, see CISG Advisory Council Opinion No. 4, Contracts for the Sale of Goods to be Manufactured or Produced and Mixed Contracts (Article 3 of CISG), available at http://cisg. law.pace.edu/cisg/CISG-AC-op4.html; Lookofsky, supra note 70, at 20.

[85] See Ferrari, supra note 42, at 126; Peter Schlechtriem, Uniform Sales Law — The Experience with Uniform Sales Law in the Federal Republic of Germany, available at http://cisgw3 .law.pace.edu/cisg/biblio.html.

[86] See Andrew J. Horowitz, *Revisiting Barter Under the CISG*, 29 J. L. & Comm. 99 (2010). See, e.g., Tribunal of International Commercial Arbitration, Ukrainian Chamber of Commerce & Trade (Ukraine), 15 April 2004, available at http://cisgw3.law.pace.edu/cases/040415u5.html; Ukraine Tribunal of International Commercial Arbitration, Ukrainian Chamber of Commerce and Trade, 10 October 2003, available at http://cisgw3.law.pace.edu/cases/031010u5.html.

the CISG to a barter transaction without any discussion of the issue.[87] Another Russian arbitration decision considered a barter transaction to comprise two contracts for the sale of goods – one in which the first party is the buyer and the other the seller, and one in which those roles are reversed.[88] A Chinese CIETAC tribunal also applied the CISG to a barter transaction.[89] Nevertheless, other Russian arbitration tribunals and courts have summarily concluded that barter transactions are excluded because they do not involve monetary payments.[90]

As for commentators, Enderlein and Maskow suggest that there are arguments that favor inclusion of barter transactions (though they don't articulate what those arguments are), but express concern that Article 53 requires the buyer to "pay the price for the goods," and that subsequent Articles imply monetary obligations, such as payment of interest. But Honnold and Flechtner observe, and we agree, that there is no definition of "price" that requires it to be paid in currency or money.[91]

Ferrari similarly contends that barter is excluded because it does not involve a payment of a "price."[92] Ferrari also notes that the pre-CISG efforts to draft uniform laws on international sales excluded barter transactions.[93] Of course, that argument cuts both ways. One might infer that the CISG was intended to follow prior conventions; alternatively, one might argue that the failure to continue the explicit exclusion is some evidence that barter transactions were intended to be included. Mistelis simply concludes that it is "widely accepted that barter … does not fall under the substantive sphere of application of the CISG."[94] Loewe is equally conclusory: "Exchange of goods against other goods is barter and not a sale. Exchange of goods against services in Roman law *do ut facias, facto ut des* is also

---

[87] See Tribunal of International Commercial Arbitration at the Russian Chamber of Commerce and Industry (Russia), 17 June 2004, available at http://cisgw3.law.pace.edu/cases/040617r1.html.

[88] See Russia Arbitration proceeding 407/1996 (Russia), 11 September 1998, available at http://cisgw3.law .pace.edu/cases/980911r1.html.

[89] CIETAC Arbitration proceeding (China), 13 June 1989, available at http://cisgw3.law.pace .edu/cases/890613c1.html.

[90] See, e.g., Russian Federation arbitration proceeding 91/2003, 9 March 2004, available at http://cisgw3.law.pace.edu/cases/040309r1.html; Federal Arbitration Court for the Moscow Region of the Russian Federation, Case No. KG-A40/3225-03, 26 May 2003, available at http://cisgw3.law.pace.edu/cases/030526r1.html. In two cases, the parties appear to have transformed a barter transaction into a monetary one, and the CISG was applied. Russian Federation arbitration proceeding 269/1997, 6 October 1998, available at http://cisgw3.law.pace.edu/ cases/981006r1.html; Russian Federation arbitration proceeding 225/2000, 22 March 2002, available at http://cisgw3.law.pace.edu/cases/020322r1.html.

[91] Ferrari also notes that the pre-CISG efforts to draft uniform laws on international sales were interpreted to exclude barter transactions. See Franco Ferrari, *Specific Topics of the CISG in the Light of Judicial Application and Scholarly Writing*, 15 J. L. & Comm. 1, 54 (1995).

[92] See Franco Ferrari, *The CISG's Sphere of Application: Articles 1–3 and 10*, in The Draft UNCITRAL Digest and Beyond 21, 63–64 (Franco Ferrari, Harry M. Flechtner & Ronald A. Brand eds., 2004).

[93] See id. at 54.   [94] Loukas Mistelis, *Article 1*, in Kröll et al, supra note 77, at 29.

considered as a barter or as a transaction sui generis, but in no event as a sale."[95] The Schlechtriem and Schwenzer treatise has changed position. The second English edition concluded that "[b]arter transactions are not covered by CISG."[96] The third English edition notes that, while prevailing opinion is against inclusion, "it is advocated here that barter contracts are not excluded from the CISG."[97] Some of the commentary is clearly influenced by domestic law, which should not be determinative given the admonition of international interpretation in Article 7(1). For instance, El-Saghir concludes that the CISG does not require that contracts under the CISG involve money, but notes that Egyptian commentators have reached the opposite conclusion based on Egyptian Civil and Commercial Code provisions that distinguish between sales and barter transactions.[98]

Some resistance to inclusion of barter transactions emanates from an early UNCITRAL report that suggest difficulties in applying some provisions of the CISG, especially those related to remedies, in barter situations. As an excellent student note demonstrates, the report is inconclusive on the issue of whether barter transactions are intended to be excluded, and arguably overstates the difficulties associated with the remedy provisions.[99]

Since neither textual nor historical arguments are determinative, one might ultimately consider whether it makes sense to include barter transactions. We conclude that it does. The objective of the CISG is to create a set of default rules for the allocation of contractual risks between commercial parties. While we do not necessarily agree with all the allocations implicit in the CISG, we see no reason to conclude that the allocation of risks that relate to issues with which the CISG is concerned – contract formation, performance, quality of goods, risk of loss, and remedies – should vary depending on whether the "price" is paid in currency or in some other form, such as goods. To the contrary, it appears odd to conclude that there is one optimal rule for determining who bears the risk of quality for goods when they are exchanged for currency and another when the same goods are exchanged for other goods. The CISG is not concerned with issues that might be unique to money in international transactions, such as exchange rates or currency exchange restrictions.

In fact, coverage of barter transactions might make even more sense in international transactions than in sales law that regulate purely domestic transactions. When goods are exchanged for "money," what is actually paid or received is frequently not the currency of the counterparty. A United States seller of goods

---

[95] Roland Loewe, *The Sphere of Application of the UN Sales Convention*, 10 Pace Int'l L. Rev. 79, 81 (1998).

[96] Rolf Herber, *Article 1*, in Commentary on the UN Convention on the International Sale of Goods (CISG) 22 (Peter Schlechtriem & Ingeborg Schwenzer eds., 2d (English) ed. 2005).

[97] Schwenzer & Hachem, supra note 23, at 33.

[98] See Hossam A. El-Saghir, *The Interpretation of the CISG in the Arab World*, in Janssen & Meyer, supra note 39, at 355.

[99] See Horowitz, supra note 86.

who is paid in euros must convert those euros into dollars in order to use them domestically. What the United States seller has received is essentially a commodity, since a euro is not currency within the seller's jurisdiction. But no one would doubt that the transaction continues to be covered by the CISG. To take the point further, assume that the American seller is a multinational corporation that desires to be paid in Australian dollars, even though the office most closely connected with the transaction for Article 10 purposes is in the United States and the buyer is located in France. The "price" is therefore paid in a medium that does not constitute "money" in either jurisdiction. Instead, the foreign money is essentially a commodity rather than a medium of exchange within either party's jurisdiction. It is unclear to us why that transaction should be covered by the CISG, but a different result would obtain if the "price" is paid in some other commodity, such as wheat.

Indeed, we suspect that numerous transactions that those who oppose inclusion of barter would include within the CISG are actually not concluded by an exchange for money. Assume that a purchasing agent for a party in Contracting State A purchases business related goods from seller in Contracting State B while visiting the seller's plant in Contracting State B. Assume that the purchasing agent gives the seller a negotiable instrument in return for the goods. A negotiable instrument is not itself money. Nevertheless, we would be surprised to discover that those who restrict the scope of the CISG to money transactions would exclude this transaction. They might respond, "but a negotiable instrument is convertible into money." Our response would be (a) "So what? If price means payable in money, then that excludes something that is not money, even if it is convertible into money," and (b) "If 'money' includes that which is convertible into money, then bartered goods qualify, as they can also be 'sold' for money."

Certainly there is no difficulty applying the CISG to the obligations of the parties to a barter transaction. If wheat is traded for chairs, the provider of each good assumes the rights and obligations of a seller with respect to what it is obligated to provide and assumes the rights and obligations of a buyer with respect to what it expects to receive. If the wheat is infested with insects before risk of loss passes, the provider of chairs has an action for breach. If the chairs are missing a leg, the provider of wheat has one.

Difficulties arise when one attempts to exclude barter transactions from the CISG. Assume for instance that the parties agree to sell an automobile for 100 bushels of wheat and $5,000, a transaction that is partial barter and partial payment. Assume further that the recipient of the automobile discovers that it does not conform to the contract description. If the CISG otherwise applies to the transaction, would it apply here? Ferrari suggests that in such a case the application of the CISG depends on whether "the price" (by which he means only money) to be paid is higher than the value of the goods to be traded.[100] Thus, on Ferrari's analysis,

---

[100] See Ferrari, supra note 91, at 64.

the CISG would apply only if the automobile is worth no more than the $5,000 payment, which leaves open the issue of why one party also transferred the wheat. We respectfully disagree with this proposed solution. Assuming that the parties intended to strike a single bargain (one automobile in exchange for the combination of 100 bushels and $5,000) and that there is no basis for invalidating the exchange, such as duress or unconscionability, there seems little basis for a tribunal or court to redefine the values intended by the parties or to assess which part of the total consideration was represented by goods and which was represented by the monetary consideration.

As another example, assume that a sales contract governed by the CISG calls for payment of the price in currency in the importing buyer's country. Later, the government of the buyer's country, concerned that it will not have enough exports to earn foreign currency, enacts legislation that requires exports to offset imports on a contract by contract basis. In response, the buyer and seller modify the price term of their contract to allow the buyer to pay in exported goods. The CISG controls the initial contract, and Article 29(1) allows the parties' agreement to modify the price term. Why is the modified contract excluded from the CISG just because it now calls for barter? Why should the change in the way the price is paid result in a change in governing law? The exclusion of the modified contract from the CISG's scope seems to us to be arbitrary and not compelled by the CISG's language or diplomatic history.

Finally, there are unfortunate occasions in which barter can become an effective "currency" of a country, typically when a government becomes so unstable that its residents are unwilling to trust its continuation and thus distrust the continuing value of the currency that the failing government issues. Residents under such circumstances traditionally use commodities other than government fiat money for transactions. If that situation were to materialize, would barter then become acceptable in international transactions with places of business located in that country, but not elsewhere? If the CISG could accommodate barter transactions in such a situation, why could it not do so in other situations?

Barter involving an exchange of services for goods presents a more difficult problem. Assume that an attorney from Contracting State A agrees to provide ten hours of legal services to a person in Contracting State B in return for a desk that the attorney intends to use in her office. Assume that the attorney finds that the desk is not as represented and that the "seller" of the desk believes that the attorney has missed an important filing deadline in the matter she was supposed to handle. Although we are confident that the CISG applies to the goods part of the transaction, we are unsure whether it also applies to services aspect of the deal. Two different positions can be taken and both seem to us defensible. One is that the CISG does not apply to services, except under Article 3(2) when the obligations of the seller of goods to provide labor or other services do not predominate. Article 3 (2)'s exception is inapplicable to the service part of the barter, because the attorney is supplying only services, not goods along with services. Thus, the disgruntled recipient of legal services would have to bring its claim under non-sales law. The opposing position is that the CISG applies to both the services and goods aspect of the barter. Article 53 requires the buyer to pay the "price" for the goods, and the "price" can include the provision of services. If the attorney's services are defective, she has not paid the price in full any more than partial payment in cash counts as payment in full in cash. Failure to pay the price is breach. Accordingly, the CISG gives the seller of the desk remedies against the attorney. True, the attorney's defective performance might be excused under particular circumstances, so that full payment might be excused. But her excuse is governed by Article 79, as is the failure to perform any obligation under the sales contract.

4. Service and hybrid contracts

The CISG applies only to contracts for the sale of goods. It therefore does not govern service contracts. This is obvious enough from Article 1's limitation. Contracts calling for the seller to supply both goods and services may or may not fall within the CISG's scope. Article 3(2) deals with these hybrid contracts. It makes clear that the CISG does not apply to contracts in which the "preponderant part of the obligations" of the seller consists in the supply of labor or other services. The seller's provision of services in manufacturing, packaging or arranging for carriage of the goods are not services to which Article 3(2) refers. Otherwise, its limitation would be superfluous.[101] Any supply of goods requires the seller to expend or arrange for some labor or other service in order to put them into the buyer's hands. The labor or other services to which Article 3(2) is labor or services called for by the contract.

The "preponderant part" exclusion of Article 3(2) causes additional difficulties. As we indicated in the earlier discussion concerning contracts for the supply of goods to be manufactured or produced, labor provided by the seller in the manufacturing process does not constitute the kind of services that would lead to the exclusion. Nevertheless, the sales contract may be attended by additional obligations on the part of the seller. Complicated goods manufactured for the buyer frequently require time-consuming installation and assembly, often at the buyer's place of business. Courts have been reluctant to define these services as amounting to a preponderant part of the seller's obligations.[102] Similarly, where the seller is obligated to provide

---

[101] See Court of Appeal Colmar (France), 26 February 2002, available at http://cisgw3.law.pace .edu/cases/080226f1.html. For agreement, see Court of Appeals Karlsruhe (Germany), 12 June 2008, available at http://cisgw3.law.pace.edu/cases/080612g1.html; Court of Appeals Paris (France), 14 June 2001, available at http://cisgw3.law.pace.edu/cases/010614f1.html.

[102] See, e.g., Court of Appeals Wein (Austria), 1 June 2004, available at http://cisgw3 .law.pace.edu/cases/040601a3.html; District Court Padova (Italy), 10 January 2006, available at http://cisgw3.law.pace.edu/cases/060110i3.html; Court of Appeals Zug (Switzerland), 19 December 2006, available at http://cisgw3.law.pace.edu/cases/061219s1.html. But see Court of Appeals Ghent (Belgium), 29 October 2003, available at http://cisgw3.law.pace.edu/cases/

training in the operation of the goods or to perform repairs, courts generally find that the agreement to provide services constitutes an ancillary obligation rather than one that amounts to a preponderant part of the seller's obligations.[103] Schwenzer, Hachem, and Kee note that some commentators conclude that a "turnkey contract" is not within the CISG's scope, but that it is generally held that the CISG governs them.[104] They ultimately determine that most turnkey contracts subordinate the sales of goods to services and thus the CISG is inapplicable. We agree that a nuanced approach is required.[105] Although there is nothing in Article 3(2) that makes the CISG inapplicable to all turnkey contracts, in most cases they will not fall within its scope. A turnkey contract obligates the contractor to design and build the project. The contractor's obligation typically makes it responsible for all work, materials, and services necessary to allow the counterparty to take over an operational facility. The design, labor, and services usually will be a preponderant part of the contractor's obligations, however "preponderance" is measured, making the CISG inapplicable to the contract under Article 3(2). In addition, turnkey contracts typically are drafted in detail and have their own governing law provisions, so that Article 3(2)'s exclusion is irrelevant.

The standard by which the "preponderant part" of the seller's obligations is measured is economic. The value of its labor and other service obligations is the "part" of the labor and other service obligations that is used in calculating "preponderance." According to most courts and commentators, "preponderant" means the majority in value.[106] Thus, under Article 3(2) the CISG is inapplicable if the value of the seller's labor and service obligations amounts to more than 50 percent of the value of all of its obligations under the contract.

At least one court, however, interprets the operative standard governing "preponderance" to include a qualitative factor. In *Sr.l. Orintix* v. *NV Favelta Ninove*,[107] a Belgian appellate court had to decide whether the CISG governed a hybrid contract

---

031029b1.html; Commercial Court Zürich (Switzerland), 9 July 2002, available at http://cisgw3 .law.pace.edu/cases/020709s1.html.

[103] See Court of Appeals Oldenburg (Germany), 20 December 2007, available at http://cisgw3.law .pace.edu/cases/071220g1.html; Civil Court Basil-Stadt (Switzerland), 8 November 2006, available at http://cisgw3.law.pace.edu/cases/061108s1.html; Court of Appeals Antwerp (Belgium), 3 January 2005, *Plessers* v. *BV Pannenclaer Vieesspecialiteiten*, available at http://cisgw3.law .pace.edu/cases/050103b1.html. But see Supreme Court (Italy) (*Jazbinsek GmbH* v. *Piberplast S.p.A.*), 6 June 2002, available at http://cisgw3.law.pace.edu/cases/020606i3.html.

[104] See Schwenzer, Hachem & Kee, supra note 74, at 120.

[105] See Ingeborg Schwenzer & Pascal Hachem, *Article 3*, in Schlechtriem & Schwenzer, supra note 45, at 72.

[106] See, e.g., District Court Zug (Switzerland)14 December 2009, available at http://cisgw3.law .pace.edu/cases/091214s1.html; District Court Forli (Italy), 16 February 2009, available at http://cisgw3.law.pace.edu/cases/090216i3.html; Tribunal of International Commercial Arbitration at the Russian Federation Chamber of Commerce 5/1997 (Russia), 22 January 1997, available at http://cisgw3.law.pace.edu/cases/980305rl.html.

[107] Court of Appeals Ghent (Belgium), 24 November 2004, available at http://cisgw3.law.pace.edu/ cases/041124b1.html.

for the sale of computer hardware and software. The sales contract required the seller to install the software and make sure that the hardware and software met a certain standard of performance. Although the court found that the price of the hardware was higher than the price of the software, it concluded that the higher price was not determinative. The parties' intentions apparently were relevant: "The will of the parties was that [Seller] would create a system for [Buyer] and make it operational ... so that the said goals would be reached." In making intentions relevant, the court effectively treats "preponderance" as a multi-factor standard, in which economic value is only one among other considerations. Although a multi-factor standard might be sensible, it has a cost.[108] Application of a standard of "preponderance" based only on economic value is relatively easy for parties to forecast in advance. By comparison, it is more difficult for parties and courts to apply a multi-factored standard, both because some factors will be difficult to gauge and combine, and because there is rarely a hierarchy that can be used when different factors point to conflicting conclusions.

5. Framework agreements: distribution and other contracts

Agreements sometimes set out the rules for future sales of goods without fixing the price or the quantity of goods that will be purchased. The rules can limit the territories and manner in which the goods are to be marketed or sold, grant exclusive rights to distribute purchased goods, or define the investments required by the parties. These "framework agreements" are varied and can include distribution, franchise, and joint venture agreements. Framework agreements by themselves are not sales contracts. While purchases made pursuant to them are contracts of sale and therefore governed by the CISG, framework agreements do not evince purchases of goods. They instead are agreements establishing the rules by which subsequent purchases will be made. Thus, the CISG does not govern the framework agreement.

It is easy to see why the CISG does not apply to framework agreements. Article 23 deems a contract to be concluded when the acceptance of the offer becomes effective. Article 14(1) in turn deems a proposal to be an offer when it inter alia fixes the quantity and price of the goods (although we will later contend that this requirement is a sufficient, but not necessary element of an offer).[109] The framework agreement does not by itself propose a quantity and price of goods for sale. Even if it does so, the offeree can agree to the terms of the framework agreement without accepting the offer with respect to quantity and price. For both reasons, the agreement is not by itself a contract for the sale of goods. To be sure, the "main"

---

[108] For endorsement of a multi-factor standard, see CISG Advisory Council Opinion No. 4, Contracts for the Sale of Goods to be Manufactured or Produced and Mixed Contracts (Article 3 CISG) ¶ 3.4 (2004), available at www.cisg.law.pace.edu/cisg/CISG-AC-opt.html; Mistelis & Raymond, *Article 3*, in Kröll et al., supra note 77, at 58–59.

[109] See Chapter 3.II.D.2.

contract can commit the offeree to purchase a specific quantity of goods at a set price in the future. In that case the main contract will be both a framework and a sales contract. However, the CISG only governs the latter contract.[110]

Most courts find that the CISG does not govern distribution or franchise agreements. They reason that these agreements organize distribution rather than transfer ownership to goods. *Amco Ukservice & Prompriladamco v. American Meter Co.*[111] is a representative case. There, a United States party created a joint venture with a Ukrainian enterprise to manufacture and distribute gas meters in the Ukraine. The United States party was to manufacture and assemble most of the components for the meters, and the Ukrainian party would assemble the remaining components provided by the United States party. When the United States party refused to ship orders, the Ukrainian enterprise sued for breach of contract. The court decided that the distribution agreement was a framework agreement to which the CISG did not apply. The absence of price and quantity terms was important to the court's characterization of the contract as a "framework" agreement. Rather than selling components to the Ukrainian party, the agreement provided a set of rules under which any future sales would occur. On similar facts, French and German courts have come to the same conclusion.[112]

Franchise agreements have been found to be outside the CISG's scope, for similar reasons.[113] The typical franchise agreement transfers know-how, a license to a trademark, and organizational protocol. It does not transfer to the franchisee any property or title in goods. As with a distribution agreement, the franchise agreement instead organizes the way in which the franchisee will sell goods.

A Swiss appellate court excluded framework agreements from the CISG's scope on a slightly narrower basis.[114] Reasoning that franchise and distribution agreements focus on distribution obligations and other "framework" commitments, the court found that labor or other services predominate. As a result, it concluded that under Article 3(2) the CISG does not apply to the agreements. Reliance on Article 3(2) will take most framework agreements outside the CISG, because the "services" component in them will predominate. However, the Article will not apply to some framework agreements. For instance, a business format franchise agreement might only

[110] See Supreme Court (France), 20 February 2007, available at http://cisgw3.law.pace.edu/cases/ 070220f1.html; *Amco Ukservice & Prompriladamco v. American Meter Co.*, 312 F. Supp.2d 681 (E.D.Pa. 2004); *Helen Kaminski PTY, Ltd. v. Marketing Australian Products*, 1997 U.S. Dist. LEXIS 10630 (S.D.N.Y. July 21, 1997) (dicta); Court of Appeals Luzern (Switzerland), 8 January 1997, available at http://cisgw3.law.pace.edu/cases/970108s1.html.

[111] 312 F. Supp.2d 681 (E.D.Pa. 2004); accord *Gruppo Essenziero Italiano, S.p.A. v. Aromi D'Italia, Inc.*, 2011 U.S. Dist. LEXIS 82217 (D. Md. July 27, 2011).

[112] See, e.g., Court of Appeals Munich (Germany), 21 January 1998, available at http://cisgw3.law .pace.edu/cases/980121g1.html; Supreme Court (France), 20 February 2007, available at http://cisgw3.law.pace.edu/cases/070220f1.html.

[113] See, e.g., Court of Appeals Luzern (Switzerland), 8 January 1997, available at http://cisgw3.law .pace.edu/cases/970108s1.html.

[114] See Court of Appeals Luzern (Switzerland), 8 January 1997, available at http://cisgw3.law.pace .edu/cases/970108s1.html.

require the franchisor to maintain the brand, protect its trademark, and provide know-how. The franchisor might be under no obligation to sell products to the franchisee. Because the franchisor does not supply goods, there is no "goods" aspect of the agreement over which its "services" aspect predominates. Or a distribution agreement could establish territories in which the supplier and distributor can distribute any of the supplier's products the distributor might order. The supplier is not obligated to provide a "service." Nonetheless, Article 3(2)'s inapplicability to either agreement is harmless here. These franchise and distribution agreements do not involve a sale of goods; they merely organize the way the franchisee is to do business. Thus, the CISG does not apply to either agreement in the first place.

Not all decisions exclude distributor agreements from the CISG. An ICC arbitral tribunal and the Italian Supreme Court have applied the CISG to distributor agreements.[115] The line between a framework agreement and discrete sales contracts concluded under it sometimes also is stretched. The French court of appeals in *Societé Romay, AG* v. *SARL Behr France*[116] arguably wrongly puts a distribution agreement on the "sales contract" side of the distinction. There the buyer and seller entered into a "collaboration agreement" for the supply of crankcases. The agreement fixed a minimum quantity of crankcases to be supplied. Relying on the agreement's minimum quantity requirement, the appellate court characterized the agreement as a sales contract rather than a distribution agreement. The court ignored the fact that the "collaboration agreement" did not obligate the purchase of the minimum quantity or fix the specific quantity to be ordered. As far as the stated facts go, the minimum quantity specified could refer to the minimum quantity available to the purchaser in the event the purchaser placed an order. To test the court's conclusion that the agreement was a "sales contract," consider a variant on the facts of the case. In the case the court concluded that the purchaser breached by ordering less than the minimum stipulated quantity of crankcases. But suppose the purchaser placed an order for more than the minimum quantity and the supplier refused to fill it. Apparently, according to the court's reasoning, the supplier would breach by not filling the entire order. After all, if the agreement committed the purchaser to order a minimum number of crankcases, it also committed the supplier to fill an order for more than the minimum number. If you are uneasy about this consequence, it might be because you do not interpret the "collaboration agreement" to commit either party to placing or filling any orders. The agreement might go on the "framework" side of the "framework/sales contract" divide.

Similarly, consignment contracts are not contracts for sale and fall outside of the CISG. The inference from the seller's obligation in Article 30 to "transfer the

---

[115] See ICC Arbitration Case No. 11849 (2003), available at http://cisgw3.law.pace.edu/cases/031849i1.html; Supreme Court (Italy), 14 December 1999, available at http://cisgw3.law.pace.edu/cases/991214i3.html.

[116] See Court of Appeals Colmar (France), 12 June 2001, available at http://cisgw3.law.pace.edu/cases/010612f1.html.

property in the goods" is that the recipient of the goods obtains title. In a consignment transaction, title does not pass. Rather, goods are delivered to a dealer who acts as an agent for the consignor in selling the goods to a third party. When the consignee makes a sale, title passes from the consignor to the buyer. The nature of the relationship between the consignor and consignee is closer to one of bailor and bailee than to one of seller and buyer.

In *Martini E Ricci Iamino S.p.A.* v. *Trinity Fruit Sale Co.*,[117] Trinity sold fruit that it received from the plaintiff, and remitted the proceeds of those sales, less a commission. The court concluded that these transactions constituted consignments and not sales between the plaintiff and the defendant. The court noted that one prior American case spoke of consignments as regulated by the CISG, but did not involve "true consignments." Another American case did apply the CISG to a true consignment, but the parties had agreed that the CISG applied so there was no analysis of whether the CISG regulated consignments where its applicability was contested. In effect, the court in *Martini E Ricci Iamino* treated the earlier case as one in which the parties had opted into the CISG. The court then concluded that the CISG's conception of "sale," which it derived from the UCC more than from provisions of the CISG itself, precluded its application to true consignments of the type involved in the case. The CISG's sole use of the term "consign," the court noted, is found in Article 32, which relates to the consignment of goods to a carrier for transport to the buyer. That "consignment" is not inconsistent with the need for a "sale" between the seller and buyer and thus is not intended to include true consignments within the general scope of the CISG. Although the court may have been involved in overkill by considering whether Article 2 of the UCC provides a basis for including consignments within the CISG,[118] such use of the UCC was harmless error, since the court ultimately concluded that those provisions did not imply that consignments fell within the CISG's scope.

B. *Opting out of and into the CISG*

1. Opting out

The CISG creates a series of default rules that govern the formation of contracts within its domain and the rights and obligations of the seller and buyer arising from

---

[117] 30 F. Supp.3d 954 (E.D. Cal. 2014).
[118] The court's understanding of Article 2 also is marred by its failure to take into account the 1999 amendments to U.C.C. § 2-326. These amendments removed § 2-326(3), which regulated consignments, and any reference to them in the section. Thus, as amended, § 2-326 no longer applies to consignments; see Comment 5 to § 2-326. California's non-uniform version of § 2-326 continues to apply to the consignment of the consignor's consumer goods; see Cal. Unif. Comm. Code § 2326(4) (2015). This limited regulation of consignments had no application in the case, because the consignment there involved non-consumer goods.

such a contract. Those default rules, however, are subject to variation by the parties. The parties may agree not only to vary from specific Articles of the CISG; they may also agree that the CISG should not apply to their transaction at all. Article 6 makes this clear. It provides that parties "may exclude the application of this Convention or . . . derogate from or vary the effect of any of its provisions." As a result, the ability to opt out of the CISG is not controversial. Indeed, studies reveal that a substantial number of transactions otherwise subject to the CISG contain opt-out clauses, although the percentage may decline as more case law and commentary make trading parties more aware of and comfortable with its provisions.[119] The broad right to opt out is seen as a manifestation of "party autonomy" that underlies the entire CISG. The only exception is that the parties may not derogate from Article 12, which preserves writing requirements where a party that has its place of business in a Contracting State that has made an Article 96 declaration.[120] Even a party that has its place of business in such a Contracting State, however, may opt out of the CISG entirely.

The issue of how to opt out is more controversial. Whether or not the parties have opted out of the CISG is a matter of their intent with respect to the governing law for their contract. Direct inquiries into intent, however, are difficult to make with accuracy. Courts, therefore, have used specific language used in the contract as a proxy for that inquiry. There are clear cases on what language will qualify as an agreement to opt out. A statement in a contract that both mentions the law to be applicable and that explicitly excludes the CISG will effectively avoid application of the latter. For instance, a clause that recites, "This contract shall be governed by the law of the State of New York, including the Uniform Commercial Code in effect in that state. The United Nations Convention on Contracts for the International Sale of Goods shall not apply to this contract." will be effective to make Article 2 of the UCC rather than the CISG the governing law of the contract.[121] Under United States cases, it is equally clear that the

---

[119] See, e.g., Ulrich G. Schroeter, To Exclude, To Ignore, or To Use? Empirical Evidence on Courts', Parties' and Counsels' Approach to the CISG (With Some Remarks on Professional Responsibility), available at http://papers.ssrn.com/sol3/papers.cfm?abstract_id=1981742; Lisa L. Spagnolo, *Green Eggs and Ham: The CISG, Path Dependence, and the Behavioral Economics of Lawyers' Choices of Law in International Sales Contracts'*, 6 J. Priv. Int'l L. 417 (2010). While the large number of opt-outs may indicate unfamiliarity, only those who are aware of the CISG in the first instance will have the capacity to opt out explicitly. It is possible that a substantial percentage of those who do not opt out are simply unaware of its existence, and thus are subsequently surprised to discover that its terms govern their contract. We are skeptical about the desirability of applying law in a manner that primarily affects the unwary. This issue should disappear as more trading parties and their attorneys gain knowledge of the CISG, but our experience with American lawyers indicates that we are far from that point.

[120] See Chapter 3.I.

[121] See *Microgem Corp. v. Homecast Co., Ltd.*, 2012 U.S. Dist. LEXIS 65166 (S.D.N.Y. April 27, 2012); *Asante Technologies, Inc. v. PMC-Sierra, Inc.*, 164 F. Supp. 2d 1142 (N.D. Cal. 2001). There also are clear cases in which a governing law clause will not be effective to opt out of the CISG. Consider a clause providing that "The rights and obligations of the parties under this contract shall be governed by the Uniform Commercial Code in effect in the State of

designation of the law of a particular state in a governing law clause, without more, will not qualify as an opt-out provision. Thus, a clause that simply states, "This contract shall be governed by the law of the State of New York" would require the court to apply the CISG if it otherwise applies.[122] The reason is that under the Supremacy Clause of the federal Constitution,[123] New York law necessarily includes federal law and the CISG is federal law. Some American courts have simply missed that point and have applied domestic law where the contract refers to the law of a particular state.[124] The court in *Roser Technologies, Inc.* v. *Carl Schreiber GmbH*[125] concluded that a governing law clause that excluded "application of laws on international sales of moveable objects and on international purchase contracts on moveable objects" was insufficient to opt out of the CISG because the Convention does not use the term "moveable objects." This goes too far in requiring a governing law clause to mimic the CISG's language. The CISG refers to "property in the goods," not "title in the goods,"[126] but no one would conclude that the Convention does not deal with property in the goods (which it does not) but does deal with title in the goods. The terms "property" and "title" are synonyms. If the parties expressly state that the CISG is not to apply, but do not indicate the governing law, that law will be selected by application of the private international law rules of the forum. Selection of the law of a non-Contracting State, however, will typically have the effect of excluding application of the CISG to a contract that would otherwise be subject to it.[127]

New York, not including the United Nations Convention on Contracts for the International Sale of Goods." The clause makes New York domestic law applicable and the CISG inapplicable only to the parties' rights and obligations under the contract. It leaves other aspects of the contract, such as its formation and interpretation, governed by the CISG.

[122] Id. at 1150. There may, however, be circumstances in which the parties will have used the quoted language with the intent to apply only the substantive contract law of the named jurisdiction, and not the CISG. Assume a transaction between a party from Contracting State A and Contracting State B. Assume further that neither the parties nor the transaction has any connection to New York, but the parties choose New York law as the governing law of the contract. Presumably they have done so because New York allows its courts to take jurisdiction over large-value cases where the parties have selected New York law, even though there are no other contacts with New York. See New York General Obligations Law § 5-1401(1). The choice of New York law in these circumstances can be interpreted to reflect an intent that New York substantive law, and not the CISG, apply. If the parties had wanted the CISG to apply, there would have been no need to select New York law, since the parties were each from a different Contracting State. One counterargument is that the parties have selected New York law only to fill the gaps in the CISG.

[123] See U.S. Const. Article VI, clause 2.

[124] For dubious opinions finding that selection of state law suffices to exclude the CISG, see *Am. Biophysics Corp.* v. *Dubois Marine Specialties*, 411 F. Supp. 2d 61, 64 (D.R.I. 2006) (excluding CISG where contract clause required construction and enforcement of contract clause "in accordance with the laws of the state of Rhode Island"); *Golden Valley Grape Juice & Wine, LLC v. Centrisys Corp.*, 2010 U.S. District LEXIS 11884 (E.D.Cal. January 22, 2010) (the CISG is inapplicable when the contract contains a choice of law clause).

[125] 2013 U.S. District LEXIS (W.D. Pa. September 10, 2013).   [126] See Articles 4(b), 30.

[127] See Court of Appeals Alicante (Spain), 16 November 2000, available at http://cisgw3.law.pace.edu/cases/001116s4.html.

Beyond the case of an explicit opt-out, however, there can be uncertainty about the parties' intentions. Although most courts require the opt-out to be affirmative or express,[128] some courts and commentators suggest that implied opt-out is possible if the parties so intended.[129] The difficulty lies in deciphering when that intention exists. As with all issues of intention under the CISG, the issue is to be determined under Article 8, which looks to the objective intent of the parties, unless one party was aware of the subjective intent harbored by the other party.[130] If the parties simply choose the law of a Contracting State and there is no evidence of a contrary intent, the CISG will be deemed to apply.[131] Thus, the CISG would apply to a contract between a party with its place of business in the United States and a party with its place of business in Ecuador, another Contracting State, where the governing law clause selects the law of Ecuador.[132] Where the contract refers to domestic law that conflicts with application of the CISG, courts are more willing to infer the intent to opt out.[133] A governing law clause that selects "the law of England" – a non-Contracting State – or "the Uniform Commercial Code in effect in the State of

---

[128] See, e.g., *Honey Holdings Ltd., I. v. Alfred L. Wolf, Inc.*, 2015 WL 337682 at *3 (S.D. Texas January 23, 2015) (selection of domestic law much show "clear intention to opt-out"); *Hanwha Corp. v. Cedar Petrochemicals, Inc.*, 760 F. Supp.2d 426, 430 (S.D.N.Y. 2011) ("The intent to opt out of the CISG must be set forth in the contract clearly and unequivocally"); *Easom Automation Systems v. Thyssenkrupp Fabco Corp.*, 64 UCC Rep. Serv.2d 106 (E.D.Mich. 2007) (courts have held that opt out must be express; citations omitted); cf. International Commercial Arbitration at the Ukraine Chamber of Commerce and Trade, 218y/2011 (Ukraine), 23 January 2012, CLOUT Abstract No. 1405 <http://cisgw3.law.pace.edu/cases/120123u5.html> (intention to exclude the CISG must be express and clear).
The implementing legislation of some Canadian provinces requires that the opt-out be express; see, e.g., Alberta, R.S.A. 200, Ch. I-6, sec. 2(3), Ontario, R.S.O., Ch. I.10, sec. 6 (Canada) (2015). Such legislation may amount to an impermissible reservation under the CISG, depending on whether Article 6 permits implicit derogations.

[129] See District Court Forli (Italy), 12 November 2012 (unpublished translation); District Court Zug (Switzerland), 27 November 2008, available at http://cisgw3.law.pace.edu/cases/081127s1.html; Court of Appeals Alicante (Spain), 16 November 2000, available at http://cisgw3.law.pace.edu/cases/001116s4.html. Many U.S. cases require express opt-out; see, e.g., *Hanwha Corp. v. Cedar Petrochemicals, Inc.*, 760 F. Supp.2d 426, 430 (S.D.N.Y. 2011); *Sky Cast, Inc. v. Global Direct Distributors, LLC*, 2008 U.S. Dist. LEXIS 21121 (E.D.Ky. March 18 2008); *Travelers Property Casualty Co. of America v. Saint-Gobain Technical Fabrics Canada, Ltd.*, 474 F. Supp.2d 1075, 1082 (D.Minn. 2007).

[130] See the discussion of Article 8 in Chapter 3.II.C.2.

[131] See Supreme Court (Austria), 2 April 2009, available at http://cisgw3.law.pace.edu/cases/090402a3.html;, Foreign Trade Court of Arbitration attached to the Serbian Chamber of Commerce (Serbia), 28 January 2009, available at http://cisgw3.law.pace.edu/cases/090128sb .html; Court of Appeals Koblenz (Germany), 17 September 1993, available at http://cisgw3.law .pace.edu/cases/930917g1.html; Court of Appeals Köln (Germany), 22 February 1994, available at http://cisgw3.law.pace.edu/cases/940222g1.html; *Asante Technologies, Inc. v. PMC-Sierra, Inc.*, 164 F. Supp.2d 1142, 1150 (N.D. Cal. 2001).

[132] See *BP Oil International, Ltd. v. Empresa Estatal Petroleos de Ecuador*, 332 F.3d 333 (5th Cir. 2003).

[133] See Supreme Court (Austria), 2 April 2009, available at http://cisgw3.law.pace.edu/cases/090402a3.html.

New York" should have that effect.[134] Nevertheless, courts that are prone to apply the CISG may construe such clauses narrowly and apply the CISG where there is any gap between it and the selected domestic law. A contract that provided for application of the "body of laws binding for the inhabitants of the Federal Republic of Germany" was deemed not to exclude the CISG because it is part of German law.[135] Additionally, courts may discover a gap in the selected domestic law that allows application of the CISG. In one case, a warranty provision explicitly referenced the Austrian commercial code for transactions with "businessmen." The court concluded that the buyer was an "entrepreneur" for purposes of Austrian law, but not a "businessman" for purposes of the commercial code. Moreover, there had been no indications that the relevant warranty clause was to apply in the event of an international transaction, since the contract did not reference any domestic law to govern such a case. As a result, the court concluded, the reference to the Austrian law in the warranty provision did not imply the requisite intent to exclude the CISG in an international transaction that did not involve a "businessman."[136]

Courts may also find an implied intent to exclude the CISG in the dealings between the parties. A California appellate court found no error in the refusal of a trial court to instruct a jury on CISG principles where the governing law clause selected California law and was silent with respect to the CISG, but there was evidence (1) that the initial draft of the contract provided for application of the CISG, and (2) that provision was removed after one of the parties expressed objections to making the CISG applicable. Some courts may infer an intent to exclude the CISG from pleadings in the dispute that refer to domestic law rather than to the CISG.[137] The French Cour de Cassation (Supreme Court) concluded that parties to an international sales transaction who had referred in their pleadings and prior proceedings only to provisions of domestic French law could not subsequently invoke the CISG.[138] The failure to use the proper name of the CISG, however, will not nullify the parties' apparent attempt to exclude it.[139] An Australian court concluded that a governing law clause providing "Australian law applicable under exclusion of UNCITRAL law" evidenced intent to exclude the CISG in favor of

---

[134] See Court of Appeals Alicante (Spain), 16 November 2000, available at http://cisgw3.law.pace .edu/cases/001116s4.html.

[135] See Court of Appeals Ghent (Belgium), 20 October 1994, available at http://cisgw3.law.pace .edu/cases/041020b1.html.

[136] See Court of Appeals Linz (Austria), 23 January 2006, available at http://cisgw3.law.pace.edu/ cases/060123a3.html.

[137] See Supreme Court (Chile) (*Industrias Magromer Cueros y Pieles S.A. v. Sociedad Agrícola Sacor Ltda.*), 22 September 2008, available at http://cisgw3.law.pace.edu/cases/080922ch .html#5; Court of Appeals Alicante (Spain), 16 November 2000, available at http://cisgw3.law .pace.edu/cases/001116s4.html.

[138] See Supreme Court (France), 25 October 2005, available at http://cisgw3.law.pace.edu/cases/ 051025f1.html.

[139] See Foreign Trade Court of Arbitration attached to the Serbian Chamber of Commerce (Serbia), 17 August 2009, available at http://cisgw3.law.pace.edu/cases/090817sb.html.

domestic Australian law.[140] In *Food Team Intn'l, Ltd.* v. *Unilink, LLC*,[141] the court noted that the defendants' most recent reply made no reference to the CISG. It concluded that the CISG was excluded, perhaps implying that the defendants had abandoned any CISG claim they might otherwise have had.

In many situations, however, the failure to reference the CISG will not be the result of a deliberate choice of the parties, even inartfully expressed, to exclude it. Rather, the parties have ostensibly been ignorant of the CISG's application when drafting their contract or their pleadings in a subsequent dispute. Here there is some variance in judicial approaches, perhaps revealing different attitudes towards the desirability of applying the CISG or the court's own familiarity with it. Some jurisdictions take the position that exclusion of the CISG cannot occur through inadvertence. Courts have the ability to apply the appropriate law, regardless of the parties' failure to plead it, under the doctrine of *iura novit curio* or "the court knows the law."[142] An opinion from an Italian court reaches just that conclusion in holding that the parties, whose failure to mention the CISG in pleadings was presumed to be the result of ignorance of its provisions, "could not have excluded – even implicitly – the application of the CISG, by choosing to make an exclusive reference to the Italian law."[143] Tribunals that hold this position would not infer the inapplicability of the CISG simply because the parties' pleadings ignored it.[144]

In other cases, failure to plead the CISG will not bar its application if the pleadings essentially make claims cognizable under the CISG. In *U.S. Nonwovens Corp.* v. *Pack Line Corp.*,[145] the court noted that the plaintiff's complaint failed to mention the CISG. Nevertheless, the breach of contract and breach of warranty claims in the complaint all had analogues to the CISG. Thus, the defendant's contention that the complaint had to be dismissed for failure to state a cause of action had to be dismissed. Moreover, the court concluded that the complaint sufficiently alleged notice of lack of conformity to satisfy Article 39's notice requirement, even though that requirement was not referenced in the complaint. Another United States District Court also has taken a more relaxed view of pleading requirements. In *Citgo Petroleum Corp.* v. *Odfjell Seachem*,[146] the defendant claimed that the CISG pre-empted the plaintiff's state law contract claims, that

---

[140] See *Olivaylle Pty Ltd.* v. *Flotweg GmbH & Co KGAA*, (No 4) [2009] FCA 522 (Australia), 20 May 2009, available at www.austlii.edu.au/cgi-bin/sinodisp/au/cases/cth/FCA/2009/522 .html?query=^Olivaylle.

[141] 872 F. Supp. 2d 405 (E.D. Pa. 2012).

[142] See Lisa Spagnolo, *Jura Novit Curia and the CISG: Resolution of the Faux Procedural Black Hole*, available at www.cisg.law.pace.edu/cisg/biblio/spanogle1.pdf.

[143] See District Court Padova (Italy), February 25, 2004, available at http://cisgw3.law.pace.edu/ cases/040225i3.html.

[144] See District Court Bamberg (Germany), 23 October 2006, available at http://cisgw3.law.pace .edu/cases/061023g1.html.

[145] 4 N.Y.S.3d 868, 872 (Sup. Ct. Suffolk Cty. 2015).

[146] 2013 U.S. Dist. LEXIS 72898 (S.D. Tex. December 10, 2014); see also *U.S. Nonwovens Corp.* v. *Pack Line Corp.*, 4 N.Y.S.3d 868, 872 (Sup. Ct. Suffolk Cty. 2015).

the plaintiff had failed to plead the CISG, and that the plaintiff could not be allowed to plead the CISG now. The court responded:

> Neither party argues that either contract at issue excludes the CISG's application. The court does not believe that the fact that Citgo did not mention the CISG in its complaint is fatal to its claim, since it asserted a breach of contract claim and the CISG is merely the law that governs that claim. Thus, the court finds that the CISG applies, a fact that the parties do not appear to dispute, and that Citgo may pursue its breach of contract claim against YPF under the CISG even though it did not specifically invoke the CISG in its complaint.[147]

In other United States cases, however, courts have treated the failure to plead the CISG until late stages of litigation as a waiver of the CISG's application,[148] even though, as we noted, a common statement of American courts is that the CISG applies unless it has been expressly excluded in the contract. Courts that have entertained waiver claims have effectively grafted onto the requirement of "explicit" exclusion an exception where the parties have assumed at some point in the litigation proceedings that domestic law governs their contract, even though one of the parties subsequently recognizes the applicability of the CISG. In *Ho Myung Moolsan, Co. Ltd. v. Manitou Mineral Water, Inc.*,[149] a South Korean buyer of mineral water filed a breach of contract action against an American seller. In its initial complaint and in all pleadings through the discovery stage – including a motion for a preliminary injunction and an appeal from denial of that motion – the buyer had relied on New York law and asserted that its claims were brought "under state law." After the close of discovery and thereafter, however, the buyer maintained (correctly it appears) that the CISG governed the transaction.

The court concluded that the buyer "by its actions" had consented to the application of the New York Uniform Commercial Code and it was "far too late" to withdraw that consent without undue prejudice to the seller. The court relied on New York law that allowed parties in litigation to consent by their conduct to the law to be applied – even though that decision was erroneous under prevailing legal principles. The court further concluded that the "course of the case would not have changed" even if the CISG applied. The decision is consistent with other cases that have precluded parties from asserting CISG claims after the commencement of litigation, although those cases often concern efforts to raise the claims for the first

---

[147] *Citgo Petroleum*, 2013 U.S. Dist. LEXIS 723898 at *13-*14; accord *St. Tropez Inc. v. Ningbo Maywood Industry and Trade Co., Ltd.*, 2014 U.S. Dist. LEXIS 96840 (S.D.N.Y. June 16, 2014) (complaint pleads facts sufficient to make the CISG applicable when the CISG not invoked).

[148] See *Eldesouky v. Aziz*, 2015 U.S. Dist. LEXIS 45990 (S.D.N.Y. April 8, 2015); *Ho Myung Moolsan, Co. Ltd. v. Manitou Mineral Water, Inc.*, 2010 U.S. Dist. LEXIS 127869 (S.D.N.Y. December 2, 2010). See also *Food Team Int'l, Ltd. v. Unilink, LLC*, 872 F. Supp. 2d 405 (E.D. Pa. 2012); *GPL Treatment v. Louisiana-Pacific Corp.*, 894 P.2d 470, 477 n.4 (Or. Ct. App. 1995) (Leeson J., dissenting).

[149] 2010 U.S. Dist. LEXIS 127869 (S.D.N.Y. December 2, 2010).

time during the appellate process.[150] In *Rienzi & Sons, Inc. v. N. Puglisi & F. Industria Paste Alimentari S.p.A.*,[151] the court found that plaintiff had waived any claim that the CISG applied by relying on New York law in all pleadings and through the pre-trial conference. The court considered any effort to change the applicable law particularly inappropriate because the absence of a parol evidence rule or statute of frauds in the CISG could affect the outcome of the case. The court thus concluded that "[t]o change course now, after the defendants have relied on New York law through the close of discovery and up until opposition of the summary judgment motion, would be prejudicial to defendants. Defendants cannot be expected to alter course on the eve of trial because plaintiff now realizes that a different law is more favorable to its position. That is gamesmanship at its worst."[152]

As these cases indicate, the situation in which parties in their pleadings or at other later points in litigation rely on domestic law raises the question as to whether litigation positions render the CISG inapplicable when it otherwise would govern their contract. If the parties have initially agreed to displace the CISG, or modified their agreement to displace it, the result is clear: the CISG does not govern the contract being litigated.[153] But the answer is controversial where one or both parties in litigation, without agreement, declare that domestic law governs the contract. Some courts have determined that the CISG is inapplicable in the circumstances, based on facts that they find gives rise to waiver, estoppel, or an untimely reliance on the CISG.[154] CISG Advisory Council Opinion No. 16[155] condemns the result in these cases. It maintains that a court, as a matter of international treaty law, is obligated to apply the CISG when the CISG governs the sale contract being litigated, even if domestic law doctrines of waiver, estoppel, or untimeliness other-wise would operate to make the CISG inapplicable.[156] We disagree. Although the law of treaties requires Contracting States to abide by their treaty obligations,[157] the CISG's provisions do not necessarily displace judicial doctrines of a forum that are procedural in character. With a single exception, the CISG says nothing about procedural rules under which it is applied. The single exception is Article 79(1), which allocates the burden of proving the requirements for exemption. An

---

[150] See, e.g., 25 October 2005, Supreme Court (France), available at http://cisgw3.law.pace.edu/cases/051025f1.html.

[151] 2014 U.S. Dist. LEXIS 41478 (E.D.N.Y. March 27, 2014).   [152] Id. at *6.

[153] See Articles 6 and 29(1).

[154] See, e.g., *Attorney General of Botswana v. Aussie Diamond Products Pty. Ltd.* (Australia), 23 June 2010, available at http://cisgw3.law.pace.edu/cases/100623a2.html (waiver); *Rienzi & Sons v. Puglisi & F. Industria Paste*, 2013 U.S. Dist. LEXIS 70196 (E.D.N.Y. May 16, 2013); *Ho Myung Moolson Co. Ltd. v. Manitou Mineral Water, Inc.*, 2010 U.S. Dist. LEXIS 127869 (S.D.N.Y. December 2, 2010) (estoppel), *GPL Treatment v. Louisiana Pacific Corp.*, 894 P.2d 470, 477 n.4 (Or. Ct. App. 1995) (dissent) (untimeliness).

[155] Exclusion of the CISG Under Article 6, available at www.cisg.law.pace.edu./cisg/CISG-AC-op16.html.

[156] See id. at ¶¶ 5.5, 6.1.

[157] See, e.g., Vienna Convention on the Law of Treaties Article 26 (1969).

exception limited to one instance itself supports the proposition that the CISG leaves the forum's procedural rules unaffected – with a single exception. Thus, the courts of Contracting States are not obligated to ignore their procedural rules when adjudicating international sales contracts. Waiver, estoppel, and untimeliness arguably are procedural doctrines that still operate when the parties litigate a contract otherwise governed by the CISG. The Advisory Council Opinion also expresses concern that adoption of domestic waiver principles will be costly in terms of undermining uniform application of the CISG. True enough. But those are not the only costs that are relevant. Requiring parties to re-litigate on a new legal theory imposes its own costs, both on the immediate parties and on the judicial system. It is not clear that uniformity costs predominate in that conflict.

2. Opting in

Article 6 allows parties to derogate from the CISG and almost all of its provisions when the CISG otherwise applies. It does not address the question concerning whether the parties can choose to make the CISG applicable to their transaction when it is otherwise does not apply. For example, a party located in the United Kingdom and a party located in South Africa might select the CISG as the rules applicable to their contract. Neither State is a Contracting State. Although the Uniform Law on International Sales expressly allowed parties to opt in to its provisions,[158] the CISG says nothing about the matter. The diplomatic history indicates that a provision allowing opting in was proposed and rejected. Apparently it was thought that the proposal was unnecessary, because parties could choose to make the CISG applicable to their transaction.[159] Is the parties' choice of the CISG effective?

Commentary and some case law allow opting in to the CISG.[160] The result clearly is defensible, because it gives the parties the rules that they choose to govern their contract. However, getting to the result is not always easy under applicable conflict of laws rules. To see this, two types of situations in which the CISG is selected by the parties need to be distinguished. In both, the CISG is inapplicable under Article 1(1). For instance, the parties do not have their places of business in different Contracting States and conflicts rules do not select the law of a Contracting State. Alternatively, the contract might be a distribution or franchise agreement, or other contract that is not for the sale of goods. In the first situation the parties'

---

[158] See Uniform Law of International Sales Article 4 (1964).
[159] See Diplomatic Conference, First Committee Deliberation, March 13, 1980, in Documentary History, supra note 20, at 473–74.
[160] See, e.g., District Court Padova (Italy), 11 January 2005, available at: http://cisgw3.law.pace.edu/cases/050111i3.html; ICC Arbitration Case 11849 (2003), available at http://cisgw3.law.pace.edu/cases/031849i1.html; Honnold/Flechtner, supra note 46, at 111–16; Loukas Mistelis, *Article 6*, in Kröll et al., supra note 77, at 116–18.; Ingeborg Schwenzer & Pascal Hachem, *Article 6*, in Schlechtriem & Schwenzer, supra note 45, at 116–18.

agreement selects the law of a Contracting State. The result here is easy. In this situation most conflicts rules will respect the choice of the parties and apply the CISG. For example, the EU Regulation on the Law Applicable to Contractual Obligations selects "the law" chosen by the parties.[161] Because the Contracting State's law includes the CISG, the EU Regulation gives effect to the parties' selection of the CISG.

The second situation is harder. Here the parties select the CISG without selecting the law of a Contracting State. The CISG is "the law" only of States that have adopted it. When parties select the CISG without selecting a Contracting State's law, they are simply choosing a term they want included in the contract. The term is not "law." Thus, strictly, most conflicts rules will not give effect to the parties' choice of the CISG. Courts and commentators that recommend that the choice nonetheless be given effect must either find that the parties implicitly have selected the law of a Contracting State or recognize a "party selected rules" exception to predominant conflicts principles. Giving effect to the parties' choice of the CISG makes good sense, for two reasons. One is that opting in gives the parties the terms they want. Parties sometimes will not want a Contracting State's domestic law to govern their contract. Allowing them to opt in to the CISG only if they select a Contracting State's law forces the parties to make the State's domestic law applicable as the price of having the CISG govern their contract. This makes the contract less valuable to the parties because it increases the parties' cost of selecting the law they prefer. Second, opting in to the CISG directly reduces the parties' cost of getting the terms they want. This is because the CISG comprises a set of default terms. As a result, by selecting the CISG the parties are selecting all of its default terms. This saves them the cost of having to replicate the CISG's terms on a term-by-term basis, which is feasible but costly. Put another way, parties still can provide in their contract for the CISG's terms even if they cannot opt in to the CISG. It is just that doing so on a term-by-term basis is inconvenient and more costly. Allowing parties to opt in to the CISG enables them to get terms they prefer at less cost than they incur if they separately incorporate terms into their contract.

Courts rarely will have to decide whether parties can opt in to the CISG directly. This is because many and perhaps most contracts governed by the CISG have arbitration clauses.[162] Institutional arbitration rules are more forgiving in their conflicts principles. They give effect to the parties' choice of law or rules. Although arbitral conflicts principles apply the "law" selected by the parties, the

---

[161] See Article 3(1); cf. Restatement (Second) of Conflicts of Law § 187(1) (law of the state selected by the parties applies if the parties could have resolved the issue by an explicit provision in their agreement); U.C.C. § 1-301(a) (where transaction bears a reasonable relation to this state and another state or nation, parties may agree that "the law" of this state or such other nation governs their rights and duties).

[162] See Mistelis, *CISG and Arbitration*, in Janssen & Meyer, supra note 39, at 375.

parties' choice of rules is binding on the arbitral tribunal.[163] This is consistent with the consensual basis of arbitration. The limitation that the parties select "law" is not present in conflicts principles effectively applied in many institutional arbitration rules.

IV. EXCLUDED ISSUES

A. *Liability for personal injury*

The CISG does not govern all aspects of sales contracts that are within its scope. It leaves a number of issues to applicable domestic law or treaty. The two primary Articles that limit the issues addressed by the CISG are Articles 4 and 5. The easier limitation is stated in Article 5. Article 5 excludes from the CISG the seller's liability for death or personal injury caused by the goods. Thus, domestic tort or other law governs the seller's liability for injury or death to the buyer or third party resulting from the goods sold. Article 5's exclusion can result in "split" law: different law applies to different types of damage resulting from the seller's breach. For example, assume that a machine sold to the buyer malfunctions, causing personal injury to the buyer's employee and forcing production in the buyer's factory to shut down. Assume also that the buyer loses sales as a result and that the seller has not disclaimed liability as to the malfunction. Article 5 makes the CISG inapplicable to the seller's liability for the personal injury resulting from the machine's malfunction. Therefore, domestic law (most likely tort law) governs this element of damage. At the same time, the shutdown of production caused the buyer to lose sales. Lost sales are economic loss and are not excluded from the CISG under Article 5. Instead, they are consequential damages that are recoverable to the extent permissible under Article 74.[164]

B. *Article 4's limited range*

Article 4's exclusion is more complicated and harder to interpret. It is unclear in many instances whether the CISG governs an issue.[165] The first sentence of the Article states the matters that the CISG explicitly controls. According to it, the CISG "governs only the formation of the contract of sale and the rights and obligations of the seller and buyer from such a contract." Thus, CISG's formation rules displace

---

[163] See id. at 382; UNCITRAL Model Law on International Commercial Arbitration Article 28(1); French Code of Civil Procedure Article 1511 (2011).

[164] Cf. Commercial Court Zurich (Switzerland), 26 April 1995, available at http://cisgw3.law.pace .edu/cases/950426s1.html (property damage from breach recoverable under the CISG); Court of Appeals Düsseldorf (Germany), 2 July 1993, available at: http://cisgw3.law.pace.edu/cases/ 930702g1.html.

[165] By one count, the CISG's applicability to more than forty issues is controversial or at least questionable; see Milena Djordjevic, *Article 4*, in Kröll et al., supra note 77, at 64, 64 n.5.

the formation rules that might otherwise govern under domestic sales law. For instance, Article 23 provides that a contract is concluded when an acceptance of an offer becomes effective. Article 18(2) in turn provides that an acceptance becomes effective when the offeror receives it. This means that the mailbox rule for acceptance, which makes an acceptance effective on dispatch, is inoperative in a transaction governed by the CISG, even in a jurisdiction that adopts the mailbox rule for domestic transactions.

A slightly less obvious application of Article 4's displacement of domestic law formation rules involves the requirement of consideration. Under the national sales law of common law countries, a contract requires, with some exceptions, support by consideration. Without consideration, an enforceable contract is not concluded. Because the CISG's formation rules do not require consideration, a contract subject to the CISG arguably is enforceable without it. Two American courts have reached different conclusions about the matter. *Geneva Pharmaceuticals Technology Group* v. *Barr Laboratories*[166] found that the requirement of consideration is a matter of validity, and thus is excluded from the CISG's scope under Article 4(a). The finding assumes that the CISG's formation rules do not displace a consideration requirement. *Shuttle Packaging Systems* v. *Tsonakis*[167] reaches the opposite conclusion. Recognizing that Article 29(1) allows a contract to the modified by the "mere agreement" of the parties, the court holds that contracts governed by the CISG are enforceable without consideration. The court's reasoning implicitly relies in part on Article 4's coverage of contract formation. [168] Because the CISG's formation rules govern the sales contract under Article 4, they displace domestic law rules that add requirements of contract formation. Since the CISG's formation rules do not require consideration, sales contracts governed by the CISG are enforceable without consideration.

Article 4 also limits the CISG's scope to the "rights and obligations of the seller and the buyer arising from" the sales contract. By its terms, the limitation makes the CISG inapplicable to two sorts of issues. One is the entitlements of the parties that arise from a source other than the contract. Setoff and recoupment are examples. Setoff is the right of parties owing mutual debts to each other to apply the debts one against the other. Recoupment gives a party a defense to payment arising from the same transaction as the other party's right to payment. Domestic decisional law or statute may give the parties the right to setoff whether or not the mutual debts arise from the same transaction. By Article 4's terms, the CISG does not govern rights arising from transactions unrelated to the sales contract. For this reason, most case law and commentary find that the CISG does not cover setoff rights.[169] Although the

---

[166] 201 F.Supp.2d 236, 284 (S.D.N.Y. 2002).

[167] 2001 U.S. Dist. LEXIS 21630 (W.D. Mich. December 17, 2001).

[168] Article 4 provides in relevant part that "[t]his Convention governs the formation of the contract of sale."

[169] See, e.g., Court of Appeals Köln (Germany), 19 May 2008, available at http://cisgw3.law.pace .edu/cases/080519g1.html; Court of Appeals Cologne (Germany), 13 February 2006, available at

sales contract can provide for a right to recoupment, none of the CISG's provisions supply the right where the contract is silent. Nonetheless, some courts and commentators find that the CISG governs the right of recoupment.[170] It is a stretch to find recoupment among the CISG's underlying principles under Article 7(2) when no provision touches on defenses to payment generally. Defenses are matters that are more plausibly left to the procedural rules of the forum. More generally, Article 4 states no standard that indicates when a right or obligation arises from the sales contract rather than from a noncontractual source. Thus, unsurprisingly, other issues such as burdens and standards of proof and attorney's fees are more controversial and may or may not be excluded by Article 4's limit.[171]

The other excluded issue concerns the rights and obligations of third parties. Because Article 4 limits the CISG's application to the rights and obligations of the buyer and seller, a third party's entitlements are governed by applicable domestic law. This means that the CISG is inapplicable to the assignment of claims and assumption of duties, and the rights of third party beneficiaries. Domestic law instead governs these matters. As a result, domestic law controls whether a third party has rights and obligations with respect to the sales contract. The CISG, however, governs the sales contract and therefore defines the rights and obligations that the assignee or third party beneficiary may obtain.

Application of Article 4's limitation is complicated when considered together with Article 1(1)(a). An example illustrates the complication. Assume that B, located in the United Kingdom, agrees to deliver a specific number of machines to C, located in France. Unknown to C, B has entered into the contract on A's instructions. A is located in the United States. France is a Contracting State and the United Kingdom is a non-Contracting State. Thus, the CISG does not govern the sales contract under Article 1(1)(a) if B and C are the parties to it. However, the CISG nonetheless still might apply to the sales contract. Two steps are required to determine whether the CISG applies. First, it is necessary to establish whether A is a party to the sales contract with C. Second, it must be determined whether the CISG applies to the contract if A is a party to the contract. As to the first step, Article 4 limits the CISG application to "the seller and the buyer" – here, B and C. The CISG therefore does not determine whether A is a party to the contract. Instead, applicable national law of agency determines whether A, as an undisclosed principal, is liable as a party to

http://cisgw3.law.pace.edu/cases/060213g1.html; District Court Padova (Italy), 25 February 2004, available at http://cisgw3.law.pace.edu/cases/040225i3.html; Peter Huber & Alastair Muller, The CISG 30 (2007); but cf. Court of Appeals Hamburg (Germany), 26 November 1999, available at http://cisgw3.law.pace.edu/cases/991126g1.html.

[170] The case law does not distinguish between setoff and recoupment by name. For the position (though not by name) that the CISG covers recoupment, see Court of Appeals Hamm (Germany), 9 June 1995, available at http://cisgw3.law.pace.edu/cases/950609g1.html; District Court Stuttgart (Germany), 29 October 2009, available at http://cisgw3.law.pace.edu/cases/091029g1.html; Djordjevic, *Article 4*, in Kröll et al. supra note 77, at 82.

[171] The scholarly debate is described and documented in *id.* 77, at 79–82, 84–85.

the contract. The forum's conflict of laws rules must select the national agency law.[172] As to the second step, A and C are located in different Contracting States. Thus, if applicable agency law finds that A is a party to the contract, the CISG applies under Article 1(1)(a). B is located in a non-Contracting State. Thus, if agency law finds that A is not a party to the contract, the CISG does not govern the contract under Article 1(1)(a).

C. Article 4(a) and (b)'s express exclusion: validity and title in the goods

Article 4's second sentence expressly excludes two issues from the CISG's scope: the validity of the contract and any of its provisions, and the effect of the contract on title (property) in the goods sold. The sentence is not a model of clarity: "In particular, except as otherwise expressly provided in this Convention, it is not concerned" with these matters. The phrase "[i]n particular" implies that there are matters other than validity and property in the goods that also are not addressed by the CISG. However, the Article gives no hint as to what these unlisted matters are. Predictably, the phrase leaves room to argue that the CISG does not address a particular matter, even when it affects the parties' rights and obligations under the sales contract. Attorney's fees, burdens of proof, and the currency in which payment is to be made are examples. With no clear limit on the issues excluded "in particular," arguments for and against exclusion are inconclusive.

Under Article 4(a), "except as otherwise provided" in the CISG, the CISG does not govern the validity of the contract or any of its provisions or any usages. The CISG does not define "validity." Although validity concerns the issues that render a contract void, voidable or unenforceable,[173] national laws differ considerably as to the matters touching on the contract that render it invalid.[174] The appearance of "validity" in the CISG and the CISG's injunction to interpret its provisions to promote uniformity in application (Article 7(1)) together suggest that the term has a meaning independent of its meaning under national law. This means that an issue is not one of validity simply because national law labels it as one. Rather, the issue is excluded from the CISG's scope only if the CISG considers it an issue of validity. Nonetheless, the precise meaning of "validity" under Article 4(a) remains unclear. Diplomatic history reveals that the CISG's drafters considered validity to touch on politically sensitive issues that prevent consensus on uniform law.[175] Rather than define the subject matter, the drafters left it entirely unaddressed. Issues of legal

---

[172] The different conflicts rules used by nations to determine applicable agency law are briefly described in Schwenzer, Hachem & Kee, supra note 74, at 176.

[173] See Geneva Pharmaceuticals Technology Corp. v. Barr Laboratories, Inc., 201 F.Supp.2d 236, 282–83 (S.D.N.Y. 2002); Milena Djordjevic, Article 4, in Kröll et al., supra note 77, at 88.

[174] See, e.g., Schwenzer, Hachem & Kee, supra note 74, at 197–202.

[175] See Working Group Session No. 1 — January 1970, in Documentary History, supra note 20, at 34 (para. 53); Helen Elizabeth Hartnell, Rousing the Sleeping Dog: The Validity Exception to the Convention for the International Sale of Goods, 18 Yale J. Int'l L. 1, 40 (1993).

capacity, duress, unconscionability and fraud easily are matters of validity. Other matters, such as certain sorts of mistake or hardship, are less easily classifiable.[176] Some American courts have implied that the CISG addresses the issue of mistake, and thus that mistake claims can be resolved under its terms.[177]

Article 4(a) excludes validity from the CISG's scope "except as otherwise expressly provided" in the CISG. The "expressly provided" qualification, although not transparent, is fairly comprehensible. "Expressly provided" does not mean "labeled a matter of validity," because the term "validity" appears in only one of the CISG's provisions: Article 55. If the CISG's drafters had intended the CISG to deal with validity only if its provisions deem a matter one of "validity," there would be an easier way to do complete the task: They simply could have made a cross reference to Article 55. There would be no need to use the clumsier "expressly provided" language of Article 4(a). By far the better inference is that the CISG "expressly provides" for an issue of validity when its provisions address the issue – even if they do not use the term "validity." Where the CISG addresses the issue, it governs the matter and displaces domestic law on the same matter.

An uncontroversial illustration concerns what are sometimes called matters of "formal validity." These are requirements of form, such as writing or signature requirements, found in some national law. Contracts or terms in them that do not satisfy such requirements are invalid and therefore unenforceable. The requirement that clauses in a contract that limit the seller's liability for consequential damages must be separately signed is an example. Another example of "formal validity" is the requirement that a contract be in writing. Article 11 by its terms allows a contract to be enforceable if it is not in written form or evidenced by a writing (unless the reservation in Article 96 and recognized by Article 12 applies). The CISG therefore expressly provides for the validity of contracts not concluded or evidenced by a writing and therefore displaces domestic law requirements of formal validity.

The hardest cases are ones in which domestic law overlaps with the CISG while giving different rights to the parties than are given by the CISG. Domestic tort and other law typically provide available remedies, measures of damages, and notice requirements that differ from the same matters dealt with by the CISG. The question is whether the CISG displaces domestic law that otherwise applies to the same set of operative facts. Consider three examples in which the question arises. In each example the CISG governs the sales contract described.

---

[176] For the debate on the classification of issues such as mistake under validity, see, e.g., Luca Bolzonello, The "Validity Exception" in the CISG and Remedies for Mistake in Domestic Contract Law: Preemption and Concurrence (2012), available at http://papers.ssrn.com/sol3/papers.cfm?abstract_id=2121714; Patrick C. Leyens, CISG and Mistake: Uniform Law vs. Domestic Law: The Interpretative Challenge of Mistake and the Validity Loophole (2003), available at http://cisgw3.law.pace.edu/cisg/biblio/leyens.html.

[177] See *Miami Valley Paper, LLC* v. *Lebbing Engineering & Consulting GmbH*, 2009 U.S. Dist. LEXIS 25201 (S.D. Ohio March 26, 2009); *Mitchell Aircraft Spares, Inc.* v. *European Aircraft Service*, 23 F.Supp.2d 915, 922 (N.D. Ill.1998).

Example 1: Seller expressly warrants the performance of the machine it sold. The machine it delivers does not perform as warranted. Buyer fails to give timely and proper notice of the nonconformity as required by the CISG (Articles 38 and 39). Although Buyer concedes that Seller did not knowingly misrepresent the machine's performance capacity, it seeks to rescind the contract based on Seller's innocent misrepresentation as to the machine's capacity. Applicable domestic tort law allows rescission in the circumstances.

Example 2: The same facts as in Example 1 except that at the time the seller expressly warranted the machine's performance Seller knew that the machine would not perform as warranted. The machine operates almost as well as warranted and Buyer is only mildly inconvenienced as a result. Although in the circumstances Buyer is not entitled to avoid the contract under the CISG,[178] applicable domestic tort law allows Buyer to rescind the contract based on Seller's fraudulent misrepresentation as to the machine's capacity.

Example 3: Seller and Buyer conclude a sales contract that violates EU competition law. The agreement is void under the Treaty on the Functioning of the European Union, which is the applicable law. Neither Seller nor Buyer breached the contract and both want it enforced.

The issue in all three examples is whether the CISG preempts non-CISG law or applies concurrently with it. In Examples 1 and 2 Buyer prefers to rely on applicable domestic tort law, if available, to rescind the contract, while in Example 3 the contracting parties prefer the contract to be enforceable under the CISG. Neither the CISG nor its diplomatic history squarely addresses the issue of the CISG's preemptive effect. One view is that when a set of facts triggers the CISG's application, so that it addresses the issue raised by them, the CISG displaces applicable non-CISG law triggered by the same facts. In Example 1 Buyer failed to give timely notice of Seller's breach of warranty. In the circumstances the CISG bars Buyer from a remedy. Domestic tort law allowed rescission of the contract based on the same facts that triggered the CISG's application. As a result, the CISG displaces remedies otherwise available under applicable tort law. It does not matter that domestic law labels Buyer's remedy as based in "tort."

In Example 2 domestic tort law is triggered by a fact not made operative by the CISG: Seller's fraud. While Seller's knowledge of the machine's nonconformity is irrelevant to Seller's liability under the CISG, it is an element of the tort of fraudulent misrepresentation. For this reason, domestic tort law is not based on the same set of facts that define Buyer's rights under the CISG. Fraud is an additional fact operative under domestic tort law. Thus, on the displacement view,

---

[178] As in Example 1, Buyer again failed to give Seller timely notice of the breach of warranty. Under Article 40 the notice is not required when the seller knows of the nonconformity in the goods, as in the example. Nonetheless under Article 49(1)(a) Buyer may avoid the contract only if Seller's breach is fundamental, and the facts show that the breach is not fundamental under Article 25's standard of "fundamentality."

the CISG does not displace applicable tort law in the example. Non-CISG law also continues to be available in Example 3. The contract's anti-competitive impact on trade within the European Union is a fact that is additional to the facts that trigger the CISG's application. It voids the contract under EU competition law. Because the EU competition law is not triggered by the same operative facts as the CISG, the CISG does not displace it. The displacement view has some basis in the CISG's diplomatic history and is advocated by some commentators, including us.[179]

The court's handling of the buyer's claims in *Electrocraft Arkansas, Inc. v. Super Electric Motors, Ltd.*[180] is consistent with the displacement view. There the court allowed the buyer to prove that the seller tortiously interfered with a business expectancy and also violated the Arkansas Deceptive Trade Practices Act (ADTPA). The tortious interference claim required a showing that the seller intentionally harmed the buyer's economic interests, while the ADTPA gives relief to a person damaged by an unconscionable, false, or deceptive business practice.[181] A breach of warranty under the CISG does not trigger either state law. Arkansas' tort law applies only when an additional fact is present: the seller's intention to harm the buyer's economic interests. For its part, the ADPTA applies only when the seller's conduct is unconscionable, false, or deceptive. Because state law was not based on the same operative facts as the CISG, the CISG does not displace it. Although the court reached this conclusion without invoking the displacement view, the view supports the result.

The displacement view is not the only position that can be taken when domestic law and the CISG overlap. Against this view Lookofsky has urged that the CISG does not invariably preempt domestic law, even when domestic law applies to the same facts as the CISG.[182] He recommends that the CISG displace domestic law only in particular cases. In other instances, domestic law competes with it, presumably allowing a party to select the law that benefits it. Lookofsky notes, fairly enough, that a State's ratification of the CISG does not signal its intent to have the CISG to displace its tort law.[183] The almost complete silence about the matter in the diplomatic history allows no inference about the participants' likely views on the matter. However, Lookofsky's case-by-case approach risks undermining the CISG's uniform application. It is hard for tribunals to

---

[179] See Secretariat Commentary, in Documentary History, supra note 20, at 407 (Article 4 para 2); Honnold/Flechtner, supra note 46, at 80–81, 96–97; Clayton P. Gillette & Steven D. Walt, Sales Law: Domestic and International 55–57 (3d ed. 2016); Peter Schlechtriem, *The Borderline of Tort and Contract—Opening a New Frontier?*, 21 Cornell Int'l L. J. 467 (1988). For a variation on this theme that advocates consideration of both a factual criterion and a legal criterion, see Ulrich G. Schroeter, *Defining the Borders of Uniform International Contract Law: The CISG and Remedies for Innocent, Negligent, or Fraudulent Misrepresentation*, 58 Vill. L. Rev. 553 (2013).

[180] 70 UCC Rep. Serv.2d 716 (E.D.Ark. 2009).   [181] See Ark. Code Ann. § 4-88-102(5) (2010).

[182] See Lookofsky, supra note 70, at 71–72; Joseph Lookofsky, *In Dubio Pro Conventione? Some Thoughts About Opt-Outs, Computer Programs and Preemption Under the 1980 Vienna Sales Convention (CISG)*, 13 Duke J. Comp. & Int'l L. 263, 279–88 (2003).

[183] See Lookofsky, *In Dubio Pro Conventione? Some Thoughts About Opt-Outs, Computer Programs and Preemption Under the 1980 Vienna Sales Convention (CISG)*, supra id. at 286.

know when the CISG preempts domestic law and when domestic law merely competes with it, and Lookofsky does not suggest a workable standard that tribunals can use. By contrast, the displacement view is relatively easy for tribunals to apply and produces greater uniformity in the CISG's application.

Article 4(b) excludes from the CISG's scope the effect that the contract may have on title ("property") in the goods sold. The exclusion is precautionary only, merely stating what is apparent elsewhere in the CISG's provisions. None of the CISG's Articles determines whether or when ownership in the goods passes from the seller to the buyer. The CISG does not, for example, determine the rights of a good faith purchaser of goods to which the seller has either void or voidable title. Although Article 30 obligates the seller to transfer the property in goods as part of its delivery obligations, the responsibility to do so is the seller's. The contract does not itself transfer title in the goods. A seller who fails to transfer ownership breaches the contract, but the breach has no effect on the location of title. Domestic law contains default rules that determine when title passes to the buyer and the effect of the seller's retention of title.[184] This means that domestic rules as to title and its passage continue to apply to sales contracts governed by the CISG. The CISG merely (and uncontroversially) requires the seller to pass ownership to the goods to the buyer. Failure to do so subjects the seller to the remedies provided by the CISG, not by domestic law.

There are two scenarios in which contracts governed by the CISG might implicate property rights in the goods governed by domestic law. One situation involves a contest between the buyer and the seller. In this case the seller retains title to secure the buyer's obligation to pay the contract price. When the buyer fails to pay the price, the seller tries to recover the goods from the buyer, arguing that it remains the owner of the goods and is therefore entitled to them.[185] The second scenario in effect involves a contest between the seller and third parties over ownership in the goods. In this case the seller again retains title to the goods it delivers to the buyer. For its part, the buyer has granted a security interest in the goods to a third party. The buyer then defaults on its payment obligations to both the seller and the third party.[186] Alternatively, the buyer goes into bankruptcy.[187] In both instances the secured creditor and the buyer's bankruptcy trustee argue that their interest in the goods is superior to the seller's interest in them. Because the CISG does not deal with the effect of the contract on ownership in the goods, applicable domestic law decides whether the seller's title retention clause is valid and gives it priority over third parties' claims to them.

---

[184] Compare U.C.C. § 2-401(2); C. civ. [Civil Code] art. 1583 (Fr.); British Columbia (Canada) Sale of Goods Act ch. 410, § 23. For a survey of national laws of important trading countries, see Transfer of Ownership in International Trade (Alexander von Zeigler, Charles Debattista, Audile Plegat & Jesper Windahl eds., 2d ed. 2011).

[185] See Foreign Trade Court of Arbitration attached to the Serbian Chamber of Commerce (Serbia), 15 July 2008, available at http://cisgw3.law.pace.edu/cases/080715sb.html.

[186] See *Usinor Industeel v. Leeco Steel Products*, 209 F.Supp.2d 880 (N.D.Ill. 2002).

[187] See Federal District Court (*Roder Zelt-und Hallenkonstruktionen GmbH v. Rosedown Park Pty Ltd., et al.*) (Australia), 28 April 1995, available at http://cisgw3.law.pace.edu/cases/950428a2.html.

3

Contract formation

I. STATUTE OF FRAUDS AND ARTICLE 12

The CISG affirmatively rejects any statute of frauds or other formality for the creation of a contract. Article 11 recites that "[a] contract of sale need not be concluded in or evidenced by writing and is not subject to any other requirement as to form. It may be proved by any means, including witnesses." In this sense, the CISG recognizes commercial practices in which parties enter binding agreements through handshakes, conduct, or simply oral understandings. Article 11 eliminates any domestic requirements not only that the contract be in writing, but also that it be evidenced by seals, notarization, or other formalities. The assertion that a contract may be proven by any means implies the absence of any parol evidence rule, a subject that we discuss in the next chapter. Of course, in accordance with the "party autonomy" principle of Article 6, parties may deviate from these rules. An offer may, for instance, require that any acceptance be in writing, and a completed contract may be governed by a "no oral modification" clause. The effectiveness of such restrictions raises issues of validity, and thus, to the extent that they are not addressed by the CISG, Article 4(a) dictates that they be governed by domestic law.

The absence of formal requirements for contract formation is a common phenomenon of civil law. But it is less frequent in common law and Scandinavian jurisdictions, and in the countries formerly within the Soviet Union. As a consequence, Article 11 was quite controversial during the drafting of the CISG. The ultimate compromise was to permit (in Article 96) Contracting States that had domestic requirements for contracts of sale to be concluded or evidenced in writing to declare that the CISG articles rendering writings unnecessary are inapplicable where any party to the contract has its place of business in one of those States. The declaration nullifies the effect of Article 11 (and of Article 29, dealing with modification or Part II of the CISG). Article 12 makes such a declaration effective by stating that Article 11 is inapplicable where any party has its place of business in a

Contracting State that has made an Article 96 declaration. To date, Argentina, Armenia, Belarus, Chile, Paraguay, Russian Federation, and Ukraine have made Article 96 reservations. China, among other Contracting States, has withdrawn its earlier declaration, perhaps in response to changes in its domestic contract law that generally eliminate writing requirements or as a concession to uniformity.[1]

The application of Article 12 has been controversial, in part due to the wording of the provision. Some commentators and early case law have suggested that a writing must exist to have an effective contract where at least one party is from a State that has made an Article 96 declaration.[2] The basis for that conclusion is the language of Articles 12 and 96 that Article 11 is inapplicable where "any party has his place of business in a Contracting State." But neither Article 12 nor Article 96 says that writing requirements will apply or, if so, whose writings will apply where a State has made an Article 96 declaration. They say only that the relevant CISG Articles (11, 29, and Part II) do not apply. Assume that Seller is located in Russia and Buyer in China. Their sales contract is not evidenced by a writing. Russia has made an Article 96 reservation while China no longer does. There are two opposing interpretations of the effect of Russia's Article 96 reservation. One is that Russia's domestic law writing requirements apply to the contract. If so, the contract is unenforceable even under the CISG. By making an Article 96 reservation, Russia declares that Article 11 "does not apply when any party has its place of business" in Russia. Russia's domestic law writing requirements therefore apply.

An opposing interpretation denies this conclusion. By making an Article 96 reservation, Russia merely declares that Article 11 "does not apply . . ." If Article 11 does not

---

[1] See Contract Law of the People's Republic of China Article 10 (1999); United Nations Treaty Collection, https://treaties.un.org/pages/ViewDetails.aspx?src=TREATY&mtdsg_no=X-10&chapter=10&lang=en. Hungary has withdrawn its Article 96 declaration as of 2016. See Press Release, United Nations Information Service, Hungary Withdraws "Written Form" Declaration Under the United Nations Convention on Contracts for the International Sale of Goods (CISG), available at www.unis.unvienna.org/unis/en/pressrels/2015/unisl219.html. Latvia withdrew its Article 96 declaration in November 2012. See Press Release, United Nations Information Service, Latvia Withdraws "Written Form" Declaration Under the United Nations Convention on Contracts for the International Sale of Goods (CISG) (November 15, 2012), available at www.unis.unvienna.org/unis/pressrels/2012/unisl177.html. Estonia and Lithuania have also withdrawn their initial Article 96 declarations. In *Weihai Textile Group Imp. & Exp. Co. v. Level 8 Apparel, LLC*, 2014 U.S. Dist. LEXIS 53688 at *18 n.1 (S.D.N.Y. March 28, 2014), the court applied China's Article 96 declaration to a contract that had been concluded when the declaration was in force, although the declaration had been withdrawn at the time of the litigation.

[2] See, e.g., High Arbitration Court of the Russian Federation (Russia), 16 February 1998, available at http://cisgw3.law.pace.edu/cases/980216r1.html; High Arbitration Court of the Russian Federation (Russia), 25 March 1997, available at http://cisgw3.law.pace.edu/cases/970325r1.html; District Court Hasselt (Netherlands), 2 May 1995, available at http://cisgw3.law.pace.edu/cases/950502b1.html; District Court Rotterdam (Netherlands), 12 July 2001, available at http://cisgw3.law.pace.edu/cases/010712n1.html; Marco Torsello, *The CISG's Impact on Legislators: The Drafting of International Contract Law Conventions*, in The 1980 Uniform Sales Law 251 (Franco Ferrari ed., 2003).

apply, the issue of the law applicable to the enforcement of a contract not evidenced by a writing is not addressed by the CISG. Instead, the issue is addressed by applicable domestic law. The forum's conflict of laws principles select this law.[3] If the applicable domestic law is the law of Russia, writing requirements under Russian law regulate the contract and therefore it is unenforceable. If applicable law is Chinese domestic law, the contract is enforceable because Chinese law has no applicable writing requirements. This does not mean that Article 11 comes back into play. It simply means that the principle of "freedom from form requirements," which is reflected in Article 11, applies through the choice of Chinese law.

The second interpretation probably is the better one. By its terms, the effect of an Article 96 reservation is simply that Article 11 "does not apply" where any party has its place of business in the Contracting State making the reservation. Article 96 does not further provide that the law governing writing requirements is the law of that Contracting State. At the same time, Article 96 does not provide that the applicable law is not that State's law. Article 96 simply is silent concerning which law is applicable. Interpreting Article 96 to make the reservation State's domestic law always applicable gives those States more than the treaty gives them: a unilateral selection of their own domestic law. Moreover, it can lead to perverse or uncertain results. Assume a contract between a party located in Russia and a party located in Argentina, each of which has made Article 96 declarations. Certainly Article 11 does not apply in such a situation. But if Russia and Argentina have different writing requirements, which one's control? An earlier proposal to the CISG that the writing requirements of the reserving State's law governed was rejected. Assuming that Contracting States that have not made an Article 96 declaration want their own domestic law to apply sometimes, Article 96 is not best read to foreclose the possibility. Thus, when an Article 96 reservation makes Article 11 inapplicable, conflict of laws rules probably select the applicable domestic law writing requirements governing the sales contract.[4]

The better position is reflected in *Forestal Guarani S.A.* v. *Daros International, Inc.*[5] There the Third Circuit applied what it considered to be the majority rule and took the "conflict of laws" route, which it concluded was appropriate under Article 7(2). Since the CISG did not expressly settle the issue of which law applied, and the principles underlying the CISG were unhelpful, the rules of private

---

[3] See, e.g., *Weihai Textile Group Imp. & Exp. Co.* v. *Level 8 Apparel, LLC*, 2014 U.S. Dist. LEXIS 53688 (S.D.N.Y. March 28, 2014); District Court Rotterdam (Netherlands), 12 July 2001, available at http://cisgw3.law.pace.edu/cases/010712n1.html; Franco Ferrari, *Writing Requirements: Articles 11–13*, in The Draft UNCITRAL Digest and Beyond 213–14 (Franco Ferrari, Harry Flechtner, & Ronald A. Brand eds., 2004).

[4] See Juzgado Nacional de Primera Instancia en lo Comercial No. 18 (Argentina), 20 October 1989, available at http://cisgw3.law.pace.edu/cases/891020a1.html (dicta); Metropolitan Court of Budapest (Hungary), 24 March 1992, available at http://cisgw3.law.pace.edu/cases/920324h1.html.

[5] 613 F.3d 395 (3d Cir. 2010).

international law would be determinative. The law of the relevant jurisdictions – New Jersey and Argentina – had different form requirements, so the choice of law mattered. A federal district court applying state law, the Third Circuit concluded, must apply the conflict of laws rules of the state in which it was located. The conflict of law rules of the forum state (New Jersey) selected the law of the jurisdiction that has the most significant relationship to the parties and to the alleged contract. Since the record did not reveal which jurisdiction played that role, the Third Circuit remanded the case to the District Court for the needed factual determinations.

Even though this resolution appears most consistent with the language of Article 12, it also can generate odd results. Assume a contract between a Russian party and a United States party in which the Russian court decides that conflict of laws rules require application of United States law. That would likely mean applying § 2–201 of the Uniform Commercial Code ("UCC"). The United States, by virtue of not making an Article 96 declaration, has presumably asserted that it is not that concerned about the inapplicability of UCC § 2–201 to a contract for the inter-national sale of goods. After all, if the dispute were between an American party and a French party, Article 11 would apply and there would be no statute of frauds. It seems peculiar to resurrect UCC § 2–201 when another jurisdiction expresses concern about the absence of a statute of frauds. Partially on this basis, one commentator suggests that UCC § 2–201 should not apply where the contract is otherwise governed by the CISG rather than by the UCC, since the inapplicability of the UCC to the CISG contract means that there is no "applicable" domestic law that requires a writing.[6] We fear that this approach proves too much. If the CISG renders the UCC inapplicable to the contract, then would a more general domestic (non-goods) statute of frauds apply? The same principle that says that the CISG displaces the UCC would seem to suggest that it also displaces other domestic law related to the necessity for writings. But if that is the case, then it is unclear to what domestic law the rules of private international law could point in order to fill the gap created by Article 12.

II. GENERAL RULES OF OFFER AND ACCEPTANCE

A. *Effectiveness of the offer and acceptance*

Contract formation under the CISG largely reflects the formal processes of offer and acceptance. Nothing in the CISG explicitly permits as open-ended of a mechanism for contract formation as we find in some domestic law that essentially allows one to discern the existence of a binding contract from conduct or other

---

[6] See Harry Flechtner in John O. Honnold, Uniform Law for International Sales Under the 1980 United Nations Convention 190 (Harry M. Flechtner ed., 4th ed. 2009) [hereinafter "Honnold/Flechtner"].

indicia of agreement.[7] Instead, the assumption of the CISG initially appears to be that bargains are struck through relatively clear signals of intent and agreement to terms by each of the parties. As we will see, that does not mean that contracts cannot be formed by informal processes, including oral contracts. It simply means that to the extent that the CISG dictates particular processes of contract formation, those processes involve the formalities of offer and acceptance.

In order to determine whether a contract has been formed through this process, we begin with the conclusion and work backwards. Article 23 recites that a contract is concluded at the moment when an acceptance of an offer becomes effective under the rules of the CISG. Thus, a contract is concluded only by an acceptance of an offer, and we need to determine when the requisite acceptance becomes effective. A series of hypotheticals can explain the operation of these seemingly straightforward rules.

Assume that on June 1, Buyer sends a purchase order to Seller that indicates its willingness to buy "1000 pairs of pajamas, style #12345 at $10 per pair." This purchase order would qualify as an offer under Article 14. That Article recites various indicia of an offer. An offer must be "sufficiently definite" and must indicate the intention of the offeror to be bound in the event of an acceptance. An offer is "sufficiently definite," in turn, if it indicates the goods and "expressly or implicitly" fixes the quantity and price or makes a provision for determining the quantity and price. Some courts contend that a proposal that does not satisfy these criteria does not qualify as an offer, even if the sender intends that it operate as one.[8] Our hypothetical, which states both a quantity and a price, satisfies these criteria, but one could imagine more ambiguous cases. An order that recites that price is to be fixed "as the market price in seller's place of business on date of shipment" would still constitute an offer, notwithstanding the absence of an explicit price, because it makes provision for determining the price. An order that simply left open the price, however, raises additional difficulties, which we discuss later under the general category of open price terms. A proposal that measured quantity by the buyer's requirements or the seller's output still provides a basis for determining quantity, and thus can qualify as an offer.

One might conclude from the fact that a proposal contains very specific terms that the sender has the requisite intention to be bound under Article 14. Nevertheless, there may be circumstances in which parties have no such intent until every detail of the transaction has been concluded. In *Hanwha Corp.* v. *Cedar Petrochemicals, Inc.*,[9] the court concluded that a Korean buyer of the petrochemical toluene had not

---

[7] See, e.g., Code civil [C. civ.] art. 1108 (Fr.) (validity of the contract requires consent of the party); U.C.C. § 2–204(1).

[8] See, e.g., Court of Appeals Frankfurt (Germany), 30 August 2000, available at http://cisgw3.law.pace.edu/cases/000830g1.html.

[9] 760 F. Supp. 2d 426 (S.D.N.Y. 2011). For a correct interpretation of the point, see Court of Appeals Frankfurt (Germany), 30 August 2000, available at http://cisgw3.law.pace.edu/cases/000830g1.html.

made an effective offer to purchase under Article 14 of the CISG because it did not reveal its intent to be bound when it made its proposal for the goods. The court determined that the parties had created a practice between themselves of a two-step process of contract formation in which neither party was to perform until there was agreement on terms that were not included in initial bids. Analysis of the circumstances in which the parties' prior transactions occurred supported the proposition that they had not entered into a final contract when they disagreed about a choice of law clause, even if they had already agreed on product, quantity, and price. The process of discerning the intent of the parties is governed by Article 8, which provides that a party's subjective intent is controlling only "where the other party knew or could not have been unaware what that intent was." Otherwise, statements and conduct of a party are to be interpreted according to the understanding that a reasonable person of the same kind as the other party would have had in the same circumstances. The court in *Hanwha* overstated the effect of "subjective intent" under the CISG. It suggested that "the CISG expresses a preference that the offeror's intent be considered subjectively." That statement incorrectly suggests that subjective intent consistently dominates objective evidence in the formation or interpretation of contracts. Such a conclusion ignores the limitations on the use of subjective intent in Article 8(1). Nevertheless, the error was harmless in the case, since neither party introduced evidence of subjective intent. Thus, only the objective intent, as revealed by the parties' past dealings, was relevant, and that intent was sufficient to negate the existence of an effective offer that could immediately be accepted.

Even proposals that are relatively specific may fail to qualify as offers. Article 14(2) provides that a proposal that is not addressed to one or more specific persons is presumed to be an invitation to make offers. Thus, mass mailings or advertisements that include a price and quantity will likely not constitute offers. The economic logic of such a restriction is that if a seller who made such a proposal were bound by any addressee who accepted the proposal, the seller would be uncertain about how large of an inventory to keep available, and could end up with more contracts than it could reasonably handle. That same logic, however, suggests that a proposal made to the public may still qualify as an offer if it contains language of restriction, such as "first come, first served," or "limited supply."

Under Article 15, an offer becomes effective when it reaches the offeree. Thus, the offer may be withdrawn if the withdrawal reaches the offeree before or at the same time as the offer. "Reaches," for these purposes, consists of an oral communication or delivery to the counterparty personally, to his place of business or mailing address or, if he does not have a place of business or mailing address, to his residence.[10] Assume in the preceding hypothetical, therefore, that Buyer has sent the offer on June 1 and it arrives at Seller's place of business on June 3, when Seller's place of

---

[10]   See Article 24.

business is closed.[11] On June 4, Buyer faxes a withdrawal of the offer. On June 5, Seller first becomes aware of both the offer and its withdrawal. The offer is effective and has not been withdrawn, because it "reached" the offeree on June 3 and was withdrawn after that date.

Even if not withdrawn, however, an effective offer may be revoked if the revocation reaches the offeree before dispatch of an acceptance.[12] One could imagine difficulties that the concept of "reaches" creates in the revocation context. Assume that the Buyer sends its offer by email on June 1. The Seller reads the email on the same date. On June 2, Buyer sends a second email that revokes the offer. At that time, however, the Seller's email server is not functioning properly, so that the Seller is unable to access and read the email until June 3. Between the time that the June 2 email was sent and the time the Seller is able to read it, the Seller dispatches an acceptance. We would conclude that the June 2 email "reached" the Seller prior to the dispatch of the acceptance.[13] Again, "reaches" means delivery to the recipient's place of business or mailing address. In the context of email, that might mean when the email hits the recipient's server, or when it is accessible to the recipient (even if not opened at that time). We would opt for the former interpretation.[14] As between the two parties, it is the recipient that is in control of its server. It would be odd to place the risk of an inoperative means of communication on the party who is not in charge of maintaining it. Even if the server were maintained by a third party on behalf of Seller, it is Seller who has contracted with that party and who therefore occupies the superior position to ensure access to communications that come through it.

Note from our earlier discussion that it is dispatch of the acceptance, not its receipt, that precludes revocation of the offer. Assume that the Buyer in our example sends its offer on June 1, which Seller receives on June 3. On that same date, Seller mails an acceptance of the offer. Now assume that on June 4, Buyer faxes Seller a

---

[11] The assumption of the example is that the business is closed for normal circumstances, such as the communication arrives on the weekend. One could imagine situations, such as a long-term closure for natural disasters, which could affect the analysis.

[12] See Article 16(1).

[13] Article 27 does not affect the result in the ongoing example. The Article in relevant part allows a party who dispatches a communication by appropriate means to rely on it if there is a delay or error in the transmission of the communication or if it fails to arrive. But that provision applies only to Part III of the CISG, which governs communications during performance of the contract, not Part II, which governs contract formation. Even if Article 27 formally applied, it would not change the result in the ongoing example. Buyer dispatched its June 2 email revoking its earlier offer. In the circumstances its dispatch was by an appropriate medium. Thus, even if the malfunction in Seller's server prevents Buyer's email from "arriving" at Seller (which we find implausible) or delayed its arrival, Article 27 allows Buyer to rely on its June 2 revocation having reached Seller prior to Seller's dispatch of its acceptance.

[14] Cf. United Nations Convention on the Use of Electronic Communications in International Contracts Article 10(2) (2005) ("The time of receipt of an electronic communication is the time when it becomes capable of being retrieved by the addressee at an electronic address designated by the addressee. ... An electronic communication is presumed to be capable of being retrieved by the addressee when it reaches the addressee's electronic address.").

revocation of the offer because another seller has offered to sell fungible pajamas for $8 per pair. Buyer is bound by the terms of its offer even though it has not received the acceptance, because the attempted revocation has occurred only after Seller dispatched an acceptance. Presumably, this rule protects the reliance interest of offerees who might begin performance immediately after dispatching an acceptance. One might think that any reliance interest could be protected by a rule that made the effectiveness of a revocation dependent on having taken steps in reliance on the contract. But the brighter-line rule of dispatch avoids the costs of having to determine the existence of reliance investments. At the same time, the dispatch rule prevents the offeror from attempting to play the market between the time it sends an offer and the time it receives an acceptance.

Now assume that it is Seller-offeree who regrets its initial decision. That is, assume that Seller has dispatched an acceptance of Buyer's offer on June 4. On June 5, Seller discovers that another buyer is willing to pay $12 for the same pajamas and Seller cannot fulfill both contracts. On that date, Seller faxes a purported withdrawal of its acceptance to Buyer. The acceptance sent on June 4 arrives at Buyer's place of business on June 6. Perhaps surprisingly, there is no contract. Under Article 22, an acceptance may be withdrawn if the withdrawal reaches the offeror before or at the same time that the acceptance would have become effective. An acceptance becomes effective when it reaches the offeror, not when it is dispatched.[15] In effect, the CISG rejects the common law mailbox rule in favor of a receipt rule. Since the fax would have reached the Buyer on June 5, the condition that withdrawal reach the offeror before the acceptance has been satisfied. Thus, although the offeree can bind the offeror by dispatching an acceptance under Article 16(1), the offeree is not itself bound until the acceptance reaches the offeror.

This combination of provisions allows the possibility of strategic behavior by offerees. Assume that the price of pajamas is sufficiently volatile that Seller would like some flexibility to decide whether to accept between the time it receives the offer from Buyer and the time that a binding contract is concluded. Seller can dispatch an acceptance by a relatively slow means of communication. That dispatch binds the offeror (Buyer) and prevents revocation of the offer. But it does not bind the offeree (Seller). Instead, the offeree can still withdraw its acceptance by a relatively fast means of communication if market conditions change in the offeree's favor. In effect, Article 16(1) provides the offeree with a zero-price option of having the offer remain open for a period of time. Offerors might want to deny such an option to offerees by stipulating in the offer that it is revocable at any time prior to receiving acceptance or by requiring immediate acceptance. Indeed, one would imagine that in markets with highly volatile prices, trade usage or contractual clauses would require all communications to occur by expeditious means and within tight timetables.

---

[15] See Article 18(2).

For the most part, the concept of acceptance will cause little difficulty. An acceptance consists of a statement made by the offeree or some conduct of the offeree that indicates assent to the offer. No acceptance can be inferred from silence or inactivity alone.[16] Although conduct can constitute acceptance, no acceptance is effective until its indication reaches the offeror. That indication must reach the offeror within the time fixed in the offer or, in the absence of a fixed time, within a reasonable time.[17] Oral offers presumptively must be accepted immediately. These rules are subject to variation if the offer or the practices of the parties so allow.[18]

The court in *CSS Antenna, Inc. v. Amphenol—Tuchel Electronics, GmbH*,[19] which we discuss in greater depth later,[20] may have been inferring an absence of intent to accept a counteroffer when it determined that a buyer did not have sufficient notice of one of its terms. In the absence of a contrary practice that the parties have established themselves or a relevant trade usage, even acceptance by conduct is effective only when the indication of assent reaches the offeror.[21] Simply beginning performance of the contract therefore will not suffice as conduct that amounts to an acceptance.[22] Thus, if Seller receives Buyer's offer to purchase a table and Seller immediately begins to manufacture the table, no contract will have been concluded until notice of Seller's conduct has reached Buyer. Under some circumstances, however, parties may generate practices in which assent is indicated in nontraditional ways that do not entail giving formal notice. One could imagine an environment in which orders must be filled immediately if at all, so taking an additional step of giving notice of acceptance becomes, at best, superfluous. If a practice has evolved between the parties or as a trade usage that allows an indication of assent to be inferred from the offeree's performance of an act without prior notice to the offeror, the acceptance is effective when the act in performed.[23] In *Urica, Inc. v. Pharmaplast S.A.E.*,[24] for example, a buyer submitted purchase orders for products that the seller immediately manufactured, produced, and shipped. The parties' prior practice of concluding contracts in that manner bound the seller to the terms of the purchase order. When the seller subsequently insisted on a price and payment terms different from those in a purchase order that the seller had already fulfilled, it failed to comply with its contractual obligations.

Notice of acceptance was not required under even broader circumstances in a recent Austrian Supreme Court case.[25] A third party placed an order on the Austrian buyer's behalf, using the buyer's stamp, for insulation material from a Romanian seller. The seller included an invoice that stated the price when it delivered the

---

[16] See Article 18(1) ("by itself").   [17] See Article 18(2).   [18] See Article 18(3).
[19] 764 F. Supp. 2d 745 (D. Md. 2011).   [20] See infra II.C.2.   [21] See Article 18(1), (3).
[22] See, e.g., *Pasta Zara S.p.A. v. United States*, 703 F. Supp. 2d 1317 (Ct. Int'l Trade 2010).
[23] See Article 18(3).   [24] 2014 U.S. Dist. LEXIS 110015 (C.D. Cal. August 8, 2014).
[25] See Supreme Court (Austria), 13 December 2012, unpublished translation by Franziska Studer.

material. The buyer processed most of the material. In rejecting the buyer's argument that no contract was concluded, the court found that the buyer had accepted the material by processing it. Processing constituted conduct indicating the buyer's assent to the seller's offer under Article 18(1). The buyer, however, never gave notice of its acceptance to the seller. This did not bother the Court. Article 18(3) allows the offeree to assent without giving notice to the offeror if the offer, practices among the parties, or usage permits it. None of the facts recited by the Court suggests that the seller's offer or that any practices between the parties or usage permitted the buyer's acceptance without notice. Thus, the Court's discussion of Article 18(3) does not support its conclusion that the buyer's acceptance concluded the contract. Instead, the Court relied on the finding that the seller's delivery of material that suited the buyer's needs, along with the invoice, waived its right to notice.

This conclusion seems right. In this case the buyer who failed to give notice of acceptance was attempting to deny the existence of the contract. The buyer should not be able to rely on its own failure to give the seller notice when it used the material delivered (whether or not the delivered material suited its needs). Such a scenario suggests opportunism by a buyer attempting to shift the risk of a third party's breach of contract with it to the seller. Nevertheless, literally understood, Article 18 (3) does not recognize an exception to the requirement of notice of acceptance in the circumstances of the case. The seller's offer did not by its terms waive the requirement, and no relevant practice or usage apparently waived it either. The Court's finding of a waiver of notice, based on the seller's performance, has no support in Article 18(3). Although Article 18(3) might have been better drafted had it made the notice requirement inapplicable when "circumstances so indicate," the Article does not include such language. The Court reached the arguably correct result by adding a sensible exception not found in Article 18(3).

Delays in receiving an acceptance can effectively be waived by the offeror, but the offeror must inform the offeree of the effective nature of the late acceptance either by immediate oral notification or dispatch of a notice.[26] This opt-in to a late acceptance changes to an opt-out system if the late acceptance shows that it has been sent in such circumstances that it normally would have reached the offeror in due time.[27] Thus, assume that an offer requires a signed acceptance by June 10. On June 9, the offeree dispatches a signed acceptance by overnight service to the offeror's proper address. Due to unexpected weather problems, the carrier cannot deliver the letter until June 11. If the letter reveals that it was sent on an overnight basis on June 9, the late acceptance is effective unless the offeror, without delay, notifies the offeree that the offer has lapsed.[28] Thus, if the offeror purchased substitute goods early on June 11 prior to delivery of the acceptance, on the understanding that no acceptance had arrived on June 10, the offeror can avoid conclusion of the original contract by notifying the offeree of the late delivery of the acceptance. But if the offeror attempts to avoid

---

[26] See Article 21(1).   [27] See Article 21(2).   [28] See Article 21(2).

conclusion of the contract several days later because it has discovered that it can purchase fungible goods elsewhere at a lower price, the intervening delay should not preclude a finding that there was a contract.

The content of the offeror's notice of a late acceptance is a matter of some debate. In *Orica Australia Pty Ltd* v. *Aston Evaporative Services, LLC*,[29] the seller had dispatched an offer (actually, a "counter-counter-counteroffer" in a long series of communications between the parties) that was conditional on the buyer placing an order by March 30. The buyer placed no order by that date, but did place one after it committed to the purchase on May 11. The buyer contended that its May 11 commitment to purchase created a new offer (or perhaps a counter-counter-counter-counteroffer). The seller, on the other hand, characterized the May 11 commitment as an acceptance of its earlier offer. It had responded to the May 11 commitment by indicating that it could expedite delivery as requested by the buyer. But the court was dubious that such an indication satisfied the criteria for ratifying acceptance of an expired offer. It recognized that Article 21(1) authorizes an offeror to ratify a late acceptance by informing the offeree or dispatching a notice to that effect. It considered commentary that the ratification must make clear that the offeror was "accepting" the late acceptance by the offeree. The seller's response to the May 11 commitment was more ambiguous. It left unclear what actions the seller had taken as a consequence of the commitment and whether the seller considered itself bound prior to receipt of the actual purchase order. Thus, there was an open question of the parties' intent, which could only be resolved by reference to Article 8. The court's willingness to allow evidence of intent, however, indicated that it was rejecting a standard that required the offeror explicitly to state its ratification of a late acceptance under Article 21(1).

B. *Revocation of an offer stating a time for acceptance*

Offers that recite a period until which they can be accepted have generated an additional issue, although it is one that has generated more academic commentary than real-world confusion. Assume, for instance, that on June 1 Buyer dispatches a letter to Seller that recites "I offer to purchase 1000 pairs of pajamas, style #12345 at $10 per pair for delivery by June 30. Let me know by June 15 whether you can fulfill the offer." On June 5, Buyer faxes a revocation of that offer. On June 6, Seller sends a letter to Buyer that recites, "We accept all the terms of your offer." Is there a contract? Article 16(2)(a) states that an offer cannot be revoked if it indicates "whether by stating a fixed time for acceptance or otherwise" that it is irrevocable. The "by June 15" term in the offer is ambiguous. Does it mean that the offer becomes irrevocable until that date merely by stating a fixed time for acceptance? That would be consistent with the rules in many civil law jurisdictions, which

---

[29] 2015 U.S. Dist. LEXIS 98248 (D. Colo. July 28, 2015).

provide that inclusion of an expiration time for acceptance implicitly indicates that the offer is irrevocable until that time. Or does the phrase mean that the offer is open until the stated date, but can be revoked prior to that time if the revocation precedes the dispatch of the acceptance? That would be consistent with the common law rule, under which an offer is generally revocable until acceptance; the inclusion of a period after which the offer lapses has no effect on the revocability of the offer prior to that time.

This was not an unintentional ambiguity in the drafting of the CISG. To the contrary, the drafters were well aware of it. Delegates from common law countries introduced an amendment to what became Article 16(2)(a) in an effort to clarify that an offer was only irrevocable only when there was a clear indication to that effect. The proposed amendment was defeated. Delegates from civil law countries then introduced an amendment to the effect that fixing a time for acceptance of itself made the offer irrevocable. This proposal was also defeated. Ultimately, the delegates settled for studied ambiguity. The result may have allowed the kinds of political compromise that facilitated agreement among the delegates.[30] But it most assuredly did nothing to advance the cause of certainty and uniformity in international commercial law. Apart from demonstrating how the CISG drafting process deviated from the interests of commercial parties, however, the provision has done little damage. To date, there are no cases that rule on which interpretation is appropriate.

Article 16(2)(b) denies revocability regardless of any timing stated in the offer if it was reasonable for the offeree to rely on the offer as being irrevocable and the offeree has acted in reliance on the offer. One American court has considered this provision to constitute a modified version of promissory estoppel, without including any requirement such as foreseeability or detriment.[31] The inclusion of such a provision, the court concluded, might preempt a claim that traditional principles of promissory estoppel could be used to circumvent the requirement of a firm offer. But the court was unwilling to generalize that decision into a conclusion that the CISG generally preempted promissory estoppel claims.

C. *Battle of the forms and Article 19*

Notwithstanding the general principle of the CISG that an acceptance must indicate an assent to the offer, rather than a modification of it, Article 19, like its notorious counterpart in United States law,[32] recognizes that commercial practice

---

[30] See Clayton P. Gillette & Robert E. Scott, *The Political Economy of International Sales Law*, 25 Int'l. Rev. L. & Econ. 446, 474–75 (2005); Gyula Eörsi, *A Propos the 1980 Vienna Convention on Contracts for the International Sale of Goods*, 31 Am. J. Comp. L. 333, 345–46, 354 (1983).

[31] See *Geneva Pharmaceuticals Technology Corp. v. Barr Laboratories, Inc.*, 201 F. Supp.2d 236 (S.D.N.Y. 2002), *aff'd in part, rev'd in part*, 386 F.2d 485 (2d Cir. 2004).

[32] U.C.C. § 2-207.

often involves an exchange of forms that match imperfectly by parties who have every intention of creating a binding agreement. The issues then become: (1) has a contract been concluded, and, if so, (2) what are its terms?

Literally read, Article 19 resolves conflicts between terms in purported offers and acceptances by finding (1) that a contract can exist even if forms are not identical, and (2) that its terms are governed largely by the common law "last shot" rule. Under the Article, a reply to an offer that purports to be an acceptance but that contains additions, limitations, or other modifications is a rejection of the offer and constitutes a counteroffer. American courts have accepted the proposition that Article 19 incorporates the "mirror image" rule by which a response to an offer operates as an acceptance only if it "mirrors" the offer in every respect.[33] Note that the inclusion of additions and other modifications under this provision eliminates the need to make the distinction between "additional" terms and "different" terms that has plagued interpreters of UCC § 2–207.[34]

The effect of the CISG rule is to transform the original offeree whose purported acceptance includes additional or different terms into a counterofferor. As a result, the original offeror who continues performance after receipt of the conflicting form is vulnerable to being deemed to have accepted the counteroffer by performance. Assume, for instance, that Buyer issues a purchase order to Seller on a form that is silent with respect to remedies for breach of contract. Seller responds with a confirmation that limits Buyer's remedies to repair or replacement of any defective goods and dispute resolution through mandatory arbitration. Assume further that Seller subsequently ships the goods and Buyer uses and pays for them. Buyer subsequently experiences complaints about the goods and seeks to recover damages from Seller. Seller's form may be deemed to be a rejection of Buyer's purchase order and a counteroffer, which Buyer accepted by acceptance of the goods. Buyer would therefore be bound by the Seller's terms.

There is one exception to Article 19(1)'s "mirror image" rule. Under Article 19(2), a reply to an offer that purports to be an acceptance but that contains additional or different terms that do not materially alter the offer operates as an acceptance. The offeror, however, may avoid that effect by giving prompt notice of objection to the new terms. If the offeror does not object, the contract that is formed includes the terms of the offer with the modifications contained in the acceptance.

One might initially think that this exception cuts broadly against the "mirror image" rule, although it still gives the original offeree its terms in the absence of an

---

[33] See, e.g., *VLM Food Trading Int'l, Inc.* v. *Illinois Trading Co.*, 748 F.3d 780 (7th Cir. 2014); *Roser Technologies, Inc.* v. *Carl Schreiber GmbH*, 2013 U.S. Dist. LEXIS 129242 (W.D. Pa. September 10, 2013); *Miami Valley Paper, LLC* v. *Lebbing Eng'g & Consulting GmbH*, 2009 U.S. Dist. LEXIS 25201 (S.D. Ohio March 26, 2009); *Travelers Prop. Cas. Co. of Am.* v. *Saint-Gobain Technical Fabrics Canada Ltd.*, 474 F. Supp. 2d 1075, 1082 (D. Minn. 2007).

[34] The details of U.C.C. § 2–207 are discussed in Clayton P. Gillette & Steven D. Walt, *Sales Law: Domestic and International* 69–77 (3d ed. 2016).

objection from the offeror. But what subsection (2) gives, subsection (3) takes away. It defines "material" terms so broadly that it is difficult to think of what kind of terms would actually fall within Article 19(2). As a result, Article 19(2)'s qualification of the mirror image rule is modest. Material terms under subsection (3) include those that relate ("among other things") to price, payment, quality and quantity of goods, place and time of delivery, extent of liability, or settlement of disputes. Perhaps the only additional or different terms that might be sufficiently immaterial to fall within Article 19(2) are corrections of typographical errors and terms that expressly add a default rule that would otherwise apply or that provide the offeror with greater rights than the offer provided. Assume, for instance, that the contract is governed by the law of a jurisdiction in which the statute of limitations for bringing contract actions is six years and the offer is silent with respect to a limitations period. If the purported acceptance contains a clause reciting that any action on the contract must be brought within six years of the alleged breach, that express statement of an implicit default should be deemed immaterial. Alternatively, assume that the offer requires the offeror-buyer to make payment in United States dollars and the acceptance permits the buyer to make payment in United States dollars or euros. The expansion of the offeror's rights should again be considered immaterial.

Some ambiguity remains, however. Assume that the buyer offers to purchase goods for $50 per unit. The seller responds with a purported acceptance that recites the price at $45 per unit. The seller then ships the goods. Prior to the time the buyer receives the goods, their market price declines. When the buyer receives the goods, it returns them on the theory that no contract has been formed. The buyer has a valid argument. Article 19(3) recites that a price term is material. Thus, the different price term in the purported acceptance constitutes a material alteration of the offer and a counteroffer by the seller that the buyer never accepted. But the seller also has a plausible argument. The different price included in the seller's purported acceptance was arguably immaterial because it favored the buyer. Thus, if the buyer did not object to the new term, the seller's reply operates as an acceptance and the buyer is bound to a contract for the goods at a price of $45 per unit. The seller can contend that Article 19 (3) should not be read to create an absolute rule that the terms listed in that provision can never be immaterial, because doing so largely reads Article 19(2) out of the CISG. If changes favorable to the offeror are inherently immaterial under Article 19(2), it should be irrelevant that the change is in one of the terms listed in Article 19(3). The buyer's best, and perhaps compelling reply, is that allowing a term deemed material by Article 19(3) to be immaterial under Article 19(2) undermines the considerable advantages of a categorical rule. Treating terms listed in Article 19(3) as material under all circumstances eliminates diffuse and indeterminate inquiries into the impact of an alteration of the offer on contract value. Although a categorical application of 19(3) will prove overinclusive on occasion, it likely has net advantages over the full range of cases.

1. The scope of Article 19

Article 19 raises a few other issues that are worth considering. First, note that nothing within the Article requires the conflicting terms to appear on written or printed forms. Oral statements that constitute offers and acceptance fit as well. But the fact that Article 19 deals with the offer and acceptance process may also limit its scope. Assume that Buyer and Seller orally agree on the telephone for the purchase and sale of 1000 pairs of pajamas, style #12345 at $10 per pair. Seller subsequently issues a confirmation of the order, and the confirmation includes a limitation on Seller's liability for any defects in the goods. Buyer does not notice the new term, accepts and pays for the goods, and subsequently seeks to impose liability on the Seller in excess of what is permitted by Seller's term. Does the limitation apply? Since Article 19 literally applies only to the offer and acceptance process, a confirmation of a preexisting contract would not be governed by the terms of the Article. Instead, the new terms included in that confirmation would constitute a proposal for modification of the contract.[35] Modifications are governed by Article 29 of the CISG, and, as we discuss later, they require "mere agreement of the parties." But even "mere" agreement requires some form of agreement, and it is unclear whether a term in a confirmation would qualify as an "agreement" to the same extent that a term in a counteroffer can be included in a contract formed through Article 19(1). Agreements formed through modifications would presumably require analysis through the Article 8 process of determining the intent of the parties. Article 19 short-circuits that process by incorporating any term in the counteroffer into the contract without further ado, as long as the original offeror has accepted the performance of the counterofferor. Under Article 18(1), conduct, such as using and paying for shipped goods, can qualify as such acceptance.

Article 19 has proven controversial. Professor Honnold has referred to its application as "casuistic and unfair."[36] He suggests, for instance, that if the offeror simply re-sent its original offer after receiving the offeree's non-identical acceptance, the offeror would get its own terms back, and such a result seems unjustifiable from the perspective of commercial intentions. Given the dissatisfaction with the common law "mirror image" rule that spawned the notorious UCC § 2–207, and the dissatisfaction with Article 19's slightly modified mirror image rule, it may be that there is simply no ideal solution to the problem of conflicting, albeit ignored terms that precede performance indicating an intent to enter into a contract. One may certainly express frustration with the ostensible inability to find a workable resolution. But the reaction of some courts applying the CISG has been simply to ignore the language of Article 19. A 2002 decision of the German Federal Supreme Court and an earlier opinion of the French Supreme Court have been read as embracing a "knock-out"

[35] See, e.g., *VLM Food Trading Int'l, Inc. v. Ill. Trading Co.*, 748 F.3d 780, 786 (7th Cir. 2014).
[36] Honnold/Flechtner, supra note 6, at 252.

rule in which conflicting terms and conditions in the parties' forms drop out and are replaced by statutory defaults.[37] Some commentators have adopted the knock-out rule explicitly.[38] That may be a reasonable interpretation of some statutory resolutions of the battle of the forms, such as § 2–207. It may even be an appropriate result. But there is absolutely no basis for it in Article 19, and courts and commentators that recommend that approach are simply ignoring the text. Of course, one limitation of the CISG is that no matter how inappropriate the results generated by application of its language, there is no mechanism for amending its provisions. Whether that limitation justifies judicial circumvention of the language that exists may depend on whether one believes that ad hoc adjudication will serve the interests of commercial actors any better. So much for uniform international commercial law.

2. The incorporation of standard terms and conditions

There is an additional issue that has haunted Article 19 analysis, though it also implicates the more general question of what terms are included in an offer or an acceptance. Numerous cases involve situations in which either the offer or the purported acceptance makes reference to the transmitting party's standard terms and conditions and attempts to incorporate them into the contract. Those standard terms inevitably deviate from terms in the counterparty's form. Do those terms and conditions become part of the offer or the acceptance and thus become part of the contract? As a formal matter, the answer should depend on the intent of the parties, determined by reference to the rules on intent in Article 8.[39] Discerning intent is always difficult. Courts have generated a set of proxies rather than make explicit investigations into the subjective intent of the parties (Article 8(1)) or the intent that would be inferred by a reasonable person in the same circumstances (Article 8(2)). Unfortunately, these proxies frequently conflict or lack much explanatory force.

---

[37] See Federal Supreme Court (Germany), 9 January 2002, available at http://cisgw3.law.pace .edu/cases/020109g1.html; Supreme Court (France) (*Les Verreries de Saint Gobain* v. *Martins-werk*), 16 July 1998, available at http://cisgw3.law.pace.edu/cases/980716f1.html. The German Supreme Court concluded that the same result would obtain under the last shot rule that appears to be embodied in Article 19, because allowing one party the benefit of its terms while omitting terms beneficial to the counterparty would violate good faith. How good faith could be violated by following the literal dictates of a provision of the CISG itself is unexplained. The same result appears to exist in a subsequent German case, Court of Appeals Frankfurt (Germany), 26 June 2006, available at http://cisgw3.law.pace.edu/cases/060626g1.html, where the court concluded that a buyer's silence in the face of the seller's standard terms and conditions could not be considered assent to those terms. But that case dealt with the existence of an agreement to arbitrate, which is subject to its own strict requirements and that therefore may require a higher level of agreement than other terms.

[38] See references in Ulrich G. Schroeter, *Article 19*, in Schlechtriem & Schwenzer: Commentary on the Convention on the International Sale of Goods (CISG) 349–350 (Ingeborg Schwenzer ed., 3d ed. 2010) [hereinafter "Schlechtriem & Schwenzer"].

[39] See *Allied Dynamics Corp.* v. *Kennametal, Inc.*, 2014 U.S. Dist. LEXIS 107920 (E.D.N.Y. August 5, 2014).

The problem arises in a variety of different contexts. Take the easiest situation, in which the terms and conditions are physically made available in a separate document that accompanies the offer or acceptance. Under those circumstances, most courts indicate that the terms and conditions are as binding as the terms on the physical offer or acceptance.[40] That is, most courts conclude that if the terms and conditions are referenced in the offer or acceptance and made physically available to the counterparty, they become part of the offer or acceptance and have the effect that any writing would have under Article 19.

There is, however, some dispute about what it means to make terms and conditions available where they do not physically accompany the offer or acceptance. The general concern underlying these decisions is whether an offeree could have intended that terms it had no reasonable opportunity to consider would be incorporated into a final contract.[41] The consensus view is that no such intent could be inferred under those circumstances. Thus, whether or not proffered terms are incorporated depends on what constitutes their accessibility to the offeree, sufficient to conclude that the counterparty had a reasonable opportunity to consider them. Some courts have suggested that nothing other than tangible copies of the standard terms and conditions will suffice.[42] Other courts have even denied effect to terms and conditions that were printed on the back of forms, unless the front of the same form made explicit reference to the terms on the back.[43] A well-known German Federal Supreme Court case observed that commentators unanimously agreed that the recipient of a contract offer based on general terms and conditions must have the ability to become aware of them in a reasonable manner, and that meant transmitting the text to the recipient or making the text available in some other way.[44] The plausible "some other way" is itself contestable, as we indicate later.

[40] See, e.g., Federal Supreme Court (Germany), 31 October 2001, available at http://cisgw3.law .pace.edu/cases/011031g1.html; District Court Trier (Germany), 8 January 2004, available at http://cisgw3.law.pace.edu/cases/040108g1.html.

[41] See Court of Appeals Naumburg (Germany), 13 February 2013, available at http://cisgw3.law .pace.edu/cases/130213g1.html.

[42] See District Court Stuttgart (Germany), 15 October 2009, available at http://cisgw3.law.pace.edu/ cases/091015g1.html; District Court Utrecht (Netherlands), 21 January 2009, available at http://cisgw3.law.pace.edu/cases/090121n1.html.

[43] See Court of Appeals Navarra (Spain), 27 December 2007, available at http://cisgw3.law .pace.edu/cases/071227s4.html; Court of Appeals Paris (France) (*ISEA Industrie* v. *Lu*), 13 December 1995, available at http://cisgw3.law.pace.edu/cases/951213f1.html. In one case, a German court allowed incorporation of terms printed on the back of a form in Italian and German and expressly referred to on the front of the form. See Lower Court Nordhorn (Germany), 14 June 1994, available at http://cisgw3.law.pace.edu/cases/940614g1.html.

[44] See Federal Supreme Court (Germany), 31 October 2001, available at http://cisgw3.law.pace .edu/cases/011031g1.html. Subsequent German decisions have followed this rationale. See Court of Appeals Naumburg (Germany), 13 February 2013, available at http://cisgw3.law .pace.edu/cases/130213g1.html.

Other cases have restricted what it means for terms to be "available" by focusing on their language rather their tangibility. German courts have concluded that in order to be effective, the general terms and conditions, and the reference to them, must be phrased in the language of the recipient or the language in which negotiations were conducted.[45] One German court refused to enforce the seller's terms and conditions, which were written in German, where the parties' dealings were conducted primarily in English, even though buyer's CEO "should sufficiently understand it."[46] Another German court, however, intimated that it would have been sufficient to incorporate terms in a language other than the language in which the contract was negotiated if the employee of the recipient who was responsible for the contract spoke the language in which the standard terms were written.[47] The Austrian Supreme Court indicated that the intent of the parties would govern the issue of whether a buyer's standard terms were incorporated. It then remanded the case for a determination of whether one party's references, in English, to the standard terms written in German on the back of a form became part of the contract in light of the parties' negotiations in English, their trading history, the presence of a bilingual representative of seller, and whether standard practices that indicated acceptance of the terms had evolved.[48]

Still other courts have placed on the recipient of the standard terms the onus of objecting if it does not understand the language in which they are written.[49] This may be closer to the American position. In the *MCC-Marble Ceramic Center Inc.* v. *Ceramica Nuova D'Agostino, S.p.A.* case,[50] the court purported to be astounded that a buyer "purportedly experienced in commercial matters, would sign a contract in a foreign language and expect not to be bound simply because he could not comprehend its terms. We find nothing in the CISG that might counsel this type of reckless behavior and nothing that signals any retreat from the proposition that parties who sign contracts will be bound by them regardless of whether they have read them or understood them." In what could be explained as either an effort at compromise or jingoism, the Austrian Supreme Court concluded that the addressee will be bound by terms if they are written in an internationally common language and he or she does not immediately indicate a lack of understanding. The court determined that English, French, and German qualify as international languages for

[45] See Court of Appeals Hamm (Germany), 6 December 2005, available at http://cisgw3.law.pace .edu/cases/051206g1.html; Court of Appeals Düsseldorf (Germany), 21 April 2004, available at http://cisgw3.law.pace.edu/cases/040421g3.html.

[46] See District Court Memmingen (Germany), 13 September 2000, available at http://cisgw3.law .pace.edu/cases/000913g1.html.

[47] See Court of Appeals Düsseldorf (Germany), 21 April 2004, available at http://cisgw3.law.pace .edu/cases/040421g3.html.

[48] See, e.g., Supreme Court (Austria), 17 December 2003, available at http://cisgw3.law.pace.edu/ cases/031217a3.html.

[49] See, e.g., Court of Appeals Köln (Germany), 24 May 2006, available at http://cisgw3.law.pace .edu/cases/060524g1.html.

[50] 144 F.3d 1384, 1387 n.9 (11th Cir. 1998).

these purposes.[51] That same case, however, took a less dogmatic view of the issue and suggested a variety of factors that would be probative of the intent of the parties to incorporate terms drafted in a language foreign to one of them. Those factors included the length, intensity, and economic importance of the business relations between the parties, as well as extent to which the foreign language is used within the society. Repeat players might be expected to invest in learning each other's language, while discrete, single-play transactors might not.

In other cases, the terms and conditions are not made physically available to the counterparty. Of course, that party could request them, once placed on notice that the other party has asserted that they apply to the contract. The German Federal Supreme Court decision previously referred to rejected the claim that the recipient had an obligation to request the terms. The court opined that the imposition of that burden would delay the conclusion of the contract, a consequence that neither party would prefer.[52] A Dutch appellate court similarly concluded that standard terms would become part of the contract if the parties implicitly agreed to their incorporation and the other party had a reasonable opportunity to review them.[53] That reasonable opportunity, however, had to arise as a consequence of the party who proposed the terms making them available to the other party. To require the other party to request them would result in both delay in contract formation and, given the relative ease with which the provider could transmit them, violate the principle of good faith under Article 7(1) and the general obligation of cooperation. Given the conclusion that the proposer of the terms was in a superior position to convey them at low cost, imposing the obligation to provide them on that party reflects the allocation to which the parties presumably would have bargained. It is not clear that the admonition of "good faith" adds much to the analysis. A Belgian court, however, concluded that a seller's standard terms could be included in a contract where the seller sent an invoice that offered to send the full text of terms, required any protest within eight days, and received no objection from the buyer within that period.[54]

---

[51] See Supreme Court (Austria), 17 December 2003, available at http://cisgw3.law.pace.edu/cases/031217a3.html.

[52] To the same effect, see Court of Appeals Naumburg (Germany), 13 February 2013, available at http://cisgw3.law.pace.edu/cases/130213g1.html ("Given that there may be considerable differences between both parties' standard terms, the recipient cannot reasonably foresee by itself which provisions the other party is about to incorporate into the contract when merely a reference is made. Even if the recipient were able to investigate the content of standard terms referred to by the other party, the process would unreasonable delay any contract conclusions to the recipient's detriment."); District Court Rotterdam (Netherlands), 25 February 2009, available at http://cisgw3.law.pace.edu/cases/090225n1.html.

[53] See Court of Appeals, The Hague (Netherlands), 22 April 2014, available at http://cisgw3.law.pace.edu/cases/140422n1.html.

[54] See Court of Appeals Ghent (Belgium), 4 October 2004, available at http://cisgw3.law.pace.edu/cases/041004b1.html.

Technological advances not anticipated during the drafting of the CISG may affect the appropriate allocation of responsibility for obtaining standard terms and conditions. In *CSS Antenna, Inc.* v. *Amphenol—Tuchel Electronics, GmbH*,[55] the court noted that the seller's confirmation form recited that general terms and conditions could be found on and downloaded from its website, and gave the relevant hyperlink. The court did not say whether reference to a website from which terms and conditions could be obtained satisfied the "availability" standard, in part because the court believed that the seller had not sufficiently indicated its intent that the terms and conditions – especially a forum selection clause contained therein – become part of the contract. But other courts have opined on what one would anticipate will become an increasingly common practice. A German court has held that a reference in seller's form that its standard terms and conditions were available at its place of business and on its website was insufficient to incorporate into the contract a jurisdictional clause found in those terms. Transmission of the terms would have been necessary.[56]

The court in *Roser Technologies, Inc.* v. *Carl Schreiber GmbH*[57] similarly concluded that references in a seller's quotations and order confirmations to a website on which standard terms could be found was insufficient to incorporate those terms into the contract, even under a "last shot" interpretation of Article 19. The court found that terms in the offer that were inconsistent with the standard terms referenced in the seller's quotations indicated a lack of intention to be bound by those terms. The confirmations did not constitute an effective counteroffer that incorporated the referenced terms because the language in those documents "merely directs the other party to a website which needs to be navigated in order for the standard conditions to be located."[58] There was no evidence that the buyer had actual knowledge of the terms or that the parties had discussed their incorporation. The court did, however, find that a material payment term that was stated on the face of the confirmation itself became part of the contract under the terms of Article 19.

The question of availability and the implications of technological advances become more complicated when considered through the lens of transaction costs. If the underlying assumption of Article 19 is that most parties do not read the forms of counterparties, then making physical copies available in all cases in order to satisfy the inquisitiveness of the idiosyncratic counterparty may be wasteful. It might be more efficient to require that idiosyncratic party to request standard terms that have been referenced. The same holds for translations. One might reasonably ask why offerors should be obligated to provide terms that will not be read, rather than simply indicate that they will be made available to the infrequent reader.

---

[55] 764 F. Supp. 2d 745 (D. Md. 2011).
[56] See Court of Appeals Celle (Germany), 24 July 2009, available at http://cisgw3.law.pace.edu/cases/090724g1.html.
[57] 2013 U.S. Dist. LEXIS 129242 (W.D. Pa. September 10, 2013).   [58] Id. at *27.

But that conclusion assumes that it is substantially more costly to provide the terms in all cases than it is for the counterparty to request and obtain them in the rare case in which it actually wants to consider them prior to concluding the contract. Technology may change that. If, as in the *CSS Antenna* and *Roser Technologies* cases, a seller sends a confirmation/acceptance that includes a hyperlink on which the buyer may easily click to open the terms and conditions, the burden on both parties – to include the hyperlink and to open the link – seems sufficiently small that neither party appears to have much of a cost advantage. If the hyperlink immediately opens to the referenced standard terms, the cost to the buyer of taking that step seems no more burdensome to the buyer than the effort it would take to review a physical copy of those terms that is attached to the seller's confirmation and that all would agree is sufficiently "available" to the buyer to satisfy the requirements of incorporation. If, on the other hand, the supplied hyperlink opens only to a home page of the seller and requires further substantial navigation through the seller's website, one might be more dubious that the relevant "availability" standard has been satisfied. The court in *Roser Technologies* noted that the website brought up by the seller's hyperlink "needs to be navigated" in order to review the terms and conditions. It would have been useful to know whether that meant an additional click, or five additional clicks to retrieve the relevant terms. Given the assumption that few commercial actors review even the terms that are physically presented to them, which do become part of the contract, the notion that terms that can be discovered with relatively equal ease are outside the contract rests on a fiction (that more readily discoverable terms would have been reviewed) that defies commercial practice.

One could imagine an evolving scenario that reduces costs of discovery even further. Assume that the seller sends an acceptance through an email to which its terms and conditions can be attached as a file or in which those terms and conditions can be embedded. Once the seller attaches or embeds the file, the buyer needs to do little more than open the relevant file or read the entire email. In short, the costs to the seller of attaching the file are likely less than the costs of including a physical copy of the terms and conditions along with the physical confirmation. A transaction cost-reducing theory would want to encourage sellers to take such action. Thus, we would expect courts to recognize the capacity of parties to exploit technology to reduce transaction costs in this manner and encourage parties to satisfy the "make available" requirement by approving the use of emailed files to send standard terms and conditions to counterparties. The minimal costs of such attachment would seem to trump even the potentially more complicated step of asking the recipient to open a hyperlink in order to find the other party's terms and conditions.

Most commentators and courts require that the proposer at least ensure that the counterparty is aware of the terms prior to conclusion of the contract.[59] Some

---

[59] See Joseph Lookofsky, Understanding the CISG 155 (4th (Worldwide) ed. 2012); Ingeborg Schwenzer, Pascal Hachem & Christopher Kee, Global Sales and Contract Law 166 (2012).

courts have gone to lengths to determine that standard terms were not incorporated into an offer or an acceptance, either because they were "surprising,"[60] or because the reference to them was insufficiently clear.[61] Other courts and commentators, however, have been willing to place the burden on the recipient of the proposal,[62] while still other cases have determined that the parties had, in prior dealings, established a practice of incorporating terms and conditions, such that continued acknowledgment of their incorporation was superfluous.[63] One United States District Court took the position that standard terms that included a warranty disclaimer and limitation on liability were effective where they appeared on the top of boxes that contained the goods, and the buyer opened the boxes and paid for the goods.[64] This determination was consistent with American decisions that recognize the incorporation of post-contract terms in "rolling" or "layered" contracts.[65] Nevertheless, the Court of Appeals in the case reversed the grant of summary judgment for the seller on the grounds that material issues of fact existed with respect to whether, under the CISG, the contested provision was part of the parties' contract.[66] Foreign commentary has criticized the district court opinion as allowing terms to be added subsequent to the formation of the original contract.[67] We are more sympathetic to the claim that terms in rolling contracts are includable. At least in relatively thick commercial markets, we anticipate that terms will be at least nonoppressive and the reference to terms and conditions often common.[68] Indeed, the district court in *Berry v. Ken M. Spooner Farms* noted that the seller introduced evidence that both the use of rolling terms and the clause on its box top were common in the trade. Nevertheless, we recognize that the more formal structures of contract formation outside of the American rolling contract cases may make that analysis appear quite radical.

---

[60] See, e.g., Court of Appeals Düsseldorf (Germany), 21 April 2004, available at http://cisgw3.law.pace.edu/cases/040421g3.html; Court of Appeals Zweibrücken (Germany), 31 March 1998, available at http://cisgw3.law.pace.edu/cases/980331g1.html, *aff'd* Federal Supreme Court (Germany), 24 March 1999, available at www.cisg.law.pace.edu/cases/990324g1.html.

[61] See, e.g., Court of Appeals Navarra (Spain), 27 December 2007, available at http://cisgw3.law.pace.edu/cases/071227s4.html; *CSS Antenna, Inc. v. Amphenol – Tuchel Electronics, GmbH*, 764 F. Supp. 2d 745 (D. Md. 2011).

[62] See, e.g., *Filanto, S.p.A. v. Chilewich Intern. Corp.*, 789 F. Supp. 1229 (S.D.N.Y. 1992).

[63] See Supreme Court (Austria), 31 August 2005, available at http://cisgw3.law.pace.edu/cases/050831a3.html; Court of Appeals Linz (Austria), 23 March 2005, available at http://cisgw3.law.pace.edu/cases/050323a3.html; District Court Coburg (Germany), 12 December 2006, available at http://cisgw3.law.pace.edu/cases/061212g1.html.

[64] See *Berry v. Ken M. Spooner Farms, Inc.*, 2006 U.S. Dist. LEXIS 31262 (W.D. Wash. April 13, 2006).

[65] See, e.g., *M.A. Mortenson Co., Inc. v. Timberline Software Corp.*, 998 P.2d 305 (Wash. 2000); *Hill v. Gateway 2000, Inc.*, 105 F. 3d 1147 (7th Cir.), *cert. denied*, 522 U.S. 808 (1997).

[66] See *Berry v. Ken M. Spooner Farms, Inc.*, 2007 U.S. App. LEXIS 26990 (9th Cir. November 16, 2007).

[67] See, e.g., Sieg Eiselen, *The Requirements for the Inclusion of Standard Terms in International Sales Contracts*, 14 Potchefstroom Electronic L. J. 234 (2011).

[68] See, e.g., Clayton P. Gillette, *Rolling Contracts as an Agency Problem*, 2004 Wisc. L. Rev. 679.

D. *Open terms*

1. Price, quantity, and intent

Nothing in the CISG requires that all final terms of the contract be embodied in the offer and acceptance that creates the contract. Article 14 explicitly allows terms to remain open. That Article defines an offer as a proposal that is "sufficiently definite and indicates the intention of the offeror to be bound in case of acceptance." A proposal in turn is sufficiently definite if it "explicitly or implicitly fixes or makes provision for determining the quantity and the price."[69] The fact that an offer can make a provision for determining quantity and price indicates that the price or quantity itself does not have to be stated in the offer. A proposal to purchase 1000 barrels of oil per month at 95 percent of the market price as reported in an industry journal on the last day of each month would certainly be sufficient. A Chinese arbitral tribunal went so far (perhaps too far) as to find that a clause in a contract that the price would be as subsequently "mutually agreed" satisfied the conditions of an offer because it required the parties to set a price through mutual negotiation, although the same tribunal concluded that a description of the goods as "basic pig iron or foundry pig iron as to be mutually agreed" was insufficiently definite to constitute an offer.[70] Of course, the intention to be bound, required for an offer under Article 14(1), might be lacking when the proposal omits a quantity or price term. A federal district court concluded that a seller's quotes were not offers when they did not fix quantity and described the quotations as being for "budgetary" purposes.[71] Although the court recited case law that required an offer to fix quantity, its conclusion is consistent with a finding that the quotes did not indicate the seller's intention to be bound in the case of the buyer's acceptance. The case does not stand for the proposition that Article 14(1) requires the offer to fix quantity.

2. The Article 55 conundrum

Some parties may fail to specify the mechanism by which an open price term is to be completed. The scope and consequences of such a term are illustrated by a German case involving the alleged sale in mid-2003 of 400,000 jars of pitted sour cherries to be delivered within the following year at a price "to be fixed during the season."[72]

---

[69] Article 14(1).

[70] See CIETAC Arbitration (China), 25 December 1998, available at http://cisgw3.law.pace.edu/cases/981225c1.html.

[71] See *Allied Dynamics Corp.* v. *Kennametal, Inc.*, 2014 U.S. Dist. LEXIS 107920 (E.D.N.Y. August 5, 2014).

[72] See District Court Neubrandenburg (Germany), 3 August 2005, available at http://cisgw3.law.pace.edu/cases/050803g1.html.

When the buyer failed to order more than about 130,000 jars, the seller brought an action to recover for damages suffered by the buyer's failure to order the balance of the jars. The buyer claimed that no contract had been concluded. The court found that the parties had acknowledged in their writings that a contract had been concluded. In addition, the parties had performed in a manner that indicated an intent to conclude a contract, as the buyer had accepted some jars under terms dictated by the parties' writings. The court dismissed the argument that the open price term precluded the finding of a contract. Instead, the court concluded, the phrase "to be fixed during the season" didn't mean that the parties would find a way of agreeing on a price during the season. Rather, it meant that the parties intended to adopt the "season price" that would come into existence during the period when the contract was to be performed, but that was unavailable at the time the contract was concluded. The court then added that the parties' implicit agreement on the season price was "thereby a determination under the standards of Article 55 CISG."

At first glance, the court's use of Article 55 to complete an open price term makes perfect sense. Article 55 provides that open price terms are presumptively completed by "the price generally charged at the time of the conclusion of the contract for such goods sold under comparable circumstances in the trade concerned." In short, one completes the open price term under Article 55 with the market price at the time of the conclusion of the contract. However, that is not what either the parties or the court did in the sour cherries case. The parties' contract called for the price to be the "season price," which the court understood to be the market price of the cherries on the date of the first delivery under the contract. Thus, if "season price" was the market price of the cherries during the season, the contract price is the market price at the first delivery – at a point after the contract's conclusion. That was also the price that the court applied. Article 55 therefore was unnecessary (and inapplicable) to the result in the case. Of course, the court may have been relying on the clause in Article 55 that makes the formula stated in that provision subject to "any indication to the contrary." But if so, then again, the court's appeal to Article 55 was unnecessary, since the parties' indication of a means of fixing the price by reference to a measure that could be determined in the future was sufficient under Article 14(1).

The court may have been on stronger ground when it argued that Article 55 could be applicable if the parties' incorporation of a price to be "fixed during the season" meant that the parties wanted to reach agreement at a later point in time. Under that interpretation, the court argued, the parties had opted out of Article 14 as a means of forming their contract. If the subsequent agreement on price did not occur, therefore, there would still be a valid contract established by the parties, and the price of the goods could be established through the use of Article 55. That seems correct, but even in that case, the market price to be incorporated would have been the one that prevailed at the time of the conclusion of the contract.[73] It would not be the market price at the time of the first delivery under the contract, as the court found.

Two points should be noted about Article 55's formula. First, it varies in its risk allocation from the parallel provision in some domestic law. Under UCC § 2–305(1), for example, open price terms are completed by reference to "a reasonable price at the time for delivery." "Reasonable price" easily equates with market price, but the risk of price changes between execution and performance of the contract are quite different. Under Article 55, the relevant market price is the one prevailing "at the time of the conclusion of the contract." Thus, the seller takes the risk of market price increases between conclusion and performance of the contract, while the buyer takes the risk of market price declines. Under the UCC provision, since the relevant market price is determined at the time of delivery,[74] sellers take the risk of market price decreases between conclusion and performance of the contract and buyers take the risk of market price increases.

But the more significant issue with Article 55 is the scope of its application. According to the terms of that Article, market price is used "[w]here a contract has been validly concluded but does not expressly or implicitly fix or make provision for determining the price." The problem lies in the ostensibly contradictory language of that provision in light of Article 14. That Article recites that a proposal for concluding a contract constitutes an offer if, among other things, it is sufficiently definite. Further, it recites that a proposal qualifies as sufficiently definite "if it . . . expressly or implicitly fixes or makes provision for determining . . . the price." Article 55's requirement that it operates only when there is a contract that has been validly concluded but that does not expressly or implicitly fix or make provision for fixing the price seems to contradict Article 14's requirement that there be a means of fixing the price before a contract can be validly concluded. The puzzle has perplexed both courts and commentators.

The Articles can be reconciled by noting that Article 14(1) does not require that all contracts comprise an offer that contains a definite price (i.e., one that fixes or makes provision for determining the price). Instead, the second sentence of Article 14(1) only states a sufficient condition for a proposal to qualify as "sufficiently definite." It says that *if* a proposal fixes price, then the proposal qualifies as "sufficiently definite" (assuming that the other criteria of Article 14 have been satisfied). As such the sentence states a safe harbor of sorts: A proposal that indicates the goods and fixes or makes provision for price will not be deemed insufficiently definite in terms. The sentence does not state a necessary condition for a proposal being sufficiently

---

[73] The court also noted that another tribunal had contended that parties who agree to reach a later agreement on price create a condition precedent to the conclusion of a valid contract. Failure to reach such an agreement, therefore, did not mean that the price was to be completed by Article 55. Instead it meant that there was no valid contract because a condition precedent to its existence had failed. See International Arbitral Court of the Chamber of Industry and Commerce of the Russian Federation (Russia), 13 March 1995, available at www.cisg.law.pace.edu/cases/950303r2.html#mr*.

[74] See, e.g., U.C.C. § 2–305(1).

definite with respect to price. It does not say that a proposal is sufficiently definite only if the proposal fixes price. Thus, as far as Article 14(1)'s second sentence goes, a proposal that indicates the goods without setting price still can count as an offer. Whether the proposal is an offer depends on whether it is sufficiently definite in terms according to Article 14(1)'s first sentence. That sentence requires the proposal to indicate the intention of the proposer to be bound in the case of acceptance. In some circumstances a proposal that omits price still might indicate an intention to be bound.[75] Article 55 can then be used to fix the price as the market price at the conclusion of the contract.

A possible alternative answer to the puzzle is to recognize that Article 14 and Article 55 speak to different situations. On this view the two Articles cover two different ways in which contracts can be formed under the CISG.[76] One way is through the mechanics of offer and acceptance described in Articles 14–24. Article 23 indicates that a contract is concluded when an acceptance of an offer becomes effective and Article 14 tells us when an offer is effective. But Article 23 does not say that the process of offer and acceptance provides the exclusive mechanism through which a contract can be concluded, and Article 14 does not define the only way in which one can make an offer. Rather, these Articles can be read as statements of conditions that are sufficient, but not necessary to have an effective contract. Another way in which contracts can be formed is through an agreement that is not the product of an acceptance of an offer. Article 55 recognizes contracts formed in this way.[77] Assume, for instance, that parties negotiate a single document over a substantial period of time, so that the signed documents contain clauses presented and dickered over by each party. It is difficult to classify the resulting document as having arisen through the process of offer and acceptance. If the resulting document was silent with respect to a means of expressly or implicitly fixing the price, but otherwise satisfied the requirements of a contract, then Article 55 would fill the price gap without violating any portion of Article 14. Another example might be an acceptance of an offer that the parties agree in advance does not require a price term.[78]

This "different routes" way of reconciling Articles 14(1) and 55 is questionable. To begin with, the CISG's explicit mechanism of contract formation is offer and acceptance. There is no explicit provision in the CISG for conclusion of a contract

---

[75] See, e.g., Commercial Court St. Gallen (Switzerland), 5 December 1995, available at http://cisgw3.law.pace.edu/cases/951205s1.html.

[76] See Franco Ferrari, *Article 14*, in UN Convention on Contracts for the International Sale of Goods (CISG): Commentary 216, 230 (Stefan Kröll, Loukas Mistelis & Pilar Perales Viscasillas eds., 2011) [hereinafter "Kröll et al."]; Harry M. Flechtner, in Honnold/Flechtner, supra note 6, at 467.

[77] Cf. U.C.C. § 2–204(1) ("A contract for sale of good may be made in any manner sufficient to show agreement including conduct by both parties which recognizes the existence of such a contract.").

[78] See Peter Schlechtriem, *Article 14*, in Commentary on the UN Convention on the International Sale of Goods (CISG) 188, 189 (Peter Schlechtriem & Ingeborg Schwenzer eds., 2d (English) ed. 2005) [hereinafter "Schlechtriem & Schwenzer 2005"].

on a basis other than an acceptance of an offer, however artificial the analysis might be in some cases. Articles 14(1) and 55 therefore appear to apply to contracts concluded by way of acceptance of an offer. We note, however, that a decent argument can be made that the CISG obliquely recognizes that contracts can be concluded other than by acceptance of an offer. Articles 14–24 state the mechanics of formation when a contract is created by offer and acceptance. However, none of these formation rules precludes a contract from being formed by other means. As far as the rules go, a contract might be concluded by any means sufficient to indicate a sales agreement. Forming a contract by a means other than through offer and acceptance simply derogates from Articles 14–23, which is perfectly permissible under Article 6. If such a contract does not set the price, Article 55 fills the gap. Article 55, which recognizes "validly concluded" contracts lacking a price term, implicitly allows a contract to be concluded other than through the mechanism of offer and acceptance. One of us finds the argument weak, because the CISG does not explicitly recognize a means of contract formation other than by acceptance of an offer.[79] The other of us, however, concludes that the CISG does not purport to limit contract formation to offer and acceptance, and thus finds no inconsistency in applying Article 55 to contracts formed through alternative procedures.

The court in the pitted sour cherries case seemed sympathetic to the application of Article 55 to contracts formed through methods other than offer and acceptance. It seemed uncertain about whether the parties' contract was formed by offer and acceptance or by some other method. The court did find that the writings between the parties expressed an intention to be bound. But the court also expressed doubt about its ability to determine who had made an offer or whether the contract had been formed through offer and acceptance, since the relevant writings appeared to refer to a preexisting oral agreement. Ultimately, the court found the relevant contract in the fact that the parties had partially performed their agreement. Thus, the contract was formed by conduct, not offer and acceptance. As we noted, the court's use of Article 55 to complete the open price term was likely a misapplication of that provision, since the contract provided for

---

[79] Article 92(1) allows Contracting States to make a reservation opting out Part II of the CISG under prescribed conditions. Part II contains Articles 14–24, which are the CISG's formation rules. Article 55 appears in Part III of the Convention. Thus, for States that have made a reservation to Article 92(1), it is possible that a contract can be concluded other than by an acceptance of an offer, in accordance with formation rules under applicable domestic law. Article 55 supplies a price term for contracts with open price terms formed in accordance with these formation rules. For the considerations behind the reservation, see Jan Kleineman, *The New Nordic Approach to CISG Part II: Pragmatism Wins the Day?*, in The CISG Convention and Domestic Contract Law 21 (Joseph Lookofsky & Mads B. Anderson eds., 2014). Denmark, Finland, Norway, and Sweden, which previously had made an Article 92 reservation, have withdrawn their reservations. See Press Release, United Nations Information Service, Norway Becomes a Party to Part II (Formation of Contracts) of the United Nations Convention on Contracts for the International Sale of Goods (CISG) (April 17, 2014), available at www.unis .unvienna.org/unis/en/pressrels/2014/unisl198.html. To date no Contracting State has an effective Article 92 reservation excluding Part II's formation rules.

the fixing of the price. Nevertheless, the court's misapplication of Article 55 was harmless because it ultimately did not fix price in accordance with that Article. Instead, it honored the parties' intentions and set price as the market price during the upcoming season, after the conclusion of the contract.

III. CONTRACT MODIFICATION

A. The "agreement" requirement

Contract modifications are governed by Article 29 of the CISG. As in the case of contract formation, the CISG eliminates any need for formal requirements to make a modification effective. Simply put, a contract "may be modified or terminated by the mere agreement of the parties."[80] As with the original contract, no consideration is required. As with the elimination of form requirements, this provision is subject to a declaration made under Article 96.[81] While China's now-withdrawn declaration spoke explicitly only about its rejection of Article 11's dispensation with formalities and evidence of a contract's conclusion, the court in *Zhejiang Shaoxing Yongli Printing and Dyeing Co., Ltd. v. Microflock Textile Group Corp.*[82] treated the declaration as referring also to modifications. Because alleged modifications to the defendant's obligations to make full payments of invoices in that case were not evidenced in writing, the court was unwilling to recognize any deviation from full payment.

What constitutes an agreement for purposes of Article 29(1) will usually be straightforward. In *Valero Marketing & Supply Co. v. Greeni Oy*,[83] the parties initially agreed that the seller would deliver goods to the buyer between September 10 and 20, 2001. When the seller could not deliver on time or conform to other contractual conditions, the parties entered a new agreement that extended the time for delivery, set a lower price for the goods, and imposed additional requirements on the seller. The district court contended that the new agreement served to extend the seller's time of performance under Article 47, and thus precluded any intervening action for breach by the buyer. But the Third Circuit found that the new agreement was not the conferral of an extension of time, but rather a modification of the original agreement, evidenced by a proposal from the buyer, an agreement by the seller, and the transmittal of a written confirmation by the buyer. As the case indicates, there is little reason to think that the concept of "agreement" is different for purposes of Article 29(1) than it is for purposes of the initial formation of the contract that is allegedly being modified.

---

[80] Accord UNIDROIT Principles of International Commercial Contracts Article 3.2 (2010); Principles of European Contract Law Articles 1:102 (parties are free to enter into a contract and to determine its contents), 1:107 (Principles apply to agreements to modify a contract) (1998).

[81] Article 12.   [82] 2008 U.S. Dist. LEXIS 40418 (S.D. Fla. May 19, 2008).

[83] 2007 U.S. App. LEXIS 17282 (3d Cir. June 27, 2007).

Nevertheless, the existence of the requisite agreement can be a matter of some dispute. Thus, assume that an oral contract is followed by a shipment that includes an invoice with a term additional to those previously agreed to by the parties. If the buyer says nothing about the new term (probably because its inclusion in the invoice was not noticed) but uses the goods and pays for them, is that conduct evidence of "agreement" to the modification, just as conduct of an offeree can constitute assent to an offer under Article 18(1)? Or is the buyer's silence as ineffective to create an agreement as silence or inactivity is to create an acceptance under Article 18(1)? Again, one would imagine that the intent of the parties as determined under Article 8 would determine the issue. But courts have provided more categorical responses, albeit conflicting ones.

There are some statements to the effect that acquiescence in behavior that is not permitted under the contract can constitute the requisite agreement, as where a buyer did not explicitly object to a shipment delay, although it did urge prompt shipment by the seller and demand status information.[84] The substance of the modification may also matter. Courts have been particularly reluctant to allow incorporation of forum selection clauses through modifications purportedly agreed to by silence. The court in *CSS Antenna, Inc.* v. *Amphenol—Tuchel Electronics, GmbH*[85] considered the distinction between a modification to a preexisting oral contract and performance of a contract without objection to a term in a counteroffer as a key difference between Article 29 and Article 19. Two American courts have rejected the notion that a forum selection clause in an invoice constituted an effective modification where the only evidence of "agreement" was the buyer's failure to object.[86] But after one of the American cases was dismissed and relitigated in Canada, an Ontario court, perhaps relying more on inferences about intent, concluded that if there were multiple deliveries under the contract, the forum selection clause could be effective at some point after the buyer became aware of it and failed to object.[87] The Ontario court did not necessarily conclude that conduct plus silence was sufficient to constitute a modification. Instead, the court concluded that (1) the issue was a triable one, to be decided by a lower court, but that (2) if forced to decide, the court would determine that subsequent shipments were governed by the contested forum selection clause, although those shipments were governed by separate contracts. Another court distinguished the "modification by conduct" cases and found an affirmative act sufficient to constitute an agreement under Article 29(1) where the buyer was required

---

[84] See American Arbitration Association, International Centre for Dispute Resolution (United States) (*Macromex Srl.* v. *Globex International Inc.*), 23 October 2007, available at http://cisgw3 .law.pace.edu/cases/071023a5.html.

[85] 764 F. Supp. 2d 745 (D. Md. 2011).

[86] See *Chateau des Charmes Wines Ltd.* v. *Sabaté USA Inc.*, 328 F.3d 528, 531 (9th Cir. 2003); *Solae, LLC* v. *Hershey Canada Inc.*, 557 F. Supp. 2d 452, 457–58 (D. Del. 2008).

[87] See Ontario Superior Court (Canada) (*Chateau des Charmes Wines Ltd.* v. *Sabaté USA Inc.*), 28 October 2005, available at www.canlii.org/en/on/onsc/doc/2005/2005canlii39869/2005can lii39869.html.

to and did sign pro forma invoices initialing the seller's general conditions of sales, including a forum selection clause.[88]

Since Article 29 covers both modifications and contract terminations, one would anticipate similar arguments with respect to conduct that suggests that a contract has ended. In an early German case, an appellate court rejected the claim that the parties had cancelled a contract for the sale of wood, since the buyer, who was apparently resisting claims for payment from the seller's assignee, did not produce any written or oral evidence from which the court could infer a mutual agreement of a cancellation requested by the buyer.[89] Nevertheless, the court concluded that the original parties had agreed, through their conduct, to cancel the contract after the buyer had complained of defects. This inference was permissible from the fact that the seller had indicated that she would come to Germany to market the goods herself and that she had found another company to market the wood. The buyer not only could treat these letters as an effort by seller to cancel the contract, but, by neither objecting to the sellers' statements nor seeking conforming goods under the contract, effectively acquiesced in the contract termination.

B. *Good faith modification*

All domestic laws allow the parties to a concluded contract to modify it by agreement.[90] However, domestic laws differ with respect to the statutory or doctrinal restrictions on modification. Two prevalent restrictions are that the modification not be against the public policy[91] of national law or be obtained in bad faith.[92] American law makes modifications in sales contracts, even without new consideration, subject to a good faith requirement. Official Comment 2 to UCC § 2–209 requires that modifications meet the test of good faith, which essentially requires that they be honest in fact and commercially reasonable. The Comment rejects any modification made to escape the original contract terms "without legitimate commercial reason." This requirement has its origins in concerns about modifications being forced through "hold up," a situation that can arise where one party has made a

---

[88] See *BTC-USA Corp. v. Novacare*, 2008 U.S. Dist. LEXIS 46714 (D. Minn. June 16, 2008).

[89] See Court of Appeals Köln (Germany), 22 February 1994, available at http://cisgw3.law.pace .edu/cases/940222g1.html.

[90] See Schwenzer, Hachem & Kee, supra note 59, at 190 n.2 (nonexhaustive list of national laws).

[91] See, e.g., Bürgerliches Gesetzbuch [BGB] [Civil Code] § 138(1) (Ger.) (void when against public policy), C.C. [Civil Code] art. 1255 (Spain) (not contrary to "the moral and the public order"); Code civil [C. civ.] art. 1131 (Fr.) (obligations with an "unlawful cause" have no effect).

[92] See, e.g., Codice civile [C.c.] [Civil Code] art. 1337 (It.) (parties in formation of contract must conduct themselves in good faith); Código Civil [C.C.] [Civil Code] art. 1158 (Spain) (contracts valid according to dictates of good faith); cf. Code civil [C. civ.] art. 1134 (Fr.) (good faith extended to contract formation by courts); Code civil (C. civ.) art. 1136 (Fr.) (agreements are binding as to consequences equity gives to them); Burgerliches Gesetzbuch [BGB] [Civil Code] § 242 (Ger.) (requirement of good faith performance extended by courts to broad array of contractual duties).

transaction-specific investment that can only be recovered by performance of the contract. The counterparty then has the capacity to refuse to perform unless terms more favorable to it are substituted for the original terms. Assume, for instance, that a party who agrees to purchase coal from a mine head at a specific price must construct a railroad spur to move the coal from the mine head to the main railway. Once the buyer constructs the spur it cannot recover that investment unless the contract is successfully performed. The seller, therefore, has the opportunity to refuse to sell unless the buyer agrees to price modifications favorable to the seller. Common law cases like *Alaska Packers Ass'n v. Domenico*,[93] in which workers who were transported to Alaska refused to perform unless their wages were raised, are frequently cited for this proposition.[94]

The response of the common law was to interpose a consideration requirement before contract modifications could be enforced. Any other modification was said to be void under the preexisting duty rule, which precluded modifications by which one party agreed to an altered performance without receiving any benefit other than what was due to it under the original contract. The malleability of that doctrine ultimately led the drafters of the UCC to reject it in favor of a "good faith" requirement that purportedly addressed the question of hold-up behavior head on. But given the difficulties that courts have in reverse engineering the reasons for proposed modifications, there has always been serious question about whether the good faith requirement can possibly provide a more objective mechanism than the consideration doctrine for distinguishing between those modifications that actually increase the surplus of a contract for the parties and those that simply seek to reallocate an existing contractual "pie."

Article 29 does not contain a good faith requirement. Again, it permits modification by "mere agreement." But Article 7(1) does require that the CISG be interpreted in a manner that promotes the observance of good faith in international trade. Is that admonition applied only to interpretation of the CISG's Articles, as a literal reading suggests, or does it incorporate into Article 29 an obligation on the part of parties to modify contracts only in good faith and thus negate bad faith modifications? If the latter, then Article 7 would transform Article 29's approval of modification by "mere agreement" into an approval of only those modifications that comport with some conception of "good faith." Alternatively, the good faith requirement could be grafted onto a contract through a conclusion under Article 7(2) that the scope of modification was a matter "governed by" the CISG, but not expressly settled in it, and thus

---

[93] 117 F. 99 (9th Cir. 1902).
[94] Whether the workers were holding up the employer is contestable. The workers complained that they received substandard equipment to perform their task. Since the workers had no alternative source of employment in Alaska and depended on the employer to transport them from Alaska, it is plausible that the employer was holding up the employees.

determinable by reference to a "general principle" of good faith.[95] Some commentators take the position that good faith permits courts to police the propriety of any modification and thus simply performs the same work as a common law consideration requirement or the good faith restriction on UCC § 2–209 modifications.[96]

As we indicated in Chapter 1 and discuss at greater length in Chapter 4, we are more dubious about extending the Article 7(1) good faith requirement or a "general principle" of good faith to the obligations of parties. Our position is that the only limitation that good faith should place on modifications is prevention of the hold-up problem that could cause a reallocation of a previously allocated contractual surplus. If the CISG is, so far as possible in light of its political origins, intended to do for commercial parties what they otherwise would have done for themselves, the reallocation of a commercial surplus without any increase in the contractual pie constitutes the kind of exploitation of a transaction-specific investment that commercial parties would want to prohibit. Other contractual behavior may be questionable from the ex post perspective of courts or arbitrators, but prohibiting that behavior does not necessarily reflect what parties would have bargained to ex ante. The problem with allowing even this degree of injection of a good faith limitation on modifications is the difficulty that courts inevitably face in their efforts to discern when parties have engaged in the kind of opportunistic behavior that characterizes bad faith exploitation of transaction-specific investments.

C. *Contractual restrictions on modifications*

Article 29(2) provides that written "no oral modification" ("NOM") clauses within contracts are effective – except when they are not. The schizophrenic effect of the provision arises from the conflict between its first sentence, which states that provisions in written contracts that modification or termination must also be in writing cannot be otherwise modified or terminated even by agreement, and the second sentence, which precludes a party whose conduct induces reliance by the counterparty from asserting the effect of the first sentence. Where a written modification is required, it may be satisfied by a unilateral confirmation of a modification or termination that the recipient fails to reject.[97] But that will still leave some cases in which even a liberal standard of "writing" is not satisfied. As a result, there will be some conditions under which conduct can constitute a waiver of the NOM clause. There is no explicit statement that the counterparty's reliance be

---

[95] See Chapters 1.III and 4.II.A.
[96] See, e.g., Andrea Björklund, *Article 29*, in Kröll et al., supra 76, at 386; cf. Ferrari, *Article 19*, in Kröll et al., supra 76, at 290–91.
[97] See Court of Appeals Innsbruck (Austria), 18 December 2007, available at http://cisgw3.law .pace.edu/cases/071218a3.html.

either reasonable or justifiable. Much of the commentary on the issue indicates that the second sentence is intended to avoid what in civil law jurisdictions is often referred to as an "abuse of rights" or "abuse of law."[98] Such an abuse allegedly may exist where one party exploits a NOM clause to deny the effect of modifications to which it has actually agreed (albeit not in writing), but which it has subsequently come to regret. Preventing such an abuse often requires characterizing the objecting party's conduct as a waiver of its ability to enforce the strict letter of the contract, including the NOM clause.

The problem with allowing waivers by conduct, especially in an international setting in which cultural differences create a broader risk of misinterpretation of the meaning of conduct, is that patterns of behavior can be misapplied to reallocate risks in ways that the actor never intended to authorize. Presumably, that is one reason why parties enter into NOM clauses in the first instance. By doing so they arguably seek to avoid a situation in which some combination of conduct by one party and reliance by the other is intended to have any legal effect. Assume, for instance, a ten-year contract between a buyer and seller that contains a NOM clause and requires the buyer to make monthly purchases of a maximum of two tons of sawdust. Assume further that after strict compliance with the contract during the first two years of the contract, the buyer begins ordering more than two tons of sawdust per month. Assume that for the first four months of this practice, the seller does nothing more than remind the buyer of its obligations under the contract, but the seller neither declares a breach nor seeks to terminate the contract. In the fifth month, however, the seller refuses to sell any additional sawdust to buyer, alleging that the contract has been breached. The buyer's response is that the seller's prior willingness to sell more than the contractually specified sum constitutes an effective modification of the contract, notwithstanding the NOM clause. Under Article 29(2), if the buyer could demonstrate that it relied on the willingness of the seller to sell a greater quantity than was contractually specified (for instance, by forgoing alternative contracts for additional sawdust on favorable terms), that conduct could be deemed an implicit "mere agreement" that effectively modified the contract. It is, of course, possible that the seller's conduct was motivated by a willingness to modify the contract in order to accommodate the buyer's increasing needs. But the seller may also have been motivated by concerns that do not reveal an intention either to alter the buyer's original obligation or to create an agreement. The seller, for example, may have considered the buyer's increased orders to constitute a breach, but one that should be ignored in order to preserve the relationship between the parties in the hope that future orders would conform to contractual requirements. Or, the seller may have considered the increased

---

[98] See Peter Schlechtriem, *Article 29*, in Schlechtriem & Schwenzer 2005, supra note 78, at 334; Rita de la Feria & Stefan Vogenauer, Prohibition of Abuse of Law (2011).

orders to constitute a breach, but one that imposed costs on the seller too small to warrant litigation costs. Neither of these motivations would mean that the seller agreed to modify the contract or to waive the right to bring an action for breach in the event that the buyer continued to comply with its contractual obligations. One reason for a NOM clause is to avoid having to make the difficult inferences from conduct about the parties' intentions and expectations by limiting any modification to those evidenced by a writing.

NOM clauses may have other beneficial functions. Employers may want to limit the consequences of rogue employees who make promises to potential customers to obtain orders from which employees get commissions. While one might think that employers should bear the consequences of their employees' misbehavior, a NOM clause that carefully signals prospective customers that the employee's statement is unenforceable when it exceeds the obligations on the written contract may be an effective way of shifting the costs to a party who can easily determine that the employee is acting in a manner inconsistent with his or her authority. These considerations suggest that a "reasonable" or "justifiable" element should be part of the inquiry into reliance. Perhaps the best way to accomplish that is by asking once more what the parties' intent was under Article 8. If a contract contains a NOM clause that has been specifically bargained for, then a customer who subsequently claims that terms of the contract have been modified by oral representations or other conduct should have a difficult time explaining how, under Article 8(2), a reasonable person in the circumstances would have the understanding that a conflicting statement or other conduct was intended to have force.

Of course, strict enforcement of a NOM clause may impose its own costs. Assume that Seller and Buyer enter into a written contract, including a NOM clause, for the purchase and sale of a computer system that is tailored to Buyer's unique needs and that thus contains specifications that vary from those used for most computer systems. Between the conclusion of the contract and the manufacture of the system, the parties orally agree to alter some of the specifications. Seller delivers a system that conforms to the modified specifications. Buyer rejects it, motivated by its changing needs rather than by any defect in the system, and claims that the modification was ineffective under the NOM clause. Both the conduct (Buyer's request for alterations) and reliance (Seller's manufacture in accordance with modification) sufficiently indicate that the parties intended that their oral agreement have legal effect, that judicial error in construing either is minimal, and that these observable and verifiable conditions make for a better check on Buyer's strategic behavior than the general conception of "good faith." Nevertheless, strict adherence to the NOM clause would deny enforcement of the modification.

The desire to secure the benefits of a NOM clause while preventing its abuse confirms Professor Schlechtriem's view that "courts will enjoy considerable discretion" in this area.[99] To date, however, courts and arbitral panels have been solicitous of NOM clauses, and have been reluctant to investigate potential conduct that might trigger exceptions under the second sentence of Article 29(2).[100]

D. *Opting out of Article 29(2)*

Given the benefits of a NOM clause, it is plausible that sophisticated commercial parties would want to signal that they not only desire to limit modifications to those embodied in a writing, but also that they really, really mean it. Imagine, for instance, that the parties agree (1) that all modifications to their contract be in writing, and (2) that Article 29(2), second sentence shall not apply to their contract. One might conclude that the exclusion of the exception (or of Article 29 in its entirety) is perfectly consistent with the admonition of Article 6 that parties may derogate from any part of the CISG. Here, commentary has focused on three possible positions, none of which is conclusively favored by either the language or purpose of Article 29 or related CISG provisions.

First, one might grant Article 6 complete priority over Article 29 and permit parties to opt out of an ability to claim "abuse" of the NOM clause. This position would elevate the concept of party autonomy and would recognize that there are valid reasons both for including a NOM clause in the contract and for avoiding judicial inquiry into whether exceptions to the NOM clause were triggered by particular conduct. After all, Contracting States that make an Article 96 declaration to the effect that writing requirements remain in effect for contract formation and modification are allowed to opt out of Article 29; why shouldn't individual parties have the same capacity?[101] But even an explicit and effective exclusion of Article 29 (2) would not mean that NOM clauses would be strictly enforced. Instead, the validity of the NOM clause in a particular situation would still be vulnerable to attack under domestic law principles. (The validity of such an exclusion would not be subject to question under the CISG itself because of Article 4.) That is, a court could still apply domestic principles of unconscionability, duress, and the like. to find that an oral modification was enforceable, notwithstanding the NOM clause. Some commentators, however, would permit the derogation under Article 6, at

---

[99] Schlechtriem, *Article 29*, in Schlechtriem & Schwenzer 2005, supra note 78, at 335.

[100] See, e.g., Tribunal of International Commercial Arbitration of the Ukrainian Chamber Commerce and Trade (Ukraine), 25 November 2002, available at http://cisgw3.law.pace.edu/cases/021125u5.html; ICC Arbitration Case No. 9117 of March 1998, available at www.unilex.info/case.cfm?pid=1&do=case&id=399&step=FullText; CIETAC Arbitration (China), 16 December 1997, available at http://cisgw3.law.pace.edu/cases/971216c1.html; *Graves Import Co., Ltd.* v. *Chilewich International Corp.*, 1994 U.S. Dist. LEXIS 13393 (S.D.N.Y. September 22, 1994).

[101] Article 12 makes those parts of Article 29, as well as of Article 11, that permit contractual consequences to be incurred without a writing inapplicable where any party has its place of business in a Contracting State that has made an Article 96 declaration.

least in the case of a NOM clause individually negotiated by relatively sophisticated and equally situated commercial actors.[102]

Second, one might conclude that the second sentence of Article 29(2) is a
mandatory rule from which the parties cannot derogate, notwithstanding
Article 6.[103] While the parties might be able to create an NOM rule, they could
not fully limit its force. For instance, they could not draft a fully enforceable,
"hard" NOM clause: a NOM clause that provides that oral modifications are
unenforceable under all circumstances, without limitation. This position is
inconsistent with Article 6, which categorically treats all of the CISG's provisions
as default rules that can be varied by the parties (unless a signatory state has made
a reservation). A hard NOM clause in effect derogates from Article 29(2), as
Article 6 permits. Parties worried about the risk of an ex post finding of reasonable reliance on an oral modification might well prefer a hard NOM clause or
opt out of Article 29(2)'s second sentence entirely. Given Article 6, there is no
reason to interpret Article 29(2) as a mandatory rule that prevents parties from
contracting for what they want.

Third, parties might be limited in their ability to opt out of Article 29 by virtue
of other obligations imposed by the CISG. Under this rationale, even if a party
does opt out of the second sentence of Article 29(2), its enforcement of the NOM
clause is subject to overriding obligations of good faith in Article 7(1) or Article 7
(2). To the extent that Article 7 is read to impose a duty of good faith in contract
performance generally (a plausible reading that we disfavor), the refusal to
recognize an oral modification would be subject to a good faith requirement,
even where a NOM clause has been included in the contract. Alternatively, even
in the face of a NOM clause, and even without the second sentence of Article 29
(2), one could use Article 8(2) to interpret an oral modification in a manner
consistent with the way a reasonable person in the listener's position would
interpret it. On this objective standard, the oral modification, when made, could
be interpreted by the other party as an agreement to waive insistence on the
NOM clause. The other party could then rely on that waiver to make the oral
modification effective.

Thus far, the debate has been of more academic than practical interest. The case
law does not reveal situations in which parties have attempted to opt out of the
conduct/reliance exception to a NOM clause. Perhaps the willingness of courts and
arbiters to enforce the clauses, noted above, makes opting out of the exception
unnecessary.

---

[102] See Schlechtriem, *Article 29*, in Schlechtriem & Schwenzer 2005, *supra* note 78, at 335.
[103] See Robert A. Hillman, *Article 29(2) of the United Nations Convention on Contracts for the
International Sale of Goods: A New Effort at Clarifying the Legal Effect of "No Oral Modification" Clauses*, 21 Cornell Int'l L. J. 449 (1988).

4

Implied terms and interpretation

Sales contracts do not specify the obligations of the parties for every possible contingency that might arise during the contract's performance. Writing a completely specified contract for even a relatively simple commercial transaction is impossible and, even if feasible, not cost-justified for the parties. Parties prefer to invest only optimally in drafting, because further investment reduces the net value of the contract. Because some contingencies are so remote that dealing with them explicitly is not worthwhile, the contract will necessarily contain gaps. Implied terms that reflect party preferences also reduce transactions costs because their existence avoids the need to supply an express term covering the same matter. Parties may also prefer implied terms to fill gaps that arise when parties believe that an attempt to fill them sends an adverse signal to the counterparty about their own quality as a contracting partner. For example, requesting an explicit damage limitation term may indicate to the counterparty that the requesting party expects to breach. The CISG supplies implied terms, including trade usage, course of dealing, and course of performance, that address some of the contingencies about which the parties leave the contract silent. The circumstances in which the CISG implies a price term and a duty of good faith are less clear and more controversial.

Implied terms apply to the contract only if it contains gaps. If the contract's express terms deal with the matter, they govern and there is no gap to be filled by an implied term. Thus, in order to determine whether implied terms apply to the contract, the contract's express terms first must be determined and interpreted. Some domestic rules, such as the parol evidence rule, control the sort of evidence a court can consider in interpreting the terms of the contract. For their part, Articles 8 and 11 prescribe the evidence a tribunal must take into account to interpret the contract's terms. The CISG is unclear as to whether (or the extent to which) the parol evidence rule applies to the interpretation of contracts governed by the CISG, although most courts have concluded that the CISG excludes the rule. This chapter describes the CISG's treatment of important implied terms and interpretation of the contract.

I. TRADE USAGE, COURSE OF DEALING, AND COURSE OF PERFORMANCE

A. *Identifying the usage*

Article 9(1) binds the parties to "any usage to which they have agreed and by any practice which they have established between themselves." Because usages to which the parties have "agreed" require an express or tacit agreement,[1] they are part of the express terms of the contract. The phrase "any practice which they have established themselves" is separated from the phrase referring to agreed usages. This fairly suggests that established practices between the parties need not be an explicit part of an agreement. Rather, the parties are bound by regularities in their behavior with respect to each other, even if their agreement does not expressly obligate them to act accordingly. There is a strong efficiency case for incorporating such customs. If the custom reflects the bargain that the parties would otherwise have struck through individual negotiations, incorporation of the custom reduces transaction costs without altering the content of the bargain. Use of custom also serves as an efficient interpretive tool to the extent that courts are able to employ trade usages to resolve ambiguities in contractual language or alleged contractual obligations.

Not all behavioral regularities should be deemed to be part of the parties' agreement, however. As we have indicated, the incorporation of usages and practices makes sense when they reflect the bargain to which parties would have agreed and thus reduce the cost of transacting by including in the contract terms that the parties consider to be mutually beneficial. Some regularities, such as waivers of breaches by the counterparty, may be intended to signal an intent to cooperate and to enhance the probability and quality of future dealings rather than to embody an understanding of the contract. Thus, parties may intend to adhere to a regular course of conduct only under certain conditions, such as when there is no evidence of intentional chiseling, when reciprocity is anticipated, or when the behavior that deviates from the contract does not justify costly enforcement of the strict requirements of the contract. If the parties intended no legal effect to follow from the practice, then the regularity should not be considered a practice that is incorporated into the contract. Third-party adjudicators often have difficulty discerning whether the behavior of a party was a consequence of a perceived contractual obligation or as a nonbinding accommodation.

---

[1]   See *Treibacher Industrie, A.G.* v. *Allegheny Technologies*, 464 F.3d 1235 (11th Cir. 2006); CIETAC Arbitration (China), 31 July 1997, available at cisgw3.law.pace.edu/cases/970731c1. html (usage part of express agreement); Supreme Court (Austria), 21 March 2000, available at http:// cisgw3.law.pace.edu/cases/000321a3.html (usage may be part of express or implicit agreement).

Article 9(1) does not specify the sort of established practices between the parties that binds them. In particular, it does not say whether repeated contracts of the same sort alone count as establishing the relevant practice or whether repeated perform-ance within a single contract suffices to establish the practice. Most courts applying the subsection have required some frequency of repeated contracts within an unspecified period of time.[2] A Swiss court held that two previous contracts do not establish a practice between the parties.[3] On other hand, the Austrian Supreme Court has held that matters discussed in preliminary negotiations can establish a "practice" between the contracting parties, even as part of the first contract between them.[4] This seems a stretch. Article 9(1)'s reference to "practices they have estab-lished between themselves" suggests that practices are established by repeated interactions between the parties. Although repeated performance within the same contract can establish a practice, negotiations prior to a first contract cannot do so. For this reason, prior negotiations leading to a first contract lack the regularity in behavior necessary to establish a practice.

Article 8(3) allows preliminary negotiations to inform the parties' interpretation of the terms of the resulting agreement. In this case the negotiations might create a usage to which the parties are bound by agreement under Article 9(1). However, they are not among the implied terms created by an established practice under Article 9(1). Although the distinction between the interpretation of express terms and supplementation with implied terms is difficult to draw in practice, preliminary negotiations may serve to interpret rather than to supplement express terms. The Uniform Commercial Code's ("UCC's") comparable provisions are clearer in their application. Under UCC § 1–303(a), repeated performance under the same contract counts as a "course of performance," while § 1–303(b) counts a sequence of comparable performance over distinct contracts as a "course of dealing." The parties' agreement includes as implied terms both course of performance and course of dealing.[5] Negotiations leading to a first contract are neither among the parties' course of performance or course of dealing.

According to Article 9(2), certain trade usages are applicable to the parties' contract, even without explicit agreement, unless their agreement provides other-wise. A trade usage qualifies for inclusion in the contract as a default term only if the

---

[2] See District Court Arnhem (Netherlands) (*Hibro Compensatoren B.V.* v. *Trelleborg Industri Aktiebolag*), 17 January 2007, available at http://cisgw3.law.pace.edu/cases/070117n1.html; Supreme Court (Austria), 31 August 2005, available at http://cisgw3.law.pace.edu/cases/05083ia3.html; Lower Court Duisburg (Germany), 13 April 2000, available at http://cisgw3.law.pace.edu/cases/000413g1.html.

[3] See Civil Court Basel (Switzerland), 3 December 1997, available at http://cisgw3.law.pace.edu/cases/971203s2.html; cf. District Court Zwickau (Germany), 9 March 1999, available at http://cisgw3.law.pace.edu/cases/990319g1.html (single previous contract does not establish a "prac-tice between the parties" for purposes of Article 9(1)).

[4] See Supreme Court (Austria), 6 February 1996, available at http://cisgw3.law.pace.edu/cases/960206a3.html.

[5] See U.C.C. § 1–201(b)(3) ("agreement").

parties knew or ought to have known of it, and if, in international trade, it is widely known to and regularly observed by parties to contracts of the type involved in the relevant trade. Even where those criteria are met, there could be some doubt whether usages should be incorporated so readily into international trade. Trade usage should be applicable to the contract, we have suggested already, where the usage reflects the bargain that the parties would otherwise have reached. During the drafting of the CISG, Chinese delegates unsuccessfully proposed that only "reasonable" usages would be binding on the parties. While some delegates responded that any usage that attracted the requisite international status would necessarily be reasonable, a regularity that arose out of a cartelized industry or by virtue of path dependence could generate inefficient customs. These concerns were expressed during the CISG drafting process when representatives of socialist countries expressed concern that commercial usages to date "had been formed by a restricted group of countries only whose position did not express worldwide opinion."[6] Perhaps a closing of the gap between developed and developing nations, and a reduction of colonial rule in which industries of the rulers arguably imposed "usages" on industries of the ruled will make the Chinese concerns less applicable.

Even if one dismisses the concern of forced usages, the effect of Article 9(2) may be restricted because its requirements limit the sort of trade usage applicable to the parties' contract. The requirements that the usage be widely known and regularly observed in international trade, as well as known to the parties, potentially restrict the application of a usage to the parties' contract. It would be the rare "unreasonable" usage that could satisfy these criteria. To apply the "usage in the particular trade" requirement, two questions must be answered: first, what is the relevant usage that is widely known and regularly observed in international trade? and second, is the relevant usage widely known and regularly observed in contracts of the type involved in the particular trade concerned? Because a custom sometimes does not have an easily identifiable content, the usage at issue can be controversial.[7] Courts and arbitral tribunals may have difficulty confirming the existence of a purported trade usage, and even if they can verify it, may be less able to identify the range of circumstances in which it applies. Do usages that arise during peacetime apply during wartime? Do conventions that are respected during a period of financial tranquility apply during periods of financial turmoil? For example, buyers and sellers may be flexible with respect to minimum purchase requirements when market prices for the commodity at issue are relatively stable. If market prices for the

---

[6] See Documentary History of the Uniform Law for International Sales 484 (John O. Honnold ed., 1989) (remarks of delegates from Yugoslavia and Czechoslovokia) [hereinafter Documentary History]. See also Michael J. Bonell, *Usages and Practices*, in Commentary on the International Sales Law 103 (Cesare M. Bianca & Michael J. Bonell eds., 1987) [hereinafter "Bianca & Bonell"].

[7] See, e.g., *Columbia Nitrogen Corp. v. Royster Co.*, 451 F.2d 3 (4th Cir. 1971); Richard Craswell, *Do Trade Customs Exist?*, in The Jurisprudential Foundations of Corporate and Commercial Law 118, 121–25 (Jody S. Kraus & Steven D. Walt eds., 2000).

commodity drop precipitously and a buyer under a fixed price contract attempts to order a quantity below the contractual minimum, a court should look askance at the existence of an alleged "custom" that permits deviation from the written requirement. Even if identifiable, Article 9(2) requires that the usage be widely known and regularly observed in the particular trade in which the contracting parties are involved. This in turn requires determining the geographic area in which the particular trade is established. The Austrian Supreme Court has concluded that a usage is widely known if a majority of businessmen in the trade acknowledges its existence.[8]

B. *Incoterms as trade usages*

An increasing number of courts maintain that Incoterms are incorporated into the CISG as trade usage under Article 9(1) where the parties have used a term that is found in the Incoterms rules.[9] The cases involve contracts that contain delivery terms such as CFR or CIF that are not defined and do not explicitly incorporate Incoterms rules by reference. Noting that Incoterms rules are frequently used in international sale contracts, the courts find that its definitions are widely known and observed in international trade.[10] Incoterms rules, they conclude, are trade usages made applicable to the contract by Article 9(2). This is an exaggeration. Delivery terms such as CFR or CIF have definitions under national law that can differ from Incoterms definitions of the terms.[11] Reference in a contract to "CFR" or "CIF,"

---

[8] See Supreme Court (Austria), 15 October 1998, available at http://cisgw3.law.pace.edu/cases/981015a3.html.

[9] See, e.g., In re World Imports, LLC, 511 B.R. 738 (Bankr. E.D. Pa. 2014); *Citgo Petroleum Corp. v. Odfjell Seachem*, 2013 U.S. Dist. LEXIS 72898 (S.D. Tex. May 23, 2013); *Cedar Petrochemicals Inc. v. Dongbu Hannong Chemical Co. Ltd.*, 2011 U.S. Dist. LEXIS 110716 (S.D.N.Y. September 28, 2011); *BP Oil International, Ltd. V. Empresa Estatal Petoleos de Ecuador*, 332 F.3d 333 (5th Cir. 2003); *St. Paul Guardian Insurance Co. v. Neuromed Medical Systems & Support*, 2002 U.S. Dist. LEXIS 5096 (S.D.N.Y. March 26, 2002); ICC Arbitration Case 7645 (1995), available at http://cisgw3.law.pace.edu/cases/957645i1.html; Tribunal of International Commercial Arbitration at the Russian Federation Chamber of Commerce and Industry (Russia), 6 June 2000, available at http://cisgw3.law.pace.edu/cases/000606r1.html. For an early case holding that the CISG is a source of trade usage, see ICC Arbitration Case 5713 (1989), available at http://cisgw3.law.pace.edu/cases/031849i1.html. "Incoterms" is a trademark of the International Chamber of Commerce.

[10] See *BP Oil International Ltd. v. Empresa Estatal Petroleos de Ecuador*, 332 F.3d 333 (5th Cir. 2003); *China North Chemical Industries Corp. v. Beston Chemical Corp.*, 2006 U.S. Dist. LEXIS 35464 (S.D. Tex. February 7, 2006); Commercial Court Buenos Aires (Argentina) (*Wacker-Polymer Systems GmbH v. Glaube S.A.*), 17 March 2003, available at http://cisgw3.law.pace.edu/cases/030317a1.html.

[11] For example, U.C.C. § 2–319(1)(b) defines "FOB place of destination," and § 2–319(1)(c) allows the FOB term to cover transportation by water and non-water borne transportation ("vessel, or other vehicle"). Neither stipulation is meaningful under Incoterms rules. Incoterms rules restrict the FOB delivery term to "FOB named port of shipment," and applies only to waterborne transportation. See Incoterms® 2010 A4 ("FOB"). The court in *BP Oil International Ltd. v. Empresa Estatal Petroleos de Ecuador*, 332 F.3d 333 (5th Cir. 2003), interpreted the delivery

without more, therefore, does not necessarily incorporate Incoterms rules. More important, Article 9(2) requires that the use of Incoterms be sufficiently prevalent ("regularly observed") in the particular trade in which the contracting parties are engaged. Merely because a usage is frequently observed in international trade does not by itself show that the usage is observed in contracts of the type involved in the particular trade concerned. For instance, some delivery terms might be interpreted differently in bulk oil trading and bulk dry goods trading. For Incoterms to be a trade usage under Article 9(2), they must be incorporated in contracts by parties in the particular trade with the requisite frequency. In fact, some Incoterms are created or revised before they are used in international commercial contracts. This was the case for the FCA delivery term ("Free Carrier named place of delivery"), which was first defined in the Incoterms 1980 rules. The term, which was created in response to the dramatic growth in containerized transport, allows delivery to the carrier at an inland point irrespective of the mode of carriage used to transport the goods.[12] Similarly, Incoterms® 2010 introduce a new delivery term, DAT ("Delivered at Terminal"), which requires delivery at the named terminal.[13] Rather than reflect trade usage, new or revised Incoterms rules definitions are introduced to alter established contracting practices.

Nevertheless, Incoterms rules are susceptible to incorporation into the contract through Article 9(2), because they have relatively clear meanings and their application does not pose the difficulties of verifiability and interpretation that might apply to putative usages with less certain content or scope. Incoterms rules are highly specific and easily accessible to nonspecialists. It takes little knowledge of the trade to determine whether goods have been delivered at a particular point. There is, for example, little discretion involved in the determination of whether the seller purchased an insurance policy or its terms. Thus, incorporation of customary terms that condition on events such as the requirement that a party purchase insurance under an Incoterms rule does not create much risk that adjudicators will reinterpret the terms on which the parties agreed to trade. Rather, courts need only determine whether the parties intended to be bound by the customary, well-understood meanings in Incoterms. Certainly there will be cases in which an issue arises as to whether the trade has adopted Incoterms rules. But the risks related to incorporation of usages are directed at far more difficult issues concerning the conditions under which they will apply, rather than at whether the parties were involved in a trade that accepted centrally promulgated rules.

Even where Incoterms are incorporated into a contract, they may coexist with obligations that cover similar territory. For example, in *Citgo Petroleum*

---

term "CFR Libertad—Ecuador" to refer to the Incoterms rules definition when the contract failed to incorporate Incoterms rules by reference.

[12] See Incoterms® 1980 (Pub. No. 350) A4 ("FCA").   [13] See Incoterms® 2010 A4 ("DAT").

Corp. v. *Odfjell Seachem*,[14] the court concluded that a CFR term in a contract incorporated the relevant Incoterms 2000 rule and required the seller to deliver the goods on board the vessel and bear the risk of loss until the good had passed the ship's rail. But the court also concluded that the CFR term was not contrary to and did not displace a concurrent responsibility of the seller under Article 32 to select an appropriate vessel for shipment.

C. *Other trade usages*

Other cases in which courts and tribunals have had to consider Article 9(2) involve more informal, unwritten practices that evolve from interactions among parties rather than the application of a well-understood set of industry rules such as Incoterms. These constitute the type of customs that might give rise to high verification costs and the risk of misapplication. Courts seem to be aware of these risks by narrowly construing the range of practices that qualify for incorporation into a contract under Article 9(2). Most of the cases where courts have applied Article 9 (2) involve the question of whether there has been compliance with an agreed-to custom rather than with its existence or scope.[15] As a result, courts have only had to focus on the presence or absence of a salient act which can be determined without technical expertise. For instance, several cases under Article 9(2) involve the need to object to terms in a contracting party's confirmation letter to avoid the inclusion of those terms in the final contract. Because those acts do not require any technical expertise or specific knowledge of the trade, however, they are verifiable to third parties (courts and arbitration tribunals) at low cost. For example, in a contract for the sale of windows and doors between an Italian seller and a German buyer, the court found that the buyer was entitled to a discount included in a confirmation letter sent to the seller.[16] The seller had not objected to the content of that letter. The court concluded:

> It is an accepted trade usage that a tradesperson who receives a letter of confirm-ation has to object to the letter's content if he does not wish to be bound by it. If he does not object, the contract is binding with the content given to it in the letter of confirmation, unless the sender of the letter has either intentionally given an incorrect account of the negotiations, or the content of the letter deviates so far from the result of the negotiations that the sender could not reasonably assume the recipient's consent. The recipient's silence causes the contract to be modified or supplemented in accordance with the letter of confirmation.

---

[14] 2013 U.S. Dist. LEXIS 72898 (S.D. Tex. May 23, 2013).
[15] See Clayton P. Gillette, *The Law Merchant in the Modern Age: Institutional Design and International Usages under the CISG*, 5 Chi. J. Int'l L. 157 (2004).
[16] See Court of Appeals Saarbrücken (Germany), 14 February 2001, available at http://cisgw3.law.pace.edu/cases/010214g1.html.

Similarly, in a case between an Austrian seller and a Swiss buyer for the sale of fiber, the court found that the seller had sent a confirmation to the buyer, thereby creating a binding contract.[17] The court concluded that the legal systems in both countries permitted formation of contracts through an exchange of confirmations for purposes of domestic contracts, and thus the parties understood that the same rule would apply "to contracts for the supply of textiles in international relationships between contractual partners established in Switzerland and Austria" under the CISG. The court may have been wrong both in its interpretation of Austrian law and about what constitutes an international trade usage under Article 9.[18] But those are errors of law, independent of the ability of the court to discern the existence of the custom (as opposed to its applicability in domestic law) or the level of compliance in the case before it.

Finally, in *Geneva Pharmaceuticals Technology Corp v. Barr Laboratories, Inc.*,[19] the court recognized an industry custom to rely on implied, unwritten supply commitments to satisfy the requirements for contract formation, notwithstanding the failure to satisfy formation obligations under the CISG. The content of such a custom does not have the provenance of Incoterms and might be thought to constitute the kind of casual, unwritten custom that generates discomfort with the incorporation of usages into contracts. Nevertheless, like the sending of a confirmation letter, it conditions on compliance with salient, nontechnical acts (here, permitting the contracting party access to a Drug Master file) that present the court with a binary choice (either there was full compliance with the custom or there was none) and requires no qualitative judgments.[20]

Courts confronted with a custom such as the need to object to confirmation letters do not face costless inquiries. The court's recitation of the relevant custom still permits exceptions that require judicial inquiry into the parties' interactions. But those investigations, which consider credibility or some deviation in terms between the order and the confirmation, involve traditional judicial inquiries in contract law.

---

[17] See Civil Court Basel, (Switzerland) (*W.T. GmbH v P. AG*), 21 December 1992, available at http://cisgw3.law.pace.edu/cases/921221s1.html.

[18] Peter Schlechtriem concluded that Austrian law had changed prior to the decision and that concurrence on domestic practices in the states of the contracting parties is not sufficient to constitute the relevant "internationality" under Article 9(2). See Remarks of Peter Schlechtriem, in Harry M. Flechtner, *Transcript of a Workshop on the Sales Convention: Leading CISG Scholars Discuss Contract Formation, Validity, Excuse for Hardship, Avoidance, Nachfrist, Contract Interpretation, Parol Evidence, Analogical Application, and Much More*, 18 J. L. & Comm. 191, 246 (1999).

[19] 201 F. Supp. 2d 236, 281–82 (S.D.N.Y. 2002).

[20] Similarly, one arbitration panel found that the practice of revising prices in post-sale invoices was a usage regularly observed in the trade that could be enforced against a buyer. The court only considered whether a usage existed (a binary decision), rather than whether the revision made by the seller was within a range permitted by the usage (a decision that would have required deeper inquiry into the technical aspects of the trade). See ICC Court of Arbitration 8324/1995—Paris (France), available at http://cisgw3.law.pace.edu/cases/958324i1.html.

Although we do not necessarily endorse such judicial intervention, we note that, where undertaken, it is triggered by general judicial policing of contractual fairness, rather than by the custom concerning confirmations.[21] While costly, these inquiries do not depend on unique industry norms and thus do not implicate the costs typically associated with a broad interpretation of the scope of custom incorporation.

D. *Ignorance of trade usage*

Article 9(2) incorporates into the contract trade usages of which the parties "know or ought to have known." If the parties actually know of the usage and do not exclude its application to their contract, they presumptively prefer to have the usage apply. The incorporation of trade usage as a term of the contract saves the parties the cost of expressly providing for it. If one or both parties are ignorant of the usage, the usage still applies to the contract if they ought to have known of it. Article 9(2)'s reference to usage of which the parties "ought to have known" suggests an objective standard of the relevant knowledge. However, the Article does not indicate when a party ought to know of the usage. The Austrian Supreme Court on two occasions has maintained that a party ought to know of a usage either when its place of business is in the geographic region in which the usage is established or when it continuously conducts business in the region where the usage applies.[22] A novice in the relevant trade located outside the region in which the usage prevails does not meet either part of the Court's standard. That party would not be charged with knowledge of the usage and Article 9(2) therefore would not incorporate it into the novice's contract.

The Austrian Supreme Court's standard is not the only possible standard for when a party "ought to know" of a usage. An alternative standard would charge a party with knowledge when the usage is established in a region among those in the relevant trade. According to this standard, an unsophisticated actor – whether a novice in the region or an outsider – ought to learn relevant usages when it contracts with a party in a region in which the usage is established, whether or not it is located in or continuously conducts business in the region. This more relaxed objective standard encourages unsophisticated actors to discover the relevant usage and determine its suitability for their contracts, because the contract incorporates the usage unless the parties provide otherwise. In addition, the more relaxed standard saves the parties the cost of making established usage applicable to their contract.

---

[21] Imagine, for instance, that there was a custom that terms of confirmation were binding unless objected to, and that the buyer failed to object to a patently unfair contractual term in a confirmation. Wholly apart from custom, courts could disregard the offensive term under a broad reading of the good faith obligation under Article 7, or under domestic law concerning the validity of terms, a subject excluded from the CISG under Article 4(a) (the validity of "any usage").

[22] See Supreme Court (Austria), 21 March 2000, available at http://cisgw3.law.pace.edu/cases/000321a3.html; Supreme Court (Austria), 15 October 1998, available at http://cisgw3.law.pace.edu/cases/981015a3.html.

Certainly it is desirable that parties be aware of the implied terms by which they are bound. The issue in deciding between the two approaches is to ensure that the parties have the relevant knowledge at the lowest cost. Those in the region where the usage prevails may not be aware that they are dealing with an unsophisticated party. If most parties in the industry and within the region are sophisticated, then it is reasonable for any one of them to presume that any other party with whom it deals in the region is aware of the usage. Under these circumstances, the least costly way of ensuring common knowledge is to impose on the unsophisticated actor the obligation to learn the relevant usages. In order to induce learning, it makes sense to apply the usage to the contract if the unsophisticated actor has been silent. If, however, the unsophisticated actor has indicated its status, then it becomes less costly for a sophisticated actor to convey the information if it wants the usage to prevail. This means that an unsophisticated actor can announce its ignorance and either obtain the relevant knowledge from the sophisticated counterparty or arguably satisfy the "unless otherwise agreed" clause of Article 9(2).

E. *The relationship among trade usage, course of performance, and course of dealing*

Article 9(1) refers to terms that parties have adopted themselves, while Article 9(2) refers to terms that are incorporated from other sources, such as industry use. It is plausible that these terms will conflict, that is, the parties will themselves adopt a term inconsistent with industry practice. When that happens, the CISG arguably creates a hierarchy that determines which practice prevails under the contract. Usages established by agreement, recognized by Article 9(1), are express terms. Express terms reflect an efficient allocation of obligations between the parties for their transaction. Allocations of obligations provided by course of performance and course of dealing are less suitable. Otherwise, the parties would have saved the cost of providing conflicting express terms. Thus, express terms prevail over course of performance or course of dealing recognized by Article 9(1). For the same reason, they also prevail over conflicting trade usage. Article 9(2) makes trade usage applicable to the contract "unless otherwise agreed," and express terms are part of the parties' agreement that provides "otherwise."

Treibacher Industrie A.G. v. *Allegheny Technologies, Inc.*[23] finds that course of performance or course of dealing prevails over conflicting trade usage. There, the contract called for delivery of tantalum carbide to the buyer on "consignment." Established trade usage defined a "consignment" in the traditional way so that a sale occurred only when and if the buyer actually used the delivered carbide. By contrast, under the parties' well established course of dealing, "consignment" meant merely that the seller would delay billing the buyer for goods delivered. The buyer

[23] 464 F.3d 1235 (11th Cir. 2006).

contended that the trade usage under Article 9(2) trumped the parties' course of dealing under Article 9(1), while the seller argued that their course of dealing trumped the trade usage. The court agreed with the seller. In doing so the court reasoned that the buyer's construction would render Article 8(3)'s reference to "practices the parties have established between themselves" superfluous and the same reference in Article 9(1) a nullity because the parties would be bound by usages even if they had established a conflicting practice. We find the court's reasoning weak, even if its conclusion on liability is correct. Its "superfluous" conclusion is questionable, because the parties' practices are useful to interpret the language of their contract where relevant trade usage does not exist or is ambiguous. For the same reason, the "nullity" conclusion is questionable: The parties' practices apply to bind them when relevant trade usage does not exist. Established practices are neither superfluous nor nonexistent merely because conflicting trade usage displaces them when such a trade usage exists. However, the *Treibacher* court's conclusion that course of dealing or course of performance prevails over conflicting trade usage is defensible. Course of performance and course of dealing are practices that allocate obligations between the parties according to their transactions with each other. Their practice amounts to an implicit bargain with respect to these obligations. The fact that these practices are inconsistent with trade usage suggests that the parties prefer the allocations made by their own practices to the allocation of obligations made by others through trade usage.

This is not to say that the parties' course of dealing or performance always will be clear, or that the parties intended a regularity in their performance to constitute a tool for interpreting the written agreement. *Treibacher* illustrates the difficulty. The seller's practice in that case was to delay billing for material purchased until the buyer used it. It is plausible that the seller was only delaying the billing for the material as an accommodation to the buyer, not as an understanding of a contractual requirement. The seller may have been willing to provide that accommodation, without being obligated to do so, as long as the buyer proved to be a good customer. Thus, delayed billing may not have been intended to serve as a "course of dealing" used to interpret the contract within the meaning of Article 9, even though it had become a regular part of the parties' dealings with each other. The case indicates that the buyer was purchasing the same material from other suppliers at a reduced price because market prices had declined after the contract was concluded. Thus, the buyer was possibly trying to evade a bad deal when it failed to use Treibacher's product. If that was the case, two things follow. First, the seller would no longer want to provide a mere accommodation, so it demanded that the buyer pay for all the goods ordered. Second, the court perhaps would want to discourage the buyer's opportunistic behavior. Applying the alleged trade usage would have allowed the buyer to avoid market price risks that the seller (and the court) believed the buyer had taken by entering into a contract for a fixed quantity of goods at a fixed price. That result could be avoided by finding that a "sale" had occurred so that the risk of post-contract market price declines fell on the buyer. The court apparently was motivated to reach that result, and was able to do so by adopting the seller's position that the delayed billing was a course of dealing that trumped the trade usage. A cleaner way of achieving that result might have been to determine that there had been a true sale when the contract was concluded, and to have avoided any discussion of the existence of a course of dealing, since delayed billing may not have been intended to constitute the kind of practice used to interpret the contract.

A similar question concerns the hierarchy among usages established by the parties or prevailing in the trade and the CISG's default terms. Do usages prevail when they are inconsistent with these terms? The Austrian Supreme Court has concluded that usages prevail.[24] The case involved a relevant trade usage that required the buyer to give notice to the seller of nonconformities in the goods within fourteen days after it examined or ought to have examined them. The buyer apparently gave notice of nonconformity after this period. According to Article 39(1), the buyer loses the right to rely on a nonconformity in the goods if he fails to give proper notice within a reasonable time after he discovers or ought to discover it. However, Article 40 bars the seller from relying on this notice period if he knew or could not have been unaware of the nonconformity and did not disclose it.[25] The issue, therefore, was whether the notice period fixed by relevant trade usage displaced Articles 39 and 40. The Supreme Court found that it did.

The Court's conclusion seems right to us, for two reasons. First, Articles 39 and 40 are default terms only; they apply unless the parties agree otherwise. Article 6 allows the parties to derogate from almost all of the CISG's provisions, including Articles 39 and 40. According to Article 9(2), parties have "impliedly made" trade usage applicable to their contract unless otherwise agreed. Because the parties in the case did not otherwise agree, the trade usage fixing a fourteen-day notice period is part of their agreement.[26] As such the parties have derogated from Articles 39 and 40 in their agreement.[27] The buyer therefore must give notice of nonconformities in the goods in accordance with the fourteen-day period, whether or not the period is reasonable and without regard to the seller's awareness of these nonconformities. Second, trade usage likely reflects an efficient allocation of obligations between participants in the trade (assuming that the usage arises from arms-length bargains

---

[24] See Supreme Court (Austria), 21 March 2000, available at http://cisgw3.law.pace.edu/cases/000321a3.html.

[25] We discuss Articles 39 and 40 in Chapter 5.C., F.

[26] Cf. Commercial Court Tongeren (Belgium) (*Scafom International BV & Orion Metal BVBA v. Exma CPI SA*), 25 January 2005, available at http://cisgw3.law.pace.edu/cases/050125b1.html ("Art. 9 lifts practices and trade usages to a source of contractual obligations that is just as important as the clauses that the parties have explicitly agreed on"). The case was subsequently reversed on other grounds. See the discussion of the decisions in Chapter 8.II.D.

[27] Accord First Committee Deliberation 13 March 1980, in Documentary History, supra note 6, at 484 (para. 73) (wording of predecessor to Article 9(2) implies that usages have precedence over the Convention).

between similarly situated participants). By comparison, Articles 39 and 40 are less likely to efficiently allocate notice obligations in contracts between participants in the trade, because they apply to sales contracts generally and do not take into account specific features of transactions in a specific trade.

II. GOOD FAITH IN INTERNATIONAL TRADE

The CISG's text nowhere states that good faith is an implied term of the contracts the CISG governs. There are two issues here. One is whether the CISG requires the parties to perform their contractual obligations in good faith. The other issue is the nature of the conduct that good faith requires, if good faith is an implied term of contracts governed by the CISG. Although some commentators and an increasing number of tribunals find in the CISG a principle of good faith conduct, they do not specify its precise content. This makes the role of good faith in decided cases difficult to determine and case outcomes in which good faith figures hard to predict.

A. *Good faith as an implied term*

Article 7(1) provides in relevant part that in the interpretation of the CISG regard is to be had for the need to promote "the observance of good faith in international trade." The reference to good faith reflects a compromise among delegates to the Vienna Conference.[28] Some delegates wanted a principle of good faith to apply to the formation of the contract. An Italian proposal would have made good faith applicable to both the contract's formation and performance.[29] Other delegates were worried that the vagueness of the principle would result in nonuniform applications if courts could interpret good faith in a manner according to their own cultural and legal backgrounds.[30] The delegates compromised and put the obligation of good faith in Article 7, which applies to the interpretation of the CISG. Thus, read literally, good faith is a principle for interpreting the CISG itself, not an obligation imposed on the contracting parties as part of the sales contract.

---

[28] See Harry Flechtner, in John O. Honnold, Uniform Law for International Sales Under the 1980 United Nations Convention 134 (Harry M. Flechtner ed., 4th ed. 2009) [hereinafter "Honnold/Flechtner"]; Michael J. Bonell, *Interpretation of Convention*, in Bianca & Bonell, supra note 6, 65, 69 (para. 3.1). The details of the compromise are described in Gyula Eorsi, *A Propos for the 1980 Vienna Convention on Contracts for the International Sale of Goods*, 31 Am. J. Comp. L. 333, 348–49 (1983). Eorsi, the president of the Vienna Conference, reports that "almost everyone thought it a strange compromise, in fact burying the principle of good faith and thus covering up the lack of a compromise;" id. at 349.

[29] See First Committee Deliberation, 13 March 1980, in Documentary History, supra note 6, at 476 (para. 44), 659 (para. 3).

[30] See UNCITRAL Review of the 1978 Draft Convention, in Documentary History, supra note 6, at 367 (para. 44); First Committee Deliberations, in id. at 479 (para. 50).

Nevertheless, commentators divide on the application of Article 7(1)'s good faith principle. Some scholars maintain that the principle is an interpretive one only.[31] It imposes an obligation on tribunals to interpret the CISG's provisions to promote good faith the observance of good faith in international trade. The principle does not apply to the contracting parties to create obligations of good faith to each other in the performance of the contract. Article 7(1)'s language, which applies to the "interpretation of this Convention," supports this position. By comparison, some domestic law imposes an obligation of good faith in the performance and enforcement of the contract.[32] Scholars who maintain that Article 7(1)'s obligation of good faith is both an interpretive principle and a standard of conduct for the contracting parties rely on diplomatic history[33] or the effect of the interpretive principle on the contracting parties' behavior.[34]

Zeller gives a structural argument in favor of construing Article 7(1)'s good faith principle as a standard of conduct for the contracting parties.[35] Article 7(1) is part of the CISG, which is a treaty. The Vienna Convention on the Law of Treaties establishes rules for interpreting treaties and therefore inter alia Article 7(1) itself. Article 31(1) of the Law of Treaties Convention requires a treaty to be "interpreted in good faith in accordance with the ordinary meaning to be given to the terms of the treaty in their context and in the light of its object and purpose."[36] Because the Article requires that treaty provisions, including the CISG's provisions, be interpreted in good faith, there is no need for Article 7(1) to impose the same obligation. The obligation already applies. Thus, Zeller concludes, to avoid rendering Article 7 (1)'s good faith principle superfluous, the principle must state a standard of conduct for the contracting parties.

The problem with Zeller's argument is that Article 7(1) does not simply mimic Article 31(1) of the Law of Treaties Convention; it adds something not in that

---

[31] See, e.g., Honnold/Flechtner, supra note 28, at 135; E. Allan Farnsworth, *Good Faith in Contract Performance*, in Good Faith and Fault in Contract Law 153, 156 (Jack Beatson & Daniel Friedmann eds., 1995); Peter Winship, *International Sales Contracts Under the 1980 United Nations Sales Convention*, 17 Unif. Comm. Code L. J. 55, 67 (1984).

[32] See, e.g., U.C.C. § 1–304.

[33] See Rolf Herber, *Article 7*, in Commentary on the UN Convention on the International Sale of Goods (CISG) 52, 63 (Peter Schlechtriem ed., 1998); Peter Schlechtriem, Uniform Sales Law 39 (1986); cf. Pilar P. Viscasillas, *Article 7*, in UN Convention on Contracts for the International Sale of Goods (CISG): Commentary 111, 121 (para. 15) (Stefan Kröll, Loukas Mistelis & Pilar Perales Viscasillas eds., 2011) [hereinafter "Kröll et al."] (better view applies good faith to the parties' rights and obligations despite legislative history); Ingeborg Schwenzer & Pascal Hachem, *Article 7*, in Schlechtriem & Schwenzer: Commentary on the UN Convention on the International Sale of Goods (CISG) 120, 136 (Ingeborg Schwenzer ed., 3d ed. 2010).

[34] See Michael J. Bonell, *Interpretation of Convention*, in Bianca & Bonell, supra note 6, at 84.

[35] See Bruno Zeller, *The Observance of Good Faith in International Trade*, in CISG Methodology 153, 136–38 (Andre Janssen & Olaf Meyer eds., 2009) [hereinafter "Jannsen & Meyer"]. For further discussion, see infra II.C.

[36] 1155 U.N. Treaty Series 331 (1969), available at http://untreaty.un.org/ilc/texts/instruments/english/conventions/1_1_1969.pdf.

Convention. Article 7(1) requires the CISG's provisions to be interpreted so as to promote good faith "in international trade." Article 31(1) does not contain the restrictive rider, probably because the Law of Treaties Convention applies to all sorts of treaties, not just to commercial treaties. The CISG is a commercial treaty and Article 7(1) instructs adjudicators to interpret its provisions to promote international trade – a goal other treaties might not have. Its injunction is not a superfluous interpretative principle. In fact, without Article 7(1)'s rider, the Article's injunction would be a bit odd. Are adjudicators set on interpreting the CISG's provisions to promote bad faith? This seems to be close to what Article 31(1) of the Law of Treaties Convention supposes. By contrast, Article 7(1)'s injunction to interpret the CISG to promote good faith in international trade has some use.

The trend in case law nevertheless understands Article 7(1)'s good faith principle to set a standard of conduct for the contracting parties. A relatively early arbitral award concluded that "[s]ince the provisions of Article 7(1) CISG concern only the interpretation of the Convention, no collateral obligation may be derived from the 'promotion of good faith.'"[37] However, most tribunals have applied Article 7(1)'s good faith principle to the interpretation of the sales contract and the parties' performance of it. A German trial court's reliance on the Article is representative.[38] The court had to decide whether the seller's standard terms became part of the contract when they were not provided to the buyer at the time the contract was concluded and the buyer was unaware of them. Relying in part on Article 7(1)'s "general obligation of good faith," it found that the seller bore the burden of supplying the buyer with its standard terms. The concluded contract therefore did not include the seller's undisclosed standard terms. A German appellate court has used the same reasoning in a similar case.[39] Courts more frequently apply an obligation of good faith to the parties' conduct without bothering to specify its basis in Article 7.[40]

An alternative basis for a principle of good faith directed at the contracting parties is Article 7(2). Article 7(2) in relevant part directs that matters not expressly addressed

---

[37] See ICC Case 8611, 23 January 1997, available at cisgw3.law.pace.edu/cases/978611i1.html.
[38] See District Court Neubrandenburg (Germany), 3 August 2005, available at http://cisgw3.law .pace.edu/cases/050803g1.html; cf. Court of Appeals Valais (Switzerland), 27 May 2005, available at http://cisgw3.law.pace.edu/cases/050527s1.html.
[39] See Court of Appeals Celle (Germany), 24 July 2009, available at http://cisgw3.law.pace.edu/ cases/090724g1.html.
[40] See, e.g., Commercial Court Aargau (Switzerland), 26 November 2008, available at http:// cisgw3.law.pace.edu/cases/081126s1.html; National Commercial Court of Appeals (Argentina) (*Sr. Carlos Manuel del Corazón de Jesús Bravo Barros v. Salvador Martínez Gares*), 31 May 2007, available at http://cisgw3.law.pace.edu/cases/070531a1.html; Tribunal of International Commercial Arbitration at the Russian Federation Chamber of Commerce and Industry (Russia), 2 June 2005, available at http://cisgw3.law.pace.edu/cases/050602r1.html; CIETAC Arbitration (China), 7 December 2005, available at http://cisgw3.law.pace.edu/cases/051207c1 .html; Court of Appeals Düsseldorf (Germany), 21 April 2004, available at http://cisgw3.law .pace.edu/cases/040421g3.html; Commercial Court Zürich (Switzerland), 30 November 1998, available at http://cisgw3.law.pace.edu/cases/981130s1.html.

by the CISG are to be settled in accordance with the general principles on which it is based. If good faith is one of the general principles of the CISG, as some suggest, then it can be used to fill gaps that otherwise exist in or to augment the CISG's substantive provisions.[41] The CISG's substantive provisions apply to the contracting parties, and these provisions might be based on a general principle of good faith. A principle of good faith is sometimes thought to underlie the following provisions (among others):[42]

- Article 16(2)(b), which deems an offer irrevocable when the offeree reasonably relies on the offer being held open.
- Article 21(2), which deems a late acceptance to be effective if its dispatch normally would have reached the offeror in due time.
- Article 29(2), which precludes a party from relying on a "no oral modification" clause in a contract when its conduct precludes it from doing so.
- Articles 37 and 46, which respectively allow the seller to cure a nonconformity in goods delivered before the date of delivery and require the seller to remedy by repair nonconformities in goods delivered, unless cure or repair is unreasonably inconvenient or expensive to the injured party.
- Article 40, which precludes the seller from relying on the buyer's failure to give notice of nonconformity in the goods in accordance with Articles 38 and 39 if it knows or ought to know of the nonconformity and does not disclose it to the buyer.
- Articles 47(2), 64(2), and 82, which limit the injured party's right to avoid the contract.
- Article 80, which bars a party from relying on the other party's breach to the extent that it caused the breach.
- Articles 85—88, which impose on the injured buyer and seller obligations to take steps to preserve the goods.

Good faith might also underlie Article 77, which requires the injured party relying on a breach to take reasonable measures to mitigate its loss. A substantial majority of

---

[41] See Joseph Lookofsky, Understanding the CISG 34 (4th (Worldwide) ed. 2012); Ulrich Magnus, *The Remedy of Avoidance of Contract Under CISG—General Remarks and Special Cases*, 26 J. L. & Comm. 423, 429 (2006) (principle of good faith underlying Article 7(2) allows reduction in exercise of a party's rights under the CISG).

[42] See Secretariat Commentary on the 1978 Draft, in Documentary History, supra note 6, at 408 (list does not include Article 16(2)); Franco Ferrari, *Articles 1–13*, in The Draft UNCITRAL Digest and Beyond: Cases, Analysis and Unresolved Issues in the U.N. Sales Convention 501, 537 (Franco Ferrari, Harry M. Flechtner & Ronald A. Brand eds., 2004) (underlying Article 16 (2)); Magnus, supra note 40, at 429 (underlying both Articles 16(2) and 29(2)); cf. John Klein, *Good Faith in International Transactions*, 15 Liverpool L. Rev. 115 (1993) (identifying additional provisions).

tribunals that find that the CISG requires the parties to perform their contract in good faith rely on Article 7(2).[43]

Our difficulty with this approach is that it is hard to extract a principle of good faith with a precise content from the CISG's provisions. A general ethical injunction to act honestly and fairly is not useful in filling in gaps in the parties' contract. Even if useful in doing so, Article 7(2) does not allow the use unless the injunction underlies the CISG. But distilling a defensible and easily applicable principle of good faith is hard, and unlikely to be successful.[44] Describing the obligation of good faith in terms close to those in a provision of good faith simply mimics the provision. It does not make the provision easier to apply. For instance, if good faith requires acting reasonably, then an offer is irrevocable when the offeree acts reasonably in reliance on the offer remaining open. But this is just what Article 16(2)(b) already provides. The principle of good faith merely restates the contents of the Article; it adds nothing. Likewise, a buyer might be said to act in bad faith when it unreasonably refuses a seller's offer to cure nonconformities in delivered goods before the date of delivery. But Article 37 gives the seller a right to cure in the same circumstances. Thus, the buyer is not entitled to prevent the seller from curing and the invocation of good faith is superfluous. On the other hand, describing good faith more generally so that it extends beyond a provision's terms risks extracting a principle that does not underlie the CISG's provisions. For instance, Klein identifies a principle of good faith that requires communication of essential information between the parties both during pre-contractual negotiations and performance of the contract.[45] The principle seemingly is broad, requiring a party to disclose information that might reduce the value of the contract to it. In addition, it goes beyond Article 8(3), which merely requires due regard be given to statements made during negotiations to determine the intent of the parties. Thus, good faith might not be superfluous in such a situation. However, the principle is not faithful to the Article, because the Article does not impose a general duty of disclosure on the contracting

[43] See, e.g., Court of Appeal Ghent (Belgium), 17 May 2002, available at http://cisgw3.law.pace .edu/cases/020515b1.html; Federal Supreme Court (Germany), 31 October 2001, available at http://cisgw3.law.pace.edu/cases/011031g1.html; Commercial Court Zürich (Switzerland), 30 November 1998, available at http://cisgw3.law.pace.edu/cases/981130s1.html.

[44] Herbert advocates the development of principles from "internationally recognized standards of honorable conduct;" see Rolf Herbert, *Article 7*, in Commentary on the UN Convention on the International Sale of Goods (CISG) 63 (Peter Schlechtriem ed., 1998). Arguably international standards of honorable conduct are insufficiently detailed to develop principles that fill gaps in contracts.

[45] See Klein, supra note 42, at 126–29. For case law finding the duty to cooperate independent of a duty of good faith, see Court of Appeals Celle (Germany), 24 July 2009, available at http:// cisgw3.law.pace.edu/cases/090724g1.html; District Court Neubrandenburg (Germany), 3 August 2005, available at http://cisgw3.law.pace.edu/cases/050803g1.html.; Court of Appeals, Koblenz (Germany), 24 February 2011, available at http://cisgw3.law.pace.edu/cases/110224g1 .html finds the duty to cooperate implicit in the duty of good faith to which the parties are subject.

parties, and – given the scope of Article 8(3) – one would imagine that a duty to disclose would be mentioned within the provision if the drafters intended that the duty apply.

Although the concept of good faith may be sufficiently developed in many legal systems to serve as an independent source of contractual obligations, we doubt that it can play that role under the CISG.[46] Indeed, given the divergent meaning of good faith among legal systems, robust use of a good faith obligation for parties could interfere with the CISG's effort to promote uniformity in international sales law.[47] Good faith does not help in applying the CISG's provisions where they do not expressly address a particular matter. It is less useful as a standard for evaluation of conduct than an inquiry in whether a party's act or omission will likely reduce transaction costs. According to the latter standard, a party is obligated to act or refrain from acting if doing so reduces the transaction costs of most contracting parties. Presumably, commercial parties would bargain for such acts or omissions because they minimize the total cost of exchange. For example, each party to a contract would presumably bar behavior by the other party that only had the effect of transferring contractual benefits to itself rather than of increasing the total contractual benefit. Thus, when exchange is not simultaneous, the party who performs first risks being exploited by the other party, who can credibly demand that the contractual surplus be renegotiated in its favor. To avoid the risk of ex post renegotiation, the first performer negotiates for contractual defensive measures, such as third-party credit enhancements, or makes fewer investments in performance. Each of these measures, however, is costly, either by increasing the cost of negotiation or reducing the value of the contract. A principle that obligates a party to reduce contracting costs saves the parties the cost of taking these defensive measures. Thus, courts that deny parties the ability opportunistically to reallocate contractual benefits are complying with the preferences of parties. But the explanation that courts are doing so because the opportunistic party fails to act in good faith adds little to the analysis. The transaction cost-reduction principle also applies before the contract is concluded, where the offer and acceptance occur in sequence. And it applies even after breach, where the injured party can take measures after breach to effect its resulting loss. In the formation of the contract, its performance and breach, the obligation to take measures that reduce contracting costs increases the net benefits of the contract.

A number of the CISG's provisions exhibit this transaction-cost-reduction principle. Article 77's mitigation requirement prevents the injured party from running up damages when it can take cost-effective measures ("reasonable" measures) to do so. Articles 85 to 88 essentially impose a mitigation requirement on injured parties in possession of the contract goods. Without the requirement, parties

---

[46] See also Steven Walt, *The Modest Role of Good Faith in Uniform Sales Law*, 33 B.U. Int'l L. J. 37 (2015).

[47] See Franco Ferrari, *The CISG's Interpretative Goals, Its Interpretative Method and Its General Principles in Case Law (Part I)*, 13 Internationales Handelsrecht 137, 153 (August 2013).

would have to bargain for it at the contracting stage or negotiate for it later, after breach. Mitigation requirements save them the expense of doing so. Article 80 prevents a party from relying on the breach of its counterparty to the extent that the party caused the counterparty's breach. This means that the counterparty is not liable when its breach is caused by the party seeking relief. Article 80 therefore does not allow a promisee to benefit from a strategy of "cause the promisor to breach, then obtain a remedy." So the promisee is unlikely to use the strategy in the first place. This saves the promisor the costs of having to take precautions against the promisee opportunistically preventing its performance. Article 37 gives the breaching seller the right to cure nonconforming deliveries before the date of delivery unless cure causes the buyer unreasonable inconvenience or expense. Without the right the seller would have to bargain for it either ex ante or after breach, incurring contracting costs in doing so. The transaction cost-reduction principle arguably also underlies Article 16(2)(b)'s irrevocability rule. By making an open offer irrevocable when the offeror prefers to revoke, the rule increases the offeror's cost of making an open offer. At the same time, the rule increases the value of the offer to the offeree, who can invest in determining the offer's worth to it. Article 16(2)(b) implicitly judges that the rule produces a net benefit for both offerors (due to the increased value offerees put on their open offers) and offerees.

The transaction-cost-reduction principle provides an explanation for many of the decisions that courts decide under the label of good faith. A case decided by the German Supreme Court holds that a buyer who is unaware of the seller's standard terms and conditions is not bound by them when they are not made available to it before the contract's conclusion.[48] The court found that requiring the buyer to make inquiries about the seller's standard terms and conditions would delay the conclusion of the contract. Both parties are harmed by the delay. As we discuss in Chapter 3, the seller easily can provide its standard terms to the buyer as part of its offer, according to the court. Based on these facts, the court concluded that principles of good faith in international trade as well as principles of cooperation and information disclosure prevented undisclosed standard terms from being included in an executed contract. The court's reasoning focuses on the comparative size of contracting costs. The court could as easily, and with greater explanatory force, have concluded that a principle of transaction-cost reduction underlying the CISG supports the result.[49]

B. *Good faith in the courts*

Case law reflects the amorphous nature of good faith in the CISG. Some of the case law takes the narrow view that the good faith obligation applies only to the

---

[48] See Federal Supreme Court (Germany), 31 October 2001, available at http://cisgw3.law.pace .edu/cases/011031g1.html.

[49] For discussion see supra II.A.

interpretation of the CISG itself and imposes no substantive obligation on the parties.[50] Other cases apply good faith both to the interpretation of the CISG and to the obligations of the parties under the sales contract. However, even in the latter cases, references to good faith overestimate the independent importance of the concept. The cases differ in the way in which good faith is applied to the parties. Tribunals use the principle of good faith in four different ways: (1) as dicta, (2) as an alternative basis for a result supported on other grounds, (3) as an additional consideration that supports a result sufficiently supported by other considerations, and (4) as grounds for a result. They rely on good faith only in the last case.

(1) *Dicta.* At times, tribunals refer to Article 7(1)'s good faith directive while deciding cases on different grounds.[51] In *ICC Case 7331*[52] the buyer refused to pay the remaining portion of the contract price after the seller denied its request to reduce the contract price in light of a depressed market for the goods. Although the buyer alleged that the goods were nonconforming, it failed to give timely notice of the nonconformity or state the price at which it later resold the goods. The tribunal noted that "general principles of international commercial practice, including good faith, should govern the dispute." However, its conclusion that the seller was entitled to the remaining portion of the contract price did not rely on these principles. The tribunal instead invoked the CISG's notice and mitigation provisions. The buyer failed to give timely notice in accordance with Articles 38 and 39, and had no reasonable excuse for not doing so. Article 44 therefore prevents it from reducing the contract price or recovering damages. In addition, the buyer did not mitigate its alleged damages as required by Article 77, according to the tribunal, because it did not establish its loss on resale. The tribunal clearly believed that the buyer acted in bad faith. Its recitation of the CISG's good faith principle immediately following the statement of the facts signals that it is dealing with a shady buyer who is attempting to avoid performing a losing contract. But the tribunal easily disposed of the case based only on the CISG's express provisions. No independent obligation of good faith figures in its reasoning.

The principle of good faith was also invoked but not relied on by the Spanish Supreme Court in *Improgess GmbH* v. *Canary Islands Car., SL and Autos Cabrera Medina, SL.*[53] There, a buyer of used cars sought recovery for the seller's delivery of damaged vehicles. A clause in the contract required the cars to be in

---

[50] See, e.g., ICC Case 8611, 23 January 1997, available at http://cisgw3.law.pace.edu/cases/ 978611i1.html.
[51] Cf. *Bobux Marketing Ltd.* v. *Raynor Marketing Ltd.*, [2002] N.Z.L.R. 506 (Thomas, J. dissenting) (referring to Article 7(1)'s language requiring good faith; the CISG inapplicable to the distribution agreement).
[52] ICC Case 7331, 1994, available at www.unilex.info/case.cfm?pid=1&do=case&id=140&step= FullText.
[53] See Supreme Court (Spain), 17 January 2008, available at http://cisgw3.law.pace.edu/cases/ 080117s4.html.

good condition. The buyer argued that the cars delivered did not conform to the contract and that it gave the seller timely and proper notice of the nonconformities. The Supreme Court disagreed. Although it remarked that Article 7's reference to the need to observe good faith in international trade "should be highlighted in resolving the present appeal," the good faith principle does not appear in the court's reasoning. Instead, the reasoning relied entirely on the CISG's warranty and notice provisions. The court found that the used cars were in good condition even with the damage alleged by the buyer. Thus, the cars conformed to the contract. In addition, the court concluded that the buyer was aware of the defects in the cars at the conclusion of the contract. Finally, the court found that the buyer's notice of the alleged nonconformities came too late and without excuse. The buyer's inspection of the cars at the point of shipment began the reasonable period within which Article 39(1) requires notice of breach to be given. This reasonable period had expired when the buyer gave notice after inspection at the point of destination, according to the court. Nothing in the court's reasoning depends on the application of Article 7's principle of good faith.

(2) *Alternative Basis.* Some tribunals have used Article 7(1)'s reference to good faith as an independent basis for a result supported by application of the CISG's provisions. Good faith here serves as an alternative ground for the result. A German trial court's reference to good faith is illustrative.[54] The case presents the somewhat common situation in which the seller fails to provide the buyer with its standard terms prior to the conclusion of the contract. When a dispute over the contract's terms later arises, the court has to decide whether the contract incorporates the seller's standard terms. The trial court followed other courts in concluding that terms of an offer not presented to the buyer and of which it unaware at the conclusion of the contract do not bind it.[55] It reached the conclusion by applying Article 8's rules of interpretation to the seller's offer. According to Article 8(2), the seller's offer is to be interpreted according to the understanding of a reasonable person in the buyer's circumstances. A reasonable offeree in the buyer's position would not have interpreted the offer to include terms of which it is not aware. Because the seller's offer did not provide its standard terms, they are not part of the concluded contract.

The court's alternative ground for the same conclusion was good faith. Good faith in international trade, according to the court, prevents burdening the offeree with terms that were not sent to it prior to the conclusion of the contract. The offeree therefore was not obligated to discover standard terms that the offeror did not send to it. This conclusion does not derive from Article 8's rules for

---

[54] See District Court Neubrandenburg (Germany), 3 August 2005, available at http://cisgw3.law
.pace.edu/cases/050803g1.html.
[55] For discussion see Chapter 3.II.A.

interpreting the terms of the offer. It derives from a separate principle that allocates the responsibility for discovering terms that do not appear in the offer. As applied by the court, good faith does not burden the offeree with the responsibility when a reasonable person in the offeree's position would not understand the offer to include the offeror's standard terms. An appellate court in Germany has adopted the same reasoning that equates the absence of good faith with the imposition of a duty to discover terms on a buyer.[56]

(3) *Additional support.* Tribunals occasionally use a principle of good faith to add support to a result supported by the CISG's provisions. Good faith also can serve to confirm the result reached on other grounds. A Spanish trial court employed good faith as additional support.[57] The court refused to enforce a forum selection clause that appeared on the back side of a contract when no reference was made on the front side to the clause. It added that the CISG's principle of good faith would be violated if the forum selection clause were enforced in these circumstances. Although the court did not state whether its refusal to enforce the clause was based on the CISG's provisions or applicable domestic law, it clearly invoked good faith as a separate consideration to support its conclusion. The court did not rely on good faith to support its refusal of enforcement. The fact that enforcing the clause would violate good faith instead confirmed its refusal to do so.

(4) *Grounds for the result.* A number of tribunals rely on good faith as the primary doctrinal basis for their decisions.[58] Good faith here figures in the rationale for the results in these cases. It does not serve merely as an alternative basis for the decision or to confirm that the result reached is warranted. One court refused to incorporate into the sales contract an arbitration clause in a guarantee issued in connection with the contract when the buyer did not expressly consent to its application.[59] According to the court, good faith required that a party be bound only by terms it could reasonably expect, and

---

[56] See Court of Appeals Naumburg (Germany), 13 February 2013, available at http://cisgw3.law .pace.edu/cases/130213g1.html ("It would run contrary to the principle of good faith (Art. 7 (1) CISG) if the recipient were under a full duty to investigate the content of any standard terms which the declaring party has not sufficiently communicated or, in other words, if the recipient was burdened with the risk of unfavourable standard terms which had never been made known to it.").

[57] See Court of Appeals Navarra (Spain), 27 December 2007, available at http://cisgw3.law.pace .edu/cases/071227s4.html (describing lower court's disposition of case).

[58] See, e.g., District Court Rotterdam (Netherlands), 25 February 2009, available at http://cisgw3 .law.pace.edu/cases/090225n1.html; Court of Appeals Navarra (Spain), 22 September 2003, available at http://cisgw3.law.pace.edu/cases/030922s4.html; Federal Supreme Court (Germany), 31 October 2001, available at http://cisgw3.law.pace.edu/cases/011031g1.html; ICC Case 8611, 23 January 1997, available at http://cisgw3.law.pace.edu/cases/978611i1.html; Court of Appeals Arnhem (Netherlands), 22 August 1995, available at http://cisgw3.law.pace.edu/cases/950822n1 .html.

[59] See Court of Appeals Navarra (Spain), 22 September 2003, available at http://cisgw3.law.pace .edu/cases/030922s4.html (Abstract).

the buyer could not expect the sales contract to be subject to the arbitration clause in the guarantee. The court could have invoked Article 8(2) to reach the same conclusion, because a reasonable person in the buyer's position would not interpret the sales contract to incorporate the arbitration clause. However, it relied on good faith, not the CISG's rules of interpretation.

In *SARL BRI Production "Bonaventure" v. Société Pan African Export*,[60] the buyer agreed to sell the goods it purchased only in South America and Africa. It breached by selling the goods in Spain. The French appellate court awarded the seller damages of 10,000 francs under the French Civil Code and an additional 10,000 francs for abuse of process. It based the latter award on the buyer's conduct at trial which, according to the court, violated Article 7(1)'s principle of good faith. This finding arguably takes the CISG's principle of good faith too far. The latter award is a fine, because the sum awarded was unrelated to the seller's loss from the buyer's breach, which is the measure of damages under Article 74. Thus, the court effectively relies on good faith to fine the buyer. However, the CISG's remedial provisions allow for compensation for breach only, and the court awarded the seller 10,000 francs in damages under French domestic law. Nothing in the CISG authorizes the award of damages in excess of the loss resulting from breach. The additional 10,000 francs awarded is punitive in character, sanctioning the buyer's abuse of process, and is not a compensatory remedy for breach of contract. Even if the CISG's good faith principle creates obligations between the parties and not merely obligations in the interpretation of the CISG's provisions, its violation cannot support a supercompensatory award under the CISG. Although domestic law might allow a sanction for abuse of process, the CISG's provisions do not.[61]

Another court relied on the CISG's good faith principle to permit avoidance of the contract to be effective without an express declaration.[62] The court found that Article 7's good faith principle does not allow a party who breaches by definitively refusing to perform to insist that the injured party electing to avoid the contract make the declaration. There is no basis for the court's position in the CISG's provisions. By its terms, Article 26 makes avoidance effective only on notice to the injured party. It does not allow for avoidance to be effective without notice, even when the breacher has definitively refused to perform. The court's limited exception to Article 26's notice requirement effectively overrides Article 26's terms. We believe that the limited exception to Article 26's declaration requirement is on the merits

---

[60] Court of Appeals Grenoble (France), 22 February 1995, available at http://cisgw3.law.pace.edu/cases/950222f1.html.

[61] Cf. District Court Trier (Germany), 8 January 2004, available at http://cisgw3.law.pace.edu/cases/040108g1.html (sanction for abuse of process as bad faith under German domestic law rejected).

[62] See Court of Appeals Munich (Germany), 15 September 2004, available at http://cisgw3.law.pace.due/cases/040101g.1.html (sanction for abuse of process bad faith under German domestic law rejected).

unjustified.[63] However, the merits of the exception aside, the court employs a good faith principle as a basis for the exception. Since the decision contradicts the explicit requirements of the CISG, however, it is difficult to contend that it deploys good faith to fill a gap under Article 7(2).

A recent decision by the German Supreme Court that relied on a principle of good faith falls into the "grounds for the result" category.[64] The seller contracted to deliver ground clay to the buyer, who used the clay in a process to grade potatoes sold as animal feed. Before the seller delivered the clay, it learned that the clay contained high levels of dioxin but did not inform the buyer. The buyer did not discover that the clay contained dioxin, although it fairly easily could have done so. The Court found that the seller had breached its obligation to deliver conforming goods while the buyer had breached its contractual duty to take reasonable care with respect to the delivered goods.[65] The buyer's duty included the obligation to verify that the goods were conforming. According to the Court, it therefore had to determine the amount of damages the buyer could recover under the CISG when the buyer's loss resulted from independent breaches by both the seller and the buyer. The Court relied on a principle of good faith underlying Articles 77 and 80, and incorporated in Article 7, to conclude that damages were to be divided according to the causal contribution of each party's breach to the loss.

The CISG does not expressly address the issue framed by the Court. Article 77 reduces the aggrieved party's recoverable damages by the amount of loss that it could have mitigated. Because the buyer did not learn that the delivered clay contained dioxin, it could not feasibly take reasonable measures to avoid its loss. Article 80 bars an aggrieved party from relying on the other party's breach to the extent that it caused the breach. The Article does not apply to preclude the buyer in the case from relying on the seller's breach to recover damages because it did not cause the seller's breach. The buyer and seller's breaches occurred independently of each other. Since none of the CISG's provisions apply to allocate the loss between the seller and the buyer, good faith is an independent and plausible basis for dividing loss according to the parties' respective causal contributions to it.

Both the Court's reasoning and reliance on good faith are questionable. The Court's finding that the buyer's duty of reasonable care with respect to the goods requires the buyer to ascertain that the goods are conforming is unsupported. The contract did not obligate the buyer to examine the goods to verify that they conformed to the contract.[66] In addition, the CISG does not impose the duty as an implied term of the contract. Article 38 requires the buyer to examine the goods as soon as practicable. However, the requirement does not impose a duty of examination, because the failure to fulfill the requirement does not give the seller

---

[63] See Chapter 5.IV.B.2.
[64] See Federal Supreme Court (Germany), 26 September 2013, available at http://cisgw3.law
.pace.edu/cases/120926g1.html.
[65] See id.   [66] For further discussion, see Walt, supra note 46, at 62–4.

a remedy against the buyer.[67] Although the buyer's failure to timely notify the seller of a nonconformity can bar it from a remedy,[68] the requirement of timely notice imposes only a sanction of sorts on the buyer. It does not impose a duty of notice. This is because the buyer does not commit a breach by failing to give the seller timely notice. The consequence of the failure is that the buyer loses its right to rely on the nonconformity against the seller. Thus, the buyer in the case did not breach by failing to ascertain that the clay it received from the seller did not contain dioxin. Only the seller committed a breach. For this reason, the issue in fact presented by the case is the amount of damages the buyer can recover under the CISG when its loss results from a breach by the seller. This is an issue expressly settled by the CISG under Article 74, which entitles an aggrieved party to recover as damages its foreseeable loss resulting from breach. Thus, the case does not present a question "not expressly settled in" the CISG and there is therefore no need to resort to a principle of good faith under Article 7(2) to resolve it.

Even if the case raised the question as to the amount of damages the buyer can recover under the CISG when its loss results from independent breaches by both the seller and the buyer, the principle the Court relies on to answer the question is not one of good faith. The Court reasoned that Articles 77 and 80 reflect a principle of good faith binding on the contracting parties.[69] The general principle apparently is that a party should not recover for loss to the extent that it could have avoided the loss (Article 77) or benefit from a breach to the extent that it caused the breach (Article 80). As applied, this principle divides damages according to the causal contribution by each breaching party to the aggrieved party's loss. However, this principle is not one of good faith. An aggrieved party can incur loss that it could have avoided even if it acted in good faith, such as by mistake or inadvertence. Similarly, an aggrieved party that causes the other party's breach may do so innocently. In both cases the general principle relied on by the Court would not allow recovery even though the aggrieved party acted in good faith. This shows that the principle at work in Articles 77 and 80 is something other than good faith.

---

[67] See Stefan Kröll, *Article 38*, in Kröll et al., supra note 33, at 560. Although courts sometimes refer to Article 38 as creating a "duty" of examination (see. e.g., District Court Reggio Emilia (Italy) (*Fliesen Kiessling v. Serenissima Cir Industrie Ceramiche SPA*), 12 April 2011, available at http://cisgw3.law.pace.edu/cases/110412i3.html.), strictly Article 38 imposes a burden on the buyer, not a duty. Cf. Kröll, *Article 38*, in Kröll et al., supra note 33, at 560.

[68] See Article 39(1). Article 40 makes Articles 38 and 39(1) inapplicable when the seller is aware or ought to have been aware of the nonconformity and fails to disclose this fact to the buyer. The facts of the case make Articles 38 and 39(1) inapplicable, because the seller was aware of the dioxin at the time it delivered the clay. For a discussion of Article 40, see Chapter 5.II.F.1.

[69] For the view that good faith underlies breach caused by the other party, see Court of Appeals Karlsruhe (Germany), 25 June 1997, available at http://cisgw3.law.pace.edu/cases/970625g1 .html; Peter Huber & Alastair Mullis, The CISG 265 (2007); Denis Tallon, *Article 80*, in Bianca & Bonell, supra note 6, at 596; First Committee Deliberations, 28th Meeting, 11 April 1980, in Documentary History, supra note 6, at 607–08 (paras. 50–64).

Once again, the operative principle is better understood as one of transaction-cost reduction. It has nothing to do with the ethical quality of the contracting parties' behavior. Article 77's mitigation limitation prevents the injured party from recovering for loss incurred after breach that it is better positioned to take measures to avoid. This gives the injured party the incentive to take these measures. Without the limitation, both contracting parties (since neither knows in advance whether it will breach) would have to incur costly measures before or after breach to prevent the injured party from driving up its damages. Article 80's preclusion rule denies any benefit to a party who regrets the contract and strategically causes the counterparty to breach. The rule thus removes the incentive to cause the breach. Without the preclusion rule, each contracting party would have to take precautions to assure that its counterparty could not cause them to breach. Taking measures to avoid increasing damages or being caused to breach is costly, and Articles 77 and 80 save parties from having to incur these costs.

Finally, it is worth noting the effort some courts make to avoid relying on good faith as a ground for a result. In *Citgo Petroleum Corp.* v. *Odfjell Seachem*,[70] the sales contract contained an Incoterms CFR delivery term. The buyer suffered loss resulting from a delay in the delivery of the contract goods due to a breakdown in the carrier's vessel. The seller knew in advance that the carrier's selected vessel had broken down in the past. In the sub-buyer's suit against the seller, the sub-buyer argued that the seller had breached its obligations of good faith and reasonableness under Article 32(2) of the CISG in its selection of the vessel. The seller argued that the parties had opted out of Article 32(2) by incorporating the CFR term into their contract. The Incoterms definition required the seller to arrange for a carriage contract on the "usual terms." According to the seller, the definition did not require it to make a reasonable carriage contract in good faith.

The court split the difference, as it were, between the seller's and buyer's arguments. It agreed with the buyer that Article 32(2) continued to define part of the seller's delivery obligation even when the agreement incorporates a CFR delivery term defined by Incoterms. However, the court limited the seller's obligation under Article 32(2) to the terms of the subparagraph. According to Article 32(2), if the seller is bound to arrange for the carriage of the goods, it must make an arrangement for transportation that is "appropriate in the circumstances." The court ruled that the subparagraph required the seller to arrange for an appropriate contract of carriage. Significantly, it did not rule that a carriage contract is appropriate only if the seller arranges for the contract in good faith. The court instead merely reported the buyer's argument that Article 32(2) requires good faith without relying on it. Nothing in the case's reasoning relies on a principle of good faith underlying Article 32(2).

---

[70] 2013 U.S. Dist. LEXIS 72898 (S.D. Tex. May 23, 2013).

C. *Good faith as a default rule*

National laws differ in their recognition of an obligation of good faith and its scope. The statutory law of many countries requires good faith in the performance of contractual obligations.[71] UCC § 1–304 imposes an obligation of good faith on the performance and enforcement of any contract subject to the UCC. The obligation is a mandatory implied term. Although UCC § 1–302(b) allows the parties to determine operative reasonable standards of good faith, it does not allow them to contract around the obligation. UCC § 1–304's obligation of good faith does not apply to the formation of the contract. The law of some common law countries either does not recognize an implied obligation of good faith or treats it as a default term that the parties can exclude by appropriate drafting.[72] By comparison, German law implies a general obligation of good faith which is mandatory and applies to both the formation and performance of the contract.[73]

Less clear is the ability of the parties to contract out of the obligation of good faith in international sales contracts. Under Article 1.7(2) of the UNIDROIT Principles of International Commercial Contracts, the obligation of good faith and fair dealing is a mandatory term. However, the term is mandatory only if the parties incorporate the UNIDROIT Principles into their agreement or a tribunal otherwise makes the Principles applicable to the contract. Otherwise, applicable domestic law determines whether good faith is a mandatory or default term. No reported case has decided whether good faith is a mandatory or default term under the CISG. We believe that it is a default term. Our argument is simple: Article 6 allows the parties to derogate from almost all of its provisions, including Article 7. Thus, parties can opt out of the obligation of good faith imposed by Article 7 either by excluding the CISG entirely or by excluding just Article 7's application to their contract. In either case the only good faith obligations that would remain are those imposed by applicable domestic law. The ability to exclude the CISG's good faith obligations therefore makes good faith a default term.

Parties might want to exclude from their agreement obligations of good faith imposed by the CISG. The CISG does not state crisp and easily identifiable principles of good faith whose application the parties can predict reliably. Even if domestic law recognizes poorly circumscribed norms of good faith, norms of good

---

[71] See Ingeborg Schwenzer, Pascal Hachem & Christopher Kee, Global Sales and Contract Law 278 n.4 (2012) (listing national codifications).

[72] See, e.g., *GEC Marconi Systems Pty Ltd.* v. *BHP Information Technology Pty Ltd.*, [2003] FCA 50 (Australia); Roy Goode, The Concept of "Good Faith" in English Law, available at www .cisg.law.pace.edu/cisg/biblio/goode1.html; Simon Whittaker & Reinhard Zimmerman, *Good Faith in European Contract Law: Surveying the Legal Landscape*, in Good Faith in European Contract Law 1, 39–48 (Reinhard Zimmerman & Simon Whittaker eds., 2000).

[73] See Burgerliches Gesetzbuch [BGB][Civil Code] § 242 (Ger.); Werner F. Ebke & Bettina M. Steinhauer, *The Doctrine of Good Faith in German Contract Law*, in Beatson & Friedmann, supra note 4, at 171.

faith in international trade (Article 7(1)) or principles of good faith underlying the CISG (Article 7(2)) are harder to identify. Parties worried about the ability of tribunals to identify these norms accurately or the suitability of the norms for the transaction might prefer to make Article 7 inapplicable to their contract. They also might prefer to opt out of all obligations of good faith, not just norms of good faith in international trade, and rely only on the literal terms of their contract. Although applicable domestic law might not allow the parties to do so, Article 6 of the CISG allows them to contract around obligations of good faith in international trade imposed by the CISG. For the parties this is better than nothing.

Arguments for finding good faith to be a mandatory term in the CISG are unconvincing. One argument relies on the consequence of opting out of Article 7 by agreement. Opting out of the Article leaves applicable the provisions of the Vienna Convention on the Law of Treaties (the "Convention"). Article 31(1) of the Convention requires treaties to be interpreted in good faith, and Article 26 requires parties to a treaty to perform their obligations under the treaty in good faith.[74] Both Articles are mandatory provisions to which reservations cannot be made. Thus, they make good faith applicable to contracts that exclude Article 7 of the CISG or the CISG entirely.[75] This argument fails to notice the entities bound by the Convention. The Convention binds states that have signed it and, according to some commentators, those required to interpret a treaty.[76] It is not directed at parties to sales contracts (unless they are states who are signatory states to the Convention). Parties to a sales contract are neither parties to treaties or called on to apply the provisions of a treaty. Article 31(1) of the Convention therefore does not impose an obligation of good faith interpretation on them.

In addition, the argument confuses a good faith interpretation of treaties, which Article 31(1) requires, with the good faith required by treaties to which it applies, about which the Article says nothing. A rule of treaty interpretation is not a rule of the treaty being interpreted. As far as Article 31(1) goes, treaties to which it applies need not require good faith or, when required, prevent parties from contracting around the requirement. Article 6 of the CISG allows contracting parties to contract around Article 7's requirements of good faith. When parties opt out of Article 7, they are no longer bound by the CISG's obligation of good faith. Article 31(1) still requires them to interpret the CISG's provisions in good faith (if Article 31(1) is directed at the contracting parties). Nonetheless, a good faith interpretation of the CISG allows the parties to contract around the CISG's good faith requirements.[77]

---

[74] See Vienna Convention on the Law of Treaties (1969), available at http://untreaty.un.org/ilc/texts/instruments/english/conventions/1_1_1969.pdf.

[75] See Zeller, *The Observance of Good Faith in International Trade,* in Jannsen & Meyer, supra note 35, at 143.

[76] See Ulf Linderfalk, On the Interpretation of Treaties 64–65 (2007); J. F. O'Connor, Good Faith in International Law 110 (1991); Ian Sinclair, The Vienna Convention Law on Treaties 120 (2d ed. 1984).

[77] Cf. *Regina v. Immigration Officer at Prague Airport ex parte European Roma Rights Centre,* [2004] UKHL 55 (para. 19) ("But there is no want of good faith [in relation to Articles 26 and 31]

According to Article 31(1), good faith is a mandatory rule of treaty interpretation. It is not a mandatory term of the CISG, a treaty to which the Article's mandatory rule applies.

III. OPEN TERMS

As noted earlier, the sales contract need not specify the rights and obligations of the parties with respect to every element of their performance. The CISG, like the UCC, fills gaps in terms left unaddressed by the parties. In addition to trade usage, course of dealing and course of performance, it supplies terms governing performance. Article 57(1)(a) calls for payment of the contract price at the seller's place of business, unless the goods or documents covering the goods are to be delivered elsewhere. The buyer has the right to inspect the goods before payment, according to Article 58(3), unless the contract provides otherwise. Article 58(1) requires the buyer to pay the contract price when the goods are placed at its disposal, and a fair implication of "pay" is that, unless otherwise agreed, payment is to be in cash. Although the CISG does not specify the currency of payment, a decent (but not conclusive) argument can be made that the currency is the legal tender of the place where delivery of the goods or documents covering them is due.[78]

A. *Open price terms*

As we indicated in Chapter 3, the CISG's treatment of open price terms is unclear. We refer to that discussion for possible ways to reconcile the ostensible inconsistencies between Article 14 and Article 55 in dealing with open price terms in contracts.[79]

B. *Open quantity terms*

The CISG allows for sales contracts that do not expressly or implicitly fix the quantity of goods. The argument for this conclusion is the same as the one we made with respect to open price terms. Article 14(1)'s first sentence requires that a proposal for concluding a contract constitutes an offer if it is sufficiently definite in terms. The terms that must be sufficiently definite obviously include the quantity of goods offered for sale. Article 14(1)'s second sentence provides that a proposal is sufficiently definite if it "indicates the goods" and provides for "determining th[eir] quantity." As with price, this sentence states only a sufficient condition of a sufficiently definite proposal. It does not say that a proposal is sufficiently definite in the

if a state interprets a treaty as meaning what it says and declines to do anything significantly greater than or different from what has been agreed" (L. Steyn)).
[78] We discuss this issue in Chapter 5.I.C.   [79] See Chapter 3.II.A.

quantity term only if it determines quantity. Thus, in principle a proposal can be an offer according to Article 14(1)'s first sentence even if it left quantity open. This can occur if the proposal leaves quantity open while being otherwise sufficiently definite and indicating the offeror's intention to be bound in the case of the offeree's acceptance. Of course, a proposal lacking a quantity term might indicate that the proposer does not intend it as an offer. Offerors usually are unwilling to risk having to buy or sell a quantity that is neither expressly nor implicitly fixed by their offer. A court ex post might supply a quantity term greater or lesser than the one the offeror would prefer. However, in some circumstances a proposal that does not state quantity could indicate the intent to be bound on the offeree's acceptance. This open quantity proposal can be an offer under Article 14(1)'s first sentence.

One court found that a telephone conversation could not conclude a sales contract when no precise quantity was discussed.[80] The court thought this followed from the fact that none of the parties' proposals fixed quantity. Article 14(1) does not support the court's assumption that a proposal is sufficiently definite only if it fixes quantity. The court mistakenly understands Article 14(1)'s second sentence to state a necessary rather than a sufficient condition of a proposal being sufficiently definite in terms. However, its conclusion that no offer had been made in the parties' telephone conversation might well be sound if the absence of a quantity term implied unwillingness to be bound by an acceptance. Article 14(1)'s first sentence therefore would not count their proposals as offers. An email sent by one of the parties after the telephone conversation, designating a proposal stating a quantity "non-committed," confirms the absence of contractual intent.

The CISG does not explicitly deal with the enforceability of output and requirements contracts. Some common law doctrine refused enforcement to such contracts on the grounds that they were insufficiently definite. In the United States, that doctrine has been overcome by UCC § 2–306(1), which requires that any output of the seller or requirements of the buyer must be supplied or demanded in good faith. Section 2–306 makes enforceable a quantity term in a contract that could otherwise be indefinite. Given the absence of a similar provision in the CISG, one might question whether a proposal to fill the buyer's requirements or to supply the buyer with all of the seller's output is sufficiently definite as to quantity. Our argument that Article 14(1) does not state a definite quantity requirement applies here: A proposal to meet a demand for requirements or to supply output may be sufficiently definite even it does not fix quantity. However, we need not rely on that argument. Even if Article 14(1)'s second sentence announces a definite quantity requirement, proposals for requirements or output meet it. That sentence requires the proposal to "indicate the goods" and make provision for "determining the quantity." A quantity term calling for requirements or output "indicates the goods." The term also

---

[80] See District Court Zug (Switzerland), 2 December 2004, available at http://cisgw3.law.pace .edu/cases/041202s1.html.

"determines" the quantity.[81] For those who find a standard of good faith in the CISG under Article 7(1), the quantity fixed is the one that meets the buyer's requirements in good faith and the output the seller produces in good faith.[82] Because we maintain that the CISG does not incorporate a good faith standard of performance, as argued in Section II, we take another position. A quantity term calling for requirements or output "indicates the goods" when trade usage or the practices of the parties, or the standard of good faith applicable by domestic law under Article 7(2), sets requirements or output. If neither trade usage or other relevant practices nor good faith determines quantity, then the quantity term in the proposal does not indicate the goods.

Courts have not required that a proposal determine a specific quantity in advance. One court found a contract on the basis of a proposal to supply "700 to 800 tons."[83] Another court found an agreement on quantity when the contract provided for the purchase of "up to 250 pounds" of the product.[84] The designation of quantity allowed in these cases is not much more specific than a designation of requirements or output. If the designations in the cases are enough to make "provision for determining the quantity," the designation of requirements or output can as well.

IV. PAROL EVIDENCE AND INTERPRETATION

A. *The parol evidence rule: retention or rejection?*

The parol evidence rule, recognized in common law systems, provides that where the parties intend a writing to represent their final statement of their agreement (the "integration"), evidence of prior negotiations or understandings ("parol evidence") is inadmissible to contradict the terms of the writing.[85] Where the parties intend the integration to be a complete expression of their agreement, parol evidence is inadmissible to supplement its terms. The CISG does not contain a parol evidence rule. However, it also does not address expressly the evidence that is admissible to prove the terms of a contract. Thus, perhaps unsurprisingly, relevant provisions can be read either as displacing the parol evidence rule or leaving unaffected the rule's application under applicable domestic law. Articles 8(3) and 7(2) are the relevant provisions. Article 8(3) states that [i]n determining the intent of a party ... due consideration is to be given to all relevant circumstances of the case including the negotiations, any practices which the

---

[81] For doubts see Franco Ferrari, *Article 14*, in Kröll et al., supra note 33, at 227; Burt A. Leete, *Contract Formation Under the United Nations Convention on Contracts for the International Sale of Goods and the Uniform Commercial Code: Pitfalls for the Unwary*, 6 Temple Int'l & Comp. L. J. 193, 201 (1992).

[82] Cf. Secretariat Commentary on the 1978 Draft, in Documentary History, supra note 6, at 411.

[83] See Supreme Court (Austria), 6 February 1996, available at http://cisgw3.law.pace.edu/cases/960206a3.html.

[84] See *Solae, LLC v. Hershey Canada, Inc.*, 557 F. Supp. 2d 452 (D. Del. 2008).

[85] See Restatement (Second) of Contracts §§ 209–210 (1981); cf. U.C.C. § 2–202 (excluding extrinsic evidence of prior agreement and contemporaneous oral agreement).

parties have established between themselves, usages. ...." Article 7(2) provides that questions governed by the CISG which are not expressly settled by it are settled by "general principles" upon which it is based or, if none do so, by applicable domestic law.

The case for finding the parol evidence rule displaced relies on Article 8(3)'s instruction to give "due consideration" to "all relevant circumstances," including the parties' negotiations in determining contractual intent. "All relevant circumstances" allows consideration of parol evidence, such as prior statements or writings, even if it contradicts or supplements the terms of the integration. Because the Article makes parol evidence admissible, the inference is made that Article 7(2) treats the question as expressly settled under the CISG. The case concludes that the parol evidence rule therefore does not apply to contracts within the CISG's scope. The view that the CISG leaves the parol evidence rule unaffected draws a different inference from the language of the same Articles. Although Article 8(3) requires giving "due consideration" to all relevant circumstances, it does not limit the way in which "due consideration" must be given to them. The parol evidence rule gives "due consideration" by making parol evidence inadmissible when a writing is found to be an integration. The view concludes that Article 7(2) leaves the admissibility of parol evidence to domestic law.

The trouble here, of course, is that the same language of the Articles supports different inferences about the CISG treatment of the parol evidence rule. The case for finding the rule displaced maintains that Article 8(3) expressly settles the admissibility of parol evidence: the evidence always is admissible to prove the terms of a contract. Thus, as expressly settled, Article 7(2) displaces the parol evidence rule otherwise applicable under some domestic law. The view that the CISG leaves the rule's application unaffected finds that Article 8(3) does not expressly settle the matter and that none of the general principles underlying the CISG does so either. We believe that the case for displacement has the stronger argument. Article 8(3) probably "expressly settles" the admissibility of parol evidence and does so in favor of including the evidence as an aid in interpreting contractual intent. The view that excluding parol evidence is a way of giving "due consideration" to all relevant circumstance seems to be a debater's point. Excluding parol evidence gives no consideration rather than due consideration to the evidence excluded. Article 8(3) requires the trier of fact to interpret the terms of the contract by taking into account all relevant circumstances and therefore evidence ("including negotiations"). For instance, English law makes inadmissible evidence of pre-contractual negotiations even to prove the meaning of terms in the integration; Article 8(3) allows the evidence.[86] The relevant diplomatic history, while not conclusive, suggests that the CISG rejects the parol evidence rule.[87]

---

[86] See *Chartbrook Limited* v. *Persimmon Homes Limited et al.*, [2009] UKHL 38. para. 39 (Article 8(3) inconsistent with English parol evidence rule, which makes inadmissible evidence of prior negotiations to prove the meaning of terms in an integration).

[87] The Australian delegate to the Vienna diplomatic conference, commenting on a version of Article 8(3), suggests that the Article required that the parol evidence rule be "amended" for contracts to which the CISG applies. See Documentary History, supra note 6, at 483 (para. 51).

That said, the impact of the CISG's likely displacement of the parol evidence rule should not be exaggerated. For one thing, the rule admits parol evidence for the purpose of proving whether a writing is an integration. Displacement of the parol evidence rule under the CISG therefore leaves this practice unaffected. More important, Article 8(3)'s treatment of parol evidence is consistent with the way in which some American courts use parol evidence to interpret terms in a contract (as opposed to adding terms to a contract). In general, courts take two different approaches to determining whether extrinsic (outside of the writing itself) evidence is admissible to interpret the terms of a writing intended as the final expression of the parties' agreement.[88] One approach determines whether the language of the contract is ambiguous from the writing itself, without recourse to other evidence. If the language is unambiguous, parol evidence is inadmissible to interpret it. This "four corners" approach limits the evidence admissible to interpret the terms of the integration. Such evidence is admissible only to resolve an ambiguity. By restricting the evidence to the terms of the integration, this approach refuses to give "due consideration" to extrinsic evidence such as prior negotiations or agreements in the absence of ambiguity. The other approach considers all evidence to determine the meaning of a contractual term; allowing the evidence is not conditioned on an initial finding that the meaning of the term is ambiguous. This approach is consistent with Article 8(3). In determining the interpretation of the integration it gives "due consideration" to all evidence. Thus, only the former approach is inconsistent with Article 8(3).

American courts, with a single exception, have concluded that the CISG displaces the parol evidence rule. They rely primarily on Article 8(3).[89] In doing so, courts have not focused on the fine points of the arguments for and against the conclusion. Rather, they reason that Article 8(3)'s instruction that "due consideration is to be given to all relevant circumstances" allows admission of prior statements or conduct of the parties to establish the terms of the contract.[90] One

---

In addition, a Canadian proposal at the conference to include in Article 11 a version of the parol evidence rule was rejected. The Austrian delegate, in rejecting the proposal, objected that it denied to the judge the "free appreciation of the evidence." See id. at 491 (paras. 82–83). Although these incidents suggest that the final version of the CISG rejected the rule, they are consistent with the delegates' belief that Article 8(3) allows domestic law to regulate the "due consideration" of parol evidence.

[88] See, Geoffrey P. Miller, *Bargains Bicoastal: New Light on Contract Theory*, 31 Cardozo L. Rev. 1475, 1506–08 (2010); Alan Schwartz & Robert E. Scott, *Contract Interpretation Redux*, 119 Yale L. J. 926, 959–60 (2010).

[89] Some cases simply state categorically that the CISG does not contain the parol evidence rule. See *Korea Trade Insurance Corp. v. Oved Apparel Corp.*, 2015 U.S. Dist. LEXIS 38214 (S.D.N.Y. March 23, 2015); *Rienzi & Sons, Inc. v. N. Puglisi & F. Industria Paste Alimentari S.P.A.*, 2014 U.S. Dist. LEXIS 41478 (E.D.N.Y. March 27, 2014).

[90] See, e.g., *MCC-Marble Ceramic Center, Inc. v. Ceramica Nuova D'Agostino*, 144 F.3d 1384 (11th Cir. 1998); *ECEM European Chemical Marketing B.V. v. The Purolite Co.*, 2010 U.S. Dist. LEXIS 7373 (E.D. Penn., January 29, 2010), *aff'd* 51 Fed. Appx. 73 (3d Cir. 2011); *Mitchell Aircraft Spares, Inc. v. European Aircraft Service AB*, 23 F. Supp. 2d 915 (N.D. Il. 1998);

American court stated the case in relatively strong terms: "the CISG does not merely lack a parol-evidence rule, it commands courts to consider extrinsic evidence that illuminates the parties' intent."[91] The single exception is an early Fifth Circuit case, *Beijing Metals & Minerals Import/Export Corp.* v. *American Business Center, Inc.*[92] The court in passing stated that the parol evidence rule applied to a contract whether it was governed by state law or by the CISG.[93] It gave no reason for the conclusion and other courts have refused to follow its finding.[94]

The leading case concluding that the parol evidence rule does not apply to contracts governed by the CISG continues to be *MCC-Marble Ceramic Center, Inc.* v. *Ceramica Nuova D'Agostino.*[95] There, the buyer, who did not speak Italian, executed an agreement on one of the Italian seller's standard forms printed in Italian. When the buyer later sued the seller for breach of contract, the seller relied on a term in the form to deny liability. The buyer argued that the term was not part of the parties' agreement and sought to introduce an affidavit to the effect that the buyer had no subjective intent to be bound by the terms of the seller's form and that the seller was aware of that intent. The court held that the parol evidence rule was inapplicable to contracts governed by the CISG and admitted the affidavit as evidence showing that the parties did not intend to include the terms in the seller's form in their agreement.

The *MCC-Marble* court based its conclusion that the CISG displaced the parol evidence rule on Articles 8(3) and 11. Article 11 is irrelevant to the admissibility of evidence going to the terms of a contract. The Article only allows a contract to be concluded and enforced without a writing. It says nothing about the admissibility of evidence to prove the terms of that contract. As far as Article 11 goes, the parol evidence rule could continue to operate to restrict the sort of evidence admissible for purpose when the contract is concluded by a writing or evidenced by one. Only Article 8(3) supports the court's conclusion. Article 8(3)'s instruction duly to consider all relevant circumstances admits evidence of prior negotiations and the like to determine the parties' intent. Strictly, the *MCC-Marble* court could have admitted the affidavit without deciding whether the CISG displaced the parol evidence rule. The buyer sought to introduce the affidavit to show that the seller's standard form was not part of the parties' final agreement. Its position was that the parties' final

Calzaturificio Claudia s.n.c. v. *Olivieri Footwear Ltd.*, 1998 U.S. Dist. LEXIS 4586 (S.D.N.Y. April 6, 1998); *TeeVee Toons, Inc.* v. *Gerhard Schubert GmbH*, 2006 U.S. Dist. LEXIS 59455 (S.D.N.Y. August 22, 2006). For a case relying on Article 8(2), see *Miami Valley Paper, LLC* v. *Lebbing Engineering & Consulting GmbH*, 2009 U.S. Dist. LEXIS 25201 (S.D. Ohio March 26, 2009).

[91] *Cedar Petrochemicals Inc.* v. *Dongbu Hannong Chemical Co. Ltd.*, 2011 U.S. Dist. LEXIS 110716 (S.D.N.Y. September 28, 2011).

[92] 993 F.2d 1178 (5th Cir. 1993).   [93] See id. at 1183 n.9.

[94] See, e.g., *ECEM European Chemical Marketing, B.V.* v. *The Purolite Co.*, 2010 U.S. Dist. LEXIS 7373 (E.D. Pa. January 29, 2010), aff'd 51 Fed. Appx. 73 (3d Cir. 2011); *MCC-Marble Ceramic Center, Inc.* v. *Ceramica Nuova D'Agostino*, 144 F.3d 1384 (11th Cir. 1998).

[95] 144 F.3d 1383 (11th Cir. 1998).

agreement was oral, not written. Thus, it was seeking to introduce the affidavit for purpose of proving that the writing was not integrated. The parol evidence rule does not bar parol evidence introduced for this purpose. The *MCC-Marble* decision, finding that the CISG displaced the parol evidence rule, left it to the jury to decide whether the seller's standard form was part of the parties' final expression of agreement. The court could have done the same even had it applied the parol evidence rule.

That said, the decision in *MCC-Marble* implicitly adopts a very strong position on the purposes for which extrinsic evidence is admissible. Even jurisdictions that allow the admission of extrinsic evidence to explain or supplement a writing do not necessarily allow that same evidence when it contradicts an integrated writing. The court in *MCC-Marble*, however, essentially permitted the latter. The buyer was attempting to introduce evidence that the parties intended that the seller be liable for quality defects, even though the writing explicitly disclaimed seller liability. Other courts have similarly interpreted the CISG to permit testimony that contradicts the written terms of an agreement.[96] Again, however, Article 8(3) mandates solely that the extrinsic evidence receive "due consideration," not that it be accepted as an accurate expression of the parties' intent. Context is important. "Due consideration" may involve giving little regard to extrinsic evidence that directly contradicts what appears to be a term in an integrated writing. The situation in which the disputed term appears in a standard form printed in a language that both parties realize one of them does not understand poses a better case for allowing extrinsic evidence of a conflicting term to show that the standard form was not an integration.

B. *Contracting into the parol evidence rule*

Parties might want to control the evidence that will be available to the fact finder to determine the terms of a contract should litigation occur. By doing so they reduce the expected cost of litigation or the variance in its possible outcomes. The parol evidence rule is a default term that saves the parties the expense of limiting by contract in advance the admissibility of certain sorts of evidence to prove the terms of the contract. As we noted previously, the predominant view is that the CISG displaces the parol evidence rule. Can parties supply the same or similar rule by agreement when their sales contract is governed by the CISG? They will have a hard time doing so. The parties could try to restrict the parol evidence applicable to their contract in either of two ways. They might include a merger clause in their agreement. The clause could recite that the writing reflects the entire agreement of the parties, and that no consideration is to be given to prior negotiations,

---

[96] See, e.g., *Alpha Prime Development Corporation v. Holland Loader Company, LLC*, 2010 U.S. Dist. LEXIS 67591 (D. Colo. August 10, 2010); *Mitchell Aircraft Spares, Inc. v. European Aircraft Serv.*, 23 F. Supp. 2d 915, 922 (N.D. Ill. 1998).

agreements or the like in determining its terms. Both the *MCC-Marble* court and the CISG Advisory Council suggest that such clauses would suffice to exclude parol evidence.[97] We are not so sure. To determine the parties' intent, Article 8(3) still applies to the merger clause. A court therefore would have to give due consideration of all relevant circumstances, including parol evidence, to reach a conclusion about the parties' intent with respect to the merger clause. Another American court reaches the same conclusion.[98] In addition, the enforceability of a merger clause might present a question of validity. If so, Article 4(a) leaves its enforceability to applicable domestic law and domestic law might refuse to enforce the clause. For both reasons, even a carefully drafted merger clause does not automatically bar parol evidence.

The second way in which parties could try to exclude parol evidence is by opting out of Article 8(3) directly. Because Article 6 permits the parties generally to derogate from the CISG's provisions, the parties' agreement might exclude application of Article 8(3). However, to determine whether the parties have agreed to opt out of Article 8(3), the terms of the agreement must be interpreted. Article 8(3) therefore seemingly applies to interpret the intent of the parties. It requires that due consideration be given to all relevant circumstances to determine whether, as applied, the parties intended to opt out of Article 8(3). As with a merger clause, parol evidence therefore is admissible to determine whether the parties intended to make parol evidence inadmissible.

---

[97] See 144 F.3d at 1391; CISG Advisory Council Opinion No. 3: Parol Evidence Rule, Plain Meaning Rule, Contractual Merger Clause and the CISG ¶ 4.6, available at www.cisg.law .pace.edu/cisg/CISG-AC-op3.html.

[98] See *TeeVee Toons, Inc.* v. *Gerhard Schubert GmbH*, 2006 U.S. Dist. LEXIS 59455 (S.D.N.Y. August 23, 2010).

5

Performance

I. THE DELIVERY OBLIGATION

Performance obligations under the CISG are set forth in deceptively simple terms. Article 30 requires the seller to deliver the goods, hand over any documents relating to them, and transfer the property in the goods, as required by the contract and the CISG itself. Those obligations are then elucidated in Articles 31 through 52. Article 53 recites that the buyer must "pay the price for the goods and take delivery of them," again in accordance with the contract and the CISG. Most disputes that arise under the CISG concern the performance and thus the interpretation of what is required by these obligations.

A. What constitutes delivery?

Delivery in international sales will frequently involve a more complicated procedure than in domestic sales because distances may be greater, multi-modal transport may be involved, and there may be additional legal requirements related to import and export of goods. Article 31 sets forth a series of default rules that govern the question of when a delivery has occurred. If the parties do not provide otherwise and the contract involves carriage of goods, delivery occurs when the goods are handed over to the first carrier for transmission to the buyer.[1] The term "carrier" implies that transportation by the seller's own vehicles does not constitute a delivery.[2] "Handing over" implies that merely making the goods available to the carrier will not constitute a delivery. Thus, placing the goods on a loading dock at the seller's place of business will not qualify. The handing over of goods sufficient to constitute a

---

[1] See Article 31(a).

[2] Cf. United Nations Convention on Contracts for the International Carriage of Goods Wholly or Partly by Sea Article 1(5) (2008) ("'Carrier' means a person that enters into a contract of carriage with the shipper.").

delivery will also frequently trigger passage of the risk of loss, since at that point the buyer assumes a superior position to avoid or insure against loss. We discuss risk of loss rules in Chapter 7. For the moment, we note that the seller completes its delivery obligations in shipment contract that involve third-party carriage by handing over the goods to the carrier, even if the seller has agreed to a term by which it pays transportation costs to the buyer's destination, as in an Incoterms rules CIF or CFR term. Once the handing over has occurred, the seller has completed its delivery obligations and subsequent delay in the buyer's obtaining the goods does not establish a failure to perform by the seller.[3] We discuss in Chapter 9 a particular conundrum about possible differences between a "handing over" by one party and a "taking over" by the other for purposes of measuring damages.[4]

The parties may, of course, deviate from these defaults. Article 31 states explicitly that its rules apply "if the seller is not bound to deliver the goods at any other particular place." The parties may specify such a place either by entering a "destination contract," which requires delivery at a "particular place" such as a specific port or ship, or by incorporating a trade term that requires delivery at some point other than transmission to the first carrier. For example, the Incoterms DAP, or "delivered at place," term obligates the seller to place the goods at the disposal of the buyer on the arriving means of transportation at the place of destination.[5] Similarly, an Incoterms DDP, or "delivery duty paid," term requires the seller to place the goods at the disposal of the buyer on the arriving means of transport ready for unloading at the named destination.[6] These contracts may still involve the carriage of goods. But "delivery" under such contracts does not occur when the goods are handed over to the first carrier. Instead, where the parties have selected a destination contract or a trade term that requires delivery elsewhere, delivery only occurs when the goods reach the particular place or are handed over in accordance with the trade term.[7]

The effect of some contractual terms, however, may be more ambiguous. Terms that require the seller to install the goods that are the subject matter of the contract in the buyer's place of business have been interpreted to mean that delivery occurs

---

[3] See Commercial Court Zürich (Switzerland), 10 February 1999, available at http://cisgw3.law .pace.edu/cases/990210s1.html.

[4] See Chapter 9.III.C.1.   [5] See Incoterms ® 2010 A4 ("DAP").   [6] Id. at A4 ("DDP").

[7] See Secretariat Commentary on the 1978 Draft, in Documentary History of the Uniform Law for International Sales 419 (paras. 6–7) (John O. Honnold ed., 1989). The 2012 CISG Digest is ambiguous on the point. It states that where the contract involves the carriage of goods, "article 31 (a) ordinarily is applicable." The Digest then states that shipment and destination contracts, including those subject to Incoterms, involve the carriage of goods. See 2012 UNCITRAL Digest of Case Law on the United Nations Convention on the International Sale of Goods Article 31 (at para. 5), available at http://cisgw3.law.pace.edu/cisg/text/digest-2012–31 .html. The implication appears to be that shipment and destination contracts are governed by Article 31(a). If that is the intended implication, we would disagree. Instead, and consistent with the Secretariat Commentary, we conclude that destination contracts require the seller to deliver at the designated place, not necessarily to the first carrier.

only at that place.[8] A term that is the equivalent of "free delivery to buyer's place of business" has been considered as only a price term by some courts,[9] but a delivery term by others.[10]

A different default rule applies when the sales contract does not involve the carriage of goods and the contract relates either to specific goods or to unidentified goods to be drawn from a specific stock or to be manufactured or produced. In this case, if the parties knew at the time of the conclusion of the contract that the goods were located at or were to be manufactured or produced at a particular place, delivery occurs when the goods are placed at the buyer's disposal at that place.[11] It is not necessary that the goods actually be handed over or be placed into the buyer's possession. Instead, the seller's obligation is satisfied when it does what is necessary to enable the buyer to obtain possession. If the sales contract does not involve carriage or the contract does not relate to unidentified specific goods or goods to be manufactured or produced, delivery occurs at the seller's place of business.

The act of delivery is not necessarily contemporaneous with the buyer's obtaining possession of the goods. Obviously, in a case involving transportation by carrier, putting the goods into the hands of the carrier occurs before the buyer receives the goods. In fact, the CISG uses other terms to indicate that the buyer has obtained physical possession of the goods. In two Articles the CISG uses the term "receives" to indicate that the buyer has taken physical possession of the goods.[12] Article 76 also refers to a party "taking over" the goods, which we conclude refers to taking physical possession or control of them.[13] The CISG's use of terms other than "delivery" to connote taking possession confirms the point that delivery need not involve receipt or taking possession.

The question as to whether the seller can deliver goods before the buyer receives them sometimes can be important. It was at issue in *In re World Imports, Ltd.*,[14] in the interplay between the United States Bankruptcy Code and the CISG. There a Chinese seller shipped goods to a U.S. buyer under a sales contract governed by the CISG. The contract contained an "FOB, country of origin" delivery term. After the buyer went into bankruptcy, the court had to decide whether the seller was entitled under the Bankruptcy Code to what the Code designates an "administrative expense" for the value of the goods delivered. An administrative expense is entitled to a high priority in the distribution of assets from the debtor's bankruptcy estate.[15]

---

[8] See Court of Appeals Köln (Germany), 21 December 2005, available at http://cisgw3.law.pace .edu/cases/051221g1.html.

[9] See, e.g., Court of Appeals Koblenz (Germany), 4 October 2002, available at http://cisgw3.law .pace.edu/cases/021004g1.html; Supreme Court (Austria), 10 September 1998, available at http://cisgw3.law.pace.edu/cases/980910a3.html.

[10] See Court of Appeals Köln (Germany), 8 January 1997, available at http://cisgw3.law.pace.edu/ cases/970108g1.html.

[11] See Article 31(b).

[12] See Articles 82(1), (2)(a) ("receives them"), 86(1) ("received the goods"); infra text.

[13] See Chapter 9.III.C.1. [14] 511 B.R. 738 (Bankr. E.D. Pa. 2014).

[15] See 11 U.S.C. § 507(a)(2).

The Bankruptcy Code gives a seller an administrative expense for "the value of any goods received by the debtor [i.e., the buyer] within 20 days before the date of the commencement of the case."[16] However, it does not define the term "received." The goods were shipped from China more than twenty days before the buyer's bankruptcy filing, and the buyer took physical possession of them at their destination within twenty days of the filing. If shipment constituted receipt by the buyer, the seller was not entitled to an administrative expense. If the buyer received the goods when it took possession of them at their destination, the seller was entitled to an administrative expense in the amount of the value of the goods received.

Most courts have applied the Uniform Commercial Code ("UCC") definition of "receipt" to define the term "received" as used in the Bankruptcy Code.[17] The UCC definition provides that receipt consists in taking physical possession.[18] The *World Imports* court, however, ruled that the CISG preempts application of the UCC and supplies the relevant definition of "receipt." Acknowledging that the CISG does not define "received," the court looked to trade usage, which the CISG makes applicable to the sales contract.[19] Trade usage includes the Incoterms definition of an FOB delivery term, according to the court. According to that definition, the seller delivers the goods when they are loaded on board the named vessel at the port of shipment.[20] Finding that the definition of the FOB term "aids in the interpretation" of the term "received" under the Bankruptcy Code, the court concluded that the goods are "constructively received" by the buyer when they are loaded on board the vessel.[21]

The court might be right that "receipt" under 509(b)(9) is defined by the applicable non-bankruptcy law governing the sales contract. This is a complicated matter that we discuss elsewhere.[22] Bankruptcy law aside, the court's inference from the Incoterms definition of delivery to the buyer's receipt of the goods is unsound. The Incoterms FOB definition, incorporated into the parties' contract, displaces Article 31(a)'s definition of delivery.[23] Under the Incoterms FOB term, the seller's obligation of delivery requires that the goods be loaded on board the designated vessel at the port of shipment. Article 31(a), which requires the seller to put the goods into the hands of the first carrier for transmission to the buyer, does not specify

---

[16] 11 U.S.C. § 509(b)(9).

[17] See, e.g., *In re Circuit City Stores, Inc.*, 432 B.R. 225 (E.D. Va. 2010); *In re Wezbra Dairy, LLC*, 493 B.R. 768 (Bankr. N.D. Ind. 2013); *In re Semcrude, LP*, 416 B.R. 399 (D. Del. 2009); cf. *In re Marin Motor Oil Inc.*, 740 F.2d 220 (3d Cir. 1984). Courts have also construed "goods" under 503(b)(9) according to UCC § 2–105(1)'s definition of the term; see *In re Goody's Family Clothing, Inc.*, 401 B.R. 131 (Bankr. Del. 2009); *In re Plastech Engineered Products, Inc.*, 397 B.R. 828 (Bankr. E.D. Mich. 2008).

[18] See U.C.C. § 2–103(1)(c).   [19] See Article 9(2).   [20] See Incoterms® 2010 A4 ("FOB").

[21] See *In re World Imports*, 511 B.R. at 745; *In re World Imports*, 516 B.R. 296, 302 (Bankr. E.D. Pa. 2014).

[22] See Clayton P. Gillette & Steven D. Walt, *Sales Law: Domestic and International* 203–05 (3d ed. 2016).

[23] Cf. Federal Supreme Court (Germany), 7 November 2012, unpublished translation by Vasileios Regkakos.

which act of placing the goods into the hands of the carrier satisfies the seller's delivery obligation. However, the Incoterms FOB definition says nothing about when the buyer receives the goods. It only defines when delivery to the carrier occurs. Thus, it is difficult to see how loading the goods on board the vessel (delivery) can constitute receipt of them.

A better inference about the meaning of the term "receives" is based on its use within the CISG's provisions that employ the term. Article 31 defines the seller's obligations of delivery, while Articles 82 and 86(1) state restrictions that apply only when the buyer has "received" the goods. The use of the different terms likely is not accidental: In the latter Articles the drafters could have referred to the buyer having "taken delivery" of the goods rather than having "received" them. Under Articles 82 (1)–(2)(a) and Article 86(1), the buyer who has received the goods possesses them. Otherwise, Article 82's requirement that the buyer make restitution of goods received and Article 86(1)'s requirement that the buyer preserve the goods received make no sense. Thus, a fair inference is that the CISG deems a buyer to receive the goods when it takes possession of them. As a result, even if bankruptcy law relies on the CISG's notion of receipt when the CISG governs the sales contract, the buyer in *In re World Imports* received the goods when it took possession of them at their destination.

B. *Time of delivery*

The parties may fix a time for delivery either explicitly or by agreeing to a determinable date. For instance, the parties could agree that trophies will be delivered "on November 1" or "three days after the opening ceremonies of the 2024 Olympic Games." If the parties have fixed a date for delivery, the seller is obligated to deliver on that date.[24] Technically, even an early delivery would not conform to the contract. Given that the buyer may have to make preparations to take delivery – an obligation of the buyer separately regulated by Article 60 – an early delivery could actually be problematic. If perishable goods are placed at the disposal of the buyer before the set delivery date, for instance, the buyer could be justifiably unprepared to accept goods that subsequently become nonconforming by the contractually established time of delivery. Thus, Article 52(1) provides the buyer the option of taking or refusing delivery of goods delivered before the date fixed by the contract.

If the parties have fixed a period for delivery, the seller may deliver the goods at any time within that period, unless the circumstances indicate that the buyer may select a date within the period.[25] The date must be agreed to by the parties, however; it cannot be unilaterally imposed by one of them.[26] A statement that the seller would

---

[24] See Article 33(a); District Court Köln (Germany), 29 May 2012, available at http://cisgw3.law .pace.edu/cases/120529g1.html.

[25] See Article 33(b).

[26] See Commercial Court Hasselt (Belgium), 20 September 2005, available at http://cisgw3.law .pace.edu/cases/050920b1.html.

"shoot for" a particular delivery date did not constitute an agreement to deliver by that date.[27] If the parties have not fixed a delivery date, the seller must deliver the goods within a reasonable time after the conclusion of the contract.[28] What constitutes a reasonable time is obviously a function of any knowledge the parties might have about the buyer's use of the goods, the time necessary for manufacture and transportation, and the period common for delivery of similar goods in other contracts. Where refurbished goods were to be delivered and the buyer indicated that it had no immediate need for the goods, an American court refused to grant summary judgment for a buyer claiming late delivery.

In one case, the buyer offered to purchase a vehicle from the seller with a time of delivery "no later than 15 March 1997."[29] The seller accepted the offer with a delivery term of "April, time of delivery remains reserved." The court concluded that the seller's term became incorporated into the contract under Article 19. Nevertheless, the court concluded that the buyer's request for delivery by March 15 became relevant to determining what constituted a reasonable time for delivery under Article 33(c). Notwithstanding the mention of "April" in the seller's acceptance, the court concluded that the "reserved" term meant that time for delivery could not be determined from the contract. Thus, delivery had to occur within a reasonable time of the conclusion of the contract. The court then found that because the buyer had indicated the importance of the March 15 date, a reasonable time for delivery expired on that date. It was irrelevant that delivery delays were common with respect to the international sale of vehicles.

C. *Place and currency of payment*

The contract usually fixes the place at which the contract price is to be paid. Where the contract is silent, Article 57 sets default rules. If the contract calls for handing over the goods or documents covering the goods at a particular place, payment is to be made at the place where they are to be handed over. If the contract does not call for the goods or documents to be handed over at a particular place, payment is to be made at the seller's place of business.[30] These default rules contain a gap when the contract calls for the goods to be handed over at place A while the documents covering them are to be handed over at place B. For example, the sales contract might call for delivery FOB Vessel X, at Long Beach, and the bill of lading to be delivered to Buyer in New York City. Article 57(1)(b) calls for payment at the place "where the handing over takes place," without addressing the possibility that the

---

[27] See *Norfolk Southern Railway Company* v. *Power Source Supply, Inc.*, 2008 U.S. Dist. LEXIS 56942 (W.D. Pa. July 25, 2008).
[28] See Article 33(c).
[29] See Court of Appeals Naumburg (Germany), 27 April 1999, available at http://cisgw3.law.pace.edu/cases/990427g1.html.
[30] See Article 57(1)(a), (b).

goods and the documents are to be "handed over" at different places. This looks like a case in which the question is "governed" by the CISG, but not settled by it. In such a case, the answer is to be determined in accordance with general principles underlying the CISG or, in their absence, applicable domestic law (both recognized under Article 7(2)). Unfortunately, it is unclear what, if any, general principles are involved or how they apply to the place of payment. Perhaps a general principle of reasonableness suggests that either place of payment would be acceptable.

It is sometimes even more difficult to determine the currency in which the price is to be paid. For example, a contract might simply call for payment at the "current price." In this case the parties' negotiations, prior course of dealing, or applicable trade usage, where present, sometimes can determine the currency in which the price is to be paid.[31] The difficult cases are those in which none of these resources aids in specifying the contract currency. The CISG has no express default rule that selects the currency in which the price is to be paid. Most of the few courts that have addressed the issue conclude that the CISG's underlying principles select it. According to these courts, the place at which the contract price is to be paid fixes the currency in which it is to be paid.[32] If the buyer is obligated to pay the price at the seller's place of business, the contract currency is the currency at that place. If it is obligated to pay against handing over the goods or documents, the contract currency is that of the place where the goods or documents are to be handed over. The contract currency is that of the place at which the contract requires payment, if the contract calls for payment at a place different from Article 57(1)'s default rules for fixing the place of payment.

Courts adopting the "place of payment" rule for currency make two assumptions: (1) that the CISG supplies a default rule for contract currency, and (2) that it selects the place of payment rule. The first assumption seems reasonable. It is plausible to conclude that the CISG also selects currency when its default rules select the time and place at which the buyer must pay the contract price. Put another way, it is unlikely that the CISG's drafters intended to leave the question of contract currency to applicable domestic law when the CISG addresses other aspects of the buyer's obligation to pay the price. The CISG supplies default rules for the time and place of payment of the contract price; it therefore probably does not leave contract currency to nonuniform applicable domestic law. In short, the subject is governed by the CISG, but not settled by it. Accordingly, one might contend that, under Article 7(2), one or more of the CISG's underlying principles arguably select a

---

[31] See Articles 8(3), 9(1), (2).

[32] See, e.g., Court of Appeals Berlin (Germany), 24 January 1994, available at http://cisgw3.law.pace.edu/cases/940124g1.html; Court of Appeals Koblenz (Germany), 17 September 1993, available at http://cisgw3.law.pace.edu/cases/930917g1.html; Metropolitan Court Budapest (Hungary), 24 March 1992, available at www.cisg.law.pace.edu/cases/920324h1.html; cf. UNIDROIT Principles of International Commercial Contracts Article 6.1.10 (2010) (where contract currency not stated, payment must be made in the currency of the place where payment is to be made).

default rule for contract currency.[33] It is easier to state that assumption, however, than to act on its implications. None of the principles that are commonly stated as underlying the CISG compel the fixing of contract currency by the place of payment of the contract price. As in other instances in which underlying principles referred to in Article 7(2) are relied on, the principles and their application are obscure.[34] At least one court that invokes the "place of payment" rule for currency relies on scholarly commentary advocating it.[35] A Hungarian court that adopted the rule gave no reason for doing so.[36] Mohs argues that Article 57(1) is a general principle that fixes the contract currency.[37] The trouble is that the Article does not state a general principle underlying the CISG; it only states a default rule governing the place of payment. For this reason, Article 57 does not compel the inference that the place of payment determines the currency of the contract price to be paid there. An underlying principle that might inform the selection of a default rule for currency is one of uniformity: a uniform default selecting currency gives effect to the CISG's international character, displacing potentially diverse domestic laws on the subject. However, the "place of payment" default is only one among many possible defaults that produces uniformity. For example, a rule that gives the buyer the option of selecting the currency in which to pay the contract price is a default that national tribunals easily can apply. Perhaps the most that can be said in favor of the "place of payment" default is that courts tend to apply it, even if the CISG could support alternative defaults for contract currency.

---

[33] Several courts conclude that applicable domestic law determines contract currency; see National Commercial Court of Appeals Buenos Aires (Argentina) (*Sr. Carlos Manuel del Corazón de Jesús Bravo Barros v. Salvador Martínez Gares*), 31 May 2007, available at http://cisgw3.law.pace.edu/cases/070531a1.html; Court of Appeals Valais (Switzerland), 30 June 1998, available at http://cisgw3.law.pace.edu/cases/980630s1.html. These courts do not believe that the CISG governs contract currency under Article 7(2). Cf. Gunter Hager, *Article 54*, in Commentary on the UN Convention on the International Sale of Goods (CISG) 620, 623 (Peter Schlechtriem & Ingeborg Schwenzer eds., 2d (English) ed. 2005); Filip De Ly, *Obligations of the Buyer and Remedies for the Buyer's Breach of Contract*, in The Draft UNCITRAL Digest and Beyond: Cases, Analysis and Unresolved Issues in the U.N. Sales Convention 468, 477 (Franco Ferrari, Harry M. Flechtner & Ronald A. Brand eds., 2004); Dietrich Maskow, *Payment of the Price*, in Commentary on the International Sales Law 393, 403 (para. 3.1) (Cesar M. Bianca & Michael J. Bonell eds., 1987) [hereinafter "Bianca & Bonell"].

[34] See, e.g., infra Chapter 4.II.A. and Chapter 9.I.A.4.

[35] See Court of Appeals Berlin (Germany), 24 January 1994, available at http://cisgw3.law.pace.edu/cases/940124g1.html.

[36] See Metropolitan Court Budapest (Hungary), 24 March 1992, available at www.cisg.law.pace.edu/cases/920324h1.html. Butler and Harindranath also assert the "place of payment" default rule; see Petra Butler & Arjun Harindranath, *Article 57*, in UN Convention on Contracts for the International Sale of Goods (CISG): Commentary 817, 824 (Stefan Kröll, Loukas Mistelis & Pilar Perales Viscasillas eds., 2011) [hereinafter "Kröll et al."].

[37] See Florian Mohs, *Article 57*, in Schlechtriem & Schwenzer: Commentary on the UN Convention on the International Sale of Goods (CISG) 792, 794–95 (Ingeborg Schwenzer ed., 3d ed. 2010) [hereinafter "Schlechtriem & Schwenzer"].

II. EXAMINATION OF GOODS

A. *"As short a period as is practicable"*

Parties to commercial contracts understand that transactions occasionally break down. This may occur notwithstanding the best efforts of the party whose conduct fails to conform to contractual expectations. When breach occurs, buyers and sellers will prefer that the related costs be as low as possible. They would prefer to use resources to engage in productive activity rather than dispute resolution. The buyer will prefer that defects in goods be addressed quickly so that it can engage in the productive activity that it anticipated when it entered into the contract. Sellers will also desire prompt resolution so they can determine whether payment will be forthcoming or whether they should attempt to resell the goods, even in a defective condition, to other buyers who can make use of them. Otherwise, goods will simply be wasted, causing a social loss as well as increasing costs for the parties.

One way in which to evaluate the CISG's rules concerning performance, therefore, is to consider whether they advance the objective of minimizing breach costs. In large part, the rules are consistent with most parties' preferences in this regard. Once goods have been made available, Article 38(1) mandates that a buyer examine them within "as short a period as is practicable under the circumstances" in order to detect any alleged nonconformity. The directive to make an examination "as soon as is practicable" leaves substantial room for interpretation. But the desire to minimize breach costs assists in the interpretive effort, as it allows a court to define an appropriate period for examination against a standard that can help to guide parties' behavior.

Some national law on periods for examination or inspection of goods is more precise. For example, the Uniform Commercial Code allows an inspection where goods are tendered or delivered or identified to the contract for sale.[38] Other provisions of the CISG, however, provide some guidance concerning the appropriate time for examination. If the contract involves carriage of the goods, examination may be deferred until after the goods have arrived at their destination.[39] As a result, even in a shipment contract the buyer is not obligated to examine the goods at the point of shipment. If the buyer discovers a nonconformity at the point of destination, but the nonconformity materialized during shipment, the rules relating to risk of loss discussed in Chapter 7 will determine whether the buyer has recourse against the seller. In this sense, risk of loss, delivery, and time for examination are entirely separate concepts. If the goods are redirected in transit or re-dispatched by the buyer without a reasonable opportunity for examination, and if the seller knew or should

---

[38] See U.C.C. § 2–513(1); cf. Handelsgesetzbuch [HGB] [Commercial Code] § 377(1) (Ger.) (in a sale between merchant the buyer must examine the goods promptly on receiving them).

[39] See Article 38(2).

have known of the possibility of such redirection or re-dispatch, examination may be deferred until after the goods have arrived at the new destination.[40]

As a general matter, the buyer is not obligated to pay the price until it has had an opportunity for an Article 38 examination.[41] Contractual terms governing delivery and payment that are inconsistent with prepayment inspection, however, may reveal an intent to deviate from that default rule.[42] For example, a documentary transaction that requires the buyer to make payment against a sight draft and bill of lading, notwithstanding that the goods are still in transit, would be inconsistent with any prepayment examination.

Notwithstanding the mandatory directive of Article 38 (the buyer "must examine the goods"), nothing in Article 38 imposes any sanction for failure to comply with the requirement. Instead, the language of "as soon as practicable in the circumstances" must be read in the context of Article 39(1)'s mandate that the buyer loses the right to rely on a nonconformity if it does not give notice to the seller specifying the nature of the lack of conformity within "a reasonable time" after it has or ought to have discovered the nonconformity. This combination of provisions can be interpreted to minimize the costs of breach. Although inspection and timely notice are technically separate requirements, their combination indicates that buyers must take appropriate action to facilitate opportunities for sellers to cure defects, return goods that are not useful for the buyer's purposes back into commerce expeditiously, and simplify the identification of the party responsible for the nonconformity. The "as soon as practicable" requirement should be read in this light. Failure to make an examination required by Article 38(1) obviously limits the capacity of the buyer to give the Article 39 notice with respect to defects that examination would have revealed. In effect, the former provision limits the time period within which the buyer must give the notice required by the latter provision.

Short of that self-inflicted wound, however, there is no sanction for failure to inspect other than the loss of the buyer's right under Article 39. The timing and degree of examination that qualify as "practicable" will depend on the nature of the goods and the nature of potential defects. Perishable goods or defects that could arise under various circumstances may demand prompt, more thorough examination. A Spanish court denied recovery where examination and notice of nonconformities in margarine was first sent five months after delivery.[43] The interpretation of "as soon as practicable" may permit a shorter period of time when the complaint is that a metal desk exhibited a nonconforming dent than when the complaint is that the same desk was two inches shorter than ordered. The dent could have arisen before or after risk of loss has passed, and the obligation of a prompt examination avoids proof difficulties that might otherwise materialize. It is less likely, however, that

---

[40] See Article 38(3).   [41] See Article 58(3); cf. U.C.C. § 2–513(1).

[42] See Article 58(3); cf. U.C.C. § 2–513(3).

[43] See Provincial Court Las Palmas Canary Islands (Spain), 16 February 2012, available at http://cisgw3.law.pace.edu/cases/120216s4.html.

someone chopped off two inches after the desk was delivered. Thus, a time period for examination that is satisfactory for the second defect may be too long for the first.

Honnold makes a similar point with respect to the characteristics of goods. He suggests that examination of containers of goods that will deteriorate quickly after being opened might be justifiably delayed until some point just prior to their use, but if the complaint about the delivery of the same goods is that an insufficient number of containers was delivered, that determination could have been made at an earlier time, so that what is "practicable" should take the characteristics of the goods into account.[44] Thus, while examination of flowers may be necessary on the day of their delivery,[45] examination of durable goods may be subject to a more liberal interpretation.[46] Moreover, the timing of an examination may depend on the characteristic of the goods for which the examination is made. Relatively prompt examination may be demanded to ensure that the goods are in the correct amount and are of the type ordered, at least where that can be done by mere visual examination, while defects in quality or operation that require more extensive testing may warrant a longer period. Other factors, such as the prior relations between the parties, may affect the appropriate timing. A German court concluded that examination of furniture within ten days of receipt by the buyer was appropriate because there had previously been problems with the conformity of goods sent by the seller to the same buyer.[47]

In a controversial case, another German court found that an examination had occurred too late to permit the buyer a remedy for nonconforming delivery of shoes.[48] The buyer had purchased the shoes under a price and delivery term of "27,000 EUR plus C&F FOB Mombassa, Kenya." The shoes were then to be transported to Kampala, Uganda, where the buyer had its place of business. The goods arrived in Mombassa on April 26, 2004, and remained there until the buyer made final payment and received the bill of lading allowing their further shipment to Kampala on May 24. The buyer examined the goods on June 16 in Kampala and found that they were defective and unusable, and included materials different from what had been ordered. The court concluded that the "contractual destination" of the goods was Mombassa, so the examination should have occurred then and there, notwithstanding the buyer's objections that any such examination would have required damage to the customs seal and would thus have caused a payment of customs duty for the goods in Kenya.

---

[44] See John O. Honnold, Uniform Law for International Sales Under the 1980 United Nations Convention 369 (Harry M. Flechtner ed., 4th ed. 2009) [hereinafter "Honnold/Flechtner"].

[45] See Court of Appeals Saarbrücken (Germany), 3 June 1998, available at http://cisgw3.law.pace.edu/cases/980603g1.html.

[46] See, e.g., District Court Forli (Italy), 16 February 2009, available at http://cisgw3.law.pace.edu/cases/090216i3.html.

[47] See District Court Darmstadt (Germany), 29 May 2001, available at http://cisgw3.law.pace.edu/cases/010529g1.html.

[48] See District Court Frankfurt (Germany), 11 April 2005, available at http://cisgw3.law.pace.edu/cases/050411g1.html.

The opinion in the shoes case implicates many of the characteristics of Article 38, and arguably gets them wrong. The court suggested that the proper place for examination was necessarily the destination indicated in the contract of sale – here, the FOB Mombassa term. The FOB term certainly allocates a variety of risks, but, as Professor Flechtner has demonstrated,[49] Article 38 does not necessarily designate the place where risk has passed as the appropriate place for examination.[50] As previously noted, making the points coterminous would minimize issues related to identification of the time when defects materialized. But parties are free to deviate from that objective, and designating different places for passage of risk and examination causes no problem where there is little doubt about the origins of the nonconformity. Certainly the latter was true in the shoes case, where the goods that were shipped bore little resemblance to the goods that were ordered. All that Article 38(1) requires is that examination occur within as short a period of time as is practicable under the circumstances. Indeed, Article 38(2) and (3) appear to contemplate that an examination may occur other than at the point designated for the passage of risk of loss. "Practicality" is a term that appears to require consideration of the burden that the buyer would have to incur to make an examination at a particular point. On that logic, the buyer's contention that it would have had to fly to Mombassa and pay additional duties perhaps deserves more attention than the court allowed. The court did, however, note that a third party could have made the examination in Mombassa and that the buyer failed to provide sufficient information about the full costs of any such examination and the effect of those costs on the profitability of the transaction. Thus, the court may have been more attentive to the buyer's plight had the buyer provided more information.

The opinion is also problematic insofar as it relies on the allegedly late examination to deny the buyer recourse. Article 38 imposes a burden on buyers, but imposes no independent sanction for failure to carry that burden. Instead, the failure to examine as soon as is practicable places on the buyer the risk that it will be unable to satisfy its obligations to give timely notice of nonconformity under Article 39(1). As discussed later, that provision does contain serious sanctions for noncompliance. But the court in the shoes case did not determine that notice of nonconformity, which was given within four weeks of delivery, was given too late. Indeed, some of the precedents suggest that it was timely. Instead, the court concluded that the delayed examination precluded the buyer from relying on the nonconformity, a proposition for which Article 38 provides no support.

[49] See Harry M. Flechtner, *Funky Mussels, a Stolen Car, and Decrepit Used Shoes: Non-Conforming Goods and Notice thereof under the United Nations Sales Convention ("CISG")*, 26 B.U. Int'l L. J. 1 (2008).

[50] A contrary statement appears in Court of Appeals Antwerp (Belgium), 22 January 2007, available at http://cisgw3.law.pace.edu/cases/070122b2.html, but that statement appears to be purely dictum and has been rejected by other commentators. See Ingeborg Schwenzer, *Article 38*, in Schlechtriem & Schwenzer, supra note 37, at 615.

B. *Extent of examination*

The obligation to examine under Article 38 is not an obligation to detect all nonconformities. Instead, the Article has been broadly interpreted to impose an obligation to make a reasonable investigation of the goods. Different measures for examination could be taken, ranging from immediate and intensive inspection of goods to delayed, less costly, casual examination. Latent defects or defects that would be revealed only by costly examinations that a reasonable buyer would not undertake are not required. Sampling or spot-checks may be appropriate where goods are ordered in bulk.[51] A purchaser of wine was not required to make an unconventional examination for the addition of water until authorities indicated the possibility of contamination.[52] If a cursory examination suggests possible defects, however, a buyer who might otherwise not be required to look further may be obligated to undertake a more thorough examination. In short, the extent of examination will depend on whether the costs of making a more thorough examination are worth incurring in light of the expected probability of detecting a defect.

Perhaps the best illustration of this principle is found in a German Supreme Court decision from 1999.[53] A manufacturer of specialized papers received a grinding device necessary for production on April 7. The device was assembled on April 13 and was put into operation as a component of another machine on April 17. The machine subsequently failed in late April, but not before the buyer had produced 120 tons of paper that were delivered to a downstream customer. In mid-May, that customer notified the buyer (its seller), that the paper contained defects. Ten days later, the buyer retained a third party to determine the source of those defects and, in early June, that party reported that the grinding device could have been the culprit. The buyer notified the seller of potential defects on June 14. The Supreme Court accepted the proposition that the defect was a latent one that could not have been detected by an inspection at the April 7 delivery, or on the April 13 installation, or even during its use prior to the failure of the machine in late April. The examination period, therefore, did not begin until the breakdown of the machine occurred. At that point, there were apparently two possible explanations for the breakdown: operator error or nonconformity of the grinding device. The Supreme Court appeared to allow the buyer an additional week after the breakdown to determine how to identify the source of the problem. Arguably, examination was not required prior to that event. The court then allowed an additional two-week period for the independent examination to occur. The opinion thus reveals that

---

[51] See, e.g., Supreme Court (Austria), 27 August 1999, available at http://cisgw3.law.pace.edu/cases/990827a3.html.

[52] See District Court Trier (Germany), 12 October 1995, available at http://cisgw3.law.pace.edu/cases/951012g1.html.

[53] See Federal Supreme Court (Germany), 3 November 1999, available at http://cisgw3.law.pace.edu/cases/991103g1.html.

there is no specific point at which examination is required. Delivery does not trigger examination where the goods must still be assembled; assembly does not trigger examination if the goods cannot then be put into operation; operation of the goods does not necessarily trigger examination if the defects are not apparent on operation; and defective outputs do not trigger an immediate examination if time is necessary to determine whether those defects are a consequence of the goods at issue or some alternative source.

C. *Giving notice of nonconformity*

1. Time of giving notice

The real work concerning the buyer's obligation to detect and provide notice of defects is done by Article 39(1). That Article provides that the buyer loses the right to rely on a lack of conformity unless notice is given to the seller within a reasonable time after the buyer has or ought to have discovered it. No particular form of notice is required. Letter, telephone, fax, email, or other communication that informs the seller of the problem will be sufficient. Nevertheless, buyers who utilize non-verifiable forms of notice may face proof problems, as was the case where a court concluded that an alleged telephonic notice was implausible.[54] The notice must specify the nature of the nonconformity. Article 39(2) contains a statute of repose. The buyer loses the right to rely on a lack of conformity if it does not give the seller notice within two years from the date on which the goods were handed over to the buyer, unless that period is inconsistent with a contractual period of guarantee.

Article 39(1) raises a number of questions that have been the source of substantial case law and commentary. The first issue involves the definition of a "reasonable time" within which notice must be given. Although the common law lawyer will find this terminology opaque, requiring consideration of such matters as the nature of the goods, the difficulty of detecting defects, and the cost of examination and notice, many early decisions applied a variety of relatively rigid periods, mostly extracted from domestic law. The 1999 German decision discussed in the prior section stated that there was a "regular" one-month period for giving notice, referring to domestic provisions that incorporated that notice period. Although the Austrian Supreme Court noted that the CISG period for notice was more lenient than the requirements of domestic law, it still appeared to use the latter as a benchmark in setting a fourteen-day period for both inspection and notice.[55] These cases have been widely criticized as inconsistent with the obligation to interpret the

---

[54] See Court of Appeals Ghent (Belgium), 14 November 2008, available at http://cisgw3.law.pace .edu/cases/081114b1.html; District Court Stendal (Germany), 12 October 2000, available at http://cisgw3.law.pace.edu/cases/001012g1.html.

[55] See, e.g., Supreme Court (Austria), 27 August 1999, available at http://cisgw3.law.pace.edu/ cases/990827a3.html.

CISG autonomously and without the risk of the homeward trend that infects appeal to analogous domestic law.

More recent cases tend to reject rigid notice periods in favor of a definition of "reasonable" that looks to the circumstances of the individual case, including the nature of the goods (such as their perishability), the likelihood that the defect could have arisen post-delivery, the difficulty of detection of the defect, and the quality of examination undertaken by the buyer.[56] The flexible approach is superior both because the variety of goods subject to the CISG makes a single period impractical and because appeals to domestic law are presumably disfavored by Article 7(1). A survey of cases in the 2004 opinion of the CISG Advisory Council[57] reveals a wide range of acceptable periods for notice, including a nineteen-day period deemed unreasonable for notice concerning defects in "seasonal" trekking shoes[58] to a six-month period deemed reasonable for notice concerning sweat suits that, on testing, were determined to be susceptible to excessive shrinkage.[59] Nevertheless, one can still find opinions that appear to measure the appropriate notice period by considering what timeframe was used in other cases, notwithstanding the different nature of the goods involved in those cases. A 2009 German decision took into account that "according to jurisprudence and the leading doctrine, the gross average is approximately one month," although its conclusion that a three-month period was too long was also predicated on earlier detection of the defects.[60]

Cases tend to conclude that the "reasonable time" period commences when an Article 38 examination is appropriate, although many cases speak in terms of "delivery," which, as we have already noted, is not necessarily coterminous with the beginning of the examination period.[61] Some defects may not be detectable until goods are processed, and notice of such defects cannot be anticipated prior that time. An Italian court speculated that defects in sheets of vulcanized rubber could not be detected until they were transformed into shoe soles, in which case notice four months after delivery might have been sufficient.[62] Once an examination is

---

[56] See District Court Forli (Italy) (*Pavital S.r.l.* v. *NV Bekaert S.A.*), 16 December 2013, unpublished translation by Arnaldo Bernardi; District Court Forli (Italy), 10 February 1994, available at http://cisgw3.law.pace.edu/cases/090216i3.html, which surveys cases to this effect.

[57] See CISG Advisory Council Opinion No. 2, Examination of the Goods and Non-Conformity Articles 38 and 39, available at www.cisg.law.pace.edu/cisg/CISG-AC-op2.html.

[58] Id.

[59] See District Court Besançon (France), 19 January 1998, available at http://cisgw3.law.pace.edu/cases/980119f1.html. See CISG Advisory Council Opinion No. 2, Examination of the Goods and Non-Conformity Articles 38 and 39 Annex, available at www.cisg.law.pace.edu/cisg/CISG-AC-op2.html.

[60] See District Court Stuttgart (Germany), 15 October 2009, available at http://cisgw3.law.pace.edu/cases/091015g1.html.

[61] See, e.g., District Court Forli (Italy), 16 February 2009, available at http://cisgw3.law.pace.edu/cases/090216i3.html.

[62] See District Court Vigevano (Italy), 12 July 2000, available at http://cisgw3.law.pace.edu/cases/000712i3.html. Nevertheless, the failure of the plaintiff to retain any of the defective shoes prevented it from satisfying its burden of proof.

appropriate, however, notice is required only when the defect is or should have been discovered. Latent or hidden defects may delay the reasonable time for notification if they could not have been revealed by an earlier examination.[63] A buyer who suspects, but is unaware of defects, may be obligated to undertake further inspection to confirm those suspicions, but is not required to give notice based on them.[64] But if defects are discovered, delay in informing the seller may preclude the claim. An Italian court concluded that where alleged defects in materials to be mixed with a cement compound were discovered within hours of their use, a notice of nonconformity that was given twenty days after the appearance of the defects and twenty-three days after delivery was untimely.[65]

2. Specificity of the notice

Article 39(1) requires that the notice specify the nature of the lack of conformity. In determining whether the specificity requirement has been satisfied, it is useful to keep in mind that the purpose of notice is to permit the seller to verify and determine the cause of the alleged defect, and then to provide a prompt remedy. A notice that allows such action by the seller should be deemed sufficiently specific, while a notice that leaves the seller without a basis for attempting a remedy should not. One court has required that "the complaint ... describe the alleged non-conformity in such detail that the seller is able to picture to himself the non-conformity in order to take the necessary measures, such as to send a representative to the buyer to examine the goods, to secure the necessary evidence for potential disputes regarding conformity of the goods, to offer exchange, additional delivery or cure the defect, or to have recourse against a supplier."[66] Relatively vague descriptions of defects may be viewed as an effort to obfuscate a problem unrelated to the good. Courts, therefore, have found insufficient specificity in notices that complain that the goods "caused problems"[67] or that software was not working properly,[68] or that the seller's general obligations have not been satisfied. Complaints about one defect will not necessarily qualify as notice about unrelated defects.[69] Some courts

---

[63] See District Court La Almunia de Doña Godina (Spain), 28 November 2013, available at http:// cisgw3.law.pace.edu/cases/131128s4.html.

[64] See District Court Vigevano (Italy), 12 July 2000, available at http://cisgw3.law.pace.edu/cases/ 000712i3.html.

[65] See District Court Forlì (Italy) (*Pavital S.r.l. v. NV Bekaert S.A.*), 16 December 2013, unpublished translation by Arnaldo Bernardi.

[66] District Court Stuttgart (Germany), 15 October 2009, available at http://cisgw3.law.pace.edu/ cases/091015g1.html.

[67] District Court Vigevano (Italy), 12 July 2000, available at http://cisgw3.law.pace.edu/cases/ 000712i3.html.

[68] See Commercial Court Zürich (Switzerland), 17 February 2000, available at http://cisgw3.law .pace.edu/cases/000217s1.html.

[69] See Supreme Court (Switzerland), 13 November 2003, available at http://cisgw3.law.pace.edu/ cases/031113s1.html.

apply Article 8(2)'s test of a "reasonable person of the same kind as the other party" in order to determine the sufficiency of the notice. On that basis, a German appellate court concluded that the recipient of a complaint that there had not been any "installation of the machines for ice cream production in ready-for-use condition for the operation of the café" was only a request for installation and not a complaint about the condition of the goods.[70] Others have noted that a common subjective meaning will govern under Article 8(1).[71]

Notwithstanding the desire to ensure that sellers have information necessary to address alleged defects, the sufficiency of any notice should be evaluated in light of the fact that buyers are likely to have less information than sellers about the causes of problems with the goods. The costs of breach are minimized where they are borne by those who can identify the defect at lowest cost. Thus, the "sufficient notice" requirement should not impose on buyers' obligations to diagnose causes that require technical knowledge within the unique expertise of the seller. If a buyer has the capacity to convey information that will allow the seller to make a prompt determination of the defect and its cure, the buyer should certainly have the obligation to convey that information. Otherwise, the seller will have to make costly investments that lead to the same determination of which the buyer was already aware. But where a buyer faces relatively high costs of determining the cause of a defect, a notice that conveys information about symptoms should be sufficient. In perhaps an overly technical reading of the requirement, the Austrian Supreme Court concluded that insufficient notice had been given where a buyer timely notified the seller that poppy seeds had been contaminated by caraway, when they had actually been contaminated by feverfew.[72]

An English case reached a result more consistent with the proper consideration of relative information. In *Kingspan Environmental Ltd & Ors v. Borealis A/s & Anor*,[73] purchasers of a polymer that was used as raw material for the manufacture of oil tanks contended that defects in the goods caused the tanks to crack and to fail prematurely. One of the issues in the case, which applied Danish law and hence the CISG, was whether plaintiffs had provided timely and sufficient notice of the alleged defects. Focusing on the sufficiency of the notice, the court began its analysis by adopting a standard that

> [the] degree of specificity required for the notice is influenced by the degree of expertise of the buyer and the fact that the buyer has processed the raw material and turned it into a different product. Greater specificity would be expected from an

---

[70] See Court of Appeals Hamburg (Germany), 25 January 2008, available at http://cisgw3.law .pace.edu/cases/080125g1.html.

[71] See District Court Zug (Switzerland), 30 August 2007, available at http://cisgw3.law.pace.edu/ cases/070830s1.html.

[72] See Supreme Court (Austria), 8 May 2008, available at http://cisgw3.law.pace.edu/cases/ 080508a3.html.

[73] [2012] EWHC 1147 (Comm).

expert than an average consumer and, also, from someone who has processed the material since, in the latter case, the buyer's knowledge of the final product will be better than that of the seller and the buyer will be expected to have some knowledge of the unprocessed product in order to be able to process it.[74]

In applying this standard, however, the court drew a rigid distinction between buyers of machinery or technical equipment and buyers of raw materials. The workings of the former might be sufficiently beyond the expertise of the buyer, so that a notice that described symptoms alone would satisfy Article 39(1). But, the court concluded, a buyer of raw materials, who then transformed those materials into a finished product, would be expected to provide notice of greater specificity than mere notice of symptoms, since the seller could not be expected to infer from a report of a failed finished product whether or how the raw material the seller had supplied was responsible. That distinction may be too categorical. It is plausible that a buyer will have sufficient knowledge of the unprocessed raw material to connect specific defects in them to specific symptoms in the finished product. But it is also plausible that a buyer who incorporates numerous raw materials into its finished product will be justifiably unaware of the properties of each of them, or of interactions among them, and thus be less able than the seller of the each of the materials to attribute symptoms to causes. If the buyer reasonably lacks knowledge of a raw material's properties that lead to a particular defect, it may be unable to provide much more information about causation than the buyer of complex machinery. Relative knowledge, not the particular type of good to which the knowledge is applied, is more appropriately the hallmark of sufficiency.

Nevertheless, the court did not require the purchaser of the raw material in the case to identify the cause of the defect with specificity. The very fact that the defect was a latent one, in the court's view, might preclude the buyer from saying more than "that the product has failed because of some defect in the material, the exact nature of which is not apparent."[75] Thus, the court deemed a letter sent by plaintiff "just sufficient" with respect to some of defendant's products where the letter raised concern about the suitability of the polymer for products that were located outdoors and guaranteed for ten years. Although the notice did not allege the exact nonconformity at issue in the lawsuit – the inadequacy of the polymer for manufacture of oil tanks to be used in Northern Europe for the guarantee period – the court concluded that the letter, which referred to test results that revealed a specific shortcoming, provided the seller with sufficient notice that the polymer was deemed unsuitable. At a subsequent meeting of the parties, the plaintiff complained of cracking in tanks attributable to a breach of contractual requirements. The court concluded that the statement of those symptoms, without any reference to "the causative mechanism," satisfied Article 39(1).[76] The court's exception for latent defects in raw materials turns on the relative knowledge of the buyer rather than the particular type of goods.

[74] Id. at para. 997.   [75] Id. at para. 1004.   [76] Id. at para. 1019.

Because the defect was latent, the buyer was not in a position to determine the cause. It could only determine that the materials were defective.

In evaluating Article 39(1)'s notice requirement, it is worth asking about the degree of specificity of notice most contracting parties would want to apply to their sales contracts. A strong argument can be made that they would not want the detail required in the information about a nonconformity to depend on the type of goods involved or the expertise of the buyer. Most parties would want the buyer to disclose details of which the seller is unaware and that the buyer can discover in a cost-effective manner. Whether the buyer's disclosure is cost-effective or the seller is ignorant of the nonconformity is independent of the nature of the goods, such as whether they are raw materials or fabricated. Thus, the specificity in the notice should not depend on the type of goods sold.

Another issue is whether sufficiency of notice depends on the buyer's expertise with respect to the goods. The seller presumptively knows more about the state and capacities of the goods than the buyer, so that detailed information disclosed about a nonconformity even by an expert buyer often will duplicate information already available to the seller. The disclosure of these details therefore usually does not produce a net expected benefit. Nevertheless, we imagine that an expert buyer will be better able to convey useful information concerning defects to a seller than a non-expert buyer. Since we want notice that cost-effectively allows sellers to determine how and whether to cure or adapt the nonconforming goods, it might make sense to induce expert buyers to convey all the information they have by making the specificity of the notice contingent on buyer expertise. But cutting against that argument is the possibility that the buyer's level of expertise may not be readily verifiable to the court and may not be susceptible to a reliable objective proxy. Indeed, expert buyers may make costly investments in hiding their level of expertise if they are held to a higher level of specificity for purposes of giving notice of nonconformity. This creates transaction costs that reduce the contract's net value. Thus, a flat rule that ignores any individual buyer's level of expertise for purposes of specificity may be advantageous, notwithstanding that it allows some expert buyers to avoid a level of notice that would facilitate seller responses to claims of nonconformity. We are uncertain whether the costs related to scrutiny of buyer expertise are sufficient to offset the benefits generated by imposing greater obligations of specificity on those buyers that are found to be experts.

The issue of specificity also implicates the limits of international uniformity in the interpretation of the CISG. The requirements of a sufficient notice are set forth differently in different versions of the CISG. As we noted in Chapter 1, the Swiss Supreme Court noted that the German version of Article 39(1) arguably contained a requirement of greater specificity than the corresponding American or French versions.[77] The latter are considered to be "official versions" of the CISG, while

---

[77] See Supreme Court (Switzerland), 13 November 2003, available at http://cisgw3.law.pace.edu/cases/031113s1.html.

the German translation was deemed to be not authoritative. The court interpreted the German version as requiring that the notice "precisely specify the nature of the lack of conformity," while the American and French versions required only notice of the "nature, type or character of the lack of conformity." Nevertheless, the court then concluded that the buyer's notice was insufficient where it stated that a delivered good was not usable, specified particular problems and missing parts, and demanded corrective measures. The court found that the failure of the buyer to include a nitrogen generator on the list of specific defects allowed the seller to assume that there was no objection with respect to that part, and thus precluded the buyer from relief when that part turned out to contain the fatal flaw in the machine. Given that sellers might be expected to have greater knowledge about their products and possible sources of malfunction than buyers, the case appears to be one in which the court recognized the more liberal notification standard of the American and French versions of Article 39, but then applied the equivalent of the more demanding German standard.

Here, again, the homeward trend may have been at work, as the court appeared to be interpreting the international requirement through a domestic lens. The court's application of the German version of Article 39 is mistaken as a construction of the CISG and probably also as a matter of policy. German is not among the six "official language" versions of the CISG, as the court acknowledged. Thus, the stricter notification standard apparent in the German version of Article 39 must yield to the more liberal standard stated in the English and French language versions of the Article. Once it acknowledged that German was not an "official language" version of the CISG, the court should have put the German translation of Article 39 aside. In addition, the seller's presumptive greater knowledge of the possible sources of nonconformities in its products than the buyer means that it requires less detailed information about the nonconformity. This knowledge allows it to infer the nature of a malfunction from the buyer's notice of the character of the nonconformity. The seller does not need the buyer's specification of particular problems to begin its own inquiry and take suitable remedial action. A notification standard that requires the buyer to specify particular nonconformities increases notification costs without an offsetting informational benefit to the seller.

3. Late notice and prejudice

Nothing in the explicit language of Article 39(1) requires that the seller be prejudiced by a late notice in order to bar the buyer's action.[78] This might seem to be an unfortunate oversight, insofar as it permits sellers who have delivered defective goods

---

[78] In one case, the fact that the seller had not suffered any prejudice was seen as a reason to allow an extended period for notice. See Court of Appeals Saarbrücken (Germany), 17 January 2007, available at http://cisgw3.law.pace.edu/cases/070117g1.html.

to obtain full payment, notwithstanding that they have suffered no harm from the buyer's delinquency. But the alternative of requiring a showing of prejudice may be worse, even if the burden of proof is placed on the seller. One would imagine that sellers would systematically claim prejudice, so that the issue would require investigation in all cases. Courts would then be required to investigate the difficult issue of prejudice, a costly inquiry that requires consideration of a counterfactual, that is, what would have happened had the seller received earlier notice. The costs of such inquiries are only worth incurring if two things are true: (1) there are a significant number of cases in which the lack of notice does not prejudice sellers; and (2) courts can easily distinguish prejudice from non-prejudice cases. We doubt that either proposition is true. Given the functions of notice to avoid waste, preserve evidence of defects, and permit early cure, we anticipate that most delayed notice cases do impose some prejudice on sellers, if for no other reason than that they must reverse what they considered to be completed transactions. Given the difficulties of proving prejudice or its absence, courts are likely to make frequent erroneous decisions, finding prejudice where there was none and none where sellers did suffer prejudice. Thus, any concerns one might have for the plight of buyers who must pay for defective goods must be balanced against the excess costs of an administrative system that invites courts to make difficult, costly, and error-prone inquiries.

D. *Consequences of failure to give notice: contract and tort*

Failure to comply with the timing or specificity requirements of Article 39(1) carries severe consequences. The buyer loses the right to rely on the nonconformity. That means that the buyer is deprived of all remedies listed under Article 45, whether for damages, demand for performance, or reduction of the price. The buyer will be responsible for full payment of the goods and unable to assert any right of setoff based on the defect.

Can a buyer who fails to satisfy the requirements of Article 39(1) overcome those consequences by bringing a similar claim in tort? After all, Article 4 limits the scope of the CISG to those issues that arise "from ... a contract." If the cause of action, say, for negligence, arises out of some other, non-contractual duty, then one might argue that CISG obligations are irrelevant and should not preempt claims under the former.

Here, the views of commentators vary widely. Honnold and Flechtner suggest that the CISG displaces tort law where the facts that would be invoked to prove a case under one cause of action are the same as the facts that would be invoked to prove a case under the other.[79] They suggest that the CISG's imposition of liability for defects regardless of fault could otherwise be circumvented by a negligence claim. Nevertheless, they would allow actions based on different facts, such as fraud claims,

---

[79] See Honnold/Flechtner, supra note 44, at 95–102; accord Gillette & Walt, supra note 22, at 55–7.

to survive. Schwenzer arguably takes a narrower view. She argues that there is "no room for domestic remedies based on the seller's negligent misrepresentation when concluding the contract to exist alongside Article 35."[80] Schlechtriem distinguished between actions that protect contractual interests created by the parties, such as an obligation to deliver goods of a certain quality, and actions that protect interests independent of contractual rights, such as health and safety interests. Thus, a claim that goods were defective because of seller negligence would be displaced, but a claim that the defective goods caused damage to the buyer's property would not be. Lookofsky concludes that where contract and tort claims are "fundamentally different, the negligence-based claims of the injured party are not 'absorbed' by the contractual breach-of-promise claim."[81] He argues that while Contracting States may have agreed to have their domestic law of sales displaced, they made no such bargain with respect to domestic law of torts. Schroeter would allow the CISG to displace alternative causes of action only where the domestic law rule is (1) triggered by the same facts that are necessary to prove an action under the CISG, and (2) the domestic law pertains to a "matter" regulated by the CISG, in the sense that the CISG allocates the risk that arises from those facts.[82] For example, the CISG would not displace a statutory cause of action that was intended to protect an interest other than contractual performance, even if that cause of action arose from the same facts necessary to a breach of contract claim.

The American cases arguably endorse a relatively narrow scope of displacement. In *Sky Cast, Inc. v. Global Direct Distrib., LLC*,[83] the court held that the buyer had given timely notice of nonconformity, but also entertained plaintiff's claim of negligent misrepresentation on the theory that a tort claim "is not controlled by the CISG, which only concerns the sales of good between merchants in different countries."[84] Similarly, in *Miami Valley Paper, LLC v. Lebbing Engineering & Consulting GmbH*,[85] the court accepted the buyer's argument that the CISG "only preempts state contract law claims, and then only to the extent that such claims fall within the scope of the treaty."[86] The court permitted the buyer to proceed on claims of negligent misrepresentation and fraudulent inducement.[87] Nevertheless, language in some cases suggests that tort claims that simply replicate rights that arise

---

[80] See Schwenzer, *Article 35*, in Schlechtriem & Schwenzer, supra note 37, at 591. Schwenzer goes on to argue that her conclusion "especially applies to negligent misrepresentation claims under Anglo-American law," notwithstanding that, as discussed later, American cases have systematically been tolerant of concurrent contract and tort claims in CISG cases.

[81] Joseph Lookofsky, *Not Running Wild with the CISG*, 29 J. L. & Comm. 141, 148 (2011).

[82] See Ulrich G. Schroeter, *Defining the Borders of Uniform International Contract Law: The CISG and Remedies for Innocent, Negligent, or Fraudulent Misrepresentation*, 58 Villa. L. Rev. 553 (2013).

[83] 2008 U.S. Dist. LEXIS 21121 (E.D. Ky. March 18, 2008).   [84] Id. at *20.

[85] 2006 U.S. Dist. LEXIS 76748 (S.D. Ohio October 10, 2006).   [86] Id. at *9.

[87] See also *TeeVee Toons, Inc. v. Schubert GMBH*, 2006 U.S. Dist. LEXIS 59455 (S.D.N.Y. August 22, 2006).

from contractual obligations, as opposed to independent claims such as bodily injury, are preempted by the CISG.[88]

After exploring the debate in exquisite detail, the Israeli Supreme Court, sitting as the Court of Civil Appeals, permitted a buyer of tiles to bring a tort claim that the seller had been negligent in their manufacture.[89] The buyer had failed to give notice of defects promptly after their discovery and thus lost the right to bring a claim under the contract. As a technical matter, the decision referred to an Israeli statute based on a predecessor to the CISG. But the relevant provisions of that treaty were sufficiently similar to the CISG provisions that the court analyzed the issues under CISG case law and commentary. Seemingly adopting Schlechtriem's distinction, the court found that the buyer's tort claim sought to protect interests that differed from those protected by international sales law. The court concluded:

> If we assume that a seller was negligent in that he did not examine the quantity of the goods that he packed, admittedly this was negligent conduct (a departure from the standard of conduct of a reasonable seller), but this negligence relates to the manner of complying with a contractual obligation, a duty that was provided in the agreement between the parties, and it is governed by the convention. By contrast, if we assume that the seller was negligent in that he shipped goods in a manner contrary to the Sanitation Regulations, the interest that was injured does not arise from the agreement between the parties, and as such it is possible that it should receive protection outside the scope of the convention. In the case before us, the claim is that Pamesa was negligent in manufacturing the tiles and it shipped a product that a reasonable manufacturer would not have marketed. If Pamesa was indeed negligent in this way, this is not a negligent performance of an obligation under the contract, but a negligent performance of a general duty of care of manufacturers that does not derive from the agreement between the parties. Therefore prima facie there should not be an absolute bar against such a claim.

Moreover, the claim here was for negligent manufacture of goods, not negligence in performing the obligations of a seller. Had the tort action been brought against an

---

[88] See, e.g., *Geneva Pharmaceuticals Technology Corp. v. Barr Labs., Inc.*, 201 F. Supp. 2d 236, 286 n.30 (S.D.N.Y. 2002), *aff'd in part, rev'd in part*, 386 F.3d 485 (2d Cir. 2004) ("Just because a party labels a cause of action a 'tort' does not mean that it is automatically not pre-empted by the CISG. A tort that is in actuality a contract claim, or that bridges the gap between contract and tort law may very well be pre-empted"); *Electrocraft Ark., Inc. v. Super Elec. Motors, Ltd.*, 2009 U.S. Dist. LEXIS 120183, at *18 (E.D. Ark. December 23, 2009) (finding that claims of negligence and strict liability – as well as claims for unjust enrichment and restitution – were preempted by the CISG because the underlying claims were not "allegations of wrongdoing that are extra-contractual or otherwise amount to a breach of a duty distinct from or in addition to the breach of contract claim at issue in this action"); *Weihai Textile Group Imp. & Exp. Co. v. Level 8 Apparel, LLC*, 2014 U.S. Dist. LEXIS 53688 (S.D.N.Y. March 28, 2014) (finding that claims for unjust enrichment, fraud, fraudulent inducement, and prima facie tort essentially constituted restated claims for breach of contract and were therefore preempted by the CISG).

[89] See Supreme Court (Israel) (*Pamesa Ceramica v. Yisrael Mendelson Ltd.*), 17 March 2009, available at http://cisgw3.law.pace.edu/cases/090317i5.html#55.

independent and distinct manufacturer, the fact that the buyer purchased the goods from a seller in a sales transaction would obviously have been no bar to an otherwise appropriate tort action. Thus, the court reasoned, there should be no bar against the manufacturer who is also the seller when the claim involves the manufacturing process rather than the obligations that attach as a function of being a seller.

E. *The two-year cutoff period*

Article 39(2) imposes an absolute bar to the buyer's claims of nonconformity unless the seller receives notice within two years from the date on which the goods were "actually handed over" to the buyer. The two-year period limits the buyer's right to recover even for latent defects and even if the buyer has otherwise reasonably failed to discover the defect. Thus, Article 39(2) operates as a statute of repose, imposing finality on the transaction, rather than as a statute of limitations, which defines a period within which an action for breach of contract may be brought. Failure to give notice within the two-year period precludes even actions otherwise brought within the applicable statute of limitations.

The reference to "handing over," as opposed to "delivery," confirms that the relevant periods for notice are triggered by opportunities for an Article 38 examination rather than mere compliance with a delivery term. The period does not begin when the defects are discovered or are discoverable.[90] Nevertheless, we recognize that there is some difficulty with this argument, because Article 60 defines the buyer's obligation to take delivery partially in terms of the buyer's "taking over the goods." That phrase might be read to imply that delivery and "taking over" – the flip side of the seller's "handing over" – are coterminous. We think that reading, though plausible, is inconsistent with the policies underlying examination. We read the buyer's obligation under Article 60 to take delivery as including the taking over of the goods, but not as defining the time of taking over as the time of delivery. Assume, for instance, that the contract calls for shipment by carrier from seller's place of business. Delivery occurs when the seller hands over the goods to the first carrier at that place under Article 31(a).[91] But the buyer does not "take over" the goods at that point. The buyer nonetheless has an "obligation" to take delivery under Article 60. If the buyer refuses to receive the goods when the carrier arrives, the buyer has, at that point, breached its obligation.

The two-year cutoff period states the outer limit for the required notice. It does not extend the required notice period under Article 39(1).[92] Thus, if earlier notice of defects should have been given, the fact that it was not should not be excused by

---

[90] See Supreme Court (France), 8 April 2009, available at http://cisgw3.law.pace.edu/cases/090408f1.html.

[91] See also supra I.A.

[92] See Provincial Court–Las Palmas Canary Islands (Spain), 16 February 2012, available at http://cisgw3.law.pace.edu/cases/120216s4.html.

compliance with Article 39(2). The court in *Sky Cast, Inc. v. Global Direct Distrib., LLC*,[93] may have missed that point. It concluded that a buyer of light poles impliedly asserted that goods were nonconforming because they were not shipped within the customary period. The court contended that this claim meant that Article 39 applied "by analogy." The court then argued that under Article 39(2), the buyer had two years to bring its claim about defective, that is, late, deliveries. But if the buyer was aware prior to the expiration of that two-year period that the deliveries were late, then it was obligated to give notice within a reasonable time of that discovery. It did not necessarily have the advantage of the full two-year period.

F. *Exceptions to buyer's loss of rights*

1. Seller's knowledge under Article 40

There are two ways in which the buyer can avoid the harsh sanctions of Article 39(1). The first involves Article 40. Under that provision, a seller who knew or could not have been unaware of the nonconformity and who failed to disclose it to the buyer may not rely on the provisions of Article 38 or Article 39. A seller who is already aware of defects cannot claim any prejudice by virtue of not having been informed about them by the buyer.

The provision generates little dispute where the seller had actual knowledge of defects that it failed to disclose. The more difficult issue involves the meaning of "could not have been unaware" of a defect. Although some commentators argue the contrary, in our view the phrase requires more than mere negligence by the seller in not detecting a defect. Negligence might be implied by a phrase such as "ought to have been aware," which is the measure of the buyer's obligation to give notice under Article 39(1). If the drafters intended a negligence standard of what a reasonable seller should or ought to have known, they knew how to say it.

It is more difficult, however, to discern what level of awareness is required. The Israeli decision mentioned earlier classified the inquiry into Article 40 as one involving good faith.[94] It considered the failure of a seller to disclose defects of which it was aware as an act of bad faith that should negate any right to rely on late examination or notice. As we have indicated elsewhere,[95] we find the invocation of good faith superfluous. It adds nothing to the analysis of when Article 40 applies or to the resolution of when the seller had the requisite level of awareness.

Certainly, the seller's mere knowledge that defects have arisen in a product that incorporated seller's goods will not satisfy the standard, since that knowledge does not mean that the seller was aware that its goods were responsible for the

---

[93] 2008 U.S. Dist. LEXIS 21121 (E.D. Ky. March 18, 2008).
[94] See Supreme Court (Israel) (*Pamesa Ceramica v. Yisrael Mendelson Ltd.*), 17 March 2009, available at http://cisgw3.law.pace.edu/cases/090317i5.html#55.
[95] See Chapter 4.II.A.,B.

nonconformity.[96] Case law seems to require at least "severe" or "gross" negligence,[97] which raises the issue of whether that standard requires anything more than negligence "with the addition of a vituperative epithet."[98] Others raise the bar to something closer to "fraud."[99] Perhaps the best one can do in these circumstances is to peruse the cases to discover some common themes that elucidate the degree of notice that a seller must have before it must disclose defects, or face preclusion from asserting Article 38 or 39. Defects that appear to have arisen from intentional acts of the seller give rise to an inference of awareness. Thus, a seller of adulterated wine could not complain of late notice by the buyer where it appeared that the nonconformity arose from willful deceit – the watering down of wine, presumably by the seller itself.[100] The Israeli case discussed earlier concluded that the standard of awareness was not satisfied where a seller of tiles did not have actual knowledge of defects in the specific shipment at issue, even if the seller was aware of problems with similar tiles in other shipments: "a general awareness of a seller that some of his products are not of the best quality does not satisfy the requirements of art. 40." But knowledge of similar defects in other goods may sometimes imply the requisite awareness. A Swedish arbitration award imposed a more liberal standard of awareness where a seller (1) was aware from other transactions that the positioning of a lock plate was critical to the proper functioning of a rail press, (2) was aware that the buyer might improperly install that part, and (3) failed to provide sufficient installation instructions to the buyer.[101] The tribunal appeared to apply something like a "conscious disregard" of facts standard.

Gross disparities between what was ordered and what was delivered may also allow inferences of the appropriate degree of awareness, or, at the very least, shift to the seller the burden of disproving awareness.[102] Failure to perform tests may satisfy the awareness standard, depending on the difficulty and expense of administering the requisite tests. Finally, the issue of awareness may ultimately boil down to one of burden of proof. Typically, the buyer bears the burden of proving the seller had the

---

[96] See *Kingspan Environmental Ltd & Ors v. Borealis A/s & Anor*, [2012] EWHC 1147 (Comm).

[97] See, e.g., Court of Appeals Ghent (Belgium), 16 April 2007, available at http://cisgw3.law.pace .edu/cases/070416b1.html; Federal Supreme Court (Germany), 30 June 2004, available at http://cisgw3.law.pace.edu/cases/040630g1.html. For a case requiring mere negligence by the seller, see Supreme Court (Spain), 8 July 2014, unpublished translation by Giovanni Ricci.

[98] See *Wilson v. Brett*, 11 M. & W. 113, 115 (1843).

[99] See, e.g., Court of Appeals Ghent (Belgium), 4 October 2004, available at http://cisgw3.law .pace.edu/cases/041004b1.html.

[100] See District Court Trier (Germany), 12 October 1995, available at http://cisgw3.law.pace.edu/ cases/951012g1.html.

[101] See Arbitration Institute of the Stockholm Chamber of Commerce (Sweden), 5 June 1998, available at http://cisgw3.law.pace.edu/cases/980605s5.html#N_7.

[102] See, e.g., Court of Appeals Ljubljana (Slovenia), 14 December 2005, available at http://cisgw3 .law.pace.edu/cases/051214sv.html (seller knew that buyer required equivalent number of doors and door jambs, but shipped disparate numbers of each); Federal Supreme Court (Germany), 30 June 2004, available at http://cisgw3.law.pace.edu/cases/040630g1.html.

requisite level of awareness. The "rule and exception" principle that we discuss in Chapter 6[103] would lead to that conclusion, since the buyer is attempting to take advantage of the Article 40 exception to the general rule stated in Article 39.

Nevertheless, in an important case, the German Supreme Court allocated to the seller the burden of proving that it did not have the requisite level of awareness that paprika was irradiated.[104] The court concluded that the buyer could not plausibly have tested for radiation, and any gross negligence occurred while the goods were within "the seller's domain." If the buyer could have demonstrated that it received irradiated paprika from the seller, then the source of radiation had to be the seller or its supplier. Hence, the seller was in the best position to determine where the radiation had occurred, and application of the "proof proximity" principle – which places the burden of proof on the party with the greatest knowledge of the issue to be proven – imposed the burden on the seller. The seller might have been able to demonstrate that it had not caused the radiation and was not grossly negligent in failing to test the goods received from its supplier. If the seller had proven that, Article 40 would have been no bar to its recovery from a buyer who gave late notice of defects. But the seller had the obligation to make that showing.

2. Excuse of late notice under Article 44

Article 44 excuses the buyer from giving notice under Article 39(1) if the buyer has a "reasonable excuse."[105] On first reading, the provision appears circular. The most plausible reasonable excuse for not giving notice is a reasonable failure to discover the nonconformity. But Article 39(1) only requires notice within a reasonable time after the buyer has or ought to have discovered the nonconformity. If Article 44 has meaning, it must apply to a situation in which it would have been unreasonable not to discover the nonconformity, but in which even the buyer who has discovered the nonconformity has a reasonable excuse for not giving notice. A German appellate court arguably conflated these issues when it propounded a relatively broad test for a reasonable excuse: "if the failure to make the required notification is so insignificant —especially with due consideration of personal circumstances affecting the buyer— that it can be waived in the course of usual and fair business dealings, and should therefore not be subject to the severe consequences of a full exclusion of liability."[106] In short, some balancing of interests, rather than a discrete event, could allow a buyer to qualify for an excuse. In that case, the interests favored allowing the buyer

---

[103] See Chapter 6.IX.

[104] See Federal Supreme Court (Germany), 30 June 2004, available at http://cisgw3.law.pace.edu/cases/040630g1.html.

[105] Note that while Article 44 applies only to Article 39(1), Article 40 excuses failure to give timely notice under both Article 39(1) and (2).

[106] See Court of Appeals Saarbrücken (Germany), 17 January 2007, available at http://cisgw3.law.pace.edu/cases/070117g1.html.

an excuse because the buyer could not know that defects in marble were attributable to the seller until it received a technical report and the buyer gave the seller notice immediately thereafter. But if lack of access to the relevant information was the cause of delay in giving notice, the buyer appears to have acted within the reasonable time provided by Article 39(1), so that Article 44 was irrelevant.

The standard examples of Article 44's application, therefore, involve communications failures that preclude the buyer from giving notice of defects it has reasonably discovered. If goods are perishable, an obvious nonconformity might require immediate notice. But a communications failure or natural disaster that prevents the buyer from sending a notice will preclude the seller from providing instructions or a cure that otherwise would have been appropriate. Article 27 would not cover such a situation because it applies only when a communication is actually given or made, but there is a delay or error in its transmission or arrival. Article 44, however, would excuse the buyer from sending an Article 39(1) notice.

A buyer who is excused under Article 44, however, does not retain the full remedies that would have been available had it given timely notice. The buyer may recover damages or reduce the price in accordance with the remedial provisions of the CISG, but is precluded from seeking loss of profit otherwise available under Article 74. Moreover, the explicit reservation of rights to price reduction and damages indicates that other remedies, such as avoiding the contract and delaying passage of the risk of loss, are denied to buyers who fail to provide timely notice under Article 39(1), even if they have an Article 44 excuse. Even where it is applicable, Article 44 only exempts a buyer who fails to provide notice under Article 39(1). It does not extend the two-year cutoff period in Article 39(2).[107]

The excuse scenario also raises a question that may be of more academic than practical interest, although it arose during the drafting of Article 44. Article 39(1) appears to incorporate an objective test with respect to notice. It limits the buyer's right to rely on a nonconformity unless the buyer gave notice within a reasonable time after the buyer did find or ought to have found the defect during an examination. Nevertheless, some subjective elements may be relevant. Assume that sophisticated technological goods are shipped from a technologically advanced country to one where such goods are relatively unknown. Assume further that the goods fail to operate properly, but the buyer attributes malfunctions to operator error. Nevertheless, the actual reason for malfunction is a defect in the goods that would have been detected earlier by a more sophisticated buyer. On a purely objective basis, the failure of the unsophisticated buyer to attribute the malfunction to a defect and to give notice to the seller may throw the buyer into the abyss of Article 39(1). But if we believe either that the seller should have known of the inferior technological level of the buyer or otherwise been responsible for ensuring the quality of the goods, then it

---

[107] See Court of Appeals Linz (Austria), 24 September 2007, available at http://cisgw3.law.pace .edu/cases/070924a3.html.

may be appropriate to employ a more subjective "ought to have discovered" test for Article 39, or to allow lack of sophistication to serve as an excuse under Article 44. Indeed, the drafting history of Article 44 suggests that it was included to permit consideration of the particular difficulties that buyers from developing countries face and thus to "excuse" them under circumstances that would not be applicable to extend the period of reasonable notice for other buyers.

III. SUSPENDING PERFORMANCE

A. *Anticipatory repudiation*

One of the common problems of commercial law concerns the question of when a breach occurs. In contracts that involve a period of time between conclusion of the contract and its performance, a promisor may indicate that it will not perform at the time required by the contract. Under those circumstances, the promisee may wish to terminate the contract in order to enter into a substitute transaction or to avoid additional losses in the event that market prices move against it after receiving indications of nonperformance. Any action by the promisee, however, may cause it to be later declared the party who breached the contract should the promisor ultimately be able and willing to perform at the time of performance. Thus, there will be uncertainty about whether the promisee can avoid the contract or seek damages prior to the time that performance was due. The doctrine of anticipatory repudiation addresses that issue by allowing a promisee to terminate a contract prior to the time of performance where it is sufficiently clear that the promisor will breach.

Article 72 recognizes the doctrine of anticipatory repudiation, though it does not bring much clarity to the criteria for determining that one has occurred. Article 72 provides only that a party may avoid a contract if "prior to the date for performance of the contract it is clear that" the other party will commit a fundamental breach. Under Article 25, a breach is "fundamental" only if it substantially deprives the promisee of what it was entitled to expect under the contract. Article 72, therefore, is consistent with other provisions of the CISG that permit avoidance of a contract only where the breach rises to the "fundamental" level.

What qualifies as a sufficient indication of impending fundamental breach, however, is left open. An overt communication of an unwillingness or inability to perform will at least resolve the clarity of the repudiation, leaving only the issue of whether the announced failure amounts to a fundamental breach.[108] But courts have allowed avoidance under Article 72 even in the absence of an explicit statement by the promisor. An American court found that a refusal to perform unless the terms of a letter of credit were amended constituted a repudiation and a

---

[108] See, e.g., ICC Arbitration Case No. 8786, available at http://cisgw3.law.pace.edu/cases/978786i1.html.

fundamental breach.[109] A buyer's failure to pay for prior shipments may establish a repudiation with respect to future deliveries.[110] A seller's communication that it was unable to locate goods required by the contract and advising the buyer to make alternative arrangements was sufficient to warrant avoidance under Article 72(1).[111] The safest conclusion one can extrapolate from the cases is that the positive and unequivocal expression of an intent not to perform can count as a repudiation.

Even where avoidance for anticipatory repudiation is justified, the promisee must, if time permits, first give notice to the other party. At least that is required if the promisor has not explicitly declared that it will not perform.[112] If the promisor responds to a notice of imminent avoidance with adequate assurances of performance, then the promisee must continue with performance.[113] These requirements have two positive effects. The obligation to give notice prevents miscommunication where a promisor does not intend to convey a refusal to perform, but the promisee has reasonably interpreted words or conduct of the promisor in a manner that gives it reason to suspect that performance is not forthcoming. Second, the opportunity both to demand and to give adequate assurances of performance helps to foreclose strategic behavior by the parties. A party who is concerned about market movements after the conclusion of the contract may wish to express an unwillingness to perform in order to induce the other party to renegotiate contract terms. The other party may be able to limit the capacity for opportunistic demands for renegotiation by insisting on compliance with contractual terms.

B. *Prospective nonperformance*

Of course, parties who seek strategic renegotiation, or parties who are actually uncertain about their capacity to perform, are likely to be ambiguous about their intentions. Only rarely will a promisor overtly declare an unwillingness or inability to perform. Instead the promisor may indicate hesitation or potential obstacles to performance. This may be because the promisor is truly uncertain about its future capacity to perform, but is sufficiently hopeful that matters will work out by the time performance is due that it does not want to terminate the contract. Alternatively, and as in the scenario of strategic behavior that might give rise to the promisee's claim of anticipatory repudiation, the promisor may be attempting to extract a greater part of the surplus generated by contractual performance than it bargained for initially. The latter possibility is greater where the parties must act sequentially. Assume, for example, that the promisor is obligated to act only after the promisee has already made an investment

---

[109] See *Magellan International Corporation v. Salzgitter Handel GmbH*, 76 F. Supp. 2d 919 (N.D. Ill. 1999).

[110] See *Doolim Corp. v. R Doll, LLC*, 2009 U.S. Dist. LEXIS 45366 (S.D.N.Y. May 29, 2009).

[111] See CIETAC Arbitration (China), 30 January 1996, available at http://cisgw3.law.pace.edu/cases/960130c1.html.

[112] See Article 72(2).   [113] See Article 72(3).

in the contract that cannot readily be used in some other transaction. Return, for instance, to our discussion in Chapter 3 in which a buyer of coal has constructed a railroad spur to the seller's coal mine, and that spur will prove useless if it is not used for that specific transaction. Knowing that the promisee has made such a relationship-specific investment, the promisor has an incentive to claim that its own performance may be more difficult or costly than initially assumed, and that renegotiation of the original contract terms is therefore necessary. The uncertainty caused by such efforts to "hold up" the promisee can be costly insofar as it raises doubts about contractual performance that parties will price into their contracts.

In either of these situations, the promisee faced with an unclear statement about prospective nonperformance faces a difficult choice. If it continues with its own performance, it may incur uncompensated losses if the promisor ultimately breaches. If it attempts to terminate the contract and withholds its own performance, it may be deemed the breaching party should the promisor ultimately be able and willing to perform. Commercial parties, therefore, would presumably prefer contractual clauses or legal doctrines that reduce the risk of hold up. As we saw in Chapter 3, clauses that make contracts non-modifiable may be viewed in this light. But other legal doctrines may have the same origins and effect. One example is a legal doctrine that allows the promisee to declare itself insecure about a promisor's prospective performance, even where the reasons for that insecurity do not rise to the level necessary to constitute an anticipatory repudiation, and to demand that the promisor either give assurances of performance or risk termination of the contract.

Article 71 addresses these concerns that arise from ambiguous expressions of prospective nonperformance. A party is entitled to suspend performance of its obligations under Article 71(1) if "it becomes apparent that the other party will not perform a substantial part of his obligations," and if that expected nonperformance will result from a serious deficiency in "his ability to perform," or in "his creditworthiness," or in "[h]is conduct in preparing to perform or in performing the contract." The effect of the provision, therefore, is to allow a party who is justifiably insecure about the other party's future performance to cease its own performance until it receives more certain information about the promisor's intentions and capabilities. The fact that Article 71 authorizes the insecure party to suspend its own obligations removes the risk that unilateral cessation of its performance will transform the promisee into the breaching party.

Article 71(1) states that the concern that the "other party will not perform a substantial part of his obligations [must arise] as a result of: (a) a serious deficiency in his ability to perform or in his creditworthiness; or (b) his conduct in preparing to perform or in performing the contract." While one could spend time attempting to think of all the potential circumstances that could arise under Article 71(1)(a) and (1)(b), it would be very difficult to think of a circumstance that affects a party's ability to perform that is outside the scope of the Article.[114] Therefore, while Articles 71(1)(a) and (1)(b) may help

---

[114] See Djakhongir Saidov, *Article 71*, in Kröll et al., supra note 36, at 931.

illustrate the type of cases that will come under Article 71, they do not limit the scope of Article 71 and thus do not have a substantial impact on its application.

The Article, however, is not a panacea for the insecure promisee. In order to avoid the possibility that suspension could itself be used strategically, Article 71 creates a series of prerequisites to its use, and limits the effect of the promisor's failure to give assurances. A party seeking the protections of Article 71 must immediately give notice of its suspension of performance, and at least one American court has implied that failure to provide such notice can preclude an effective suspension.[115] Unlike Articles 72 and 73, Article 71 does not give the invoking party the right to avoid the contract. Instead, Article 71(1) only allows the invoking party to "suspend the performance of his obligations." This essentially allows the invoking party to put the contract on hold until (1) the other party gives "adequate assurance of his performance" under Article 71(3), (2) the conditions that justified suspension no longer exist, or (3) there is a right to declare an anticipatory breach under Articles 72 and 73.[116] Thus, Article 71 "does not authorize a seller to dispose of goods held for the buyer nor does it authorize a buyer to purchase goods to replace goods to be supplied by the seller ..."[117] As one court put it, Article 71(1) only gives a party the right to "unilaterally modify the time of performance ..."[118] The party who has suspended performance but not received assurances will, of course, claim that the absence of assurances makes it "clear" that a fundamental breach will ensue. The result, however, is that Article 71 provides less certainty about the rights of the parties than they might have preferred, even though it creates a rough framework for permitting parties to resolve suspicions and rumors concerning contractual performance.

Article 71 applies to both buyers and sellers. While an explicit statement of prospective nonperformance will qualify,[119] it is not necessary. A buyer who has been informed that delivery will be delayed may defer a promised pre-delivery payment.[120] A seller whose buyer fails to obtain a required letter of credit may suspend delivery.[121] Since Article 71(1) only deals with future breaches, it does not grant a party the right to deny delivery or to refuse payment for delivery once the

---

[115] See *Weihai Textile Group Imp. & Exp. Co. v. Level 8 Apparel, LLC*, 2014 U.S. Dist. LEXIS 53688 at *37-*38 (S.D.N.Y. March 28, 2014).

[116] See District Court Stendal (Germany), 12 October 2000, available at http://cisgw3.law.pace .edu/cases/001012g1.html; UNICITRAL Digest of Case Law on the U.N. CISG, Art. 71 ¶ 1, available at www.uncitral.org/pdf/english/clout/CISG-digest-2012-e.pdf.

[117] See Honnold/Flechtner, supra note 44, at 386.

[118] District Court Stendal (Germany), 12 October 2000, available at http://cisgw3.law.pace.edu/ cases/001012g1.html.

[119] See Federal Supreme Court (Germany), 27 November 2007, available at http://cisgw3.law .pace.edu/cases/071127g1.html.

[120] See Court of Appeals Auserrhoden (Switzerland), 10 March 2003, available at http://cisgw3.law .pace.edu/cases/030310s1.html.

[121] See Supreme Court of British Columbia (Canada), 21 August 2003, available at http://cisgw3 .law.pace.edu/cases/030821c4.html. In that case, however, the court concluded that an eight-week suspension by the seller was unreasonably long.

seller has breached an obligation. For example, if a seller delivers nonconforming goods, a buyer cannot invoke Article 71 to justify refusing to pay a portion of the contract price.[122] Therefore, if the buyer does not have any obligations before the seller has performed, there will be little for it to suspend. In some situations, the buyer will be able to revoke a revocable letter of credit,[123] withhold a down payment, or not secure a delivery method for an FOB contract.[124]

1. After the conclusion of the contract

Article 71(1) specifies that only information about a potential nonperformance that becomes apparent after the conclusion of the contract is relevant to whether a party can justifiably suspend its performance. Therefore, a party who is aware before the contract is made that circumstances could impede the other party's performance cannot later use this information as a reason to suspend its own obligations.

A Swiss case[125] illustrates this point. A Chinese seller entered into a contract to sell scooters to a Swiss buyer. The seller suspended its obligation to deliver the goods due to outstanding unpaid debt amounting to more than $7 million. The buyer avoided the contract, claiming that suspending the delivery constituted a fundamental breach of contract. The court stated that the creditworthiness of the buyer was to be evaluated based on the "deterioration of the financial situation in comparison to the conclusion of the contract ... If the vending party knew that the solvency was poor prior to the conclusion of the contract and the solvency had not deteriorated since then, it was not entitled to stop the goods." The court held that the seller was unable to prove that the buyer's creditworthiness had seriously declined since the conclusion of the contract. Therefore, the seller did not have a right to suspend performance, and the buyer was justified in avoiding the contract.

This rule makes sense. Article 71(1) primarily serves to protect the non-breaching party from damages when it faces performance risks greater than those that it anticipated at the time the contract was concluded. Risks of which it was or ought to have been aware at the time of contracting should already be priced into the contract.[126] An example helps illustrate Article 71's operation. Assume that seller knows in advance that there is an 85 percent chance that buyer, who contracts to purchase unique custom-made furniture at a price of $10,000, will pay and a 15 percent chance that the buyer will go bankrupt. Assume also that the seller's cost of producing the furniture is $9,000. In addition, assume that the seller was able to charge $12,000 for the goods because the buyer is at a high risk of bankruptcy. Therefore, assuming a zero distribution in the buyer's bankruptcy, the seller's

---

[122] See Christiana Fountoulakis, *Article 71*, in Schlechtriem & Schwenzer, supra note 37, at 952.

[123] See Saidov, supra note 114, at 931.   [124] Id.

[125] See Supreme Court (Switzerland), 17 July 2007, available at http://cisgw3.law.pace.edu/cases/070717s1.html.

[126] See Saidov, *Article 71*, in Kröll et al., supra note 36, at 924.

expected profit from the sale is $1,200, or ($12,000 x .85) + (0 x .15) - $9,000. Suppose that two weeks after entering into the contract the seller's cost increases to $11,000, but no other changes occur. The seller now has an expected loss of $800 on the transaction. In this situation, the seller may strategically attempt to use Article 71 to suspend its performance and then avoid the contract, even though buyer's financial situation has not changed.

Parties should assume the risk of information known about their counterparties before entering into a contract. In applying Article 71, therefore, courts should inquire whether the seller has acquired information about the buyer after the conclusion of the contract that diminishes the contract's value, and that could not reasonably have been discovered previously. For example, assume a seller enters into a contract with a buyer to deliver $5,000 worth of apples in two months. Assume at the time of contracting the seller knows the buyer has an unpaid debt of $5,000 that is one week past due. Assume that it is now two months later, and the seller suspends delivery because the buyer still owes $5,000.

While some might argue that the seller is not entitled to suspend delivery because he was aware of the debt at the time of contracting, there has been a significant change in the circumstances during the two-month period. Despite knowing that the buyer owed $5,000 before entering the contract, a one–week–old debt may not be cause for concern. However, by the time the delivery was due the $5,000 was nine weeks overdue, which is a much stronger indicator that the buyer will not pay for goods under the suspended contract.

2. "Becomes apparent"

How does it become apparent that the counterparty will not perform a substantial part of its obligations? Comparing the nature and the language of Article 71 to that of Articles 72 and 73 and case law provides some guidance. Article 72 states that it must be "clear that one of the parties will commit a fundamental breach of contract" before the counterparty can declare the contract avoided prior to the date of performance. Article 73 requires one party's failure to perform its obligations in one installment of an installment contract to give "good grounds to conclude that a fundamental breach of contract will occur" with respect to future installments before the latter can avoid the future elements of the contract. The three different standards – "clear," "good grounds," and "becomes apparent" – suggest that "becoming apparent" requires a lower probability that a breach will occur. This is consistent with the function of the Articles. Since Article 71 primarily functions to generate information and does not allow the insecure party immediately to avoid the contract, one would suspect that Article 71 would have a lower threshold than Articles 72 and 73.[127] One court has

---

[127] See Fountoulakis, *Article 71*, in Schlechtriem & Schwenzer, supra note 37, at 958; Honnold/ Flechtner, supra note 44, at 428; Saidov, *Article 71*, in Kröll et al., supra note 36, at 922–23; Mercédeh A. da Silveira, Anticipatory Breach under the United Nations Convention on

referred to the standard for Article 71 as a "high probability"[128] of breach, while another has stated that there needs to be "a substantial probability of non-performance."[129] Additionally, commentators agree that whether it "becomes apparent that the other party will not perform a substantial part of his obligations" must be viewed from the perspective of a reasonable person in the party's situation.[130]

Case law also clarifies the circumstances under which it is apparent that the other party will not perform a substantial part of its obligations. In one case, a Hungarian seller contracted with an Austrian buyer for several shipments of mushrooms.[131] The parties agreed that the buyer would open up a bank guarantee. After the seller had delivered the first shipment, the buyer neither paid for the goods nor obtained the guarantee. The seller refused to make any further deliveries. The court found that the seller was allowed to suspend performance under Article 71 because the failure to obtain the bank guarantee made it apparent that the buyer would not pay for the goods.

A similar result was reached in a 1996 Chinese arbitration,[132] where a seller from Macau (at the time a Portuguese colony for choice of law purposes) and a Chinese buyer entered into a contract for wool. The goods were to be shipped to a port in Vietnam. However, the contract required the buyer to obtain a letter of credit, which it failed to do. The seller therefore changed the shipping destination to Hong Kong, the closest port, for fear that it would not receive payment after delivery to Vietnam. The arbitral tribunal determined that the seller had validly suspended his obligation to deliver goods due to a legitimate concern about the buyer's ability to pay. Therefore, the tribunal held that the buyer was responsible for any cost associated with storing the goods in Hong Kong and excess shipping.

Additionally, courts have frequently found it apparent that a buyer will not be able to pay when it has not paid for previous deliveries. In an American case, a Korean seller entered into a contract for garments with an American buyer.[133] The parties agreed that the buyer would pay for all goods within fifteen days of delivery. The buyer consistently failed to make timely payments. The buyer subsequently placed a

---

Contracts for the International Sale of Goods, available at www.cisg.law.pace.edu/cisg/biblio/azeredo.html (noting that Article 71 has a lower threshold than Article 72).

[128] Supreme Court (Austria), 12 February 1998, available at http://cisgw3.law.pace.edu/cases/980212a3.html.

[129] Honnold/Flechtner, supra note 44, at 429.

[130] See Fountoulakis, *Article 71*, in Schlechtriem & Schwenzer, supra note 37, at 958; Honnold/Flechtner, supra note 44, at 429; Saidov, *Article 71*, in Kröll et al., supra note 36, at 923; Silveira, supra note 128.

[131] See Hungarian Chamber of Commerce and Industry (Hungary), 17 November 1995, abstract available at www.unilex.info/case.cfm?pid=1&do=case&id=217&step=Abstract.

[132] See CIETAC Arbitration (China), 27 February 1996, available at http://cisgw3.law.pace.edu/cases/960227c1.html.

[133] See *Doolim Corp.* v. *R Doll, LLC*, 2009 U.S. Dist. LEXIS 45366 (S.D.N.Y. May 29, 2009). See District Court Hasselt (Belgium) (*J.P.S.* v. *Kabri Mode*), 1 March 1995, available at http://cisgw3.law.pace.edu/cases/950301b1.html.

large order, which the seller agreed to fulfill because the buyer promised both to reduce its debt and to provide a letter of credit for the new order. The buyer failed to make payments for prior orders or to provide the letter of credit. The court held that the seller was justified in suspending his obligation because "it was apparent that [the buyer] would be, at the very least, seriously deficient in its performance of its remaining contractual obligations."

However, in an Austrian case,[134] the court held that the seller was not justified in suspending its obligations. In that case, a Czech seller entered into multiple contracts with an Austrian buyer for umbrellas. After the seller made several deliveries of umbrellas, the buyer claimed the goods were defective, and the parties agreed to reduce the price for those deliveries. The parties subsequently entered into additional contracts for umbrellas, but the buyer failed to pay for those deliveries, and apparently revoked an order for its bank to make a payment to the seller. During this time, the parties entered into yet another contract for umbrellas. When the seller attempted to suspend its obligation to produce those umbrellas until the buyer paid for the previous deliveries, the court – in what may be too strict of an interpretation of Article 71[135] – held that "singular delayed payments or a sluggish mode of payment are normally not sufficient to show a serious loss of creditworthiness. ... Furthermore, the revocation of the payment order does also not show a serious lack of creditworthiness on the part of the [buyer] with high probability." In a recent American case, the court denied summary judgment to a seller who contended that it was entitled to the protections of Article 71 where a buyer had made payments pursuant to a payment schedule, but had made those payments several days late.[136]

"Apparent" seller nonperformance may be more difficult to discern. In an Austrian case,[137] a German seller had entered into a contract for natural gas with an Austrian buyer through a series of telephone calls and faxes. The court interpreted the agreement between the parties to require the buyer to obtain a letter of credit after the seller named the place at which the gas would be loaded. The seller never informed the buyer of the place of loading, and the buyer suspended its obligation to open a letter of credit. After the buyer repeatedly asked for the loading location, the seller informed the buyer that, due to restrictions from its supplier, the goods could not be delivered to Belgium, where the buyer planned on taking delivery. The court concluded that it had become apparent that the seller was not able to fulfill his obligations under the contract.

---

[134] See Supreme Court (Austria), 12 February 1998, available at http://cisgw3.law.pace.edu/cases/980212a3.html.

[135] See Saidov, *Article 71*, in Kröll et al., supra note 36, at 926–27.

[136] See *Weihai Textile Group Imp. & Exp. Co. v. Level 8 Apparel, LLC*, 2014 U.S. Dist. LEXIS 53688 at *38 (S.D.N.Y. March 28, 2014).

[137] See Supreme Court (Austria), 6 February 1996, available at http://cisgw3.law.pace.edu/cases/950523a3.html.

3. "Will not perform"

Article 71(1) deals exclusively with anticipated nonperformance. When a party has breached an obligation under the contract, such as by making delivery of defective goods or not making a delivery, Article 71(1) no longer applies and the aggrieved party is restricted to its remedies granted under Article 45 and 61.[138]

Nevertheless, an Austrian court held that the general principles on which the CISG is based allow a party to withhold performance or give partial performance after the other party has breached the contract.[139] An Italian buyer and an Austrian seller had entered into a contract for a recycling machine. After claiming that the machine was defective and had caused consequential damages, the buyer withheld a portion of the contract price. The court attempted to determine whether the CISG allowed "one party to withhold its performance . . . in case of the other party's breach of contract." The court held that such a right existed under a general principle discerned from Articles 58, 71, 80, 85, and 86 that a buyer that received nonconforming goods could withhold part of the payment.[140]

4. "Substantial part of its obligations"

Article 71 operates only when the prospective nonperformance affects a "substantial part" of the promisor's obligations. Ambiguities in the term "substantial part" may be addressed by comparisons to the language and purposes of Article 72 and 73, and by case law. Articles 72 and 73 give a party the right to avoid the contract in the event of a "fundamental breach" rather than the failure to perform a "substantial part" of the party's obligations. If we view the function of Article 71 as a means of generating information that might avoid strategic behavior or misunderstandings about promisor's intentions, then one would expect that it should be available more readily than avoidance. Thus, an apparent failure to perform a "substantial part" of one's obligations need not amount to an apparent "fundamental breach."[141]

This rationale was adopted in a German District Court opinion concerning a contract for shoes.[142] The contract stipulated that payment was required within sixty days of delivery. A portion of the delivered shoes contained defects. The buyer paid for the conforming goods approximately seventy-five days after the goods were

---

[138] See Fountoulakis, *Article 71*, in Schlechtriem & Schwenzer, supra note 37, at 952.

[139] See Supreme Court (Austria), 8 November 2005, http://cisgw3.law.pace.edu/cases/051108a3 .html

[140] See also Supreme Court (Poland), 11 May 2007, available at http://cisgw3.law.pace.edu/cases/ 070511p1.html (supporting the view of the Austrian Supreme Court).

[141] See Gillette & Walt, supra note 22, at 215–16; Fountoulakis, *Article 71*, in Schlechtriem & Schwenzer, supra note 37, at 954; Saidov, *Article 71*, in Kröll et al., supra note 36, at 918; Silveira, supra note 128, at § 2(a).

[142] See District Court (Germany), 15 September 1994, available at http://cisgw3.law.pace.edu/ cases/940915g1.html.

delivered but refused to pay for the defective goods. The seller sued for payment and interest for the defective shoes and interest for the fifteen-day late payment on the non-defective shoes. The court held that delivering the defective shoes was a fundamental breach of the contract and that the buyer had effectively avoided the contract. The court found that the seller, therefore, was not entitled to any compensation for delivery of the defective goods. With respect to the non-defective shoes, the court held that the buyer was entitled to suspend its payment under Article 71 because it had become apparent during the course of performance that the seller was not going to fulfill a substantial part of its obligation. It concluded that the buyer was justified in suspending payment for the non-defective shoes as well, despite the fact that there was no fundamental breach of contract with respect to those shoes.

Article 51(1) supports the court's determination to separate the defective from the non-defective shoes. That Article makes Article 49(1)(a) applicable with respect to nonconforming parts of delivered goods, and Article 49(1)(a) in turn allows the buyer to avoid the contract only if the nonconformity amounts a fundamental breach of contract. Taken together, Article 51(1) and Article 49(1)(a) allow avoidance of the nonconforming part of a delivery when the nonconformity is a fundamental breach of that part of the contract. The court apparently found that the delivery of the defective shoes constituted a fundamental breach with respect to them and that the buyer therefore could (and did) avoid the contract with respect to those shoes. So far the court was on solid ground. However, the court also allowed the buyer to invoke Article 71 despite the fact that the seller delivered the shoes – albeit defective shoes. At this point, the buyer would no longer be anticipating nonconforming goods. Instead, it has actually received nonconforming goods. Article 71 only deals with anticipated breaches, so it should not apply. Article 81(1), not Article 71, allows the buyer to withhold the portion of the contract price representing the defective shoes delivered.

The District Court for the Western District of Michigan concluded that suspension of performance was appropriate in the event of a fundamental breach, without determining whether a lesser nonconformity would be sufficient.[143] A Greek seller had entered into a contract with an American buyer for manufacturing equipment for plastic gardening pots. The seller maintained that it was justified in violating a non-competition clause in the agreement because the buyer failed to make payments. The buyer responded that it had suspended payments under Article 71 because the seller's goods were nonconforming. The court, in an effort to determine whether the buyer was entitled to a preliminary injunction, concluded that, notwithstanding the buyer's "legitimate complaints" concerning the goods, those complaints did not relate to either a fundamental or even a substantial breach of the contract.[144] The court also concluded that the buyer's failure to pay did

---

[143] See *Shuttle Packaging Sys., L.L.C. v. Tsonakis*, 2001 U.S. Dist. LEXIS 21630 (W.D. Mich. December 17, 2001).
[144] Id. at *28.

constitute a fundamental breach, which justified noncompliance with the non-competition clause.

While the "substantial part" condition entails a lower threshold than fundamental breach, a 1994 German case illustrates the lower bounds of the requirement. In that case, the buyer refused to accept the last of four shipments of bacon, claiming that he could suspend his obligation to accept the goods under Article 71 because the goods were nonconforming. The seller proceeded to resell the goods for a lower price on the market and sued for damages. The court established that the vast majority of the goods were conforming and that only 420 kg out of the 22,400 kg of bacon in the fourth shipment were nonconforming. This was insufficient to qualify as a "substantial part" under Article 71. The buyer's unjustified suspension of its obligation to accept the goods amounted to a fundamental breach on its part, so the seller was justified in avoiding the contract. Note that, notwithstanding that the case illustrates a deficiency that would not amount to "substantial part," the court applied Article 71, and did so despite the fact that a breach had already occurred.

IV. AVOIDANCE AND ITS CONSEQUENCES

A. *General principles*

To avoid the contract is to put it to an end based on the other party's breach. Avoidance is the counterpart of doctrines such as "cancellation" of contracts in domestic law.[145] The CISG uses avoidance as the condition to the availability of particular remedies. Avoidance ends the contract while non-avoidance keeps it in effect. Thus, if the contract is avoided, the parties' continuing obligations to perform are terminated. In this case the goods remain the seller's responsibility and the price, if paid previously, must be returned to the buyer. It does not matter whether the goods have been delivered or whether the buyer has accepted or rejected them. Under Articles 74–76, as applicable, the avoiding party can recover damages. If the contract is not avoided, the performance obligations of the parties remain in spite of the breach. Accordingly, the injured party can compel the breaching party's performance, in appropriate circumstances, and recover damages under Article 74 or (if the buyer is the injured party) reduce the price in accordance with Article 50. The details of these avoidance-based remedies are described in Chapter 9.[146]

Before exploring the requirements and consequences of avoidance under the CISG, it is useful to understand the implications of defining a standard for permitting avoidance. Some legal systems permit cancellation or avoidance of a contract for any nonconforming tender. In the United States, for example, the buyer enjoys the benefits of a "perfect tender" rule that permits rejection of tendered goods for

[145] See U.C.C. § 2–106(4).   [146] See Chapter 9.II.A.–C.

any nonconformity, regardless of the degree of deviation from contractual requirements.[147] The effect of this rule is to allow buyers to reject goods for any technical
nonconformity. Thus, buyers may reject nonconforming tenders even though they
are actually dissatisfied with the deal that they made rather than with the quality of
the goods delivered. If market prices have fallen between the time of contracting and
the time of performance, for example, a buyer may seize on a technical nonconformity to get out of a fixed price contract and purchase the goods at the lower
market price. Doctrines such as "good faith" and the seller's right to cure nonconformities may constrain the buyer's ability to avoid a contract for technical reasons,
but the possibility of strategic behavior remains. Given that possibility, it may seem
peculiar that any jurisdiction would adopt a perfect tender rule. But the alternative
rule, which would allow avoidance of the contract only when a more substantial
nonconformity occurred, also invites strategic behavior. In that event, it is the seller
who can seize on the legal standard to act opportunistically. A seller whose contract
can only be avoided if a tender substantially deviates from contractual requirements
may make an imperfect tender in the expectation that either the buyer will not
notice – in which case the seller receives full payment for less than full performance – or that the seller will compensate for any shortfall with a price adjustment or
low-cost cure – in which case there was "no harm in asking." Unless there is reason
to believe that buyers or sellers are systematically more strategic than the other,
opportunism is simply a risk inherent in the choice of a standard for avoidance. It
cannot be the basis for choosing one standard over another.

   Once breach has occurred, however, avoidance addresses a new set of risks.
Avoidance allocates the responsibility for salvaging the goods after a breach. If the
contract is not avoided, the buyer must take delivery of the goods despite the breach.
Although the injured party can recover damages, the buyer who cannot avoid the
contract must dispose of the goods or adapt them to its purposes. If the contract is
avoided, the seller has the responsibility of disposing of or adapting the goods. The
decision to impose the responsibility for salvage on the buyer or the seller, and
thus the standard for avoidance, must take two different risks into account. The
injured party faces the risk that a remedy will not fully compensate its loss.
The breaching party faces the risk that the injured party will act opportunistically
to receive more than the value of its injury. Sales law rules that allocate responsibility to salvage goods must trade off the risk of under-compensation against the risk
of strategic manipulation of damages. Where a breaching seller's cost of retrieving
and replacing nonconforming goods is low, the injured buyer has little ability to act
opportunistically. The seller will retrieve and replace the goods if the cost of doing so
is less than the amount of the buyer's damages. Otherwise, the seller will pay
damages. Where the seller's costs of retrieving and replacing nonconforming goods
is high, the buyer can credibly demand more than the value of its injury. The seller

---

[147] See U.C.C. § 2–601; cf. Sales of Goods Act 1994 § 15A (United Kingdom).

will meet the buyer's demand if the sum demanded is less than the cost of retrieving and replacing the goods. For this reason, high retrieval costs enable the injured buyer to act opportunistically. The buyer's exploitation of these costs creates bargaining costs, which are wasteful. Thus, one would expect that commercial actors would want the buyer's right to avoid to be limited where the seller's salvage costs are high. By limiting salvage costs in those circumstances, commercial law reduces the possibility that the injured buyer will be able to act strategically by placing salvage costs on sellers.

The CISG is somewhat responsive to these concerns. For the most part, avoidance under the CISG is available only in the event of a "fundamental breach."[148] In order to satisfy that standard, the breach must substantially deprive the other party of what it expected to receive under the contract.[149] Thus, the CISG rejects the perfect tender rule. Although the CISG does not formally endorse a "substantial performance" rule, the definition of a fundamental breach means that a seller who has deviated in only minor ways from contractual requirements may be liable for damages, but does not face the risk of having the contract avoided. This rule makes sense in light of the desire to minimize the costs of breach. A perfect tender rule may be sensible for domestic sales, which typically involve goods traveling comparatively short distances. The breaching seller therefore can retrieve nonconforming goods at tolerable expense. Thus, the seller's risk of being exploited by the buyer is slight. By comparison, international sales typically send goods over long distances, and may require additional costs, such as customs duties and tariffs, which make the cost of retrieving them high. Thus, unlike the typical domestic sale, the costs to the seller of recovering defective goods or finding a substitute buyer in a foreign jurisdiction are substantial. As a result, the risk of the injured buyer's strategic manipulation of its damages is serious. Hence, the fact that avoidance is available only when a breach is "fundamental" reflects the CISG drafters' implicit judgment that the risk of the aggrieved buyer acting opportunistically is greater than the risk that the aggrieved buyer's inability to avoid the contract will lead to under-compensation. Where the breach is not fundamental, the injured party cannot shift the responsibility to salvage the goods to the breaching party. The injured buyer therefore cannot exploit the high cost of retrieving or reselling the goods to bargain for compensation above its injury. The injured buyer instead must salvage the goods and obtain a remedy or bargain to have the breaching party salvage them.

B. *Avoidance: grounds and requirements*

As we have noted, the CISG permits the injured party to avoid the contract in either of two circumstances. One is where the breach of the contract is "fundamental."

---

[148] As we discuss later, avoidance may also be available if the aggrieved party has set a further period for performance and that period has expired without receiving the required performance. See Article 49(1)(b).

[149] See Article 25.

Avoidance also is permitted if the seller fails to deliver any goods at the time of performance and fails to perform within the additional period of time for performance that the injured party is allowed to stipulate.[150] Where the seller or buyer is late in its respective performance, the injured party loses the right to avoid the contract if it does not do so within a reasonable time after it has discovered the breach. For breaches other than late performance, termination of the contract must come within a reasonable time after the injured party discovered or ought to have discovered the breach.[151]

1. Grounds of avoidance: fundamental breach

Article 25 provides that a breach is fundamental if it results in such detriment to the injured party as substantially to deprive it of what it is entitled to expect under the contract. The definition contains a limitation of foreseeability. A breach is not fundamental even if it substantially deprives the injured party of what it was entitled to expect under the contract if the result was unforeseeable. The general terms in which Article 25 definition is cast give little guidance to contracting parties ex ante or to courts and arbitral tribunals ex post. As a result, determining the fundamentality of a breach can be difficult. Given the costs of reversing an international sales transaction, courts tend to disfavor a finding of fundamental breach. A 2009 opinion of the Swiss Supreme Court articulated a common position when it concluded: "The term 'fundamental breach' under Art. 25 CISG is to be interpreted narrowly. If it is doubtful whether or not a breach may qualify as fundamental, it should generally be assumed that no fundamental breach is existent."[152] Obviously enough, to be fundamental the breach must be serious in extent;[153] it must "substantially deprive" the injured party of what he reasonably expected had the contract been performed. The extent of injury that counts as a "substantial deprivation" is not self-evident. The court in the Swiss case found that a fundamental breach had occurred where a packaging machine performed at only 29 percent of its required capacity. However, such quantitative measures will not always be available, and the seriousness of breach is inevitably contestable in particular cases. Contractual recitations of aspects of performance the parties consider essential can make the inquiry easier, supplying evidence of the value the parties place on performance.

A more significant difficulty is that it is unclear whether the criteria of fundamentality include factors other than the extent of breach. One such potential factor is the injured party's ability to resell or adapt the goods following breach. Article 25's definition of fundamentality does not say whether the ability to resell-or-adapt makes

---

[150] See Article 49(1)(b).   [151] See Articles 49(2)(a), (b), 62(2)(a), (b).

[152] Supreme Court (Switzerland), 18 May 2009, available at http://cisgw3.law.pace.edu/cases/090518s1.html.

[153] See Federal Supreme Court (Germany), 3 April 1996, available at http://cisgw3.law.pace.edu/cases/960403g1.html.

the breach not fundamental. Two opposing positions can be taken, both consistent with Article 25's language. On the one hand, Article 25's focus on the results of breach might suggest that the extent to which breach reduces the value of the contract to the injured party alone is relevant ("A breach … is fundamental if it results …"). The injured party's ability to resell-or-adapt does not affect the seriousness of the breach. The opposing position is that the result of breach takes into account the injured party's ability to resell-or-adapt. An injured party who reasonably can resell or adapt the goods following breach can reduce its net loss. The loss might leave the injured party only insignificantly less well off than it would be without breach. According to this position, the "result" of breach referred to in Article 25 includes measures that can be taken to mitigate loss.

The case law reflects these two positions. German and Swiss courts have relied on the injured party's ability to resell or adapt goods conveniently to find a breach not fundamental.[154] Some commentary favors the position.[155] On the other hand, the Second Circuit in *Delchi Carrier S.p.A v. Rotorex Corp.*[156] appeared to determine the character of a breach without regard to the injured party's ability to resell or adapt nonconforming goods. There the seller delivered air conditioning compressors that did not conform to a sample and specifications. The compressors delivered had lower cooling capacity and higher energy use than the contract required. In upholding the district court's finding of a fundamental breach, the *Delchi Carrier* court determined that cooling capacity and energy use are important to the product's value.[157] The court did not ask whether the buyer could have resold or adapted the compressors delivered or require record evidence to this effect. Apparently the extent of breach, not the injured party's ability to undertake remedial action, alone determines fundamentality. There are too few cases on the issue to discern a noticeable trend in the position taken by courts or arbitral tribunals.

2. Notice of avoidance

Even where the nonconformity amounts to a fundamental breach, the injured party must take certain steps in order to make an effective declaration of avoidance. Article 26 requires the injured party to give notice to the breaching party declaring the contract avoided. Efforts to avoid a contract without notice are ineffective. The CISG does not require the notice to be in a specific medium or take a particular form. A declaration of avoidance need not state the grounds the injured party is

---

[154] See Federal Supreme Court (Germany), 3 April 1996, available at http://cisgw3.law.pace.edu/cases/960403g1.html; Supreme Court (Switzerland), 28 October 1998, available at http://cisgw3.law.pace.edu/cases/981028s1.html; Court of Appeals Köln (Germany), 14 October 2002, available at http://cisgw3.law.pace.edu/cases/021014g1.html; Commercial Court Zurich (Switzerland), 26 April 1995, available at http://cisgw3.law.pace.edu/cases/950426s1.html (repair).

[155] See, e.g., Joseph Lookofsky, Understanding the CISG 109–115 (4th (Worldwide) ed. 2012); Honnold/Flechtner, supra note 44, at 281.

[156] 71 F.3d 1024 (2d Cir. 1995).   [157] Id. at 1030.

relying on to terminate the contract.[158] Article 26 merely requires that the declaration give notice of avoidance. To be effective, and consistent with the notion that avoidance is to be disfavored in international sales, the notice must unambiguously indicate that the contract is being avoided.[159]

At least one court has recognized an exception to the notice requirement where, given the conduct of the other party, notice would be superfluous.[160] The court found that to be the case where the breaching party "seriously and conclusively refused to perform its contractual obligations by disputing the existence of a binding contract." The court reasoned that a declaration of avoidance in the circumstances would serve no purpose: "[if the breaching party] unambiguously and definitively indicates that it will not perform its contractual obligation, it would be mere formality to require a separate declaration of avoidance."[161] The result seems contestable because the injured party's declaration is not a "mere formality" even where, as here, the breaching party denies that it is in a contractual relationship at all. The declaration still provides useful information to the breaching party by indicating that the injured party intends to avail itself of avoidance-based remedies.[162] To reduce its damages, the breaching party might in response undertake measures it would not undertake if the injured party does not avoid the contract. For example, it might propose to salvage the goods by reselling or purchasing them at a reduced price rather than having the injured party salvage the goods. In addition, requiring a declaration of avoidance avoids later litigation over whether the breaching party's statements indicated an unambiguous and definitive refusal to perform. Lastly, even if notice of avoidance sometimes is not useful, Article 26 nonetheless expressly requires it. Other courts and some commentary reject the claim that notice of avoidance can be disposed with as superfluous.[163] This view seems to us to have the stronger argument.

---

[158] Several scholars have taken the contrary position; see Christopher M. Jacobs, *Notice of Avoidance Under the CISG: A Practical Examination of Substance and Form Considerations, the Validity of Implicit Notice, and the Question of Revocability*, 64 U. Pitt. L. Rev. 405, 409 (2003); Henry Deeb Gabriel, *General Provisions, Obligations of the Seller and Remedies for Breach of Contract by the Seller*, in The Draft Digest and Beyond: Cases, Analysis and Unresolved Issues in the UN Sales Convention 336, 340 (Franco Ferrari, Harry Flechtner & Ronald A. Brand eds., 2003). Their position assumes that Article 39(1)'s requirement of notice, which does require specification of the nature of the nonconformity, extends to the notice required by Article 26. We argue later (infra page 199) that Article 39(1)'s notice requirement does not apply to Article 26. Case law and most commentary agree; see, e.g. 2012 UNCITRAL Digest of Case Law on the United Nations Convention on the International Sale of Goods 122 (at para. 5), available at www.uncitral.org/pdf/english/clout/CISG-digest-2012-e.pdf (collecting cases); Christiana Fountoulakis, *Article 29*, in Schechtriem & Schwenzer, supra note 37, at 441.

[159] See Supreme Court (Austria), 28 April 2000, available at: http://cisgw3.law.pace.edu/cases/000428a3.html.

[160] See Court of Appeals Munich (Germany), 15 September 2004, available at http://cisgw3.law.pace.edu/cases/040915g2.html.

[161] Id.   [162] See, e.g., Articles 75, 76, 81(2).

[163] See, e.g., Court of Appeals Graz (Austria), 29 July 2004, available at http://cisgw3.law.pace.edu/cases/040729a3.html; Peter Huber & Alastair Mullis, The CISG 210 (2007).

Although other provisions of the CISG might appear to require the avoiding party to state the grounds of avoidance, in fact they do not. Article 39(1) provides that the buyer loses the right to rely on a nonconformity that has not been specified in a notice to the seller. Seemingly, an injured buyer who is avoiding the contract is relying on a nonconformity in the goods.[164] However, Article 39(1) is better read as not applying to the act of avoidance. One reason is that Article 26's requirements for avoidance are self-contained: "A declaration of avoidance of the contract is effective only if made by notice to the other party." Because the Article contains no other requirements, effective notice of the declaration does not require a statement of the grounds of avoidance. For this reason, Article 39(1)'s notice requirements are separate and apply only to the notice that informs the seller of nonconformities. In addition, Article 39(1)'s notice requirements apply only to buyers, not to sellers. By contrast, Article 26's notice requirement for avoidance is general, applying to both avoiding sellers and buyers. This again suggests that Article 39(1)'s requirements do not apply to avoidance.

Finally, separate notice requirements for avoidance and other remedies make economic sense. Avoidance terminates the contract while other remedies keep the contract in force. The specificity requirements of Article 39(1) allow a seller that has delivered nonconforming goods to have a basis for curing the nonconformity, and thus to maintain the value of the contractual performance. When the contract is put to an end, on the other hand, a statement of the grounds of termination has less value to the breaching party. Although the breaching party might find information about the nature of the nonconformity justifying avoidance valuable in deciding how to salvage the goods, the information has no use to it in preserving the deal. This is because any remedial action the breaching party might undertake would come too late. At the same time, notice of the declaration of avoidance benefits the breaching party by saving it the costs of further, possibly wasteful performance at little cost to the avoiding party. Thus, a notice of avoidance is cost-justified while a statement of the grounds of avoidance is not. By contrast, where the contract is not terminated, notice of the grounds of the injured party's complaint is valuable to the injured party. It can use the information to take remedial action or reach an accommodation with the injured party.

This leaves the question of the sorts of declarations that count as notice of avoidance. Article 26 does not say. Obviously, an injured party's notice to the effect "I hereby avoid the contract" suffices, as does "I hereby terminate the contract."

---

[164] At least where the goods do not conform to the contract or default terms supplied the CISG. It is arguable that cases of other breaches, such as late or other improper delivery, improper documentation or the establishment of credit enhancements, the buyer is not relying on a nonconformity in the goods. If so, in such cases Article 39(1) does not even require the avoiding buyer to state the grounds on which it avoiding the contract. The argument in the text against Article 39(1)'s applicability to avoidance assumes that Article 39(1)'s reference to "lack of conformity in the goods" applies to all breaches of the seller's contractual obligations, not just to its obligations with respect to the goods.

"I intend to avoid" or "I will avoid" equally obviously does not count as avoidance; the statements express only an intention to avoid and do not declare the contract avoided.[165] Harder cases fall in between these paradigms of "avoidance" and "no avoidance" declarations. *Roder Zelt und Hallenkonstrucktionen GmbH v. Rosedown Pty Ltd. & Eustace,*[166] an Australian decision applying the CISG, is a difficult case. The seller sold goods to the buyer while retaining title in them. When the buyer later went into bankruptcy after breaching the sales contract, the seller filed a claim in the bankruptcy proceeding to recover the goods. The court found that the filing gave notice of avoidance. Filing a claim by itself is not a declaration of avoidance, because it is consistent with a request for remedies other than avoidance such as damages. The filing alone therefore does not notify the buyer that the seller is terminating the contract. However, the seller's filing in *Roder Zelt* did not merely ask for a remedy against the buyer. It demanded the return of the goods. A demand for the return of goods unmistakably indicates to a buyer that the seller considers the contract ended. Thus, the *Roder Zelt* court's finding that the seller gave effective notice of avoidance might well be correct. On the other hand, a buyer's return of goods to the seller did not qualify as "implied" notice, at least where the buyer simultaneously expressed a willingness to pay for goods that it had resold.[167] Nor will an option granted to the buyer either to reduce the price or to take back the goods.[168]

C. *Cure and fundamental breach*

The CISG gives the seller an opportunity to cure any failure in its performance. Both the right to cure and the circumstances in which cure is allowed are broad. Article 37 grants the seller the right to remedy "any lack of conformity" in the goods delivered as long as the date of delivery has not passed. The only limitations on the right are that the cure must occur by the date for delivery and the cure may not cause the buyer unreasonable inconvenience or unreasonable expense. Since the cure must occur by the delivery date, it would be the rare case in which cure by performance would trigger harm to the buyer, unless the buyer had to expend additional sums to receive two deliveries instead of one. Cure under these circumstances may take the form of delivering missing goods, delivering conforming goods

---

[165] Cf. CIETAC Arbitration (China), 1 February 2000, available at http://cisgw3.law.pace.edu/cases/000201c1.html.

[166] See Federal District Court (Australia), 28 April 1995, available at http://cisgw3.law.pace.edu/cases/950428a2.html.

[167] See District Court Frankfurt (Germany), 16 September 1991, available at http://cisgw3.law.pace.edu/cases/910916g1.html. But it appears that a Swiss court interpreted a request by the buyer for the seller to take back a machine as sufficient to constitute a declaration of avoidance. Court of Appeals Valais (Switzerland), 21 February 2005, available at http://cisgw3.law.pace.edu/cases/050221s1.html.

[168] See Lower Court Zweibrücken (Germany), 14 October 1992, available at http://cisgw3.law.pace.edu/cases/921014g1.html.

to replace nonconforming ones, or repairing nonconforming goods. Article 34 explicitly extends the right of cure to defects in documents covering the goods up to the date of delivery, as long as cure does not cause the buyer unreasonable inconvenience or expense.

Article 48(1) extends the seller's right to cure past the date of delivery. Again, the seller must cure without unreasonable delay and without causing the buyer unreasonable inconvenience or uncertainty in reimbursement of expenses advanced. Because it occurs after the date of delivery, it is easier to imagine how a proposed cure under Article 48 could be unsatisfactory to the buyer. The buyer may need the goods to fill downstream contracts by a certain date or may suffer a loss waiting for goods that need to be incorporated into an ongoing manufacturing process. Because the Article allows the breaching seller to remedy its breach without limiting the form the remedy may take, cure apparently can include repair, tender of substitute goods, or a financial accommodation. Article 48(2) allows a seller to request the buyer to make known whether it will accept a cure; if the buyer fails to comply with the request within a reasonable time, the seller may perform within the time stated in its request. During that period of time, the buyer may not resort to any remedy inconsistent with the seller's performance. Essentially that precludes the buyer from avoiding the contract and pursuing avoidance-based remedies. Both Articles 37 and 48 allow the buyer to recover damages even when cure is affected.

The right to cure initially seems fully consistent with minimizing the costs of breach. If a breach can be cured at a cost lower than what would be required for either the buyer or seller to enter a substitute transaction or to leave the goods unused, then it appears to be most desirable way of dealing with nonconformity. But looking at the possibility of cure only at the time of breach ignores the incentive effects that the opportunity to cure creates and that may vary with the underlying rules about what constitutes a breach. Recall that some national laws adopt a perfect tender rule, which permits the buyer to reject goods for any nonconformity. Cure makes sense in that context because a buyer who has a right to reject even for a technical nonconformity may use that power to cancel a contract due to dissatisfaction with the deal rather than dissatisfaction with the seller's performance. A buyer, for instance, may reject goods for a minor nonconformity simply because post-contract price movements allow the buyer to purchase equivalent goods at a lower price. The seller's right to cure constrains the buyer's strategic behavior by allowing the seller an additional opportunity to provide conforming goods. That opportunity, in turn, reduces the buyer's incentive to exploit market price changes that cause regret about the deal that the buyer now wishes to avoid. There is little reason for the buyer to reject goods strategically if the seller can simply keep the transaction intact by offering cure.

But, as we have noted, the CISG's requirement of a "fundamental breach" before a contract can be avoided already removes the buyer's incentive to reject goods for minor nonconformities. Cure is unnecessary to constrain buyer opportunism where the buyer can only avoid a contract if the seller's breach is fundamental. If anything, the fundamental breach requirement induces sellers, not buyers, to chisel on performance because the minor (nonfundamental) defects may be overlooked and, if noticed, may still be redressed by price adjustments rather than by cancellation of the contract. The seller's ability to cure any defect exacerbates the possibility of seller opportunism by giving the seller who performs imperfectly an additional opportunity to deal with the nonconformity, and thus reduces the seller's incentives to ensure an initial conforming delivery.

The seller's right to cure under Article 48 is expressly constrained by Article 49 ("Subject to Article 49 ..."). Article 49(1)(a) allows the buyer to avoid the contract when the seller's breach is fundamental, and an avoided contract cannot be cured. However, the meaning of Article 48's "subject to Article 49" language is opaque, so that the relation between Articles 49(1)(a)'s right of avoidance and Article 48's right to cure is unclear. Inconveniently, Article 48's drafters themselves seem uncertain about its interpretation.[169] One possibility is that the injured buyer may avoid the contract for fundamental breach only when the seller's right to cure has ended or likely will not be forthcoming. This seems a questionable understanding of the relation of cure to avoidance because it gets things backwards: The position makes the right of avoidance "subject to" the right to cure, not the right to cure "subject to" the right of avoidance, as Article 48(1)'s language requires. A second possibility is that Article 49(1)(a) gives the injured buyer a right of avoidance without regard to the seller's right to cure. In this case the seller can cure only if the buyer has not avoided the contract. Correspondingly, the buyer cannot avoid if the seller cures or makes a credible offer to do so before the buyer declares the contract avoided. This is a plausible understanding of Article 48(1)'s "subject to Article 49" language.

Most courts, arbitral tribunals, and commentators endorse the former possibility. They require that the curability of a breach be taken into account in determining whether the breach is fundamental.[170] This interpretation of "fundamentality" has a practical consequence. It means that unless the buyer has a sufficient interest in the seller's immediate conforming performance to preclude cure under Article 48, or the seller has refused to cure, the breach does not become fundamental until the period for cure has ended without the seller having cured. The position makes some sense, notwithstanding the injury it does to the wording of Article 48. Assume that a buyer contracts to receive goods on January 15, although it will not suffer any injury if it receives the goods by January 20. Assume that the seller delivers seriously

---

[169] See First Committee Deliberations, 24 March 1980, in Documentary History for the Uniform Law of International Sales 562–65 (paras. 40–76) (John O. Honnold ed., 1989).

[170] See Court of Appeals Köln (Germany), 14 October 2002, available at http://cisgw3.law.pace .edu/cases/021014g1.html; Court of Appeals Koblenz (Germany), 31 January 1997 available at http://cisgw3.law.pace.edu/cases/970131g1.html; Commercial Court Aargau (Switzerland), 5 November 2002, available at http://cisgw3.law.pace.edu/cases/970131g1.html; Huber & Mullis, supra note 163 at 222; Honnold/Flechtner, supra note 44, at 427; Peter Huber, *Article 49*, in Kröll et al., supra note 36, at 727.

nonconforming goods on January 15. The seller offers to cure by January 20. Can the buyer say that the seriously nonconforming delivery on January 15 entitles it to avoid the contract, even though it believes that the seller will cure the nonconformity before it suffers harm? We would allow the cure and deny the buyer's power to avoid, notwithstanding the wording that makes cure subject to avoidance. We are moved to this result in part by the desire to minimize avoidance, as the notion of "fundamental breach" suggests is appropriate. But we also believe that allowing cure in this situation is likely to prevent buyer opportunism. After all, if the buyer truly does not need the goods until the time of cure, the buyer's desire to resist cure is likely based on its desire to take advantage of market price shifts in its favor between the time of contracting and the time of performance rather than on concerns about the ultimate quality of performance.

Other courts reach a similar conclusion, albeit by different reasoning. They maintain that a fundamental breach can be defined apart from the right to cure, but that even a fundamental breach is subject to the seller's right to cure under Article 48. In a case involving inflatable "arches" to be used for advertising during car races, the seller offered to cure defects that caused the arches to collapse.[171] The court concluded that this was sufficient to preclude the buyer from avoiding the contract under Article 48(2), notwithstanding the fundamental nature of the breach: "the buyer does not have the right to avoid the contract even in case of an objective fundamental defect as long as and as far as the seller comes up with a remedy (subsequent cure of the defect) and such is still possible." The result seems to stretch the scope of a seller's right to cure, insofar as it fails to consider that Article 48(2) follows from Article 48(1), which is subject to the right to avoid under Article 49.

While the prevailing interpretation of "fundamentality" is attractive, it has its own shortcomings. Making cure relevant to the fundamental character of a breach in effect makes the buyer's right of avoidance subject to the seller's right to cure. This consequence conflicts with the Article 48(1)'s reference to "subject to Article 49," which seemingly gives priority to the buyer's right to avoidance over the seller's right to cure. Another problem is that the prevailing interpretation makes administration of the sales contract difficult. The problem is that sometimes the contracting parties cannot know whether a breach is fundamental unless they know whether cure is forthcoming. Whether cure is forthcoming might be itself uncertain. For example, suppose Buyer orders oranges it plans to resell after receipt but has no customers to date. The oranges Seller delivers are seriously nonconforming, as recognized by Buyer. Because Buyer does not have an immediate need for conforming oranges, Article 48(1) gives Seller a reasonable amount of time in which to cure. What is that time? Buyer knows that the oranges delivered are seriously nonconforming, and it might be able to arrange a resale of conforming oranges at undetermined dates after

---

[171] See Commercial Court Aargau (Switzerland), 5 November 2002, available at http://cisgw3.law .pace.edu/cases/021105s1.html.

receipt. But Buyer cannot forecast with any confidence the reasonable time within which Seller can tender conforming oranges. If the curability of breach must be taken into account to determine the fundamental character of a breach, Buyer is uncertain about whether Seller's breach is fundamental. It therefore also remains uncertain about whether it has a right to avoid the contract.

The ability of the seller to "remedy . . . any failure to perform his obligations" states a right of cure that is arguably broad enough to encompass cure by repair of defects, as well as by providing substitute goods, again assuming that the seller can do so without unreasonable delay and without causing the buyer unreasonable inconvenience. Article 36(1), which gives the seller the right to cure before the date of delivery, confirms this right. The Article allows the seller to deliver missing parts, make up for deficiencies in quantities delivered, replace nonconforming goods, "or remedy any lack of conformity in the goods delivered." Given the types of cure other than repair, the last "remedy" clause clearly includes cure by repair. The close similarity in phrasing between Article 36(1) and Article 48(1)'s reference to a cure "remedy" makes it likely that the latter Article allows cure by repair.

But it is not clear that repair alone provides the buyer with the benefit of its bargain. Assuming that the buyer is willing to pay $x for a new good, one might infer that the buyer would anticipate paying something less than $x for a "repaired" good. Thus, if the buyer must pay the full contract price for a repaired good, the buyer is paying for something that it did not receive. While the differential between a new good and a repaired one may be insufficient to qualify as a fundamental breach that gives rise to a right of avoidance, we would allow the buyer to recover from the seller an amount that reflects the difference between the market price of new goods and the market price of used or repaired goods that fit the contract description. Doctrinal support for this proposition can be found in Article 48(1), which retains for the buyer the right to claim damages, notwithstanding the seller's right to cure.

Article 48(1) imposes a limit on cure by repair: The repair must "remedy" the nonconformity in the goods. The Article allows the seller to "remedy . . . any failure to perform his obligations." A repair that diminishes the ex ante value to the buyer of the seller's performance is not a "remedy." Otherwise, the seller could make any repair, however inadequate, and take the position that it counts as a remedy. In this case the buyer would be left to recover as damages the diminution in the value of the repaired goods to it. Article 48(1) does not support the seller's position. To count as cure, the repair must remedy the nonconformity in the goods. Article 48(1)'s last sentence retains the buyer's right to recover damages. However, the buyer need rely on these damages only when the seller's repair remedies the nonconformity. For instance, repair might be effected without causing the buyer unreasonable delay, inconvenience, or expense. The buyer must rely on damages for compensation for injury resulting from the seller's repair. This does not give the seller the right to cure by repair when the repair substantially reduces the value of the repaired goods to the buyer.

D. *Grounds of avoidance: additional time for performance*

The CISG confers on the injured party, whether buyer or seller, the right to give the breaching party an additional period of time within which it must perform. In a case where failure to perform means failure to deliver (in the case of a seller) or to pay or take delivery (in the case of a buyer), an additional failure within the additional period fixed permits the injured party to avoid the contract, even without additional proof of of a fundamental breach.[172] This is the one situation in which a fundamental breach is not necessary for avoidance. In effect, the CISG adopts a "one bite at the apple" rule that makes a second failure to deliver (or pay or take delivery) presumptively a fundamental breach. The procedure and consequences of fixing the time period is the *Nachfrist* ("extended period" or "grace period") procedure, adapted from German law.[173]

The procedure for extending the time for performance gives the injured party a remedy somewhat similar to specific relief. Just as an order for specific relief demands that the breaching party perform, the notice of additional time demands that the breaching party perform within a fixed period of time. However, unlike specific relief, the procedure for additional time is nonjudicial: The injured party gives the notice and fixes the extended period for performance. The breaching party can elect not to perform, while a breaching party subject to an order of specific relief is compelled to perform. The breaching party's failure to perform within the additional period merely gives the injured party the power to avoid the contract without showing the existence of a fundamental breach. In addition, unlike specific relief, the extended period is subject to a "reasonable time" limit. The party providing such notice binds itself to accept the subsequent requested performance within the stated period and not to resort to remedies for breach of contract until that period has passed.

Since the grant of an additional time to perform can be conferred unilaterally by the non-breaching party, fixing such a time does not constitute a modification of the contract subject to Article 29. This has two consequences. First, even if the original contract contains a clause prohibiting modifications or terminations other than in writing, the notice fixing an additional time need not be in writing. Second, because the original contract has not been modified, the grant of an additional time for performance does not imply the absence of a breach of the original contract. It is true that Article 47(2) and Article 63(2) specify that the aggrieved party may not resort to any remedy for breach of contract within the extended period. But the aggrieved party retains any right to claim damages for delay in performance. Assume, for instance, that a seller is obligated under the contract to deliver goods on July 1. The buyer requires the goods to fulfill a downstream contract on July 10. Assume the

---

[172] See Articles 49(1)(b), 64(1)(b).
[173] See Bürgerliches Gesetzbuch [BGB] [Civil Code] § 281(1) (Ger.).

seller informs the buyer on June 25 that it will be unable to fulfill the contract on July 1, and the buyer grants an additional period of time for delivery until July 5. If the delayed delivery prevents the buyer from meeting its full obligations to the downstream buyer on July 10 and the buyer must compensate the downstream buyer for that failure, the buyer retains the right to recover damages from the seller, notwithstanding the grant of an additional time.

There can, however, be situations in which it is difficult to distinguish between the grant of an additional time under Article 47 and a modification under Article 29. Assume in the preceding example that on June 25 the seller informs the buyer of its inability to deliver the goods on July 1. The buyer states, "I can accept the goods if you deliver them by July 3." The seller responds, "I can't do any better than July 5." The buyer says, "okay," and accepts the goods on July 5. Does the exchange between the parties constitute an offer and acceptance of a modification to the original contract that would preclude any damages for the buyer's delay in performing its downstream contract? Or does the buyer's assent to the seller's indication of inability to perform prior to July 5 simply constitute an accommodation in the seller's unilateral fixing of an additional time of performance under Article 47? Perhaps, like any issue of interpretation under the CISG, the answer to these questions can be given only through an investigation of the parties' intent consistent with the dictates of Article 8. A similar situation arose in the case of *Valero Marketing & Supply Company v. Greeni Trading Oy*.[174] Greeni had contracted to sell naphtha to Valero. Greeni sent the naphtha on a ship that Valero had rejected and could not deliver within the contractual window. Valero proposed that it would accept the oil only through a more complicated delivery process, only up to a certain date, and only at a price discount. Greeni accepted the proposal, but still could not deliver within the extended period. The district court held that the prohibition in Article 47 on a buyer's ability to seek a remedy for breach after providing an additional period for performance foreclosed Valero's right to insist on its more stringent delivery requirements. But the Third Circuit concluded that even if the new agreement was inappropriate under Article 47, it was a perfectly permissible modification of the original agreement under Article 29 and had been assented to by Greeni.

The injured party is not obligated to fix an additional period for performance. Indeed, in one case, the court implied that the breaching party's assertion of a date for delayed performance precluded any need for the aggrieved party to fix an additional time.[175] However, if a party elects to do so, the period fixed must be reasonable in duration.[176] The failure to set a reasonable time, however, does not mean that the notice fixing an additional time is ineffective; rather it means that the court may substitute a reasonable time for the additional period during which

---

[174] 2007 U.S. App. LEXIS 17282 (3d Cir. July 19, 2007).
[175] See Court of Appeals Düsseldorf (Germany), 21 April 2004, available at http://cisgw3.law.pace.edu/cases/040421g3.html.
[176] See Articles 47(1), 63(1).

performance can occur. Thus, where delivery was due on March 15, and the buyer provided the defaulting seller with an option to deliver by March 24, a German appellate court noted that any reasonable time would have expired by April 11, which was the date when the buyer gave notice of avoidance.[177] During the reasonable period, the injured party cannot resort to a remedy, but may recover damages for the breaching party's delay in performance.[178]

As noted previously, a fundamental breach is not a requirement of the procedure for an additional time. Although the seller's failure to deliver goods or the buyer's failure to pay the contract price or take delivery often constitutes a fundamental breach, it need not always be one. Likewise, although the breaching party's failure to perform within the additional period often will be a fundamental breach, the failure sometimes does not seriously injure the aggrieved party. Nonetheless, in the case of non-delivery, the breaching party's failure to perform within the period fixed gives the injured party the right to avoid the contract under Article 49(1)(b) (in the case of a buyer) and Article 64(1)(b) (in the case of a seller) without a showing that the failure to perform amounted to a fundamental breach. Given the vagueness in the notion of a fundamental breach, the procedure for additional time is useful because it enables the injured party to reliably determine when it can avoid the contract without having to determine the fundamentality of a breach.

"Non-delivery," while a seemingly simple condition of the CISG's procedure for an additional time, potentially can cause problems. Non-delivery exists only when the seller has breached by not delivering any goods or the buyer has breached by not paying the contract price or taking delivery. Article 49(1)(b)'s reference to "non-delivery" and Article 64(1)(b)'s reference to the buyer's failure to "perform the obligation to pay the price or take delivery of the goods" expressly state these respective limitations. Thus, the procedure for an additional time does not apply where the seller has delivered goods, but the goods delivered are nonconforming. The trouble is that it is not always self-evident when the seller has not delivered or the buyer not taken delivery. Suppose the contract calls for the seller to deliver oranges. The seller instead delivers apples. Or suppose the contract calls for the contract to be paid in dollars. The buyer pays in euros. Has the seller "delivered" the goods? Has the buyer "performed its obligation to pay the price"? One might conclude that delivering "something" is still a delivery that makes Article 49(1)(b) inapplicable. Alternatively, one might conclude that, at some point, a nonconforming delivery is so far removed from what was required by the contract that it cannot count as a delivery at all. Of course, often a delivery of different goods than were called for by the contract amounts to a fundamental breach. In these cases, the buyer does not need to invoke Article 49(1)(b)'s additional period to avoid the

---

[177] See Court of Appeals Naumburg (Germany), 27 April 1999, available at http://cisgw3.law.pace .edu/cases/990427g1.html.
[178] See Articles 47(2), 63(2).

contract. It can do so under Article 49(1)(a).[179] However, there are cases in which the distinction between non-delivery and nonconforming delivery makes a difference. In rare cases the seller's delivery of different goods might not amount to a serious breach. For example, assume that the buyer ordered apples and the seller delivered oranges. If the apples had the same market value as the oranges the seller promised to deliver, the breach might not be fundamental. In such cases a buyer wanting to avoid the contract can do so under Article 49(1)(b) only if the case is one of "non-delivery."

Commentators agree that the delivery of goods entirely different from the contracted goods still counts as delivery.[180] A 1996 German Supreme Court case that squarely addressed the issue is a bit less unequivocal. There the buyer argued that the seller's delivery of nonconforming goods amounted to non-delivery. The Court disagreed: "[Buyer's] position is incorrect. Contrary to German domestic law,[181] the CISG does not differentiate between delivery of different goods, and delivery of goods that do not conform to the contract . . . The Court does not need to resolve whether, in the event of a blatant divergence from the contractual condition, a non-delivery [within] the meaning of Art. 49(1)(b) CISG can arise. Such a violation of contract did not occur in the present case."[182] If the Court believed that the CISG does not count delivery of different goods as "non-delivery," the extent to which the delivered goods "diverged" from the contracted goods would not matter. The Court could simply have deemed the seller's tender to be delivery and stopped. Its refusal to consider the issue based on the facts about the extent of the seller's breach presented to it might signal that in some cases delivery of different goods could count as non-delivery. On the other hand, the Court might merely be offering an additional reason for not considering the seller's tender to be "non-delivery" for purposes of Article 49(1)(b).

The distinction between non-delivery and nonconforming delivery does not mean that Article 47 does not apply at all to the latter cases. The language of Articles 47 and 49 indicates that, at least as a technical matter, the buyer can fix a time for remedy of non-conformities. Article 47 provides for the buyer to fix the additional period "for performance by the seller of his obligations." It does not limit the availability of a grant of additional time to situations in which the seller has failed to deliver. Situations of nonconforming deliveries in which Article 47 is important

---

[179] If the buyer does not want to avoid the contract, it can rely on Article 46(2) to require the seller to deliver substitute goods (subject to Article 28's limitation). The availability of specific performance under the CISG is discussed in Chapter 9.I.C.

[180] See, e.g., Markus Muller-Chen, *Article 49*, in Schlechtriem & Schwenzer, supra note 37, at 753.; Honnold/Flechtner, supra note 44, at 419; Michael Will, *Right to Avoid the Contract*, in Bianca & Bonell, supra note 33, at 363–64.

[181] German law after 2001 no longer distinguishes between a nonconforming delivery and delivery of different goods. See Bürgerliches Gesetzbuch [BGB] [Civil Code] § 434(3) (Ger.).

[182] See Federal Supreme Court (Germany), 3 April 1996, available at http://cisgw3.law.pace.edu/cases/960403g1.html; see also Lower Court Viechtach (Germany), 11 April 2002, available at http://cisgw3.law.pace.edu/cases/020411g1.html.

implicate Article 49(2). That Article places limitations on the buyer's right to avoid, notwithstanding that the requirements of avoidance under Article 49(1) have been satisfied. Under conditions prescribed in Article 49(2), the aggrieved party loses the right of avoidance if it fails to give timely notice of avoidance.

Assume, for example, that the contract calls for the seller to deliver a machine that performs ten functions on December 1. On that date, the seller delivers a machine that performs only five of the designated functions, and that the nonconformities constitute a fundamental breach. Nevertheless, the buyer needs the machine for those five functions and, under Article 47, grants the seller an additional week in which to remedy the defects. The seller fails to remedy the defects within the additional week. If the buyer then attempts to avoid the contract, the seller may claim that the buyer failed to avoid the contract within a reasonable time after it knew of the breach, and thus is deprived of the right to avoid under Article 49(2)(b)(i). But the fact that the buyer was entitled to and did fix an additional week for performance under Article 47 allows the buyer to avoid the contract under Article 49 (2)(b)(ii).[183] That provision denies the buyer the right to avoid a contract where the seller has delivered goods and has breached by means other than late delivery, unless the buyer declared the contract avoided within a reasonable time after the expiration of the additional period. A case in which the goods have been delivered and there has been a breach other than late delivery necessarily includes a delivery of nonconforming goods, and excludes the case of non-delivery. Thus, the invocation of the additional period in Article 49(2)(b)(ii) would make no sense if Article 47 were restricted to non-delivery cases. The buyer in our example may avoid as long as it acts promptly after the expiration of the additional period. In such a case, however, the buyer must still demonstrate that it suffered a fundamental breach.

Nevertheless, the consequences of invoking Article 47 in a case where nonconforming goods have been delivered are quite limited. Unlike the case of non-delivery, a buyer who suffers a nonconforming delivery but who allows an additional time for performance still cannot avoid the contract unless the nonconformity amounts to a fundamental breach. Mere failure to deliver conforming goods within the additional period after delivery of nonconforming goods will not allow avoidance. That seems clear from the admonition in Article 49(1)(b) that avoidance is possible without a showing of a fundamental breach only in non-delivery cases. Moreover, as Article 49(2) (b)(ii) indicates, the buyer's failure to declare the contract avoided within a reasonable time after expiration of the additional period deprives the buyer of its avoidance right.

Finally, this scenario illustrates some additional features of Article 49(2). That provision removes the buyer's right to declare the contract avoided, even if the buyer otherwise would have that right under Article 49(1). Article 49(2), therefore, does not come into play unless the requirements of Article 49(1) have already been satisfied.

---

[183] This assumes that where the buyer has invoked Article 47 Article 49(2)(b)(ii) ("fixed by the buyer in accordance with paragraph (1) of Article 47") trumps Article 49(2)(b)(i).

Moreover, Article 49(2) only removes the buyer's right to avoid the contract in cases where the goods have been delivered. Since Article 49(2) speaks of situations in which goods have been delivered but a right to avoid exists, Article 49(2) is only speaking of cases in which there has been a nonconforming delivery (delivery of defective goods or a late delivery) and the nonconformity is sufficient to constitute a fundamental breach. Thus, Article 49(2) removes the buyer's right to avoid where the buyer suffered a fundamental breach but failed to take appropriate action necessary to avoidance, such as by issuing a timely Article 26 notice of avoidance. In those cases, the buyer loses the right to avoid if it fails to do so within a reasonable time of the events specified in Article 49(2). If the nonconformity takes the form of a late delivery, the buyer must declare the contract avoided within a reasonable time after becoming aware that the delivery has been made. If the nonconformity takes the form of defects in the goods, the buyer must declare the contract avoided within a reasonable time (1) after it knew or should have known of the breach, (2) after the expiration of the additional period for performance granted under Article 47 (or after the seller has declared that it will not perform within that period), or (3) after the additional period indicated by the seller who purports to cure under Article 48 (or after the buyer has declared that it will not accept such cure). We address in Chapter 9.I.B.3 the interesting debate about whether one who fails to satisfy the requirements of Article 49(2) can still attain the benefits of avoidance by reducing the amount payable for defective goods to zero.

Article 49(2) does not address the time within which the aggrieved buyer who has not received delivery and wants to avoid the contract must act. The same gap exists in Article 64(2) when a seller who has not received payment wants to avoid the contract. By their terms, the Articles do not apply to avoidance based on non-delivery or nonpayment. The CISG does not lay down a notice period in these cases. Some commentators maintain that, where the CISG does not state a time limit, the statute of limitations of applicable non-CISG law (treaty or domestic) controls.[184] We do not see how. A statute of limitations sets a time period within which suit may be brought without regard to the timeliness of notice. Its broad purpose is to conserve judicial resources and give the breaching party repose. By contrast, timely notice requirements have a different purpose (reducing the loss from breach) and operate independently of a statute of limitations. For this reason, rules prescribing the timeliness of notice can apply to bar a remedy even if the applicable statute of limitations has not run. Article 39(2)'s two-year cutoff period for giving notice of nonconformity is an example of such a rule.[185] The more likely applicable non-CISG rules governing the timeliness of notice in non-delivery and nonpayment cases involving avoidance are substantive rules of notice, not statutes of limitations.

---

[184] See Ulrich Magnus, *The Remedy of Avoidance of Contract Under CISG—General Remarks and Special Cases*, 26 J. L. & Comm. 423, 429 (2006); Andrea Bjorklund, *Article 26*, in Schlechtriem & Schwenzer, supra note 37, at 357–58 (mentioned as an option).

[185] See supra II.E.

6

Liability for nonconformity

I. INTRODUCTION

Articles 35(1), 35(2), 41, and 42 of the CISG allocate to the seller the risk that goods will fail to conform either to the express requirements of the contract or to certain implied terms. Thus, in everything but name, the Articles describe warranties as to the goods. The language of those Articles will be familiar to the lawyer conversant with the warranties that are called "express warranty," "implied warranty of merchantability," or "implied warranty of fitness for a particular purpose," and "warranty of good title." One backs into the requirements of Articles 35, 41, and 42 by starting with the statement in Article 36 that the seller is liable in accordance with the contract and the CISG for a nonconformity that exists at the time that the risk passes to the buyer. Articles 35, 41, and 42 effectively indicate what constitutes a lack of conformity by stating certain conditions that the seller must satisfy. Article 35 requires that delivered goods are conforming only if they comply with contractual descriptions, quantities, and qualities required by the contract, only if they are contained or packaged in the manner required by the contract, and only if they meet the implied obligations of Article 35(2). The last of these obligations, by virtue of being incorporated into the contract through the CISG, need not be explicitly set forth by the parties. Instead, they will apply "[e]xcept where the parties have agreed otherwise." Those implied obligations require conforming goods to be fit for the purposes for which the described goods would ordinarily be used, to be fit for any particular purpose of which the seller was aware if the buyer reasonably relied on the seller, to possess the qualities of any sample or model held out by the seller, and to be contained or packaged in the manner usual for such goods. Article 41 requires that the goods delivered be free of any claim or right of a third party to them. Article 42 imposes similar requirements with respect to conflicting claims and rights that arise from industrial property or intellectual property law.

Article 35 presents a variety of interpretive difficulties. Whether or not goods satisfy the qualitative requirements of the CISG depends on issues such as the meaning of a contractual "description," the purposes for which the goods ordinarily are used, and any particular purpose of which the seller was aware. We would resolve these ambiguities by defining the scope of liability in a manner consistent with the function of warranty law generally, which we define as placing on a seller the risk of defects that the seller either is or holds itself out to be in the superior position to avoid, reduce, or price. Imposing liability on such a seller makes sense insofar as it reflects the allocation for which the parties themselves otherwise would have bargained. Sellers will make warranties to signal the quality of their goods and to indicate that buyers need not make further investigations into the qualities of goods. If sellers were not responsible for the statements that they make, then buyers either would be lulled into complacency about products whose characteristics turn out to be different than as stated, or would make superfluous and costly investigations into product quality that affect their willingness to transact about otherwise desired goods. Neither sellers (at least honest ones) nor buyers would prefer that state of affairs. As a result, we believe that both sellers and buyers would prefer that the seller bear the obligation to provide goods that conform to contract descriptions and meet implied obligations that arise out of the sellers' superior knowledge. True, warranties may add to sellers' liability and thus to the price of goods. But buyers less well positioned to discern defects or to predict them should be willing to pay the additional price because, assuming that the warranty is priced competitively, they would otherwise incur greater overall costs in making independent investigations or bearing the risk of product quality.

Nevertheless, this rationale for warranty also suggests the limits of the doctrine. If sellers do not have or hold themselves out as having superior information about the product, there is no reason to believe that they are better positioned to avoid or insure against defects. In those circumstances, the buyer would presumably not want to pay the additional premium for a warranty, because the buyer is at least equally able to avoid or insure against defects, and the seller would not want to bear the corresponding liability because it would have insufficient information about how to price it. The meaning of Article 35 should, as we will discuss, be understood in these terms.

II. REQUIREMENTS OF CONFORMING GOODS

A. *The function of "warranties" of quality*

Article 35(1) recites that "the seller must deliver goods which are of the quantity, quality and description required by the contract and which are contained or packaged in the manner required by the contract." The Article essentially transforms the contractual terms into an express warranty, although Article 35 does not formally distinguish between express and implied obligations. Instead, Article 35(1) speaks of terms that are "required by the contract," and Article 35(2) requires that goods satisfy certain conditions in order to "conform with the contract." Presumably, the seller is in a superior position to provide information about the quality of the goods and an accurate description of them because it has manufactured them or is a repeat player in transactions involving similar goods. Buyers will tend to know less about the quality risks or defect rates of goods that they purchase only occasionally. The different levels of knowledge possessed by buyers and sellers represent a problem known in the economics literature as asymmetric information. In the absence of an obligation to provide conforming goods, sellers might exploit their informational advantage by representing that their goods have characteristics that buyers cannot easily evaluate or verify. Under those circumstances, buyers may be unwilling to trust sellers' representations and thus might avoid transactions that, if sellers' representations were trustworthy, would be mutually beneficial. Ideally, a legal default rule would encourage sellers to reveal their superior information by informing buyers about the characteristics of their goods so buyers could make informed purchasing decisions and rely on those representations. A rule that places on the seller liability for nonconformities with its representations achieves that objective, especially in international transactions where the buyer may have difficulty assessing the quality of the goods prior to delivery.

Indeed, sellers of high-quality goods should prefer to bear liability in order to signal the quality of their goods. A simple example will illustrate the analysis that leads to that conclusion.[1] Assume that a buyer is contemplating purchasing a car from a used car dealer at the offered price of $1,000. Also assume that the buyer places a value of $1,200 on the car if it possesses a particular level of quality, but only $600 if it does not. Assume in addition that there are two kinds of sellers of cars: high-quality sellers who sell cars that would be worth $1,200 to the buyer and low-quality sellers who sell cars that would be worth only $600 to the buyer. Assume also that high and low quality sellers are evenly divided, so that the buyer faces a 50 percent chance of purchasing the good from a high-quality seller and a 50 percent chance of purchasing it from a low-quality seller. Finally, assume that at the time of purchase the buyer is unable to determine whether a car it is considering is of high quality or low quality. If there were no law holding sellers liable for their statements, sellers of low-quality cars would advertise their cars as high quality and attempt to sell them at the same price as high-quality cars. If the buyer cannot distinguish between the types of cars prior to purchase, it will treat every car as having an expected value of only $900, that is, a 50 percent chance of having a $1,200 value and a 50 percent chance of having a $600 value. The buyer will not purchase the car at the offered price of $1,000, even though there is a 50 percent chance that the car is

---

[1] Here we draw on Clayton P. Gillette & Franco Ferrari, *Warranties and "Lemons" Under CISG Article 35(2)(a)*, 10 Internationales Handelsrecht 2 (2010).

worth $1,200. If high-quality sellers are unable to convince buyers of their status, they will lose sales that both parties would prefer be made.

Article 35(1) solves this problem by supporting representations made by the seller with a legal commitment that allows buyers to have confidence in the veracity of sellers' statements. Sellers of low-quality goods cannot replicate the statements of sellers of high-quality goods because they would have to pay too much in breach of contract claims to make selling their goods profitable. Armed with a legal commitment, sellers of high-quality goods can credibly represent the character of their goods, and buyers can trust that the description accurately reflects the quality of the goods.

Of course, even sellers who genuinely believe that their goods are of the quality they describe and invest optimally in product quality may still occasionally produce or sell goods that fail due to defects that occur without negligence or fault. In the event that those defects materialize, either the buyer or the seller must bear the related cost. Presumably, if either the seller of the buyer enjoys a cost advantage in insuring against these defects, we would want that party to bear the risk of defects in order to minimize the costs related to the transaction.

Here too, possession of superior information indicates that the seller is better able to bear the risk of defects. Sellers who make repeated sales of the same good typically have better information about defect rates, and thus are better able to incorporate an accurate expected cost of defects into the price of every good that is sold. That cost essentially becomes an insurance premium that buyers pay when they purchase the good. Because buyers, who only buy the goods occasionally, typically do not have the same knowledge of defect rates that sellers have, buyers could not as easily determine whether to insure against obtaining a defective unit.

Again, an example may illustrate the general insurance function of Article 35(1). Assume that a seller of goods expects to sell 1,000 units of a good every year for $1,000 each. The seller knows from historical experience that even if it takes optimal precautions against defects in the manufacturing process, five units every year will be turn out to be worthless. Neither sellers nor buyers, however, can detect which goods are the worthless ones until they are purchased and put into use. Since the total cost of the defects is $5,000 (5 defective units x $1,000 price), sellers would presumably be willing to incur the risk of defects by selling the components to the same 1,000 buyers for $1,005 each. As long as buyers believe that the additional $5 they are paying for the good accurately reflects the expected cost to them of receiving a defective good, buyers would presumably be willing to pay the $5 premium in order to avoid the risk that the good they are purchasing for $1,000 is worthless. Because buyers do not know defect rates as well as sellers, buyers could not easily self-insure against obtaining a defective unit, since they will not know what reserves to create for potential defects. Thus, if buyers and sellers were to bargain explicitly about the allocation of risk of defective goods, one would antici-pate that the majority of contracts would allocate the risk that goods do not meet the seller's description to the seller. Article 35(1) makes these negotiations unnecessary by placing the risk on the seller as the default rule.

B. *Characteristics "required by the contract"*

The inclusion of five characteristics – quantity, quality, description, container, and packaging – indicate that Article 35(1) is intended to include all factual and legal characteristics of the good expressly or impliedly agreed on by the parties. In theory, each one of these terms has a separate meaning. However, in practice, it is often difficult to distinguish among them. Take, for example, the ostensibly separate characteristics of the quality and description of a good. Where a buyer asks for green widgets and a seller delivers blue widgets, the delivered goods differ from the contract description even though their quality, that is, their capacity to function in the way that the buyer anticipated, may be the same. Quality may also include non-physical conditions, such as compliance with industry standards of production, or, in the view of some, compliance with labor regulations.[2] However, the terms "quality" and "description" will often be conflated.[3] For example, when a buyer asks for a metal desk, the term "metal" is both a description and a quality term.

The phrase "required by the contract" following both clauses in Article 35(1) directs courts to interpret the terms of the contract to determine the descriptions, quantity, quality, or packaging to which the parties have agreed and to which the goods as delivered must conform. Unlike some domestic law, however, Article 35(1) contains no requirement that the descriptions or representations made by the seller form the basis of the bargain or that the buyer rely on the statement.[4] Instead, the CISG assumes that any term in the contract relating to quantity, quality, or description of the goods, or any term concerning packaging and containers is a relevant term for purposes of a conforming delivery. Therefore, courts need not delve into the difficult question of whether a statement of the seller constituted a basis of the bargain. The buyer is presumably purchasing the seller's representations, which would be factored into the price in a well-operating market, even if the buyer is not necessarily relying on their accuracy.

Assume, for example, that the buyer is purchasing a good that the seller represents has characteristics, such as a corking machine that is described as capable of corking a specified number of wine bottles per hour. Assume further that at the time of sale

---

[2] See Stefan Kröll, *Article 35*, in UN Convention on Contracts for the International Sale of Goods (CISG): Commentary 495 (Stefan Kröll, Loukas Mistelis & Pilar Perales Viscasillas eds., 2011) [hereinafter "Kröll et al."]; Ingeborg Schwenzer, *Article 35*, in Schlechtriem & Schwenzer: Commentary on the Convention on the International Sale of Goods (CISG) 573 (Ingeborg Schwenzer ed., 3d ed. 2010) [hereinafter "Schlechtriem & Schwenzer"].

[3] See René Franz Henschel, The Conformity of Goods in International Sales: An Analysis of Article 35 in the United Nations Convention on Contracts for the International Sale of Goods 159 (2005).

[4] Compare U.C.C. § 2–313(1).

the buyer does not anticipate utilizing the machine to full capacity and therefore is indifferent to that representation. Subsequent to the purchase, the buyer increases its production and discovers that the corking machine does not satisfy the represented capacity. The buyer would have an action under Article 35(1), notwithstanding that it did not rely on or otherwise base its purchase on the nonconforming characteristic.

Nevertheless, it is still essential to ask whether the purported representation with which the goods do not conform constitutes a term of the contract. There is substantial room for parties to debate about what terms are actually incorporated into a contract governed by the CISG.[5]

1. Extrinsic evidence to determine contract terms

Article 35(1) is not limited to express terms. In that sense, the phrase "required by the contract" may vary from the express warranty created by a writing. Because the CISG does not contain a parol evidence rule,[6] extrinsic evidence can be used to determine the terms of the contract. Descriptions of goods that are found in advertisements or that are made during negotiations or that can be inferred from conduct of a party will also become part of the contract if, in accordance with Article 8, they are deemed to have been intended by the speaker or actor to be incorporated.[7] Failure to provide compressors that conformed to specification sheets provided by the seller constituted a violation of Article 35 in one of the earlier American CISG cases.[8] A Russian arbitration tribunal concluded that, notwithstanding the absence of quality requirements both in the contract itself and appendices to it, quality descriptions in documents sent by the seller prior to execution of the appendices created obligations of conformity under Article 35.[9] Descriptions "required by the contract" may be implied from the statements or conduct of the parties, even though no affirmative description is provided. A Swiss appellate court concluded that a seller who made a series of statements that lulled the buyer into believing that it was purchasing a packaging machine that could perform a certain number of operations per minute could not later claim that the contract did not call for satisfaction of that requirement, even if it was impossible to produce such a product.[10]

---

[5] See Clayton P. Gillette & Steven D. Walt, Sales Law: Domestic and International 370–71 (3d ed. 2016).

[6] See Chapter 4.IV.

[7] See, e.g., Court of Appeal (New Zealand) (*RJ & AM Smallman v. Transport Sales Ltd.*), 22 July 2011, available at http://cisgw3.law.pace.edu/cases/110722n6.html.

[8] See *Delchi Carrier SpA v. Rotorex Corp.*, 71 F.3d 1024 (2d Cir. 1995).

[9] See Tribunal of International Commercial Arbitration at the Russian Federation Chamber of Commerce and Industry (Russia), 6 June 2003, available at http://cisgw3.law.pace.edu/cases/030606r1.html.

[10] See Court of Appeals Basel-Stadt (Switzerland), 26 September 2008, available at http://cisgw3.law.pace.edu/cases/080926s1.html.

Similarly, terms implied from trade usage and prior practices between the parties can become a part of the contract under Article 9.[11] Assume, for instance, that the seller and the buyer enter into a contract for 100 cartons of apples. Assume further that it is widely known and regularly observed in international trade that a seller can deliver a quantity of apples within 5 percent of the agreed on amount due to the variability of harvests. When the seller delivers ninety-five cartons of apples, the buyer may argue that the delivery is nonconforming. But Article 9(2) states that "the parties are considered, unless otherwise agreed, to have impliedly made applicable to their contract or its formation a usage of which the parties knew or ought to have known and which in international trade is widely known to, and regularly observed by, parties to contracts of the type involved in the particular trade concerned." If the buyer ought to have known about this trade usage, the goods conform to the contract under Article 35 because the trade usage became a term of the contract.[12]

This was the approach taken by the Austrian Supreme Court, although the case formally involved Article 35(2)(c) rather than Article 35(1).[13] A Dutch seller offered to ship frozen fish to an Austrian buyer. Before reaching an agreement, the buyer had pouches of similar fish, not drawn from the bulk offered for sale, tested. The buyer then ordered twenty-four tons of the fish. The buyer failed to inspect the goods on delivery to its own plant, because the goods were expected to be shipped immediately to their ultimate destination in Latvia. When the container of fish arrived in Latvia, it was not allowed through customs because the fish had been caught more than a year earlier. The buyer complained that the goods were nonconforming in that they had come from a prior year's catch and, according to the buyer, commercial custom within the international fish business required that the fish come from the most recent year's catch. The trial court had determined that such a custom did exist, but an appellate court had rejected some of those findings. The Supreme Court found that the appellate court had followed an improper procedure in rejecting the findings related to the trade usage and remanded the case to the appellate court for "concrete determinations regarding the existence of the claimed trade custom." But the Supreme Court's opinion made clear that if the seller had knowledge that such a custom existed, its violation constituted a nonconformity.

2. Opinions and other representations not included as contractual obligations

Some representations made by parties during negotiations will not be "required by the contract," because those representations were not intended to be part of the

---

[11] See Henschel, supra note 3, at 161; Peter Huber & Alastair Mullis, The CISG 131 (2007); Stefan Kröll, *Article 35*, in Kröll et al., supra note 2, at 499–501; Gillette & Walt, supra note 5, at 362.

[12] See Ontario Superior Court of Justice (Canada), (*La San Giuseppe* v. *Forti Moulding Ltd.*), 31 August 1999, available at http://cisgw3.law.pace.edu/cases/990831c4.html; Schwenzer, *Article 35*, in Schlechtriem & Schwenzer, supra note 3, at 572; Gillette & Walt, supra note 5, at 125; Henschel, supra note 3, at 151; Stefan Kröll, *Article 35*, in Kröll et al., supra note 2, at 494.

[13] See Supreme Court (Austria), 27 February 2003, available at http://cisgw3.law.pace.edu/cases/030227a3.html.

contract at all. Statements that are reasonably understood as puffery or mere opinion are, therefore, not necessarily "descriptions" of the goods. Thus, a claim that the buyer is getting a "good deal" will not constitute a misrepresentation even if the buyer pays an above average amount for the good, because the claim merely amounted to an opinion of the seller.[14] Statements of substantial generality or that are commonly understood as "sales talk" typically will not serve as descriptions to which the goods must conform. A seller who remarks "This is the best drill press ever made," should be understood to be saying something quite different from one who specifies a particular speed or rate of operation. If we return to the function of "warranty" as a solution to the problem of asymmetric information, it is improbable that the buyer will have a basis for believing that the seller has superior information about every drill press ever made. But a buyer is likely to conclude that a seller who represents that "this drill press contains a 1/3" HP 120V motor that will drive the chuck from 500 to 3,100 rpm" has made specific investigations necessary to support the statement, and thus has the kind of superior information that justifies the imposition of liability for nonconformity in the first instance.

Making the distinction between expressions of opinion and expressions of fact may be difficult. As a general matter, the greater the detail in a statement alleging specific and verifiable characteristics of the goods ("this corking machine will cork 200 bottles per hour") rather than general comparisons or recommendations ("this corking machine is faster than most of its competitors"), the more likely it is reasonable for the party at whom the statement is directed to interpret it as a description under Article 35. If liability for nonconformity is justified in part on reducing search costs for buyers, then the more verifiable a statement is, the more it is appropriate to incorporate that statement into the requirements of conformity, since the statement implies that the seller has already undertaken any inquiries necessary to support it.

One additional problem that arises in international trade is that language or cultural differences may lead the party who makes the statement to have a different view of its meaning than the recipient of the statement. Cultural differences or difficulties in translation may complicate efforts to determine whether information conveyed by the seller is mere puffery or was an agreed term of the contract.[15] One could easily imagine a statement made by the speaker in his or her native language with an element of sarcasm, exaggeration, or humor being interpreted as a sincere representation by a non-native listener unfamiliar with linguistic nuances. Article 8 places the risk of such misinterpretation on the speaker. Under Article 8(1), the speaker's subjective intent or meaning will apply only if the other party knew or could not have been unaware of it. Under Article 8(2), where the other party

---

[14] See *Miami Valley Paper, LLC* v. *Lebbing Engineering & Consulting GmbH*, 2006 U.S. Dist. LEXIS 25201 (S.D. Ohio October 10, 2006) (claim of negligent misrepresentation in CISG case).

[15] See Gillette & Walt, supra note 5, at 370–71.

reasonably is unaware of the speaker's intent, a speaker's statement is interpreted according to the understanding that a reasonable person of the same kind as the other party would have had in the same circumstances. Article 8(3) instructs a court to consider "all relevant circumstances" when determining the intentions of the party making the statement or the understanding a reasonable person would have, and the cultural or linguistic background of the buyer would serve as one of those circumstances.

C. Scope of nonconformity

Courts tend to read the conformity requirement of Article 35(1) strictly. If the parties have agreed on a specified quantity, delivering less or more than that quantity will constitute a nonconformity.[16] In the absence of any trade usage to the contrary, the seller is liable for even the smallest discrepancies from the contract quantity.[17] If the parties have agreed to a certain quality or description of the goods, any failure to conform to that quality or description will constitute nonconformity.[18] The degree of the discrepancy will, of course, be relevant when assessing the correct remedy. Because an immaterial discrepancy would not likely amount to a fundamental breach of contract under Article 25, the buyer would not be able to avoid the contract. Therefore, an immaterial breach would only entitle the buyer to repair, reduction in price, or damages in accordance with the impact of the discrepancy on the buyer.[19] Similarly, if parties agree to an approximate quantity of goods, delivering outside the range dictated by application of Article 8 and Article 9 would constitute a nonconformity.

If the seller delivers the goods before a fixed delivery date, the buyer may accept delivery or refuse the goods.[20] In the event that the seller delivers more goods than were agreed to, the buyer may take delivery of or reject the excess goods. A buyer who desires to reject the excess goods must treat that excess as a nonconformity and comply with the notice requirements of Article 39, and must preserve them under

---

[16] See Supreme Court (Switzerland), 7 July 2004, available at http://cisgw3.law.pace.edu/cases/040707s1.html; Commercial Court Zürich (Switzerland), 21 September 1998, available at http://cisgw3.law.pace.edu/cases/980921s1.html; Court of Appeals Koblenz (Germany), 31 January 1997, available at http://cisgw3.law.pace.edu/cases/970131g1.html.

[17] See Henschel, supra note 3, at 35; Stefan Kröll, *Article* 35, in Kröll et al., supra note 2, at 493; Ingeborg Schwenzer, *Article* 35, in Schlechtriem & Schwenzer, supra note 2, at 585.

[18] See *Delchi Carrier SpA v. Rotorex Corp.*, 71 F.3d 1024 (2d Cir. 1995); District Court Paderborn (Germany), 25 June 1996, available at http://cisgw3.law.pace.edu/cases/960625g1.html; Western High Court (Denmark), 10 November 1991, available at http://cisgw3.law.pace.edu/cases/991110d1.html; Federal Supreme Court (Germany), 8 March 1995, available at http://cisgw3.law.pace.edu/cases/950308g3.html; Court of Appeals Köln (Germany), 21 May 1996, available at http://cisgw3.law.pace.edu/cases/960521g1.html; ICC Case No. 6653, 26 March 1993, available at http://cisgw3.law.pace.edu/cases/936653i1.html and www.unilex.info/case.cfm?pid=1&do=case&id=36&step=Abstract.

[19] See Kröll, *Article* 35, in Kröll et al., supra note 2, at 493.   [20] See Article 52(1).

Article 86. The buyer would presumably then have a right to return or store the excess goods and claim reimbursement for its expenses under the damage provisions of the CISG. A buyer who fails to give notice under Article 39 or who accepts the excess goods must pay for them at the contract rate.[21]

If the parties have agreed on how the goods should be contained or packaged, delivering goods that do not conform to that agreement will constitute a nonconformity.[22] Clearly this would be the case if the nonconformity causes damage to the goods that would have been avoided by conforming packaging. Wholly apart from Article 35 (1), improper packaging that causes damage to the goods will render the seller responsible even if the damage materializes after the risk of loss has passed to the buyer, since the improper packaging would constitute an act or omission of the seller.[23] But the obligation to deliver conforming goods is violated even if the packaging or container does not affect the actual quality or description of the goods. Typically, a technical nonconformity that does not affect the goods will not give the buyer any rights to remedies. One could imagine, however, a situation in which the packaging has independent value such as the packaging of brand name electronics. In such a case, the nonconformity may have substantial effect on the value of the good.

D. *Nonconformity or non-delivery?*

Assume that a contract calls for the delivery of five carloads of corn and the seller delivers five carloads of cotton. Is this a nonconforming delivery or a total failure to deliver? The question is by no means a purely academic one. If the delivery of completely different goods were construed as a non-delivery of goods, for instance, Article 39(1) would not require the buyer to give notice of the breach. But if the same delivery were considered a delivery – albeit of nonconforming goods – the buyer would be obligated to give notice of breach in accordance with Article 39(1). Moreover, Article 49(1)(b) provides a buyer with an alternative right to avoid the contract in the case of non-delivery, and Article 49(2) limits the buyer's right to avoid in the case of delivery. Thus, even though substantial deviations from contract requirements will likely constitute a fundamental breach regardless of whether the seller is considered to have made a nonconforming delivery or no delivery, the differences in the buyer's rights may be significant.

The domestic law of some Western European countries treats the delivery of a wholly different good, or *aliud*, as a failure to deliver rather than a delivery of nonconforming goods.[24] There is some support in the Secretariat's Commentary

---

[21] See Article 52(2).

[22] See Compromex Arbitration Proceeding (Mexico), 29 April 1996, available at http://cisgw3.law .pace.edu/cases/960429m1.html.

[23] See Article 66.

[24] See Schwenzer, *Article 35*, in Schlechtriem & Schwenzer, supra note 2, at 574; Cagdas Evrim Ergun, Comparative Study of the 1980 Vienna Sales Convention and Turkish Sales Law,

for the proposition that the distinction is incorporated into the CISG. The Secretariat's Commentary on Article 29 (now Article 31) states that "[i]f the contract calls for the delivery of corn, the seller has not delivered if he provides potatoes."[25] The Secretariat's Commentary on Article 33 (now Article 35) states, "[u]nder this convention if the seller has handed over or placed at the buyer's disposal goods which meet the general description of the contract, he has 'delivered the goods' even though the goods do not conform in respect of quantity or quality."[26] The Secretariat's Commentary could be interpreted to say that courts should apply Article 35 to small differences in the goods delivered and apply Article 30 when the seller delivers wholly different goods. Other commentators, however, reject this view and conclude that even a delivery of different goods falls into the category of nonconforming delivery, thus triggering notice requirements.[27]

An early case of the German Supreme Court appeared to adopt the latter view when it ruled, in a case involving a delivery of cobalt sulfate of different composition and origin than was required, that "the CISG does not differentiate between delivery of different goods and delivery of goods that do not conform to the contract."[28] But the court then muddled the issue by proclaiming that it did not have to decide "whether, in the event of a blatant divergence from the contractual condition, a non-delivery in the meaning of Art. 49(1)(b) CISG can arise." Thus, it left open the possibility that Article 35 would not apply to "blatant" differences. Subsequent courts appear to have adopted the view that even goods with substantial deviations constitute "deliveries" under the CISG, although those comments appear to be dictum because the cases involved "insignificant" defects.[29]

available at www.cisg.law.pace.edu/cisg/biblio/ergun.html (Turkish law); Ingeborg Schwenzer & Pascal Hachem, *The CISG—Successes and Pitfalls*, 57 Am. J. Comp. L. 457, 465 ns. 43&44 (2009) (Swiss law). German law no longer recognizes the *aliud*; it considers the delivery of different goods as delivery of nonconforming goods. See Burgerliches Gesetzbuch [BGB] [Civil Code] § 434(3) (Ger.) ("a material defect").

[25] Secretariat Commentary on the 1978 Draft, in Documentary History of the Uniform Law on International Sales 419 (now Article 31, para. 3) (John O. Honnold ed., 1989) [hereinafter Documentary History].

[26] Secretariat Commentary on the 1978 Draft, in Documentary History, supra note id. at 422 (former Article 33, para 2).

[27] See Schwenzer, *Article 35*, in Schlechtriem & Schwenzer, supra note 2, at 574; Franco Ferrari, *Applicability and Applications of the Vienna Sales Convention (CISG)*, Int'l Legal Forum 137, 231 n. 843 (1998); Kröll, *Article 35*, in Kröll et al., supra note 2, at 492, 497; John O. Honnold, Uniform Law for International Sales Under the 1980 United Nations Sales Convention 368–69 (Harry M. Flechtner ed., 4th ed. 2009) [hereinafter "Honnold/Flechtner"].

[28] Federal Supreme Court (Germany), 3 April 1996, available at http://cisgw3.law.pace.edu/cases/ 960403g1.html. A previous decision by a German appellate court did treat the delivery of fabrics in a color not ordered by the buyer as an *aliud*, or non-delivery. See Court of Appeals Düsseldorf (Germany), 10 February 1994, available at http://cisgw3.law.pace.edu/cases/ 940210g2.html.

[29] See, e.g., Court of Appeals Düsseldorf (Germany), 21 April 2004, available at http://cisgw3.law .pace.edu/cases/040421g2.html. See also Lower Court Viechtach (Germany), 11 April 2002, available at http://cisgw3.law.pace.edu/cases/020411g1.html.

We agree with those commentators who conclude that the burden on the buyer of noticing such a substantial discrepancy is typically small enough that it should be obligated to give notice.[30] Requiring notice of nonconformity in these cases facilitates the reintroduction into commerce of goods unwanted by the buyer in the disputed transaction. In the case of "different" goods, there is less reason to suspect that the tendered goods are defective rather than inappropriate for the buyer's purposes. As a result, they may be perfectly appropriate for some other buyer, such as a purchaser of cotton in our earlier example. Timely notice that the goods are "different" from those contracted for facilitates the prompt resale to another buyer. Treating the "different" goods as nonconforming within the meaning of Article 35 triggers the notice requirement and thus expedites the transfer of the goods to those who can make use of them. Article 38(1) requires the buyer to examine "the goods" delivered within a practicable period, and Article 39(1) bars the buyer from relying on a remedy if it fails to notice of the nonconformity of "the goods" within a reasonable time after it discovered or ought to have discovered the nonconformity. "The goods" in both Articles easily include delivered goods that are completely different from those called for by the contract.

III. FITNESS OF GOODS FOR THEIR ORDINARY USES

Article 35(2)(a) requires sellers to deliver goods that "are fit for the purposes for which goods of the same description would ordinarily be used."[31] The language creates an obligation similar to an implied warranty of merchantability that often arises under domestic law and that requires the merchant seller to deliver goods that satisfy certain standards.[32] Article 35(2)(a) shifts the losses arising from both fraudulent and unintentional defects onto the seller. As in the case of Article 35(1), this allocation of risk is appropriate where the seller has superior information concerning the quality of the goods and thus is better positioned to avoid defects or to insure against them, and to take the defect rate into account when determining the price of the goods. And, as in the case of Article 35(1), the allocation reflects the bargain that informed parties would otherwise reach because it allows high-quality sellers to signal the quality of their goods in a reliable manner, while low-quality sellers will tend to disclaim the obligation in order to avoid liability.

---

[30] See, e.g., Kröll, *Article 35*, in Kröll et al., supra note 2, at 492; Schwenzer, *Article 35*, in Schlechtriem & Schwenzer, supra note 2, at 574.

[31] See ICC, Arbitral Award No. 10377, available at http://cisgw3.law.pace.edu/cases/020377i1.html; Court of Appeal Grenoble (France), 15 May 1996, available at http://cisgw3.law.pace.edu/cases/960515f1.html; Supreme Court (France), 23 January 1996, available at http://cisgw3.law.pace.edu/cases/960123f1.html.

[32] See, e.g., U.C.C. § 2–314.

A decision by the German Federal Supreme Court helps to explicate the meaning of "ordinarily be used."[33] A German seller agreed to sell ground clay to a Dutch buyer under the contract description "Potato Separation Clay A01." The clay was to be used to grade potatoes in a process that involved passing the potatoes through water in which the clay was mixed. Certain grades of the potatoes put through the process were sold by the buyer as animal feed to feed producers. After the seller discovered elevated levels of dioxins in its clay, it delivered a shipment to the buyer. The court found that the clay did not conform to the contract under Article 35(1) and Article 35(2)(a). In concluding that the clay did not meet Article 35(2)(a)'s requirement of fitness for ordinary purposes, the court determined that the presence of dioxins was inconsistent with the expectations of an average purchaser of ground clay, based on common use of the product. But the court also noted that uses outside of that range do not give rise to Article 35(2)(a) warranties: "The goods, in order to fulfill these user expectations, do not have to be fit for all theoretically perceivable forms and possibilities of use, but only for such uses that suggest themselves in light of the material and technical specificities of the goods and reasonable market expectation based thereon." Here, it was common knowledge that the seller's clay would be used to separate the potatoes and that potatoes not fit for human consumption would be sold for animal feed.

Once the seller was aware that its clay was not appropriate for one of the obvious uses to be made of the goods, failure to disclose the dioxin contamination meant that Article 35(2)(a) had been breached. Moreover, the fact that the buyer could have remedied the situation at low cost, by simply rinsing the potatoes, did not excuse the seller's failure to disclose the nonconformity, even though the buyer had general knowledge of the need to avoid impurities in the animal feed that it delivered. Since rinsing was not required by any regulation and the buyer had no reason to be aware of the dioxin contamination, the buyer was under no obligation to take steps that would have alleviated the situation. The court's conclusion is consistent with the use of warranty liability to solve the problem of asymmetric information. The seller, who had superior knowledge about the presence of the dioxins, was better able to bear the risk that its clay contains them – or to disclose the situation – than the buyer. The seller's comparatively better position does not change even if the buyer later could take measures to avoid the risk or its impact. Had the seller taken advantage of its position and disclosed the information, the buyer could have either bargained for dioxin-free material or for a price reduction that reflected the buyer's need to incur additional costs to avoid contamination. The fact that the buyer likely would have demanded a lower price for goods with the characteristics that it received indicates that it received goods of a different description than what it bargained for and what the contract price suggested.

---

[33] See Federal Supreme Court (Germany), 26 September 2012, available at http://cisgw3.law.pace.edu/cases/120926g1.html.

The case does contain an interesting anomaly, however. After concluding that the buyer was not obligated to alleviate the problem by rinsing the potatoes, the court went on to find that the buyer had breached its contractual duty to ascertain that the clay did not pose health risks for humans or animals. The court appears to have meant a contractual duty to the seller, rather than to the clay buyer's own downstream buyers of potatoes for animal feed. Accordingly, the court saw the issue raised by the case as one of how the CISG calculates the buyer's damages when both contracting parties contribute to the buyer's loss by breaching the contract. This misunderstands the economic purpose served by obligations to comply with descriptions of goods. Articles 35(1) and 35(2)(a) allocate the risk of nonconformity to the seller and away from the buyer. Where the seller has sold clay used for sorting potatoes and that sale carries a commitment that the clay is usable for its ordinary purpose, the buyer is relieved of the responsibility of verifying that the clay can safely be used to produce animal feed. The seller therefore is liable if the delivered clay contained dioxins even if the buyer later could have avoided loss by rinsing its graded potatoes. The CISG provides the limitations on Article 35 liability. Articles 38 and 39 relieve the seller of responsibility where the buyer fails to provide timely notice of nonconformities of which the buyer should have been aware. But neither of those provisions deviates from the principle that sellers bear liability for nonconformities in the situation that was before the court.[34] Article 38 requires the buyer to timely inspect the goods, and Article 39(1) requires it to give the seller timely notice of nonconformities in them. However, neither Article applies when the seller is aware of the nonconformities before delivery, as the seller was in the case.[35]

The remaining limitations on Article 35 liability are found in the explicit language of the Article itself. As we discuss later, Article 35(3) absolves the seller of liability where the buyer knew or could not have been unaware of the nonconformity, that is, where there is no asymmetric information problem for liability to solve. But that provision arguably draws the limit of the conditions under which the seller can avoid liability for nonconformities. Moreover, liability under Article 35 is strict. The absence of fault is irrelevant. To the extent that the court's analysis of the contribution of each party to the damage reflects principles of comparative fault, such concerns do not enter into the equation. The court, by finding that the buyer breached its duty of reasonable care with respect to the clay, leaves the risk that the clay contains dioxins on the buyer. This is inconsistent with its previous finding that the seller had warranted that the clay did not contain dioxins.

However, even if sellers should bear the risk for product defects generally, the justifications for liability indicate that sellers should not necessarily bear the risk of every nonconformity. In a situation where the buyer has superior information we would expect the parties to place the risk of default on the buyer. One would imagine that sellers have superior information when their goods are being used in

---

[34] See Chapter 5.II.F.   [35] See Article 40.

the same manner by a large number of buyers. It is under those circumstances that sellers will receive feedback about the utility of their goods and it is with respect to common uses that sellers will provide qualitative protections during the manufacturing process. The limitation of Article 35(2)(a) to "purposes for which goods of the same description would ordinarily be used" can be understood in these terms.

Conversely, there are two common circumstances in international sales where the buyer has information equal to or superior to that of the seller concerning potential defects with the good: (1) when the buyer plans to use the good for an idiosyncratic purpose; and (2) where the regulatory standards of the buyer's jurisdiction differ from those in the seller's jurisdiction. In the first situation, the buyer has unique requirements for the goods that the seller is not likely to consider during the manufacturing process or in pricing the risk of product defects. Sellers will only take into account the normal or ordinary use to which the good is put and thus the normal risks to which the good is subjected. The buyer occupies the best position to ensure that the goods are fit for its purposes by informing the seller of any unique requirements. For instance, a buyer who needs an underwater camera cannot expect the seller of an average camera to impliedly warrant that the camera is waterproof. Thus, while it is sensible for sellers to make warranties with respect to the ordinary use of the good, no efficiency gain is likely to arise when the sellers are responsible for unanticipated uses of the good.

A. Compliance with regulatory standards in the jurisdiction of use

The preceding analysis also suggests the proper resolution of those cases that concern an alleged breach of Article 35(2)(a) in the second situation identified: where a seller delivers goods that satisfy product standards in the seller's jurisdiction but not those of the buyer's jurisdiction. These cases have proven controversial. But assuming that buyers of goods have superior information about the prevailing regulations in their jurisdictions, most buyers and sellers would negotiate for a warranty that only guaranteed that the goods would comply with the regulations in the seller's country, unless the buyer has disclosed its relevant domestic regulations. The reasoning fits the model of asymmetric information that we have suggested underlies Article 35. Most buyers are in a better position than their sellers to discover information about regulatory standards that are applicable in their jurisdictions but not their sellers' jurisdictions. Thus, it will be less costly for buyers to convey that information to sellers than for sellers to obtain it on their own. The appropriate legal rule should therefore induce buyers to convey the information. Imposing liability on the seller only if it violates regulations of which it has or should have knowledge induces the buyer to convey the information, because the buyer otherwise bears the risk that the goods will not be usable in its jurisdiction. Armed with the relevant information, the seller can make the necessary determination of its own product (about which it has superior information) and, if appropriate, adjust the goods or the contract price. The buyer's disclosure eliminates any asymmetric information about the requirements in its own jurisdiction.

But the argument applies only where the buyer has superior information about regulatory requirements. Thus, the argument does not hold when there is reason to believe that the seller has or should have knowledge of the requirements of the buyer's jurisdiction. This may be the case, for example, where the seller is a repeat player in the buyer's jurisdiction and can be expected to have learned the relevant regulatory requirements or where it can amortize the cost of discovering them over numerous transactions, so that such investigation becomes more worthwhile than if the seller entered into a single transaction in the buyer's jurisdiction. In this case the seller and buyer would likely negotiate for a warranty that guaranteed conformity with regulatory standards in the buyer's jurisdiction.

This analysis is consistent with the approach of the famous (or infamous) "mussels" case decided by the German Supreme Court.[36] A Swiss seller and a German buyer entered into a contract for mussels. The mussels were delivered with a sufficiently high concentration of cadmium that a governmental agency in Germany declared them "not harmless," although the seller maintained that the cadmium content did not exceed the permitted limit. The Supreme Court determined that the cadmium contamination alleged by the buyer did not prevent the goods from conforming to contract requirements. The court admitted that there might be reservations about the quality of the mussels if German public law provisions concerning cadmium were relevant. But, the court concluded, that was not the case. Sellers were not expected to comply with "specialized public law provisions of the buyer's country or the country of use." The regulations of the buyer's country would apply only where the same standard exists in the both the seller's country and the buyer's country or where the buyer had specified the applicable standards and relied on the seller's expertise to satisfy them. Additionally, the court raised four special circumstances where the regulations of the destination may apply: (1) the seller maintains a branch in the importing country; (2) the seller had a long-standing business connection with the buyer; (3) the seller often exported goods in the buyer's country; or (4) the seller has promoted products in that country.

The exceptions cited in the case are consistent with the asymmetric information rationale for implied obligations of conformity, since they describe situations in which the seller is more likely to have information about regulations in the buyer's jurisdiction. Indeed, a decision of the New Zealand Court of Appeal explained a refusal to incorporate the regulations of a buyer's jurisdiction into Article 35(2)(a) explicitly on that rationale.[37] That case involved a sale from New Zealand to

---

[36] See Federal Supreme Court (Germany), 8 March 1999, available at http://cisgw3.law.pace.edu/cases/950308g3.html.

[37] See Court of Appeal (New Zealand), (*RJ & AM Smallman* v. *Transport Sales Ltd.*), 22 July 2011, available at http://cisgw3.law.pace.edu/cases/110722n6.html.

Australia of trucks that did not comply with requirements of the latter necessary to permit full registration and use. The court concluded that although the seller had made previous sales to Australian buyers, the buyers "were in a much better position than [the seller] to know the registration requirements of their own country." Indeed, the prior sales had occurred without difficulty, so there was no reason for the seller to be aware that its goods were noncompliant. Moreover, the seller had provided the buyer with names of persons who could assist with the importation process, thereby signaling that the seller itself lacked the requisite knowledge.

The majority of courts have followed this approach, holding that the term "ordinarily be used" under Article 35(2)(a) will be determined from the perspective of the seller's country, while maintaining the exceptions discussed in the mussels case.[38] For instance, when the same standard exists in both countries, compliance with that regulation will be required under Article 35(2)(a). This may have special significance in trade between countries of the European Union. Numerous regulations have been harmonized within the EU, and in those cases courts are likely to apply the uniform regulation rather than limit the seller's obligation to compliance with domestic regulations.[39] Nevertheless, there are decisions that conflict with or limit the reach of the "mussels" case, and leading commentators find it controversial.[40] An American district court confirmed an arbitral award that was based on the case, but that found one of the German court's exceptions to be applicable.[41]

One of the leading commentators on the CISG has convincingly argued with the rationale more than with the result of the mussels case.[42] Schlechtriem concluded that a seller that has been made aware of the country of use of the goods must observe the applicable public laws in that country, because the seller is impliedly aware of the particular purpose to which the buyer is going to put the goods. Schlechtriem, therefore, would analyze the case under Article 35(2)(b) rather than Article 35(2)(a). That analysis would not necessarily lead to the seller's liability, however. As we will discuss, the seller in such a situation is only liable if the buyer reasonably relied on the seller's skill and judgment. If the buyer was not aware that a seller had reason to be familiar with the domestic regulations in the place of use, the

---

[38] See Federal Supreme Court (Germany), 2 March 2005, available at http://cisgw3.law.pace.edu/cases/050302g1.html; Supreme Court (Austria), 13 April 2000, available at http://cisgw3.law.pace.edu/cases/000413a3.html; District Court (Netherlands), 15 October 2008, available at http://cisgw3.law.pace.edu/cases/081015n2.html; Court of Appeals Versailles (France), 13 October 2005, available at http://cisgw3.law.pace.edu/cases/051013n1.html; *Medical Mktg. Int'l, Inc. v. Internazionale Medico Scientifica, S.R.L.*, 1999 U.S. Dist. LEXIS 7380 (E.D. La. May 17, 1999).

[39] See Court of Appeals Versailles (France), 13 October 2005, available at http://cisgw3.law.pace.edu/cases/051013f1.html.

[40] See Court of Appeals Grenoble (France), 9 September 1995, available at http://cisgw3.law.pace.edu/cases/950913f1.html.

[41] See *Medical Mktg. Int'l, Inc. v. Internazionale Medico Scientifica, S.R.L.*, 1999 U.S. Dist. LEXIS 7380 (E.D. La. May 17, 1999).

[42] See Peter Schlechtriem, Uniform Sales Law in the Decisions of the Bundesgerichtshof, available at http://cisgw3.law.pace.edu/cisg/biblio/schlechtriem3.html.

buyer would have difficulty demonstrating that it exercised the requisite reasonable reliance on the seller. The situations in which a buyer could reasonably rely on the seller's judgment basically reflect the exceptions stated in the "mussels" case, that is, where the seller was a repeat player in the buyer's jurisdiction or otherwise had substantially invested in that jurisdiction. In essence, this conclusion means that compliance with regulations becomes a matter of construing the intent of the parties. Rather than woodenly applying a rule that the regulations of the seller's jurisdiction is applicable, proper analysis requires determining under Article 8 whether the negotiations and documents that constitute the contract reveal an intent that the seller take the risk of compliance with the regulations of the destination jurisdiction.

B. *The scope of "ordinary use"*

Ordinary use need not be restricted to a single type of use. The asymmetric information justification for the implied obligation indicates that ordinary use will include any use that is common for the goods at issue. Bottles used for soft drinks must be produced in a manner that allows their contents to be consumed, even if those contents range from soft drinks to alcoholic beverages.[43] On the same logic, not all discrepancies in goods constitute a violation of the Article 35(2)(a) obligation. Tribunals have determined that technical nonconformities that do not diminish the average buyer's valuation of the good do not violate the warranty.[44] Thus, printed materials containing misplaced text that does not render its meaning illegible may still conform to the contract.[45] Plants that are healthy, but not fit for the climate in which the buyer uses them, do not violate the obligation.[46] Used goods that exhibit normal wear and tear are fit for the purposes for which goods of that description would ordinarily be used, especially if their price reflects those imperfections.[47] A small number of nonconforming goods within a larger shipment do not render the entire shipment nonconforming if a similar shipment from any other seller would include a similar amount of defects, where the remaining defects reflect optimal efforts by sellers to avoid nonconformities and only idiosyncratic buyers would

---

[43] See Supreme Court of New South Wales (Australia), (*Fryer Holdings* v. *Liaoning MEC Group*), 30 January 2012, available at www.globalsaleslaw.org/content/api/cisg/urteile/2325.pdf.

[44] See Ontario Superior Court of Justice (Canada) (*La San Giuseppe* v. *Forti Moulding Ltd.*), 31 August 1999, available at: http://cisgw3.law.pace.edu/cases/990831c4.html; see also Commercial Court Hasselt (Belgium), 28 June 2006, available at http://cisgw3.law.pace.edu/cases/060628b1.html; International Chamber of Commerce, Arbitral Award No. 8247, available at http://cisgw3.law.pace.edu/cases/968247i1.html; Commercial Court Zürich (Switzerland), 21 September 1998, available at http://cisgw3.law.pace.edu/cases/980921s1.html.

[45] Id.

[46] See District Court Coburg (Germany), 12 December 2006, available at http://cisgw3.law.pace .edu/cases/061212g1.html.

[47] See Supreme Court (Spain), 17 January 2008, available at http://cisgw3.law.pace.edu/cases/ 080117s4.html.

demand a higher level of quality. In a case decided by the Ontario Superior Court of Justice, an Italian seller had a long-term business relationship with a Canadian buyer for picture frame moldings.[48] The buyer contended that many of the seller's deliveries had been defective. The court found that a small percentage of the goods contained minor defects. However, the court determined that the deliveries had no more defects than goods delivered from any other supplier, and that in the supply for picture frame moldings "some level of tolerance for defects is to be expected." Thus, the court determined that the goods were fit for their ordinary purposes.

C. *Average quality, reasonable quality, or merchantable quality*

An interpretation of "ordinary use" that is made against the background of the seller's informational advantage still requires some understanding of when a particular good is "fit for the purposes for which goods of the same description" are used. Adjudicators and commentators have variously interpreted the obligation on which the CISG language is based as referring to "average quality," "reasonable quality," "merchantable quality," or "satisfactory condition."[49] We conclude that "merchantable quality" is the best standard to apply.[50]

"Reasonable quality" has been endorsed by commentators and some tribunals.[51] Nevertheless, it suffers from its inherent vagueness that prevents parties from knowing in advance whether they have satisfied the obligation and requires tribunals subsequently to define the term against some other standard.[52] Thus, even those tribunals that embrace a reasonableness standard ultimately must make reference to some more concrete basis for determining whether a proffered good is satisfactory. In the most thorough analysis of the issue in the case law, for instance, an arbitral tribunal from the Netherlands rejected the merchantable standard (in part because it believed that standard was inconsistent with the drafting history of Article 35) and instead applied a reasonableness standard (even though nothing in the drafting history suggested that standard was intended).[53] But in concluding that the tendered goods were not of reasonable quality, the tribunal relied primarily on the fact that the price at which the sellers were required to resell the goods reflected a deep

---

[48] See Ontario Superior Court of Justice (Canada) (*La San Giuseppe* v. *Forti Moulding Ltd.*), 31 August 1999, available at: http://cisgw3.law.pace.edu/cases/990831c4.html.

[49] See Schwenzer, *Article 35*, in Schlechtriem & Schwenzer, supra note 2, at 577.

[50] For a more detailed analysis of the issue, see Gillette & Ferrari, supra note 1.

[51] See Joseph Lookofsky, Understanding the CISG 74 (4th (Worldwide) ed. 2012); Arbitration Institute, Stockholm Chamber of Commerce (Sweden), 5 June 1998, available at http://cisgw3.law.pace.edu/cases/980605s5.html.

[52] For criticisms of the "reasonableness" standards along these lines, see Clayton P. Gillette & Robert E. Scott, *The Political Economy of International Sales Law*, 25 Int'l Rev. L. & Econ. 446 (2005); Michael P. Van Alstine, *Dynamic Treaty Interpretation*, 146 U. Pa. L. Rev. 687, 750 (1998).

[53] See Netherlands Arbitration Institute, Arbitral Award No. 2319 (Netherlands), 15 October 2002, available at http://cisgw3.law.pace.edu/cases/021015n1.html.

discount from the contract price. That is the very essence of the merchantability standard: Goods are unmerchantable if no buyer with knowledge of their actual characteristics will pay the contract price for them. So the tribunal was essentially applying merchantability in the guise of reasonableness. Finally, reasonableness describes a range of quality that arguably induces sellers to produce goods of minimally acceptable quality, because doing so allows them to save costs that would have to be incurred to produce goods of higher quality, while still satisfying their legal obligations with respect to conformity.

Average quality is often used in civil law countries as the measure of fitness for ordinary use and has been adopted by some commentators and tribunals – not surprisingly, those from civil law countries.[54] During the drafting of Article 35, the Canadian delegation generously (since common law countries traditionally adopt a merchantability standard) proposed to include an average quality rule.[55] That amendment, however, was subsequently withdrawn.[56] Literal interpretation of the standard would create a moving target, so that sellers would have difficulty knowing what standard of performance they were promising and buyers would have difficulty knowing the standard of performance they were receiving. To see why this is the case, assume that the plausible quality of goods ranges from "high" to "low," and that goods delivered in the absence of a legal warranty of quality are randomly distributed over this range. Thus, taken literally, the "average" quality of a good would approximate the mean between "high" and "low" quality. Once we use an implied warranty of quality to require that conforming goods be of "average" quality, however, all goods of a quality below the average would fail to satisfy the warranty. As a result, sellers could not satisfy contractual obligations by tendering goods of that quality, unless they explicitly disclaim the warranty. Sellers of below average quality goods who did not want to disclaim warranties would drop out of the market. The effect of that move, however, would be to shift the "average quality" of goods upwards, as the disappearance of below average quality altered the definition of average quality for the goods that remained. Of course, that equilibrium would be short-lived, as the new "below average" quality goods would now fail to satisfy legal requirements. Once the previously "below average" goods disappear, goods that are tendered would all be between the "high" point of quality and the former "average" point of quality. As a result, the actual "average" of tendered goods would move to some point between the old average and the high point. "Average" quality becomes costly to determine because of the constant change in the standard.

One might contend that this discussion of "average" misunderstands the signifi- cance of that term. Instead, "average" could mean a level of quality that would be acceptable to the "average" buyer and thus translate into something closer to a

---

[54] See, e.g., District Court Berlin (Germany), 15 September 1994, available at http://cisgw3.law .pace.edu/cases/940915g1.html.
[55] See Diplomatic History, *supra* note 25, at 676.   [56] See id., at 536 (para. 45).

reasonable expectations test. While that is a more coherent standard, there needs to be a means of determining in any given case whether that standard has been satisfied. The most plausible test of whether reasonable expectations of the average buyer are satisfied would be whether the good, with the alleged defect, was marketable at the price of other goods of similar description. Buyers who expect a good to have certain characteristics would not pay the same price for a good without those characteristics. But once appeal to market price is used as the measure of "average," that test also becomes indistinguishable from "merchantable." Appeal to market price may be unnecessary where the deviation from expectations is so significant that the good substantially fails to fit its contract description. But the cases in which choice among "reasonable," "average," and "merchantable" standards make a difference tend, as in the Netherlands arbitration, to involve allegations of less substantial nonconformities.

The merchantability test has been employed explicitly by some tribunals, although again there appears to be a homeward bias in that the relevant tribunals tend to be located in common law countries that adopt the test for purposes of domestic law. Indeed, these decisions sometimes expressly adopt the test from domestic law, seemingly unaware of the international nature of the CISG provision that they are applying.[57] Other cases use terms that are essentially synonymous with "merchantable." For instance, the German Supreme Court concluded that "an important part of being fit for the purposes of ordinary use is resaleability (tradability)."[58] A Swiss court found that a buyer of catalogues with misprints suffered no compensable damages where the defect did not cause a "devaluation" of the goods – an apparent reference to the absence of a decline in its market value.[59] We interpret "merchantability" for Article 35(2)(a) purposes, and for warranty purposes generally, to require that the goods that are the subject of the dispute can be sold in the same market in which the original transaction occurred to a buyer who is aware of the characteristics complained of at a price that is substantially similar to the contract price.[60] As the Netherlands Arbitral Tribunal mentioned earlier concluded, "a merchantability test under CISG based on English common law, if any, would raise the question whether a reasonable buyer would have concluded contracts for [the goods at issue] at similar prices if such a buyer had been aware of the mercury concentrations." The fact that the goods could only be resold at a deep discount

---

[57] See, e.g., Supreme Court of New South Wales (Australia) (*Fryer Holdings* v. *Liaoning MEC Group*), 30 January 2012, available at www.globalsaleslaw.org/content/api/cisg/urteile/2325.pdf.

[58] Federal Supreme Court (Germany), 2 March 2005, available at http://cisgw3.law.pace.edu/cases/050302g1.html.

[59] See Commercial Court Zürich (Switzerland), 21 September 1998, available at http://cisgw3.law.pace.edu/cases/980921s1.html.

[60] See CIETAC Arbitration (China), 3 June 2003, available at http://cisgw3.law.pace.edu/cases/030603c1.html (using the merchantability standard). For a somewhat different definition of merchantability, which, however, is also price-related, see Thomas M. Beline, *Legal Defect Protected by Article 42 of the CISG: A Wolf in Sheep's Clothing*, 7 U. Pitt. J. Tech. L. & Pol'y. 6 (2007), stating that "the threshold is merchantability such that the goods could be resold at the price in which the buyer expected to resell them."

relative to their contract price indicated that they were not merchantable. Merchantability thereby avoids the problems of the "reasonableness" and "average quality" standards insofar as it permits the quality of the good at issue to be measured against a standard – market price[61] –that is sufficiently verifiable to avoid the gross classifications about quality that generate difficulties of application associated with "reasonable" or literal interpretations of "average" quality.

For instance, shoes of a wide variety of quality can be fit for the ordinary purpose of walking. But shoes that cost $500 are expected to have characteristics different from shoes that cost $50. Thus, price may do a significant amount of work in segmenting markets for goods that might otherwise seem fungible. This graduated warranty avoids the pitfalls of "reasonableness" and "average quality" because it recognizes the diversity of quality among goods used for the same purpose and does not induce strategic play by sellers or buyers.

More importantly, price is likely to reflect informational advantages that justify warranty liability in the first instance. Assuming relatively competitive markets, price should reflect the inputs that the seller invests in product quality. If price incorporates the seller's informational advantage about quality, then the good that is the subject matter of the contract should be saleable to another buyer in the same market at the contract price if the information at issue was made explicit. The inability to command the same price for the good once the disputed characteristic is known reveals a qualitative difference between the good and other goods that purport to be used for the same purpose.

As a result, a merchantability standard that asks whether the good at issue could be resold in the same market at a price similar to the one charged in the contract for conforming goods assumes that the seller is signaling product quality in the very manner that economic theory suggests sellers would want to do in order to avoid the problem of asymmetric information. A low-quality seller trying to mimic high-quality sellers by charging the same price, therefore, should be held responsible for the quality of good indicated by the price. On the other hand, a seller who charged significantly less than the market price for a similar good should be held to a lower standard and therefore may well not be liable (assuming no other basis for liability), since the low price signaled that its good was of inferior quality.

IV. FITNESS OF GOODS FOR ANY PARTICULAR PURPOSE KNOWN TO THE SELLER

A. Scope and justification

Article 35(2)(b) states that the goods must be "fit for any particular purpose expressly or impliedly made known to the seller at the time of the conclusion of the contract,

---

[61] For price as a relevant factor in determining whether the Article 35(2)(a) threshold is met, see also Willhelm-Albrecht Achilles, Kommentar zum UN-Kaufrechts Übereinkommen 95 (2000).

except where the circumstances show that the buyer did not rely, or that it was unreasonable for him to rely, on the seller's skill and judgment."[62] Article 35(2)(b) deals with the situation where the buyer has superior information about its particular purpose for the good while the seller has superior information about the qualities of the good at issue and thus of the suitability of the good for the proposed use. The term "particular purpose," unlike the "ordinary purpose" in Article 35(2)(a), suggests that courts should consider the subjective requirements of the buyer rather than the requirements of the average consumer. The Article encourages the buyer to convey information to the seller about intended use and encourages the seller to convey information to the buyer about the utility or disutility of a product for that use. This exchange facilitates productive trade since sellers who have and provide information about the utility of products can save buyers the cost of searching for appropriate goods. However, buyers will only rely on sellers' recommendations and avoid costly searches if they can trust the accuracy of those recommendations. Otherwise, statements by sellers may simply lull into complacency buyers who would otherwise make their own investigations and purchase appropriate products. Imposing liability on the seller provides buyers who justifiably rely on representations from sellers with the assurance necessary to induce trade. At the same time, there is little reason to impose liability on the seller where the buyer already knows the characteristics of the goods and thus is not relying on the seller for information about their appropriateness for the buyer's purpose.

The buyer's requirements are taken into account, therefore, only where they have been made known to the seller at the time of the conclusion of the contract. The fact that the purpose can be made known to the seller "expressly or impliedly" indicates that the purpose need not be recited in the contract as long as the seller has become aware of it.[63] Because the justification for the obligation is rooted in informational advantage, it should not matter whether the seller obtains that information directly from the buyer or indirectly, and implicitly, from other circumstances. But debate remains over when the seller has sufficient information. A term that requires a seller to deliver plants to a particular jurisdiction has been held to provide notice to the seller that the plants will be used in that jurisdiction,[64] though one might reasonably infer that delivery in one jurisdiction does not preclude resale to another and thus falls short of giving the seller the requisite information to trigger Article 35(2)(b).[65] Although there is some support in the Secretariat Commentary for

---

[62] For examples see *Schmitz-Werke Gmbh Co. v. Rockland Indus., Inc.*, 37 F. App'x 687, 689 (4th Cir. 2002); Court of Appeals Grenoble (France), Case No. 93, April 1995, available at http://cisgw3.law.pace.edu/cases/950426f2.html.

[63] See District Court Munich (Germany), 27 February 2002, available at http://cisgw3.law.pace.edu/cases/020227g1.html.

[64] See District Court Coburg (Germany), 12 December 2006, available at http://cisgw3.law.pace.edu/cases/061212g1.html.

[65] See Kröll, *Article 35*, in Kröll et al., *supra* note 2, at 520 (citing Franco Ferrari, *Article 35*, in *Internationales Vertragsrecht* (Franco Ferrari et al. eds., 2007)).

the proposition that the seller must have actual knowledge of the buyer's particular purpose,[66] commentators have indicated that it is sufficient that a reasonable seller would have known of that purpose from the circumstances.[67] Perhaps the more liberal construction provides a means of giving Article 35(2)(b) meaning independent of Article 35(1), since any requirement of which the seller has actual knowledge and to which the seller did not object would presumably become a description of the goods. It is perhaps on this ground that some conclude that Article 35(2)(b) may have been unnecessary given the breadth of Article 35(1).[68] Of course, even in a case in which the seller learns of the buyer's purpose from other sources, Article 35(2)(b) requires that the buyer rely on the seller's expertise. Once the buyer has established that the seller was aware of the buyer's particular purpose, however, commentators have inferred from Article 35(2)(b)'s language that the seller bears the burden of proving that the buyer did or should not have relied on the seller's skill and judgment.[69] We discuss later the extent to which Article 35 allocates the burden of proof.[70]

B. *The scope of "particular purpose"*

A "particular purpose" need not be an idiosyncratic or atypical one. A good of a general description may have a broad range of purposes, and different forms of the good may be appropriate for different purposes within the range. For example, a buyer who purchases a computer to use it as a doorstop would be using it for a particular purpose. But so would a purchaser who uses the computer for photo editing, even though that purchaser is not making a rare or extraordinary use of the computer. A computer seller who is aware that a buyer will be using the computer for photo editing with a memory-consuming photo editing program is still aware of the buyer's "particular purpose" and will be subject to Article 35(2)(b) if the buyer makes its requirements known and is relying on the seller to select an appropriate computer. A United States District Court concluded that there was no violation of Article 35(2)(b) where a manufacturer of mesh with a chemical that caused dissolving of an insulation board was only aware that its product would be used in an exterior insulation and finish system.[71] The manufacturer was not aware that the specific building for which the mesh was purchased contained materials that would dissolve if used with the specific chemical in the mesh. Since the mesh was compatible with some exterior insulation and finish systems, and the manufacturer

---

[66] See Secretariat Commentary on the 1978 Draft, in Documentary History, supra note 25, at 422 (former Art. 33, para. 8).

[67] See, e.g., Schwenzer, *Article 35*, in Schlechtriem & Schwenzer, supra note 2, at 581; Kröll, *Article 35*, in Kröll et al., supra note 2, at 519.

[68] See Honnold/Flechtner, supra note 27, at 336.   [69] Id.   [70] See infra X.

[71] See *Travelers Property Casualty Company of America* v. *Saint-Gobain Technical Fabrics Canada Ltd.*, 474 F. Supp. 2d 1075 (D. Minn. 2007).

was aware that its product would be used with such a system, the manufacturer was only aware of the ordinary purpose for its mesh. Presumably, had the seller been aware that its product would be used in combination with insulation board prone to dissolving, it would have been aware of the buyer's particular purpose, even though that purpose was common within the industry.[72]

The fact that a particular purpose need not be idiosyncratic means that there can be significant overlap between Article 35(2)(a) and Article 35(2)(b): A party's particular purpose will often correspond to an ordinary use of the good that is the subject of the contract.[73] Where a party's particular purpose also is ordinary, presumably the party will prefer to proceed under subsection (2)(a) rather than (2)(b), because (2)(b) requires proof of reliance while (2)(a) does not. However, cases arising out of Article 35(2)(b) will typically deal with an occasional or rare use of the good in question rather than the good's ordinary use, because the seller warrants the ordinary use whether or not that use was "made known" to him or the buyer reasonably relied on his skill and judgment. Case law has generated a few examples of non-ordinary uses of goods: using the goods in unique climatic conditions;[74] needing the good to last for an unusually long duration;[75] and needing the goods to meet public law provisions in the buyer's state that are different from the seller's.[76]

C. *Proving reliance on a particular purpose*

Unlike Article 35(1), Article 35(2)(b) contains a reliance requirement. Goods that do not satisfy a particular purpose fail to conform to the contract only if the buyer relied, and it was reasonable for it to rely, on the seller's skill and judgment. Again, the rationale is consistent with allocating losses to parties with superior information about the quality of the goods. If the buyer knows as much as the seller, there is little reason to shift the risk of inappropriateness to the latter. An example from a German case illustrates the point.[77] A Dutch seller entered into a contract for plants with a German buyer. The plants did not survive in the climate to which they were delivered. The buyer claimed that the plants were not fit for the climate, and it was the seller's responsibility to assure the plants would survive at their delivery destination. The court acknowledged that the seller was aware of the local climate in

---

[72] See *TeeVee Toons, Inc. v. Gerhard Schubert GmbH*, 2006 U.S. Dist. LEXIS 59455 (S.D.N.Y. August 23, 2006).

[73] See Lookofsky, *supra* note 51, at 71; but see Henschel, *supra* note 3, at 222 ("For Article 35(2)(b) to apply, the goods must be used for a purpose while lies outside what is considered the ordinary use of the goods …").

[74] See District Court Coburg (Germany), 12 December 2006, available at http://cisgw3.law.pace.edu/cases/061212g1.html.

[75] See District Court Munich (Germany), 27 February 2002, available at http://cisgw3.law.pace.edu/cases/020227g1.html.

[76] See *supra* III.A; *infra* IV.A.

[77] See District Court Coburg (Germany), 12 December 2006, available at http://cisgw3.law.pace.edu/cases/061212g1.html.

which the plants were to be used and that the plants were unfit for that location. Nevertheless, the buyer specialized in gardening and landscaping. It operated in the area to which the plants were sent and was "equally or even better acquainted with the peculiarities of the particular locations" than the seller. Under those circumstances, it was unreasonable for the buyer to rely on the seller's skill and judgment.

As a general principle, there is no reliance where a buyer asks for a specific product. Some commentators have suggested that a seller who knows that the requested product is not fit for the buyer's purpose still has an obligation to inform the buyer of that fact. This obligation is typically stated to arise under the requirement of good faith in Article 7(1), and there is some support for the proposition in the Secretariat's Commentary.[78] For example, if a buyer asks for bleach, a seller who knows the buyer plans on using it to clean colored clothing would be obligated to explain the unsuitability of the product to the buyer. Notwithstanding our general doubt about an expansive reading of good faith,[79] a buyer seems to have some redress from a seller who is aware of the buyer's error and exacerbates it by supplying an unfit good where a low-cost corrective would be possible. Even under the catchall conception of good faith, however, the seller would have no further duties if the buyer still insists on the goods. For instance, even if a seller has a duty to disclose the buyer's impending error, a seller is not obligated to refuse to sell the goods that the buyer demands.[80]

V. CONFORMITY TO SAMPLES AND MODELS

Article 35(2)(c) states that goods must "possess the qualities of goods which the seller has held out to the buyer as a sample or model." Characteristics of goods as tendered that deviate from the characteristics in a sample or model, therefore, constitute nonconformities for purposes of Articles 35 and 36.[81] Although the terms "model" and "sample" are not defined, the assumption of commentators and case law is that a sample is drawn from the bulk of goods that are the subject of the sale while a model involves a prototype or other representation of the goods that will actually be sold.[82] The distinction is important because the inference to be drawn about the characteristics of the goods actually sold will be stronger where a sample is involved than where a model is involved. Nevertheless, at least in their translations, many cases

---

[78] See Henschel, supra note 3, at 237; Kröll, *Article 35*, in Kroll et al., supra note 2, at 522; Schwenzer, *Article 35*, in Schlechtriem & Schwenzer, supra note 2, at 582; Secretariat Commentary on the 1978 Draft, in Diplomatic History, supra note 25, at 422 (former Article 33, para. 9 and n.5).

[79] See Chapter 4.II.A., B.

[80] See Henschel, supra note 3, at 237; Schwenzer, *Article 35*, in Schlechtriem & Schwenzer, supra note 2, at 582.

[81] See *Delchi Carrier SpA v. Rotorex Corp.*, 71 F.3d 1024 (2d Cir. 1995).

[82] Compare, e.g., U.C.C. § 2–313, Official Comment 6.

appear to conflate the terms and treat what clearly is a model as a sample.[83] In some situations, the distinction becomes clouded. For instance, a buyer agreed to purchase wooden doors in "Tulipwood" for one of its customers, but indicated that it was unfamiliar with the wood and requested what the court referred to as a "sample."[84] The sample provided was of uniform color. Apparently full doors of tulipwood show differences in color and thus the wood was considered unfit for use unless the doors with which they are made are intended to be painted or treated to hide color variations. The buyer's order indicated that the doors were to be "blank permanently untreated," by which the buyer intended to convey that its customer would not be coloring them. The doors arrived with differences in color, and the buyer contended that they therefore did not conform to the sample. The court rejected the claim on the grounds that what it referred to as a "sample" was too small for the buyer to infer that the final product would not contain differences in color. Nor could the buyer reasonably have anticipated that the seller would deliver a complete door as a sample. The latter statement may be true enough. But it perhaps indicates that what was provided was not a sample at all, but the less reliable prototype implied by a model.

In either case, holding out the sample or model creates an implied understanding between the parties that the goods will match the characteristics in the sample or model, although the required degree of "matching" may vary according to whether a sample or model is involved and the extent to which the sample or model was intended by the parties to constitute a representation of the goods sold under the contract. In a CIETAC arbitration, the seller sent samples of mushrooms that were rejected by the buyer. The seller responded by indicating that mushrooms sent in fulfillment of the contract would be of better quality than the samples. The samples therefore created a baseline for the goods that were tendered under the contract. The fact that the seller ultimately tendered mushrooms of lower quality than the samples meant that the mushrooms did not conform to contractual requirements.[85] Even where a sample is provided, it may offer only a limited representation of the characteristics of the goods actually sold. For example, a sample of buckwheat may be relied on for the size and color of the goods actually delivered, but not their

---

[83] See, e.g., Commercial Court Hasselt (Belgium) (*Bruggen Deuren BVBA* v. *Top Deuren VOF*), 19 April 2006, available at http://cisgw3.law.pace.edu/cases/060419b1.html (small "sample" of type of wood used in complete door); Court of Appeals Graz (Austria), 9 November 1995, available at http://cisgw3.law.pace.edu/cases/951109a3.html ("sample" consisted of marble blocks shown to the buyer). Neglect of the difference between samples and models is not limited to foreign cases; see *Delchi Carrier SpA* v. *Roterex Corp.*, 71 F.3d 1024, 1028 (2d Cir. 1995) (agreement based on "sample" compressor supplied by the seller).

[84] See Commercial Court Hasselt (Belgium), (*Bruggen Deuren BVBA* v. *Top Deuren VOF*), 19 April 2006, available at http://cisgw3.law.pace.edu/cases/060419b1.html/.

[85] See CIETAC Arbitration (China), 18 September 1996, available at http://cisgw3.law.pace.edu/cases/960918c2.html.

sanitary quality.[86] Where the goods do conform to a sample or model, that fact can be used as a shield by the seller, rather than as a sword by the buyer, to indicate that no nonconformity exists.[87]

Article 35(2)(c) requires conformity to a sample or model of the "goods which the *seller* has held out" (emphasis added). Literally read, the language indicates that Article 35(2)(c) does not apply when a buyer holds out to a seller a sample or model of what the buyer expects to receive. But that distinction is immaterial if the buyer can demonstrate that the qualities of the sample or model that it provided implicitly or expressly became a part of the contract under Article 35(1).[88] In the absence of such a showing, however, the limitation to sellers may be justified because a seller who provides a sample or model is presumably aware of its characteristics and its capacity to reproduce them under the conditions specified by the buyer. Where a buyer shows the sample or model, the seller is less likely to be aware of any potential variations that might materialize in fulfilling the buyer's order. As a result, one might draw an inference about the seller's obligation to provide conforming goods only where the seller has actually acknowledged that it can comply with the buyer's sample or model.[89]

Courts tend to treat Article 35(2)(c) as having priority over all subparagraphs within Article 35(2).[90] For example, if a seller delivers goods that conform to a sample but the good is not fit for its ordinary purpose or not fit for the buyer's particular purpose, the seller is not responsible. The effect of the sample is essentially to provide the buyer with sufficient information about the fitness of the good for the buyer's purpose that it is no longer appropriate to place the risk of nonconformity on the seller. The Belgian decision concerning wooden doors discussed previously illustrates that principle, since the buyer had better information about the requirements of its own customer, and the model could have provided information about whether the goods that the seller proposed to deliver would satisfy those

---

[86] See ICC Arbitration Case No. 9773 of 1999, available at http://cisgw3.law.pace.edu/cases/999773i1.html.

[87] See District Court Regensburg (Germany), 24 September 1998, available at http://cisgw3.law.pace.edu/cases/980924g1.html.

[88] See District Court Aschaffenburg (Germany), 20 April 2006, available at http://cisgw3.law.pace.edu/cases/060420g1.html; District Court Paderborn (Germany), 25 June 1996, available at http://cisgw3.law.pace.edu/cases/960625g1.html; Court of Appeals Graz (Austria), 9 November 1995, available at http://cisgw3.law.pace.edu/cases/951109a3.html; Henschel, supra note 3, at 250–51; Huber & Mullis, supra note 11, at 140; Schwenzer, *Article 35*, in Schlechtriem & Schwenzer, note 2, at 584; but see Commercial Court (Belgium), 14 September 2005, available at http://cisgw3.law.pace.edu/cases/050914b1.html (applying 35(2)(c) despite the fact the buyer held out the samples).

[89] See Henschel, supra note 3, at 251.

[90] See Helsinki Court of Appeals (Finland), 30 June 1998, available at http://cisgw3.law.pace.edu/cases/980630f5.html ("if it is held that this was a case of sale by sample, there would be no need to refer to particular purpose made known to the [s]eller. A reference to a sample excludes the application of the criteria in Article 35(2)(b) .... ."); Huber & Mullis, supra note 11, at 140; Schwenzer, *Article 35*, in Schlechtriem & Schwenzer, supra note 2, at 583.

purposes. Of course, in that case, the buyer overestimated the significance of the model ("sample"), and thus concluded that the goods would serve its customer's purposes when, in fact, they did not. In other situations the sample or model will not be amenable to testing or an amateur buyer will not be able to discern the manner in which the sample or model may deviate from the tendered goods. Therefore, in these circumstances the seller may have more information than the buyer about the good's fitness for the buyer's purposes. This may indicate that the seller should be liable in some situations for goods that are nonconforming under one of the subparagraphs of Articles 35(2), even though the goods conform to the sample.[91] In this respect, courts need to determine the level of inspection required by the buyer to discover defects in the sample and whether, in the circumstances, a buyer should be held responsible for inadequately inspecting a sample where the buyer had not revealed its lack of skill.

An example from a German case illustrates these issues.[92] An Italian seller entered into a contract with two buyers for large globes that would be displayed at the buyers' rental agencies. The buyers contended that the globes were not conforming because their motors only allowed them to operate for one year. The court determined that the buyers had made it clear to the seller that the globes were intended for long-term use. Therefore, the court held that, under Article 35(2)(b), the globes needed to have a longer operational lifetime than one year. The seller contended that Article 35(2) (b) was inapplicable to this situation because it had provided a prototype of the goods that permitted inspection by the buyers, and the globes that were ultimately delivered contained the same motor that was present in the sample. The court concluded that the prototype was intended only to indicate the design of the final product and that the parties never intended that the buyers would perform tests that would indicate the duration of the motors' viability. Therefore, provision of the sample did not preclude liability for nonconformity. Implicit in the decision was an assumption that the seller, rather than the buyers, had the capacity to determine the longevity of the motor. Had that characteristic been more susceptible to determination by the buyers, a different result would have been appropriate.

VI. RELATIONSHIP BETWEEN ARTICLE 35(1) AND ARTICLE 35(2)

Since Article 35(2)(b) requires the buyer to make its particular purpose known to the seller, it will be rare that the particular purpose of the goods, once communicated, will not become a description "required by the contract" under Article 35(1).[93]

---

[91] See District Court Munich (Germany), 27 February 2002, available at http://cisgw3.law.pace .edu/cases/020227g1.html.

[92] See id.

[93] See Honnold/Flechtner, supra note 27, at 336 ("Thus, paragraph 2(b) of Article 35 may not have been necessary, but may help to reduce uncertainty …"); see also District Court Coburg (Germany), 12 December 2006, available at http://cisgw3.law.pace.edu/cases/061212g1.html;

Assume a buyer informs the seller that the buyer needs a cell phone while on assignment in France. The seller tells the buyer that a specific cell phone will work in France, and the buyer purchases the phone. The scenario fits the requirements of Article 35(2)(b), so that the cell phone will not conform to the contract unless it is suitable for operation in France. But the description that the cell phone will operate in France could also be interpreted as having become a term of the contract under Article 8. The seller would then be required to provide goods that conform to this description under Article 35(1). As a result, it is difficult to think of any circumstance in which Article 35(2)(b) applies and Article 35(1) does not. Any such case would have to involve the theoretical lacunae between the requirements of Article 35(1) that a term be contractually agreed on and the potentially less restrictive requirements for making a particular purpose known to the seller.[94]

Perhaps one can find a different scope for Article 35(2)(b) than for Article 35(1) through the requirement of the former that the particular purpose be "made known" to the seller. At times, even in the absence of a direct statement, a buyer may provide information from which a reasonable seller would infer the buyer's particular purpose. That information will be sufficient to trigger the seller's obligation under Article 35(2)(b), but may not rise to the level of a description of the goods under Article 35(1).[95] Assume in this hypothetical that the buyer only tells the seller that his phone broke while he was on assignment in France, and he needs a new phone shipped to his hotel in Paris. In this situation, the buyer may have made his particular purpose known to the seller without making a contractual agreement that the phone would work in France. Of course, the buyer would still have to demonstrate reliance on the seller in order to assert an Article 35(2)(b) claim. One court concluded that requirements stated in documents and faxes concerning the composition of skin care products were sufficient to bring to the seller's attention the need to comply with the buyer's desire to have a product that retained vitamin content for a specified shelf life.[96]

The fact that both Article 35(1) and Article 35(2)(b) can apply in the same situation poses a potential conflict, however, because the former does not require the buyer reasonably to rely on the seller's skill and judgment. For instance, assume in the cell phone hypothetical that the buyer requests a particular phone and informs the seller that she (the buyer) intends to use it in France. Assume that the seller provides the cell phone, but it is inappropriate for the specified function. Given that the buyer

Helsinki Court of Appeals (Finland), 30 June 1998, available at http://cisgw3.law.pace.edu/cases/980630f5.html.

[94] See Schwenzer, *Article 35*, in Schlechtriem & Schwenzer, supra note 2, at 581.

[95] See Supreme Court (Austria), 19 April 2007, available at http://cisgw3.law.pace.edu/cases/070419a3.html ("A seller is obligated to deliver goods complying with the buyer's specifications of which the seller knew or ought to have known, irrespective of whether the parties have expressly incorporated these specifications into the contract").

[96] See Helsinki Court of First Instance (Finland), 11 June 1995, *aff'd* Helsinki Court of Appeals, 30 June 1998, available at www.cisg.law.pace.edu/cisg/wais/db/cases2/980630f5.html.

requested the good, it would be difficult to establish that the buyer exhibited the kind of reasonable reliance on the seller's skill and judgment that is necessary to recover under a claim that the good was not fit for its particular purpose under Article 35(2)(b).[97] However, the information provided by the buyer, combined with the conduct of the seller, could imply, under Article 8, that the functionality of the cell phone in France was an implied term of the contract. In that event, the seller's provision of a good that did not satisfy that term could be interpreted as the provision of a nonconforming good under Article 35(1).

A similar problem arises in the relationship between Article 35(1) descriptions and Article 35(2)(c) samples and models. If the parties understand that the goods as delivered will possess the qualities of a sample or model, that understanding indicates that the characteristics of the sample or model have become an implied term in the contract for purposes of Article 35(1).[98] Thus, as with Article 35(2)(b), it will rarely be that case that Article 35(2)(c) applies and Article 35(1) does not. Assume that a seller shows a buyer a sample of the goods that are ultimately to be sold under the contract. Some domestic law would treat the sample in the same manner that it treats oral or written statements about the goods, that is, as a description of the goods to which they must ultimately conform.[99]

Under any regime, there may be a question of the extent to which parties who have contracted with respect to a sample intend to permit variation from it in the goods that are delivered. In a case involving the sale of stone, an Austrian appellate court noted that even if one assumed that Article 35(2)(c) was inapplicable because the relevant "sample" was offered by the buyer from a brochure, there remained a question of whether the parties agreed that the color of the stone in the brochure became a description of the goods under Article 35(1).[100] The characterization has significance under the CISG, in part because a strict reading of Article 35(3), which precludes recovery by a buyer who is aware of nonconformities, applies only to Article 35(2).[101]

One might distinguish between the stricter requirements for the qualities of a good to be contractually agreed on under Article 35(1) and the less restrictive requirements that a seller "has held out" the sample or model to the buyer. One court has interpreted the term "held out" in Article 35(2)(c) as requiring an implicit or explicit agreement between the parties that the delivered goods will conform to

---

[97] See District Court Coburg (Germany), 12 December 2006, available at http://cisgw3.law.pace .edu/cases/061212g1.html; Kröll, *Article 35*, in Kröll et al., supra note 2, at 521.

[98] See Court of Appeals Graz (Austria), 9 November 1995, available at http://cisgw3.law.pace.edu/ cases/951109a3.html (noting the minor distinction between Article 35(1) and Article 35(2)(c) in a case where the buyer held out a sample); Honnold/Flechtner, supra note 27, at 337; Lookofsky, supra note 51, at 75–6; see also *Delchi Carrier SpA v. Rotorex Corp.*, 71 F.3d 1024 (2d Cir. 1995).

[99] See, e.g., U.C.C. § 2–313(1).

[100] See Court of Appeals Graz (Austria), 9 November 1995, available at http://cisgw3.law.pace.edu/ cases/951109a3.html.

[101] We discuss the possibility of applying Article 35(3) to Article 35(1) cases later.

the sample.[102] This interpretation, however, leaves Article 35(2)(c) indistinct from Article 35(1), which, assuming that the drafters intended to give each Article independent meaning, cannot be the correct interpretation. Instead, "held out" should be given a less restrictive interpretation.

This view is also consistent with the history of Article 35(2)(c). Article 33(1)(c) of the Uniform Law on the International Sale of Goods (ULIS), on which Article 35(2) (c) is based, required an implicit or explicit agreement between the parties that the goods would conform to the sample. However, this requirement was deleted from Article 35(2)(c), which some commentators interpret as creating a presumption that the goods will conform to the sample or model whether or not there is an implicit agreement between the parties that they will.[103] This presumption puts the burden on the seller to indicate that the goods will not conform to the sample. It creates a small distinction between Article 35(1) and Article 35(2)(c) and reduces the burden of proof on the party who attempts to show that the goods conformed or did not conform to the sample.

We are reluctant to interpret Article 35(1) in a manner that conflicts with results that would be dictated in the situations that Article 35(2) was intended to cover. Instead, and in order to avoid rendering Article 35(2)(b) superfluous, we would read that provision to require reliance to establish liability whenever a buyer claims that the nonconformity arises out of a failure of the goods to satisfy a particular purpose. Kröll similarly states that to avoid a conflation of Article 35(1) and 35(2) "an implicit agreement should not be assumed lightly" in defining the scope of the former.[104] But the possibility that a single scenario fits both subsections of Article 35 and plausibly leads to different results under them suggests that some clarification would have been appropriate. In any event, and given the substantive consequences, the CISG's drafters should have drawn a sharper distinction between Article 35(1) descriptions and characteristics of the goods that become part of the contract under Article 35(2).

VII. THE REQUIREMENT OF ADEQUATE PACKAGING

Article 35(2)(d) states that goods must be "contained or packaged in the manner usual for such goods or, where there is no such manner, in a manner adequate to preserve and protect the goods." Article 35(2)(d) applies when the parties have not agreed to the method of shipping explicitly or impliedly, in which case the applicable provision would be the last clause of Article 35(1).[105] It sets the minimum

---

[102] See District Court Berlin (Germany), 15 September 1994, available at http://cisgw3.law.pace .edu/cases/940915g1.html.
[103] See Henschel, supra note 3, at 243; Kröll, *Article 35*, in Kröll et al., supra note 2, at 522–23.
[104] See Kröll, *Article 35*, in Kröll et al., supra note 2, at 501.
[105] See Court of Appeals Saarbrücken (Germany), 17 January 2007, available at http://cisgw3.law .pace.edu/cases/070117g1.html.

standard for packaging and containers unless the parties agree to less protective packaging. The Article also applies to packaging labels such as expiration dates and handling instructions.[106] If the obligation is breached, then the seller will be responsible for damage caused by the improper container or packaging, even if the damage materializes after the risk of loss has passed to the buyer.[107]

A. The "usual" manner of packaging

The term "usual" in Article 35(2)(d) is similar in many ways to the term "ordinary" in Article 35(2)(a) and therefore requires reference to the measures taken by similarly situated sellers in international trade.[108] However, if there is no "usual" method found in international trade, courts must determine whether the standard in the buyer's or seller's country should apply. For instance, if the seller's and buyer's country have different packaging or label requirements, but the goods only conform to the seller's country's standards, a court will have to decide what country's standards must be met to fulfill Article 35(2)(d).[109] This is obviously a variation on the issue of whether health and safety requirements of the buyer's country or the seller's country prevail under Article 35(2)(a).[110] As in that situation, and notwithstanding occasional statements that the regulations of the seller's jurisdiction apply,[111] clear rules may be less appropriate than an analysis of which party was best positioned to ascertain the relevant rules. The same analysis, aided by the circumstances surrounding the contract, helps determine the parties' intent as to which country's regulatory standards control.

This was the approach that a French appeals court took in a case involving an Italian seller and French buyer of cheese.[112] The cheese arrived without the proper composition and expiry labeling required by French law. The court found that, due to the ongoing relationship between the parties for at least several months, the seller knew that the cheese would be marketed in France. In light of that relationship, the

---

[106] See Henschel, supra note 3, at 269; Schwenzer, *Article 35*, in Schlechtriem & Schwenzer, supra note 2, at 584.

[107] See Article 66; Court of Appeals Koblenz (Germany), 14 December 2006, available at http://cisgw3.law.pace.edu/cases/061214g1.html.

[108] See CIETAC Arbitration (China), 30 March 1994, available at http://cisgw3.law.pace.edu/cases/940330c1.html; Arbitration Chamber of Paris No. 9926 (France), 2007, available at http://cisgw3.law.pace.edu/cases/079926f1.html; Henschel, supra note 3, at 271; Huber & Mullis, supra note 11, at 141; Kröll, *Article 35*, in Kröll et al., supra note 2, at 525; Schwenzer, *Article 35*, in Schlechtriem & Schwenzer, supra note 2, at 584.

[109] See Court of Appeals Grenoble (France), 9 September 1995, available at http://cisgw3.law.pace.edu/cases/950913f1.html.

[110] See supra III.A.

[111] See Court of Appeals Saarbrücken (Germany), 17 January 2007, available at http://cisgw3.law.pace.edu/cases/070117g1.html.

[112] See Court of Appeals Grenoble (France), 13 September 1995, available at http://cisgw3.law.pace.edu/cases/950913f1.html.

court concluded that the contract should be construed to incorporate the parties' intent that the seller assume an obligation to comply with French packaging regulations

For the same reasons we noted in our discussion of Article 35(2)(a), in the absence of additional conditions, such as repeat play by the seller in the buyer's jurisdiction, the usual method of packaging should be viewed from the perspective of the seller's jurisdiction. In the typical situation, the buyer has superior information about the requirements in his own jurisdiction and should be obligated to convey those to the seller, so that, absent evidence of an intent to shift the risk to the seller, the parties' should be assumed to have limited the seller's obligation to compliance with its regulations.[113] However, when the seller is more likely to know the "usual" packing method in the buyer's jurisdiction, the standards of that jurisdiction should apply. The exceptions discussed in the "mussels case" will be relevant for determining whether the goods must comply with the standards of the buyer's jurisdiction: the seller knew the standard, should have known the standard, or the same standard exists in both countries.[114] The French appellate court appears to have assumed that repeat play and knowledge that the goods would be marketed in France provided ample reason for the seller to have adequate information about the regulations in the buyer's jurisdiction. Perhaps; but the case involved shipments of multiple kinds of cheese and there was a labeling problem with the parmesan cheese in one shipment. One would like to know whether the regulations that were applicable in the case before the court were also applicable in the prior interactions of the parties and whether those prior shipments had been accepted without difficulty.

Determining the "usual" method of packaging will also depend on the mode of transportation used by the buyer, assuming it is made known to the seller.[115] For example, the "usual" packaging method of a product might be different depending on whether it is traveling by boat or by train. In *Dingxi Longhai Dairy, Ltd.* v. *Becwood Technology Group, L.L.C.*,[116] the plaintiff appeared to be making a claim under Article 35(2)(d) when it contended that shipment of inulin in unenclosed trucks exposed the goods to moisture and was contrary to instructions and acceptable practices in the industry. The plaintiff made a more direct claim under the Article by alleging that shipping personnel had to repackage some of the inulin prior to transportation to the United States due to Dingxi's improper packaging techniques. That claim failed because it appeared that after buyer rejected the shipments, it

---

[113] See Court of Appeals Saarbrücken (Germany), 17 January 2007, available at http://cisgw3.law.pace.edu/cases/070117g1.html ("In general, the standards in the seller's country determine the adequacy for usual purposes."); Henschel, supra note 3, at 271; Kröll, *Article 35*, in Kröll et al., supra note 2, at 525.

[114] See Henschel, supra note 3, at 271; Kröll, *Article 35*, in Kroll et al., supra note 2, at 525.

[115] See Henchel, supra note 3, at 172–74; Kröll, *Article 35*, in Kroll et al., supra note 2, at 525.

[116] 2010 U.S. Dist. LEXIS 59997 (D. Minn. July 1, 2008).

repurchased them at salvage, repackaged them, and resold them without providing customers any notice of defects.

The term "usual" implies packaging that most buyers would accept and thus suggests that what a seller believed would be a reasonable deviation from that majoritarian standard will not necessarily be adequate. An idiosyncratic buyer would have to signal a preference for either higher or lower quality packaging. A recent French arbitral award illustrates the point, although it involves the ancillary task of loading goods rather than the form of packaging.[117] A Cypriot seller and a French buyer entered into a contract for a chemical compound. After the goods were loaded onto a boat, a third party again inspected the goods on behalf of the buyer and found the goods to be of substandard quality. When the goods arrived at their final destination, they were rejected for lack of conformity. The buyer contended that the nonconformities were attributable to the process that the seller had used to load the chemical compound onto the ship. The arbitrator determined that the seller had employed the usual method for moving goods in a warehouse and loading them, that the buyer was aware of the process and had not requested any alternative, and that the method was "usual and well known by professionals."

B. *"Adequate" packaging*

If no usual usage can be established, then conforming goods must be contained or packaged in a manner adequate to preserve and protect them.[118] This will be relevant in situations where there is a new or a custom-made good. To determine whether the packaging is adequate, the court must consider the "type of goods, the means and length of transport, [and] the climatic conditions likely to be encountered . . ."[119] The relevant considerations are apparent in a case that involved a Mexican buyer of fruit from an Argentine seller.[120] There the buyer gave the seller a sample of cardboard boxes that were to be used to transport the product, and the seller gave the buyer a sample of tin cans and labels. The products arrived by sea with significant water damage that was partially due to the seller's use of low quality packaging, which was different from the packaging in the samples. The court found

---

[117] See Arbitration Chamber of Paris, No. 9926 (France), 2007, available at http://cisgw3.law.pace .edu/cases/079926f1.html.

[118] See Henschel, supra note 3, at 277; Schwenzer, *Article 35*, in Schlechtriem & Schwenzer, supra note 2, at 585.

[119] Huber & Mullis, supra note 11, at 141; see also Court of Appeals Saarbrücken (Germany), 17 January 2007, available at http://cisgw3.law.pace.edu/cases/070117g1.html; Compromex Arbitration Proceeding (Mexico), 29 April 1996, available at http://cisgw3.law.pace.edu/cases/ 960429m1.html.

[120] See Compromex Arbitration Proceeding (Mexico), 29 April 1996, available at http://cisgw3.law .pace.edu/cases/960429m1.html.

that the goods did not conform to the contract under Article 35. Although the case could have been decided under any of several Article 35 subsections, the court invoked Article 35(2)(d) when it stated that "[i]t is evident that a great part of the goods were damaged because of the inadequate containers and cardboard boxes that were used, especially when taking into account that their transportation would be by sea, a fact of which the respondents were fully aware."

The decision to contain or package goods necessarily implicates the cost of the transaction. As a result, in determining whether the seller has taken adequate measures, the parties would presumably consider whether additional or alternative precautions would have been cost-justified in light of the risks posed by factors such as the type of goods, the means and length of transport, and the climatic conditions likely to be encountered. In short, the inquiry into "adequacy" is guided by a risk/benefit standard that considers the costs of avoiding damage to the goods, the damages that will materialize should those precautions not be taken, and the probability that the damage will materialize. Assume, for example, that there are two buyers who wish to purchase a $1,000 custom-made bay window. Buyer 1 is a contractor who needs the window in perfect condition; a window in a lesser condition will slow down his construction job for three days. The delay will cost him an estimated $4,000. Buyer 2 is making repairs to his home and can continue working on other projects if the window arrives in a defective condition. Therefore, the delay will cost him only $1,000. Assume further that there are two packaging methods: a cardboard box packaging that reduces the probability of a broken window arriving to 2 percent, and a wooden crate that reduces that probability to 1 percent. The packaging methods cost $50 and $75, respectively. For the first buyer, using the wooden crate costs an additional $25 and reduces the risk of losing $4,000 by 1 percent, or $40. A seller who is aware of all this information would only comply with the adequacy requirement if it shipped in the wooden crate. The second buyer, however, would presumably be unwilling to pay an additional $25 for a reduction in expected loss of only $10.

Of course, in most situations, a seller will not be aware of damages that the buyer will suffer beyond the loss of the goods, and thus will make calculations based solely on that value. The buyer who has idiosyncratic needs would have to convey that information to the seller, in which case the packaging requirements might become an explicit term of the contract covered by Article 35(1). Indeed, the fact that the buyer in the Mexican case provided sample packaging may be read in that light. In our example, a seller aware only that the loss of the window would materialize if it arrived broken, either because it was not aware of the contractor's additional losses or because it was shipping to the homeowner who would not bear those additional losses, would be justified in using the cardboard packaging. The additional $25 for the wooden crate would not be worth the additional expected loss, which would now be only $10. In terms of Article 35(2)(d), the cardboard packaging in such a case would be "adequate."

C. *Relationship of packaging requirements to risk of loss*

The seller can be liable for failure to package the goods in the usual or adequate manner even if there are no defects in the goods at the time the risk passes to the buyer. Any unusual or inadequate packaging would constitute a nonconformity that existed at the time the risk transferred under Article 36(1), and the seller is therefore liable for any damage that occurs to the goods, due to unusual or inadequate packaging, after the risk passes to the buyer.[121] In fact, Article 35(2)(d) is most relevant in this circumstance because, if damage is done to the goods before the risk passes to the buyer, buyers will likely be able to bring a claim under Article 35(1), 35(2)(a), and 35(2)(d). However, if damage is done to the goods after the passing of the risk due to inadequate packaging, only Article 35(2)(d) can be used to get remedies for the damage.

An example from a recent German case illustrates this point.[122] A buyer obtained wine bottles from the seller's place of business. The bottles were packaged in an inadequate manner, which caused them to break or lose their sterility while the buyer was traveling back to his country. The buyer successfully sued for damages because the goods had inadequate packaging at the time the risk passed to the buyer despite the fact that the bottles themselves were not defective when the risk passed. If the bottles had lost their sterility prior to the time that the risk had passed to the buyer, the seller would be responsible under Articles 35(1) and 35(2)(a) as well as Article 35(2)(d). There would be no need, therefore, to prove that the packaging was unusual or inadequate.

VIII. ARTICLE 35(3)'S LIMITATION ON LIABILITY

Article 35(3) provides that "the seller is not liable under subparagraphs (a) to (d) of the preceding paragraph for any lack of conformity of the goods if at the time of the conclusion of the contract the buyer knew or could not have been unaware of such lack of conformity."[123] This rule fits the underlying goal of placing losses from nonconformity on the party in the best place to bear the risk. A buyer who has knowledge about the quality of the goods can no longer claim an informational disadvantage that would justify shifting the risk of quality to the seller.

A. *"Could not have been unaware"*

One area of scholarly debate is how to interpret the term "could not have been unaware." Some scholars contend that a buyer who acts with gross negligence

---

[121] See Court of Appeals Koblenz (Germany), 14 December 2006, available at http://cisgw3.law .pace.edu/cases/061214g1.html; Huber & Mullis, supra note 11, at 141.

[122] See Court of Appeals Koblenz (Germany), 14 December 2006, available at http://cisgw3.law .pace.edu/cases/061214g1.html.

[123] See CIETAC Arbitration (China), 20 January 1994, available at http://cisgw3.law.pace.edu/ cases/940120c1.html.

"could not have been unaware" of the defect.[124] Others would require a higher standard, such as proving that an obvious defect existed in the good.[125] While this debate has been largely confined to the academic sphere, at least one case has supported a gross negligence standard.[126] Other circumstances may indicate the conditions under which "awareness" can be attributed to the buyer. A Chinese arbitral panel denied relief to a buyer of a defective hydraulic press where the buyer had purchased the same product from the seller previously and had suffered the same difficulties of which it was currently complaining.[127] A Finnish decision was more forgiving of buyers. In a case involving the content of skin care products, the seller maintained that the buyer was aware that vitamin A decomposes over time, so that it could not have expected that the required concentration of that element would be retained over the shelf life of the goods. The Court of First Instance, in a decision upheld on appeal, concluded that once the seller gave assurances about vitamin A concentrations, "it was not the business of the buyer to find out as to how the seller will take care of the manufacturing. This being the case, it appears that the buyer counted on the seller's expertise in terms of how the seller reaches the required vitamin A content and how the required preservation is carried out."[128]

The limited immunity that sellers receive under Article 35(3) also means that the buyer bears the quality risk only with respect to the particular defect of which it has knowledge. As the Federal Court of Australia has reasoned: "It would also be quite uncommercial to read Article 35(3) as excluding liability for loss suffered by reason of a lack of conformity where the buyer knew of, and was content to accept, a particular defect (such as an absence of software which the buyer intended to obtain and install itself) but did not know of a different defect (such as faulty wiring) which was also present when the contract was made. Knowledge of the first defect would not relieve the seller from liability for loss resulting from the second."[129]

Satisfying the requirement that one "could not have been unaware" of nonconformities, however, is different from satisfying a requirement that one "should have known" of those same nonconformities. The latter phrase expresses something like a negligence standard, while the former assumes something closer to actual or constructive knowledge. "Could not have been unaware" sounds something like a

---

[124] See Henschel, supra note 3, at 293–95.
[125] See Henschel, supra note 3; Huber & Mullis, supra note 11, at 142; Stefan Kröll, *Article 35*, in Kröll et al., supra note 2, at 529; Schwenzer, *Article 35*, in Schlechtriem & Schwenzer, supra note 2, at 586.
[126] See Court of Appeals Köln (Germany), 21 May 1996, available at http://cisgw3.law.pace.edu/cases/960521g1.html.
[127] See CIETAC Arbitration (China), 20 January 1994, available at http://cisgw3.law.pace.edu/cases/940120c1.html.
[128] See Helsinki Court of First Instance (Finland), 11 June 1995, *aff'd* Helsinki Court of Appeals, 30 June 1998, available at www.cisg.law.pace.edu/cisg/wais/db/cases2/980630f5.html.
[129] Federal Court (Australia) (*Castel Electronics Pty Ltd* v. *Toshiba Singapore Pte Ltd.*), 20 April 2011, available at www.austlii.edu.au/cgi-bin/sinodisp/au/cases/cth/FCAFC/2011/55.html?stem=o&synonyms=o&query=cisg#disp9.

definition of "notice" that includes a situation in which a person has reason to know a fact exists from all the facts and circumstances that the person actually does know.[130] The difficulty is likely to arise when, during pre-contractual negotiations, the seller informs a buyer that there may be a defect in the good or invites the buyer to inspect the goods. Requests for inspection may be more prevalent with respect to used goods, where the seller's request for inspection may be intended to allow the buyer to discover patent defects prior to setting a price for the goods.

Assume that, notwithstanding such a request, a buyer fails to inspect and then complains about defects that might have been apparent on inspection. From the perspective of placing losses on the party best positioned to avoid them, the buyer who failed to make the inspection should bear the loss, unless the costs of inspection are substantial in light of the risk – potentially a common occurrence in international transactions. But the buyer may have a broader range of defenses. First, notwithstanding the seller's request, the buyer may appeal to the majority opinion that there is no obligation under the CISG for the buyer to examine the goods.[131] Even those opinions, however, are subject to exceptions. Some commentators take the position that the seller may not be liable when it requests the buyer to inspect the goods and there is an obvious defect that the buyer would have noticed had it made an inspection.[132] Others suggest that Article 35(3) would preclude the seller's liability if an invitation to inspect the goods is combined with a warning that there may be defects in the goods.[133] Still others are more equivocal and maintain the that buyer's right to complain will "depend on the circumstances of the particular case, such as the nature of the goods, the skill and experience of each party, the reasonableness of an examination by the buyer, etc.,"[134] or on the degree of specificity with which the seller describes the potential defect.[135] The more precise the seller's admonition, the more likely it is that inspection will be

---

[130] See, e.g., U.C.C. § 1–202(a)(3).

[131] See Huber & Mullis, supra note 11, at 143; Honnold/Flechtner, supra note 27, at 339; Richard Hyland, *Conformity of Goods to the Contract Under the United Nations Sales Convention and the Uniform Commercial Code*, in Einheitliches Kaufrecht Und Nationales Obligationenrecht 305, 324 (Peter Schlechtriem ed., 1987); Schwenzer, *Article* 35, in Schlechtriem & Schwenzer, supra note 2, at 587.

[132] See Schwenzer, *Article* 35, in Schlechtriem & Schwenzer, supra note 2, at 587; Henschel, supra note 3, at 296 (stating that the decision is not clear under the CISG); see also Hyland, supra note 130, at 325 (concluding that under American and French law a buyer has a duty to inspect the goods if invited).

[133] See Arbitration Chamber of Paris, No. 9926 (France), 2007, available at http://cisgw3.law.pace .edu/cases/079926f1.html (holding that the seller was excluded from liability under 35(3) because the seller was aware that the goods were of subpar quality and refused to inspect the goods more thoroughly); see also Hyland, supra note 131, at 324–25 (concluding that under German law the invitation must be combined with a warning in order to exclude liability for the seller). For the contrary view, see Huber & Mullis, supra note 11, at 143 (seller would need to inform buyer of the specific defect not just generally warn him).

[134] Id.   [135] Id.

worth its cost because the buyer will discover a feature that could determine the desirability of completing the transaction.

The use of the phrase "could not have been unaware" supports a broader standard of seller immunity. Perhaps a standard that compares the cost of inspection with the probability of discovering defects would be appropriate if the relevant phrase were "should have been aware." Indeed, that phrase may have been more appropriate given the objective of placing the risk of nonconformity on the party with superior knowledge, since that criterion should not be read to allow one with easy access to knowledge to stick its head in the sand and avoid obtaining the relevant information. But to say that one "could not have been unaware" is to suggest that one already had information from which it could conclude that nonconformities existed. Thus, a buyer who simply refuses to inspect on invitation may be "unaware," even if the inspection would have been efficient. Nevertheless, if a seller has informed a buyer of a high probability of a defect, the buyer already knows something from which it is easier to conclude that it "could not have been unaware" of the nonconformities of which it subsequently complains.

B. *The limited application of Article 35(3)*

By its terms, Article 35(3) only applies to Article 35(2)(a)–(d). It does not immunize a seller where the nonconformity derives from a violation of Article 35(1). Thus, a strict reading of Article 35(3) would permit a buyer to obtain relief for nonconformities that constitute deviations from contractual requirements concerning quality, quantity, or description even if at the time of the conclusion of the contract the buyer knew or could not have been unaware of such lack of conformity. The Secretariat's Commentary to what became Article 35 similarly states that "this rule does not go to those characteristics of the goods explicitly required by the contract."[136] Under such circumstances, the buyer who is aware that the goods fail to conform to the contractual quality, quantity, or description may have the expectation that the nonconformity will be remedied before delivery or that the seller will pay damages.[137] In short, the provision in the contract of a particular quality, quantity, or descriptive term entitles the buyer to a good that conforms to that term.

Nevertheless, the relationship between Article 35(1) and Article 35(3) is more complicated than a literal interpretation of the provisions implies. First, recall that Article 35(1) implicates terms that become part of the contract both explicitly and implicitly. Thus, the Secretariat's Commentary may be too narrow insofar as it provides that Article 35(3) is inapplicable to characteristics "explicitly" required by the contract. Of course, those terms of the contract that are implicitly included as a

---

[136] Secretariat Commentary on the 1978 Draft, in Documentary History, supra note 25, at 422 (former Article 33, para. 14).

[137] See Schwenzer, *Article 35*, in Schlechtriem & Schwenzer, supra note 2, at 588.

consequence of Articles 35(2)(a) through (d) are subject to Article 35(3). But terms that are implicitly incorporated into the contract as a consequence of contract interpretation under Article 8 or by virtue of usages under Article 9 are also exempt from Article 35(3). For example, if a court concludes that parties have established a practice between themselves that, under Article 9(1), becomes a part of the contract or that, under Article 8(3), a reasonable person would infer was intended to constitute part of the contract, that term will be subject to Article 35(1) and exempt from Article 35(3), even though it was not explicitly stated in the writing.

But the same concept of implied terms may also limit the extent to which Article 35(1) immunizes buyers from the reach of Article 35(3). One might contend, for instance, that the buyer's awareness of a defect, or even a failure to discover a defect after a thorough examination of the goods, means that the existence of a discrepancy from express requirements has become a term of the contract. If that is the case, then tender of a good that contains that discrepancy is not "nonconforming" and Article 35(3) never comes into play.[138] Assume, for instance, that the buyer is aware both of a defect and of the physical impossibility of remedying it prior to the time of tender, but nevertheless proceeds to conclude the contract. Even if one does not formally invoke Article 35(3) in such a situation, it would be difficult to argue that the buyer has not waived compliance with the unachievable requirement. Indeed, despite the clear wording of the Article, courts have applied Article 35(3) to Article 35(1) either expressly or by apparent analogy.[139] No precise test distinguishes between situations in which a buyer may ignore a known discrepancy and take advantage of Article 35(1) and those situations in which the buyer is subject to a principle that looks a lot like Article 35(3), even though that provision does not apply directly. Relevant factors include the ease with which the seller can remedy the known defect and the price of the good, the latter of which may implicitly indicate imperfections in performance.[140]

In some cases, Article 35(1) may be even less forgiving of buyer inattention to defects than Article 35(3). The possibility that a contract description includes defects may be implied with respect to characteristics of which the buyer should have known or took the risk of not knowing. In short, Article 35(1) does not limit the seller to claims that the buyer "knew or could not have been unaware" of the claimed nonconformities. The reasoning in *Mitchell Aircraft Spares, Inc.* v. *European Aircraft Service AB*,[141] is instructive. A seller of used airline parts listed integrated drive generators (IDGs) for sale and represented that they might be of a type

---

[138] See Supreme Court (Spain), 17 January 2008, available at http://cisgw3.law.pace.edu/cases/080117s4.html; Copenhagen Maritime Commercial Court (Denmark), 31 January 2002, available at http://cisgw3.law.pace.edu/cases/020131d1.html.

[139] See Court of Appeals Vaud (Switzerland), 28 October 1997, available at www.unilex.info/case.cfm?pid=1&do=case&id=311&step=Abstract; Court of Appeals Sion (Switzerland), 29 June 1998, available at www.unilex.info/case.cfm?pid=1&do=case&id=366&step=Abstract.

[140] See Henschel, supra note 3.   [141] 23 F. Supp. 2d 915 (N.D. Ill. 1998).

that was identified through a unique descriptive number that the buyer desired. The buyer determined from documents sent by the seller that the parts did have the required number, although the documents did not mention that number, and issued a purchase order describing the parts as being of that number. The seller's invoice and Material Certification Form also contained the descriptive number. The IDGs turned out not to be of that number. The buyer maintained that it had agreed to purchase IDGs of the specified number, while the seller argued that it had agreed to sell the IDGs that it had available for sale, regardless of their descriptive number. The court denied both parties' motions for summary judgment. True, the purchase order and invoice contained the relevant number. That sounds as though compliance with that number was required. But there was evidence that the seller had sent the pre-contractual documents in order to allow the buyer to determine whether the parts were of the required number and the buyer had decided to purchase the parts after making that determination for itself. The court, therefore, was suggesting that, notwithstanding an explicit description of the goods in the purchase order and invoice – which would appear to implicate Article 35(1) – the need for the buyer to confirm the accuracy of that description could mean that the seller was not obligated to tender goods that complied with it.

The scope of 35(3) is also limited to some extent by Article 35(2)(c). Sellers could use Article 35(2)(c) as a shield by claiming that the goods complied with a sample even though there are defects. In this way, Article 35(2)(c) is very similar to Article 35 (3). However, under Article 35(2)(c) the seller is claiming immunity because there is no lack of conformity, while under Article 35(3) the seller is claiming he is not liable despite the lack of conformity. If the buyer is aware of a defect in the sample, then there is no need to invoke Article 35(3) for tender of goods containing the same defect, because those goods will conform to the sample and be conforming under Article 35(2)(c). Of course, Article 35(3) remains relevant with respect to characteristics of the goods that are not evident in the sample and that must be satisfied under other provisions of Article 35.

C. *Nonconformity involving fraud*

There is some question regarding the ability of a seller to take advantage of Article 35 (3) where the nonconformity results from fraud. In a case decided by a German appellate court, an Italian seller sold a used car with documents that fraudulently concealed the mileage and date of first registration.[142] The seller argued that the buyer could not have been unaware that the car did not conform to the contract because his wife had actual knowledge of the facts. The court concluded that, even

---

[142] See Court of Appeals Köln (Germany), 21 May 1996, available at http://cisgw3.law.pace.edu/ cases/960521g1.html. The court could have dealt with the issue by simply saying that Article 35 (3) does not apply to Article 35(1).

if the buyer could not have been unaware of the defects, Article 35(3) is inapplicable where the seller acts fraudulently. The court inferred this result from Article 40, which states that a seller cannot claim failure to notify under Articles 38 and 39 as a defense to a claim under Article 35 if the seller was aware of the lack of conformity and did not inform the buyer, as well as from the general obligation of courts under Article 7(1) to "promote . . . the observance of good faith in international trade." The court noted that "[e]ven a grossly negligent unknowing buyer appears to be more protection-worthy than a seller acting fraudulently." That statement, however, may also limit the scope of the exception. Some commentators suggest that Article 35(3) continues to apply where both seller and buyer have actual knowledge, but does not apply where the seller has actual knowledge and the buyer only "could not have been unaware" of the defect.[143]

IX. OBLIGATIONS TO DELIVER GOODS FREE FROM THIRD-PARTY RIGHTS AND CLAIMS

A. *Conflicting rights and claims to the goods*

Article 41 requires the seller to deliver goods which are free from any right or claim of a third party. The requirement applies unless the buyer has agreed to purchase the goods subject to the right or claim. Ownership, a lien, a bailment, or a possessory interest may give a third party rights in the goods. Under Article 41 the seller must deliver goods that are not subject to such rights. In everything but name, the Article obligates the seller to make an implied warranty of good title in the goods that are the subject of the contract.

The CISG's regulation of the Article 41 obligation runs parallel to its regulation of the Article 35 requirement of conformity. While Article 35 requires that the seller delivers goods that conform to the contract, Article 41 requires that it deliver goods free from the rights or claims of third parties to them. Just as Article 39(1) bars a buyer's reliance on nonconformities when it fails to give the seller timely and sufficient notice, Article 43(1) bars the buyer's reliance on Article 41 when it fails to give the seller timely and sufficient notice of the rights or claims of third parties. In addition, the standard for proper notice under both Articles is the same: The buyer must specify the nature of the nonconformity or third party's right or claim within a reasonable time after it becomes aware or ought to have become aware of them.[144] Finally, Article 44 limits the buyer's remedies when it has a reasonable excuse for giving tardy notice of a nonconformity under Article 39(1) or a third party's right or claim under Article 43. The CISG regulates the two sorts of obligations differently in one respect. Article 39(2)'s two-year cutoff date applies only to

---

[143] See, e.g., Kröll, *Article 35*, in Kroll et al., supra note 2, at 530.
[144] See Chapter 5.II.C.1., 2.

nonconformities.[145] There is no similar time limit for the buyer's assertion of third party rights or claims under Article 43.

Article 41's construction is for the most part straightforward. The Article requires the seller to deliver the goods free of "any right or claim" of a third party. Determining whether the goods are delivered free of a third party's "right" in them is in principle unproblematic. A third party's rights in the goods are created or recognized by applicable law other than the CISG. For instance, applicable domestic law determines who has title to the goods and when title in them passes.[146] More generally, because the CISG only governs the rights and obligation of the contracting parties arising from the sales contract,[147] it has nothing to say about whether the buyer takes the goods subject to a third party's rights in them. Law other than the CISG therefore determines these rights. Thus, the Austrian Supreme Court found that the seller had breached Article 41's requirement when it delivered propane subject to a restriction created by its supplier limiting the countries in which propane could be resold.[148] In another case, a bus that had been sold was impounded by Russian customs authorities when the bus lost its temporary import status.[149] The delivery term in the sales contract made the seller responsible for expenses in clearing the bus for export, including paying customs fees for doing so. In the circumstances the rights of Russian customs authorities to the bus meant that the seller had violated Article 41's requirement.

Article 41's limiting language, "unless the buyer agreed to take the goods subject" to the third party's right or claim, must be considered in connection with Article 30. Article 30 in relevant part obligates the seller to deliver title ("property") to the goods as required by the contract. A German court found that a seller that had effectively disclaimed its Article 41 requirement by agreement nonetheless had violated its Article 30 obligation to deliver title to the goods.[150] In so finding, the court ruled that Article 30's requirement is independent of Article 41's requirement. The ruling is mistaken. The buyer's agreement to take the goods subject to a third party's rights relieves the seller of having to deliver goods meeting Article 41's requirement. As a result, the contract does not require the seller to deliver title to the goods, to the

---

[145] See Chapter 5.II.E. Courts applying Articles 39(1) and Article 43(1) refuse to set a rigid time limit within which notice must reasonably be given; see, e.g., District Court Forli (Italy), 16 February 2009, available at http://cisgw3.law.pace.edu/cases/090216i3.html (Article 39(1)); Federal Supreme Court (Germany), 11 January 2006, available at http://cisgw3.law.pace.edu/cases/060111g1.html (Article 43(1)).

[146] Article 4(b).   [147] Article 4.

[148] See Supreme Court (Austria), 6 February 1996, available at http://cisgw3.law.pace.edu/cases/960206a3.html.

[149] See Tribunal of International Commercial Arbitration at the Russian Federation Chamber of Commerce and Industry (Russia), 21 January 1998, available at http://cisgw3.law.pace.edu/cases/980121r1.html.

[150] See Court of Appeals (Dresden), 21 March 2007, available at http://cisgw3.law.pace.edu/cases/070321g1.html.

extent of the buyer's agreement. The court's ruling wrongly ignores Article 30's qualifying phrase, "required by the contract."

A 2002 Russian Federation case took a relaxed view of Article 41's limiting language, "unless the buyer agreed to take the goods subject" to the third party's right or claim.[151] A seller sold combines to a buyer that apparently it was leasing to others. Based on the buyer's knowledge that the purchased combines were being leased, the court concluded that the buyer had agreed to purchase combines subject to the leases. The inference from the buyer's knowledge, without more, to its implicit agreement seems too quick.

One interpretive difficulty in Article 41 concerns its reference to "claim." Does the term refer to any claim by a third party to the goods, however frivolous? Or does it refer only to colorable claims made by them to the goods? Although most American courts construe § 2–312(1) of the Uniform Commercial Code ("UCC") to extend the implied warranty of good title to a warranty against only colorable claims,[152] Article 41's language does not suggest the same limitation. For one thing, the Article's reference to "right or claim" means that a third party's claim does not have to be based on a legal interest in the goods. A claim based on a legal interest in them gives the third party a "right." Thus, apparently a claim to the goods, however unmeritorious, is enough for the seller to be in breach of Article 41. In addition, "claim" is unqualified, so that the seller breaches its obligation even when a third party's claim to the goods is frivolous. The little diplomatic history on point agrees.[153] Thus, the best understanding of Article 41 is that it avoids the need for the line-drawing exercise of distinguishing colorable from frivolous claims to the goods.

Although Article 41's allocation to the seller of the risk of colorable third party claims to the goods might be efficient, its allocation of the risk of non-meritorious third party claims is not. Given its familiarity with the goods and dealings affecting them, the seller might be in a comparatively better position than the buyer to anticipate and resolve colorable claims to the goods by third parties. By contrast, many non-meritorious claims are potentially unpredictable and may not depend on the seller's dealings with respect to the goods. Once they arise, the seller may not be able to convince the third party making the claim that it has no legal basis. In this respect a non-meritorious claim is similar to an exogenously caused event that neither the seller nor the buyer can do anything to avoid or overcome. The contractual surplus therefore is not increased by making the seller responsible for frivolous third-party claims to the goods.

---

[151] See Federal Arbitration Court for the Western Siberia Circuit of the Russian Federation (Russia), 6 August 2002, available at http://cisgw3.law.pace.edu/cases/020806r1.html.
[152] See *Saber v. Dan Angelone Chevrolet*, 811 A.2d 644 (R.I. 2002); *Colton v. Decker*, 540 N.W.2d 172 (S.D. 1995); cf. U.C.C. § 2A-211(1)(b) (leases of goods).
[153] See Secretariat Commentary on the 1978 Draft, in Diplomatic History, supra note 25, at 426 (Comment 3 to then-Article 39) ("It is the seller's responsibility to remove [the burden of litigation against the buyer based on a frivolous claim to the goods] from the buyer").

B. *Conflicting rights and claims based on industrial property or intellectual property*

A buyer's ability to use goods may be limited not only by competing claims to them, but also by claims that they infringe on patent, trademark, trade secret, or other rights based in the law of industrial property or intellectual property. Article 42 obligates the seller to deliver goods free from any such rights or claims. That Article, however, imposes more limited liability on the seller than does Article 41 with respect to conflicting title claims. The seller bears liability for rights and claims based on industrial property or intellectual property only if, at the time of the conclusion of the contract, the seller knew or could not have been unaware of them. Liability, therefore, is less strict than in the case of competing claims of title. In addition, the seller bears liability for the relevant right or claim only if it is asserted under the law of the State where the goods will be resold or used – and then only if the parties understood at the time of contracting that the goods would be resold or used in that State, or under the law of the State where the buyer has its place of business. Presumably the CISG's drafters were concerned that the wide variance of intellectual property law among States could generate substantial exposure for a seller if it were vulnerable to claims of infringement made under the law of States that had little connection with the transaction and thus that posed risks that the seller could not easily price into the contract.

The seller, moreover, bears no liability for conflicting industrial property or intellectual property rights or claims where the buyer knew or could not have been unaware of them at the time of the contract. A buyer with such actual or constructive knowledge will be deemed to have contracted for the goods subject to such rights or claims.

In an early case that applied the CISG, an Israeli court concluded that both buyer and seller were aware at the time of the conclusion of the contract that the goods that were the subject of the sale bore a trademark of a company whose goods were marketed worldwide.[154] Knowledge of the trademark was imputed because both parties were within the trade of the trademark holder and knew that manufacturers in the trade normally register marks for their products. The court noted that both parties not only had the requisite knowledge of the infringement to trigger the seller's liability under Article 42(1) and the buyer's assumption of risk under Article 42(2)(a), but also that, under Israeli law, the parties had failed to deal with each other in good faith. As a consequence, the court concluded that it should divide liability for the damages evenly between the parties and require each of the parties to pay equal costs to the State Treasury.

Finally, the seller bears no liability if the right or claim arises out of the seller's compliance with specifications furnished by the buyer. In the Israeli case just discussed, the court assumed that the seller's immunity applies only if the buyer

---

[154] See Supreme Court (Israel) (*Eximin v. Textile and Footwear Italstyle Ferarri Inc.*), 22 August 1993, available at http://cisgw3.law.pace.edu/cases/930822i5.html.

asked to seller to comply with the specifications, not if compliance was left to the seller's discretion.[155]

X. DISCLAIMERS OF LIABILITY FOR NONCONFORMITY

Various provisions in the CISG make it clear that the obligations created by Article 35 may be disclaimed. Article 6 allows parties to "exclude the application of [the] Convention or . . . derogate from or vary the effect of any of its provisions," and this language certainly includes the provisions that create obligations of conformity to the contract.[156] Thus, in theory, parties may agree that Articles 35(1) and 35(2) are inapplicable to their agreement. In addition, Article 35(2) states that the Article does not apply when "the parties have agreed otherwise."[157] Article 35(3), as discussed, can be treated as a disclaimer of liability where the buyer knew or could not have been unaware of the lack of conformity. Finally, to the extent that disclaimer is a question of the content of a contract, Article 8 provides the applicable rules for interpreting the terms the parties intended to incorporate into their agreement. A warranty disclaimer allocates to the buyer the risk that the goods do not conform to the contract. Therefore, whether the contract disclaims warranties is a matter of contract interpretation. If, for example, one party makes statements that a reasonable person would interpret as language of disclaimer, then Article 8 would presumably incorporate that statement into the meaning of the contract.

Nevertheless, there is disagreement on how to determine the effectiveness of those disclaimers. Problems may arise when disclaimers are written in fine print, written vaguely, written by a seller who has knowledge of specific defects, or written in a way that is extremely favorable to the seller. A buyer under these circumstances is likely to claim that the seller's purported disclaimer is ineffective. That claim may be interpreted as an assertion that the disclaimer is invalid, and therein lies the rub. Issues of validity are outside the CISG; thus, some commentators and courts contend that the issue of the validity of a disclaimer is governed by national law.[158] The CISG does not define "validity," and the sparse relevant diplomatic

---

[155] Id.

[156] See *Ajax Tool Works, Inc. v. Can-Eng Manufacturing Ltd.*, 2003 U.S. Dist. LEXIS 1306 (D.Il. January 20, 2003).

[157] Similarly, Article 41 immunizes the seller from liability for delivering goods subject to a competing right or claim if the buyer agreed to take the goods subject to that right or claim.

[158] See *Norfolk S. Ry. Co. v. Power Source Supply, Inc.*, 2008 U.S. Dist. LEXIS 56942 (W.D. Pa. July 25, 2008); *Geneva Pharm. Tech. Corp. v. Barr Labs.*, 201 F. Supp. 2d 236, 282–83 (S.D.N.Y. 2002) *rev'd on other grounds*, 386 F.3d 485 (2d Cir. 2004). See, e.g., Court of Appeals Köln (Germany), 21 May 1996, available at http://cisgw3.law.pace.edu/cases/960521g1.html; cf. Supreme Court (Austria), 7 September 2000, available at http://cisgw3.law.pace.edu/cases/000907a3.html (validity of standard clauses restricting right to withhold payment governed by applicable domestic law); Laura E. Longobardi, *Disclaimers of Implied Warranties: The 1980 Convention on Contracts for the International Sale of Goods*, 53 Fordham L. Rev. 863 (1985); Schwenzer, *Article 35*, in Schlechtriem & Schwenzer, supra note 2, at 589.

history suggests that the term includes matters of contractual capacity, duress, fraud, and illegality.[159] It is unclear whether the term extends to warranty disclaimers. Of course, if it does, and if domestic law therefore applies to the question of validity, the result will be a reduction in the extent of uniformity that the CISG produces. This is especially true when it comes to disclaimers, where there "is extreme diversity in comparative law."[160]

The diversity and complexity of national laws governing validity may make sellers fearful that they are leaving themselves open to significant liability, which could lead to difficulties because obligations of conformity are likely to be priced. A seller who believes that it has disclaimed those obligations, only to be informed that under applicable domestic law it has not is likely to face liability beyond what it charged for when setting the price for the goods. A seller who knows of defects may be able to reveal them to the buyer and avoid liability under Article 35(3), or by ensuring that the presence of the defects become part of the contract under Article 35(1),[161] but that will not help the seller with respect to defects unknown at the time the contract is executed and for which the seller remains liable under Article 36. An opposing view asserts that the enforceability of a purported disclaimer is a function of interpreting the terms of the contract under the formation rules in Part II of the CISG and Article 8.[162] For example, a court may determine whether a statement made by a seller during negotiations becomes a part of the contract. Assuming the terms are part of the contract, courts will then interpret the terms to fix their scope using Article 8.[163] Under Article 8(1), courts look to the intent of the parties with respect to the disclaimer. If Article 8(1) is inapplicable because the buyer was unaware of the seller's intent, the court should assess the understanding of a reasonable person in the position of the buyer according to Article 8(2). In either circumstance, the court would, under Article 8(3), take account for "all relevant circumstances of the case including the negotiations, any practices which the parties have established between themselves, usages and any subsequent conduct of the parties."

This approach was followed in *TeeVee Toons, Inc. v. Gerhard Schubert GmbH,*[164] where a German seller entered into a contract with an American buyer for a system that would mass-produce packaging for audio and video cassettes. The system malfunctioned frequently and failed to produce packaging at the proper rate and quality. The buyer claimed the goods did not conform under Article 35(2)(a) and Article 35(2)(b). The seller argued that the terms and conditions, found in the fine

---

[159] See Secretariat Commentary on the 1978 Draft, in Documentary History, *supra* note 25, at 254–55; Helen Elizabeth Hartnell, *Rousing the Sleeping Dog: The Validity Exception to the Convention on Contracts for the International Sale of Goods* 18 Yale J. Int'l L. 1, 69–73 (1993).

[160] Hyland, *supra* note 131, at 312; Kröll, *Article 35*, in Kröll et al., *supra* note 2, at 531.

[161] See Kröll, *Article 35*, in Kroll et al., *supra* note 2, at 532.

[162] See Joseph Lookofsky, *The 1980 United Nations Convention on Contracts for the International Sale of Goods*, in International Encyclopedia of Laws—Contracts 95–6 (Roger Blanpain & J. H. Herbots eds., 2000).

[163] Id. at 96.   [164] 2006 U.S. Dist. LEXIS 59455 (S.D.N.Y. August 23, 2006).

print of the written contract, waived the existence of any liability under Article 35. The court interpreted the enforceability of the waiver by determining the intent of the parties under Article 8. The seller had told the buyer on multiple occasions that the fine print was not important for their agreement. Since there is no parol evidence rule in the CISG, the court concluded that even statements that contradict the text could be used to determine the intent of the parties. Further complicating the issue, the agreement had a merger clause, which, if effective, would have excluded all oral statements made by the parties. The court, however, determined that it was also necessary to discern the intent of the parties with respect to the effectiveness of the merger clause. The fact-dependent nature of these inquiries meant that summary judgment on the issue of the disclaimer had to be denied.

There is some support for this approach in the language of Articles 4 and 35. According to Article 4, validity rules are omitted from the Convention "except as otherwise expressly provided." It could be said that Article 35 specifically deals with questions of validity by stating that Article 35(2) applies unless "the parties have agreed otherwise." Thus, the key question of whether the parties agreed to the disclaimer is provided for by Article 35, which can be handled within the CISG framework by determining and interpreting the terms of the contract. However, this approach leaves much to be desired. In particular, it does not instruct courts how to deal with clear substantive validity rules with respect to disclaimers, such as disclaimers procured through fraud, duress, and unconscionability.[165] Moreover, reading "validity" too broadly threatens to limit the scope of CISG rules generally. Any time we interpret a contract term under Article 8, we might limit the enforceability of the literal term in ways that might be construed as affecting its "validity."

The third option distinguishes between issues of validity on the one hand and, what Kröll calls issues of "effectiveness" on the other.[166] The theory distinguishes between those issues relating to disclaimers to which national law should apply and those issues that should be handled through contract formation and interpretation rules of the CISG. As Kröll distinguishes the issues, "a narrow understanding of validity should be adopted, which is largely restricted to the question of whether a disclaimer is as such permissible and if so to what extent, but does not cover issues related to the effectiveness of such clauses."[167] It is not entirely clear what the issue of "a disclaimer as such" refers to. Does national law deal with a disclaimer "as such" only when it allows a disclaimer at all? Or does that law deal with a disclaimer "as such" when it allows a disclaimer that has the same substance and form of presentation as the disputed disclaimer? If the latter, it is not clear what is left for the inquiry into "effectiveness." As Lookofsky, who also endorses a hybrid approach, concludes:

---

[165] See Court of Appeals Köln (Germany), 21 May 1996, available at http://cisgw3.law.pace.edu/cases/960521g1.html (resorting to German law to determine that disclaimers were not applicable if the seller acted fraudulently); Honnold/Flechtner, supra note 27, at 340 (describing validity rules where courts should resort to national law).

[166] See Kröll, *Article 35*, in Kröll et al., supra 2, at 531–32. [167] Id.

In [the] future, courts may have to struggle with the fact that the line between (domestic) validity and (CISG) substance is not always clear. To take one clear example, under both German and Austrian law an unusual clause does not become "part of the contract" if the other party did not have reason to expect it under the "circumstances," especially as regards the *"appearance"* of the contract. This provision functions as a validity rule and should (when otherwise applicable) supplement— and not be displaced by—the CISG substantive regime. On the other hand, under § 2-316(2) of the American Uniform Commercial Code, a warranty disclaimer is without effect unless it is *conspicuous* and mentions the *word* 'merchantability'. And while it might well be argued that this too is a validity rule (in some respects similar to the German and Austrian ones just noted), the "merchantability" requirement is so closely tied to *American substantive* law (UCC § 2-313) that it renders the rule highly inappropriate—and arguably also ineffective—in the CISG context.[168]

We conclude that a hybrid approach is appropriate, but that the theories stated to this point generate too much confusion and fail to distinguish the relevant issues. A better theory of disclaimers sharply distinguishes between the contractual allocation of risk and the legal recognition of that allocation. Whether a warranty disclaimer is enforceable requires asking two questions: (1) has the contract allocated the risk of the relevant nonconformity to the buyer? and (2) if so, will this allocation be given legal effect? Question (1) is a matter of contract interpretation, answerable by reference to the CISG contract formation and interpretation rules, while question (2) a matter of validity. Question (1) simply asks whether the purported disclaimer is part of the contract at all. That was the issue addressed by the court in *TeeVee Toons*. If it had answered that question in the affirmative, it would then have to determine whether the intended clause was effective, or valid, to accomplish what the parties intended. That issue would properly be decided under domestic law.

Although there is a risk that national laws may have different standards of validity, this is an inevitable consequence of Article 4(a)'s limitation on the CISG's scope. Still, the risk of limited uniformity with respect to the second, "legal effect" question may be less problematic than some suggest.[169] The fact that domestic law applies to validity does not necessarily entail that specific domestic provisions intended for situations contemplated by domestic law will apply to transactions governed by the CISG. For instance, as Flechtner notes, the specific requirements in UCC § 2-316 for disclaimer of the warranty of merchantability do not necessarily apply to Article 35, because the warranty of merchantability as provided under the UCC does not exist in the CISG.[170] UCC § 2-316 is a provision that limits the application of UCC §§ 2-313, 2-314, and

---

[168] Lookofsky, supra note 51, at 93.

[169] See Kröll, *Article 35*, in Kroll et al., supra note 2, at 531 ("Given the varying and sometimes very detailed requirements for validity and effectiveness of such declaimers under national laws, and approach which would require that a disclaimer would have to meet the various nations provisions in regards to their appearance or wording to be valid would constitute a serious threat to the uniform application of the CISG").

[170] See Honnold/ Flechtner, supra note 27, at 230-31.

2–315. Those provisions, however, do not apply to contracts governed by the CISG. Instead, liability for nonconformities is created by Article 35. As a result, there is no basis for applying § 2–316 directly. Common law disclaimer rules apply instead. Nevertheless, it would be disingenuous to claim that there is no analogue between UCC § 2–314 and Article 35, or that the requirements of § 2–316 do not provide an appropriate metric for determining whether, as a general matter, purported disclaimers are effective. For example, issues of conspicuousness and use of language commercially understood as constituting a disclaimer, such as "as is" or "with all faults," should be relevant to any general proposition about the validity of a disclaimer. That is, the fact that indicia of validity or invalidity are also part of a specific domestic law may be testimony to their generality rather than to their irrelevance to determining effectiveness for purposes of the CISG. But because those characteristics of a disclaimer are appropriate, we would expect less variance to result from applying a "validity" analysis to the question of enforceability than some might fear.

The analysis can be illustrated through *Norfolk Southern Railway Co. v. Power Source Supply, Inc.*,[171] which involved a contract for the sale of locomotives between a Virginia seller with a Pennsylvania presence and a Canadian buyer. The purported disclaimer on the second page of the two-page document was in capital letters in the same font size as the rest of the document. It expressly disclaimed warranties of merchantability and fitness for a particular purpose. When the seller demanded the full contract price, the buyer alleged breach of the implied warranties of merchantability and fitness for a particular purpose. After determining that the CISG governed the sales contract, the court found that the contract effectively disclaimed the implied warranties. The court reasoned that Article 4 took the validity of the disclaimer out of the CISG, so that it had to look to national law. It then considered the explicit provisions of the UCC in Pennsylvania and Alberta sales law concerning disclaimers of warranties, and found that the purported disclaimer in the contract before it would be valid under either of those regimes.

There was little doubt in the court's view that the contract contained a disclaimer. The court did not undertake an Article 8 analysis of the term. It easily could have done so. Having decided that the contract included a disclaimer of warranties, the next issue was its enforceability. The step in the court's reasoning relying on Pennsylvania's UCC § 2–316(2) or the specific Alberta Sale of Goods Act provision[172] is more questionable. Article 4(a) directs a court to the applicable domestic law governing the validity of the disclaimer. However, which part of domestic law controls is a separate and harder question to answer. In testing the disclaimer by § 2–316(2) and Alberta sales law, the *Norfolk Southern* court assumed that either

---

[171] 2008 U.S. Dist. LEXIS 56942 (W.D. Pa. July 25, 2008).
[172] See Alberta Sale of Goods Act, R.S.A 2000, Ch. S-2, § 54 ("Where any right, duty or liability would arise under a contract of sale by implication of law, it may be negatived or varied by express agreement or by the course of dealing between the parties or by usage if the usage is such as to bind both parties to the contract.") (2015).

Pennsylvania's Article 2 of the UCC's disclaimer provision or Alberta's Sale of Goods Act provision governing disclaimers applies to a contract governed by the CISG. That is not necessarily the case. Article 2's disclaimer provisions apply to sales contracts governed by the UCC. The UCC did not govern the contract at issue. Thus, general contract principles governing disclaimers under Pennsylvania common law instead might apply. The selection of different Pennsylvania law matters because Pennsylvania's common law might enforce a disclaimer that does not mention "merchantability" or meet the other requirements of § 2–316(2) or (3). The same, we speculate, would be true under Alberta law.

To decide which part of domestic law applies, perhaps the following counterfactual question should be asked: If the sales contract were not governed by the CISG and were otherwise governed by domestic law, which part of applicable domestic law would govern it? Alternatively, a different, non-counterfactual question might be asked: Given that the sales contract is governed by the CISG, which part of applicable domestic law that the CISG does not displace governs the enforceability of the disclaimer? If the first, counterfactual question were asked on *Norfolk Southern's* facts, the answer would be Pennsylvania's Article 2 of the UCC (or Alberta's Sale of Goods Act). Thus, although the *Norfolk Southern* court does not ask the question, it tested the warranty disclaimer by the correct part of potentially applicable domestic law. If the second, non-counterfactual question had been asked by the *Norfolk Southern* court, the answer would be Pennsylvania's (or Alberta's) common law of disclaimers. Although the result in the case might be the same, the test for the effectiveness of the warranty disclaimer would be different. In other cases, the two different questions can give different results. For instance, assume that the parties' contracts expressly disclaimed all express warranties. Unlike UCC § 2–316(1), Article 35(1) does not prevent the parties from doing so, and Article 6 allows the disclaimer. Given the disclaimer, the parties have allocated the risk that the goods do not conform to the quantity, quality, and description required by the contract to the buyer. Nonetheless, applicable domestic law might treat the disclaimer as invalid and therefore ineffective. If the domestic law is state statutory law, the counterfactual question would be answered in the negative: If the contract were governed by Article 2 of the UCC, § 2–316(1) would make the disclaimer of the express warranties ineffective. There is no similar result guaranteed under the common law of warranty disclaimers. Thus, if the non-counterfactual question were asked the answer might be in the affirmative: The common law of disclaimers applied to a contract governed by the CISG might enforce a disclaimer of express warranties.

XI. BURDEN OF PROOF FOR NONCONFORMITY

We have dealt elsewhere with the extent to which the CISG governs the allocation of the burden of proof on specific issues.[173] Here, we deal with the application of

---

[173] See Chapter 5.II.F.1; Chapter 8.IX; Chapter 9.I.A.4.

those principles to the question of proving nonconformity. Although our general contention is that the CISG allocates the burden of proof only in the single area where it is mentioned explicitly, the majority of commentary and case law is to the contrary.[174] A few courts have resorted to national law to allocate the burden of proof, perhaps on the view that the CISG is silent on the issue.[175] Some commentators suggest that, according to customary rules, the ultimate buyer will have the burden of proving that the risk materialized prior to the conclusion of the contract.[176] Articles 4 and 7 might be read in a manner consistent with this conclusion. Article 4 provides that the CISG governs the rights and obligations of the contracting parties arising from the contract. One could include among these "obligations" the burden of the buyer to persuade the trier of facts that the goods do not conform to the contract. However, even this conclusion is not ineluctable. Article 4 limits the "obligations" governed by the CISG to those arising from the sales contract. Burdens of proof are created and assigned by the procedural rules of the forum, not by the contract (unless the contract itself assigns burdens of proof). Thus, it quite plausible that Article 4 leaves burdens of proof to national law.

Most of the commentary supporting the majority view rests on the assumption that, pursuant to Article 7(2), burden of proof allocations can be discerned from the general principles on which the CISG is based. We are unconvinced that those general principles have been identified with sufficient precision to allow such a broad allocation. The basic principle on which commentators rely is that each party must prove the existence of the factual prerequisites in the legal provision on which it is relying, but where one finds that in the CISG remains somewhat mysterious. Ferrari is perhaps being quite candid about the difficulties of finding a precise textual predicate when he states that, in the case law, "the prevailing view is that [burden of proof] is somehow governed by the CISG."[177]

The debate appears to be dominated by continental views, which have a rich tradition of rules for allocating burden of proof replete with Latin maxims,[178] though those rules often vary from jurisdiction to jurisdiction.[179] As Kröll demonstrates, many of the positions that commentators endorse in apparent support of underlying general principles are heavily influenced by the author's domestic law. To the extent

---

[174] See Franco Ferrari, *Burden of Proof Under the CISG*, in 2000–2001 Review of the Convention on Contracts for the International Sale of Goods (CISG), at § II, available at www.cisg.law .pace.edu/cisg/biblio/ferrari5.html; Kröll, *Article 35*, in Kröll et al., supra note 2 at 532. For the view that the CISG does not govern burden of proof issues that are not explicitly allocated, see Honnold/Flechtner, supra note 27, at 86–7.

[175] See *Chicago Prime Packers, Inc. v. Northam Food Trading Co.*, 408 F.3d 894 (7th Cir. 2005); Federal Supreme Court (Germany), 9 January 2002, available at http://cisgw3.law.pace.edu/ cases/020109g1.html; International Chamber of Commerce, Case No. 6653, 26 March 1993, available at http://cisgw3.law.pace.edu/cases/936653i1.html and www.unilex.info/case.cfm? pid=1&do=case&id=36&step=Abstract.

[176] See, e.g., Fritz Enderlein & Dietrich Maskow, International Sales Law 270 (1992).

[177] See Ferrari, supra note 2.   [178] Id.

[179] See Kröll, *Article 35*, in Kröll et al., supra note 2, at 534.

that principles are identified, they consist of broad propositions such as those identified by Ferrari: (1) a party that seeks to derive beneficial legal consequences from a legal provision must prove the existence of the factual prerequisites of that provision; (2) a party that seeks an exception from application of a general legal rule must prove the existence of the factual prerequisites of that exception; and (3) a party in superior possession of factual information must prove those facts.[180] The first two propositions are frequently combined in what is referred to in continental literature as the "rule and exception" principle or the maxim of *onus actori probandi incumbit.* It places on each party the burden of proving the factual prerequisites of the legal provisions for which it relies for either a claim or a defense.[181] For example, Hager and Schmidt-Kessel maintain that "a person who relies on a rule in his favour must prove that the preconditions of the application of that rule are satisfied."[182] The third proposition is often referred to as the "proof proximity principle."[183] Under that principle, the burden of proof lies with the person who is the most proximate to the evidence.[184] As Ferrari puts it, "[t]hose facts that are exclusively in a party's sphere of responsibility and which therefore are, at least theoretically, better known to that party have to be proven by that party, since it is that party who exercises the control over that sphere."[185] Most scholars and courts seem to view this as an exception to the "rule and exception principle." The exception shifts the burden of proof to the seller when the buyer rejects goods or notifies the buyer of nonconformity immediately after inspection.[186] This exception is similar to that embodied in UCC § 2–607 (4), which imposes on the buyer the burden of proving breach with respect to accepted goods. Where the buyer fails to accept goods, the seller is likely to have superior information about the conditions under which any nonconformity materialized and thus bears the burden of proving conformity. Where the buyer has

---

[180] See Ferrari, supra note 174.

[181] See Stefan Kröll, *The Burden of Proof for the Non-Conformity of Goods under Art.* 35 CISG, 59 Belgrade L. Rev. 162, 170 (2011); Supreme Court (Switzerland), 13 November 2003, available at http://cisgw3.law.pace.edu/cases/031113s1.html.

[182] Günter Hager & Martin Schmidt-Kessel, *Article 67*, in Schlechtriem & Schwenzer, supra note 2, at 932.

[183] Kröll, *Article 35*, in Kröll et al., supra note 2, at 533; Schwenzer, *Article 35*, in Schlechtriem & Schwenzer, supra 2, at 592.

[184] See Supreme Court (Switzerland), 7 July 2004, available at http://cisgw3.law.pace.edu/cases/040707s1.html; Federal Supreme Court (Germany), 8 March 1995, available at http://cisgw3.law.pace.edu/cases/950308g3.html; Kröll, supra note 181, at 170; see also Schwenzer, *Article 35*, in Schlechtriem & Schwenzer, supra note 2, at 592.

[185] Ferrari, supra note 174.

[186] See Supreme Court (Austria), 12 September 2006, available at http://cisgw3.law.pace.edu/cases/060912a3.html; Kröll, *Article 35*, in Kröll et al., supra note 2, at 533; S.A. Kruisinga, (Non-) conformity in the 1980 Convention on Contracts for the International Sale of Goods: A Uniform Concept? 164 (2004); Thomas Neumann, *Features of Article 35 in the Vienna Convention: Equivalence, Burden of Proof and Awareness*, 11 Vindobona J. Int'l Com. L. & Arb 81, at ¶ 39 (2007) available at www.cisg.law.pace.edu/cisg/biblio/neumann.html; Schwenzer, *Article 35*, in Schlechtriem & Schwenzer, supra note 2, at 593.

accepted the goods, there is a risk that nonconformities arose subsequent to delivery. As a result, a preference to place the burden of proof on the party with superior access to information about the evolution of the defect would impose on the buyer of accepted goods the obligation of proving nonconformities.

Certainly these may be principles that are widely adhered to in different legal systems. But that fact alone does not entail that they are implicated in the CISG. Indeed, the principles may conflict, as where a party who seeks an exception is not in superior possession of facts which, if true, would justify the exception. In spite of Kröll's advocacy of finding burden of proof within the CISG, he recognizes that the commonly proposed principles do not necessarily generate clear answers: "Notwithstanding the broad consensus as to the existence and relevance of these two principles [which essentially embody the three principles recited previously], completely divergent views exist as to their consequences in relation to the allocation of the burden of proof for non-conformity of the goods."[187] If the objection to using domestic law is that it will decrease uniformity in application of CISG rules, the response is that application of the underlying principles that have been suggested are so vague and contradictory that their application provides no greater certainty or uniformity.

The difficulties inherent in treating burden of proof under Article 36 as an issue determinable from Article 7(2) is clear from a review of the positions that courts and commentators have taken on the issue. Article 36 makes the seller liable for any lack of conformity that exists at the time when the risk passes to the buyer and for any lack of conformity that occurs after that time, and that is due to a breach of any of its obligations. The burden of proof issue, therefore, entails the question of whether the seller must demonstrate conformity at the relevant time or whether the buyer must prove nonconformity. In theory, at least, the burden need not be borne completely by a single party. Kröll, for instance, suggests that the buyer should have the burden of proving that the goods are not in conformity at the time notice of breach is given, but that a buyer's satisfaction of that burden should create a presumption that the goods were not in conformity at the time the risk passed. Thus, the burden would shift to the seller to prove that the goods were in conformity at the time the risk passed.[188] However, this view could potentially put the burden of proof on a seller for a substantial period after the goods left the seller's possession. The seller would then have no way to determine what the buyer had done with the goods between delivery and notification of nonconformity.[189]

The Seventh Circuit's decision in *Chicago Prime Packers, Inc.* v. *Northam Food Trading Co.,*[190] is the primary American contribution to the issue, though the decision creates more confusion than clarity. An American seller had entered into

---

[187] See Kröll, supra note 181, at 171.
[188] See Kruisinga, supra note 186, at 169–70; Kröll, *Article 35*, in Kröll et al., supra note 2, at 535.
[189] See Kröll, supra note 181, at 177.   [190] 408 F.3d 894 (7th Cir. 2005).

a contract with a Canadian buyer for ribs. The ribs were picked up from a processor by the buyer's agent and delivered directly to the buyer's costumer. Thus, neither the buyer nor the seller ever had physical possession of the goods. The deliverer and the customer who received the ribs said the contents were in good order, although neither the deliverer nor the customer examined the contents of the boxes. Later inspection revealed that the ribs were not in satisfactory condition, and the buyer refused to pay. There was, however, no way to determine at what point the ribs had gone bad and records concerning the maintenance of the ribs were probative at best. The party bearing the burden of proof would unlikely be able to satisfy it, and thus would lose the case. The buyer maintained that the seller had that burden because proving conformity was an essential element of its contract claim. The seller maintained that nonconformity was an affirmative defense that placed the burden on the buyer. The court looked to general principles of the CISG under Article 7(2) to resolve the matter, but concluded that UCC provisions analogous to CISG provisions provided at least some evidence of those principles. The relevant provisions of the UCC, including the warranty provisions, would place the burden of proof on the buyer in the situation.[191] The court thus concluded that the buyer had the same burden under the CISG. In effect, the court applied domestic law to the burden of proof issue, but did so in guise of applying a principle inherent in the CISG. The result of placing the risk of loss on the buyer may make sense in that it induces buyers to make expeditious inspections of goods or to ensure, in a case where the buyer does not physically receive the goods, that their downstream purchasers make such inspections. But neither the fact that the result is sensible nor that the analysis reflects the UCC outcome entails that it expresses an underlying principle of the CISG. Indeed, the very robustness of the debate about the burden of proof in nonconformity cases reveals the absence of uniformity among commentators and decreases the concerns that would materialize if the issue were treated as a matter subject to domestic law.

Kröll has advocated the most interesting and complex system for allocating the burden of proof under Article 35 in an approach that considers the different contexts in which the issue of conformity arises.[192] He suggests that conformity issues raise questions about (1) the proper standard for measuring nonconformity, (2) the present condition of the goods, and (3) the condition of the goods at the time the risk passed. He would apply the rule and exception standard to the first inquiry, so that, for instance, the buyer who seeks to benefit from the requirement that goods be fit for their ordinary purpose must bear the burden of proving what that purpose is, while a seller who is attempting to demonstrate that the buyer is not using the goods for their ordinary purpose would bear the definitional burden. The burden of proving the present state of the goods would be allocated in accordance with the "proof proximity principle."[193]

---

[191] See U.C.C. § 2–607(3).   [192] See Kröll, supra note 181.   [193] Id. at 176.

One problem with Kröll's proposal is finding its basis in Article 7 or elsewhere else in the CISG's provisions. Again, it is difficult to discern in the general principles underlying the CISG provisions different burden assignments. In addition, on its own terms the proposal presents difficulties. One is that Kröll has peculiar conceptions of what it means to be proximate to the relevant proof. He would, for instance, place on the seller the burden of proving conformity where the buyer accepted the goods but did so with a complaint or reservation about their quality. This seems to us an ad hoc exception to the "proof proximity principle." The buyer's physical possession of the goods and recognition of a defect at the point of acceptance allows it to memorialize proof of their nonconformity. An awareness of the nonconformity and proximity to the goods puts the buyer in a comparatively better position to preserve evidence of the defect. Kröll expresses concern that leaving the burden on the buyer with respect to such goods would "de facto punish the buyer for accepting the defective goods with reservations," and would run contrary to what he views as a general objective of the CISG to minimize returns in international sales. But defining the imposition of a burden of proof as a de facto punitive measure to be avoided appears to ignore the principle, inherent in proof proximity, of placing the burden on the party with superior information. Moreover, any allocation of burden of proof to the seller will have the effect of facilitating returns and thus run counter to the general objective of minimizing them.

Perhaps for these reasons, Kröll limits the cases in which the seller necessarily bears the burden to situations in which the buyer complains at the time of delivery. But he justifies this limitation not on the grounds that post-delivery the buyer occupies the best position to explain what has happened to the goods – or as a manifestation of the proof proximity principle. Rather, he does so the grounds that after delivery the burden of proving the condition of the goods at the time that the risk passed should be allocated on the basis of the rule and exception principle. He contends that this would place the burden of proof on the buyer, assisted by a presumption of nonconformity at the time risk of loss passed if the buyer can demonstrate that they are currently defective. The rationale for this position is that, in the absence of Articles 35(1) and 35(2), the seller would have no duty to provide conforming goods. Therefore, only the buyer receives the legal benefit from Articles 35(1) and 35(2) and must bear the burden of proving entitlement to that benefit.[194] Other commentators interpret the rule and exception principle as imposing the burden of proving conformity on the seller claiming payment,[195] although the buyer would bear it if the buyer had paid but sought damages.[196]

---

[194] See Kruisinga, supra note 182, at 171; Schwenzer, *Article* 35, in Schlechtriem & Schwenzer, supra note 2, at 592–93; Neumann, supra note 186, at ¶ 38.

[195] See Hager & Schmidt-Kessel, *Article* 67, in Schlechtriem & Schwenzer, supra note 2, at 932.

[196] Id. See also Court of Appeals Valais (Switzerland), 27 April 2007, available at http://cisgw3.law .pace.edu/cases/070427s1.html ("As a general matter, the party who claims a right based on a rule has the burden to prove that the rule's conditions are met; in contrast, the other party has to

While Kröll's system and those of other contributors to the interesting debates about burden of proof are perfectly logical, the CISG likely does not reflect their results. The complexity and indefiniteness of results their application would generate make it difficult to conclude that the drafters intended the CISG to govern the issue of burden of proof without more explicit incorporation of rules that would apply to particular situations. It is counterintuitive to conclude that the CISG simultaneously incorporates principles that assign burdens of proof on such different bases as the "rule and exception principle" and the "proof proximity principle." Because the different principles risk inconsistent burden assignments, one would expect a treaty adopting them to signal their incorporation and give some guidance about their application. Combined with the uneasy basis for discovering underlying principles that would inform the burden of proof,[197] we find little basis for discerning implicit burden of proof allocations within the CISG itself. Indeed, the discovery of such allocations could cause other difficulties, since the allocation of burdens of proof will necessarily interact with other procedural doctrines, such as what satisfies that burden, that no one argues are governed by the CISG. To append one externally determined procedural rule into a regime otherwise governed by domestic law is to risk distorting carefully balanced doctrines within the domestic procedural system.[198]

---

prove the facts that exclude or are opposed to the application of the rule. If the buyer rejects the goods by invoking their non-conformity the seller must prove that the goods are in conformity with the contract; if the buyer already accepted the goods the buyer would have to prove their non-conformity" (citations omitted)).

[197] Some commentators draw support from Articles 2 and 25.

[198] Kröll recognizes this. He concludes his advocacy for including the burden of proof within the CISG by noting that the "obvious connection between the standard of proof and the importance of the burden of proof provides good arguments that they should not be regulated completely independent from each other." Kröll, supra note 181, at 179.

7

Risk of loss

I. CONSEQUENCES OF PASSING THE RISK OF LOSS

International sales governed by the CISG are likely to involve transport of goods over substantial geographical distances, and frequently involve transportation through multiple carriers and types of carriage, or multimodal transport. Shipping goods from a landlocked seller across water to a distant buyer is likely to comprise on-loading and off-loading from trucks, ships, and railways, each operated by a different entity. The consequences include both increased likelihood of damage or loss for the goods and increased difficulties in identifying the point at which any damage occurred. As a result, the default rules allocating the financial responsibility for loss or damage to the goods take on additional importance in these transactions. They inform buyers and sellers of the effects of damage or loss on their underlying obligations to pay or to deliver conforming goods and determine which of them is entitled to pursue remedies against the carriers involved in the transaction.

Legal systems differ in their default rules allocating risk of loss. They tend to allocate risk in three different ways. Some national law based on Roman law passes risk from the seller to the buyer at the conclusion of the contract.[1] A second group of legal systems passes risk with respect to the goods sold when title (property) to them passes.[2] The third group of national laws passes risk of loss on delivery of the goods to the buyer.[3] The CISG's risk of loss rules are closest to the third group. They do not and cannot pass risk based on passage of title, because the CISG does not determine title in the goods,[4] and with a single exception do not pass risk to the buyer at the

---

[1] See, e.g., Schweizerisches Obligationenrecht [OR] art. 185 (Switz.); W.W. *Barrett* v. *Ngazana*, (1901) NLR 223 (South Africa).

[2] See, e.g., Sales of Goods Act 1979 sec. 20(1) (United Kingdom); Code civil [C. civ.] art. 1138 (Fr.).

[3] Bürgerliches Gesetzbuch [BGB] [Civil Code] § 446 (Ger.); cf. U.C.C. 2–509(3).

[4] See Article 4(b); supra Chapter 2.

conclusion of the contract.[5] Instead, under the CISG's basic risk of loss rule risk generally passes when the buyer takes over the goods or is in a position to do so.[6] The details of the CISG's risks of loss rules are described and evaluated in the sections that follow.

The CISG's treatment of risk of loss begins with a statement of the consequences of the passage of that risk. The primary consequence results from a negative implication. Article 66 recites that "[l]oss of or damage to the goods after the risk has passed to the buyer does not discharge him from his obligation to pay the price, unless the loss or damage is due to an act or omission of the seller." Article 66 does not itself indicate when the risk of loss passes; it only provides that the buyer's liability to pay the price continues if loss or damage materializes after the risk of loss has passed to the buyer. The negative implication is that any loss or damage that materializes prior to the time that the risk has passed has the effect of discharging the buyer from its obligation under Article 53 to pay the price of the contracted goods. This is consistent with the statement in Article 36(1) that the "seller is liable in accordance with the contract and this Convention for any lack of conformity which exists at the time when the risk passes to the buyer."

Assume, for instance, that a German seller S sells widgets to an Italian buyer B. The widgets are shipped by sea from S to B by carrier C. While the goods are on C's ship, the widgets sustain water damage. B receives damp widgets, which are completely unusable, and refuses to pay for them. B can avoid the obligation to pay for the goods based on the nonconformity if, but only if, the risk of loss had not passed to it when the damage occurred.[7] Assuming that the risk of loss passed when the goods were loaded onto the ship, B is required to pay notwithstanding its receipt of useless goods. If, on the other hand, the damage had occurred while the goods were still in S's possession, B would be discharged from its obligation to pay for the goods and, if the damage constituted a fundamental breach, B would be entitled to avoid the contract. For instance, in a German case,[8] plants were damaged on an overseas voyage. The court found that some of the nonconformity was due to the plants being poorly grown, rather than damaged during the shipping, so the seller was liable for the nonconformity.

Since Article 66 says nothing about when risk of loss does pass, and only indicates the consequences of that event, determination of the time when risk passes requires consideration of contractual provisions and of Articles 67–69. Before addressing that issue, however, it is necessary to examine one exception to the general rule of Article 66.

---

[5] Article 68(1) is the exception.   [6] See Article 69(1)–(2).

[7] See, e.g., CIETAC Arbitration (China), 5 June 1997, available at http://cisgw3.law.pace.edu/cases/970625c1.html.

[8] See District Court Bamberg (Germany), 23 October 2006, available at http://cisgw3.law.pace.edu/cases/061023g1.html.

A. *"Act or omission" of the seller*

Article 66 contains one noteworthy exception: the buyer will be discharged from its obligation to pay if the loss or damage is due to the seller's "act or omission," even if the risk has passed to the buyer. That proviso generates some interpretive difficulties. An easy case involves the failure of the seller to package the goods appropriately. If the goods are damaged because the seller did not provide proper packaging, that failure will constitute an act or omission that precludes the seller from obtaining the price of the goods. But even without the Article 66 exception, the seller in such a case should ultimately be liable for such a failure. This is because improper packaging is a breach of the seller's obligation under Article 35(2)(d) to deliver goods that are contained or packaged in the manner usual for such goods or, where there is no such manner, in a manner adequate to preserve and protect the goods. Goods that fail to comply with that standard are deemed nonconforming by Article 35(2)(d). Thus, the seller would be liable under Article 36(1) because the nonconformity existed at the time the risk passed to the buyer, even though the result of the inadequate packaging only materialized later.

In a 2006 case from a German appellate court, the contract for the sale of wine bottles called for delivery to take place "ex factory," which formally would have shifted the risk of loss to the buyer at the seller's place of business.[9] Apparently the bottles arrived in a condition that made them unsuitable for wine, either because they were broken or had lost their sterility. The seller demanded the price, claiming that any defects had arisen during transport by truck. The court, however, concluded that the seller retained liability under Article 66, because the defects that materialized were caused by the seller's use of a particular porous and unsuitable foil. As a result, even though the risk of loss had formally passed, the seller's act of improper packaging discharged the buyer's obligation to pay. Presumably, the improper packaging had occurred at the time when the goods were shipped, so the seller was responsible under Article 36 for the nonconformity that existed at the time that the risk passed. Similarly, if nonconformities in the plants case discussed previously had been due to their being poorly grown, and the buyer complained that they lived a shorter period than was anticipated and guaranteed by the seller, rather than that damage had occurred during shipment, the seller would remain responsible even without the exception in Article 66.[10] The seller would be liable under Article 36(2). That provision imposes liability on the seller for any lack of conformity that occurs after the risk has passed to the buyer if the lack of conformity is due to the seller's breach of its obligations, including a guarantee by the seller that the goods will retain specified qualities or characteristics for a specific period.

---

[9] See District Court Koblenz (Germany), 14 December 2006, available at http://cisgw3.law.pace .edu/cases/061214g1.html.

[10] See District Court Bamberg (Germany), 23 October 2006, available at http://cisgw3.law.pace .edu/cases/061023g1.html.

If the proviso of Article 66 includes only cases in which the seller has conducted itself in a manner that constitutes a breach of contract, the provision seems superfluous. Because in these cases the injured buyer who bears the risk of loss can recover damages for breach of contract, the seller would ultimately be unable to recover the full price of the goods. Indeed, the drafting committee rejected a proposal that the exception should apply only if the act or omission amounted to a breach of contract.[11] The key interpretive issue, therefore, is what acts or omissions, if any, that do not entail an independent breach of contractual obligations still discharge a buyer to whom the risk has passed from his obligation to pay the price.

One set of cases involves negligence on the part of the seller independent of its contractual obligations. These cases might implicate some extra-contractual failure to disclose information concerning the goods to the carrier charged with transporting them to the buyer. In a Chinese arbitration, the seller failed to notify the carrier that the cargo, piperonal aldehyde, had to be stored at cold temperatures and failed to arrange for nonstop shipment. When the goods subsequently spoiled, the buyer was absolved from liability for payment, notwithstanding that under the applicable CIF shipment term risk would have passed when the goods were loaded onto the ship.[12] The seller's failure to notify the carrier of the characteristics of the cargo constituted an omission under the Article 66 proviso. Even in that case, however, the tribunal concluded that the buyer had notified the seller of the requirements and the parties had reached a "special agreement" about shipping requirements. As a result, even this case may be viewed as an application of Article 36 in which the seller failed to provide a delivery that conformed to contractual specifications.

Other acts or omissions might involve the commission of a tort unrelated to contractual requirements. For example, a seller who loads goods onto a carrier and thereby completes its delivery obligations so that risk has passed to the buyer may damage the goods in the process of removing its loading equipment. In this situation, most commentary would impose the loss on seller.[13] Alternatively, assume that the seller invalidly seizes the goods for an alleged nonpayment and the goods suffer damage while they are in the seller's possession. Here, too, we would find that the damage discharged the buyer, notwithstanding the technical passage of the risk to that party. The effect of the Article 66 discharge in these cases is simply to provide a shortcut to the same result that would obtain if the buyer was required to pay the price,

[11] See UNCITRAL Yearbook VIII (1977), A/32/17 at ¶ 531, available at www.cisg.law.pace.edu/cisg/legislative/B01-66.html.

[12] See CIETAC Arbitration (China) (1999), available at http://cisgw3.law.pace.edu/cases/990000c1.html. For a similar case, see CIETAC Arbitration Award (China), 23 February 1995, available at http://cisgw3.law.pace.edu/cases/950223c1.html.

[13] See, e.g., Zoi Valioti, Passing of Risk in International Sale Contracts: A Comparative Examination of the Rules on Risk under the United Nations Convention on Contracts for the International Sale of Goods (Vienna 1980) and INCOTERMS 2000 (September 2003) (unpublished LL.M. thesis, University of Kent), available at http://cisgw3.law.pace.edu/cisg/biblio/valioti1.html.

but then could either recover the price in a tort action against the seller or exercise a right of recoupment to reduce the price by the amount of its damages.

Nevertheless, not every "act or omission" triggers the Article 66 proviso. Assume, for instance, in the German bottles case discussed before, that the seller had used state-of-the-art packaging, but the sterility of the bottles was still compromised. Assume further that the seller could have avoided that result by using an alternative that no seller uses because its cost exceeds the value of the expected loss. One might argue that the failure to use the inefficient packaging still triggers the proviso, because the seller's "omission" caused the damage. We do not read the proviso to create a regime of strict liability. Instead, the relevant act or omission "must be derived from the violation of some binding standard."[14] Although Article 66 speaks only of an "act or omission," not an act or omission the avoidance of which would have been cost-justified, any alternative conclusion would lead to an anomaly. With some expenditure, sellers almost always can do something to avoid a later loss to the goods. Unless an "act or omission" is limited to acts or omissions worth avoiding, a seller who failed to use an inefficient method of protecting goods from loss or damage would remain responsible for them, even if the risk had passed to the buyer. This result would be inconsistent with the pattern of risk of loss rules in the CISG. (It would also be inconsistent with the allocation of liability the parties would bargain for if they faced no transaction costs.) As we discuss later, those rules tend to place the risk of loss on the party best positioned to avoid the loss from materializing or to insure against the loss that does materialize. A buyer appears to occupy that position once it obtains control or possession of the goods. Placing loss on the seller because of that party's failure to utilize inefficient accident-avoidance measures disrupts the implicit objective of allocating losses in accordance with risk-avoiding capacity.

The "binding standard" of conduct implies that the act or omission be remediable under tort law. But the potential incorporation of tort liability into the Article 66 proviso raises the issue of what tort law applies. Some concern has been raised that the incorporation of domestic tort law into the Article threatens uniformity. Honnold, for example, concludes that the "vagaries and inappropriateness for international trade of scraps of domestic law" require the primary standard of the parties' obligations to be the requirements established under the contract and the CISG.[15] Hager and Schmidt-Kessel contend that the proviso requires something like "reasonable care."[16] Assume that the contract did not require protective packing and such packing was unusual in the circumstances. The seller's failure to provide protective packing therefore would not breach the seller's obligations under Articles

---

[14] John O. Honnold, Uniform Law for International Sales Under the 1980 United Nations Convention 515 (Harry M. Flechtner ed., 4th ed. 2009) [hereinafter "Honnold/Flechtner"].

[15] Id.

[16] See Günter Hager & Martin Schmidt-Kessel, *Article 66*, in Schlechtriem & Schwenzer: Commentary on the UN Convention on the International Sale of Goods (CISG) 921, 925 (Ingeborg Schwenzer ed., 3d ed. 2010) [hereinafter "Schlechtriem & Schwenzer"].

35 and 36. Nonetheless, if the seller was in a position to place the goods in protective packing at relatively low cost but decided not to do so, that failure arguably is an "omission" under most domestic standards of tort law.

But if these commentators mean that the definition of "act or omission" necessarily requires the application of some international standard of care, we would disagree. The seller who acts in a jurisdiction is typically liable for its torts committed while in that jurisdiction, and we see no reason to relieve the seller of that liability because it is in the process of performing an international sale of goods. Indeed, we conclude that the incorporation of domestic tort law would provide a clearer standard of liability or non-liability than the incorporation of some vague international norm of appropriate conduct. Assume, for instance, that the seller causes damage to the goods after the risk has passed because of the seller's involvement in an activity that is considered sufficiently dangerous in the relevant jurisdiction that it falls under the category of strict liability. A seller engaged in dynamiting activities, for example, might non-negligently cause an explosion that damages the goods after the risk of loss has passed to the buyer. Although we do not advocate a strict liability regime for all the seller's activities, we would invoke the Article 66 proviso in this case to discharge the buyer of its obligations if strict liability applied to dynamiting in the jurisdiction in which the seller was engaged in the activity. If, on the other hand, the seller non-negligently engaged in the same activity and its conduct damaged the goods in a jurisdiction that did not adopt strict liability for the activity (dynamiting), we would not apply the proviso.

Where the buyer has been discharged of its obligation to pay the price due to the seller's act or omission that causes damage, there remains an issue of the extent of that discharge. In a case in which the proviso is applied to conduct that constitutes a breach of contract (and again we are dubious about whether such a case is intended to fall within the proviso), and if the subsequent loss is less than total, the buyer may be discharged of its obligation to pay the price, but is not necessarily entitled to avoid the contract entirely. The right to avoid would still depend on whether the loss or damage attributable to the seller's act or omission constituted a fundamental breach. If it did not, then the buyer may recover damages for seller's breach under Articles 35(2)(d) and 36, but would still be responsible for payment for that part of the goods that were conforming. In the German wine bottles case previously discussed, for example, the court interpreted the discharge under Article 66 as a means of denying to the seller the right to receive the full purchase price for goods that were defective due to his own noncompliance with the contract. The court concluded that the buyer could reduce the price under Article 50, even if the buyer had lost the right to avoid by failing to give timely notice, and could even reduce the price to zero where that amount reflected the value of the goods at the time of delivery. The seller in that case contended that the value of the wine bottles at that time – prior to when they were broken or lost their sterility – amounted to their full market value, since the bottles conformed to the contract in all respects other than their defective packaging. As a result, the seller maintained, damages should be calculated as the difference at the time when risk passed to the buyer between the value of the bottles that were poorly packed and the value of those that had been properly packed. Where the bottles otherwise conformed to the contract, the seller suggested, damages calculated in that manner would be zero. But the court determined that the proper calculation required consideration of the value that improperly packaged goods would have at the time that they arrived at their destination. The court concluded that the goods had no value at that time and thus, far from the seller's assertion that damages were zero, the buyer was entitled to reduce their value to zero.[17]

B. *Loss or damage*

What constitutes loss or damage to the goods is usually a straightforward inquiry. The relevant loss or damage usually consists of physical defects that reduce the value of the goods below what they would otherwise command or the disappearance or destruction of the goods. A Chinese arbitration tribunal rejected a claim that a delay in delivery caused by shipping goods on a vessel that was seized as unseaworthy was the type of damage that fell within the risk of loss provisions. The tribunal limited the covered risks to "damages by accident, such as loss or damages by natural or fortuitous accidents."[18] But a decision in the Belgian case of *Mermark Fleischhandelsgesellschaft mbH* v. *Cvba Lokerse Vleesveiling*,[19] suggests a somewhat broader view. The buyer in that case contended that it did not have to pay for pork that had been delivered to it under contract, but that it could not resell because of a governmental order related to concerns about dioxin contamination of pork. The relevant order was issued subsequent to the delivery of the pork to the buyer. The court accepted the seller's contention that the chronology meant that the seller was entitled to the price under Article 66 because the relevant loss of, or damage to the goods had occurred after the risk had passed to the buyer. The pork itself had not suffered any physical change between the time of shipment and time of delivery. Thus, the relevant "loss of, or damage to" the goods apparently consisted of the reduction in value due to issuance of the governmental order prohibiting resale of the pork. Even if this were seen as a case of force majeure, it was one that materialized after the risk had passed to the buyer. The court, however, also noted that the buyer could not maintain that the goods were nonconforming at the time of delivery, because the buyer had failed to conduct an examination that might have revealed an absence of contamination, and thus might have indicated that the pork was fit for resale. We are less convinced that the kinds of

[17] See District Court Koblenz (Germany), 14 December 2006, available at http://cisgw3.law.pace.edu/cases/061214g1.html.

[18] See CIETAC Arbitration (China), 1 April 1997, available at http://cisgw3.law.pace.edu/cases/970401c1.html.

[19] See Court of Appeals Ghent (Belgium), 16 June 2004, available at http://cisgw3.law.pace.edu/cases/040616b1.html.

risk that the case involved – what some call "legal risk" – falls under Article 66 at all. The possibility of government intervention to disrupt contractual expectations is more appropriate for treatment under Article 79, which deals with impediments to the performance of a contract.[20] The risks referenced by Article 66 appear to involve physical consequences (disappearance or damage) rather than external events that reduce the value of the transaction or that make it more difficult to perform.[21]

II. CONTRACTING FOR PASSAGE OF RISK: INCOTERMS RULES

Articles 67 through 69 provide a comprehensive set of rules that determine when risk of loss passes, and thus that determine the point at which the effects of Article 66 are triggered. But passage of risk is one of the primary examples of when parties take advantage of Article 6 and "derogate from" or opt out of the CISG default rules. Commercial parties frequently include within their contracts terms that specify the passage of risk. In international trade this is frequently accomplished by incorporation of Incoterms into contracts. Incoterms, or international commercial terms, consist of various trade terms that are promulgated by the International Chamber of Commerce and govern a variety of issues common to commercial contracts, including risk of loss. The first version of Incoterms was published in 1936 and they have been revised on a regular basis. The most recent version is Incoterms® 2010.[22] These rules comprise the most common set of international trade rules that define the rights and obligations of the seller and buyer in contracts that involve international transportation of goods. These rights and obligations are bundled into various designations, which are known by three-character designations: EXW, FAS. FOB, FCA, CFR, CPT, CIF, CIP, DAP, DAT, and, DDP. The designations in turn are classified into two categories organized according to the mode of transport. Group 1 (EXW, FCA, CPT, CIP, DAT, DAP, and DDP) consists of delivery terms applicable to any mode of transport, while the terms in Group 2 (FAS, FOB, CFR, and CIF) apply only to waterborne transport. Within each group, in the order of the listed terms, the obligations of the seller increase and the obligations of the buyer decrease. Thus, the E-term "EXW," or Ex Works, simply requires the seller to place the goods at the disposal of the buyer at the place of shipment, while D-terms impose on the seller obligations of arranging for carriage and bearing the risk of loss

---

[20] See Chapter 8.II.
[21] See Johan Erauw, *Delivery Terms and the Passing of Risk: Drafting Clauses Related to CISG Articles 66–70*, in Drafting Contracts Under the CISG 383, 392 (Harry M. Flechtner, Ronald A. Brand & Mark S. Walter eds., 2008) [hereinafter "Flechtner et al."]. For a different view, see Sylan Bollée, *The Theory of Risks in the Vienna Sale of Goods Convention 1980*, Pace Review of the Convention on Contracts for the International Sale of Goods 245, 273 (1999–2000) (distinguishing between confiscation of goods through an act of state, such as export or import bans (not within Article 66), and confiscation of goods by an enemy state in wartime (within Article 66).
[22] Incoterms® 2010 (Pub. No. 715).

until the goods are placed at the disposal of the buyer. Depending on the specific D-term, these obligations may include unloading the goods, paying import duties and taxes, and having the goods delivered to the buyer at the ultimate destination. In each case, Incoterms rules define the delivery obligations of the seller and connect the transfer or risk of loss with the completion of those obligations. As in the CISG, the passage of title is irrelevant to the issue of passage of risk.

Where the parties explicitly incorporate Incoterms rules into their contract, courts have used that reference to displace or augment CISG rules that deal with the same issue, such as risk of loss or place of delivery.[23] This may cause some deviation from or add some precision to the rules that would apply under the CISG. For instance, use of an FOB term under Incoterms® 2010 entails that the risk passes when the seller places the goods on board the vessel nominated by the buyer at the named port of shipment. The risk does not pass until the goods are loaded on board;[24] "passing the ship's rail" does not satisfy the obligation. This rule places some meat on the bones of Article 67(1), which shifts the risk to the buyer when the goods are "handed over" to the first carrier. A German decision has interpreted "handing over" as requiring the carrier to take custody of the goods. Thus, the court concluded that handing over occurs only when loading is completed.[25]

Where parties have not explicitly referenced Incoterms, but have incorporated into their contract a term that is defined in Incoterms, tribunals have used the Incoterms definitions to interpret the contract language.[26] The convincing rationale for this conclusion is that, under Article 9(2), contractual terms have the meanings attributed to them in widely accepted international trade, and Incoterms constitute the best evidence of those meanings.[27] As long as Incoterms are used in the relevant trade in which the parties are engaged,[28] the meaning that Incoterms give to the

---

[23] See Tribunal of International Commercial Arbitration at the Russian Federation Chamber of Commerce and Industry (Russia), 24 January 2002, available at www.cisg.law.pace.edu/cisg/wais/db/cases2/020124r1.html; Court of Appeals (Argentina), *Bedial S.A. v. Paul Müggenburg and Co. GmbH*, 31 October 1995, available at http://cisgw3.law.pace.edu/cases/951031a1.html.

[24] See Incoterms® 2010 A4 ("FOB").

[25] See District Court Bamberg (Germany), 23 October 2006, available at http://cisgw3.law.pace .edu/cases/061023g1.html; cf. *BP Int'l Ltd. v. Impresa Estatal Petroleus Ecuador*, 332 F.2d 333, 337 (5th Cir. 2003) (CISG incorporates Incoterms rules through Article 9(2)).

[26] See, e.g., Federal Supreme Court (Germany), 7 November 2012, unpublished translation by Vasileios Regkakos; Tribunal of International Commercial Arbitration at the Russian Federation Chamber of Commerce and Industry 406/1998 (Russia), 6 June 2000, available at www.cisg.law.pace.edu/cisg/wais/db/cases2/000606r1.html#* (use of Incoterms rules to define contractual CIF term in order to calculate appropriate insurance and appropriate amount of lost profits); Commercial Court Buenos Aires (Argentina), *Autoservicio Mayorista La Loma S.A.*, April 2003, available at www.cisg.law.pace.edu/cisg/wais/db/cases2/030400a1.html.

[27] See *China North Chemical Industries Corp. v. Beston Chemical Corp.*, 2006 U.S. Dist. LEXIS 35464 (S.D. Tex. February 7, 2001); *St. Paul Guardian Ins. Co. v. Neuromed Medical Systems & Support, GmbH*, 2002 U.S. Dist. LEXIS 5096 (S.D.N.Y. March 26, 2002); *BP Oil Int'l Ltd. v. Empresa Estatal Petroleos de Ecuador*, 332 F.3d 333 (5th Cir. 2003).

[28] See supra Chapter 4.I.B. for a discussion of the proviso.

delivery terms controls. For example, in *Xinsheng Trade Company* v. *Shougang Nihong Metallurgic Products*,[29] the court found that goods had been damaged by ice[30] and water while awaiting resolution of a dispute that had deferred loading onto a ship. The court concluded that the parties had effectively modified the contract to permit the goods to remain unloaded at the harbor. The contract used an FOB price term, which, under the relevant Incoterms® 2000 rule, applied exclusively to water-borne transport[31] and shifted the risk of loss to the buyer only after the goods passed the ship's rail. Since that had not occurred, the risk of loss remained with the seller.

Similarly, assume that a seller of goods in California agrees to sell goods to a buyer in Italy. The terms of contract are "CIF Rome (Incoterms® 2010)." The goods are to be shipped by independent trucker from California to New York and shipped by boat from New York to Rome. Assume further that a fire breaks out on the ship in the Atlantic and the goods are destroyed. The seller demands payment from the buyer. Article 66 tells us that the buyer is discharged from its payment obligation if the risk of loss has not passed at the time of damage, and the negative implication is that the buyer is obligated to pay, even for destroyed goods, if the damage materialized subsequent to the passing of the risk of loss. Here, the selection of the CIF term governs the passing of risk. Under a CIF contract, the seller is obligated to bear the risk and cost of loading the goods on board the designated vessel at the port of shipment.[32] Since the loss materialized after the goods were loaded on board, while they were in transit, the risk had passed and the buyer must pay for the goods. If the same loss had materialized when the goods were destroyed while in the possession of the truck that brought them to the port, the seller would bear the risk of loss under the CIF term, even though the seller would have passed the risk to the buyer when they were handed over to the truck (the first carrier) under Article 67. Placing the risk on the buyer might initially seem anomalous, because it has not arranged for carriage or had control of the goods. But careful consideration of the CIF term reveals that the seller's obligation in this respect is to obtain an insurance policy for the benefit of the buyer. Thus, it is perfectly sensible that the buyer bear the risk of loss, as it is the insured party with respect to the goods subsequent to shipment by sea.

---

[29] High People's Court of Ningxia Hui Autonomous Region (China), 27 November 2002, available at http://cisgw3.law.pace.edu/cases/021127c1.html.

[30] The Pace translation refers to damage by "breeze," which might mean "wind." But since the opinion refers to "1–3 mm thickness of breeze" on the goods, we have assumed that ice or frost was intended.

[31] Note that this differs from the use of the term under U.C.C. § 2–319, which permits its use in any transportation contract. The proposed amendments to Article 2 of the U.C.C. would have remedied the inconsistency by eliminating § 2–319, but that is now part of legal history. See John A. Spanogle, *Incoterms and UCC Article 2 — Conflicts and Confusions*, 31 Int'l L. 111 (1997). The FOB term under Incoterms® 2010 continues to apply only to waterborne transport.

[32] See Incoterms® 2010 A4, A5 ("CIF").

The express incorporation of Incoterms rules, however, has not been interpreted as an attempt to opt out of the CISG entirely.[33] The use of Incoterms rules only displaces the provisions of the CISG that would otherwise define when risk of loss passes or when delivery occurs. Most importantly, Incoterms rules do not state the consequences of the passing of risk. The effect of that passing is still regulated by Article 66. For instance, in a CIETAC decision,[34] the tribunal determined that the parties had used a CIF price term. Under Incoterms® 1990 (then applicable), that meant that the risk of loss passed to the buyer when goods pass the ship's rail at the port of loading.[35] The goods were damaged as a result of being maintained at improper temperatures during shipping. The parties had reached an independent agreement under which the seller was obligated to ensure that the carrier maintained the goods at the proper temperatures during the period of shipment. Since the seller failed to fulfill that obligation, the tribunal reasoned, the damage to the goods was attributable to an act or omission of the seller, and the seller would therefore bear the loss under Article 66, notwithstanding that the risk had passed to the buyer under the CIF term.

III. RISK OF LOSS RULES UNDER THE CISG

A. *The residual rule of Article 69*

1. Risk of loss without third-party transportation

In the absence of the selection of an alternative point for passage of risk, by reference to Incoterms rules or otherwise, CISG provisions will allocate the risk of loss. For the most part, those provisions embody a principle consistent with the efficient allocation of risks, that is, to place the loss on the party who can avoid or insure against it at lowest cost. Presumably, parties would bargain for this assignment in order to reduce the costs of their transaction. Thus, title to or ownership of the goods plays no role in the allocation of risk of loss.[36] Possession or control of the goods, on the other hand, will play a major role, since the party who holds or controls the goods typically is best positioned to protect them from loss or to have an insurable interest in them.

---

[33] See Supreme Court (Austria), 22 October 2001, available at www.cisg.law.pace.edu/cisg/wais/db/cases2/011022a3.html.

[34] See CIETAC Arbitration (China), 23 February 1995, available at http://cisgw3.law.pace.edu/cases/950223c1.html.

[35] See Incoterms A5, B5 ("CIF") (1990). Under Incoterms® 2010, risk would pass when the goods were loaded onto the ship. See id, A4, A5 ("CIF").

[36] Court of Appeals Schleswig-Holstein (Germany), 29 October 2002, available at http://cisgw3.law.pace.edu/cases/021029g1.html. The last sentence of Article 67(1) confirms this conclusion in reciting that the passage of risk is not affected by the fact that the seller is authorized to retain documents that control the disposition of the goods. Article 4 notes that the CISG is not concerned with the effect that the sale contract may have on the property in the goods sold.

Article 69 provides the residual rule for the passage of the risk of loss. Thus, Article 69 applies where the criteria for the special cases of Article 67 and Article 68 have not been satisfied. Typically, Article 69 applies because the contract calls for the buyer to take delivery at the seller's place of business, or calls for the seller itself to deliver the goods to the buyer rather than through a carrier, or calls for the buyer to take delivery of the goods being held by a bailee. For the first case, the basic rule is set forth in Article 69(1). Risk of loss passes when the buyer takes over the goods. Taking over the goods requires that the buyer obtain possession of them, either directly or through an agent. A buyer who obtains possession of the goods has control of them and therefore is in a position to minimize risks to them. Assume, for instance, that the contract calls for the seller to provide the goods to the buyer at the seller's loading dock and requires the buyer to retrieve them by October 1. The seller places the goods on the loading dock on September 29. On September 30, the goods are destroyed in a fire. The seller may claim that the goods have been placed at the buyer's disposal and thus the buyer should bear the risk of loss. But under the rule of Article 69(1), the buyer will not yet have taken over the goods and thus will not bear the risk of loss. This is a sensible rule, since the goods remained within the seller's dominion and control at the time of their loss.

Assume the same contract, except that the buyer fails to retrieve the goods by October 1. On October 5, the goods are destroyed in a fire at seller's plant. Now the buyer bears the risk of loss. Article 69(1) provides that if the buyer does not take over the goods "in due time," risk of loss passes when the goods are (1) placed at his disposal, and (2) he commits a breach of contract by failing to take delivery. Since the seller had placed the goods on the loading dock on September 29, the goods were placed at the buyer's disposal on that date. Because the contract required the buyer to retrieve the goods by October 1, the buyer breached the contract by failing to pick up the goods by that date. Thus, when the fire occurred on October 5, the buyer had the risk of loss. This result might initially seem anomalous in light of the objective of placing the loss on the party in control of the goods. The seller would appear to occupy that position in this case. But given the buyer's breach of contract in failing to pick up the goods, the seller presumably could have recovered the price of the goods from the breaching buyer if the goods had not been destroyed. Thus, placing the loss on the buyer just gets to the same result that would be achieved if the risk of loss had never passed but the buyer was responsible for payment as a consequence of its breach.

Assume in the preceding case that the fire did not occur until November 1. Would the seller still be able to place the risk of loss on the breaching buyer? The issue is complicated by Article 85, which places a kind of mitigation requirement on the seller where the buyer has not taken delivery when due. Under those circumstances, the seller who remains in possession of the goods is obligated to take such steps as are reasonable in the circumstances to preserve them. Thus, if the seller should have retrieved the goods from the loading dock and placed them in a location that would have protected them from the fire, the seller will not be able to shift the loss on the buyer. The seller will, however, be able to recover his reasonable expenses from the buyer.[37]

2. Risk of loss when buyer obtains goods from party other than seller

Article 69(2) allocates risk of loss when the buyer "is bound to take over the goods at a place other than the place of business of the seller." It therefore covers the case in which the seller delivers the goods personally to the buyer (since other Articles deal with third-party transportation to the buyer) or when the buyer retrieves them from a third party, such as an independent warehouse or other bailee. Under Article 69(2) the risk passes when delivery is due and the buyer is aware that the goods have been placed at its disposal at the designated location. By explicitly requiring that the buyer be aware that the goods have been placed at its disposal, Article 69(2) avoids a difficult issue concerning the proper recipient of an acknowledgment that goods are available to the buyer.[38] Once it receives the acknowledgement, the buyer is in control of the goods in the sense that it can decide whether to leave the goods at the warehouse or with the seller, or retrieve them. It thus makes sense to place the risk of loss on the buyer at that point.

To see the operation of Article 69(2), assume that an American seller maintains a large amount of goods in a public warehouse and sells goods stored in the warehouse by selling negotiable warehouse receipts to buyers. A Canadian buyer purchases a negotiable warehouse receipt covering two loads of goods. Possession of the warehouse receipts entitles the buyer to obtain the goods, so they are put at buyer's disposal at the time that it comes into possession of the warehouse receipts. Before the buyer

---

[37] Article 85's mitigation requirement is limited to preservation of the goods. By its terms, the Article does not require the party subject to the requirement to act to preserve their value. By contrast, Article 77's mitigation requirement, which reduces the damages recoverable by the injured party by the amount of avoidable loss, can "require" the party to act to preserve the value of breached goods. These different mitigation requirements can affect the amount of an injured party's recovery, depending on the remedy it seeks. For example, assume in the ongoing example that fire did not destroy the goods. Rather, the seller retained them and made no attempt to resell them when it easily could have done so. Assume also that the market price of the goods declined during this time. Because risk of loss passed to the buyer, the seller is entitled to the contract price under Article 62. Article 77 requires the seller to mitigate its loss by taking reasonable measures to do so. In the circumstances of the example, reselling the goods in a declining market is a reasonable measure. However, Article 77's mitigation requirement applies only if the seller recovers damages. It does not apply when the seller is recovering the price, because a price recovery is not "damages." The CISG's careful distinction between damages and non-damage remedies confirms as much; see Articles 49(1)(a),(b), 61(1)(a),(b). Thus, a seller recovering the price is subject only to Article 85's mitigation requirement. The CISG therefore gives it no incentive to avoid reasonably avoidable loss in the value of breached goods when risk of loss has passed to the buyer.

[38] Compare U.C.C. § 2–509(2); *Jason's Foods, Inc.* v. *Peter Eckrich & Sons, Inc.*, 774 F.2d 214 (7th Cir. 1985); *O.C.T. Equipment, Inc.* v. *Shepherd Machinery Co.*, 95 P.3d 197 (Okla. Ct. Civ. App. 2004).

can obtain goods from the warehouse, the warehouse catches fire and the goods are destroyed. Under Article 69(2), risk of loss is on the buyer because goods were put at its disposal at a place other than the place of business of seller and the buyer was aware of this fact. The operative assumption seems to be that the buyer would have insured after obtaining possession of the warehouse receipts, which implicitly indicated that the goods were in the warehouse. If, on the other hand, the seller had instructed the buyer and the warehouse that the goods could be retrieved as of a certain date, the risk of loss would not pass to the buyer until that date because that is when the goods were put at its disposal. In a Danish case, the seller delivered a grain dryer to the buyer, whose employees helped unload it using their own tractor and chain.[39] After the dryer was unloaded from the truck and was being towed to the buyer's plant, the chain holding the dryer broke, causing substantial damage to it. The court found that when the dryer was unloaded the buyer had taken possession, thus transferring the risk under Article 69. Given that delivery occurred at a place other than the seller's place of business, the court appears to have been proceeding under Article 69(2).

The time when the buyer takes over the goods is not always clear. In *Alpha Prime Development Corporation v. Holland Loader Company, LLC*,[40] the court denied summary judgment to a buyer of coal mining equipment because there were genuine issues of material fact with respect to whether nonconformities existed at the time that the risk passed to the buyer, as required under Article 36(1). The alleged nonconformities consisted of the seller's failure to refurbish the equipment prior to its shipment to Mexico. The court noted that Article 69(2) applied where the buyer was bound to take over the goods at a place other than the seller's place of business, and that in such a case the risk would pass when delivery was due and the buyer was aware that the goods had been placed at its disposal. But the court concluded that there were unresolved issues with regard to whether buyer was to take over the equipment at its point of origin or at the delivery point, whether buyer was to take over the equipment before or after it was refurbished, and whether the equipment had ever been placed at buyer's disposal.

In all Article 69 cases, the goods are not deemed to have been placed at the buyer's disposal, and thus the risk does not pass, until the goods have been identified to the contract, such as by marking them or otherwise connecting them with the contract.[41] Where goods are to be delivered from a warehouse, the requirement will be satisfied if the goods identified to the contract are stored separately from other goods. But the time of identification is more questionable when the goods subject to

---

[39] See Randers County Court (Denmark), 8 July 2004, available at http://cisgw3.law.pace.edu/cases/040708d1.html.

[40] 2010 U.S. Dist. LEXIS 67591 (D. Colo. July 6, 2010).

[41] Article 69(3). Article 67(2) indicates that identification for purposes of that Article can be made "by markings on the goods, by shipping documents, by notice given to the buyer or otherwise." There is no reason to believe that identification carries an alternative definition for purposes of Article 69(3).

the contract for sale are part of a fungible store of goods. Assume, for instance, that a buyer purchases 1,000 gallons of oil to be removed from a storage tank containing 10,000 gallons of oil. If the buyer has received all the documentation and notice necessary to obtain delivery of the oil when the entire storage tank had been destroyed, who bears the risk of loss? A literal reading of Article 69(3) suggests that the seller retains the risk of loss because the goods were part of a fungible mass rather than separately identified to the contract. Nevertheless, a strict reading of Article 69 (2) suggests that the criteria of that subsection were satisfied so that the risk has passed. Nicholas has suggested, based on provisions of earlier efforts to create a body of international sales law, that where identification is for practical purposes inseparable from the taking of delivery, the goods have been sufficiently identified when the seller has done everything necessary to enable the buyer to take delivery.[42] The case for concluding that the risk has passed is even stronger where the contract identifies the precise bulk of fungible goods from which the buyer's allocation is to be taken and the entire bulk of goods is destroyed. Assume, for example, that the contract specifies that the buyer has purchased 1,000 gallons of oil from the tanker S.S. Titanic. If the Titanic is holding 10,000 gallons when it is lost at sea, there is little doubt that the buyer's goods have suffered damage and thus little is to be gained by imposing a strict identification requirement.[43] We deal below in the discussion of Article 67 with the possibility that only part of the bulk of goods is destroyed.

B. *Passage of risk in transportation cases*

1. Shipment contracts

Article 67 governs the passage of risk where the goods must be transported from the seller to the buyer. If the contract of sale requires carriage of the goods from the buyer to the seller, and the seller is not bound to hand the goods over at a particular place, the risk passes to the buyer when the goods are handed over to the first carrier. This rule is consistent with Articles 30 and 31. Article 30 imposes on the seller an obligation to deliver the goods. Article 31 provides the default place of delivery. Unless the seller is bound to deliver the goods at a particular place, delivery under a contract that involves carriage of goods occurs when they are handed over to the first carrier for transmission to the buyer. "Handed over" requires that the goods be put into the possession or control of the carrier.[44]

---

[42] See Barry Nicholas, *Residual Rules on Risk*, in Commentary on the International Sales Law 502, 504 (Cesare M. Bianca & Michael J. Bonell eds., 1987) [hereinafter "Bianca & Bonell"].

[43] See Honnold/Flechtner, supra note 14, at 525.

[44] See District Court Bamberg (Germany), 23 October 2006, available at http://cisgw3.law.pace .edu/cases/061023g1.html.

Shifting the risk to the buyer when the first carrier obtains the goods makes sense in an international transaction that is likely to involve multimodal transportation. At the very least, the rule avoids difficulties involved in proving when the damage materialized. Assume, for instance, that goods are brought by truck from the seller's plant to a port, by ship from that port to a port in the buyer's jurisdiction, and by truck from that port to the buyer's plant. When the goods arrive, they are unpacked and found to have been damaged. Assume that the damage clearly occurred during transit, notwithstanding adequate packaging by the seller. But during which part of the transit? Shifting the loss from the seller to the buyer at the first transportation point avoids the need for a dispute between the buyer and seller with respect to that difficult inquiry. In addition, the buyer, who ultimately receives the goods, has better access than the seller to evidence (which might not be much) that could identify the part in the transit at which the loss occurred.

"First carrier" in Article 67(1) is considered by most commentators to mean the first "independent" carrier.[45] If the seller uses its own trucks to bring goods to a port for shipment to the buyer, the risk passes only when the goods are handed over to the ship. The language of "carriage" and "handing over" to a "carrier" in the CISG typically implies a third party, such as where the seller is bound to arrange a contract of carriage under Article 32 or to hand goods to a carrier who issues documents embodying the contract of carriage under Article 68. Certainly it would be odd to require the buyer to bear the risk of loss while the goods remained in the control of the seller's own employees.

2. Transportation to a particular place

The second sentence of Article 67(1) governs the case excluded from the first sentence, that is, where the seller is bound to hand the goods over to a carrier "at a particular place." In this situation, the risk passes to the buyer only when the goods are handed over to the carrier at that place. But what does the "particular place" designation mean? Every contract of carriage must include some destination to which the goods are ultimately to be transported. Thus, a contract that requires that the goods be sent to 50 Main Street, Omaha, Nebraska names a particular place as a final destination for the goods. But Article 67(1) refers to situations in which the goods are to be handed *to the carrier* at a particular place.

Thus, assume that the sales contract requires that the goods be shipped "on the S.S. Titanic, Port of New York." That designation would constitute a particular place at which the seller was to hand the goods to the ocean carrier. Assume that the contract

---

[45] See Honnold/Flechtner, supra note 14, at 520–21; Johan Erauw, *Article 67*, in UN Convention on Contracts for the International Sale of Goods (CISG): Commentary 890, 892 (Stephan Kröll, Loukas Mistelis & Pilar Perales Viscasillas eds., 2011) [hereinafter "Kröll et al."]; cf. United Nations Convention on Contracts for the Carriage of Goods Wholly or Partly by Sea Article 1(5) (2008) ("Carrier") ("[p]erson that enters into a contract of carriage with a shipper").

with that instruction involves a seller located in California and that the goods are ultimately to be transported to Italy. Also assume that nothing is said about how the goods are to be transported to the Port of New York. The seller sends the goods by independent truck from California to the Port of New York and they are destroyed when the truck is involved in an accident. One might argue that the risk of loss falls on the buyer because the situation is governed by the first sentence of Article 67(1), given that the independent truck was the first carrier and thus the risk had passed when the goods were handed over to it. That interpretation, however, would restrict the scope of the second sentence to situations in which the goods were handed over to the carrier at a particular place by the seller *personally*. There is nothing in the drafting history or logic to support such a constrained scope for the second sentence. Instead, the loss in the example remains on the seller because the designation of a particular place for handing over the goods keeps the risk on the seller until the goods are handed over at that place. It is certainly true that this allocation of risks could cause the very kind of uncertainty in multimodal transport that the first sentence of Article 67(1) appears intended to avoid. Assume, for instance, that the goods in the example are not destroyed, but are delivered in Italy in damaged condition. If the source of the damage is unclear, then the application of the second sentence can generate a dispute about whether the damage occurred prior to or after the handing over of the goods in New York. Nevertheless, that is the preferred and understood allocation assumed by the parties. The common understanding of the FCA term under Incoterms is consistent with that understanding of the "particular place" designation. The FCA rule requires the seller to deliver the goods to the carrier or to another person nominated by the buyer at an agreed point or at a named place, and imposes on the seller the risk of loss until they have been so delivered.[46]

Article 67(2) puts a restriction on the passage of risk. It provides that risk does not pass until the goods are identified to the contract. Identification requires that the goods be particularized as being the subject of the sales contract. According to Article 67(2), identification can occur by marking the goods, shipping documents or by notice given to the buyer "or otherwise." The restriction of identification usually is not a problem when the sales contract involving carriage covers goods segregated or ascertainable as devoted to the contract. However, identification can be difficult when goods are sold in bulk. For example, assume that the seller contracts to ship to the buyer by carrier 1,000 of 5,000 pounds of wheat held in bulk. Assume also that the contract requires the seller to have the wheat delivered by carrier to the buyer, not to another carrier at a particular place. A lot of 1,000 pounds of the 5,000 pounds held in bulk is destroyed after the seller delivered the entire bulk to the carrier. Can the seller claim that the buyer bears the risk of loss because the destroyed lot represents the "buyer's" wheat? The risk of loss passes to the buyer under Article 67(1)'s first sentence only if the 1,000 pounds of wheat shipped is identified to the sales contract. Unless the destroyed wheat has been identified to the

---

[46] See Incoterms® 2010 A4, A5 ("FCA").

contract by being marked, covered by the bills of lading, by notice to the buyer or "otherwise," the risk of loss remains with the seller. Identification by notice to the buyer requires ascertaining exactly when notice was given. Risk passes only when this difficult-to-verify event occurs. By comparison, some domestic law is more forgiving. Uniform Commercial Code ("UCC") § 2-105(4)'s identification requirement allows a sold share of an undivided bulk to be identified to the contract. In this case the buyer becomes the owner in common of the agreed portion of the 5,000-pound bulk of wheat sold to the buyer (1,000 pounds).

C. *Risk of loss of goods sold in transit*

1. Conclusion of the contract

Sometimes goods will be resold after they have already been put in transit to an initial buyer (who becomes the seller in the resale contract). For example, shipments of commodities often are resold in various quantities multiple times, in "string sales," before being delivered to the final buyer at the port of destination. In these circumstances, Article 68 sets forth rules for the passage of risk. For the most part, risk passes on the conclusion of the resale contract. Assume, for example, that on December 1, Buyer 1 arranges for the purchase of a barge-load of grain from Seller and Seller immediately ships the grain to Buyer 1. On December 2, while the goods are en route to Buyer 1, Buyer 1 sends Buyer 2 an offer to sell the same grain to Buyer 2. On December 3, Buyer 2 dispatches an acceptance to Buyer 1. On December 5, Buyer 1 receives the acceptance. Unknown to both Buyer 1 and Buyer 2, the goods have been destroyed at sea on December 4. Who bears the risk of loss? Article 68 says that the risk in respect of goods sold in transit passes to the buyer from the time of the conclusion of contract. Article 23 states that a contract is concluded only when an acceptance becomes effective, and Article 18 requires receipt, not dispatch, for an acceptance to become effective. Buyer 1 did not receive the acceptance until December 5. As a result, Buyer 1 still had the risk of loss on December 4 when the damage occurred.

That example makes it clear when the damage occurred. More difficult issues will arise when that assumption is relaxed. Assume, for instance, that damage to goods is discovered on December 5, but the damage materialized from a slow leak in the ship's hold that started some time before that date, and the time of damage cannot be fixed with precision. The issue of who bears the risk of loss will now be indeterminate and liability will likely depend on the issue of who has the burden of proof, a subject that we discuss later and at greater length in Chapters 6 and 9.

2. Retroactive transfer of risk to the ultimate buyer

Although Article 68 establishes the time of the conclusion of the contract as the point at which risk passes with respect to goods sold in transit, it provides for an exception where "the circumstances so indicate." In those special cases, the risk is assumed by the ultimate buyer from the time the goods were handed over to the carrier that issued the documents embodying the contract of carriage.[47] What would constitute sufficient circumstances to place the risk on the buyer in that case? While the vagueness of the statement threatens to undermine some of the specificity involved in making risk pass with the conclusion of the contract, the exception appears primarily directed at the situation in which the re-seller conveys to the buyer an insurance policy that covers the goods and that has been endorsed by the latter to the ultimate buyer. That endorsement means that the ultimate buyer is the party with the interest in the insurance policy. As a result, even if it could be determined that the risk materialized prior to the conclusion of the contract, the ultimate buyer is the appropriate party to bring the insurance claim. Under those circumstances, it makes sense to treat the ultimate buyer as bearing the risk of loss from the outset.

This limited rule of retroactivity, however, is itself subject to an exception, though perhaps one of more academic than practical significance. Under the last sentence of Article 68, if the seller knew or ought to have known that the goods were lost or damaged at the time the contract was concluded and did not inform the buyer, the risk remains with the seller. This allocation introduces an element of fault into the assignment of risk of loss, and it is not clear that it gives the buyer anything that the buyer would not have under Article 35, that is, a cause of action for delivering nonconforming goods. The last sentence does, however, introduce an additional ambiguity. Assume that the initial buyer knew or had reason to know that one-tenth of the grain on a barge whose contents were resold in transit had become rotten prior to the conclusion of the contract and failed to disclose that damage to the ultimate buyer. In fact, unknown to the initial buyer, one-fifth of the goods had become rotten. The goods then suffer additional damage unrelated to the rot when the carrier is involved in an accident en route to the ultimate buyer. The initial buyer is liable for the undisclosed damage of which it did or should have had knowledge, notwithstanding the retroactive risk allocation rule of the second sentence. But is the initial buyer also liable for the additional damages? In short, is the initial buyer liable only for the undisclosed damage, one-tenth of the grain, or for *any* damage that materializes, whether that is one-fifth of the grain attributable to the same cause as the undisclosed damage, or to damage from an unrelated cause? Nicholas contends that the legislative history suggests an intent to make the non-disclosing party liable for any undisclosed damage and any additional damage that is "causally connected" to the original damage. He suggests that such a rule is preferable insofar as it avoids division of the transit risks.[48] That rule appears to cover all the damage caused by the rot (one-fifth in our example), but not the damage caused by the unrelated accident. Hager and Schmidt-Kessel reach a contrary conclusion that

[47] The UCC does not transfer risk retroactively when goods are sold in transit; see Official Comment 2 to U.C.C. § 2-509.
[48] See Barry Nicholas, in Bianca & Bonell, supra note 42, at 499–500.

the drafting history indicates "that the intention is to make the seller liable only for loss which has already occurred at the time of the conclusion of the contract and of which he knew or ought to have known."[49] Honnold would go further. He suggests that the qualifying nondisclosure would amount to a fraud that justifies avoidance of the contract, and thus prefers not to impose on the ultimate buyer the obligation to undertake the complicated inquiry that would apply if causal connections had to be proven. It is less clear that Honnold would apply this same principle where the damage complained of was entirely unrelated to the undisclosed risk.[50]

We agree with the minority view that looks to a causal connection on the grounds that it is most consistent with the underlying principles for allocating risk of loss. As we suggested earlier, the exception introduces the issue of fault or breach into the allocation of risk of loss. One of the advantages of the CISG is that it generally does not conflate those two issues.[51] Instead, it tends to keep the risk of loss on the party best positioned to avoid or insure against loss while providing remedies for that party if the counterparty has breached its obligations (as discussed later). The third sentence of Article 68 poses an interesting test of that principle. It operates to keep the loss on the seller, even though the buyer is the insured party. It is arguable that the non-disclosing party had control over the goods when the damage first materialized, and might have been able to avoid additional damage by disclosing what it knew. Thus, keeping the risk on the seller may minimize total damage related to the original damage. There is no reason, however, to believe that the seller is best positioned to protect against unrelated damage that materializes before or after the conclusion of the contract and about which it neither has nor should have knowledge.

IV. BURDEN OF PROOF IN RISK OF LOSS CASES

Cases involving risk of loss frequently arise when the buyer receives goods that have been damaged in transit. In those cases, buyers assert that they are not liable for payment because they have received nonconforming goods. Under Article 36(1), the success of that argument depends on whether the nonconformity existed at the time the risk passed to the buyer. If it did, the seller is liable and cannot recover the full price of the goods. But as our discussion to this point demonstrates, the ability to determine the point at which damage occurred can approach the impossible. As a result, the assignment of the burden of proof in such cases is crucial.

---

[49] See Gunter Hager & Martin Schmidt-Kessel, *Article 68*, in Schlechtriem & Schwenzer, supra note 16. This appears to be the majority opinion within the European commentary. See Anjanette Raymond, *Article 68*, in Kröll et al., supra note 45, at 903.

[50] See Honnold/Flechtner, supra note 14, at 529–30. Enderlein and Maskow appear to agree that the retroactivity principle continues to apply where the undisclosed risk is entirely unrelated to the risk of which the ultimate buyer is complaining. See Fritz Enderlein & Dietrich Maskow, International Sales Law 271–72 (1992).

[51] Compare U.C.C. § 2–510. Breach does enter affect risk of loss in Article 69(1). Breach does not alter risk of loss in the situation covered by Article 70.

We have discussed the general issue of the allocation of burden of proof in Chapters 6 and 9. The CISG does not expressly allocate the burden of proof with respect to risk of loss. One might readily conclude, therefore, that burden of proof issues are governed by the law of the contract.[52] Nevertheless, some commentators maintain that because burden of proof issues are so intertwined with the rights and obligations of the parties, the CISG governs the evidentiary issues as well. Burden of proof is implicated in resolving three sorts of issues: (1) whether risk passed to the buyer; (2) whether the seller delivered conforming goods at the time risk passed to the buyer; and (3) whether the buyer is liable for price even after risk passed to it. The sparse case law is divided concerning the burden of proving that the goods were conforming at the time risk passed to the buyer. Some courts put the burden on the seller while other courts put it on the buyer, at least when it has taken delivery.[53] Courts allocating the burden to the seller rely on a general principle to the effect that the party benefitting from a legal provision must prove the factual elements of the provision.[54] According to Article 66, the buyer must pay the price after risk has passed to it, unless the loss or damage is due to the seller's act or omission. Thus, the general principle presumably requires the seller to demonstrate that the loss materialized after risk had passed, but requires the buyer that resists payment of the contract price after the risk has passed to prove that the seller's act or omission caused the loss or damage to the goods. The United States Court of Appeals decision that placed the risk on the buyer awkwardly referred to the CISG as "the international analogue to Article 2 of the Uniform Commercial Code."[55] In the name of applying the "general principles" on which the CISG is based pursuant to Article 7 (2), the court then inferred that the UCC standard relating to an action for delivery of nonconforming goods was sufficiently similar to CISG Article 35(2) that the corresponding UCC allocation of risk of loss to the buyer should also apply. This strikes us as placing too much weight on the similarities of domestic and the CISG to incorporate the former into the latter. While throughout this text we have expressed doubt about efforts to deploy the general principles underlying the CISG, we conclude that any such principles must be discerned from the CISG itself, rather than imported through any domestic law, which could easily conflict with the domestic law of some other Contracting State.

[52] See Sylan Bollée, *The Theory of Risks in the Vienna Sale of Goods Convention 1980*, Pace Review of the Convention on Contracts for the International Sale of Goods, 245, 278 (1999–2000); Johan Erauw, in Flechtner et al., supra note 21, at 389.

[53] Compare District Court Kortrijk (Belgium), 6 October 1997, available at http://cisgw3.law .pace.edu/cases/971006b1.html (burden on seller) with *Chicago Prime Packers, Inc. v. Northam Trading Food Co.*, 408 F.3d 894 (7th Cir. 2005) (burden on plaintiff-buyer).

[54] See Supreme Court (Austria), 12 September 2006, available at http://cisgw3.law.pace.edu/cases/ 060912a3.html; Franco Ferrari, *Burden of Proof Under the CISG*, 2000–2001 Review of the Convention on Contracts for the International Sale of Goods (CISG), available at www.cisg .law.pace.edu/cisg/biblio/ferrari5.html.

[55] *Chicago Prime Packers, Inc.*, 408 F.3d at 898. We discuss the case at greater length in Chapter 6.X.

The assignment of the burden of proving that risk has passed is a separate issue. In a German case,[56] a German buyer of furniture was to take possession at the manufacturer's place of business and load the furniture for transportation. A practice between the parties developed in which completed furniture was stored in a warehouse until the buyer requested delivery. The buyer was not expected to pay for the goods until it requested delivery. After the manufacturer went bankrupt, the furniture disappeared from the warehouse. The plaintiff (seller's assignee) requested payment. It contended that the risk of loss had passed to the buyer because the seller had placed the furniture at the buyer's disposal at the warehouse and notified the buyer of that fact through statements on storage invoices. The court found first that the burden of proving the passage of risk of loss was on the party asserting it. In this case, that would be the plaintiff. Here, the plaintiff could not satisfy that burden because it was not clear that delivery was yet due, and thus that the requirements of Article 69(2) had been satisfied. Under the contracts, delivery dates were determined by the buyer, and the seller presented no evidence about when the buyer had requested delivery of the missing furniture. Indeed, the plaintiff failed to prove even that the seller had performed its obligation to deliver the furniture under Article 31. Delivery required the seller to take all steps necessary under the contract, including loading the furniture on railway wagons or the buyer's trucks. Without performance of that obligation, the seller had failed to place the goods at the buyer's disposal. Finally, the plaintiff failed to prove when the goods had disappeared. As a result, it was impossible to find out whether the loss of the furniture has occurred before or after the passing of risk.

V. EFFECT OF BREACH OF CONTRACT ON RISK OF LOSS

For the most part, the fact that one party has breached the contract does not prevent the passing of the risk of loss where it would otherwise occur. As a result, under Article 66, a buyer is not discharged from its obligation to pay for goods damaged or destroyed after the risk has passed to it, even though the goods fail to conform to the contract. But that does not mean that the buyer will ultimately be responsible for the price of the goods. According to Article 70, the buyer retains its remedies for breach of contract notwithstanding the passage of the risk under Articles 67, 68, and 69, if the seller's breach is fundamental. Thus, if the seller's breach was fundamental, the buyer may avoid the contract.[57]

To see how these Articles operate, assume that the parties have entered into a contract for the purchase and sale of fifty cases of chardonnay wine worth $100 per case with a term under which risk passes to the buyer on shipment. When the wine

---

[56] See Court of Appeals Hamm (Germany), 23 June 1998, available at http://cisgw3.law.pace.edu/cases/980623g1.html.

[57] See Article 49(1)(a); Chapter 5.IV.B.1.

arrives at the buyer's place of business, the buyer discovers that the seller has shipped fifty cases of cabernet worth $100 per case. Before the buyer can return the goods to the seller, the wine is destroyed in a fire at the buyer's place of business. The shipment of cabernet presumably would constitute a fundamental breach under Article 25, since it substantially deprives the buyer of what it expected to receive under the contract (fifty cases of chardonnay). Thus, although the buyer continues to bear the risk of loss under Article 67, under Article 70 the buyer retains its remedies for breach. Those remedies include the right to avoid the contract under Article 49(1)(a) where the breach is fundamental. As a result, even though Article 66 provides that passage of risk does not discharge the buyer "from his obligation to pay the price," the buyer who avoided the contract would have no obligation to pay, since no contract requiring payment exists after avoidance. While this might seem peculiar from the perspective of placing the risk of loss on the party in the best position to avoid the risk or to insure against it, keep in mind that the buyer that received a nonconforming delivery would retain an action against the seller for breach if the goods had not been destroyed. Thus, one effect of Article 70 is to preserve for the buyer of destroyed or lost goods the same rights it would have had in the absence of the risk's materialization.

Now assume that buyer discovers that the seller had shipped forty-five cases of chardonnay worth $100 per case and five cases of cabernet sauvignon worth $100 per case. Again, the nonconforming wine is destroyed in a fire at the buyer's place of business prior to the time when the buyer can return those cases to the seller. The buyer bears the risk of loss and, under Article 66, is therefore not discharged from its obligation to pay the price of the goods. The breach in this case presumably would not be fundamental, so the buyer cannot avoid the contract. But the buyer still retains its rights under Article 35 and Article 36(1) with respect to the nonconforming delivery. The statement in Article 70 to the effect that the buyer retains its remedies in the event of a fundamental breach does not imply that the buyer loses its rights where the breach is not fundamental. Article 70 only makes clear that the buyer who has suffered a fundamental breach can avoid the contract notwithstanding passage of the risk to it. Thus, the buyer may – by offset, counterclaim, or separate action – recover for the nonconforming tender. In our example, however, the recovery becomes complicated by the fact that the buyer has received goods that, while nonconforming, were perfectly good as cabernet. Arguably, the buyer ordered goods with a value of $100 per case and received goods worth $100 per case, albeit not the goods that were ordered. As a result, the buyer's damages arguably would be zero and the buyer arguably would be liable to pay the entire contract price to the seller. Nevertheless, the nonconforming nature of the goods indicates that the buyer has suffered a breach and can collect damages if it could not make use of the nonconforming goods that had the same value as the use it could have made of conforming goods. If the goods had been defective (for example, the wine had spoiled), rather than the wrong goods, so that their value was less than the contract price, buyer would have an action for damages suffered as a consequence of the nonconformity, and that cause of action would survive the destruction of the goods.

There are two other points worth mentioning about the consequences of the buyer's ability to avoid the contract under Article 70. First, note that avoidance effectively shifts market risks around the price of the goods, as well as the risk of their loss, back to the seller. Assume that the seller had shipped chardonnay, as required, but that the chardonnay shipped was undrinkable. In the interim the market price of drinkable chardonnay plummeted. If the shipped chardonnay had been drinkable, the buyer could not have avoided the contract and therefore would bear the loss from the decline in market price. But in the event of a fundamental breach, the ability to avoid the contract under Article 70 allows the buyer to shift the risk of the market price decline to the seller, notwithstanding that the fixed price of $100 per case in the contract assigned it to the buyer.

Second, the fact that avoidance is conditioned on a fundamental breach returns us to the discussion in Chapter 5 concerning the interaction between fundamental breach and cure. Assume again that the buyer ordered fifty cases of chardonnay wine at $100 per case and the seller shipped fifty cases of cabernet wine with a value of $100 per case. Assume also that when the buyer discovers the discrepancy, it notifies the seller, who agrees to replace the cabernet with chardonnay and to pick up the former when delivering the latter. Before the seller delivers the replacement wine, but within a reasonable period of its promise to do so, the cabernet is destroyed in a fire at the buyer's place of business. Can the buyer avoid the contract? Certainly the buyer initially received a delivery that substantially deprived it of what it expected to receive under the contract. Thus, one might conclude that the buyer suffered a fundamental breach. But if the buyer did not have an immediate need for the chardonnay, then the seller's offer to cure within a reasonable time deprived the buyer of its ability to claim that a fundamental breach occurred. If that is the case, then the buyer would not be entitled to avoid the contract under Article 49 and would be limited to damages for nonconformity. Again, assuming that the chardonnay and the cabernet had equal market value to the buyer, those damages arguably would amount to zero.

8

Exemption from performance

I. INTRODUCTION: LEGAL CONSEQUENCES OF CHANGED CIRCUMSTANCES

Virtually all legal systems provide some basis for allowing parties to deviate from contractual performance with impunity when circumstances substantially change between the time the contract was concluded and the time that it is to be performed. The relevant changes usually implicate a significant unanticipated increase in one party's costs of performance or the occurrence of some unanticipated physical or regulatory obstacle that destroys the subject matter of the contract or the rationale for performing it. Legal doctrine recognizes that commercial parties enter into contracts that each believes will be personally profitable to perform, and that those beliefs are based on assumptions made at the time of the conclusion of the contract about the conditions that will exist at the time performance is due. Sellers, for instance, assume that they can procure the goods necessary for performance at a price lower than the contract price, while buyers assume that they can profitably use the goods for which they have contracted. Both parties assume that they will be physically able to perform the contract. Less certain, at least where the contract is silent, is how parties intend to allocate the risk that those assumptions prove incorrect. Different legal systems apply very different default rules that allocate that risk by defining the range of conditions under which nonperformance does not constitute a breach. Some legal systems permit adjustments when the equilibrium of the contract has been disturbed or when performance is possible but unexpectedly burdensome, while others essentially prohibit deviations from the contract unless performance is virtually impossible.[1] These doctrines reflect the attitudes that different legal systems have towards the propriety of enforcing the literal terms of a contract, attitudes that are often

---

[1] See Peter Mazzacano, *Exemptions for the Non-Performance of Contractual Obligations in CISG Article 79* 7–10, 26–30 (2014); Elena Christine Zaccaria, *The Effects of Changed Circumstances in International Commercial Trade*, 9 Int'l Trade & Bus. L. Rev. 135 (2005).

summarized as embracing one of two Latin maxims. Doctrines that restrict the adjustment of contractual obligations are often associated with the principle of *pacta sunt servanda*, or "promises ought to be kept," while doctrines that permit more liberal adjustment are associated with the principle of *rebus sic stantibus*, roughly translated to condition performance on circumstances remaining the same over the contractual term. American lawyers will think in terms of Uniform Commercial Code ("UCC") § 2–615, which excuses the seller from a contract when performance has been rendered "impracticable" by the occurrence of a contingency that the parties assumed would not materialize and the risk of which was not assumed by the seller.

The CISG's entry into this debate is Article 79. The provision "exempts" the buyer or seller from liability for failure to perform "any of its obligations" if the party seeking exemption can prove that the conditions set forth in that Article have been satisfied. For the seller, exemption is available when the requirements of Article 79 are satisfied regardless of whether seller's failure consists of a failure to deliver goods at all, a failure to deliver part of the goods, or failure to deliver in a timely manner. As we will discuss, whether the Article also covers delivery of defective goods is a more complicated issue. For a buyer, Article 79 may exempt liability for failure to take delivery or to pay in a timely manner. The range of changed circumstances that qualify for an exemption is less certain. We argue later in the chapter that, although physical impossibility is likely not required, additional financial burdens of performance may not be sufficient. While a party could not successfully claim that it was excused from any of its obligations simply by demonstrating that it used all reasonable efforts to comply with contractual requirements, the availability of Article 79 means that contract liability under the CISG is not altogether "strict." Finally, it is an important element of the CISG scheme that exemption applies only to "liability for damages." Performance is not excused in the sense that the disappointed party is without remedy. A party who is exempt still commits a breach of contract. A party who has not received a performance because the requirements for exemption have been satisfied may still seek relief that does not entail a demand for damages, such as avoidance of the contract.

A party seeking exemption from performance under Article 79 must demonstrate that (1) its failure to perform was due to an impediment that was beyond its control, (2) it could not reasonably be expected to have taken the impediment into account at the conclusion of the contract, and (3) once the impediment occurred, the party could not reasonably have avoided it or its consequences. Article 79, by its terms, applies to both buyers and sellers, while some domestic law applies only to sellers.[2] The language of Article 79 ("if he proves") makes clear that the party seeking the

---

[2] See, e.g., U.C.C. § 2–615. Comment 9 to UCC § 2–615 goes past the text of § 2–615(1) in excusing the buyer based on the section. Courts generally have relied onto the Comment to extend § 2–615's excuse to buyers. See, e.g., *Lawrence v. Elmore Bean Warehouse, Inc.*, 702 P.2d 930, 932 (Idaho App. 1985); *Nora Springs Coop. Co. v. Brandau*, 247 N.W.2d 744 (Iowa 1976); but cf. *Northern Indiana Public Service Co. v. Carbon County Coal Co.*, 799 F.2d 265 (7th Cir. 1986).

exemption bears the burden of proving that these conditions have been satisfied. The party seeking exemption must give notice of the impediment and its effect,[3] and any exemption is only available during the period when the impediment exists. Finally, Article 79 restricts the ability of a party to obtain an exemption based on the failure of a third person to perform part of the contract.

These conditions indicate that the core issues underlying Article 79 involve considerations of assumption of the risk, foreseeability, and the consequences of the alleged impediment. But Article 79's terms raise a series of interpretive issues. As a result, Article 79 has brought little clarity to the issue of when deviations from contractual requirements can occur without liability. It has been the subject of substantial and conflicting commentary, and the cases that have arisen under the provision serve primarily to reveal disagreement on interpretation and a general reluctance by courts to permit exemption. Perhaps the best lesson to be garnered from study of Article 79 is that parties would be well advised to fashion an explicit force majeure clause or similar provision in their contract that defines with more precision the conditions for exemption from performance. Indeed, the possibility of utilizing a force majeure clause may justify parsimonious use of Article 79 insofar as it reveals that parties may be better positioned than courts to allocate the risks associated with remote events that may disrupt initial contractual expectations.

II. AN IMPEDIMENT BEYOND THE CONTROL OF THE PARTY SEEKING EXEMPTION

A. *The scope of "impediment"*

The requirement that the party seeking exemption prove an "impediment beyond his control" presents several interpretive difficulties. The first involves the meaning and scope of the necessary impediment. Although there is some argument for the proposition that the impediment must render performance impossible,[4] that definition seems too strict to encompass all the conditions for exemption that the drafters had in mind. Impossibility cases might arise where a designated source of materials has become unavailable, either due to its nonexistence (such as where crops from a designated piece of land fail) or because regulatory intervention prevents access to the goods (such as where a government places an embargo on importation or sale of goods required by the contract). This interpretation would eliminate the availability of an exemption for obligations that either have become substantially more costly

---

[3] See District Court Komarno (Slovak Republic), 24 February 2009, available at http://cisgw3 .law.pace.edu/cases/090224k1.html. If the notice is not received by the other party within a reasonable time after the party who fails to perform knew or ought to have known of the impediment, it is liable for damages resulting from such nonreceipt.

[4] See Dionysios Flambouras, Comparative Remarks on CISG Article 79 & PECL Articles 6:111, 8:108 (May 2002), available at http://cisgw3.law.pace.edu/cisg/text/peclcomp79.html#er.

than originally anticipated, or obligations that are possible but that have become worthless because of a change in circumstances that has negated the initial reason for concluding the contract ("frustration of purpose" cases).

Other commentators find the restriction to cases of impossibility too strict, both because the standard categorization of events that are "impossible," such as government prohibitions, often are not physically impossible to perform, and because the drafting history to some extent reveals an intent to permit a somewhat more liberal inclusion of events as impediments.[5] While impossibility may be too harsh a test, not every exogenous event that interferes with performance qualifies as an impediment. A mere reluctance to perform based on events that do not affect the capacity to perform fall outside of Article 79. For instance, a nonbinding regulation would not qualify,[6] even if violating it might expose the buyer to some reputational reprisal. The events that qualify as impediments reflect those that one would expect to find in a contractual force majeure clause. Natural disasters such as earthquakes, floods, hurricanes, and the like are standard examples of eligible impediments. They also include such matters as war, terrorist acts, state interventions and regulations, or perhaps labor disturbances. Indeed, the frequency with which events are included in force majeure clauses may be an appropriate standard to employ in defining the scope of the "impediment" term, because the regularity with which they indicate contractually based reasons for nonperformance suggests that they constitute usages that, pursuant to Article 9(2), are "widely known to, and regularly observed by, parties to contracts of the type involved in the particular trade concerned."

A New York federal court concluded that the Republic of Iraq had not breached its contractual obligations to purchase yarn where imminent wartime activities led to the withdrawal of the parties responsible under the contract for inspection of the yarn and issuance of documents required by a letter of credit.[7] That opinion was somewhat peculiar, since it is typically the nonperforming party who invokes the impediment claim. In this case, the seller was seeking performance by contending that Iraq was required to cure its failure to take delivery of the yarn at the earliest opportunity. The court concluded that the war had made seller's performance impossible, and thus the buyer bore no legal duty to compensate seller for goods that were never delivered as a consequence of the impediment.

Impediments to performance may include the destruction of unique goods subsequent to manufacture but prior to delivery, as well as situations that prevent manufacture.[8] There is some debate about whether an impediment for purposes of

5 See John O. Honnold, Uniform Law for International Sales Under the 1980 United Nations Convention 627 (Harry M. Flechtner ed., 4th ed. 2009) [hereinafter "Honnold/Flechtner"].

6 See CIETAC Arbitration (China), May 2006, available at http://cisgw3.law.pace.edu/cases/060500c1.html.

7 See *Hilaturas Miel, S.L. v. Republic of Iraq*, 573 F. Supp.2d 781 (S.D.N.Y. 2008).

8 See Secretariat Commentary on the 1978 Draft, in Documentary History of the Uniform Law for International Sales 445 (former Article 65, Example 65A) (John O. Honnold ed., 1989) [hereinafter Diplomatic History].

Article 79 exists if the goods have been destroyed prior to conclusion of the contract and the parties reasonably were unaware of their destruction. That situation would be handled by the doctrine of mistake under some legal systems, and mistake arguably affects the validity of the contract. As a result, Article 4 might require any dispute arising from such a case to be resolved under non-CISG domestic law.[9] But some commentators note that Article 4 does not exclude cases where the CISG expressly addresses an issue that might fall under the rubric of "validity," and consider claims of impediment due to pre-contract destruction of the goods as an example.[10] The broadest interpretations of events include financial "hardship," which we treat later as a special case.

In short, even if all agree that the notion of "impediment" for purposes of Article 79 requires an autonomous definition, the range of domestic doctrines governing excused performance make the definition of the requirement in any given case highly susceptible to the possibility of a "homeward trend."[11] Perhaps one can only reiterate Honnold's observation that, in light of the various national rules concerning the scope of excuse for nonperformance, the use of a phrase as ambiguous as "impediment beyond his control" suggests that "Article 79 may be the Convention's least successful part of the half-century of work toward international uniformity."[12]

B. *"Beyond his control"*

The ambiguity of "impediment" is exacerbated by the requirement that, in order to generate an exemption, its occurrence must be "beyond his [the party seeking exemption] control." There is little case law that elucidates the meaning of that requirement. As the CISG Advisory Council Opinion on exemption concluded, "a court finding a party exempted under Article 79 may be presumably satisfied that the alleged impediment was beyond the control of that party, yet one finds not much discussion in the available judicial decisions as to when that requirement should be deemed to have been met."[13] The requirement might initially be thought to refer to the ability of that party to control the materialization of the impediment. But that issue appears to be addressed more directly by the explicit requirement elsewhere in Article 79(1) that the party claiming exemption could not have reasonably avoided the impediment. Thus, the "beyond his control" requirement must impose some additional constraint on the availability of an exemption.

---

[9] See, e.g., Denis Tallon, *Exemptions*, in Commentary on the International Sales Law 577–78 (Cesare M. Bianca & Michael J. Bonell eds., 1987) [hereinafter "Bianca & Bonell"]; Wanki W. Lee, *Exemptions of Liability Under the 1980 United Nations Convention*, 8 Dickinson J. Int'l L. 386–87 (1990).

[10] See, e.g., Peter Schlechtriem, Uniform Sales Law 32 (1986); Fritz Enderlein & Dietrich Maskow, International Sales Law 323 (1992).

[11] See Mazzacano, supra note 1, at 33–6.   [12] Honnold/Flechtner, supra note 5, at 627.

[13] CISG Advisory Council Opinion No. 7, Exemption of Liability for Damages Under Article 79 of the CISG ¶ 4, available at www.cisg.law.pace.edu/cisg/CISG-AC-op7.html.

Nevertheless, several courts have proceeded by conflating the concepts of avoidability and control. For example, a French court determined that theft of railroad ties was not beyond the seller's control where their disappearance occurred over a six-month period and in such quantities that the theft could not have remained unnoticed.[14] But the court also concluded that the same facts implied that the seller had been negligent in the supervision of the goods, and that Article 79 was therefore unavailable because the seller had the reasonable ability to foresee or overcome the loss. In that case, it is difficult to understand what the "beyond his control" analysis adds. In a German case involving contaminated powdered milk, the court noted that the seller had been unable to demonstrate whether the contaminants originated merely from "unfortunate events" or from seller's failure to comply with "optimum standards in the course of its production of powdered milk."[15] That statement suggests that, contamination notwithstanding, compliance with optimum standards could have served as the basis for an exemption, presumably because buyers accept the risk that normal processes will produce anomalies ("unfortunate events"), but sellers bear the risk of failure to comply with cost-effective processes. But if that is what the court means, then its analysis of the seller's "control" appears only to replicate what would be necessary under the analysis of what would be necessary to "avoid the impediment" under Article 79(1).

Finally, consider a German appellate decision in which the court concluded that a seller who, in good faith, had sold a stolen car could not invoke Article 79 in a breach of contract action.[16] The court held that Article 79 exemptions are limited to situations in which there are "objective circumstances, which prevent the fulfillment of the contractual obligation, that show no connection to the person of the seller." Failure to transfer property in the goods to the buyer as required by the contract was, in the court's view, a "personal circumstance" of the seller, and thus not an impediment beyond its control. As we discuss later, commentators have agreed that matters of personal circumstance are not beyond the control of the party seeking exemption. While the distinction seems oblique, some sense of the rationale becomes clearer in the court's discussion of why the seller's personal circumstances were implicated. The court found that the car in question was of a type that was subject to a high degree of theft, that the purchase price was low, and that the seller's inquiries into the origins of the car and other conditions surrounding the sale indicated some question about its status. In short, the court appeared to imply that the seller, even if acting in good faith, had enough reason to be suspicious that it

---

[14] See Court of Appeals Lyon (France), 27 March 2014 (unpublished translation by Elena Hadjimichael).

[15] See Court of Appeals Dresden (Germany), 23 October 2000, available at http://cisgw3.law.pace .edu/cases/001023g1.html.

[16] See Court of Appeals Munich (Germany), 5 March 2008, available at http://cisgw3.law.pace .edu/cases/080305g1.html.

could reasonably be expected to have avoided the theft or its consequences.[17] It is therefore unclear whether the ultimate rationale of the court depended on the "control" or "avoidability" element of Article 79, since the court appeared to be assessing each claim by reference to the same facts. Again, the appeal to what was beyond the party's control appears to be redundant of the avoidability condition.

Any independent meaning for the phrase "beyond his control" appears to be directed at removing several categories of impediments from consideration for exemption. It reiterates the commonly understood requirement that the relevant impediment must arise from a source exogenous to the conduct of the party claiming the exemption. Certainly a supplier should not be entitled to burn down its factory and then seek excuse from supplying goods that it was to manufacture. A party who negligently fails to apply for an export license cannot claim an exemption when its inability to ship goods depends on the absence of that document. But beyond confirming what no one would doubt, the phrase does mischief. Honnold appears to be referring to the "control" requirement when he proposes that an impediment refer to "a barrier to performance, such as delivery of the goods or transmission of the price rather than an aspect personal to the seller's performance."[18] This seems a rather anodyne, if not overly enlightening, definition. The most recent commentary by Schwenzer finds Honnold's remark "troubling," presumably because it is too narrow. Nevertheless, her substitute of "'external' circumstances or circumstances of the external sphere which also encompasses the object of the obligation"[19] hardly brings clarity to the phrase. A party's "sphere of influence," a term that many continental commentators use to define the concept of "control," is not necessarily restricted to those factors over which the party has physical oversight. For instance, as we will discuss, several courts have determined that a seller's selection of a supplier for raw materials or finished products places those goods within the seller's control, even if the seller cannot inspect them prior to providing them to the buyer. Some commentators seek to draw more distinct lines between those impediments that are or are not within the obligor's control. Atamer, for example, contends that an obligor must conduct its business to avoid even rare interruptions, including failure of equipment or management, or "internal labour disputes," and must "take all precautions to ensure that production is not hampered

---

[17] The decision also makes clear the broad scope of Article 79 in those cases in which it does apply. Note that the language of Article 79 allows an exemption from any of the claiming party's obligations. Here, the seller contended that Article 79 exempted it from the obligation under Article 30 to transfer the property in the goods to the buyer.

[18] See Honnold/Flechtner, supra note 5, at 617. Nicholas uses the phrase "external barrier to performance" to denote the scope of impediment. See Barry Nicholas, *Impracticability and Impossibility*, in the U.N. Convention on Contracts for the International Sale of Goods, in International Sales: The United Nations Convention on Contracts for the International Sale of Goods 5-1, 5-10 (Nina M. Galston & Hans Smit eds., 1984) [hereinafter "Galston & Smit"].

[19] See Ingeborg Schwenzer, *Article 79*, in Schlechtriem & Schwenzer: Commentary on the UN Convention on the International Sale of Goods (CISG) 1067 (Ingeborg Schwenzer ed., 3d ed. 2010) [hereinafter "Schlechtriem & Schwenzer"]).

by such malfunctions."[20] The language of "all precautions," however, reveals the inherent conflict between the control requirement, which appears to apply a categorical approach, and the unavoidability requirement, which, as we will discuss, is subject to a reasonableness limitation.

Indeed, the entire effort to define "control" through a distinction between what is external and internal to the firm is problematic because it ignores the general problem that the extent to which a party controls circumstances that might affect performance is a function of effort. With enough investment one can avoid adverse events or their consequences, which implies that their materialization is always within the control of the affected party. Labor disturbances at the seller's own plant (as opposed to a labor strike at the port from which goods are to be shipped) may impede performance, and that impediment obviously could be avoided by conceding the demands of the laborers. For that reason, commentators have divided on the inclusion of discrete labor disturbances as a basis for exemption.[21] Some distinguish between a labor disturbance at the obligor's plant and a general strike, which may be due to more general economic conditions and thus more readily deemed to be outside the obligor's control.[22] On this rationale, an unforeseeable internal strike isolated to the seller's plant would not qualify for an exemption, even if the employer is acting reasonably in not yielding to employee demands. Rather, labor disputes are deemed to be part of the risk that the seller assumes when it contracts to provide goods.

Certainly each party takes risks with respect to its personal characteristics, such as financial instability or health (including death of a key party to the contract), so that any impediments to performance that arise from those characteristics are within the control of each party to the contract and outside the realm of an exemption. But the scope of "personal characteristics" is less helpful than might seem the case unless one simply takes a strict categorical approach. Some do. Atamer distinguishes between a discrete illness or death of an obligor and an epidemic.[23] She classifies the latter as exogenous and thus beyond the control of the obligor, although the source of illness may bear little relationship to the ability of the obligor to perform. The same logic applies to characteristics of the firm, such as the functionality of its manufacturing or data processing equipment.[24] But the definition of "personal

---

[20] See Yesim Atamer, *Article 79*, in UN Convention on Contracts for the International Sale of Goods (CISG): Commentary 1043 (Stefan Kröll, Loukas Mistelis & Pilar Perales Viscasillas eds., 2011) [hereinafter "Kröll et al."]; Joseph Lookofsky, Understanding the CISG 134 (4th (Worldwide) ed. 2012).

[21] Compare, e.g., Enderlein & Maskow, supra note 10, at 323, with Tallon, supra note 9, at 584.

[22] See Atamer, *Article 79*, in Kröll et al., supra note 20, at 1043; Schwenzer, *Article 79*, in Schlechtriem & Schwenzer, supra note 19, at 1073.

[23] See Atamer, *Article 79*, in Kröll et al., supra note 20, at 1043. See Schwenzer, *Article 79*, in Schlechtriem & Schwenzer, supra note 19, at 1070–71 (epidemics may constitute impediments, but unforeseen illness, death, or arrest will not).

[24] See Hans Stoll & Ulrich Huber, *Article 79*, in Commentary on the UN Convention on the International Sale of Goods (CISG) 815 (Peter Schlechtriem & Ingeborg Schwenzer eds., 2d (English) ed. 2005).

circumstances" seems sufficiently flexible that sharp distinctions between the "personal" and the "general" should be avoided. Moreover, the categorical approach ignores the fact that the reason why a particular risk will fall within a category (such as "risks commonly assumed by each party") is that a particular risk either is or is not more readily avoided or redressed by that party. If that is the case, there is little reason not to use that analysis directly rather than to try to fit the risk into some categorical proxy.

A similar inference can be made from those cases that involve government regulations introduced after the conclusion of the contract and that implicate both the scope of impediment and the meaning of "control."[25] One court affirmed an arbitrator's finding that government regulations that prohibited the importation of the goods under dispute constituted the necessary impediment to seller's delivery of goods.[26] The arbitrator relied on the unprecedented speed and scope of the regulations to conclude that the parties would not have anticipated their imposition during the period of the contract.[27] In a similar case, government prohibitions on the importation of goods into the buyer's country exempted the buyer from liability for failure to take delivery.[28]

Perhaps a better way to think about "control" is in terms of whether the alleged impediment constituted one of the risks that those in the position of the party seeking exemption is usually deemed to take in similar transactions. That may be because that party is in a superior position to know of the risk, or to calculate its probability. Being able to identify or calculate a risk may serve as a proxy for being in a superior position to avoid it. Even if the risk is not worth avoiding, the relative capacity to consider it has value, since it helps to determine whether cost-effective means of avoiding it either exist or are worth developing.[29] Thus, being in a superior position to identify the risk helps explain why an understanding that a particular party should bear the risk might materialize within the trade. Thinking of control in

---

[25] See Secretariat Commentary to the 1978 Draft, in Documentary History, supra note 8, at 445 (former Article 65, para. 10). A government prohibition on the export of coal did not provide an exemption where the restrictions were in effect prior to conclusion of the contract in Bulgarian Chamber of Commerce and Industry Arbitration Case 56/1995 (Bulgaria), 24 April 1996, available at http://cisgw3.law.pace.edu/cases/960424bu.html. See also District Court Hertogenbosch (Netherlands) (*Malaysia Dairy Industries* v. *Dairex Holland*), 2 October 1998, available at http://cisgw3.law.pace.edu/cases/981002n1.html.

[26] See *Macromex Srl.* v. *Globex International, Inc.*, 2008 U.S. Dist. LEXIS 31442 (S.D.N.Y. April 16, 2008), *aff'd* 330 Fed. Appx. 241 (2d Cir. 2009). Nevertheless, exemption under Article 79 was denied because the seller could have avoided the consequences of the impediment.

[27] See *Macromex Srl.* v. *Globex International, Inc.*, American Arbitration Association, International Centre for Dispute Resolution, Case No. 50181T 0036406 (October 23, 2007), available at http://cisgw3.law.pace.edu/cases/071023a5.html.

[28] See Tribunal of International Commercial Arbitration at the Russian Federation Chamber of Commerce (Russia), 22 January 1997, available at http://cisgw3.law.pace.edu/cases/970122r1.html.

[29] See Atamer, *Article 79*, in Kröll et al., supra note 20, at 1041–42.

those terms avoids the seeming arbitrariness or indeterminacy of categories such as external/internal or "sphere of influence."

Some of the commentary and the case law is consistent with the view that the "beyond his control" requirement considers the usual risks taken by each party, even if the reasoning of the court is not expressed in those terms. Schwenzer justifies the distinction between personal and other characteristics in part on her understanding of the risks commonly assumed by each party in a transaction, though she does not discuss why the common trade understanding would arise.[30] The difference is perhaps best illustrated by the rationale in a decision of the High Court of Arbitration of the Russian Federation to the effect that a buyer was not exempt from performance where money that it had paid to a foreign bank in exchange for goods was stolen.[31] Although it is difficult to conclude that the buyer had control over the security measures taken by the foreign bank to which it made payment, it seems less plausible that, had the parties bargained about the risk of theft, they would have allocated it to the seller.

C. "Hardship" as an impediment

Parties who enter into long-term transactions at prices that are either fixed by the contract or that are pegged to a particular index may discover that market prices of the goods have shifted between the time of contracting and the time of performance in a manner that makes the contract less profitable for one party and more profitable for the other than initially anticipated. Market prices that have long been correlated to a particular index may suddenly deviate from that index because of shortages, surpluses, or government regulations. Sellers who agreed to sell goods at $x in six months will be chagrined to discover that the market price for the same goods on the delivery date is $2x. For their part, buyers are likely to complain that they should not have to pay contract prices for goods that have dramatically decreased in value at the time of delivery and that they will be unable to resell profitably. In these circumstances, it is not impossible or even physically difficult to perform the contract. Performance under the new economic conditions would, however, allegedly cause a financial "hardship" to the party adversely affected by the price shift. In common parlance within the continental literature, the original "equilibrium of the contract" has been disturbed.[32] In economic terms, market shifts have caused an

---

[30] Id. at 1071.

[31] See High Arbitration Court (Russia), 16 February 1998, available at http://cisgw3.law.pace.edu/cases/980216r1.html.

[32] See, e.g., Joseph Lookofsky, *Not Running Wild with the CISG*, 29 J. L. & Comm. 141, 156 (2011). The language of the "equilibrium of the contract" is used in the UNIDROIT Principles of International Commercial Contracts (PICC) Article 6.2.2 (2010), which applies hardship principles where "the occurrence of events fundamentally alters the equilibrium of the contract either because the cost of a party's performance has increased or because the value of the performance a party receives has diminished, and (a) the events occur or become known to the disadvantaged party after the conclusion of the contract; (b) the events could not reasonably have been taken into account by

unanticipated and unpriced reallocation of the "surplus" or joint gain to be created by the contract.

Legal systems vary in their reaction to claims of financial hardship.[33] Indeed, reactions to claims of hardship serve as a prime example of variation in international commercial law, and thus frustrate efforts to infer efficient rules from legal practice. Legal principles in numerous domestic laws provide for judicial adjustment or contract termination, albeit typically under limited circumstances that recognize the possibility that parties have allocated risks arising from unforeseen events, and that deny adjustment where the contract reveals such a risk allocation.[34] The United Kingdom recognizes no duty to renegotiate in the presence of economic hardship. Nor apparently does France, at least in matters of civil and commercial law, although French courts may apply the concept in contracts with the French government and may apply a principle of force majeure in contracts with private parties.[35] In the United States, the Uniform Commercial Code excuses performance when an event the nonoccurrence of which was a basic assumption of the contract causes the contractual obligation of a party to whom the risk of occurrence was not allocated to become impracticable. Dramatic price variations in sales contracts have been a staple of the cases in which the relevant provision, UCC § 2–615, has been invoked, and the claims have failed with very few exceptions.[36] Several civil law countries, on the other hand, have adopted a broad doctrine of hardship, either by statute[37] or in case law.[38]

the disadvantaged party at the time of the conclusion of the contract; (c) the events are beyond the control of the disadvantaged party; and (d) the risk of the events was not assumed by the disadvantaged party." UNIDROIT, an acronym for the International Institute for the Unification of Private Law, is an independent intergovernmental organization. The PICC therefore comprises general principles, not legal rules that are binding law in any jurisdiction. Nevertheless, the PICC contains a preamble that provides: (1) that they shall apply when the parties have agreed that their contract is to be governed by them; (2) that they may apply when the parties have agreed that their contract be governed by general principles of law, the *lex mercatoria* or the like; (3) that they may be applied when the parties have not chosen any law to govern their contract; (4) that they may be used to interpret or supplement international uniform law instruments; (5) that they may be used to interpret or supplement domestic law; and (6) that they may serve as a model for national and international legislators. Clause 3 in the Preamble is potentially misleading. Because the PICC is not law, its principles may be applied to a contract that does not incorporate them only if permitted by applicable law. See Ralf Michaels, *Purpose, Legal Nature, and Scope of the PICC*, in Commentary on the UNIDROIT Principles of International Commercial Contracts (PICC) 34, 38–9 (Stefan Vogenauer ed., 2d ed. 2015).

[33] For a review of the reactions of different legal systems, see Mazzacano, supra note 1, at 85–92.

[34] See Rodrigo Momberg Uribe, *The Duty to Renegotiate an International Sales Contract in the Case of Hardship—International Case Note*, 19 Eur. Rev. Private L. 119, 124 (2011).

[35] See Mazzacano, supra note 1, at 100.

[36] See, e.g., *Northern Indiana Public Service Co. v. Carbon County Coal Co.*, 799 F.2d 651 (7th Cir. 1986).

[37] See, e.g., C.c. [Codice civile] art. 1467 (It.); Nieuw Burgerlijk Wetboek [NBW] 6.258 (Netherlands); C.C. [Codigo Civil] art. 478 (Brazil); Burgerliches Gesetzbuch [BGB] [Civil Code] § 313 (Ger.).

[38] See Cristoph Brunner, Force Majeure and Hardship Under General Contract Principles 403 (2008).

Article 79 brings little clarity to the issue of whether hardship qualifies as an impediment. Little can be authoritatively discerned from the drafting history. Flechtner notes that incorporation of a specific provision that would allow contract adaptation in the event of hardship was rejected during the drafting of Article 79.[39] The Advisory Council's Opinion notes that the report of the Working Group that considered avoidance or adjustment of a contract to escape "excessive damages" was "not adopted," and concludes that even if one accepts the proposition that the drafting history is relevant, "such history evidences that the discussions were not conclusive on this question."[40]

Schlechtriem's report of the deliberations in Vienna that led to the CISG provides fodder for all sides of the debate. He writes:

> One of the controversial points in the preliminary UNCITRAL discussions was whether economic difficulties — "unaffordability" — constitute a ground for exemption. In the end, the general view was probably that both physical and economic impossibility could exempt an obligor. It cannot be concluded, therefore, on the basis of the change in terminology from "circumstances" in ULIS Article 74(1) to "impediments" that an impediment in the sense of Article 79(1) of the Convention is only an occurrence that absolutely bars performance, but — under very narrow conditions — impediment also includes "unaffordability". As a rule, however, since the obligor generally guarantees his financial capability to procure and produce the promised goods, increased procurement and production costs do not constitute exempting impediments.[41]

In light of this uncertainty, there are at least four plausible interpretations of the CISG's treatment of the question. First, one might contend that hardship cases are governed by the CISG and settled in favor of including hardship within the terms of Article 79. As a result, financial distress that causes radical price changes may, in a proper case, constitute an impediment that exempts the adversely affected party from liability if it also satisfies the other criteria of Article 79. Second, one may contend that hardship cases are governed by the CISG, but that Article 79 is intended to exclude such cases. That interpretation would deny relief under Article 79 to the adversely affected party because hardship does not qualify as an impediment necessary for exemption. Third, one may contend that hardship cases are governed by the CISG, but are not settled expressly by Article 79 or any other explicit provision. As a result, under Article 7(2), the issue of hardship is to be settled in conformity with the general principles on which the CISG is based. Article 7(1) dictates that those principles include regard for the international character of the convention, uniformity in its application, and the observance of good faith in international trade. Thus, if those principles would be served by taking hardship into account, then the CISG

---

[39] See Honnold/Flechtner, supra note 5, at 629.
[40] CISG Advisory Council Opinion No. 7, supra note 13, at ¶¶ 29–30.
[41] Schlechtriem, supra note 6, at 102.

should be interpreted as incorporating such a principle. That might mean allowing an exemption on terms similar to those that exist under Article 79, or allowing some alternative redress, such as mandating renegotiation of contracts that are the subject of radical price changes.[42] Fourth, one may contend that the CISG has absolutely nothing to say about hardship cases. That is, they are neither governed by nor settled expressly by the CISG or by its general principles. In that situation, Article 7(2) mandates that courts analyzing a hardship issue in a case otherwise governed by the CISG should look to principles of private international law and apply the law concerning hardship of the jurisdiction that those principles make applicable to the transaction.

Each of these positions, often with some epicycles or variations, has its supporters. Although some commentators reject the notion that Article 79 addresses the issue,[43] there appears to be an emerging consensus among commentators, at least those from civil law jurisdictions where domestic law is more sympathetic to claims for adjustment, that hardship qualifies as an impediment within Article 79, albeit one to be employed sparingly.[44] That is the position taken by the CISG Advisory Council in its opinion on Article 79. In a bit of a non sequitur, Advisory Council Opinion No. 7 concludes: "The language of Article 79 does not expressly equate the term 'impediment' with an event that makes performance absolutely impossible. Therefore, a party that finds itself in a situation of hardship may invoke hardship as an exemption from liability under Article 79."[45] At the same time, the Advisory Council Opinion Comment provides that price fluctuations are "a normal risk of commercial transactions in general," and reserves the hardship case for the "wild and totally unexpected market fluctuations in goods or currency."[46] Honnold expresses the view that Article 79(1) "seems to leave room for exemptions based on economic dislocations" where those dislocations constitute a barrier to performance comparable to qualifying physical impediments.[47] Nevertheless, Flechtner's additional commentary on Honnold notes that the "exemption" remedy of Article 79 does not fit well with the standard remedy for hardship cases in civil law. That remedy involves adaptation of the contract, either through renegotiation by the parties or judicial imposition of a new price.[48] Lookofsky, on the other hand, suggests that hardship should be subsumed within validity, and therefore falls outside the CISG entirely under Article 4.

---

[42] Flechtner appears to endorse something close to this view to claim that Article 7(2), by incorporating standards in Article 79, would allow exemption from liability if a very extreme loss of value, amounting to frustration of purpose, resulted from developments that were beyond the control of the party seeking relief. See Honnold/Flechtner, supra note 5, at 622. But Flechtner distinguishes that situation from hardship cases, where he concludes that Article 79 not only governs the hardship issue and resolves it in favor of its inclusion, but also pre-empts domestic rules that might allow a renegotiation remedy. Id. at 630.

[43] See, e.g., Carla Spivack, *Of Shrinking Sweatsuits and Poison Vine Wax: A Comparison of Basis for Excuse under U.C.C. § 2-615 and CISG Article 79*, 27 Pa. J. Int'l Econ. L. 757 (2006).

[44] See, e.g., Schwenzer, *Article 79*, in Schlechtriem & Schwenzer, supra note 19, at 1076.

[45] CISG Advisory Council Opinion No. 7, supra note 13, at ¶ 3.1.   [46] Id. at ¶ 39.

[47] See Honnold/Flechtner, supra note 5, at 628.   [48] See id. at 628–29.

Indeed, he contends, quite reasonably, that such a resolution makes sense because it permits parties to choose among competing domestic treatments of hardship.[49] The Advisory Council Opinion, on the other hand, rejects the inclusion of hardship within the nebulous category of validity.[50]

D. *Hardship exemption: case law and assessment*

The few cases that deal with the issue do little to resolve the question of hardship, though most reveal an aversion to finding the circumstances necessary to grant an exemption. An early Italian decision rejected a seller's defense that a 43.7 percent increase in the market price of the contracted for goods justified nonperformance (although the court also concluded that the CISG did not apply to the case).[51] A 2005 CIETAC Arbitration decision that applied the CISG but that did not explicitly mention Article 79 concluded that a buyer of iron ore was bound by the contract price when negotiations between the parties after a dramatic decrease in the market price of iron ore failed to result in a modified price.[52] In a Bulgarian arbitration, it was the buyer who contended that a seller should have suspended deliveries of steel ropes because market conditions had worsened, the price had increased, and the construction industry was in depression. The tribunal concluded that conditions of Article 79 were not satisfied because performance was not objectively impossible, the facts did not represent force majeure, and the described events were foreseeable.[53]

The most discussed recent case of hardship took a different view. In *Scafom International* v. *Lorraine Tubes S.A.S*,[54] the Belgian Supreme Court displayed sympathy both to the concept and to a broad remedy of renegotiation when hardship materializes. Scafom International, a Dutch firm, had entered into a contract to purchase steel tubes to be used for the production of scaffolds from a French firm that was a predecessor to the Belgian seller involved in the litigation. Later, the seller notified the buyer that the contract prices would have to be modified due to an unpredictable 70 percent increase in steel prices. The buyer refused and litigation ensued. An initial decision from the Commercial Court was a model of the "no adjustment for hardship" theory.[55] That court first concluded that the matter was not

---

[49] See Lookofsky, supra note 32, at 160.
[50] See CISG Advisory Council Opinion No. 7, supra note 13, at ¶ 36.
[51] See District Court Monza (Italy) (*Nuova Fucinati SpA* v. *Fondmetall International A.B.*), 14 January 1993, available at http://cisgw3.law.pace.edu/cases/930114i3.html.
[52] See CIETAC Arbitration (China), 25 May 2005, available at http://cisgw3.law.pace.edu/cases/050525c1.html.
[53] See Arbitration Tribunal of Bulgarian Chamber of Commerce & Industry, Case No. 11/1996 (Bulgaria), 12 February 1998, available at http://cisgw3.law.pace.edu/cases/980212bu.html.
[54] Supreme Court (Belgium), *Scafom International* v. *Lorraine Tubes S.A.S.*, 19 June 2009, available at http://cisgw3.law.pace.edu/cases/090619b1.html.
[55] See Commercial Court Tongeren (Belgium), *Scafom International* v. *Lorraine Tubes S.A.S.*, 25 January 2005, available at http://cisgw3.law.pace.edu/cases/050125b1.html.

expressly settled in Article 79 or elsewhere in the CISG. It then turned to domestic law without considering whether any of the CISG's underlying principles settled the matter. Belgian law, in the court's view, rejected theories of hardship, or *imprévision*, on the theory that it would undermine the legal certainty inherent in the doctrine of *pacta sunt servanda*. Price increases, domestic Belgian decisions had implied, are always foreseeable and financial loss was simply a risk of the transaction. Thus, there was no good faith obligation that precluded the obligee from demanding a promised performance simply because it had been rendered more costly by changed circumstances. Moreover, the court concluded, the seller could have protected itself against a dramatic price increase by inserting a price adjustment clause in its contract. Indeed, the seller did include such a clause in its standard terms and conditions, but, for reasons that were unclear, those terms had not been incorporated into the Scafom contract. The reasoning of those domestic law principles (though not the substantive laws themselves) could be applied to cases governed by the CISG.

If the commercial court's decision was a model of strict application of contractual language, the Supreme Court's logic was a model of confusion. It began by asserting that unforeseen changes in circumstances that increase the burden of performance in a disproportionate manner for one party could form an impediment under Article 79. The court then concluded that the 70 percent increase in the price of steel was unforeseeable (contrary to the commercial court's view) and that the increases had "rendered the further performance of the contracts under unchanged conditions exceptionally detrimental" to the seller. Thus, the court might be read as concluding that Article 79 included financial hardship cases. But the court also quoted Article 7(1) and (2) for the proposition that general principles that govern international trade should fill any gaps in the CISG, which implied that the hardship issue was not resolved or "expressly settled" by Article 79 after all, but that it was still governed by the CISG. The court required the renegotiation sought by the seller. The imposition of that remedy implies that the court was not interpreting Article 79 to incorporate a principle of adjustment in hardship cases, since that remedy is not found in Article 79 – or elsewhere in the CISG. Thus, the court appeared to find a "gap" in the CISG, and created a preference for filling it with general principles of international trade in order to promote uniformity. From there, the court made the leap to declare that the relevant principles were to be found in the UNIDROIT Principles of International Commercial Contracts (PICC), which permits a party aggrieved by changed circumstances that fundamentally disturb the equilibrium of the contract to seek not only exemption from damages, but also renegotiation of the contract.[56]

Each of these steps is questionable. We have already indicated the diversity of opinion on the issue of whether, and how, Article 79 incorporates hardship cases. As

---

[56] See UNIDROIT Principles of International Commercial Article 6.2.3(1) (2004) ("In case of hardship the disadvantaged party is entitled to request renegotiations."), in effect at the time of the decision.

we indicated previously, most commentators are currently of the view that the conditions for exemption from performance include cases of hardship. If that opinion is correct, then no appeal to Article 7 would be necessary. Perhaps, however, the court was interpreting Article 79 to mean that hardship provided an exemption and Article 7 provided its consequences, such as the need to renegotiate.[57] But if that were the case, then one would have expected the court to deal with Article 79(5), which itself deals with the consequences of exemption.

If Article 79 does not deal with hardship, but the issue is "governed by" the CISG, the court misread the instruction of Article 7(2) about how to proceed. That Article mandates that gaps be filled by reference to the "general principles on which" the CISG is based, which is not necessarily the same as the general principles of international trade. Indeed, the absence of any hint within the CISG of a remedy of renegotiation suggests some divergence between the two. Article 7(1) includes within the interpretive principles of the CISG the desire to promote uniformity in its application and the observance of good faith in international trade. But, as we have indicated, the range of reactions in domestic law to claims of hardship is too great to infer much in the way of what "good faith in international trade requires" of parties whose contractual expectations have been disappointed by financial disruptions.

The PICC does recognize the possibility of hardship as an excuse. But the Belgian Supreme Court stated the proposition too strongly when it concluded that the party adversely affected by changed circumstances "is also entitled to claim the renegotiation of the contract" under those principles. The PICC provides more moderately that a hardship that fundamentally alters the equilibrium of the contract permits the disadvantaged party to request renegotiations, and that a court may subsequently terminate the contract or adapt it. Perhaps the court viewed the PICC as playing a more complicated role, as a statement of some of the "general principles" that underlie the CISG. This position requires some explanation, however. Certainly it cannot mean that the drafters of the CISG took the PICC into account, since the first version of the PICC appeared in 1994 and thus post-dated the CISG by more than a decade. The claim, therefore, at most means that the PICC provides a convenient set of principles that happens to coincide with principles underlying the CISG, and that therefore can be incorporated through the language of Article 7(2). The PICC invites this interpretation when it states in its Preamble that the principles "may be used to interpret or supplement international uniform law instruments," a phrase that clearly includes the CISG. If one follows the admonition of Article 7(1) that the CISG is to be interpreted in a manner that promotes uniformity, then the statement of uniform principles may facilitate that purpose.

This appears to be the position of the French Supreme Court (Cour de Cassation) in a recent case involving a claim of hardship due to increased prices for

---

[57] See Lookofsky, supra note 32, at 166–67.

materials and a subsequent decrease in the profitability of the transaction.[58] The court held explicitly that the CISG does not exclude hardship, defined in the PICC. Perhaps more importantly, even if a non-sequitur, the court concluded that because the PICC applies to all contracts, and thus has a "larger sphere of application" than just the sale of goods, it could be used "to complete and interpret" the CISG, presumably because the PICC represents the general principles that underlie it. For the court, the use of the PICC to fill gaps in the CISG itself would satisfy the Article 7 objectives of promoting internationality, applying law uniformly, and adhering to good faith in international commerce. Nevertheless, the court refused to conclude that hardship existed in the case before it or that renegotiation was required. The court based its refusal on the grounds that the appellate court had not determined whether the increase in the price of raw materials that was the basis for the hardship claim exceeded the normal risks taken by the parties.

The court's rationale that the PICC clarifies the general principles underlying the CISG seems questionable, at least with respect to claims of hardship. As we have noted previously,[59] it is difficult to find or generate any definitive set of general principles to which Article 7(2) refers. At the very least, one might expect that a principle that qualified as sufficiently general to underlie the CISG must reflect widespread and relatively uniform practice. The availability of a hardship exception to contractual obligations – especially one combined with a renegotiation require-ment – is one area in which there is substantial diversity among legal systems. As we will explain, there is good reason for that diversity, since the advantages of a hardship exception and a renegotiation requirement are contestable, and parties have con-tractual mechanisms for dealing with post-contract price shocks. To elevate a "soft law" principle of renegotiation from the PICC into a default rule enforceable by courts in the name of uniformity seems to ignore both the variations in domestic law and the intentions of parties who omitted, perhaps intentionally, a renegotiation clause from their contract.

The reluctance of other courts to recognize a hardship exemption reflects the view that market price risks are inherent in long-term contracts. The party who wishes to avoid or minimize risks, under this view, is obligated to do so expressly, even with respect to price fluctuations outside historical parameters. While there is something intuitively attractive about the notion that parties have only contracted with respect to a discrete set of financial risks, including a range of prices, and thus did not intend their contract to apply outside of those parameters, we are sympa-thetic to the reluctance demonstrated by these cases to allow an exemption under Article 79 directly or through an alternative analysis based on general principles of the CISG or international commercial law. There are multiple reasons for this

---

[58] Supreme Court (France), 17 February 2015, unpublished translation by Clemence Whitney Alice Marie Ploix.

[59] See Chapter 1.V; Chapter 4.II.A.; Chapter 5.I.C., Chapter 9.I.A.

conclusion. First, radical price fluctuations do not appear without reason. Rather, they arise because of some exogenous event that creates surpluses or shortages that are reflected in prices. If the underlying event was within the risk contemplated by the parties, then the fact that its consequences took the form of disturbing the equilibrium of the contract is irrelevant. The effect should be subjected to the same analysis as the cause, so that its foreseeability should render the consequences to be within the risk taken by each of the parties. The foreseeability analysis is perhaps more telling in the case of hardship claims, because parties to long-term arrangements not only can foresee that market prices could change dramatically between the conclusion of the contract and the time of performance. They can also protect themselves relatively easily against ahistorical price shifts. A party concerned about such a shift can always set parameters beyond which the contract will cease to operate. Assume, for instance, that parties are negotiating a long-term supply contract for a commodity that within recent history has a range of ± 20 percent of its current price. Price fluctuations within that range would presumably reflect the assumptions of the parties about the price of the commodity during the life of their contract. It would, therefore, be plausible to insert into the contract a clause that obligates the parties to renegotiate prices should market prices for the commodity fall outside that range. The precise cause of such an ahistorical shift, and thus its foreseeability, would be irrelevant. Of course, one might contend that the parties only intended their contract to operate within the historical range of market prices. Thus, hardship could presumptively apply when market prices fall outside that range. But judicial determination of the appropriate range will be a far more difficult task (what period of time should be considered? what are normal fluctuations?) than inducing the parties to set appropriate parameters ex ante. One might expect, therefore, that if parties had expressly negotiated about whether historical parameters were presumed to apply, they would not have negotiated for the higher cost solution of ex post judicial adjustment.

Even beyond contractual clauses, at least some parties disadvantaged by price shifts need not bear the ultimate loss. Relatively large firms can deploy strategies for dealing with the unknown by having a diverse portfolio of contracts that provides insurance or hedges against price shocks. Where a firm constantly sells or purchases the same good, a combination of long-term, short-term, fixed price, and spot price contracts is likely to provide a shield against shocks that frustrate the purpose of any one contract. It would be odd to allow such a firm to keep the "winners" within its portfolio and obtain exemptions from performance of the "losers."

Indeed, the availability of strategies for dealing with risks in long-term contracts explains why parties frequently assume risks implicit in the price terms of the contracts they enter. Parties may, for instance, allocate risk by agreeing to a fixed-price contract and an escalator that contains a floor but no ceiling.[60] Alternatively,

---

[60] See *Northern Indiana Public Service Co. v. Carbon County Coal Co.*, 799 F.2d 265, 278 (7th Cir. 1986) ("[A] fixed-price contract is an explicit assignment of the risk of market price

parties may insert clauses that require price adjustment either under very specific circumstances or under some vaguer standard, such as the materialization of a change in economic circumstances that causes one party to suffer financial hardship.[61] Similarly, if a party enters into a forward contract at one side of the transaction and a spot market contract on the other side of the transaction, a perfectly appropriate inference would be that the party has impliedly taken the risk of price movements between the period of contract execution and performance. Assume, for instance, that a middleman seller agrees to sell steel at $x per metric ton in two months. The seller could have purchased the steel at the time of the resale contract and thus fixed its profit at that time. If the seller instead plans to purchase the steel just before it is required to perform the resale contract, there seems little reason to conclude that the seller has done something other than bet on the movement of steel prices in the intervening period. Thus, if the price of steel at the time of performance is $2x, the situation is essentially identical to an explicit bet on price movements. One commercial party's liability should not depend on a counterparty's erroneous guess about subsequent market movements.

In addition, the application of a hardship exemption requires judgments for which ex post analysis may do worse than ex ante planning. Even those who favor a hardship exception recognize that it has the capacity to destabilize contractual relationships. These commentators therefore restrict application of a hardship exemption to a vague standard, such as "a 'limit of sacrifice' beyond which the obligor cannot be reasonably expected to perform."[62] Some commentators have attempted to quantify the degree of deviation from normal prices necessary to constitute hardship. But those very efforts instead reveal the complexity and uncertainty inherent in any such effort. Thus, a now-withdrawn official comment to the PICC assumed that a hardship defense was available when there was "an alteration amounting to 50 percent or more of the cost or the value of the performance is likely to amount to a 'fundamental' alteration."[63] Brunner implies that a 100 percent

---

increases to the seller and the risk of market price decreases to the buyer, and the assignment of the latter risk to the buyer is even clearer where, as in this case, the contract places a floor under price but allows for escalation. If, as is also the case here, the buyer forecasts the market incorrectly and therefore finds himself locked into a disadvantageous contract, he has only himself to blame and so cannot shift the risk back to the seller by invoking impossibility or related doctrines. . . .").

[61] See, e.g., *Sudbrook Trading Estate* v. *Eggleton*, [1983] 1 A.C. 444.

[62] CISG Advisory Council Opinion No. 7, supra note 13, at ¶ 38.

[63] See UNIDROIT Principles of International Commercial Contracts Official Comment 2 to Article 6.2.2. (1994). Maskow also contends that that a 50 percent increase in the cost of performance or a 50 percent decrease in value of the performance to be received would trigger valid claims for hardship. See Dietrich Maskow, *Hardship and Force Majeure*, 40 Am J. Comp. L. 657, 662 (1992). The portion of Comment 2 setting the 50 percent threshold was withdrawn from the 2004 edition of Official Comment 2, apparently because the threshold was thought too low and arbitrary. See Ewan McKendrick, *Article 6.2.2.*, in Commentary on the UNIDROIT Principles of International Commercial Contracts (PICC) 816 (Stefan Vogenauer ed.,

increase would qualify, though he is more careful than most in specifying that cost increases do not necessarily translate into commensurate profit decreases.[64] Schwenzer contends that cost increases are likely to have higher fluctuations in international markets than in domestic markets and thus advises a 150–200 percent margin for invocation of hardship.[65] The sources of these figures appear to be little more than speculations by their authors, or inferences from domestic law, as opposed to conclusions predicated on some reasoned economic theory of parties' expectations about the "equilibrium" of the contract they have negotiated. Without a theory that identifies these expectations, all standards for determining whether an alteration of this "equilibrium" is fundamental are arbitrary.

Percentage increases may also be less material to the profitability of the affected party than initially appears. Even dramatic price increases for inputs do not necessarily translate into commensurate losses for outputs of the disadvantaged party. Assume, for instance, that a seller must pay twice the contract price to supply the buyer with a good, x, that has become scarce subsequent to the time that the supply contract was executed. As an economic matter, the increase does not necessarily translate into an increase in the price of a finished product, y, into which the buyer was going to incorporate x. Thus, it is not clear that a buyer will be able to recover the additional price that it would have to pay to the seller if required to renegotiate the price of x. The buyer will be able to recover that amount only if it can commensurately increase the price that it charges for its finished product, y. Whether the price of y increases depends on the supply and demand for it in the marketplace, and the availability of substitutes for x in the production of y. It cannot be assumed, therefore, that even a dramatic increase in the cost of x will cause an alteration in the equilibrium of the contract, because, assuming that "equilibrium" implies consequences for both parties, cost increases to the seller have no predictable effect on the buyer. Whether or not the cost increase to the buyer reduces its profit from the sale of y depends on the facts of each case – a task that hardship doctrine would require courts to undertake by analyzing the market conditions of each contract.

All these considerations lead us to conclude that hardship should be excluded from the scope of impediments under Article 79, and indeed from the CISG itself. We base that conclusion on the belief that most parties would not bargain to permit nonperformance for unspecified price risks and would not agree to the rules stated in the PICC concerning judicially imposed renegotiation. Our review of the arguments for and against adjustment for hardship reveals that the dispute largely

---

2d ed. 2015). Whether the 50 percent threshold is too low or arbitrary depends on the parties' expectations about the contract's "equilibrium," about which the PICC says nothing.

[64] See Christoph Brunner, *Force Majeure and Hardship Under General Contract Principles: Exemption for Non-Performance in International Arbitration* 426–27 (2008).

[65] See Ingeborg Schwenzer, *Force Majeure and Hardship in International Sales Contracts*, 39 Vict. U. Wellington L. Rev. 709, 717 (2008).

focuses on an empirical claim. Implicit in the argument for a default hardship rule is the belief that extreme pricing risks must be outside the contract because they arise infrequently and parties are largely incapable of dealing with the resulting uncertainty about their materialization. On this view, a default hardship rule does not impinge on contractual autonomy, since, in the absence of an express assumption or allocation, parties would want the legal regime to impose on them obligations to assess and manage remote risks. By contrast, implicit in the argument against a default rule allowing hardship adjustment is the belief that commercial parties both can and do deploy strategies for assessing and managing even remote price risks with sufficient skill that their presumed intent is to allow each party to deal with potential disadvantageous events rather than to invite ex post judicial intervention. We conclude that parties can and do contract in a manner that allocates price risks when they intend those risks to be covered by their agreement and would be reluctant to leave the determination of unforeseeable price risks and their consequences to an arbiter that examines the situation ex post.

The lack of uniformity across jurisdictions about the legal principles that govern hardship also indicates a diversity of opinion too great to conclude that the drafters of the CISG intended to resolve the issue without addressing it explicitly. For the same reason, we doubt that one can resolve the issue under Article 7(2) by reference to "the general principles" on which the CISG is based, because those principles, at least with respect to the issue of hardship, are too varied to provide a clear answer to the question.[66] While we are sympathetic to the view that the issue can be handled as one of validity under Article 4, and thus addressed outside the CISG, the nebulous nature of "validity" makes that a more difficult route. Thus, we would resolve the hardship issue under the last clause of Article 7(2). That is, we conclude that the issue of hardship in any individual case should be resolved in conformity with the law applicable to the contract by virtue of the rules of private international law. The legal rule concerning hardship, if any, would be dictated by the governing law that applied to the contract under rules of private international law. While such a result may not advance internationality as urged in Article 7(1), that goal is only one of several that inform international commercial law. There seems little reason to advance internationality over the commercial objective of minimizing the costs that parties must incur to obtain and enforce their desired contract. The absence of a default hardship rule may actually advance the latter objective by inducing parties to specify the parameters under which their contract operates. Although specification may increase ex ante negotiation costs, it dramatically reduces the costs of ex post resolution of disputes that would otherwise be subject to the vagaries of "hardship."

Certainly we are reluctant to find the remedy of mandated renegotiation adopted in the *Scafom* case inherent in Article 79 or in the principles that underlie

---

[66] To the same effect, see Christina Ramberg, *Swedish Case Note on* Scafom, 19 Eur. Rev. Private L. 116, 117 (2011).

the CISG generally. As Flechtner implies, Article 79(5) provides for the consequences of exemption, and renegotiation is not among them.[67] The difficulty of
enforcing a renegotiation requirement undermines its propriety. Even the PICC
provides no sanction for parties who fail to achieve agreement after renegotiation.
Schwenzer makes the more questionable claim that a party that rejects a reasonable
offer of adjustment would be unable to avoid the contract if a court concludes that
the party should have consented to the adjustment on the basis of good faith.[68]
A court could, of course, reach such a decision, but its basis in the CISG is unclear.

None of this suggests that parties to a transaction that is vulnerable to changed
circumstances will fail to cooperate when a remote risk materializes. To the
contrary, reputational concerns, the desire to continue an ongoing relationship, or
norms of commercial behavior are all likely to create incentives for cooperation. But
the fact that parties ex post desire to cooperate does not entail that they would ex
ante agree that cooperation is required. Indeed, one can imagine reasons why parties
would avoid such an obligation that have nothing to do with the desire to secure
what some see as windfall gains from price shifts. Obligations to renegotiate can
create perverse incentives that rational commercial parties would wish to avoid.
These incentives may distort behavior during the performance of the contract.

Consider two possible scenarios in which renegotiation creates both personal and
social losses. In the first scenario, a seller enters into a long-term supply contract for
goods that require the buyer to make substantial relationship-specific investments,
that is, investments that cannot readily be transferred to other transactions. Imagine,
for example, a seller who sells coal from a coal mine at a fixed price to a buyer who is
obligated to build a railroad spur from the main track to the mine head in order to
transport the coal. If production costs spike, the seller may demand renegotiation of
the fixed price. The buyer will be vulnerable to demands for price increases because
it cannot otherwise recover its investment in the railroad spur. We have cited the
possibility of this type of holdup as the motivation for legal restrictions on contract
modification. But it similarly explains why parties would want to avoid renegotiation
generally, and certainly would want to avoid a legal obligation to renegotiate. Any
assumption that a renegotiation default rule reflects the preferences of parties
vulnerable to holdup appears to be misguided.

Alternatively, consider the effects of mandated renegotiation or judicially imposed
adjustments on the ex ante incentives of the parties to avoid remote risks from
materializing. Assume, for instance, that one party identifies a remote risk (say, a .001
probability), that, if it materializes, will cause the party to suffer a $1,000,000 loss and
that can be avoided with a current expenditure of $800. Presumably, a risk neutral

---

[67] See Honnold/Flechtner, supra note 5, at 629.

[68] See Schwenzer, supra note 65, at 724. Elsewhere, Schwenzer notes that some agreements allow
for third-party adaptation of contracts or for a right to avoid in the event renegotiation fails.
These could be effective enforcement mechanisms. See Schwenzer, *Article 79*, in Schlechtriem & Schwenzer, supra note 19, at 1086.

actor would invest in avoiding the risk because precaution costs of $800 are less than the expected loss of $1,000 (.001 x $1,000,000). Now assume that the party believes that if the risk materializes the legal regime will cause the parties to renegotiate or will impose loss sharing on the parties, so that the disadvantaged party anticipates that it would bear half the costs of the risk. Presumably the disadvantaged party would not take the precaution to avoid the risk, even though precaution costs are less than its expected value. That is because the expected value of the loss to the party is now only half of the total expected loss, or $(.5)(.001)(1,000,000) = 500. A risk neutral actor will not invest the $800 necessary to avoid the risk in order to save an expected personal loss of $500. In short, allowing opportunities for ex post modification of contracts in light of remote risks can induce parties to invest suboptimally in their avoidance.

III. IMPEDIMENTS AND DEFECTIVE GOODS

A. *The availability of exemption*

The availability of an exemption from liability for delivery of nonconforming goods, rather than non-delivery or late delivery, has been a source of some controversy. There is some textual support for the more expansive interpretation because the language of Article 79 refers to an exemption from liability for a party's failure to perform "any of his obligations." Nevertheless, the consequences of including defective goods within Article 79 argue against such a reading.

The debate about the inclusion of defective goods in Article 79 involves defects that materialize because the seller was unaware of them, notwithstanding the use of state of the art procedures in their manufacture. The underlying assumption is that the defects arose non-negligently, and thus could not reasonably have been avoided by the seller. In this sense, either the defect or the seller's reasonable ignorance of it constitutes the "impediment" that is beyond his control and that causes a failure to satisfy contractual obligations. Some commentators, including those involved in the drafting process, have expressed surprise at the continuing claims that such cases can qualify for an exemption since, they note, the term "impediment" was deliberately selected to distinguish prior uniform sales proposals that used the term "circumstances" to define the conditions for an exemption. The shift was thought (at least by some) to avoid any inference that "circumstances" included a defect, as opposed to an externally caused barrier to performance.[69]

---

[69] See Barry Nicholas, *Impracticability and Impossibility in the U.N. Convention on Contracts for the International Sale of Goods,* in Galston & Smit, supra note 18, at 5–10; Honnold/Flechtner, supra note 5, at 617–8. Nicholas, however, had earlier expressed doubt that the change in terminology would have the intended effect. See Barry Nicholas, Force Majeure *and Frustration,* 27 Am. J. Comp. L. 231 (1979).

Those who continue to urge application of an exemption to cases of defects tend to come from civil law jurisdictions in which domestic law identifies liability with fault. In those jurisdictions, the non-negligent failure to avoid defects would not lead to liability, and that particular lens ostensibly influences an interpretation of Article 79 that similarly allows an exemption from liability where defects arise "faultlessly."[70] Common law commentators, who are comfortable with the standard imposition of strict liability for breach of warranty, are more sympathetic to the interpretation of Article 79 that imposes liability on a seller who has taken optimal precautions but still produces defective goods. We believe that the common law lawyers have the better of the argument, notwithstanding Schwenzer's position that the civil law position has prevailed in the case law. Our position, possibly influenced by our own backgrounds as American lawyers, is that the drafting history is clear with respect to the intent of the drafters. Schwenzer suggests otherwise and points to an example in the Secretariat's Commentary in which goods are required to be packaged in plastic containers which have become unavailable for reasons that the seller could not have avoided.[71] That commentary states that if substitute packing materials were available, then the seller must use them to avoid the impediment rather than refuse to deliver, and is exempt from damages if it does use them. The example, therefore, deals with packing containers that are unavailable to the seller, not with defects in either the containers that are available or defects in the goods themselves. The delivery of goods with substitute packing materials is described as an example of overcoming an impediment (the containers' unavailability), not as a delivery of defective goods. It is difficult to see how the example supports the general proposition that nonconforming goods fall within Article 79.

More to the point, the introduction of fault into the concept of an impediment is inconsistent with the rest of the scheme of the CISG, and, as Honnold notes, inconsistent with other parts of Article 79.[72] Notwithstanding the absence of the language of warranty, Article 35(1) provides that a seller "must deliver goods which are of the quantity, quality and description required by the contract." This is language of strict liability that tolerates no inquiry into the fault of the seller of nonconforming goods. Articles 45(1) and 65(1) are to the same effect. They provide remedies for the counterparty if a party "fails to perform any of its obligations," and make no concession for non-negligent failure.[73]

---

[70] See, e.g., Schwenzer, *Article 79*, in Schlechtriem & Schwenzer, *supra* note 19, at 1065–66.

[71] Id. at 1066, referring to the Secretariat Commentary on the 1978 Draft, in Documentary History, *supra* note 8, at 446 (former Article 65, para. 9, Example 65D).

[72] Honnold suggests that Article 79(4), which requires a party seeking exemption to give notice to the counterparty is "absurd" in connection with delivery of goods with a hidden defect, since, by definition, the seller would not know of the defect. Honnold/Flechtner, *supra* note 5, at 427. He also suggests that the difficulty that the buyer would have in proving seller negligence argues against allowing fault to be the basis of an exemption.

[73] See Joseph Lookofsky, *Fault and No-Fault in Danish, American and International Sales Law: The Reception of the United Nations Sales Convention*, 27 Scan. Stud. L. 109, 128–30 (1983).

Perhaps the debate represents much ado about nothing. Even those who suggest that defective deliveries can theoretically fall within Article 79 note that there will be few cases in which such a claim is ultimately successful. Schwenzer's position on Article 79's application to defects is modified (or contradicted) by her acknowledgement that sellers are strictly liable for the conformity of goods and thus will rarely be able to rely on Article 79 with respect to nonconformities.[74] Lookofsky agrees that Article 79 could apply to defective deliveries, but finds the conditions under which an impediment that both damaged, but did not destroy goods, and that was unforeseeable to the seller to be so limited as to make the applicability of the exemption trivial in defective delivery cases.[75] Nicholas also contends that sellers of defective goods are unlikely to satisfy the requirements of unforeseeability and unavoidability.[76] Atamer makes the reasonable point that a defect due to some internal manufacturing or other process at the seller's own plant may not be an "impediment beyond his control" in the first instance, because the defect did not arise from some exogenous event.[77] Consistent with that argument, a German case that involved Spanish paprika that contained levels of contaminants in excess of safety regulations in the buyer's jurisdiction was decided on the grounds that the seller was responsible for its performance "independently of whether the goods were contaminated with ethylene oxide through a treatment in the plant of the [seller] or in any different way," which appears to be an allusion to the alleged impediment being within seller's control.[78] A Spanish case that also involved contaminated paprika (there must be a lot of contaminated paprika floating around) similarly rejected the seller's claim of an impediment, based on the excessive burden required to detect the defect, on the grounds that the risk was reasonably under the control of the party that failed to comply with the contract.[79] Given our position that the scope of "beyond his control" reflects an allocation of risks between the parties, we accept the argument that defective goods cases are outside of Article 79 completely, because it is unlikely that a buyer would accept the risk of latent or unknown defects, except in the case where goods are manufactured to buyer's specifications.[80] The strict liability rule of Article 45(1) makes sense in this context, even where the process giving rise to the defect was state of the art, primarily because the seller occupies the best position to monitor its processes and to develop improvements where it is cost-effective to do so, and thus should be assumed to have taken the risk of occasional defects in its current processes.

---

[74] See Schwenzer, *Article 79*, in Schlechtriem & Schwenzer, supra note 19, at 1066.

[75] See Lookofsky, supra note 73, at 135–37.

[76] See Nicholas, Force Majeure *and Frustration*, supra note 70.

[77] See Atamer, *Article 79*, in Kröll et al., supra note 20, at 1057.

[78] District Court Ellwangen (Germany), 21 August 1995, available at http://cisgw3.law.pace.edu/cases/950821g2.html.

[79] Supreme Court (Spain), 9 July 2014, available at http://cisgw3.law.pace.edu/cases/140709s4.html.

[80] Atamer, *Article 79*, in Kröll et al., supra note 20, at 1057.

Admittedly, there is a certain logic to permitting exemption in the case of nonconformity due to some external disaster, at least when the same event would have satisfied the conditions of Article 79 had it completely destroyed the goods. Assume, for instance, that goods are caught in a hurricane that could have destroyed them, but instead only caused damage that reduced their value by one-half. There is something peculiar about saying that the seller's ability to provide useful, but defective goods should subject it to damages liability, which could include consequential damages, whereas it would have been liable for no damages had it simply discarded the defective goods. Such a rule encourages waste, because the seller might prefer not to deliver the goods at all and claim an exemption rather than deliver useful, if imperfect goods that generated liability for damages. Of course, if exemption were available in the defective delivery case, the buyer would still have an action for price reduction or for repair or replacement, or, in a proper case, be able to avoid the contract.

The expansive interpretation is more problematic when the seller is not the manufacturer, but simply resells goods manufactured by others. Here, the seller often will have no opportunity to inspect the goods if they are pre-packaged by the manufacturer. In this sense, the manufacturer's failure to comply with contractual specifications might qualify as the kind of external impediment with which Article 79 is concerned, though the distinction between the discoverable defect created by a seller's own processes and a non-discoverable one created by the seller's supplier does appear to introduce into the analysis an element of fault that Article 45(1) makes superfluous. Of course, one can only make so much of these fine linguistic niceties. At bottom, the issue is one of risk allocation for the imperfections of the seller's supplier. Since one would anticipate that, as between the buyer and seller, the latter – who is likely a repeat player with respect to the goods and the supplier – is best positioned both to know defect rates and to price the risk into the contract with the buyer, exemption seems inappropriate. The same analysis supports the proposition that upstream suppliers are not beyond the control of sellers, as discussed earlier, because the seller takes the risk that it has acquired goods from a third party that produced them in a manner that fails to conform to contractual specifications.

B. *Judicial treatment of delivery of defective goods*

The cases on exemption for defective goods are mixed. Many of them ultimately fail to distinguish between the questionable applicability of Article 79 to such cases and the failure of the seller to satisfy the "impediment beyond his control" criterion for allowing the exemption. The German and Spanish paprika cases are of this nature. The best known case of this type is the so-called Vine Wax case.[81] There, the

---

[81] See Federal Supreme Court (Germany), 24 March 1999, available at http://cisgw3.law.pace .edu/cases/990324g1.html.

plaintiff, an operator of a vine nursery, had purchased from the defendant a wax used to protect vines from drying out and from infection. The defendant, in turn, had purchased the product from a third party. A fourth party actually manufactured the vine wax. The defendant had specifically ordered the manufacturer's wax but never accepted or inspected it, as it was shipped directly to the plaintiff. When the wax turned out to be defective, the seller contended that Article 79 exempted it from liability because it was merely an intermediary in the transaction, and the cause of the damage was beyond its control. The German Supreme Court disagreed. The court noted the conflict in opinion about the applicability of Article 79 to defective goods. It did not attempt to resolve that debate, but instead indicated that no Article 79 exemption could apply because the defect was not beyond the seller's control. The buyer, the court implied, bargains for conforming goods and is indifferent about the source of supply of those goods. Just as the contract would allocate to the seller the risk of nonconforming delivery if the seller were the manufacturer – in which case the seller would clearly have control of the processes that generated the defect – the same risk allocation prevails if the seller obtains the goods from a third party. Only if the seller can demonstrate that the defect was beyond its control in the narrower sense that some external event precluded delivery could the seller take advantage of Article 79. Short of that, it was within the responsibility, and hence the control, of the seller to see that its supplier delivered conforming goods. Here, the manufacturer had used an inappropriate raw material. As that event was within the manufacturer's control, it was necessarily also within the acquisition risk assumed by the seller.[82] That the seller had no ability to inspect the goods manufactured by another party was irrelevant. At the very least, therefore, the court implied that even if Article 79 could apply to a defective goods case, the eligible defect could not be one that arose from the manufacturing process because the choice of supplier falls within what continental writers frequently refer to as the seller's "sphere of influence" that defines the contours of the seller's "control."

More broadly, the decision stands for the proposition that the question of exemption is essentially a question of contractual risk allocation, rather than an inquiry into fault or ex post judicial loss allocation. In a subsequent case involving contaminated powdered milk, the same court implied that defective deliveries could qualify for an Article 79 exemption.[83] The court noted that the seller could only be exempt from damages "if it can prove that any lipase infestation of the delivered milk would not have been detectable, even upon the careful use of the necessary methods of analysis [that is, using state of the art detection procedures] before any further processing, and that a possible infestation in the manufacture of the powdered milk was based

[82] The court relied on Article 79(2) to assert that a seller could only claim exemption for defects in goods provided by its supplier if the supplier also qualified for exemption under Article 79(1). See infra IV.A. for a discussion of whether Article 79(2) is intended to apply to suppliers.

[83] See Federal Supreme Court (Germany), 9 January 2002, available at http://cisgw3.law.pace.edu/cases/020109g1.html.

on grounds that were outside of its sphere of influence." While that decision suggests a narrow basis for exemption in a defective goods situation, there would have been no need for the remand if Article 79 did not apply to nonconforming goods at all.

Compare with the Vine Wax case a French decision that considered a claim by the buyer of judo suits that shrank more than permitted by contractual specifications. The material used for the suits was manufactured by a third party. It was apparently this feature that led the court, in somewhat conclusory and enigmatic fashion, to note that the defendant was "in the position of a seller of a product whose manufacture and notably whose elaboration of the fabrics are beyond [seller]'s control."[84] Thus, absent a showing of bad faith, the seller was entitled to take advantage of Article 79, although it could only recover a reduced price and was required to reimburse customs fees. The French court's conclusion was subsequently rejected by a Finnish appellate court in a decision that found that a seller typically takes the risk that its suppliers will provide nonconforming goods.[85] In that case, the buyer received goods that had been subjected to radiation and were thereby nonconforming. Although one of the seller's suppliers could have irradiated the goods, the court concluded that an Article 79 impediment must be restricted to unpredictable events outside the "sphere of influence" of the party in breach, and the selection of a supplier was within the seller's sphere.

IV. FORESEEABILITY OF THE IMPEDIMENT

Article 79(1) excludes from eligibility for exemption any impediment that was foreseeable at the time the contract was concluded. That limitation can be inferred from the requirement that the impediment be one that the party seeking exemption could not reasonably be expected to have taken into account at the time of the conclusion of the contract. The underlying assumption of the requirement is that if the intervening event was foreseeable, then the adversely affected party had an opportunity to contract out of liability, or to demand a price for assuming liability, should the event materialize. The negative implication is that if the event was unforeseeable, the parties could not have considered the risk in their negotiations. Thus, any gain enjoyed or loss suffered as a consequence of the event was neither deserved nor priced into the contract terms. Since the parties did not contemplate or bargain with respect to the risk that materialized, the agreement that they reached and the allocation of risks incorporated within it were presumably not intended to operate in the circumstances that have arisen. Imposition of an obligation to perform or to perform on the original terms, therefore, allocates to the obligor a

---

[84] Commercial Court of Besançon (France) (*Flippe Christian v. Douet Sport Collections*), 19 January 1998, available at http://cisgw3.law.pace.edu/cases/980119f1.html.

[85] See Court of Appeals Turku (Finland), 24 May 2005, available at http://cisgw3.law.pace.edu/cases/050524f5.html#573.

risk that it was not compensated to take. Instead, the argument goes, had the parties considered the conditions that have materialized, they would have produced either a radically different bargain or no bargain at all. In short, the response to the argument that exemption violates the maxim of *pacta sunt servanda* ("promises ought to be kept") is that the *pactum* that must be performed is different from the *pactum* to which the parties agreed, so that enforcement of the original terms no longer reflects either the expectations of the parties or a reasonable allocation of the benefits and burdens of the transaction.

A. *The foreseeability standard*

"Foreseeability," of course, is a notoriously malleable concept, so that ex post manipulation of what was ex ante predictable may often seem unprincipled. Whether an event was foreseeable depends on the level of generality with which it is described. Take, for instance, the classic cases in which parties claimed excuse from nonperformance due to increased shipping costs after wartime sinking of ships in the Suez Canal required transit through longer, more expensive routes.[86] Resolution of those cases frequently rested on the foreseeability of the events that led to closure of the Canal. But those events can be variously described as (1) sinking ships that blocked the Canal; (2) closure of the Canal; (3) war in the Middle East; (4) or political unrest in the Middle East. Although some of the descriptions are more specific than others, all are in some sense accurate descriptions of the cause of changes in the cost of performance. There is no a priori reason for selecting one of these descriptions over the others. Yet the reaction of rational actors to the first might be, "I never could have imagined that would happen," while the reaction to the last would be "so what else is new?" To make legal rights dependent on the fortuitous selection of one of these descriptions over the others is to permit judges substantial discretion about whether adjustments are appropriate.

The description problem is exemplified by *Raw Materials Inc.* v. *Manfred Forberich GmbH & Co., KG,*[87] in which an American firm had contracted to purchase railroad rail from a German partnership. The rail was to be shipped from the port in St. Petersburg, Russia, which "unexpectedly" froze over in December 2002. The parties disputed whether the rail was to be loaded in St. Petersburg or delivered to the buyer by December 31, 2002. The buyer argued that delivery was required by that date, and that the necessary period for transport (3–4 weeks) meant that the freezing of the port was irrelevant, since proper shipment would have had to have occurred prior to the freezing of the port in order to comply with contractual deadlines. The seller contended that only loading was required by the end of

---

[86] See, e.g., *Transatlantic Financing Corp.* v. *United States,* 363 F.2d 312 (D.C. Cir. 1966); *Tsakiroglou & Co. Ltd.* v. *Noblee Thorl GmbH,* [1962] A.C. 93.

[87] 2004 U.S. Dist. LEXIS 12510 (N.D. Ill. July 6, 2004).

December, so that the unexpected freezing, which accompanied the worst winter in sixty years, exempted the seller from performance. The court denied buyer's motion for summary judgment because material facts remained in dispute concerning the time when the port was closed to shipping and the timing of the delivery obligation. But the court also concluded that the foreseeability of the port's freezing was similarly in dispute and should be resolved by a jury.[88]

What the jury might decide, however, depends on the description of the event that it would be asked to evaluate. The buyer maintained that "it hardly could come as a surprise to any experienced shipping merchant (or any grammar school geography student) that the port in St. Petersburg might become icy and frozen in the Russian winter months." Thus, the buyer was attempting to describe the alleged impediment at a level of generality that made its foreseeability more plausible. One could even describe the relevant event as "closing of the port at St. Petersburg," an event that might have been precipitated by labor or political strife in addition to extreme weather, and thus rendered the event more foreseeable than a focus on weather alone would suggest. The court, however, implied that the alleged impediment should be described at a more refined level of specificity. It suggested that the relevant event should be described as a severe winter that was attended by an inability of icebreakers to free the port for normal shipping, thus leading to the closing of the port at an earlier point in the winter than usual. The more a court is willing to accept highly specific characteristics to define the impediment, the less likely it is that a determination of foreseeability can be sustained. Nevertheless, it is difficult to justify one description as a more accurate account of the relevant events than an alternative.

B. *Finding foreseeability*

The frequency with which an event materializes is an obvious element in determining its foreseeability. History is assumed to repeat itself. But quantifying the necessary degree of repetition is an elusive task. The court in *Raw Materials* was at least receptive to the claim that a frost that occurred only every sixty years could be unforeseeable. A Dutch court was less willing to specify the requisite incidence of the impediment. In *Agristo N.V. v. Macces Agri B.V.,*[89] a seller of potatoes claimed that extreme weather conditions caused it to harvest fewer potatoes than anticipated

---

[88] The case has been frequently criticized for the court's use of UCC § 2–615 to interpret Article 79. See, e.g., Joseph Lookofsky & Harry M. Flechtner, *Nominating* Manfred Forberich: *The Worst CISG Decision in 25 Years?*, 9 Vindobona J. Int'l Comm. L. & Arb. 199 (2005), available at www.cisg.law.pace.edu/cisg/biblio/lookofsky13.html; Francesco G. Mazzotta, *Why Do Some American Courts Fail to Get It Right?*, 3 Loy. U. Chi. Int'l L. Rev. 85 (2005). Nevertheless, no one doubts that both provisions require foreseeability or that the meaning of that term is equivalent in the two regimes.

[89] District Court Maastricht (Netherlands), 9 July 2008, available at http://cisgw3.law.pace.edu/cases/080709n1.html.

and prevented storage of potatoes that it did harvest. Those conditions, seller maintained, exempted it from performance under forward contracts that it had concluded with buyer. As a result, seller contended, it was not liable for the damages that the buyer incurred when entering into cover contracts. The court accepted the proposition that severe weather had diminished the potato harvest. The court also rejected the buyer's claim that seller could have obtained sufficient potatoes elsewhere. But the court was wary of the proposition that the diminution in supply justified an exemption. The court noted that it is commonly known that weather can be unsettled and can affect growers' production. Diligent growers, the court opined, will take this into account. Indeed, the court suggested that diligent growers will not enter forward contracts for their entire expected harvest in order to be able to adjust for variations in production due to weather, and appointed an appraiser to evaluate whether the seller had overcommitted in light of prudent practices. In effect, the court revealed skepticism about allowing an exemption because it believed that the seller could have made ex ante adjustments to its practices to deal with the potential materialization of unlikely, but plausible weather conditions. But the court, without explanation, assigned exactitude to the seller's deliberations. The court assumed that a reasonable seller would only enter into forward contracts in an amount of potatoes that it could have delivered in 90 percent of the years.[90]

The court arguably was adopting the kind of "reasonably foreseeable" standard that some commentators have endorsed and that is explicit in the language of Article 79(1). The language of the Article requires that the impediment be one that the party claiming exemption "could not reasonably be expected to have taken into account."[91] What constitutes reasonable foreseeability is controversial. Foreseeability is a function of the investment made in predicting the future. Given time and effort, parties could "foresee" almost any impediment that could materialize during the contract period. Of course, at some point, the investment in prediction is not worthwhile because the cost of analyzing and allocating the remote risk exceeds the expected value of the loss that would occur if the risk materialized. It makes no sense to invest $100 to analyze a risk that has a 1:1,000 chance of occurring and that will cost $10,000 if it does materialize. Thus, risks defined as "unforeseeable" may essentially constitute nothing more than those that are not worth addressing at the

---

[90] A similar analysis appears to have been made by other courts. See, e.g., Court of Appeals Murcia (Spain), 25 May 2012, available at http://cisgw3.law.pace.edu/cases/120525s4.html (seller of chili powder denied Article 79 exemption because contamination of food colorants was not unusual); Court of Appeals Lamia (Greece), [no date] 2006, available at http://cisgw3.law.pace.edu/cases/060001gr.html#* (seller of sunflower seeds not exempt under Article 79 on the grounds that failure to deliver sunflower seeds due to drought and the consequent inability to load goods should have anticipated the difficulty since the same event had occurred several years previous).

[91] See Hans Stoll & Ulrich Huber, *Article 79*, in Commentary on the UN Convention on the International Sale of Goods (CISG) 817 (Peter Schlechtriem & Ingeborg Schwenzer eds., 2d (English) ed. 2005); Tallon, *Exemptions*, in Bianca & Bonell, supra note 9, at 579–80.

time of contracting under normal time and resource constraints. That would be the effect of a "reasonably foreseeable" limitation.

But there are reasons to expand "foreseeability" beyond its relationship to efficient investment in predicting the future. First, a decision not to invest resources in identifying and avoiding remote risks or in shifting them may not mean that the parties intended to exclude them from the contract. It may instead mean that the adversely affected party reasonably determined that it would assume the risk of the remote event. When such an event materializes, that party should not be entitled to avoid liability for performance on the grounds that it was inefficient to predict the event's occurrence. In Article 79, that same inquiry may be implicit in the possibility that the impediment was "taken into account" at the time of contracting. The Secretariat Commentary to the draft version of Article 79 recites that in some cases exemption will not apply because "it is clear from the context of the contract that one party has obligated himself to perform an act even though certain impediments might arise."[92] Indeed, numerous decisions have implied that one party assumed the risk of the remote event, not by virtue of having estimated its probability of occurrence, but by virtue of being well positioned to do so. For instance, in *Société Romay AG v. SARL Behr France*,[93] the court found that a buyer was precluded from applying Article 79 because its status as a professional in the field of international trade and its failure to include contractual provisions relating to modification or revision of terms meant that it had accepted the risk of nonperformance. In effect, these courts appear to be allocating risks to the party in the best position to avoid them or to limit their effects should they materialize. That analysis does not necessarily imply that the party could have made a cost-effective investigation that would have revealed the risk's likelihood. It implies only that where one party occupies the superior position to determine whether to avoid the risk there might be an assumption that the parties assigned the risk accordingly.

Some recurrent situations provide consensus on whether certain kinds of events will be deemed foreseeable. Regulations or other impediments will typically be deemed to have been foreseeable or otherwise susceptible to being taken into account if they were in place at the time of the conclusion of the contract.[94] A Bulgarian buyer who failed to open a documentary credit required by its contract with an Austrian seller could not claim exemption due to a Bulgarian governmental order suspending payment of foreign debts, because that order had been declared at

---

[92] Secretariat Commentary on the 1978 Draft, in Documentary History, supra note 8, at 445 (former Article 65, para. 5).

[93] Supreme Court (France), June 30, 2004, available at http://cisgw3.law.pace.edu/cases/040630f1 .html.

[94] See Tribunal of International Commercial Arbitration at the Russian Federation Chamber of Commerce and Industry, Arbitral Award (Russia), 16 March 1995, available at http://cisgw3.law .pace.edu/cases/950316r1.html; Bulgarian Chamber of Commerce and Industry (Bulgaria), 24 April 1996, available at http://cisgw3.law.pace.edu/cases/960424bu.html.

the time that the contract was concluded.[95] Certainly, a buyer is in a superior position to be aware of its own jurisdiction's regulations, so that it should not be permitted to contend that domestic prohibitions on imports exempt it from performance. An American buyer who ordered semi-automatic weapons manufactured to its specifications had little basis for complaint when the manufacturer complied with the buyer's requirements, but the Bureau of Alcohol, Tobacco, and Firearms denied import approval.[96] Even if the party was unaware of the impediment, exemption is unavailable if the party should have been aware. A buyer of coal was therefore unable to rely on government regulations on coal export that were in effect before the conclusion of the contract.[97] Indeed, the "regulation" cases appear to be a specific application of a more general principle that the buyer takes the "utility risk," that is, the risk that the buyer will be able to use the goods for which it has contracted.

V. AVOIDING THE IMPEDIMENT AND OVERCOMING ITS CONSEQUENCES

Under Article 79(1), exemption is permitted only if the obligor could not have avoided or overcome the impediment or its consequences once it arose. The term "reasonably be expected," which precedes the phrase "to have taken the impediment into account" in Article 79(1), is best read as also modifying the part of the sentence that deals with avoiding and overcoming the impediment or its consequences. A party is not obligated to expend $10,000 to avoid the materialization of a risk with an expected value of only $5,000 or to spend that amount on an alternative source of supply for goods with a contract price of $5,000. But if destroyed goods that had been identified to the contract are easily replaceable with a commercially reasonable substitute, their destruction will not justify an exemption.[98] "Reasonableness," however, must take into account the consequences to all the parties. Assume, for instance, that a seller could only replace destroyed goods with a contract price of $1,000 through an additional expenditure of $1,100. One might conclude that the expenditure is unreasonable. But now assume further that the seller is aware that failure to deliver the goods will cause the buyer a loss of $5,000 on a downstream contract. Now the net benefit of making the replacement justifies the additional cost because it maximizes the joint value of the transaction to the parties. We would

---

[95] See ICC Arbitration Case No. 7197 of 1992, available at http://cisgw3.law.pace.edu/cases/927197i1.html.

[96] See CIETAC Arbitration (China), August 1993, available at http://cisgw3.law.pace.edu/cases/930807c1.html.

[97] See Arbitration Tribunal of Bulgarian Chamber of Commerce & Industry (Bulgaria), 24 April 1996, available at http://cisgw3.law.pace.edu/cases/960424bu.html.

[98] See Secretariat Commentary on the 1978 Draft, in Documentary History, supra note 8, at 446 (former Article 65, para. 9, Example 65B).

conclude that it would be unreasonable for the seller not to obtain the replacement goods, notwithstanding the additional expenditure that the seller would incur.

The cases that have arisen provide some basis for predicting the lengths to which sellers must go to satisfy their obligations once an impediment arises. A German decision rejected the seller's assertion that Article 79 exempted it from the obligation to deliver good title to the stolen car it had sold.[99] In doing so, the court noted that the seller's suspicion could have been aroused by the metal plate containing the vehicle identification number that had been affixed to the original identification number. An arbitration tribunal rejected an Article 79 claim by a Chinese seller of canned oranges on the grounds that, even though flooding occurred in that part of Hunan province from which the seller intended to procure the oranges, the contract did not stipulate that the goods had to come from that area, and oranges from elsewhere were available.[100] A seller of tomato concentrate was unable to use the reduction of a tomato harvest due to heavy rains as a basis for exemption, because the crop was not entirely destroyed and the seller failed to indicate an ability to deliver even a proportionate amount of the goods to the buyer.[101] Goods to be made from specified materials that have become unavailable may be substituted for with goods made from different materials.

These cases reveal a common concern of courts when sellers seek exemption in the face of impediments that reduce the supply of fungible goods. Courts may be suspicious that a party is using a change in circumstances to avoid a bad deal rather than to avoid an obligation that has become unexpectedly onerous. The court in the tomato concentrate case concluded that the evidence revealed that the seller was attempting to exploit the higher market prices that prevailed in the face of crop shortages after the rains. That same assumption about strategic behavior by sellers is apparent in an arbitration case involving a seller's effort to exempt itself from liability for failure to deliver chicken to Romania after that nation banned chicken imports due to a feared avian flu epidemic.[102] After the ban went into effect, the buyer suggested that delivery could be made to an alternative port. The seller refused, pleading that the governmental action constituted the requisite impediment, and resold the chicken at a substantial profit over what it would have earned under the original contract. The tribunal, suspicious that the seller was motivated more by the subsequent increase in chicken prices than by its inability to ship, indicated that the seller could have overcome the impediment with reasonable efforts.

---

[99] See Court of Appeals Dresden (Germany), 21 March 2007, available at http://cisgw3.law.pace .edu/cases/070321g1.html.

[100] See CIETAC Arbitration (China), 30 November 1997, available at http://cisgw3.law.pace.edu/ cases/971130c1.html.

[101] Court of Appeals Hamburg (Germany), 4 July 1997, available at http://cisgw3.law.pace.edu/ cases/970704g1.html.

[102] See *Macromex Srl. v. Globex International, Inc.*, AAA Case No. 50181T 0036406, 23 October 2007, available at http://cisgw3.law.pace.edu/cases/071023a5.html; aff'd 2008 U.S. Dist. LEXIS 31442 (S.D.N.Y. April 16, 2008); *aff'd* 330 Fed Appx. 241 (2d Cir. 2009).

Although some alternatives were unnecessary because they required Herculean efforts, alternative delivery points were possible, as evidenced by the conduct of other traders of chicken during the relevant period.

Even in the case of non-fungible goods, however, parties are required to take cost-effective measures to avoid the consequences of an impediment. In one case, the seller of roller mills appeared to be raising something in the nature of an Article 79 defense by contending that the manufacturer specified in the contract was no longer producing the goods. The court concluded that because the contract concerned used equipment of a type that the seller typically refurbished and overhauled, the buyer would have expected a machine containing components that the seller had reworked as opposed to "a foreign imitation" with "a Russian product."[103] The existence of an impediment, in short, does not permit the party seeking exemption to refrain from any performance or to provide just any substitute. A seller of goods intended for operation of a café and production of ice cream could not avoid liability simply by refusing to take any steps towards installation once it discovered that the place designated for installation lacked access to water and electricity supply. Instead, the seller was obligated to assemble the goods and prepare them for operation to the extent possible.[104]

The obligations imposed on parties by the contract, however, may limit the extent to which a professed exempt party must go to provide substitute performance. In *Agristo N.V. v. Macces Agri B.V.*,[105] the court determined that a contract for potatoes was intended to limit the seller's obligations to provide only those goods that he grew on his land. Thus, when weather conditions allegedly impeded delivery of those potatoes, the seller was not obligated to obtain similar goods from other growers.

VI. ARTICLE 79(2): FAILURE OF A THIRD PARTY TO PERFORM

Article 79(2) deals with the situation in which a party contends that its right to exemption derives from the failure of a third party who has been "engaged to perform the whole or a part of the contract" to meet its obligations. In such a situation, the party seeking an exemption can avoid liability only if (1) it satisfies the requirements of Article 79(1), and (2) the third party also satisfies the requirements of Article 79(1). The objective of Article 79(2), therefore, is to impose additional requirements on the party seeking exemption and thus to limit its availability where the alleged impediment directly affected a third party. It prevents the seller from contending that the default of some third party on whom the seller was relying in

[103] See Court of Appeals Zweibrücken (Germany), 2 February 2004, available at http://cisgw3.law .pace.edu/cases/040202g1.html.

[104] See Court of Appeals Hamburg (Germany), 25 January 2008, available at http://cisgw3.law .pace.edu/cases/080125g1.html.

[105] District Court Maastricht (Netherlands), 9 July 2008, available at http://cisgw3.law.pace.edu/ cases/080709n1.html.

order to perform its own contract with the buyer itself constitutes an impediment that qualifies the seller for an exemption. Instead, the seller must demonstrate that, in every respect, that third party would be eligible for an exemption if the criteria of Article 79(1) were applied to it. For example, temporary inability of a third party carrier to transport goods will provide an exemption only for the period of the suspension, and the seller remains liable for failure to deliver the goods within a reasonable time thereafter.[106]

The primary interpretive difficulty with Article 79(2) involves the definitional scope of a "third party" who has been "engaged to perform the whole or a part of the contract." If the party who fails to perform does not meet that criterion, then the case is properly analyzed under Article 79(1) alone and Article 79(2) never comes into play. The effect seems somewhat odd, because some parties who are not considered third parties are more closely connected to the seller than other parties who are considered third parties. One might have assumed that it was the default of the first group that would be most likely to increase the liability of the seller. Nevertheless, the fact that the first group falls outside of Article 79(2) means that a seller who claims exemption based on a closely connected third party need only satisfy Article 79(1), rather than both subsections. As we discuss next, the case law frequently avoids this apparent anomaly by holding that defaults by parties in the first group are not "beyond the control" of the seller, and thus do not qualify for exemption under Article 79(1).

A. *The narrow construction of "third party"*

Both commentary and case law suggest that the term "third party" should be construed more narrowly than might initially appear to be the case. Firms, of course, operate through employees, but a party's employees are not considered third parties for purposes of this clause, even though they may act with a degree of independence.[107] Perhaps more surprisingly, general suppliers of goods also are not considered third parties who perform the contract. As in the interpretation of the "beyond his control" requirement of Article 79(1), a seller is deemed to assume the "acquisition risk" or "procurement risk" related to its choice of suppliers or manufacturers.[108] A CIETAC panel concluded that even though a manufacturer

---

[106] See, e.g., CIETAC Arbitration (China), 9 August 2002, available at http://cisgw3.law.pace.edu/cases/020809c1.html.

[107] See CISG Advisory Council, Opinion No. 7, supra note 13, at ¶ 16; Court of Appeals Lugano (Switzerland), 29 October 2003, available at http://cisgw3.law.pace.edu/cases/031029s1.html.

[108] See Court of Appeals Turku (Finland), 24 May 2005, available at http://cisgw3.law.pace.edu/cases/050524f5.html#573; Court of Appeals Hamburg (Germany), 28 February 1997, available at http://cisgw3.law.pace.edu/cases/970228g1.html; CIETAC Arbitration (China), 30 January 1996, available at http://cisgw3.law.pace.edu/cases/960130c1.html; Tribunal of International Commercial Arbitration at the Russian Federation Chamber of Commerce and Industry (Russia), 9 April 2004, available at http://cisgw3.law.pace.edu/cases/040409r1.html.

suffered a technical problem that reduced its production capacity by 35 percent, the seller who anticipated receiving the goods from that manufacturer could not claim exemption because its contract with the buyer did not specify the precise manufacturer to be used.[109] Conversely, some commentators have concluded that a seller lacks control where there is no effective choice of a supplier, perhaps because one firm has a monopoly on the goods to be supplied or because the buyer insisted on a particular supplier, either by name or by specifying a product available from only one manufacturer.[110] In that event, a default by the supplier may, if Article 79(2) is satisfied, permit the seller to claim an exemption.[111] Other commentators find the case of the subcontractor who is to manufacture the goods to be the quintessential Article 79(2) case, if the subcontractor is engaged for a particular contract rather than one who generally produces goods for the seller. Honnold, for example, suggests that the subsection applies where a seller turns over to a third party the performance of the seller's duty to manufacture goods to the buyer's specifications.[112] In a widely cited commentary, Tallon requires that there be an "organic link" between the subcontract and the main contract, by which he appears to mean that both the seller and the subcontractor understood that the latter was performing an obligation of the former for the particular contract.[113]

The doctrinal fiction that supports these results is that general suppliers do not perform the contract; instead they satisfy preconditions for the seller to perform or assist in the preparation of performance. This principle applies to manufacturers of components and suppliers of raw materials or of completed goods that are simply resold by the party seeking exemption. It applies whether non-delivery is the result of production problems with the third party or other problems, such as financial difficulties.[114] The anomaly of this principle is that if one wanted to place the acquisition risk on the seller, then one might think it appropriate to make it *more* difficult to obtain an exemption by making the seller prove both subsections (1) and (2) where it selected, or had control over, the third party. Indeed, there is some argument that the whole existence of subsection (2), along with all the confusion it generates, is due to a misunderstanding concerning the meaning of subsection (1).[115] There are occasional cases in which tribunals vary from the principle and either allow a seller an exemption under Article 79(1), notwithstanding that the alleged

---

[109] See CIETAC Arbitration (China), 17 June 1994, available at http://cisgw3.law.pace.edu/cases/940617c1.html. See Supreme Court (Hungary), 1992, available at http://cisgw3.law.pace.edu/cases/920000h1.html.

[110] But see Tallon, *Exemptions*, in Bianca & Bonell, supra note 9, at 584. Tallon would find that the "engaged to perform" language is satisfied because "though not chosen by the seller, has been accepted by him as part of the bargain and he is under the technical control of the seller."

[111] See CISG Advisory Council, Opinion No. 7, supra note 13, at ¶ 18.

[112] See Honnold/Flechtner, supra note 5, at 635.

[113] See Tallon, *Exemptions*, in Bianca & Bonell, supra note 9, at 584.

[114] See, e.g., Arbitral Tribunal Hamburg (Germany), 21 March 1996, available at http://cisgw3.law.pace.edu/cases/960321g1.html.

[115] See CISG Advisory Council, Opinion No. 7, supra note 13, at ¶ 16.

impediment consists of a supplier's failure to deliver,[116] or apply Article 79(2) to suppliers.[117]

Similar principles apply on the buyer's side. While buyers may also obtain exemptions when the criteria of Article 79(1) are satisfied, a failure to make payments because the buyer's own customers failed to pay their bills or a financial institution contracted by the buyer failed to forward a payment when due will likely not allow the buyer to claim an exemption. The buyer in such cases will have difficulty contending that Article 79(1) was satisfied.[118] That, at least, was the result in a Russian case in which a tribunal rejected a buyer's claim for an exemption, even though its default was based on an inability of its own customers to make payments for goods because of a severe drought.[119]

B. *Third parties covered by Article 79(2)*

If suppliers to sellers do not qualify, then who are the relevant "third parties" covered by Article 79(2)? They include carriers who transport the goods from the seller to the buyer, or subcontractors who complete "finish" work.[120] Assume, for instance, that a ship transporting the goods suffers an unexpected disaster and the goods end up on the ocean floor. If the disaster was unforeseeable, the carrier qualifies for an exemption under Article 79(2)(b), and the seller likely would be exempt from liability under Article 79(1). As a result, the seller would be exempt from performance under Article 79(2). Of course, like suppliers, these parties are also frequently selected by the seller, so that the justification for distinguishing among the various third parties is somewhat suspect. The CISG Advisory Council's Opinion on the subject reflects much of the commentary when it classifies these parties as "not merely separate and distinct persons or legal entities, but also economically and functionally independent from the seller, outside the seller's organizational structure, sphere of control or responsibility."[121] But why a carrier fits that description more than a supplier whose ownership structure and decisions are wholly independent of the seller is a puzzle that is not easily solved. Perhaps the best one can do is to agree with that part of the Opinion that concludes,

[116] See, e.g., District Court Besançon (France) (*Flippe Christian* v. *Douet Sport Collections*), 19 January 1998, available at http://cisgw3.law.pace.edu/cases/980119f1.html.

[117] See, e.g., ICC Arbitration Case No. 8128 of 1995; available at http://cisgw3.law.pace.edu/cases/958128i1.html. While the tribunal applied Article 79(2), its reasoning for denying exemption was essentially the same as would be used under Article 79(1) to the effect that a seller who selects a supplier is responsible for the latter's performance.

[118] See District Court Alsfeld (Germany), 12 May 1995, available at http://cisgw3.law.pace.edu/cases/950512g1.html.

[119] See Tribunal of International Commercial Arbitration at the Russian Federation Chamber of Commerce and Industry (Russia), 15 November 2006, available at http://cisgw3.law.pace.edu/cases/061115r2.html.

[120] See Court of Appeals Lugano (Switzerland), 29 October 2003, available at http://cisgw3.law.pace.edu/cases/031029s1.html.

[121] CISG Advisory Council, Opinion No. 7, supra note 13, at ¶ 19.

"[i]t is not easy to ascertain the precise meaning of '. . . a third person whom [the party claiming exemption] has engaged to perform the whole or part of a contract . . .'"[122]

The inclusion of carriers as third parties reveals how the scope of Article 79 must be distinguished from the scope of risk of loss. In a Swiss case,[123] art catalogues were delivered after the exhibition for which they had been ordered. The buyer sought to apply Article 79(2) in order to limit the seller's attempt to avoid the contract by attributing the delay to the carrier. But the court concluded that the seller had satisfied its obligations when it made timely delivery to the carrier. Any error by a forwarding agent therefore did not constitute part of the seller's contractual performance. As a result, the carrier had not been contracted to perform any of the seller's obligations, and any delay after delivery to the first carrier was at the risk of the buyer. Assume, however, that the goods had suffered damage when being transported by the carrier to the buyer, but during a period when the risk of loss remained on the seller. Assume further that the loss of the catalogues also caused foreseeable consequential damages to the buyer. Even if the destruction of the goods was due to a natural disaster, seller bears the risk of their loss and cannot recover their price from the buyer. But Article 79 may insulate the seller from liability for damages that might otherwise apply under Article 74.

VII. RELIANCE ON ARTICLE 79 BY BUYERS

Buyers have attempted to deploy Article 79 when inaction by banks has frustrated payment. These claims tend to be determined under the Article 79(1) language of "control" rather than under Article 79(2). In one arbitration, the buyer claimed that it could not pay its seller after its bank became bankrupt. The tribunal appeared to resolve the case under Article 79(1) by holding that bank insolvency did not qualify as an impediment beyond the buyer's control.[124] A Russian arbitration panel reached a similar result where the buyer contended that it was exempt after the funds it paid to a foreign bank for transmission to the seller had been stolen.[125] Another Russian tribunal denied relief to a buyer whose payment to the seller was prohibited by currency regulations, and who claimed that seller's claim should be brought against the Bank for Foreign Economic Affairs of the USSR.[126] Although that bank had assumed liability for certain debts affected by its regulation, the tribunal appeared to

---

[122] Id.

[123] See Commercial Court Zürich (Switzerland), 10 February 1999, available at http://cisgw3.law.pace.edu/cases/990210s1.html. For a similar risk of loss analysis, see CIETAC Arbitration (China), 25 June 1997, available at http://cisgw3.law.pace.edu/cases/970625c1.html.

[124] See Tribunal of International Commercial Arbitration at the Russian Federation Chamber of Commerce and Industry (Russia), 6 October 1998, available at http://cisgw3.law.pace.edu/cases/981006r1.html.

[125] See High Arbitration Court (Russia), 16 February 1998, available at http://cisgw3.law.pace.edu/cases/980216r1.html.

[126] See Tribunal of International Commercial Arbitration at the Russian Federation Chamber of Commerce and Industry (Russia), 13 December 1995, available at http://cisgw3.law.pace.edu/cases/951213r1.html.

conclude that the payment could have been made before the regulation went into effect. But the tribunal also appeared to rely on domestic law under which a debtor remains responsible for nonperformance by a third party who has been engaged to perform the debtor's contractual obligations. The fact that the seller could direct its claims to the bank did not automatically exempt the buyer from its obligations. In another arbitration, the tribunal did appear to apply Article 79(2) to reach a similar conclusion that an order of the Russian Central Bank that prohibited currency payments to nonresidents was an impediment that nullified liability for nonpayment under a contract.[127] Although the court concluded that the buyer's claim was "not grounded in Article 79," that language appears to indicate that the claim was not valid under that Article rather than that the claim did not arise under it. The tribunal thus rejected the claim because the buyer was essentially contending that the actions of a third party, the central bank, constituted the impediment, and the buyer had failed to establish that the third party was relieved from liability.[128]

Buyers have also invoked difficulties in obtaining a letter of credit as the basis for an exemption. In a Chinese arbitration, the buyer claimed that the bank's decision not to issue a letter of credit constituted force majeure and qualified as an exemption under Article 79(1) because it was beyond the buyer's control. The tribunal did not cite Article 79, but concluded that the decision was not unforeseeable and that the bank's decision was based on the questionable solvency of the buyer and therefore could not be attributed to force majeure.[129]

VIII. EFFECTS OF SATISFYING THE ARTICLE 79 EXEMPTION

A. *Effects on rights of parties*

Article 79(5) recites that nothing in the Article prevents either party from exercising any right other than to claim damages. The consequence is that the parties retain substantial rights both under the contract and outside the contract, even when an impediment sufficient to trigger Article 79 has been established. Perhaps most importantly, the failure of the exempt party to perform still amounts to a breach of

---

[127] See Tribunal of International Commercial Arbitration at the Russian Federation Chamber of Commerce and Industry (Russia), 30 July 2001, available at http://cisgw3.law.pace.edu/cases/010730r1.html.

[128] Bank insolvencies can also affect seller's obligations in ways that implicate Article 79. In yet another Russian arbitration, a seller instructed the buyer to wire funds to a particular bank for prepayment of goods. After the buyer did so, the seller's bank became insolvent and the seller's account was frozen. The tribunal concluded that insolvency did not constitute force majeure and that the buyer had satisfied all its contractual obligations. Thus, the buyer was entitled to recover a contractual penalty for late delivery or non-delivery. See Tribunal of International Commercial Arbitration at the Russian Federation Chamber of Commerce and Industry (Russia), 12 January 1998, available at http://cisgw3.law.pace.edu/cases/980112r1.html.

[129] See CIETAC Arbitration (China), 29 September 1997, available at http://cisgw3.law.pace.edu/cases/970929c1.html.

contract, and if that breach is a fundamental one, the nonexempt party is entitled to avoid the contract. The nonexempt party, therefore, may be able to cancel its own performance.

Read literally, the preservation of non-damage remedies in Article 79(5) appears to retain the right of the nonexempt party to demand specific performance under Article 46 or 62. Specific performance, after all, is not a damages remedy. Of course, where the exemption derives from destruction of unique goods or otherwise completely impairs performance, such a result would be, in Honnold's phrase, "absurd."[130] It is difficult to think of the circumstances in which one would seek such a remedy from a party who had already demonstrated that it satisfied the conditions of Article 79(1). The failure to provide explicitly that specific performance is unavailable may be viewed as recognition of the obvious, rather than a grant of the remedy.[131] Even if specific performance were theoretically available, some commentators contend that Article 28 would allow a court to refuse to order it, since the domestic law of most jurisdictions would not apply that remedy to a party excused from performance on other grounds.[132]

Some commentators maintain that specific performance is available where the exemption is only a temporary one or where substitute performance is available.[133] That certainly seems a plausible way of reconciling the literal language of Article 79 (5) with the absurdity of allowing performance in impossibility cases. But the better way to think about such cases is to conclude that the exemption is not available once the impediment has disappeared, so the default remedy of specific performance naturally applies. As we have noted already, if a substitute performance is available, then the consequences of the impediment can be avoided and the criteria of Article 79(1) are not satisfied. Similarly, Article 79(3) makes clear that any exemption ends when the impediment ends.

Even if an exemption does not give rise to a fundamental breach, a buyer whose seller qualifies for an exemption may still obtain a reduced price under Article 50. Assume, for instance, that an impediment prevents a seller from delivering more than 90 percent of the goods required by the contract. Assume further that the missing 10 percent does not constitute a fundamental breach but causes the buyer to

---

[130] Honnold/Flechtner, supra note 5, at 641.

[131] The Uniform Law on International Sales did not include specific performance among the remedies preserved in spite of an exemption. See ULIS Article 73(3) (1964). Some commentators have suggested that the failure to exclude specific performance in Article 79(5) therefore indicates that it was intended to be included. A German proposal to make it clear that specific performance could not be invoked was apparently rejected, but on the grounds that in the case of a continuing impediment, there would be no practical problem with an aggrieved party actually seeking specific performance. See Schwenzer, supra note 65, at 720.

[132] See Lookofsky, supra note 20, at 139 (using example of court refusing to order specific performance of a contract deemed subject to Article 79 because of supervening and unforeseen illegality); Honnold/Flechtner, supra note 5, at 642; Peter Schlechtriem, Uniform Sales Law 102 (1986).

[133] See, e.g., Schwenzer, *Article 79*, in Schlechtriem & Schwenzer, supra note 19, at 1084.

suffer consequential damages. The buyer would neither be able to avoid the contract nor to recover consequential damages, but would be responsible only for payment of 90 percent of the contract price. Either party may claim restitution under Article 81, even where the contract has been avoided. In the prior example, if the buyer had prepaid the full contract price, it would be entitled to restitution of the excess 10 percent.

A French court addressed many of these issues in a case involving sweat suits that suffered excess shrinkage after use.[134] The buyer sought avoidance of the contract, plus reimbursement of the contract price and customs fees, as well as interest. The court concluded (notwithstanding the multiple cases that place suppliers within the seller's "sphere of influence") that an exemption applied because the defects in manufacture were beyond the seller's control. Without any analysis under Article 79 (2), the court appeared to reach that conclusion because neither the seller nor the seller's supplier had manufactured the goods. The court found that not all the goods were nonconforming and that buyer had derived some profit from their sale. Thus, the court ordered a price reduction of 35 percent of the invoiced amount and restitution of the excess amount that had been paid. Fair enough. But the court also ordered reimbursement of customs fees. Those sound like damages, which should have been excluded.

The court also awarded interest on the amounts to be reimbursed to the buyer. Most commentators and courts agree that the general obligation to pay interest for delayed payments under Article 78 and the seller's obligation to pay interest on refunded amounts, which is set forth in Article 84, is an obligation separate from one to pay compensatory damages under Article 74. As a result, interest on overdue amounts is payable, even if the party is exempt from liability for nonpayment.[135] A German lower court denied interest on a payment that was delayed due to an impediment that warranted exemption. An appellate court affirmed the denial of interest, but predicated that holding on the buyer's right to suspend performance under Article 71(1)(b) rather than Article 79.[136]

B. *Effect of exemption on payment clauses*

Assume that the contract provides for a payment by the breaching party in the event of nonperformance. Can that clause be enforced notwithstanding that the nonperforming party qualifies for an exemption? It seems inadequate, but possibly

---

[134] See District Court Besançon (France) (*Flippe Christian v. Douet Sport Collections*), 19 January 1998, available at http://cisgw3.law.pace.edu/cases/980119f1.html.

[135] See Tribunal of International Commercial Arbitration at the Russian Federation Chamber of Commerce and Industry (Russia), 13 May 2008, available at http://cisgw3.law.pace.edu/cases/080513r1.html; County Court Willisau (Switzerland), 12 March 2004, available at http://cisgw3.law.pace.edu/cases/040312s1.html.

[136] See District Court Berlin (Germany), 15 September 1994, available at http://cisgw3.law.pace.edu/cases/940915g1.html.

doctrinally true that the answer depends on the vagaries of classification. If the required payment is deemed a liquidated damages clause, then Article 79(5)'s preclusion of liability for damages prevents enforcement. An early ICC Arbitration Case apparently concluded that a clause that provided for payment of a fee for nonperformance even in the event of force majeure was invalid as inconsistent with Article 79.[137] Perhaps that same clause, however, could have been construed as an effort by the parties to opt out of Article 79(5). That same logic could be used to allow enforcement of a clause characterized as a termination fee or even a penalty clause. But in the latter cases, the same result may obtain by classifying them as non-damages payment obligations, although penalty clauses may be invalidated as excessive, under domestic law and Article 4.

The Secretariat Commentary on the 1978 Draft of the CISG took a different position. It stated: "It is a matter of domestic law not governed by this Convention as to whether the failure to perform exempts the non-performing party from paying a sum stipulated in the contract for liquidated damages or as a penalty. . . ."[138] Thus, the Commentary appears to place liquidated damages clauses outside the CISG completely, and to allow their enforcement to be determined even when they arise in a context governed by the CISG. The language of the CISG's remedial provisions supports the Commentary's position. Articles 45 and 61 carefully distinguish between "damages" and remedies other than "damages," and Articles 74–77 define or measure the amount of recoverable damages. A liquidated damages clause does not measure damages when it provides for an amount different from the sum recoverable according to Articles 74–77. There is no more reason to consider this sum "damages" for purposes of Article 79(5)'s limitation on exemption than to consider the sum a non-damages remedy defined under the CISG. In fact, the CISG does not deem a liquidated damages clause as either damages or as a non-damages remedy. It simply does not regulate damages stipulations, thereby leaving their regulation to domestic law. Thus, because Article 79(5)'s effect is limited to exemption from damages, a liquidated damages clause continues to operate when a party is exempt under Article 79. It becomes inoperable in the circumstances only if invalid under applicable domestic law.

IX. BURDEN OF PROOF IN EXEMPTION CASES

In a rare moment of providing clarity on the allocation of burden of proof, the drafters of Article 79 explicitly assign the burden with respect to the existence of an

---

[137] See ICC Arbitration Case No. 7585/1994. The case is not translated from the French. We rely on the account in Dionysios P. Flambouras, *The Doctrines of Impossibility of Performance and clausula rebus sic stantibus in the 1980 Vienna Convention on Contracts for the International Sale of Goods and the Principles of European Contract Law: A Comparative Analysis*, 13 Pace Int'l L. Rev. 261 (2001), available at www.cisg.law.pace.edu/cisg/biblio/flambouras1.html#76.

[138] Secretariat Commentary on the 1978 Draft, in Documentary History, supra note 8, at 446 (former Article 65, para. 9, Example 65D).

impediment on the party seeking an exemption. Both tribunals and commentators have concluded that the language that a party is exempt "if he proves that the failure [to perform] was due to an impediment beyond his control ..." constitutes an express allocation of the burden of proof.[139] Others contend that the language demonstrates that, even outside of Article 79 cases, burden of proof is an issue within the scope of the Convention, or that the burden of proof is, as a general matter, assigned to the party who asserts a claim or an exception or objection.[140] We discuss burden of proof issues generally in Chapters 6 and 9.[141]

X. CONTRACTING AROUND ARTICLE 79

The applicability of Article 79 to a contract is at issue when it contains a force majeure clause. Certainly Article 6, which allows parties to derogate from any of the CISG's provisions, allows parties to opt out of Article 79. The issue where a force majeure clause appears, therefore, is whether its presence signifies the intention to exclude Article 79 in favor of the contractual clause. A force majeure clause might modify, supplement, or displace Article 79. Unless the contract expressly displaces Article 79, two different inferences are possible. The presence of a force majeure clause might indicate the intent to cover explicitly the risks that the clause addressed, and to leave other risks for treatment through default rules, including Article 79. Or the contractual clause might signify an intent to limit the range within which adjustment is appropriate, and thus to derogate from Article 79. The choice between these inferences is not necessarily the same for all such clauses; Article 8 might require different conclusions depending on whether the clause was simple or complex, boilerplate or negotiated, or limited or extensive in scope.[142]

In one case, the court found that a contractual force majeure clause had the same effect as Article 79.[143] Thus, it was unnecessary to determine whether the contractual clause displaced, expanded or restricted Article 79. (The court does not explain why the parties would provide by contract for a result already provided for by Article 79.) Given the finding, the court did not have to address the relationship between the force majeure clause and Article 79. The decision is a bit puzzling, because the

---

[139] See, e.g., Court of Appeals Zweibrücken (Germany), 2 February 2004, available at http:// cisgw3.law.pace.edu/cases/040202g1.html. See Schwenzer, *Article 79*, in Schlechtriem & Schwenzer, supra note 19, at 1087.

[140] See, e.g., Federal Supreme Court (Germany), 9 January 2002, available at http://cisgw3.law .pace.edu/cases/020109g1.html.

[141] See Chapter 6.X; Chapter 9.A.4.

[142] The ICC Force Majeure Clause 2003 excuses a party's performance when (1) the force majeure event is beyond the party's control, (2) not foreseeable at the time the contract is concluded, and (3) could not reasonably be avoided or overcome. See ICC Force Majeure Clause 2003 (Pub. No. 650) (2003). The Clause follows Article 79 closely, so that its incorporation into a contract might not signal the intent to displace Article 79.

[143] See Court of Appeals Hamburg (Germany), 28 February 1997, available at http://cisgw3.law .pace.edu/cases/970228g1.html.

contractual clause arguably provided for a broader right of nonperformance than Article 79. The contractual clause stated that "The Seller shall not be held responsibility if due to force majeure, Seller fails to make delivery within the time stipulated in this sales contract or cannot deliver the goods." It contained no restriction on whether the seller's inability was due to the act of a third party. When the seller failed to deliver because its own supplier demanded a substantially higher price for the product under contract, the court applied the default rules of Article 79, including the restriction on exemption contained in Article 79(2). The court thus concluded that a seller bore the risk that its own supplier would fail to deliver the contracted-for goods, at least where the contract did not require goods for which there was no available replacement, and that increases in market price did not qualify for exemption. All this seems correct as a matter of interpreting Article 79. The more interesting, and less analyzed issue, was whether the parties intended to incorporate that same analysis into their rather vague force majeure clause, or whether they intended a broader basis for excuse that might have exonerated a seller whose own supplier defaulted in light of higher market prices. We would not sanction such a risk allocation, but the relevant issue is what the parties intended, not whether they allocated the risk appropriately. The court avoided that more difficult inquiry.

If one adopts the view that Article 79 covers hardship cases, the effect of a force majeure clause complicates the analysis. Does the contractual clause incorporate the hardship doctrine, displace it by adopting a narrower range of exemptions, or imply the parties' silence on the issue? The answer is the same: It depends on the intent of the contracting parties. For this reason, the question is one of contract interpretation. As with most contract clauses, no universally applicable inference can be drawn as to whether parties intend to displace or merely limit the application of hardship doctrine to their contract. A reliable inference instead depends on the circumstances of the parties and the language of the force majeure clause itself. Notwithstanding the possibility that parties intended to include hardship, as we indicated in our discussion of that issue, we would treat certain clauses in contracts between sophisticated commercial actors, such as renegotiation clauses, clauses that link price increases during the contract term to explicit indices, or clauses that set parameters within which the contract operates, as implicit allocations of price risks and thus as rejection of the hardship doctrine to their contracts.

9

Remedies

The CISG allows the injured party to choose among a set of remedies. The party may avoid the contract, recover damages, obtain specific relief, or suspend its own performance.[1] In addition, Article 50 permits the buyer to reduce the contract price. Articles 44 and 61 list these remedies for the buyer and seller, respectively. Both Article 45(2) and 61(2) make explicit that certain damages remain recoverable even when the injured party obtains a remedy other than damages. A remedy not included in Article 44 and 61's list is restitution, available under Article 81. The following is an index that collects the CISG's remedies:

TABLE 9.1: *Remedies*

	Seller (Article 61)	Buyer (Article 45)
1. Avoidance	Article 64(1)	Article 49(1)
2. Specific relief	Article 62	Article 46
3. Price reduction	Inapplicable	Article 50
4. Damages:		
General rule	Article 74	Article 74
Substitute transaction	Article 75	Article 75
Market price measure	Article 76	Article 76
5. Restitution	Article 81(2)	Article 81(2)

Some of the CISG's remedies can be obtained without judicial intervention while others require judicial recognition. Suspension of performance, avoidance of the contract, and reduction of the contract price do not require a judicial order. The non-breaching party can obtain these remedies, where applicable, unilaterally. We have therefore discussed avoidance in Chapter 5 as part of the rights and

---

[1] We discuss the right to suspend performance in Chapter 5.III.B.

obligations of parties with respect to performance of the contract. Recall from that chapter that avoidance means that the contractual obligations of both parties come to an end, and that avoidance in international sales transactions is disfavored.[2] On the other hand, damages or specific relief requires judicial determination. Some remedies are available only if the non-breaching party avoids the contract. Others are available only if the contract is not avoided. Finally, several remedies remain available whether or not the non-breaching party avoids the contract.

I. NON-AVOIDANCE-BASED REMEDIES

As we explain in Chapter 5, the injured party may not have a right to avoid the contract unless the breach is fundamental and other requirements of avoidance have been satisfied.[3] Even if it has a right to do so, the party may prefer a remedy other than avoidance. In this case the CISG makes available both substitutional and specific relief. The injured party who either cannot or has not avoided the contract can recover damages, reduce the contract price, or (subject to limitation) compel the breaching party to perform. Although the calculation and elements of damages mostly track recoverable damages under the Uniform Commercial Code ("UCC") and common law principles for remedies, price reduction and specific relief do not.

A. *Article 74's general rule for recoverable loss*

Article 74 states the general rule for recovering damages for breach. It provides that damages "consist of a sum equal to the loss, including the loss of profit, suffered by the other party as a consequence of breach." The Article initially appears to provide for full compensation to the aggrieved party, including consequential and incidental damages. Because the Article includes lost profits among "loss," it aims to put the injured party in the position that it would have been in had there been full performance. Thus, Article 74's rule protects the injured party's expectation interest.[4]

Article 74 does not state a formula for calculating damages. Nor does it state the conditions under which an injured party can rely on its rule. Other Articles do. Article 45(1)(b) allows the buyer to recover damages under Article 74 if the seller "fails to perform any of his obligations" under the contract or the CISG, while Article 61(1)(a) does the same for the seller if the buyer "fails to perform any of his obligations" under the contract or the CISG. Article 74 is best thought of as prescribing a general rule or principle of compensation by which damages are to be awarded. The general rule does

---

[2] See Chapter 5.IV.A.   [3]   See Chapter 5.IV.B.1.
[4] See *Profi-Parkiet Sp. Zoo v. Seneca Hardwoods LLC*, 2014 U.S. Dist. LEXIS 71289 (E.D.N.Y.-May 23, 2014); Court of Appeals St. Gallen (Switzerland), 13 May 2008, available at http://cisgw3.law.pace.edu/cases/080513s1.html; CISG Advisory Council Opinion No. 6: Calculation of Damages Under CISG Article 74 ¶ 1 (2006), available at www.cisg.law.pace.edu/cisg/CISG-AC-op6.html.

not state a trivial requirement. It requires that damages be calculated to protect the injured party's expectancy ("lost profit") rather than its reliance or restitution interests. For the same reason, Article 74's general rule does not allow the award of punitive damages. Punitive damages, if available, may be awarded only under applicable domestic law. By awarding damages "as a consequence of breach," Article 74 also signals that damages are available for breach even if the breaching party is not at fault in breaching. Thus, Article 74 deviates from some domestic law that awards damages only when there is fault or does not allow damage awards to reflect lost profits.[5]

An injured party who has not avoided the contract can recover damages only under Article 74. Although Articles 75 and 76 have their own calculations of damages, these Articles are available to calculate damages only if the contract has been avoided. In determining damages recoverable under Article 74's general rule, two other Articles must be taken into account. Article 77 requires damages to be reduced to the extent that the injured party has not mitigated its loss. Article 78 allows the award of interest, increasing the damages recoverable under Article 74.

1. The limitation of foreseeability

Although it initially appears to provide for full compensation to the aggrieved party, Article 74's second sentence limits recoverable damages according to their foreseeability. Damages may not exceed the loss the breaching party "foresaw or ought to have foreseen at the time of the conclusion of the contract, in light of facts and matter of which he then knew or ought to have known, as a possible consequence of the breach." Although stated in slightly different terms, this limitation essentially embodies the *Hadley* v. *Baxendale* foreseeability requirement for recoverable consequential damages. As with the *Hadley* rule, facts that the breaching party knew or ought to have known at the conclusion limit its liability. Facts it discovers or ought to have discovered after the contract's conclusion have no effect on recoverable damages.

The foreseeability limitation, which is common in domestic law – even if stated in somewhat different terms than Article 74 – makes sense. Parties cannot easily price into their contracts risks that they did not foresee. The result is that without a limitation unforeseen risks will expose breaching parties to a risk of liability for which they have not been compensated and that they may be ill-equipped to bear. Parties exposed to unforeseen damages might avoid entering into what would otherwise be mutually valuable contracts, because they would risk liability for loss that they were not paid to bear and that the other party was better able to avoid.

Nevertheless, Article 74 leaves open some vital issues concerning the scope of the limitation. Article 74 does not say whether the requirement of foreseeability applies

---

[5] See, e.g., Burgerliches Gesetzbuch [BGB] [Civil Code] § 280(1) (Ger.); Reinhard Zimmerman, The New German Law of Obligations 50–1 (2005); cf. Kobeloven [Sale of Goods Act] § 23 (Den.) (seller of specific goods liable for damages for untimely delivery unless untimeliness is not its fault).

to both the type and extent of loss.[6] It might be that it was unforeseeable that a buyer intended to resell the goods that it contracted to purchase from a breaching seller, so that lost profit (a type of loss) was unforeseeable. But it might also be foreseeable to the seller that the goods that cost $10 would be resold, but unforeseeable that they would be used in a product that would be so successful as to generate many millions of dollars of profits (the extent of loss). Article 74 seems to preclude recovery in the first case. It is unclear whether the Article precludes recovery in the latter.

There is some argument that Article 74's foreseeability limitation differs from the traditional test of *Hadley* and related domestic law in one respect.[7] As a matter of technical formulation, Article 74 excludes loss that the breaching party did not or could not reasonably foresee, in the light of the facts and matters of which he then knew or ought to have known, as a "possible consequence" of its breach. American law concerning contracts other than for sales of goods excludes recovery of losses the breaching party did not have reason to foresee as a "probable result" of the breach.[8] Fewer types of loss are excluded by Article 74's language than under domestic law doctrine, because loss can be foreseeable as a possible consequence of breach, even if not a probable consequence of it. But the UCC, rather than general contract principles, provides the closest analogue to the CISG, and the relevant UCC provision, § 2–715(2)(a), permits recovery of consequential damages resulting from the seller's breach for any loss resulting from general or particular requirements and needs of which the seller has "reason to know" at the time of contracting. That limitation appears far closer to the "possible" loss standard of the CISG than to the "probable" one in general contract law. If there is a substantial difference between the CISG and the UCC on this score, it lies in the fact that the UCC appears to permit recovery of consequential damages only for the buyer,[9] while Article 74 applies to both parties.

Two American cases that have focused on Article 74's foreseeability limitation both understand it as stating the foreseeability limitation in terms of "probable" consequences,[10] while a third case adheres to the "possible" language.[11] We believe

---

[6] The Austrian Supreme Court requires foreseeability with regard to both the type and extent of loss, see Supreme Court (Austria), 14 January 2005, available at http://cisgw3.law.pace.edu/cases/050114a3.html; see also Ingeborg Schwenzer, *Article 74*, in Schlectriem & Schwenzer: Commentary on the UN Convention on the International Sale of Goods (CISG) 999, 1020 (Ingeborg Schwenzer ed., 3d ed. 2010) [hereinafter "Schlechtriem & Schwenzer"].

[7] See Franco Ferrari, Hadley v Baxendale *v Foreseeability Under Article 74 CISG*, in Contract Damages: Domestic and International Perspectives 305 (Djakhongir Saidov & Ralph Cunnington eds., 2008).

[8] See Restatement (Second) of Contracts § 351(1) (1981).

[9] See U.C.C. § 2–715(2); cf. U.C.C. § 2–710.

[10] See *Delchi Carrier SpA* v. *Rotorex Corp.*, 71 F.3d 1024, 1029 (2d Cir. 1995) ("The CISG requires that damages be limited by the familiar principle of foreseeability established by *Hadley v. Baxendale*"); *TeeVee Toons, Inc.* v. *Gerhard Schubert GmbH*, 2006 U.S. Dist. LEXIS 59455, at *40 (S.D.N.Y. August 12, 2006). Cf. Supreme Court (Switzerland), 28 October 1998, available at http://cisgw3.law.pace.edu/cases/981028s1.html (limitation traceable to Anglo-American law); District Court Gelderland (Netherlands), 30 July 2014, available at http://cisgw3.law.pace.edu/cases/140730n1.html.

[11] See *Al Hewar Environmental & Public Health Establishment* v. *Southeast Ranch, LLC*, 2011 U.S. Dist. LEXIS 128723 (D. Fla. November 8, 2011).

that these verbal formulations do not translate into significant differences in result. Taken literally, a "possible" consequences formulation imposes something close to strict liability rather than a limitation, because an even moderately informed breaching party can forecast a huge range of possible losses that can result from its breach. In short, virtually anything is "possible" from the ex ante perspective that Article 74 embraces. The very fact that a result materialized indicates that it was "possible" that it could materialize, and given sufficient time and effort, a party could have foreseen that such a result could possibly materialize. Thus understood, the foreseeability requirement of Article 74 does not foreclose recovery for any damage suffered. While the requirement that the breaching party is only charged with what was foreseeable in the light of the facts and matters of which he knew or ought to have known at the time of contracting, the flexible characterization of those facts and circumstances limits the effect of that constraint. That result becomes more likely as one expands the description of the consequence. The loss of down-stream contracts from breach that lead the aggrieved party to declare bankruptcy may be described as either foreseeable lost revenues or as less readily foreseeable insolvency. Neither the CISG's drafters nor the delegates who approved the CISG likely intended this result. Nor do the cases that apply the "possible consequences" test appear to allow such a broad standard of foreseeability. At the same time, a probability test arguably demands too much if it means a greater than 50 percent probability that the consequence complained of would materialize. Certainly the current cases make no inquiry into whether foreseeability transcends some probabilistic threshold. The court in *Delchi Carrier SpA v. Rotorex Corp.*[12] concluded that the transactions for which the buyer sought consequential damages were "objectively foreseeable" at the time the contract was concluded. Similarly, the court in *TeeVee Toons, Inc. v. Gerhard Schubert GmbH*[13] inferred foreseeability from evidence that the buyers intended to resell the goods that defendant agreed to manufacture and made no inquiry into probability.

We conclude, therefore, that notwithstanding differences in technical formulations, in practice the Article 74 test and the "probable consequences" test converge on something like a "reasonably foreseeable consequences" test. Consequences that are remote, although possible, should be excluded because the likelihood that they would materialize has not been priced into the contract. The breaching party, that is, would not have been paid to take the risk that the aggrieved party would suffer the loss complained of. On the other hand, the breaching party would have had an opportunity to price a risk of a reasonably foreseeable loss, even if that risk did not rise above a 50 percent threshold. We conclude that this interpretation is consistent with the practice of courts as well as with a theory of consequential damages that places loss on the party best positioned to avoid or insure against them.

---

[12] 71 F.3d 1024 (2d Cir. 1995).
[13] 2006 U.S. Dist. LEXIS 59455 (S.D.N.Y. August 22, 2006).

Al Hewar Environmental & Public Health Establishment v. *Southeast Ranch, LLC*[14] illustrates the convergence. There a buyer contracted with its seller for a large quantity of hay. The buyer in turn arranged to sell a portion of the hay to a sub-buyer. As part of the arrangement, the buyer posted a forfeitable bond to assure delivery. The buyer had entered into the same arrangement with the sub-buyer over the previous several years. When the seller breached by failing to deliver the hay, the buyer had to cancel its contract with the sub-buyer and forfeited its bond. The court awarded the buyer consequential damages, including the amount of the bond. In doing so it relied on Article 74's "ought to have known" language, finding that these damages were foreseeable to the seller at the time of the conclusion of the contract. Given the quantities of hay the buyer was purchasing and the buyer's past contracting practices, the seller could have reasonably foreseen that the buyer would resell some of it. The seller therefore also could have reasonably foreseen that its breach might result in a loss to the buyer in those resale transactions. Although the court makes no specific findings as to why the seller ought to have known that this loss was a foreseeable result of breach, the facts it recites suggest that the result was reasonably foreseeable to the seller. The court did not decide (and did not need to decide) whether the loss was a probable result of breach.

But the court in *CITGO Petroleum Corp.* v. *Odfjell Seachem*[15] reached what is arguably an alternative conclusion, and did so in a manner that demonstrates, perhaps to a fault, the ineffectiveness of Article 74's language of the "possible." Tricon had contracted for the purchase of cyclohexane from YPF. It then contracted to resell the cyclohexane to CITGO, and CITGO in turn contracted to resell to BASF. Each of the resale contracts would generate significant profit for the reseller. But those resales were negated when delivery of the cyclohexane to Tricon was delayed. Through a series of intermediate transactions, CITGO brought a claim for damages on behalf of both Tricon and itself, and contended that lost profits were recoverable as a foreseeable consequence of the delay in delivery because YPF had reason to know that Tricon was merely a reseller. The court, arguably ignoring the language of Article 74, applied a version of *Hadley* that permitted recovery of lost profits only if YPF could foresee that Tricon would suffer a delay in reselling as a consequence of the breach. To satisfy this standard, the court concluded, YPF would have needed to understand that Tricon was a reseller, not a company that purchased and used cyclohexane itself, and that Tricon had a short-term deal to resell the product. Moreover, the burden was on CITGO to demonstrate that YPF had the requisite understanding, even though YPF and Tricon's prior dealings indicated that Tricon was a trader, not a user, of cyclohexane. The lack of evidence on foreseeability was fatal to CITGO's efforts to attempt to demonstrate that Article 74 was or could be satisfied. As the court concluded, "[w]hile certainly YPF *may*

---

[14] 2011 U.S. Dist. LEXIS 128723 (D. Fla. November 8, 2011).
[15] 2014 U.S. Dist. LEXIS 170843 (S.D. Tex. December 10, 2014).

have known [that Tricon was a reseller], such supposition does not rise to the level necessary to survive summary judgment."[16] That inquiry, however, misunderstands a literal reading of Article 74. Under that reading, the relevant issue was not whether YPF may have known that Tricon would resell the goods, but whether, given what YPF did or ought to have known, YPF could foresee the possibility that Tricon would resell the goods.

The Austrian Supreme Court's application of Article 74's foreseeability limitation is consistent with the "reasonable foreseeable consequences" test.[17] According to the court, consequential damages are recoverable if at the conclusion of the contract a reasonable person in the breaching party's position could view the loss as a "sufficiently probable consequence" of breach. It concluded that Article 74 therefore requires determining the degree to which a reasonable person in the breaching party's position at the conclusion of the contract could foresee the loss from its breach. The court remanded the case to the lower court for it to make this determination. A "probable consequences" test for foreseeability requires that the loss be probable, not merely sufficiently probable as the court requires. The court's concern with the degree to which the loss is foreseeable suggests that the loss must be reasonably foreseeable at the conclusion of the contract. A Russian arbitral tribunal, in denying the buyer lost profits on a sale to its sub-purchaser, reached a similar conclusion.[18] It concluded that the breaching seller had "no obligation" to foresee the buyer's lost profits when it was not informed of the buyer's sale to the sub-purchaser.

There is one additional technical distinction between the foreseeability limitation expressed in *Hadley* and in Article 74. Traditionally, *Hadley* speaks in terms of what was foreseeable to both parties at the time the contract was concluded,[19] while Article 74 speaks only in terms of what the party in breach foresaw. As a practical matter, the difference is likely to be immaterial because it is highly improbable that the party in breach would foresee a consequence that might befall the aggrieved

---

[16] Id. at *20 (emphasis in original).

[17] See Supreme Court (Austria), 14 January 2002, available at http://cisgw3.law.pace.edu/cases/020114a3.html.; cf. Tribunal of International Commercial Arbitration (Russia), 6 June 2000, available at http://cisg3.law.pace.edu/cases/000606r1.html (buyer denied consequential damages when breaching seller was not informed of buyer's sale to a sub-purchaser).

[18] See Tribunal of International Commercial Arbitration (Russia), 6 June 2000, available at http://cisg3.law.pace.edu/cases/000606r1.html.

[19] According to the *Hadley* court, "[w]here two parties have made a contract which one of them has broken, the damages which the other party ought to receive in respect of such breach of contract should be such as may fairly and reasonably be considered either arising naturally, i.e., according to the usual course of things, from such breach of contract itself, or such as may reasonably be supposed to have been in the contemplation of both parties, at the time they made contract, as the probable result of the breach of it." *Hadley* v. *Baxendale*, 156 Eng. Rep. 145, 151 (Ex. 1854). Only the second of *Hadley's* two "rules" refers to what was foreseeable to both parties ("in the contemplation of both parties"). The Restatement (Second) of Contract's statement of the *Hadley* rule refers only to what was reasonably foreseeable to the breaching party when the contract was made; see Restatement (Second) of Contracts § 351 (1) (1981).

party and that the aggrieved party itself did not foresee. More likely is the circumstance in which the breaching party, with limited information available to it, would not foresee a consequence that is foreseeable to the aggrieved party.

2. Calculation of loss under Article 74

According to Article 74, recoverable damages are equal to the loss resulting from breach. The aggrieved party does not have to rely on Article 75's cover measure or Article 76's market price measure to calculate damages, even when available.[20] In fact, sometimes the aggrieved party can only rely on Article 74 to recover damages. This will be so when it has not avoided the contract under either Article 75 or Article 76. Since Article 74 does not require avoidance, it will be the primary source of damage recoveries under Article 36 when the buyer retains goods that fail to conform to the contract.

Notwithstanding its broad applicability, Article 74 does not state how loss from breach is to be calculated. Nonetheless, its reference to "loss . . . as a consequence of breach" suggests that damages are to be calculated to protect the aggrieved party's expectation interest. This is because awarding damages for loss from breach puts the victim in the position it would be in had the contract been performed. Protecting the aggrieved party's expectancy interest requires determining two positions. One is the aggrieved party's position as a result of the breach. The other is the position that party would have been in had the contract been performed. A damage calculation that gives a monetary award ("a sum") equal to the difference between these two positions measures the aggrieved party's loss from breach. For example, in one case the seller delivered nonconforming goods and sued the buyer to recover the remaining portion of the contract price.[21] The court calculated the buyer's damages under Article 74 as equal to this portion of the price and denied the seller recovery. In effect it measured these damages as the difference between the value that conforming goods would have had at the time of delivery and the value of the delivered goods at that time.

That measure of damages appears to be correct in light of the objective of retaining the aggrieved party's benefit of the bargain. Assume, for example, that a buyer enters into a contract with a seller for the purchase of Grade A sawdust at a price of $100,000, with delivery to occur in six months. Assume that at the time of delivery, Grade A sawdust in the quantity required by the contract has a market value of $110,000. Finally, assume that the seller instead delivers the same quantity of Grade B sawdust, which has a value at the time of delivery of $90,000. The buyer has suffered a loss measured by the difference between the value of what it expected

---

[20] See Articles 45(1)(b), 61(1)(b).
[21] See District Court Trier (Germany), 12 October 1995, available at http://cisgw3.law.pace.edu/cases/951012g1.html.

to receive (sawdust worth $110,000) and what it did receive (sawdust worth $90,000), or $20,000. If the buyer receives $20,000 in damages, it will be in the same position it would have occupied had there been performance, because it will have $90,000 in sawdust and $20,000 in damages for a total value of $110,000 – the value it would have received had there been performance.

Although the reference to the aggrieved party's loss suggests that there is a single amount that satisfies Article 74, there are different ways of measuring loss, and they could give rise to different amounts. The cost of repair measures the buyer's loss from the seller's nonconforming tender, unless the buyer suffers loss not compensated by repair.[22] If nonconforming goods have a prevailing market price at the time delivery is due, the market price differential can measure loss from breach.[23] Likewise, the cost of funds measures the seller's loss as a result of the buyer's delay in paying the contract price. All these measures calculate damages consistent with Article 74's general rule for recoverable loss. Occasionally, establishing loss directly can be difficult. Loss is not directly observable, and the party bearing the burden of proving loss might not have the evidence needed to establish it directly. In this event the party might prefer to rely on repair costs or the market differential to prove its loss.

3. Consequential and incidental damages

Under Article 74 loss from breach includes incidental loss and consequential damages. Article 74's reference to "loss ... as a consequence of breach," because unqualified, covers both sorts of loss. Incidental loss is out of pocket expense incurred as a result of breach. Storage and transportation costs that would not have been incurred had the contract been properly performed are incidental expenses. Consequential damages include liability to third parties as well as opportunity costs incurred as a result of breach. Although domestic law sometimes makes the distinction between incidental loss and consequential damages important,[24] the CISG does not. Both are recoverable under Article 74. As types of recoverable damages, both incidental loss and consequential damages are subject to Article 74's limitation of foreseeability. Finally, they are recoverable under Article 74 even when the

---

[22] See District Court Stuttgart (Germany), 29 October 2009, available at http://cisgw3. law.pace .edu/cases/091029g1.html; CIETA Arbitration Award (China), 31 May 2006, available at http:// cisgw3.law.pace.edu/cases/060531c1.html; ICC Case 8740 (1996), available at http://cisgw3.law .pace.edu/cases/968740i1.html; Court of Appeals Köln (Germany), 8 January 1997, available at http://cisgw3.law.pace.edu/cases/970108g2.html.

[23] See Secretariat Commentary on the 1978 Draft, in Documentary History of the Uniform Law for International Sales 449 (para. 7) (John O. Honnold ed., 1989) [hereinafter "Documentary History"]; Court of Appeals Zweibrucken (Germany), 2 February 2004, available at http:// cisgw3.law.pace.edu/cases/040202g1.html.

[24] For instance, Article 2 of the UCC allows the seller to recover only incidental loss, not consequential damages; see U.C.C. §§ 2–710, 2–715. The buyer may recover both sorts of loss; see § 2–715(1), (2).

aggrieved party measures its damages under Articles 75 or 76, as both Articles make explicit. In a Spanish case the aggrieved seller sought to measure its damages for wheat it resold under Article 75's resale measure, and for unsold wheat under Article 76's market measure.[25] The Spanish Supreme Court upheld the trial court's damage award under Article 74, which included the warehousing costs the seller incurred before it resold the wheat the breaching buyer had refused. The Court, however, also upheld the lower court's refusal to include in the damage award under Article 74 additional financing costs the seller allegedly incurred while arranging resale. It found that the seller had not sufficiently proven these costs. Financing costs incurred as a result of breach, if proven, easily are recoverable as "loss...as a consequence of the breach."

4. Burden of proof

The CISG is unclear about the assignment of the burden of proving damages. There are two issues here. One is whether the CISG or the forum's law governs burden of proof. The second issue is the assignment made by applicable law, either by the CISG or the forum's law. Courts and commentators tend[26] to conclude that the CISG assigns the burden of proving loss from breach and that the party claiming damages under Article 74 bears that burden.[27] Although both parts of the conclusion are reasonable, the case for it is far from compelling. Article 74 does not deal with burdens of proof. In fact, apart from Article 79(1), none of the CISG's provisions expressly address the question. Thus, the CISG must deal with burdens of proof, if at all, implicitly.

Commentators find that Article 7 implicitly addresses the matter. We are not so sure. By its terms, Article 7(1) requires the CISG to be interpreted to promote uniformity in its application. Uniformity in interpretation only demands that tribunals interpret the CISG's provisions in the same way.[28] As far as the instruction goes, they may interpret the CISG to assign or not to assign the burden of proving

---

[25] See Supreme Court (Spain), 1 July 2013, unpublished translation by Santiago J. Teran.

[26] See *Delchi Carrier SpA v. Rotorex, Corp.*, 71 F.3d 1024 (2d Cir. 1995); Court of Appeals Helsinki (Finland), 26 October 2000, available at http://cisgw3.law.pace.edu/cases/001026f5.html; District Court Saan (Switzerland), 20 February 1997, available at http://cisgw3.law.pace.edu/cases/970220s1.html.

[27] See Peter Huber & Alastair Mullis, The CISG 36, 281 (2007); CISG Advisory Council Opinion No. 6: Calculation of Damages Under CISG Article 74 ¶ 2 (2006), available at http://cisgw3 .law. pace.edu/cisg/CISG-AC-op6.html; Schwenzer, *Article 74*, in Schlechtriem & Schwenzer, supra note 6, at 1025; Franco Ferrari, *Burden of Proof Under the United Nations Convention on Contracts for the International Sale of Goods*, 2000 Int'l Bus. L. J. 665, 666; *Chicago Prime Packers, Inc. v. Northam Trading Food Co.*, 408 F.3d 494, 899 (7th Cir. 2005); Supreme Court (Austria), 12 September 2006, available at http://cisgw3.law.pace.edu/cases/060912a3.html; Court of Appeals Hamm (Germany), 31 March 1998, available at http://cisgw3.law.pace.edu/cases/980331g1.html; District Court Vigevano (Italy), 12 July 2000, available at http://cisgw3.law.pace.edu/cases/000712i3.html.

[28] Cf. CISG Advisory Council Opinion No. 6, Calculation of Damages Under Article 74 ¶ 2.5 (2006), available at www.cisg.law. Pace.edu/cisg/CISG-ACop6.html.

damages. Tribunals follow Article 7(1)'s instruction as long as they converge on the interpretation of the relevant provision. Thus, Article 7(1)'s requirement of uniformity in interpretation does not implicitly deal with burden of proof. According to Article 7(2), matters not expressly settled by the CISG are to be settled according to general principles underlying it. The trouble is that it is hard to identify these principles. Although some commentators have found a large number of underlying principles,[29] it is difficult to see how principles bearing on burden of proof are embedded in the CISG. For instance, the principle is sometimes offered to the effect that a party wanting to benefit from a provision bears the burden of proving the provision's factual requirements.[30] Article 74 gives the aggrieved party a right to recover its loss and places limits on the loss it may recover. However, it suggests nothing about whether the aggrieved party must introduce evidence to establish that loss. Although the principle might be a good one, it has no basis in a provision that merely grants remedial rights.

Ultimately, the question as to whether the CISG assigns burdens of proof with respect to damages is not of major importance. This is because, according to those who find that it does so, the party claiming damages under Article 74 bears the burden of proving its loss.[31] Domestic law tends to assign the burden in the same way.[32] We would expect that to be the case, since the aggrieved party has better access to the relevant information than the breaching party.

5. Lost profits and the standard for recovery

Article 74 expressly includes lost profits as an element of recoverable damages. The express inclusion probably is intended to signal that the Article counts lost profits as recoverable "loss;" it does not under some domestic laws. Article 74 does not state how lost profits are to be calculated. Unsurprisingly, courts calculate it as they would under applicable domestic law. Unfortunately, this tendency provides more potential for divergence between the CISG and domestic law than one finds with respect to standards of proof. National laws differ concerning the required likelihood of loss

---

[29] See, e.g., Ulrich Magnus, *The General Principles of UN Sales Law*, 3 Int'l Trade & Bus. L. 33 (1997) (26 general principles); Camilla B. Anderson, *General Principles of the CISG – General Impenetrable?*, in Sharing International Commercial Law Across National Boundaries 13, 28 (Camilla B. Anderson & Ulrich B. Schroeter eds., 2008) (reporting 14 general principles identified by the CISG Digest).

[30] See, e.g., Magnus, supra note 32, at 33, 52; Ferrari, supra note 28, at 667–68.

[31] See, e.g., Huber & Mullis, supra note 27, at 36, 281; Ingeborg Schwenzer, *Article 74*, in Schlechtriem & Schwenzer, supra note 6, at 1025; Victor Knapp, *Damages in General*, in Commentary on the International Sales Law 541 (Cesare M. Bianca & Michael J. Bonell eds., 1987) [hereinafter "Bianca & Bonell"].

[32] See Ingeborg Schwenzer, Pascal Hachem & Christopher Kee, Global Sales and Contract Law 646 (2012).

supported by the evidence.[33] For instance, they differ about whether the aggrieved party must prove its damages with reasonable certainty, clear and convincing evidence, or some other standard of proof. An unfortunate example of reverting to domestic standards can be found in *Orica Australia Pty Ltd* v. *Aston Evaporative Services, LLC*.[34] The court concluded that Article 74 allowed lost profits, but – considering only American decisions – then observed that "[c]ourts applying this have often imported lost-profits standards similar to [the standard of the relevant state in the United States]."[35] That standard, which requires proof of the fact that damages will accrue in the future and sufficient admissible evidence to compute a fair approximation of the loss, may be perfectly appropriate. But the inference that domestic principles should be imported into the CISG simply proves too much. If courts from jurisdictions with different standards each import their own standards, no autonomous CISG standard can evolve. Perhaps the best one can say of the approach in *Orica Australia Pty Ltd* is that the party seeking lost profits did not argue for a different standard, leaving the court with an unquestioned assumption.

The CISG Advisory Council advocates a standard of reasonable certainty: The evidence must allow a reasonable estimate of damages.[36] It bases its recommendation on the CISG's international character and Article 74's policy of full compensation. Although selection of a standard of proof is complicated, it is not clear that a reasonable certainty standard is efficient. This is because a standard of proof has two opposite effects on the contracting parties. One occurs at the point of breach, when the aggrieved party must decide to litigate. Lower standards of proof increase the incentive of the aggrieved party to sue, because they make it more likely that evidence will show loss from breach. The other effect occurs prior to breach, at the point of contracting. At this point lower standards of proof increase the expected liability of a party, because they increase the likelihood that loss will be found in the event it breaches. By increasing the likelihood that the aggrieved party can recover its loss, the reasonable certainty standard increases the value of the contract to that party. At the same time, the standard increases the expected cost of the contract by increasing the expected liability from breach. By contrast, higher standards of proof decrease the contract value because the loss on breach is harder to establish. However, these standards also decrease the cost of the contract by reducing the expected liability from breach. Thus, in general, the two effects point in different directions. Their respective sizes are unknown and hard to estimate. Without a basis

---

[33] See, e.g., Kevin M. Clermont, *Standards of Proof in Japan and the United States*, 37 Cornell J. Int'l Law 263 (2004); Kevin M. Clermont & Emily Sherwin, *A Comparative View of Standards of Proof*, 50 Am. J. Comp. L. 243 (2002).

[34] 2015 U.S. Dist. LEXIS 98248 (D. Colo. July 28, 2015).   [35] Id. at *23.

[36] See CISG Advisory Council Opinion No. 6, Calculation of Damages Under Article 74 ¶. 2.6 (2006) available at www.cisg.law.pace.edu/cisg/CISG-AC-op6.html; see also Ingeborg Schwenzer, *Article 74*, in Schlechtriem & Schwenzer, supra note 6 at 1026.

for estimating their size, a reasonable certainty standard (or any other standard) seems difficult to support as an optimal basis for proving damages.

The buyer's profit is the difference between the value to it of the seller's performance and the contract price. For the seller, profit is the difference between the contract price and its cost of performance. Rational buyers and sellers expect a profit from performance, so that the difference between value and price (buyer) and price and cost (seller) is positive. To date both German and American courts calculate lost profits under Article 74 in the same way.[37] Costs that the aggrieved party would incur in performance are variable costs. Variable costs that the victim saves by breach are deducted from the value of performance (buyer) or the price (seller) to arrive at its lost profit. Costs that the aggrieved party incurs whether or not the contract was entered into are fixed costs. In calculating lost profits, fixed costs are not deducted from the value of performance.[38]

The aggrieved party sometimes will prefer to recover lost profits directly under Article 74. This can occur when proving the prevailing market price at the time of delivery or the resale price is difficult. To establish its lost profits under Article 74, the aggrieved party must prove the value of performance to it and its performance costs. The burden of doing so can be easier than proving market or resale price, even when Articles 75 or 76 are available to measure damages.

Al Hewar Env. & Public Health Est. v. Southeast Ranch, LLC[39] is likely an example. There the buyer contracted with the seller to purchase bales of hay for a total price of $5,166,000. The contract called for a $787,500 down payment, which the buyer paid the seller. The buyer in turn contracted to sell the hay to a downstream buyer for $6,806,000. This contract required the buyer to post a forfeitable performance bond in the amount of $452,000. When the seller failed to deliver the hay to the buyer, the buyer avoided the contract. The buyer in turn cancelled its contract with the downstream buyer, who, in turn, called on the buyer's performance bond. Although the buyer could have measured its damages under Articles 75 or 76, it elected to recover its lost profit under Article 74.

The court calculated the lost profit at $2,427,500 as follows: The value of the seller's performance to the buyer was the $6,806,000 contract price due from the downstream buyer. The buyer's variable costs were the $5,166,000 breached contract price. Because the buyer had made a $787,500 down payment on the price, the seller's breach saved it $4,378,500 ($5,166,000 - $787,500 = $4,378,500). Thus, the buyer's lost profit under Article 74 equaled the difference between $6,806,000 and

---

[37] See Court of Appeals Hamburg (Germany), 26 November 1999, available at http://cisgw3.law .pace.edu/cases/991126g1.html; *Delchi Carrier SpA v. Rotorex Corp.*, 71 F.3d 1024 (2d Cir. 1995); *TeeVee Toons, Inc. v. Gerhard Schubert GmbH*, 2006 U.S. Dist. LEXIS 59455 (S.D.N.Y. August 12, 2006).

[38] See *Profi-Parkiet Sp. Zoo v. Seneca Hardwoods LLC*, 2014 U.S. Dist. LEXIS 71289 (E.D.N.Y. May 23, 2014).

[39] 2011 U.S. Dist. LEXIS 128723 (S.D. Fla. November 8, 2011).

$4,378,500 or $2,427,500. In addition, the $452,000 performance bond that the buyer forfeited on canceling its contract with the downstream buyer was a foreseeable consequential damage resulting from the seller's breach. Article 74 therefore includes it in the buyer's recoverable loss. Thus, the buyer's total recoverable loss under the Article is $2,879,500. The court noted that the same calculation would be made under United States domestic law.

6. Lost volume sellers

Article 74 does not directly address whether a "lost volume" seller can recover its lost profit on the breached contract. A seller loses volume when its available supply of the goods exceeds its available customers at any time. If the buyer breaches and the seller resells the same goods to another buyer at the breached contract price, Article 76's market measure gives the seller no damages. This is because the market price of the second sale will equal the contract price. Thus, the contract price- market price differential is zero. Nevertheless, the seller may have suffered damages that should be compensated: Given that the seller had sufficient goods to serve all available customers, the seller may claim that it would have made the second sale even if the first buyer had performed. Thus, the second sale was an additional sale, not a substitute sale. The seller will have lost a profit on the breached contract and should be entitled to recovery of that profit as a "sum equal to the loss . . . suffered by the other party as a consequence of breach."

The Austrian Supreme Court has accepted this reasoning and allowed a lost volume seller to recover its lost profit under Article 74.[40] The CISG Advisory Council takes the same position.[41] Although supported by some domestic case law, their reasoning is questionable. Both accept the traditional notion of a "lost volume" seller as one who has the capacity to supply all its customers. According to the Austrian Supreme Court: "[B]usinesspersons, who regularly trade with goods as the ones involved in the avoided contract, will—as a general rule—always be in a position to replace the failed transaction by a substitute transaction selling the goods of the avoided contract or different goods on the basis of the current market price."[42]

Although a seller who loses a sale due a breach should receive its lost profit, the availability of sufficient goods to make sales to additional customers notwithstanding the breach should not, of itself, constitute lost volume. To lose volume, it must be the case that the seller not only could have made the additional, sale; it must also be true that the seller would have made the additional sale.[43] There are at

[40] See Supreme Court (Austria), 28 April 2000, available at http://cisgw3.pace.law.edu/cases/000428a3.html.

[41] See CISG Advisory Council Opinion No. 6, Calculation of Damages Under CISG Article 74 ¶ 3.20 (2006), available at http://cisgw3.law.pace.edu/cisg/CISG-ACop6.html.

[42] Id.

[43] See District Court Gelderland (Netherlands), 30 July 2014, available at http://cisgw3.law.pace.edu/cases/140730n1.html.

least two reasons why a seller who has the capacity to make an additional sale would not do so. First, the effort to make the additional sale might require incurring costs that render the additional sale unprofitable. To earn a profit from making a sale in addition to the breached contract, the seller's marginal costs in supplying the additional good must equal its marginal revenue from the sale. The seller maximizes its profit by making sales up to the point where the marginal cost of the sale equals its marginal revenue. In a relatively competitive market, sellers will occupy that position. For this reason, unless the market is noncompetitive or the seller has a peculiar reason for not operating at its profit-maximizing capacity, any sale the seller makes with the breached goods is a substitute sale, not an additional one. As a result, the seller does not lose volume from the breached sale.[44]

In addition, by its breach, the buyer has indicated that it no longer has productive use for the goods. As a result, if it had performed the contract and accepted the goods, the buyer presumably would have attempted to resell them. Arguably, any such resale would have occurred within the seller's market, since the buyer purchased the goods in that market. As a result, the seller would have been deprived of the sale made to the party who purchased the goods from the performing buyer. On that logic, resale of the breached goods only occurred because of the breach; it was, therefore, a substitute for the breached contract, not an additional sale. As a consequence, the seller did not lose volume when the buyer failed to accept the goods and the seller resold them to a party that the buyer otherwise would have serviced.[45]

7. Litigation costs

Article 74 does not say whether attorney's fees and other litigation costs are recoverable as damages. Unsurprisingly, courts and commentators divide over the issue,[46] although in some cases it is unclear whether an award of attorney's fees has been made under Article 74 or under some domestic law principle.[47] Both sides

---

[44] American domestic case law shows a similar divide over the definition of the lost volume seller; compare *Neri v. Retail Marine Corp.*, 285 N.E.2d (N.Y. 1972) with *R.E. Davis Chemical Corp. v. Diasonics, Inc.*, 826 F.2d 678 (7th Cir. 1987). Indeed, *R.E. Davis Chemical* imposes on the seller the burden of proving that it would have lost volume.

[45] See *A. Lenobel, Inc. v. Senif*, 252 App. Div. 533 (N.Y. 1938).

[46] Compare *San Lucio S.r.l. v. Import & Storage Services LLC*, 2009 U.S. Dist. LEXIS 31681 (D.N.J.); *Hermanos Succesores v. Hearthside Baking Co.*, 315 F.3d 385 (7th Cir. 2002); Harry Flechtner & Joseph Lookofsky, *Viva Zapata! American Procedure and CISG Substance in a U.S. Circuit Court of Appeals*, 7 Vindobona J. Int'l L. & Comm. Arb. 93 (2003) (CISG silent on attorney's fees), with Court of Appeals Turku (Finland), 12 April 2002, available at http://cisgw3 .law.pace.edu/cases/020412f5.html; Lower Court Augsburg (Germany), 29 January 1996, available at http://cisgw3.law.pace.edu/cases/960129g1.html; Fritz Enderlein & Dietrich Maskow, International Sales Law 298–99 (1992) (Article 74's compensation principle allows recovery of attorney's fees).

[47] See Court of Appeals Turku (Finland), 12 April 2002, available at http://cisgw3.law.pace.edu/ cases/020412f5.html.

have respectable arguments in their favor. According to one position, Article 74 allows the aggrieved party to recover damages equal to its "loss," and litigation costs are a type of incidental expense resulting from breach. If the aggrieved party cannot recover its litigation expenses, damages do not put it in the same position as performance would have. Article 74 therefore would not protect its full expectancy interest. Although Article 74 does not expressly address litigation costs, Article 7(2) directs that general principles underlying the CISG settle matters that the CISG implicitly addresses. A relevant underlying principle, supported by Article 74, is one of full compensation: the principle that a damage award fully protects the aggrieved party's expectancy interest. The principle of full compensation argues for construing Article 74 to allow recovery of litigation costs.

The opposing position relies on Article 74's language to the effect that damages equal the "loss . . . as a consequence of breach." Loss that results from events other than breach therefore is not recoverable under the Article. Arguably, litigation costs are the consequence of litigation, not breach.[48] If the breaching party had posted a forfeitable bond equal to the loss breach caused the aggrieved party, the victim would not have to litigate. It could call on the bond instead. Or the breaching party might have fully compensated the aggrieved party without litigation. These possibilities arguably show that litigation costs are the result of the victim having to sue to get paid, not the breach itself.

American courts have systematically refused to award attorney's fees in litigation governed by the CISG.[49] *Zapata Hermanos Succesores v. Hearthside Baking Co.*[50] remains the best judicial discussion of the matter. There, Judge Posner concluded that attorney's fees are unavailable under the CISG; they are recoverable, if at all, only under the procedural law of the forum. Posner notes an odd consequence of interpreting damages under Article 74 to cover litigation costs. Article 74 allows recovery for loss resulting from breach. Thus, although litigation costs would be recoverable by the prevailing plaintiff (the aggrieved party), the prevailing defendant could not recover its litigation costs in the event it is found not to have breached.[51] True, the law of a forum that has a "loser pays" rule would award the prevailing defendant its litigation costs. But the prevailing defendant would not be made whole in a forum that adopts the American rule ("each side bears its own litigation costs"). Judge Posner conjectured that the United States, with its American rule, would not likely have signed the CISG had Article 74 allowed for the recovery of litigation costs.[52] Contracting States with a "loser pays" rule, he speculated, likely did not

---

[48] See John Gotanda, *Article 74*, in UN Convention on Contracts for the International Sale of Goods (CISG): Commentary 1010 (Stefan Kröll, Loukas Mistelis & Pilar Perales Viscasillas eds., 2011) [hereinafter "Kröll et al."].

[49] See, e.g., *Profi-Parkiet Sp. Zoo v. Seneca Hardwoods LLC*, 2014 U.S. Dist. LEXIS 71289 (E.D.N.Y. May 23, 2014); *Chicago Prime Packers, Inc. v. Northam Food Trading Co.*, 320 F.Supp.2d 702, 717 (N.D.Ill. 2004), *aff'd*, 408 F.3d 894 (7th Cir. 2005).

[50] 313 F.3d 385 (7th Cir. 2002).   [51] Id. at 389.   [52] Id.

think about the matter at all. His first conjecture seems plausible to us, given the reservations that the United States expressed with respect to other proposed provisions. The second seems less certain. Because Article 74 only awards damages for loss resulting from breach, even Contracting States with a "loser pays" rule could not construe the Article to allow a prevailing defendant to recover its litigation costs. They plausibly also concluded that litigation costs are recoverable, if at all, by the prevailing party only under the law of the forum.

Nothing in the recent case of *Stemcor USA, Inc. v. Miracero, S.A. de C.V.*,[53] changes the American view of attorney's fees, even though their award in an arbitration was upheld under Article 74. Stemcor sold steel coils to Miracero, a Mexican steel importer and distributor. When Stemcor failed to provide Mexican authorities with documentation that would have permitted preferential tax treatment of the sales, Miracero was assessed an additional $2.6 million in taxes and fees, and Miracero incurred $340,000 in costs to overturn those assessments. Miracero was ultimately awarded $819,437.86 for its attorneys' fees and costs in both the Mexican legal proceedings and the New York arbitration. Stemcor sought to vacate the arbitration award on several bases, including the non-arbitrability of the dispute and the allegedly *ultra vires* award of attorneys' fees.

On the issue of fees, the court noted that the relevant arbitration rules allowed the arbitral panel to award the costs of the arbitration to a prevailing party. But Stemcor contended that the CISG provided the substantive law applicable to the arbitration, and that damages under Article 74 are limited to the loss suffered as a consequence of the breach. Implicitly, Stemcor was contending that attorneys' fees are a consequence of the decision to bring an arbitration proceeding or litigation, not a consequence of the breach itself, and thus were unrecoverable under Article 74. The court, however, rejected the contention that the applicability of the CISG to the dispute meant that attorneys' fees were disallowed. The court concluded that choice of law provisions do not override arbitrators' ability to award fees otherwise available under the relevant arbitration rules.[54] In essence, therefore, the court appears to have been agreeing with Judge Posner's position that the issue of attorneys' fees fits more comfortably within the realm of procedural rules that fall outside the CISG than substantive rules that are created by it. But the court also confirmed the award of attorneys' fees in the case because the CISG itself does not "unambiguously" bar recovery of fees and costs.[55] One might initially read this claim as inconsistent with the holding in *Zapata*. But context matters. The court in *Stemcor* did not decide whether Article 74 either allowed or disallowed attorneys' fees. Instead, it recognized that *Zapata* had found attorneys' fees to fall outside of Article 74, that other courts included such fees within Article 74, and that commentators deemed the matter unresolved. As a result, the legal status of attorneys' fees under the CISG remained open. In that context, the court concluded that the

[53] 2014 U.S. Dist. LEXIS 140058 (S.D.N.Y. September 30, 2014).   [54] Id. at 14.   [55] Id. at 16.

decision of the arbitral panel to permit attorneys' fees had a "colorable" basis in law. This is the deferential standard that the court deemed necessary to surmount in order to overturn the arbitral award.[56]

Essentially, the court was simply deciding that an arbitral panel that either awarded or disallowed attorney's fees could be said to be acting reasonably. Neither decision would satisfy the standard for reversal. Viewed from that perspective, *Stemcor* detracts only minimally from *Zapata*. Assume, for example, that the arbitral panel in *Stemcor* had decided not to award attorneys' fees and that the disappointed plaintiff sought judicial reversal of the arbitral decision on the grounds that such costs were required by Article 74. Presumably, the court in *Stemcor* also would have denied that claim, again because it was only deciding that, given the disputed status of attorneys' fees under Article 74, an arbitrator picking either position will not have committed the degree of error necessary to overturn the arbitral award. Thus, the deferential standard of review of arbitral awards, not a construction of Article 74, was decisive in *Stemcor*. *Stemcor* does, however, vary from *Zapata* in one interesting respect. Judge Posner's decision has been criticized for its inattention to what commentators have viewed as contrary case law from other jurisdictions on the availability of attorneys' fees under Article 74.[57] The *Stemcor* court's recognition of the division in opinion is worthy of attention and approval insofar as it takes seriously the admonition to interpret the CISG in light of its international character and to consider opinions and commentary from outside the forum. To the extent that the ambiguity about the issue arises from conflicting views of courts from different jurisdictions, the court successfully avoided any accusation of a homeward trend in deciding CISG cases.

8. Interest

Article 74 clearly allows the recovery of interest on damages for breach of an obligation to pay the contract price or other sums of money. Breach deprives the injured party of the use of the money owed, and damages therefore compensate for this loss. Bearing the burden of proving its damages, the injured party must establish the amount of interest due on sums owed. The cost of capital to the party over the relevant period accurately measures interest owed.[58]

---

[56] Id. ("At most, then, Stemcor has identified an ambiguity in the law, which the arbitrators here resolved in favor of granting fees. Since that decision was at least reasonable, and certainly 'barely colorable,' this Court will not disturb it.").

[57] See, e.g., David B. Dixon, *Que Lastima Zapata — Bad CISG Ruling on Attorneys' Fees Still Haunts U.S. Courts*, 38 U. Miami Inter-Amer. L. Rev. 405, 422–24 (2007); John Felemegas, *An Interpretation of Article 74 CISG by the U.S. Circuit Court of Appeals*, 15 Pace Int'l L. Rev. 91, 119–21 (2003); cf. Harry Flechtner & Joseph Lookofsky, *Viva Zapata! American Procedure and CISG Substance in a U.S. Circuit Court of Appeals*, supra note 46, at 103 (endorsing result but criticizing opinion for failure to refer to relevant foreign case law).

[58] See, e.g., Court of Appeals Düsseldorf (Germany), 14 January 1994, available at http://cisgw3 .law.pace.edu/cases/940114g1.html.

Interest can be recovered under Article 78 independently of interest on damages. Article 78 provides: "If a party fails to pay the price or any other sum that is in arrears, the other party is entitled to interest on it, without prejudice to any claim for damages recoverable under Article 74." The provision's vagueness or incomplete character has divided courts and commentators. Clearly interest is recoverable under Article 78 without proof of loss under Article 74, as the last clause in Article 78 expressly allows. More generally, interest awardable under Article 78 is not awarded as damages.[59] It is not compensation for the loss of the use value of money or other sum due. Article 78 appears in Section III ("Interest") of Chapter V of the CISG, while the CISG's damages appear in Section II ("Damages") of the same chapter. The separation by different sections reinforces the different bases on which interest is awarded.

This difference between interest and damages has a practical consequence. Interest is not recoverable under Article 74 when the parties' contract effectively excludes damages. That would be the situation, for example, when the contract contains an exclusive liquidated damages clause. Even when the contract does not exclude damages, Article 79(5) does not allow recovery of interest as damages when the party's liability for nonperformance is exempted under Article 79. Nonetheless, in both cases the injured party still is entitled to interest under Article 78. Interest is not recoverable under that Article only when a contractual provision effectively excludes Article 78's application to the contract.

The distinction between interest and damages means that the injured party can recover interest as damages under Article 74 in addition to interest recovered under Article 78.[60] Further, the availability of interest under Articles 78 and 74 allows the injured party to choose the Article under which to recover interest. This is because Article 78 allows interest on the price or other sum that is "in arrears." Although we think that allowing interest as damages under Article 78 stretches the meaning of the phrase "in arrears" too far, adjudicators and some commentators disagree.[61] So, for

---

[59] See ICC Case No. 7585 (1992), available at http://cisgw3.law.pace.edu/cases/927585i1.html (Article 78's purpose is to distinguish between interest and damages).

[60] See District Court Padova (Italy), 31 March 2004, available at http://cisgw3.law.pace.edu/cases/040331i3.html; Lower Court Oldenburg (Germany), 24 April 1990, available at www.cisg.law.pace.edu/cases/900424g1.html.

[61] See, e.g., Supreme Court of Western Australia, (Australia) (*Ginza Pte Ltd* v. *Vista Corporation Pty Ltd.*), 17 January 2003, available at http://cisgw3.law.pace.edu/cases/030117a2.html; Court of Appeals (Finland), 26 October 2000 available at http://cisgw3.law.pace.edu/cases/001026f5.html; District Court Landshut (Germany), 5 April 1995, available at http://cisgw3.law.pace.edu/cases/950405g1.html. For commentary maintaining that Article 78 allows interest on any damage claim, see Klaus Bacher, *Article 78*, in Schlechtriem & Schwenzer, supra note 6, at 1052; for commentary expressing some doubts, see John O. Honnold, Uniform Law for International Sales Under the 1980 United Nations Convention 608 (Harry M. Flechtner ed., 4th ed. 2009) [hereinafter "Honnold/Flechtner"]; Francesca G. Mazzotta, CISG Article 78: Endless Disagreement Among Commentators, Much Less Among the Courts, available at www.cisg.law.pace.edu/cisg/biblio/massotta78.html.

example, the damage award obtained by a buyer who receives nonconforming goods apparently represents a sum "in arrears." Accordingly, Article 78 allows interest on the award.

To recover interest as damages under Article 74, the injured party must prove its loss from the breaching party's failure to pay obligated sums. Such proof is unnecessary under Article 78, because the Article awards interest independently of loss. On the other hand, although Article 78 does not specify the interest rate applicable to interest awarded under the Article, the interest rate recoverable under Article 74 is measured by the injured party's loss of the use of obligated sums. Thus, the interest rate used to calculate recoverable interest under Article 74 in principle can be higher than the benchmark rate used to calculate interest awarded under Article 78. A Swiss court concluded that an injured seller could recover interest calculated at a higher interest rate under Article 74 than at the legal rate of interest allowable under applicable domestic law.[62] A German appellate court awarded the injured seller interest under Article 74 calculated by the interest rate payable on the bank loan it used to finance the sale.[63] The award is consistent with allowing interest recoverable under Article 78 to be calculated using a different interest rate. A tribunal in an early ICC Arbitration concluded that the interest rate awarded under Article 78 was independent of any claim for damages under Article 74 CISG, and could be higher than the legal rate applicable to Article 74 losses.[64] The tribunal awarded the non-breaching seller interest based on its borrowing costs. On the other hand, an Austrian arbitral tribunal used the interest rate due on the seller's bank loan to calculate interest under Article 78.[65] This is the same benchmark used to award interest under Article 74.

As noted, Article 78 does not set the interest rate applicable under the Article. It could be the LIBOR, the EURIBOR, the Fed Funds rate or another official discount rate, the prime rate, or some other benchmark.[66] One United States federal court applied a federal interest rate based on the average rate of return on one-year Treasury bills for the relevant time period between the time the plaintiff's claims arose and the entry of judgment.[67] The omission of an interest rate reflects the inability of the

---

[62] See Commercial Court Zurich (Switzerland), 10 July 1996, available at http://cisgw3.law.pace
.edu/cases/960710s1.html.

[63] See Court of Appeals Düsseldorf (Germany), 14 January 1994, available at http://cisgw3.law
.pace.edu/cases/940114g1.html.

[64] See ICC Court of Arbitration–Paris, 7197 (1992), available at http://cisgw3.law.pace.edu/cases/
927197i1.html.

[65] See Arbitral Tribunal (Austria), 15 June 1994, available at http://cisgw3.law.pace.edu/cases/
940615a4.html.

[66] See e.g., District Court Gelderland (Netherlands), 30 July 2014, available at http://cisgw3.law
.pace.edu/cases/140730n1.html (assigning the statutory interest rate in accordance with
Dutch law).

[67] See *Profi-Parkiet Sp. Zoo v. Seneca Hardwoods LLC*, 2014 U.S. Dist. LEXIS 71289 (E.D.N.Y.
May 23, 2014).

CISG's drafters to reach a consensus on a uniform rate.[68] Although some adjudicators find that the matter is addressed by the CISG's underlying principles, a significant majority of courts and arbitral tribunals deem the applicable interest rate to be outside the CISG's scope.[69] In their view, under Article 7(2) the rate is determined instead by the applicable national law selected by the forum's conflict of laws principles. There is much less agreement about the national law selected by these principles. Adjudicators have selected the law of the breaching party's place of business, the injured party's place of business, the place where payment was to be made, and the place of the forum.[70] Several courts even select the law of the injured party's place of business without relying on conflict of laws principles.[71] Given the uncertainty about the interest rate applicable under Article 78 in the case law, the parties do well to provide for one in their contract.

Article 78 says little about elements of calculations that will determine whether interest payments are fully compensatory. It says nothing about the date from which interest begins to accrue either on the contract price due or on any amount owing ("any other sum that is in arrears"). With respect to price, the date from which interest begins to run seems clear: the date on which the price is due. The date from which interest on other amounts due accrues, such as carriage costs or an insurance policy taken for the breaching party's benefit, is harder to determine. Where the amount due is damages,[72] different dates are plausible. Does interest on damages run from the date of the breach, the date the cause of action accrues (if different), the entry of a judgment, or some other point? An American appellate court faced

---

[68] See 11th Plenary Meeting, April 8, 1980, in Documentary History, supra note 23, at 761 (para. 3).

[69] See, e.g., *Chicago Prime Packers, Inc. v. Northam Trading Co.*, 320 F. Supp.2d 702, 716 (N.D.Ill. 2004); ICC Case No. 10274 (1999), available at http://cisgw3.law.pace.edu/cases/990274i1.html; Francesco G. Mazzotta, CISG Article 78: Endless Disagreement Among Commentators, Much Less Among the Courts, available at www.cisg.law.pace.edu/cisg/biblio/massotta78.html (appendices collecting cases from different national or arbitral fora as of 2004); 2012 UNCITRAL Digest of Case Law on the United Nations Convention on the International Sale of Goods 377 (at para. 13), available at http://uncitral.org/pdf/english/clout/CISG-digest-2012-e.pdf. For cases finding that the interest rate is within the CISG's scope, see, e.g., *Zapata Hermanos Sucesores, S.A. v. Hearthside Baking Co., Inc.*, 2001 U.S. Dist. LEXIS 15191 (N.D.Ill. August 28, 2001), *partially rev'd* 313 F.3d 385 (7th Cir. 2002); Arbitral Tribunal (Austria), 15 June 1994, available at http://cisgw3.law.pace.edu/cases/940615a4.html.

[70] See 2012 UNCITRAL Digest of Case Law on the United Nations Convention on Contracts for the International Sale of Goods 377 nn. 46–50, available at http://uncitral.org/pdf/english/clout/CISG-digest-2012-e.pdf (collecting cases).

[71] See, e.g., Commercial Court Koophandel (Belgium), 20 September 2005, available at http://cisgw3.law.pace.edu/cases/050920b1.html; District Court Arbon (Switzerland), 9 December 1994, available at http://cisgw3.law.pace.edu/cases/941209s1.html 1994; District Court Frankfurt (Germany), 16 September 1991, available at http://cisgw3.law.pace.edu/cases/910916g1.html.

[72] For the view that Article 78 covers interest on recoverable damages, see District Court Zug (Switzerland), 21 October 1999, available at http://cisgw3.law.pace.edu/cases/991021s1.html; John Gotanda, *Article 78*, in Kroll et al., supra note 48, at 1044. For the distinction between interest recoverable on damages under Articles 74 and 78, see supra text accompanying notes 57–58.

with the issue of whether prejudgment interest was governed by domestic law or the CISG concluded that it did not have to decide the question, because the trial court's award of such interest was permitted by each.[73] But in doing so, the court made the unfortunate leap that the CISG's status as a treaty permitted it to decide the issue as matter of domestic federal law rather than to discern an answer from within the CISG itself.

Finally, the CISG does not determine whether the interest that is payable is calculated as simple or compound interest. These gaps have led to conflicting decisions. For example, courts have concluded that compound interest is available if granted under domestic law,[74] unavailable under the CISG (with an analogy to domestic law),[75] and available if the claimant can prove that it had to make additional interest payments because of the other party's default.[76]

B. *Reduction of the price*

Article 50 allows the buyer a form of substitutional relief that has no counterpart in common law systems. It gives a money allowance by way of a reduction in the contract price owed the seller. Article 50's measurement of recovery is familiar in civil law systems.[77] The term "price reduction" suggests to a common lawyer an offset or counterclaim to the contract price, where the offset or counterclaim is in the amount of damages. This is its meaning under the UCC.[78] "Price reduction" has a different meaning under Article 50. The reduction in price is stated in terms of a proportion, rather than an amount that reflects the difference between the monetary value of expected performance and actual performance. Moreover, the CISG does not consider a reduction in price a form of damages. Articles 74 through 76 give damage measures, and these measurements differ from the measurement given by Article 50. In addition, the CISG throughout carefully distinguishes between damages and a reduction in price. For instance, Articles 45(1) makes available to the aggrieved buyer as alternatives damages under Articles 74–77 and

---

[73] See *ECEM European Chem. Mktg. B.V. v. Purolite Co.*, 451 Fed. Appx. 73 (3d Cir. 2011).

[74] See Commercial Court Versailles (France), 12 March 2010, available at www.cisg.fr/decision .html?lang=fr&date=10-03-12.

[75] See Court of Appeals Brandenburg(Germany), 18 November 2008, available at http://cisgw3 .law.pace.edu/cases/081118g1.html.

[76] See Court of Appeals Antwerp (Belgium), 24 April 2006, available at http://cisgw3.law.pace .edu/cases/060424b1.html.

[77] See, e.g., Code civil [C. civ.] art. 1644 (Fr.); Burgerliches Gesetzbuch [BGB] [Civil Code] § 441 (3) (Ger.). For background, see Reinhard Zimmerman, The Law of Obligations: Roman Foundations of the Civilian Tradition 318, 327–29 (1990); A.M. Honore, *The History of the Aedilitian Actions from Roman to Roman-Dutch Law*, in Studies in the Roman Law of Sale 132 (David Daube ed., 1959). The place of the remedy in the CISG is described in Eric E. Bengston & Anthony J. Miller, *The Remedy of Price Reduction*, 27 Am. J. Comp. L. 275 (1979).

[78] See, e.g., U.C.C. § 2–717.

a price reduction under Article 50.[79] For its part, Article 44 allows an aggrieved party who has a reasonable excuse for failing to give the requisite notice of breach to reduce the price or claim damages (except for lost profits). This choice among remedies reflects the difference between damages and a reduction in price.

Three consequences follow from Article 50's remedy not being a form of damages. First, because the CISG does not consider a reduction in price to be damages, limits on recoverable damages do not apply to Article 50's remedy. Article 77 states a mitigation requirement: The breaching party may "claim a reduction in the damages" to the extent the aggrieved party could have mitigated them. As price reduction under Article 50 is not "damages," a buyer relying on the Article is not subject to a mitigation requirement. Likewise, Article 74 limits the loss recoverable as damages to loss that the breaching party foresaw or could reasonably have foreseen at the conclusion of the contract as a result of the breach. Again, as Article 50's price reduction is not damages, its recovery is not restricted by a foreseeability limitation.

Second, restrictions on the occasions in which damages may be recovered do not apply to Article 50. In particular, Article 79's exemption from liability, when it applies, exempts the breaching party only from liability for damages. An aggrieved buyer can still reduce the price in accordance with Article 50. This is because, according to Article 79(5), "[n]othing in this article prevents either party from exercising any right other than to claim damages under this Convention." A buyer is prevented from claiming damages against a seller whose liability for nonperformance is exempted by Article 79. However, Article 79(5) expressly preserves the buyer's right to exercise its non-damages remedies, such as reducing the price in accordance with Article 50.

Third, recovery under Article 50 can be combined with a recovery of damages. Article 45(2) provides that the buyer is not deprived of a right to claim damages by exercising his right to other remedies. Consequential damages are recoverable by the buyer under Article 74, as loss resulting from breach. Although a price reduction is not damages, the buyer relying on Article 50 may also recover consequential damages (subject to Article 74's foreseeability limitation). Article 50's remedy therefore is cumulative with Article 74's damage remedy. Of course, the injured buyer cannot claim both damages and a price reduction for the same portion of loss, as this would result in a duplicative recovery. Thus, the buyer cannot rely on both remedies for loss representing a nonconformity in the goods. However, consequential damages are not recoverable directly under Article 50, because the Article's remedy reduces price based on the nonconformity in the goods, not on loss resulting from the nonconformity.[80] Consequential damages therefore compensate for loss not

---

[79] See Article 45(1)(a) ("exercise the right provided in Articles 46 to 52"), (b) ("claim damages as provided in Article 74 to 77").

[80] See Article 50 ("If the goods do not conform with the contract ... the buyer may reduce the price in the same proportion as the value that the goods delivered had at the time of the delivery bears to the value that conforming goods would have had at that time").

recoverable under Article 50. For this reason, a price reduction along with consequential damages is not duplicative.

1. Conditions of price reduction

Article 50 gives the buyer the right to reduce the price when the seller breaches by delivering nonconforming goods. The breach need not be fundamental under Article 25 and, even if fundamental, the buyer may choose to reduce the price rather than avoid the contract. If the buyer has already paid the contract price, Article 50 entitles him to recover the amount of the reduction in price.[81] As a prerequisite of any remedy, the buyer must give the seller timely and proper notice of breach.[82] The right to a price reduction is made subject to the seller's right to cure the nonconformity in the goods, according to the Article's second sentence ("the seller ... remedies any failure to perform his obligations in accordance with article 37 or article 48 ..."). Thus, the buyer loses the right to reduce the price if the seller either cures the nonconformity or the buyer refuses to allow the seller to do so.

According to the majority of commentators, the buyer must declare a reduction in price.[83] This requires the buyer to state its intention to reduce the price. Both German and Swiss courts have required a declaration as a condition of exercising the remedy, with the German court relying on commentary to this effect.[84] There is no basis in Article 50 for the requirement,[85] and no good reason to impose one.

[81] The buyers' right to restitution of the price paid derived from Article 50 itself, not Article 81. Article 81 allows restitution only in the case of avoidance. See Article 81(2) and "Section V: Effects of Avoidance." A buyer who reduces the price in accordance with Article 50 has not avoided the contract.

[82] See Article 39(1). Article 44 allows the buyer to reduce the price even when it has not given the requisite notice, if it has a reasonable excuse for not doing.

[83] See Huber & Mullis, supra note 27, at 250; Markus Muller-Chen, *Article 50*, in Schlechtriem & Schwenzer, supra note 6, at 772; Ivo Bach, *Article 50*, in Kröll et al., supra note 48, at 756; UNCITRAL Digest 243 (para. 6) (2012).

[84] See Court of Appeals Munich (Germany), 2 March 1994, available at http://cisgw3.law.pace .edu/cases/940302g1.html; Court of Appeals Geneva (Switzerland), 15 November 2002, available at http://cisgw3.law.pace.edu/cases/021111. The German court relied on Peter Huber, *Article 50*, in Commentary on the UN Convention on the International Sale of Goods (CISG) 439 (Peter Schlechtriem ed., 2d (English) ed. 1998).

[85] The available diplomatic history relevant to the matter is inconclusive. At one point the British delegate to the Vienna Conference proposed that the phrase "the buyer may declare the price to be reduced" in an earlier version of Article 50 be eliminated because it seemed too weak. "May," according to the delegate, suggested that the buyer's entitlement was conditional rather than a unilateral right. See First Committee Deliberations, 23rd Meeting, 26 March 1980, in Documentary History, supra note 23, at 580 (para. 56). In response the delegates agreed that Article 50 gave the buyer the unilateral right to declare the price reduced. Id. at 581 (para. 62). This response is ambiguous. The delegates could have agreed that the buyer had the unilateral right which it may, but need not, exercise by a declaration. Or the consensus could have been that the buyer had the unilateral right which is exercised by a declaration of a reduction in price. The only safe inference from the incident is that the delegates agreed that Article 50 gave the buyer a unilateral right to reduce the price.

The CISG is careful to require a declaration, as Articles 49(1) and 61(1) do with respect to avoidance of the contract. The absence of a similar condition from Article 50 suggests that the buyer can reduce the price without declaring in advance its intention to do so. As important, there is no purpose served by requiring a declaration. To rely on any remedy, the buyer must give the seller notice of the fact and basis of its breach.[86] This breach-related information puts the seller in a position to cure the nonconformity in the goods, if it chooses do so. The seller does not benefit from the buyer's declaration that it intends to reduce the price. It has all the information it needs to decide whether or not to cure. Rather than give a good reason for the demand of a declaration, the commentary and slight case law simply assert the requirement. Nonetheless, it is a good bet that developing case law will follow the German and Swiss courts.

A more difficult question concerns the meaning of "nonconformity in the goods." Article 50's remedy applies only if the goods do not conform to the contract. Clearly goods that do not fit the description, packaging, quality, or quantity required by the contract are nonconforming.[87] Equally clear, a delay in delivery or defects in documents required by the contract constitute defects in performance, not in the goods. The performance is defective, even if the goods conform to the contract. Accordingly, the buyer can reduce the price for goods that do not meet the standards required by the contract but not for delay in delivery or defective documents.[88] The difficult case involves delivery of goods with defective title or that are subject to claims by third parties. The seller's delivery breaches its obligations imposed by Article 41 or Article 42. Are goods with defective title or subject to competing claims nonconforming? Or does their delivery constitute another sort of defective performance?

The diplomatic history reveals that delegates were aware of the problem of characterizing the breach. Rather than resolve it, they decided to leave its resolution to courts.[89] To date no court has done so. Most commentators take the position that goods subject to third party claims are not goods that "do not conform to the contract."[90] They construe "conformity" narrowly, limiting its reference to matters the CISG refers to by the term. Articles 35 and 36 refer to the respects in which the goods must conform to the contract, while Article 41 and Article 42 deal with third parties' claims to or concerning the buyer's right to use the goods. The narrow construction of "conformity" has support in the CISG's Section titles. Section II to Chapter II, Part III's heading reads: "Conformity of the goods and third party

---

[86] See Article 39(1).   [87] See Article 35(1).

[88] See District Court Düsseldorf (Germany), 5 March 1996, available at http://cisgw3.law.pace .edu/cases/960305g1.html (price reduction not available for late delivery).

[89] See Documentary History, supra note 23, at 582; Michael Will, *Reduction of Price*, in Bianca & Bonell, supra note 31, at 373 (para. 3.4).

[90] See, e.g., Markus Muller-Chen, *Article 50*, in Schlechtriem & Schwenzer, supra note 6, at 771; Huber & Mullis, supra note 27, at 248.

claims." The heading recognizes the distinction between a breach of Articles 35 and 36 ("conformity") and a breach of Article 41 or Article 42 ("third party claims").

The predominant view of commentators has textual support. Articles 35 and 36 refer to "conformity," and it therefore seems reasonable to limit "conformity" to standards for the goods set by those Articles. By giving the term a narrow meaning, the CISG's drafters might have made price reduction available only when delivered goods do not conform under Articles 35 and 36. True, Article 50's remedy is unavailable in other instances of defective performance, even though the breach can be as serious as the delivery of nonconforming goods. But this arguably is a restriction on the remedy made by the CISG's drafters.

One consideration, however, does not support the predominant view: legal certainty.[91] Delivered goods subject to third party claims are nonconforming in a nontechnical but recognizable sense. They fail to meet a standard of quality as clearly as when the goods fail to satisfy the contract description, for instance. This failure is unlike late delivery or tender of defective documents covering the goods, which clearly do not make the goods nonconforming. Finally, this failure is just as easy (or difficult) to verify as other standards with respect to the goods. For these reasons, legal certainty is not jeopardized by allowing third party claims to the goods to count as a "nonconformity" for purposes of Article 50's remedy.

2. Calculation of price reduction

Article 50 allows the buyer to reduce the contract price in the same proportion that the value of the nonconforming goods on the date of the delivery bears to the value that the goods would have had on the same date if they conformed to the contract. The proportional reduction in price allows the calculation of the reduced price the buyer owes. A simple formula calculates the reduced price directly, as follows:

Reduced price/Contract price = Value of the nonconforming goods delivered/ Value of conforming goods

Rearranging terms:

Reduced price = Value of nonconforming goods delivered/Value of conforming goods x Contract price

Article 50's remedy is stated in terms of the proportion by which the contract price may be reduced. This last formula calculates the reduced price the buyer owes. The difference between the contract price and the reduced price is the amount by which the buyer may reduce the contract price under Article 50.

An example may clarify the application of the formula. Assume that the seller and buyer agree to a sale of goods at a contract price of $60. At the time of delivery, the market price of the goods has decreased, so that conforming goods would only be

[91] For reliance on this consideration, see Huber & Mullis, supra note 27, at 248.

worth $40. The seller delivers goods that are nonconforming. As a result, at the time of delivery, they are only worth $30. Thus, they are worth only $30/$40, or ¾ of what they would have been worth had they been conforming. Assume the buyer needs the goods even in their defective state and therefore does not avoid the contract even though the nonconformity amounts to a fundamental breach. The buyer does not have to pay the full contract price or pay the contract price less damages for breach. Instead, it may invoke Article 50 to pay that part of the contract price that represents the fractional value of the goods relative to what they would have had if the delivery had conformed to the contract. Since that fractional value here is ¾, the buyer need only pay ¾ of the contract price or ¾ of $60, or $45. Thus, the buyer may reduce the price by $15.

To calculate the price reduced under Article 50, the date at which delivery occurs must be determined. Article 31 states the seller's obligations of delivery, and presumably the delivery occurs when the seller fulfills its obligations.[92] Under Article 31(a), when the sales contract involves carriage, the seller completes its delivery obligation when it hands the goods over to the first carrier for transmission to the buyer. In this case, therefore, delivery occurs before the buyer takes possession of the goods. Under Articles 31(b) and (c), when the sales contract does not involve carriage, the seller fulfills its delivery obligation when it places the goods at the buyer's disposal. Delivery here too can and usually will occur before the buyer takes possession of the goods.

3. Price reduction to zero: worthless goods

Assume that the seller delivers nonconforming goods that have no value at all. Courts that have considered the question have allowed the buyer to whom worthless goods have been delivered to reduce the price to zero.[93] Presumably, use of the price reduction formula would be unnecessary in such a case. The buyer could achieve the same result by simply avoiding the contract. A seller who has delivered worthless goods fundamentally breaches the contract in all but the most atypical cases. As a result, the buyer can avoid the contract, which relieves the buyer of the obligation to pay the contract price.

Given the relative ease of avoidance, the use of Article 50 in a "zero value" case suggests that the buyer is invoking the remedy because it has failed to comply with the requirements of avoidance. This may be, for example, because the buyer failed

---

[92] See Ivo Bach, in Kröll et al, supra note 48, at 760–61 for a summary of different points of delivery advocated by scholars.

[93] See, e.g., Federal Court (Australia) (*Castel Electronics Pty. Ltd. v. Toshiba Singapore Pte. Ltd.*), 28 September 2010, available at http://cisgw3.law.pace.edu/cases/100928a2.html; Federal Supreme Court (Germany), 2 March 2005, available at http://cisgw3.law.pace.edu/cases/050302g1.html; Supreme Court (Austria), 23 May 2005, available at http://cisgw3.law.pace.edu/cases/050523a3.html.

to give timely notice and is barred from avoiding the contract under Article 49(2). Some scholars are bothered by this result. They believe that allowing the buyer to reduce the price to zero permits an aggrieved party to circumvent the requirements of avoidance.[94] For instance, a buyer who fails to provide a timely notice of avoidance may be precluded from avoiding the contract and thus from recovering damages under Article 75 or 76. But that same buyer would, under the more liberal view of Article 50, still be entitled to pay a reduced price under Article 50. Nevertheless, the antipathy of some commentators to this result does not have much going for it. To begin with, Article 50's language does not limit the remedy to the delivery of nonconforming goods having some value. Its stated formula refers to the "value" of nonconforming goods, which can be zero. Article 50's terms aside, the limitation produces an arbitrary result without good reason. Suppose goods with a contract price of $100 are delivered at the time the market price of conforming goods remains at $100. Suppose too that Article 50's remedy applies only when nonconforming goods delivered have some value. If the nonconforming goods have a market value of 1 cent, the reduced price is 1 cent (1 cent/$100 x $100 = 1 cent), so that the buyer can reduce the $100 contract price by $99.99. However, if the nonconforming goods have no value, the buyer cannot reduce the price at all. The difference between nonconforming goods having no value and their having a value of one cent is negligible. The buyer is harmed in both cases. It is arbitrary to allow price reduction in the "some value" case but not in the "zero value" case. Allowing price reduction only in the former case introduces a discontinuity in remedy without justification. There is no good reason to deny the buyer in the zero value case the right to reduce the $100 contract price by $100, so that the reduced price is zero.

Finally, the charge that reliance on Article 50 in a zero value case "circumvents" the CISG's requirements for avoidance begs the question. The buyer circumvents these requirements only if the CISG does not allow the buyer access to Article 50. Avoidance requires the buyer to give notice of avoidance within a reasonable time.[95] Although Article 50 does not state a time limit within which the buyer must exercise its right to reduce the price, the right arguably must be exercised within a reasonable time too. However, the two periods need not be the same. Thus, it is possible that the buyer is too late to avoid the contract while not too late to timely exercise its right to reduce the price. Article 45's index of remedies suggests that Article 50's remedy is an alternative to avoidance. The different time periods for avoidance and the exercise of price reduction plausibly correspond to these alternatives. An argument therefore is needed to show that the appearance is deceptive and that Article 50's remedy is unavailable in zero value cases. The argument will be hard to make. If avoidance somehow displaces the

---

[94] See Ivo Bach, in Kröll et al., supra note 48, at 761–62 for a concise summary of the objections.
[95] See Article 49(2)(b).

remedy of price reduction in a zero value case, the same likely is true in an "almost zero value" case. Put another way, if allowing price reduction in a zero value case circumvents the requirements for avoidance, the same is true in an "almost zero value" case.

To be sure, avoidance and price reduction give nominally different results in a zero value case. If the buyer avoids the contract, Article 81(1) requires it to return the goods. If the buyer reduces the price, it retains them. However, this difference in outcome is unimportant because in a zero value case the goods are worthless. Neither party therefore can benefit from the goods, so that it does not matter who ultimately retains them. Thus, even if price reduction allows the buyer to circumvent avoidance in a zero value case, the possibility is harmless.

4. Damages versus price reduction

Article 74's damage measure calculates the loss to the aggrieved buyer who has retained the goods as the difference between the value of the conforming goods and the value of the nonconforming goods. The measure is sometimes described as "linear": damages are equal to loss from breach, so that damages increase directly with loss. By contrast, Article 50's reduction in price is a "proportional" measure. It reduces the contract price by the proportion of the value of the nonconforming goods delivered to value of hypothetical conforming goods to the contract price. Because the value of goods may deviate from the contract price, Article 50 may reduce the price by a different amount than a damage measure.

When would an aggrieved buyer prefer to reduce the price under Article 50 rather than recover damages? As Article 50's formula suggests, the desirability of price reduction depends on the value of the goods as compared to the contract price. Measuring value by market price, three cases are possible: (1) the market price remains stable and equal to the contract price, (2) the market price increases above the contract price, and (3) the market price declines below the contract price.

(1) *Stable market price.* When the market price at the time of delivery remains equal to the contract price, Article 50 gives the same recovery as damages under Article 74. For example, if the contract price is $100, the market price of conforming goods at the time of delivery remains $100 and the value of nonconforming delivered goods is $95, Article 74 gives $5 in damages ($100 - $95 = $5). Article 50 reduces the contract price by $5, so that the reduced price the buyer must pay also calculates to $95 ($95/$100 x $100 = $95).

(2) *Increased market price.* When the market price at the time of delivery has increased above the contract price, Article 74 gives a higher recovery in damages than Article 50's remedy. Assume again that the contract price is $100, but now

assume that the market price of conforming goods on delivery increases to $105 and the market price of the nonconforming goods delivered is $100. Now, damages under Article 74 again would be $10 ($105 value as expected - $100 value as delivered = $5). The aggrieved buyer would pay the contract price of $100, less Article 74 damages of $5 for a net price of $95. However, Article 50 reduces the contract price by only $4.77, so that the reduced price the buyer must pay is $95.23 ($100/$105 x $100 = $95.23). As a result, the buyer in the increasing market will choose Article 74 over Article 50.

(3) *Decline in market price.* When the market price of the goods at the time of delivery has declined below the contract price, the buyer's remedy under Article 50 is greater than the amount of recoverable damages under Article 74.[96] Assume again that the contract price is $100, but that the market price of conforming goods on delivery is $95 while the market price of the nonconforming goods delivered is $90. The buyer's damages under Article 74 are $5 ($95 - $90 = $5). It would be required to pay the contract price of $100, but is entitled to Article 74 damages of $5 for a net price of $95. By comparison, Article 50 allows the buyer to pay a reduced price of $94.73 ($90/$95 x $100 = $94.73) for the nonconforming goods. Accordingly, while Article 74 allows the buyer to deduct $5 in damages from the $100 contract price, Article 50 allows it to reduce the contract price by $5.27 ($100 - $94.73 = $5.27) – a greater amount.

Article 50 does not measure the buyer's expectation interest in either case (2) or case (3). In case (3) the buyer of course would most prefer to get out of the contract, because the market price is below contract price. By keeping the contract in place and reducing the price according to Article 50, the buyer still pays $94.73 for goods worth $90. The buyer is better off avoiding the contract and purchasing conforming goods at the now-prevailing market price of $95 (or nonconforming goods at the now-prevailing price of $90). Avoidance allows the buyer to shift back to the seller the risk of the decline in market price. However, the buyer will not always be able to avoid the contract or want to do so. Avoidance is not possible if the nonconformity is not serious enough to constitute a fundamental breach. Even if the breach is fundamental, the buyer may fail effectively to declare the contract avoided. Finally, the buyer might need the goods immediately even if they are substantially nonconforming Rather than avoiding the contract and having to return the goods,[97] it will want to retain them and rely on a non-avoidance-based remedy. In these instances, the buyer will prefer to reduce the price in accordance with Article 50 rather than obtain damages.

---

[96] A decline in market price is not necessary for Article 50 to give a greater recovery than damages. The same result follows if market price remains constant but the contract price is above it.

[97] See Article 81(1).

5. Evaluation

It is worth asking whether the remedy of price reduction is defensible. Although the remedy has long been available in civil law systems, we are dubious about its justification. A reduction in price does not always protect the buyer's expectation interest. Where the market price on delivery and the contract price are equal, Article 50's measure gives the same recovery as damages under Article 74. These damages assure the buyer its expectation. However, where market price goes above the contract price, Article 50 gives the buyer less than its expectation. For instance, in the example where the market price of conforming goods on delivery increases to $105, the contract price is $100 and the value of the nonconforming goods on delivery is $100, Article 50 reduces the price by $4.77, so that the buyer pays $95.23. The buyer's recoverable damage under Article 74 is $5, so that it pays $95 ($100 - $5) for nonconforming goods with a market value of $100. And where the market price on delivery declines below the contract price, as when the market price declines to $95, contract price is $100, and the value of the nonconforming goods is $90, Article 50 reduces the price by $5.27, while the buyer's damages under Article 74 are $5.00. Price reduction in this case therefore awards the buyer more than its expectation. In this way the remedy gives the seller an inefficient incentive to breach or perform. Where the reduction in price awards the buyer less than its expectation, the seller is encouraged to inefficiently breach the sales contract; where the remedy awards the buyer more than more its expectation, the remedy encourages the seller to inefficiently perform the contract.

Article 50's measure might be defended as a way of allocating the risk of fluctuations in market price ex post. The measure forces the buyer to share part of the risk of an increase in market price and the seller to share part of the risk of a market decline. This defense based on risk sharing is unconvincing. For one thing, the way in which Article 50 shares risk seems arbitrary. In the case of the above-market price increase, the seller obtains 4.6 percent of the market increase ($ .23 divided by $5 = 4.6 percent). However, the seller bears 5.4 percent of the market decrease in the case of the market decline above ($.27 divided by $5 = 5.4 percent). The asymmetric character of the sharing of gains and losses appears ad hoc.

In addition, the seller does not share any of the benefit of an increase in the market price of the goods. This is because Article 50 does not operate alone. The buyer also has the option of electing to recover damages. It will do so when damages give a greater recovery than is provided by Article 50's reduction in price. Article 45 (2) allows the buyer to recover damages rather than rely on Article 50's remedy. Thus, in the case of the example of a market price increase, damages give the buyer the entire $5 increase in market price. The seller does not get a share of the increase. When the buyer's other available remedies are taken into account, the risk sharing rationale therefore does not justify Article 50's remedy.

Finally, and most important, a fixed contract price allocates the risk of market price fluctuations: The seller bears the cost of market price increases and the buyer bears the cost of declines in price. It is unclear what therefore justifies Article 50's reallocation of risks already allocated by a fixed contract price. Because there is no reason to believe that most parties prefer to reallocate market risk ex post, reallocation is not a majoritarian default. If atypical parties want to shift the risk of changes in market price, their contract easily can provide for a different price term. In any case, Article 79 insulates the buyer from liability when its performance is exempted. The exemption, when it applies, already reallocates the risk of intervening events on contract performance. There is no justification for a further ex post reallocation of the risk of changes in market price when the buyer's performance is not exempted from liability.

Sometimes it is said that Article 50's reduction in price is a restitutionary measure. Restitution is noncontractual in nature. The measure's purpose is to eliminate the amount by which the breaching seller has been enriched by delivering nonconforming goods.[98] If so, a reduction in price does not achieve this restitutionary aim. This is because in a market decline Article 50 gives the buyer more than the seller benefitted by its breach. In the earlier example, the seller gained $5 by delivering nonconforming goods: the difference between the $95 market price for conforming goods on delivery and the $90 market price for the nonconforming goods. However, Article 50 allows the buyer to reduce the price by $5.27– $.27 more than the seller was enriched by its breach. The measure therefore, at best, only approximates a restitutionary measure.

C. *Specific relief*

The CISG gives the aggrieved party a right to require performance of the contract. Article 46(1) provides that "[t]he buyer may require performance by the seller of his obligations, unless [it] has resorted to a remedy which is inconsistent with this requirement." Article 62 gives the seller the same right to the buyer's performance of the contract. It provides that the seller may require the buyer to pay the contract price, unless the seller has resorted to a remedy inconsistent with this requirement.

In several respects the right to specific relief is broad. The relief is available at the request of the aggrieved party. Subject to the Article 28 proviso that we discuss later, a tribunal to which the request is directed does not have the discretion to refuse specific relief and award damages instead. Articles 46(1) and 62 give the aggrieved party the right to compel the breaching party to perform its obligations ("his obligations"). The breaching party therefore can be required to perform all of its obligations under the contract, not just obligations of delivery or payment. For example, Article 62 entitles the seller to compel the buyer to have established a

---

[98] See, e.g., Gunter H. Treitel, Remedies for Breach of Contract: A Comparative Account 108 (1988).

letter of credit naming the seller as beneficiary, as required by the contract.[99] Article 46(3) even entitles the injured buyer to require the seller to repair nonconforming goods, unless repair is unreasonable in the circumstances.

Finally, Articles 46(1) and 62 impose only one restriction on specific relief: The aggrieved party cannot have already resorted to a remedy inconsistent with obtaining the relief. The operative terms in the restriction are "resorted" and "inconsistent." Avoidance of the contract is inconsistent with specific relief, because avoidance ends the contract while specific relief enforces it. Likewise, a buyer who has reduced the price under Article 50 is compensated for the seller's breach. Specific performance would force the seller to perform an obligation, even though it already has compensated the buyer for the failure to perform. On the other hand, an injured buyer who has not acted to avoid the contract or reduce the price has not "resorted" to a remedy at all. Accordingly, Article 46(1) does not prevent the buyer from requesting specific performance as an alternative to avoidance or a price reduction. Damages can compensate the injured party for loss from breach even when the breaching party is later forced to perform its contractual obligations. A request for damages therefore is consistent with a request for specific relief.[100] Damages can be sought either as an alternative to specific relief or in addition to it. Of course, a party who already has recovered damages for loss from breach cannot obtain specific relief to avoid the loss.

It is worth noticing a requirement that does *not* apply to specific relief: mitigation. Although Article 77 requires the injured party to mitigate its loss, the requirement by its own terms applies only to "damages." Accordingly, if the injured party fails to take reasonable measures to reduce its loss from breach, Article 77 entitles the breaching party to "claim a reduction in the damages . . ." Because specific relief under Articles 46(1) and 62 does not constitute "damages," Article 77's mitigation requirement does not apply to it. The inapplicability of mitigation to specific relief is not an oversight. Article 45 and 61's respective lists of remedies both carefully distinguish between "damages" and "rights." The latter include the right to specific relief given by Articles 46 and 62. Applying a mitigation requirement to specific relief ignores the CISG's articulated divide between substitutional relief ("damages") and non-substitutional relief ("rights"), which includes specific relief. Both the relevant diplomatic history and commentary support the inapplicability of mitigation to specific relief.[101]

---

[99] See ICC Case No. 7197 (1992), available at www.cisg.law.pace.edu/cases/927197i1.html.

[100] See ICC Case No. 12173 (2004) (para. 53), available at http://cisgw3.law.pace.edu/cases/041217i1.html; Secretariat Commentary on the 1978 Draft, in Documentary History, supra note 23, at 426 (paras. 4, 6).

[101] See Steven Walt, *For Specific Performance Under the United Nations Sales Convention*, 16 Texas Int'l L. J. 211, 227–28 (1991); cf. Honnold/Flechtner, supra note 61, at 598 (applying the mitigation requirement to specific performance as not making a "serious inroad" to the rule requiring specific performance).

1. Article 28's limitation on specific relief

The CISG makes specific relief generally available to the injured party. This reflects its routine availability in civil law systems, at least as a matter of formal law.[102] By contrast, common law systems and UCC § 2–709 and § 2–716 treat specific relief as an exceptional remedy.[103] The remedy is awarded in the discretion of the court only when damages are inadequate to compensate for the injured party's loss, perhaps because the unique nature of the goods or a thin market for cover renders damages difficult to ascertain. The difference in the approaches to specific relief among legal systems reflects in part differences in judgment about the nature of contractual obligation. Some legal systems implicitly view the contractual obligation of performance as sufficiently sacrosanct as to permit its enforcement, even against an unwilling trading partner. Hence, the maxim *pacta sunt servanda*. Other legal systems reject the notion that unwilling parties should be judicially coerced to perform if they are willing to compensate the injured actors, or construe the "promise" as one to perform or to pay, rather than only to perform.

The division among legal systems with respect to specific performance also implicitly reflects the degree of concern about the effect of the remedy on efficient breach. Requiring a party specifically to perform discourages breaches that may be socially desirable. If a breaching seller, for example, is willing fully to compensate the aggrieved buyer for its losses, including any lost profits, reputational injury from losing downstream contracts, or any other losses imaginable, then presumably the seller is breaching because it can provide the same goods to an alternative buyer who is willing to pay an amount that allows the seller to compensate the first buyer fully and still profit from fulfilling the second contract. That scenario suggests a social gain if the seller fulfills the second contract, not the first. Under these circumstances, it is unclear why we would want to require the seller to perform the first contract. One might contend that the second buyer should be required to obtain the goods from the first buyer or from alternative seller. But if the second buyer is offering an idiosyncratically high price to the seller, presumably each of those alternative avenues would require it to incur additional transaction costs. If the first buyer is in a better position than the breaching seller or the second buyer to enter into a replacement for the breached contract, then costs are saved by denying specific performance and granting compensatory damages. That result places the first buyer in the same position as performance after it enters the cover contract that it is best situated to conclude.

---

[102] See, e.g., Burgerliches Gesetzbuch [BGB] [Civil Code] § 241 (Ger.); Code civil [C.c.] art. 1142 (Fr.); Schweizerisches Obligationenrecht [OR] [Code of Obligations] art. 97 (Switz.); Codigo Civil [C.C.] art. 475 (Braz.).

[103] For the discrepancy between doctrine and case law, see Douglas Laycock, The Death of the Irreparable Injury Rule (1991).

For example, a buyer of mass produced goods may readily enter into a cover contract for fungible goods if the original seller fails to perform. Requiring the seller either to perform or to find another seller of the same goods may simply impose additional costs that could be avoided by an award of damages. Some legal systems, particularly common law systems, appear to take this view and award specific performance only where the aggrieved party is poorly positioned to enter a replacement contract. A contract for unique goods is the standard example of a contract in which the aggrieved party cannot easily enter a replacement contract. Other legal systems, particularly civil law systems, take a different view. They allow more liberal use of specific performance, perhaps based on the belief that promises should be performed and that damages are not an appropriate substitute for promise-keeping.

That is not to say, however, that an award of specific performance necessarily produces an inefficient result. Damages can induce inefficient breach if the loss from breach is measured inaccurately, so that the injured party is undercompensated. In this case a party might breach even when performance yields greater gains than breach. Whether specific relief or damages is the preferred default remedy depends on whether the risk of inefficient performance is greater than the risk of inefficient breach. This ultimately is an empirical matter. There is almost no relevant data collected to decide the question.[104]

As a compromise between civil and common law approaches to specific relief, Article 28 limits its availability under the CISG. The Article provides:

> If, in accordance with the provisions of this Convention, one party is entitled to require performance of any obligation by the other party, a court is not bound to enter a judgment for specific performance unless the court would do so under its own law in respect of similar contracts of sale not governed by this Convention.

The limitation stated in the Article is that the forum court is not required to order specific relief, unless it would order the relief in like contracts governed by its own law. To apply Article 28's limitation on specific relief, the forum court must ask two questions. First, is the specific relief sought by the party available under the CISG? Second, if the relief is available, would the court order it for like contracts ("similar contracts") otherwise governed by its own law? If affirmative answers are given to both questions, the forum court must order specific relief. Otherwise, Article 28 permits, but does not require, the court to refuse.

The English language version of Article 28 refers only to "specific performance." Specific performance is the buyer's right to obtain performance from the seller. The

---

[104] For an event study measuring the effects of specific relief on share price, see Yair Listokin, *The Empirical Case for Specific Performance: Evidence from the IBP-Tyson Litigation*, 2 J. Emp. Legal Stud. 469 (2005); for experimental evidence on the effect of specific relief as a default remedy, see Ben Depoorter & Stephan Tontrup, *How the Law Frames Moral Intuitions: The Expressive Effect of Specific Performance*, 54 Ariz. L. Rev. 673 (2012).

Article does not refer to "specific relief," which includes the seller's right to the buyer's performance, such as paying the contract price. Nonetheless, there is no reason to think that the phrase limits only the buyer's right to obtain performance from the seller.[105] Such a limitation is arbitrary, because there is no principled reason why Article 28 would limit only one sort of specific relief. After all, the Article responds to the concerns of delegates from common law systems who opposed the free availability of all types of specific relief under the CISG.[106] The few tribunals that have mentioned the Article appear to believe that it applies to the seller's right to obtain performance from the buyer as well.[107]

The phrases, "its [i.e., the court's] own law" and "similar contracts of sale not governed by this Convention," are a bit opaque. "Its own law" likely refers to the substantive domestic law of the judicial forum. Not only do other interpretations strain the plausible meaning of the phrase. They also frustrate the purpose served by Article 28: to allow the forum court not to order specific performance when doing so would not be required under its own domestic law with respect to a like contract. For instance, suppose that "its own law" refers to the law selected by the forum court's conflict of laws rules applicable to sales contracts not governed by the CISG. Because the law selected varies depending on the particular sales contract and the circumstances of the transaction, "its own law" is indeterminate in reference. The phrase might pick out the law of a civil law system that makes specific relief routinely available or the law of a common law system which restricts its availability. Unless "its own law" refers to the substantive domestic law of the judicial forum, Article 28's limitation cannot guarantee that a common law court will not have to order specific relief when it would not do so under its own domestic law. The few courts that have applied Article 28 understand the phrase to refer to the judicial forum's substantive domestic law.[108]

"Similar contracts of sale not governed by this Convention" is harder to interpret. The phrase is ambiguous, giving different possible results. "Similar contracts of sale" might refer to contracts for the sale of goods governed by the forum court's substantive domestic law. Specific aspects of these sales contracts, or the circumstances in which they are concluded, need not be "similar" to the sales contracts governed by the CISG. For instance, suppose the forum court's substantive domestic sales law is Article 2 of the UCC. Article 2 governs a range of sales of goods contracts, some of

---

[105] For the suggestion that it might, see E. Allan Farnsworth, *Specific Relief and Damages*, 27 Am. J. Comp. L. 247, 249 (1979). Farnsworth does not explain why Article 28's drafters might have intended to limit its application to specific performance.

[106] See First Committee Deliberation, 19 March 1980, in Documentary History, supra note 23, at 525–26 (paras. 43–44).

[107] See Commercial Court Bern (Switzerland), 22 December 2004, available at http://cisgw3.law .pace.edu/cases/041222s1.html.

[108] See, e.g., Commercial Court Bern (Switzerland), 22 December 2004, available at http://cisgw3 .law.pace.edu/cases/041222s1.html; *Magellan Int'l Corp. v. Salzgitter Handel GmbH*, 76 F. Supp.2d 919 (N.D.Ill. 1999).

which do not have features similar to sales contracts governed by the CISG. Specific relief with respect to these contracts might not be permitted by UCC § 2–716(1) or § 2–709(1)(a). Alternatively, "similar contracts of sale" might refer to sale of goods contracts governed by the forum's substantive domestic law that share specific aspects of sales contracts governed by the CISG. Such aspects might include sales of goods with few close local substitutes and high transportation costs. The lack of close substitutes or the presence of high transportation costs makes cover or resale difficult. Given these facts, UCC § 2–716(1) or § 2–709(1)(a) might require specific relief (if requested) in the circumstances. To date no tribunal has focused on the ambiguity in the phrase "similar contracts of sale not governed by this Convention."

Magellan International Corp. v. *Salzgitter Handel GmbH*[109] illustrates Article 28's application. There, an American buyer ordered steel bars according to its specifications from a German seller. When the parties disputed the terms of the contract and the seller refused to deliver, the buyer sued in an Illinois federal district court asking for specific performance of the contract. The seller moved to dismiss for failure to state a claim. The court denied the motion. It noted that the forum court's own law is § 2–716(1) of the UCC. Under § 2–716(1) a court may order specific performance if the goods are unique or "in other proper circumstances." Official Comment 1 to § 2–716 states that the inability to cover is "strong evidence" of "other proper circumstances." Relying on the Comment, the court concluded that the buyer had sufficiently pled its complaint for specific performance.[110]

The procedural posture of the case limits the lessons that can be drawn from the *Magellan* court's application of Article 28. The court was considering the Article only in connection with a motion to dismiss the complaint. Thus, it did not have to decide whether the buyer in fact was unable to obtain from other suppliers the specially manufactured steel bars it had ordered from the seller. The court only had to determine whether the buyer had alleged facts which, if true, entitled it to specific performance: "Given the centrality of the replaceability issue in determining the availability of specific relief under the UCC, a pleader need allege only the difficulty of cover to state a claim under that section [§ 2–716(1)]. Magellan [the buyer] did that."[111] The case therefore does not stand for the proposition that specific performance is routinely available in American courts to enforce contracts governed by the CISG. A more straightforward application of Article 28 is provided by a Swiss case.[112] Swiss law gives the seller the unqualified right to recover the contract price from the buyer. Relying on this law, the Swiss court concluded that Article 28's restriction "can be disregarded in the case at hand." It awarded the seller the price under Article 62.

One plausible effect of the compromise struck by the interaction of Articles 28, 46 (1), and 62 is to generate a race to the courthouse or forum shopping to enforce

---

[109] 76 F. Supp.2d 919 (N.D.Ill. 1999).   [110] Id. at 926.   [111] Id. at 926.
[112] See Commercial Court Bern (Switzerland), 22 December 2004, available at http://cisgw3.law .pace.edu/cases/041222s1.html.

contracts without forum selection clauses. Assume that an American buyer and a German seller are in a dispute concerning a breach of a contract for the sale of goods governed by the CISG. If the German seller desires to avoid a decree of specific performance, it might rush to file a lawsuit in the United States before the American buyer is able to file a lawsuit in Germany, on the theory that American law is more restrictive on the issue than German courts. One can also imagine the opposite preference operating: The buyer, anticipating the seller's breach, might file suit in Germany seeking to order the seller to deliver according to the contract. The contractual response to this prospect is to include a forum selection clause and a governing law clause in the sales agreement to prevent forum shopping for a remedy. Parties will select a forum selection clause, taking into account the effect of specific relief on the cost of performance and therefore on the contract price. Specific relief increases the cost of performance because it allows the aggrieved party to require performance even when the gains from breach exceed that party's loss. At the same time, the remedy avoids the risk that a damage award undercompensates the aggrieved party for its loss from breach. If the parties value specific relief by an amount more than the increase in the contract price associated with the remedy, the contract will contain forum selection clause designating a forum that makes specific relief routinely available. If they value specific relief by an amount less than this increase in the contract price, the forum selection clause will designate a forum that makes specific relief available only as an extraordinary remedy or not at all.

2. Specific relief in arbitration

Article 28's limitation does not apply to arbitration. According to the Article, "a court" is not required to order specific performance if its own law would not require it do so with respect to like contracts not governed by the CISG. Arbitral tribunals are not courts. Thus, Article 28 does not restrict the availability of specific relief in arbitration. The only limits on the relief imposed by the CISG are those stated in Articles 46(1) and 62. This reflects the predominant preference of parties to international sales contracts for arbitration. In addition, few disappointed buyers seek specific performance, and relatively few sellers pursue an action for the price.[113] Most injured parties do better making other arrangements and recovering damages from the breaching party. Given the frequency of arbitration under the CISG and

[113] See Alan Schwartz, *The Myth that Promisees Prefer Supercompensatory Remedies: An Analysis of Contracted for Damage Measures*, 100 Yale L. J. 468, 488 (1990); for the sparse use of specific performance even when the remedy is available by right, see Heinrik Lando & Caspar Rose, *On the Enforcement of Specific Performance in Civil Law Countries*, 24 Int'l Rev. L. & Econ. 473 (2004); Treitel, supra note 96, at Remedies for Breach of Contract: A Comparative Account 53. For the same observation with respect to arbitral awards, see Sigvard Jarvin, *Non-Pecuniary Remedies: The Practices of Declaratory Relief and Specific Performance in International Commercial Arbitration*, in Contemporary Issues in International Arbitration and Mediation: The Fordham Papers 2007 167, 182 (Arthur W. Rovine ed., 2007).

infrequency of actions for specific relief, the dearth of decisions applying Article 28 is unsurprising. UNCITRAL cites six court cases that discuss Article 28 in its 2012 Digest of CISG case law. By comparison, the 2012 Digest cites thirty-one cases that discuss Article 46 and 132 cases that discuss Article 62.

Arbitral tribunals occasionally (but without being required to) invoke Article 28. The arbitral tribunal in *ICC Case 12173* had to decide whether a liquidated damages clause and a clause calling for specific performance in a contract were mutually exclusive remedies.[114] In determining that the buyer could rely on both remedies, the tribunal mentioned but did not rely on Article 28. Similarly, a 2006 Russian arbitral tribunal denied the buyer's request for specific performance.[115] In reaching its conclusion that the seller was not obligated to deliver when the buyer failed to pay on an unrelated contract, the tribunal found that its result "corresponds with" Article 28. Apparently the arbitral tribunal determined that a Russian court would not be required to order specific performance in a similar contract governed by Russian domestic law. Article 28 is an irrelevant legal limitation in both arbitrations, because the tribunals are not courts. The invocation of the Article therefore is dictum.

Rules outside the CISG do not limit the authority of arbitrators to order specific relief. The rules of arbitral institutions rarely deal with the remedies an arbitral award may provide.[116] The prevailing view is that arbitrators may award specific relief if the remedy is within the scope of the arbitration agreement and not prohibited by applicable law. Awards issued in arbitrations conducted under the major arbitral institutions have included specific relief.[117] For instance, *ICC Case 7453* included an award of specific performance when the arbitration agreement called for all disputes arising in connection with the contract to be "finally settled" by the arbitrator.[118] In *ICC Case 7197*, a sales contract governed by the CISG called for the buyer to have established a letter of credit.[119] The buyer failed to do so. Noting that Article 62 gave the seller the right to require the buyer to perform its contractual obligations, the arbitral tribunal's award ordered the buyer to establish the letter of

[114] See ICC Arbitration Case No. 12173 (2004), available at http://cisgw3.law.pace.edu/cases/041217311.html.

[115] See Tribunal of International Commercial Arbitration (Russia), 30 June 2006, available at http://cisgw3.law.pace.edu/cases/06063011.html.

[116] An exception is the American Arbitration Association Commercial Arbitration Rule 43(a), which expressly allows for specific performance; cf. 1996 English Arbitration Act § 48(5)(b) (arbitrator has power to order specific performance of a contract other than a contract relating to land); Ontario Arbitration Act § 31 (1991) (power to order specific relief).

[117] See Performance as a Remedy: Non-Monetary Relief in International Arbitration (Michael E. Schneider & Joachim Kröll eds., 2011) (case studies of awards under major arbitral institutions); cf. 2 Gary B. Born, International Commercial Arbitration 2480 (2009) (courts routinely uphold arbitral awards of specific performance).

[118] See ICC Case No. 7453 (1994), Collection of ICC Awards: 1996–2000 109 (Jean-Jacques Ardaldez, Yves Derains & Dominque Hascher eds., 2003).

[119] See ICC Case No. 7197 (1992), available at http://cisgw3.law.pace.edu/cases/927197i1.html.

credit provided in the contract. The tribunal (properly) did not mention Article 28's limitation on specific relief.

Unsurprisingly, arbitral tribunals will not order specific relief if the remedy is impractical or impossible to enforce. A Zurich Chamber of Commerce arbitral award refusing specific performance relies on the constraint of practicality.[120] The arbitration involved the Russian seller's failure to deliver under a series of long-term contracts for the sale of aluminum governed by the CISG. The arbitral tribunal gave two reasons for refusing the buyers' request that the seller be required to deliver shipments under the contracts. One was that the CISG does not provide for specific performance in the circumstances. This is clearly mistaken; Article 46(1) provides for the relief. The tribunal's second reason was that specific performance is an impractical remedy even if the CISG provides for it: The buyers cannot expect "to have an award enforced in Russia providing the [seller] must specifically perform its obligations under the various contracts for the next eight to ten years ..."[121] The difficulty of supervising long-term contracts, not Article 28's limitation, restricts the availability of an award of specific performance.

II. AVOIDANCE-BASED REMEDIES

If the injured party can avoid the contract and chooses to do so, it can recover damages. The CISG allows the injured party to choose among three options for measuring damages. It can recover damages for its loss from breach under Article 74. Alternatively, it can obtain substitute performance and recover damages under Article 75. Substitute performance for the buyer is the purchase of replacement goods, and for the seller the resale of the breached goods. The injured party's third option is to forgo substitute performance and recover damages under Article 76 measured by the market price ("current price") of the contract goods. Article 74 gives the injured party damages equal to its foreseeable loss. Article 75 gives damages equal to the difference between the contract price and the price of the substitute transaction. Article 76 gives damages equal to the difference between the contract price and the "current" price of the goods. Articles 75 and 76's damages measures have close counterparts under some domestic sales laws. Article 75 corresponds to a cover measure of damages, and Article 76 to a "market price" measure.[122]

---

[120] See Zurich Chamber of Commerce (Switzerland), 31 May 1996, available at http://cisgw3.law
.pace.edu/cases/960531s1.html.

[121] For another instance of the constraint of practicality, see ICC Case 8032 (1995), 21 Yr. Bk. Comm. Arb. 113 (A.J. van der Berg ed., 1996) (specific performance rejected because practically impossible to enforce); see also Jarvin, supra note 106, at 180–81.

[122] See, e.g., §§ U.C.C. 2–712, 2–713; Nieuw Burgerlijk Wetboek [NBW] arts. 7.36, 7.37 (Nether.); Burgerliches Gesetzbuch [BGB] [Civil Code] §§ 249, 252, Handelgesetzbuch [HGB] [Commercial Code] § 376(1), (2) (Ger.); Schweizerrisches Obligationenrecht [OR] [Code of Obligations] art. 191(2), (3) (Switz.); Code civil [C. civ.] art. 1144 (Fr.).

In principle the CISG's damage measures all protect the injured party's expectation interest. Article 74 measures damages directly according to loss from breach, so that damages put the injured party in the position it would be have been in had the contract been performed. Articles 75 and 76 measure loss from breach indirectly, as the difference between the price of a substitute transaction or market price, respectively, and the contract price. In practice these damage measures can yield different recoveries. The remedies in Articles 74–76 use different formulae to measure damages. For instance, Article 75's substitute performance formula uses the price of the substitute transaction, while Article 76's current price differential uses (as a general matter) the market price at the place of delivery and at the time of avoidance. Because these formulae measure the price of goods at different times, they may not give the same damages. Assume, for example, that the seller breaches a contract for the sale of goods at a contract price of $100. Assume that on the day of the breach, the current price of the goods is $105 and that the next day the buyer reasonably purchases goods in substitution at the reasonable price of $106. The Article 75 measure would give damages of $5, while the Article 76 measure would give damages of $6. In addition, the remedies provided by Articles 74–76 require proof of different elements and therefore have different proof costs associated with their use. For this reason, the injured party who bears the burden of proving these elements may not be indifferent between damage measures.

A. *Substitute performance measure: Article 75*

Article 75 measures the injured party's damages as the difference between the price of a substitute transaction and the contract price. If the injured party is the seller, the price of the substitute transaction is the price at which it has resold the contract goods. For the injured buyer, it is the price at which it has covered by making an alternative purchase of comparable goods. Article 75's last clause ("as well as . . .") allows the injured party to recover additional damages under Article 74. The most common sort of additional damages will be incidental expenses associated with making a substitute transaction, such as negotiation costs and transportation expenses, and consequential damages.

The CISG does not allow the non-breaching party to elect between measuring its damages under Article 75 or under Article 76. Although some domestic law is unclear about the election of remedies,[123] the CISG clearly bars an election between Article 75's substitute performance formula and Article 76's market price formula. According to Article 76, the injured party who has avoided the contract

---

[123] Compare U.C.C. §§ 2–703, 2–711 with §§ 2–712 comm. 3 (first paragraph), 2–703 comm. 1. See John A. Sebert, *Remedies Under Article 2 of the Uniform Commercial Code: An Agenda for Review*, 130 U. Pa. L. Rev. 360, 380–83 (1981); Ellen Peters, *Remedies for Breach of Contract Relating to the Sale of Goods Under the Uniform Commercial Code: A Roadmap for Article 2*, 73 Yale L. J. 199, 203–06 (1963).

may recover damages according to its market price formula "if he has not made a purchase or resale under Article 75." Thus, an injured party who has obtained substitute performance that meets Article 75's requirements may not use Article 76 to calculate its damages. Because Article 76's exclusion is limited to substitute performance under Article 75, the aggrieved party still has the option of measuring its damages by Article 74, in accordance with its general rule.[124] Of course, before the injured party obtains substitute performance it retains the option of obtaining substitute performance and calculating its damages by Article 75 or not doing so and calculating its damages by Article 76.

To apply the bar against election of remedy, the party bearing the burden of proving damages must establish that the injured party did not obtain substitute performance under Article 75. Courts and commentators maintain that the injured party bears the burden of proving its damages under Articles 74–76.[125] This means an injured party relying on Article 76's market price formula must establish that it has not obtained substitute performance in accordance with Article 75. For the same reason, the injured party calculating its damages under Article 75 must prove the elements needed to calculate them. Thus, the injured party must show that the transaction it entered into was a substitute for the breach contract. For example, the injured seller is required to show the goods it resells are those identified to the breached contract.[126] Similarly, the injured buyer must establish that the purchase it makes is a cover purchase for the breached contract.

B. *Article 75's requirements*

Article 75 requires that the substitute performance be obtained "in a reasonable manner" and "within a reasonable time." The former requirement sometimes is

---

[124] See Court of Appeals Graz (Austria), 29 July 2004, available at http://cisgw3.law.pace.edu/cases/040729a3.html; Rechtbank Limburg (Netherlands) 16 April 2014, available at http://cisgw3.law.pace.edu/cases/140416n1.html.

[125] See CISG Advisory Council Opinion No. 6, Calculation of Damages Under CISG Article 74 ¶ 2 (2006), available at www.cisg.law.pace.edu/cisg/CISG-AC-op6.html; Federal Supreme Court (Germany), 9 January 2002, available at http://cisgw3.law.pace.edu/cases/020109g1.html; District Court Vigevano (Italy), 12 February 2000, available at http://cisgw3.law.pace.edu/cases/000712i3.html; Court of Appeals Zweibrucken (Germany), 31 March 1998, available at http://cisgw3.law.pace.edu/cases/980331g1.html. It is unclear whether the CISG or applicable domestic law allocates the burden of proving damages to the injured party. Most commentators assert that the CISG governs the burden of proving damages. See Ingeborg Schwenzer, *Article 74*, in Schlechtriem & Schwenzer, supra note 6, at 1025 ("nearly undisputed" that burden of proof allocation governed by the CISG); Franco Ferrari, *Burden of Proof Under the CISG*, Review of the Convention on Contracts for the International Sale of Goods (CISG) 1 (2000–2001), available at www.cisg.law.pace.edu/cisg/biblio/ferrari5.html; Magnus, supra note 30, at 51–2 (1997). For a critical assessment of this view, see infra IX.

[126] See, e.g., CIETAC Arbitration Award (China), 27 April 2000, available at http://cisgw3.law.pace.edu/cases/000427c1.html; CIETAC Arbitration Award (China), 30 November 1997, available at http://cisgw3.law.pace.edu/cases/971130c1.html.

particularly difficult to apply. Article 75 does not even provide measures of reasonable cover purchase or resale found in UCC § 2–706, such as requirements of notice of an intent to resell or reasonable identification to the broken contract. Nor does it distinguish between private sales and public sales as does UCC § 2–706.

A "reasonable manner" connotes the means by which a substitute performance is obtained. As one arbitral tribunal a bit unhelpfully put it, acting in a reasonable manner requires acting as a "prudent and reasonable" party would act.[127] Presumably "reasonableness" provides sufficient latitude that the aggrieved party does not have to resell or cover on the exact terms as the original contract. Article 75 requires only that the substitute goods be purchased "in replacement" for the original goods. If the repurchased goods are of somewhat higher quality, and thus of higher cost than the original goods, a buyer who can demonstrate a need to obtain the replacement goods in a timely manner and the relative unavailability of identical goods should be able to recover the difference between the contract price and the price of the substitute transaction.

Importantly, reasonableness allows some flexibility in the price of the substitute transaction. In principle goods can be resold in a reasonable manner at a low price or replacement goods can be purchased in a reasonable manner at a high price. As far as Article 75's language goes, the high or low price of substitute performance does not by itself affect the reasonableness of the performance.

Courts nonetheless have relied on the price of a substitute transaction to determine its reasonableness. In an early case a German appellate court found that a resale price about a quarter of the contract price made the resale unreasonable.[128] A more recent French case concluded that the manner of the buyer's cover was unreasonable when the buyer paid close to double the price the breaching seller offered.[129] The results in these cases can be understood in two different ways. The courts could be assuming that the reasonableness of a substitute transaction includes price, so that a price significantly above or below contract price makes the transaction unreasonable. Article 75's "reasonable manner" requirement does not allow price to figure in the way in which a substitute transaction is obtained. Alternatively, price can be circumstantial evidence that bears on the reasonableness of the manner of the substitute transaction. A very high or very low price, without countervailing evidence, makes it likely that the substitute transaction was unreasonable. Using price merely as evidence of the reasonableness of a transaction does not go beyond Article 75's "reasonable manner" requirement. *ICC Award 8128*[130] appears to use

[127] See ICC Case No. 10274 (1999), available at http://cisgw3.law.pace.edu/cases/990274i1.html.

[128] See Court of Appeals Hamm (Germany), 22 September 1992, available at http://cisgw3.law.pace.edu/cases/920922g1.html.

[129] See Court of Appeals Rennes (France), 27 May 2008, available at http://cisgw3.law.pace.edu/cases/920922g1.html.

[130] See ICC Case No. 8128 (1995), available at http://cisgw3.law.pace.edu/cases/958128i1.html.

price in this way. There the injured buyer made a cover purchase at a much higher price than could have been paid with a more leisurely purchase. Noting that the buyer had to cover quickly in order to meet a deadline with its sub-buyer, the arbitral tribunal concluded that the higher price did not make the cover unreasonable. The tribunal relied on the circumstances in which the buyer covered to determine the reasonableness of the cover transaction. Price was only one piece of evidence bearing on the reasonableness of the cover.[131]

The "reasonable time" requirement obviously limits the discretion of the aggrieved party to play the market in response to the other party's breach. If, for example, a buyer believes that market prices will decline after the breach, the buyer may wait before entering into a cover transaction in the expectation that it will be able to obtain the same goods at a price lower than the contract price. If prices do in fact decline, the buyer will be quite pleased that the seller breached. If prices increase, however, the buyer bears no risk because it is entitled to recover the difference between the contract price and the cover price from the breaching seller. In effect, the buyer is gambling with the seller's money. The "reasonable time" requirement constrains the ability of the buyer (or the seller) to act in that manner. The concept of "reasonable time," therefore, should be construed in light of its objective of reducing strategic behavior by the aggrieved party. That is, what constitutes a reasonable time in any case should depend at least in part on the volatility of prices in the relevant market.

One clear condition of "reasonable time," however, is that it is measured from the time "after avoidance." In *Profi-Parkiet Sp. Zoo v. Seneca Hardwoods LLC*,[132] a purchaser of wood flooring claimed damages for a substitute transaction at a price in excess of the contract price. The court noted that the invoice submitted by the buyer was dated prior to the time when the breach was discovered by the buyer. The court concluded, quite logically, that "plaintiff could not have replaced goods that it was unaware were deficient," and denied recovery for that alleged replacement. The court did, however, allow the same buyer to recover Article 75 damages for the difference between the price paid to the breaching seller and the price paid to another seller from whom the buyer made a replacement purchase three months after discovering the breach.

In calculating damages under Articles 74–76, the injured party's duty to mitigate must be taken into account. Article 77 requires the party to take reasonable measures to mitigate its loss. The breaching party may reduce damages for which it is liable by

---

[131] To the same effect is ICC Case 10274 in which the seller resold breached goods for 20 percent less than the contract price after unsuccessfully trying to resell them at a higher price. The tribunal found that in the circumstances the seller had acted in a reasonable manner and awarded damages calculated according to Article 75. See ICC Case No. 10274 (1999), available at http://cisgw3.law.pace.edu/cases/990274i1.html. Cf. Supreme Court (Spain), 28 January 2000, available at http://cisgw3.law.pace.edu/cases/000128s4.html (inferior price obtained through a quick sale made after refusing offer for a higher price unreasonable).

[132] 2014 U.S. Dist. LEXIS 71289 (E.D.N.Y. May 23, 2014).

the amount of mitigable loss if the injured party fails to mitigate. Accordingly, mitigable loss is deducted from damages calculated under Articles 74–76 to arrive at the damage award. This creates a problem, because Article 77's application here assumes that a substitute transaction can meet Article 75's requirements when the injured party fails to mitigate. Arguably the circumstance is rare. It is unlikely to occur in the typical range of cases.

To see this, notice that to measure its damages under Article 75 the injured party must have acted in a reasonable manner and time in obtaining substitute performance. If the party has not acted reasonably, it must calculate its damages by either Article 74 or 76, not Article 75. However, a party who fails to mitigate its loss has not acted reasonably in the circumstances according to Article 77 (". . . must take such measures as are reasonable in the circumstances to mitigate . . ."). For this reason, the injured party does not obtain a substitute transaction in a reasonable manner. There might be cases in which the failure to mitigate is unrelated to the substitute transaction, so that the non-breaching party acts unreasonably in not avoiding loss while acting reasonably in effecting substitute performance. But such cases will be rare. More typically the failure to mitigate takes the form of failing to make a reasonable and timely substitute transaction. In these cases the failure to mitigate prevents the injured party from measuring its damages under Article 75. Although the party can recover damages under Articles 74 or 76, with a deduction of mitigable loss from damages calculated under those Articles, Article 75 is unavailable to it.

A simple numerical example illustrates this point. Assume that Buyer breaches a sales contract with a contract price of $80 before Seller delivers the contract goods. After Seller effectively avoids the contract, it waits an unreasonably long period of time to resell them. It receives $60 for the goods, the stable market price, when it eventually resells the goods. Had Seller resold in a reasonable and timely manner, it would have gotten $75 for the goods. Under these facts, Seller's mitigable loss is $15, the difference between the $75 it would have received on a reasonable and timely resale and the $60 it received on actual resale. Thus, Article 77 allows Buyer to deduct $15 from a damage award against its damages calculated under Articles 74 or 76. Seller's recoverable damages under both Articles is $20 ($80 - $60 = $20), assuming that its loss is measured by market price and that the market price was $60 at the time of avoidance. Deducting the $15 mitigable loss from these damages gives Seller a net recovery of $5. However, on the facts Seller cannot calculate its damages under Article 75's formula, because its resale was not made in a timely manner.

The facts in the example essentially are those presented in a case decided by the Spanish Supreme Court in 2000.[133] There, the buyer breached and the seller avoided the contract, according to the Court. The seller then quickly resold the goods "for a very inferior price." Because the seller had previously rejected an offer

[133] See Supreme Court (Spain), 28 January 2000, available at http://cisgw3.law.pace.edu/cases/000128s4.html.

from the buyer for the goods at a higher price, the Court deemed it to have failed to mitigate under Article 77. Nonetheless, the Court allowed the seller to measure its damages by Article 75 while ordering that the damages be reduced by the amount of mitigable loss. Although the Court's finding of net damages is correct on the facts, its reliance on Article 75 is mistaken. The seller's failure to accept the earlier, higher priced offer for resale made the later, lower-priced resale unreasonable. (We might disagree with the court's conclusion on that point, since a once-disappointed seller's refusal to deal with a breaching buyer might not be unreasonable.) Thus, the seller cannot calculate its damages under Article 75 as the difference between the resale price and the higher contract price. Put simply, given the facts in the case, Article 75 and 77 cannot both apply.

The Spanish Supreme Court's reliance on Article 75 probably is harmless on the facts of the case. After all, forcing the seller to measure its damages under either Article 74 or Article 76 while deducting mitigable loss yields the same net damage award. But in other cases the calculation of damages under Articles 74 or 76 might give different damages. This is because the facts that need to be proven under these Articles are different and might have different proof costs associated with them. For instance, Article 76 requires proof of the market price ("current price") at the time of avoidance if the seller has not delivered the goods. The market price at that time might be higher than the price at which the seller resells. In addition, the seller might have difficulty proving this price or incur higher proof costs than are incurred in proving a reasonable resale. For a similar reason, it might have difficulty proving the amount of its loss directly under Article 74, particularly if it values the goods above their market price. In such cases the Article under which damages are measured can matter.

C. *Market price measure: Article 76*

An injured party who has avoided the contract need not calculate its damages by reference to Article 75's formula. If it has not obtained a substitute transaction that satisfies Article 75, the injured party may measure its damages by Article 76's market price formula. Under Article 76, damages are equal to the difference between the "current price" for the goods and the contract price. The "current price" is the prevailing price – the market price. It is determined under Article 76(2) by reference to the price prevailing at the place where delivery of the goods should have been made. If there is no current price at that place, the price at such other place as serves as a reasonable substitute may be used, but due allowance must be made for differences in the cost of transporting the goods from the original and the substitute place. Article 76's formula obviously is available to the injured party only if the contract goods have a market price.[134] If the goods of the kind are not traded with sufficient regularity to establish a prevailing price, the non-breaching party cannot

---

[134] See ICC Case No. 8740 (1996), available at http://cisgw3.law.pace.edu/cases/968740i1.html.

use Article 76 but must rely instead on either Articles 74 or 75 to measure its damages. An injured party using Article 76's market price measure can recover additional damages, such as incidental expenses or consequential damages, under Article 74.

ICC Case 8740[135] conveniently illustrates the application of Article 74–76's damage remedies. The arbitration involved a contract for the sale of a quantity of coal. The seller breached its obligations under Article 35 by delivering nonconforming coal and failing to deliver the required quantity. In response the buyer avoided the contract and covered by making a substitute purchase for part of the undelivered coal. When the buyer tried to set-off its damages from the contract price, the arbitral tribunal had to determine how those damages were properly measured. The tribunal found that the buyer could calculate its damages under Article 75 only for the portion of undelivered coal it covered. There was no "substitute transaction" with respect to the remaining portion. In addition, the tribunal found that the buyer's damages could not be measured under Article 76 because there was no current price for the contracted coal. Given attributes of coal and diverse needs of its buyers, together with the absence of a coal exchange, no market price existed. Finally, the tribunal found that Article 74's measure also could not be used to measure the buyer's damages with respect to the portion of undelivered coal for which it had not covered.

The tribunal's first two findings are unobjectionable. They appear to be fairly straightforward applications of Articles 75 and 76, given the stated facts. However, the tribunal's last finding is questionable. Article 74 allows the injured party to recover of damages equal to the foreseeable loss from breach. The Article is silent about the evidence of loss and therefore does not prevent the use of cover price in calculating loss. The buyer made a partial cover of the undelivered quantity of coal, and the price of this cover could be extrapolated as the price at which the entire quantity of undelivered coal could be purchased.[136] Thus, the buyer's loss from breach under Article 74 is equal to the difference between the cover price for the entire quantity of undelivered coal and the contract price. For this reason, the buyer should have been able to calculate its damages under Article 74 even if Article 76 was unavailable to it. Any other result fails to satisfy the objective of compensating the buyer for its loss.

---

[135] Id.

[136] It is hard to see how cover price does not meet the tribunal's standards of proof with respect to loss under Article 74. Article 75's formula uses a substitute transaction to calculate damages, and there is no reason why the same measure cannot be used under Article 74. Commentators disagree about whether standards of proof are governed by the CISG or by applicable domestic law. Compare CISG Advisory Council Opinion No. 6, Calculation of Damages Under CISG Article 74 ¶ 2 (2006), available at http://cisgw3.law.pace.edu/disg/CISG-AC-op6.html. (CISG governs) with Peter Schlechtriem, *Non-Material Damages — Recovery Under the CISG*, 19 Pace Int'l L. Rev. 89, 97 (2007) (forum law governs).

1. "Taking over" the goods

For purposes of Article 76's formula, the price is current as of the time of avoidance if avoidance occurs before the goods have been delivered. If, on the other hand, the injured party avoids the contract after taking over the goods, the current price is as of the time of "such taking over."[137] The CISG does not define "taking over." One might define it as the time of delivery, especially in light of the fact that Article 60 defines the buyer's obligation to take delivery as including "taking over the goods." We reject that conclusion. When the drafters of the CISG meant "delivery," they knew how to say it (e.g., Articles 30, 31, and 33). Thus, we conclude that when they used the term "taking over" the goods, they intended it to have independent meaning. The difficulty lies in defining that meaning. We conclude that, in the context of Article 76 at least, "taking over" is best understood as the receipt of actual possession of the goods by the buyer or the buyer's agent under circumstances that permit the buyer to examine them. We believe that this understanding is most consistent with the reasons for Article 76's distinction between measuring damages at the time of avoidance in non-delivery cases and at some alternative time in other cases. Presumably, we want to fix the buyer's market-price damages at the time when the buyer can determine whether the goods conformed to the contract. This induces the buyer to make a prompt examination under Article 38 and a prompt decision whether to avoid or not, because the buyer would bear the risk of subsequent market price movements. Any alternative time permits the buyer to play the market between the time that it discovers the defect and the time it is allowed to fix its damages. Under our reading, the buyer who delays declaring avoidance will only be able to recover an amount equal to the difference between contract price and the current price at the time it was able to examine the goods, even if the market price of the goods subsequently increased and the buyer would be able to obtain higher damages if it avoided at that later time. Thus, there is no strategic reason for the buyer to delay the avoidance decision and speculate about market prices.

We conclude that this is an appropriate result because we interpret the requirement that current price be set as of the time of "taking over" as an effort to constrain buyers' strategic behavior. Flexibility is built into the decision to avoid. In the event of a late or defective delivery, Article 49 permits a buyer a reasonable time to avoid. Assume that the buyer purchases goods at a contract price of $100 and receives goods sufficiently defective to constitute a fundamental breach. Assume further that at the time of the defective delivery, conforming goods have a market price of $105. The buyer who recognizes the defect can immediately avoid and recover Article 76 damages of $5. But the buyer can delay avoidance for a reasonable time to "play the market." If the market price continues to increase and damages are fixed as of the time of avoidance, the buyer suffers no harm, because it can avoid at a later point

---

[137] See Article 76(2).

within the reasonable period and recover the difference between market price and contract price when it does avoid. If the market price declines, for example to $95, the buyer can simply avoid the contract and purchase the goods at the lower price, pleased that the seller breached. In effect, and as we discussed with respect to the "reasonable time" requirement under Article 75, the buyer is gambling with the seller's money. Some domestic law deals with this problem by fixing market price damages at the time of tender in the case of an aggrieved seller[138], or at the time when the buyer learned of the breach in the case of an aggrieved buyer.[139] If the buyer who receives defective goods were able to fix damages as of the time of avoidance, the greater discretion that benchmark provides would increase the risk that the buyer would make the substance and timing of the avoidance decision based on predicted market price movements rather than on satisfaction with the goods or capacity to fix damages at an earlier point. Of course, the breaching party could make a claim that the aggrieved party had failed to mitigate damages under Article 77, but that claim comes replete with its own difficulties of proof.

A reading of "taking over" that equates it with delivery may avoid strategic behavior, but it fails to induce efficient decision making, because it includes no requirement that the aggrieved party be able to detect the nonconformity at the time its damages are fixed. Assume, for instance, a shipment contract in which the seller is required to deliver the goods to a carrier for transportation to the buyer. The goods are handed over the first carrier in accordance with Article 31(a) on March 1. They reach the buyer one month later, but are sufficiently defective to justify avoidance. Assume that the contract price for the goods is $100, that the current price at the time they were handed over to the first carrier was $105 and that the current price at the time that the buyer receives possession of the goods is $110. Even if the buyer avoids the contract immediately on receipt of the nonconforming goods, equating "taking over" with delivery limits the buyer to damages of $5 ($5 = $105 - $100). That is the case even though at the time that the buyer had an opportunity to examine the goods and avoid the contract, the market price of the goods was $110. Thus, defining "taking over" as referring to a time prior to when the buyer could know of the fundamental breach permits the breaching party to impose some breach costs onto the aggrieved party. We recognize that the buyer could simply make a cover purchase at $110 and invoke Article 75 to be made whole. But aggrieved parties may have reasons not to enter into cover purchases, and the ambiguities of Article 75 that we discussed above may force use of Article 76. As we noted in Chapter 6, the inclusion of "taking over" within Article 60's definition of "delivery" does not necessary make the two periods coterminous.

Consistent with our definition of "taking over," we read the buyer's obligation to take delivery under Article 60 as including the taking over of the goods, but not as defining the time of taking over as the time of delivery. Assume that the contract

---

[138] See, e.g., U.C.C. § 2–708(1).   [139] See, e.g., U.C.C. § 2–713(1).

calls for shipment by carrier from the seller's place of business. Delivery occurs at that point under Article 31(a). On our reading, the buyer does not "take over" the goods at that point. The buyer nonetheless has an "obligation" to take delivery under Article 60. If the buyer refuses to receive the goods when the carrier arrives, the buyer has, at that point, violated its obligation. That is different from defining the taking over as of the time of the delivery. We also recognize that one argument against our position is that if the drafters intended a "receipt" term, which may be more consistent with our concerns, they knew how to say so, since they use that term in Articles 65, 79, and 97. Nevertheless, we conclude that defining "taking over" in terms of the time when examination becomes plausible as the best fit with the policies of Article 76.

As this discussion suggests, Article 76's damage measure can give different damages than under Article 75, whether current price is set as of time of avoidance or the time of delivery. This is because current price can differ from the price at which the injured party obtains substitute performance. Article 76 gives the party a reasonable period in which to effect the substitute performance. This period, even when short, ends after the avoidance or delivery of the goods. During this time market price can fluctuate.

Finally, notwithstanding that the "taking over" exception in the second sentence of Article 76(1) is written in terms of "the party," there is reason to believe that it applies only to buyers. As a practical matter, circumstances will rarely permit such a claim by a seller. Perhaps a seller who, for example, recovers goods from a breaching buyer would be considered to have "taken over" the goods for purposes of Article 76 and would have to fix its damages as of that time rather than at the time of avoidance.[140]

2. Establishing current price

By its terms, Article 76's measure requires determination of the current price of goods of the kind at the time of avoidance of the contract or taking over the goods. While Article 76(2) establishes the relevant market for fixing the price (the place of delivery, even though that might vary from the place of avoidance or of taking over), establishing market price at these times can be difficult, particularly in highly volatile markets. An injured party unable to prove market price at these times cannot rely on Article 76 to measure damages.[141] Nonetheless, several Chinese arbitral awards are particularly forgiving in their determination of market price and its timing. One award allowed the international market price of the goods of the kind to serve as the current price rather than the domestic market price at the place the

---

[140] See Honnold/Flechtner, supra note 61, at 588–89.
[141] U.C.C. § 2–723(2) allows for evidence of prevailing market price within reasonable times before prescribed times when evidence of market price is not readily available for the prescribed times. Article 76(2) does not contain a similar allowance under the CISG.

goods were to be delivered.[142] Another award considered an offer to sell, although not accepted, sufficient to establish current price when the offer came within six days of the buyer's avoidance.[143] A third award allowed the price of resold goods to serve as a "reasonable reference of" the market price at the time of avoidance.[144] The tribunal nonetheless also acknowledged that Article 75's resale-contract differential would yield lower damages than Article 76's market price-contract differential. Another award used the contract price in the modified agreement as the market price when the current price at the time of avoidance was otherwise unavailable.[145] The tribunal apparently assumed that the market price at the time of avoidance remained the same as when the modified contract was concluded earlier.

D. *Restitution following avoidance*

After the contract has been avoided, the CISG gives a party the right to restitution of the goods it supplied or payment made under the contract. Restitution is not listed among the buyer and seller's respective remedies appearing in Articles 45 and 61. Instead its availability and restrictions on the relief are treated separately, in Articles 81–84. Labels aside, restitution gives a party a remedy: the right to recover goods it supplied or payments it made. The separate treatment of restitution makes the remedy available independently of a right to recover damages or specific relief. Restitution is useful when the injured party cannot or prefers not to prove its damages or establish its entitlement to specific relief. It is also helpful when Article 79 exempts a party from liability for breach. In this case Article 79(5) does not allow the recovery of damages. Restitution is not damages. Thus, if the breach permits avoidance of the contract, the right to restitution allows the non-breaching party to recover goods it supplied or payment made.

Under Article 81(2) a party who has wholly or partly performed the contract may claim restitution from the other party for what it has supplied or paid under the contract. Article 81(2)'s second sentence requires that the restitution be concurrent. This requirement in effect gives a contracting party a security interest in the other party's obligation to make restitution. Thus, a buyer who has prepaid the contract price and taken delivery of the goods is not obligated to redeliver the goods to the

---

[142] See CIETAC Arbitration Award (China), 2 May 1996, available at http://cisgw3.law.pace.edu/cases/960502c1.html; but cf. CIETAC Arbitration Award (China), 12 September 1994, available at http://cisgw3.law.pace.edu/cases/940919c1.html; CIETAC Arbitration Award (China), 20 January 1994, available at http://cisgw3.law.pace.edu/cases/940220c1.html (market price at place goods should have been delivered).

[143] See CIETAC Arbitration Award (China), 20 January 1993, available at http://cisgw3.law.pace.edu/cases/930120c1.html.

[144] See CIETAC Arbitration Award (China), October 2007, available at http://cisgw3.law.pace.edu/cases/071000c1.html.

[145] See CIETAC Arbitration Award (China), 30 June 1999, available at http://cisgw3.law.pace.edu/cases/990630c1.html.

seller if the seller refuses or is unable to remit the contract price. In this case the goods can serve as a source of repayment of the contract price. The concurrent requirement for restitution also in effect secures other obligations the seller owes the buyer. Avoidance of the contract leaves unaffected a party's liability for damages, as Article 81(1) makes explicit. Accordingly, the goods the buyer retains can also serve as a source of payment of any damage award the buyer may obtain against the seller.

Article 81(2)'s right of restitution is limited by the CISG's scope. The Article only gives a party the right against its counterparty. Two limitations restrict the restitution right. First, Article 81(2) does not give the seller or buyer title in the goods or payment that can be recovered by restitution. Because Article 4(b) excludes from the CISG's scope issues of the effect of the sales contract on title ("property") in the goods, the right to restitution says nothing about title to the goods or payment recovered. Thus, applicable domestic law, not the CISG, determines whether their recovery reinvests title in the seller or buyer. Second, the right to restitution provides no right against third parties. Article 4 limits the CISG's scope to the formation of the sales contract and the rights and obligations of the contracting parties arising from it. An unpaid seller has no rights under the CISG, for example, to recover goods that the buyer has resold to third parties. A prepaying buyer who never received goods has no rights under the CISG to recover the payment from a bankrupt seller's estate. Instead applicable domestic law, including bankruptcy law, governs the rights of the creditors and the buyer's bankruptcy trustee to the contract goods or payment.[146] Thus, applicable domestic law may restrict or eliminate the contracting parties' rights to restitution when third parties have claims to them.

Even with its limitations, Article 81(2)'s right to restitution is broader than similar rights given under some domestic law. By comparison, UCC § 2–507(2) and § 2–702 (1) impose greater restrictions on the seller's right to reclaim goods delivered under the contract. Section 2–507(2) allows the seller to reclaim the goods only when the buyer fails to make payment on delivery,[147] and § 2–702(1) allows reclamation from buyers who have received the goods on credit while insolvent. Neither of these limitations applies under Article 81(2). Under Article 81(2), after avoidance of the contract the seller may demand restitution of goods delivered whether or not payment is due on delivery or the buyer received the goods on credit. The parties' rights to restitution displace domestic law rules that affect restitution, unless the parties have opted out of Article 81(2) or the CISG entirely.

---

[146] See 11 U.S.C. § 546(c); *Usinor Industeel* v. *Leeco Steel Products, Inc.*, 209 F. Supp.2d 880 (N.D.Ill. 2005); Federal District Court (*Roder Zelt-und Hallenkonstruktionen GmbH* v. *Rosedown Park Pty Ltd. et al.*) (Australia), 28 April 1995, available at http://cisgw3.law.pace.edu/cases/950428a2.html.

[147] See Comment 3 to U.C.C. § 2–507 (subsection (2) codifies the cash seller's right of reclamation).

1. The place and costs of restitution

The CISG does not expressly provide for the place of restitution of the goods, or for the price or costs of restitution. Almost all courts and commentators maintain that they are determined under Article 7(2), which incorporates general principles underlying the CISG.[148] There is some disagreement over the general principles that select the place of restitution as well as the place selected. Three different positions appear in the case law or commentary.

(1) *The reverse role rule.* One position views the restitution transaction as the reverse of the original transaction. Accordingly, the seller in the original transaction who is to recover the goods is in the position of the buyer in the restitution transaction, and the buyer in the original transaction who is to recover the contract price paid is in the seller's position in the restitution transaction.[149] The reverse role rule therefore deems the buyer's place of redelivery of the goods in the restitution transaction to be at the place of delivery in the original transaction. Likewise, the seller's place of repayment of the price in the restitution transaction, according to the rule, is the place of payment in the original transaction. Under Article 31(c)'s default rule, the place of delivery of the goods is the seller's place of business, and under Article 57(1)(a)'s default the place of payment also is the seller's place of business. Accordingly, in the restitution transaction the goods are redelivered and the price repaid at the buyer's place of business. If the contract governing the original transaction requires different places of delivery or payment, the reverse role rule requires redelivery and repayment in the restitution transaction at those places.

Although courts and commentators tend to favor the reverse role rule (also called the "mirror image" rule), the rule and its consequences can be questioned. For one thing, it is unclear which of the CISG's underlying principles supports the rule. Rather than being backed by these principles, the rule rests on an

---

[148] See Supreme Court (Austria), 29 June 1999, available at http://cisgw3.law.pace.edu/cases/ 990629a3.html; CISG Advisory Council Opinion No. 9, Consequences of Avoidance of the Contract ¶¶ 3.12, 3.16 (2008), available at www.cisg.law.pace.edu/cisg/CISG-AC-op9.html; Rainer Horning, *Article 81*, in Commentary on the UN Convention on Contracts for the International Sale of Goods (CISG) 860 (Peter Schlectriem & Ingeborg Schwenzer eds., 2d (English) ed. 2005). For application of domestic law to the place of restitution, see Court of Appeal Paris (France), 14 January 1998, available at http://cisgw3.law.pace.edu/ cases/980114f1.html.

[149] See Supreme Court (Austria), 29 June 1999, available at http://cisgw3.law.pace.edu/cases/ 990629a3.html (restitution obligations "mirror image" of obligations under the original transaction); Court of Appeals Karlsruhe (Germany), 19 December 2002, available at http://cisgw3 .law.pace.edu/cases/021219g1.html; Court of Appeals Valais (Switzerland), 21 February 2005, available at http://cisgw3.law.pace.edu/cases/050221s1.html; Christiana Fountoulakis, *Article 81*, in Schlechtriem & Schwenzer, supra note 6, at 1110.

analogy, as one court acknowledges.[150] The buyer in the restitution transaction is in a similar position to the seller in the original transaction (it is obligated to deliver the goods), and the seller in the restitution transaction is in a similar position to the buyer in the original transaction (it is obligated to pay the price). Thus, by analogy the buyer has the delivery obligations of the original seller, and the seller has the repayment obligations of the original buyer.

As applied, the reverse role rule can inefficiently allocate costs in the restitution transaction. This is because, if Article 58(1)(a)'s place of delivery default applies to the original transaction, the rule requires redelivery of the goods to the seller at the buyer's place of business. However, between the date the goods are delivered and date the contract is avoided, the buyer might have moved them elsewhere for storage or processing. The reverse role rule therefore requires the buyer to bear the costs of having the goods shipped back to its place of business. These costs are wasted, because the seller likely does not benefit from retrieving them there. It can resell the goods in a local market where they are located initially as high a price. The more general point is that the efficient allocation of delivery costs as part of the original transaction may not be efficient with respect to the restitution transaction.

(2)   *Delivery and payment at the innocent party's place of business.* Several European commentators find that the CISG's underlying general principle of good faith determines the place of delivery of payment in restitution.[151] Apparently a party acts in bad faith or at least is at fault by breaching the contract; fault obligates it to redeliver the goods or repay the price at the non-breaching party's place of business. If the buyer breaches and the contract is avoided, it must redeliver the goods at the seller's place of business and the seller must make repayment there. If the seller breached, it must retrieve the goods at the buyer's place of business and be repaid there too.

This position is weak and no courts have adopted it. Although some commentators find a principle of good faith in the performance of contracts among the CISG's underlying principles,[152] breach need not be in bad faith or the result of fault. For instance, Article 35 makes warranty liability strict, and Article 74 gives damages even when the breaching party is not at fault in breaching. Even where

---

[150] See District Court Giessen (Germany), 17 December 2002, available at http://cisgw3.law.pace .edu/cases/021217g1.html. ("... one may look at Art. 57(1)(a) by analogy"). It is worth emphasizing that the reverse role rule is based only on an analogy. The parties' performance under the original transaction is called for by the sales contract; the restitution obligations in the reverse transaction are not. They instead are imposed to unwind certain obligations created by the contract. The buyer in the restitution transaction is not really selling the restitution goods, and the seller in the transaction is not really buying the goods. The analogy by itself does not convincingly select the place of performance of the restitution obligations.

[151] See Christiana Fountoulakis, *Article 81*, in Schlechtriem & Schwenzer, supra note 6, at 1112 n.78.

[152] See, e.g., Magnus, supra note 30, at 33; Honnold/Flechtner, supra note 61, at 135; Michael J. Bonell, *Interpretation of Convention*, in Bianca & Bonell, supra note 31, at 84.

breach is the result of fault, determining the place of restitution by fault can inefficiently allocate the costs of reversing the original transaction. This is because the party at fault might be in an inferior position to the innocent party with respect to redelivery or repayment. For example, the innocent seller might face lower carriage costs in reshipping the goods or be able to resell the goods in the at-fault buyer's local market. The costs of redelivering the goods are lower when the seller retrieves them from the buyer's place of business. Somewhat more unusual, an innocent buyer who is a beneficiary on the seller's standby letter of credit might be able to draw on the letter for repayment of the contract price rather than obtain payment from the seller at its place of business. Setting the place of repayment at the at-fault seller's place of business is the more expensive route.

(3) *The locus on avoidance rule.* A third position is that the place of delivery of the goods in the restitution transaction is their location at the time the contract is avoided.[153] If the goods are at the buyer's place of business when the contract is avoided, the buyer must make them available to the seller there. If they are stored or being fabricated elsewhere at the time of avoidance, the buyer must make them available to the seller at the place of storage or fabrication. If the goods are in transit at the time the contract is avoided, the buyer must make any documents covering them available to the seller to allow it to take delivery of the goods. This "locus on avoidance" rule is more or less the one recommended by the CISG Advisory Council.[154] The rule is attractive because it efficiently allocates the costs of redelivering the goods. The costs of retrieving the goods from locations other than the buyer's place of business do not favor the buyer. In addition, the seller might prefer to resell the goods in a market near to the location of the goods. For this reason, requiring the buyer to incur costs in returning the goods to its place of business is wasteful. Because the locus on avoidance rule efficiently allocates the costs of delivering restitution goods (and the CISG is otherwise silent), we favor it over its two competitors.

The locus on avoidance rule with respect to repayment of the contract price is more difficult to apply. The CISG Advisory Council recommends that repayment be at the buyer's place of business, subject to an exception. The exception applies when payment under the original transaction was made at a different place, such as at a bank. In that case the Advisory Council recommends that the place of repayment in the restitution transaction be at the same place.[155] This exception to the locus rule should not be recognized. At the time the contract is avoided the seller has received payment, even if the payment initially was made to a bank or other payment intermediary. The fact that payment under the original contract was made

---

[153] See CISG Advisory Council Opinion No. 9, Consequences of Avoidance of the Contract ¶¶ 3.12–3.13 (2008), available at http://cisg-law.pace.edu/cisg/CISG-AC-op9.html.
[154] Id.   [155] See id. at ¶ 3.15.

through an intermediary is irrelevant to the preferred location for repayment after the contract is avoided.

The remaining question is whether the locus of repayment should be at the seller's or the buyer's place of business. We have no views that lead us to favor one repayment locus rather than the other. As far as we can see, the choice is a coin toss. The locus rule could select the buyer's place of business, as courts do,[156] or the seller's place of business. There seems nothing objectionable about requiring repayment at the seller's place of business while requiring redelivery of the goods at their location. Article 81(2)'s concurrence requirement only obligates the seller and buyer to perform their respective obligations of restitution at the same time. It does not require that their obligations be performed at the same place.

Where the goods are redelivered to the seller at the buyer's premises or other proper location, the seller often will incur costs in retrieving and disposing of them. These include the expense of transporting, meeting applicable regulatory requirements and reselling the goods. Although the CISG does not expressly allocate the costs of restitution between the seller and buyer, its damages provisions apply to allocate them.

If the buyer's breach is exempted by Article 79 after the goods have been delivered, Article 79(5) does not allow the seller to recover damages. The seller nonetheless retains the right to avoid the contract (if avoidance is permitted) and restitution of the goods delivered. Costs that the seller incurs in retrieving them are the consequence of the buyer's breach and therefore damages under Article 74. Retrieval costs therefore are damages; however they are labeled. Because Article 79 (5) limits the buyer's liability to remedies other than damages, the seller cannot recover its retrieval costs. A French court exempted the seller's delivery of nonconforming goods under Article 79 while awarding the buyer customs fees it incurred in importing them.[157] Customs fees are among the buyer's (foreseeable) loss resulting from the seller's breach and therefore damages in everything but name. They are not recoverable from the exempted seller.

Where a party's liability for breach is not exempted by Article 79, the costs of restitution are borne by the breaching party. If the buyer breaches and the seller retrieves the goods after avoiding the contract, the seller's retrieval costs are loss resulting from the breach. As such they are recoverable damages. If the seller breaches and retrieves the goods after the buyer avoids the contract, the seller's retrieval costs result from its own breach. They are not damages and the breaching seller therefore cannot recover the retrieval costs. Finally, as recoverable loss, the

---

[156] See District Court Giessen (Germany), 17 December 2002, available at http://cisgw3.law.pace .edu/ases/012117g1.html; cf. Supreme Court (Austria), 28 June 1999, available at http://cisgw3 .law.pace.edu/cases/990629a3.html ("The place of performance for the obligations concerning restitution should mirror the place of performance for the primary contractual obligations").

[157] See District Court Besançon (France), 19 January 1998, available at http://cisgw3.law.pace.edu/ cases/980119f1.html.; Chapter 8.III.B.

expenses of retrieving and disposing of the goods are subject to Article 77's mitigation requirement. Thus, if the non-breaching seller chooses to ship the goods back
to its premises when it could have more cheaply sold them in the buyer's local
market, the costs of shipment are not recoverable to the extent they exceed the costs
of making a local sale.

2. The benefits of restitution of goods

Article 81(2) gives the party the right to restitution of what it supplied or paid the
other party. Article 84(2)(b) goes further and obligates the buyer to account to the
seller for all benefits which it derived from the goods if it is impossible for the buyer
to make restitution of them. If the buyer resells delivered goods before the seller
makes a claim for restitution, it is impossible for the buyer to return the goods. The
buyer nonetheless has "benefitted" from the goods to the extent that the sub-buyer
has no claims against it arising from the sale.[158] In this case the Article 84(2)(b)
entitles the seller to what a Finnish court calls a "monetary surrogate":[159] the
resale price.

Article 84(2) enables the seller sometimes to recover more in restitution than it
could in damages. This is because Article 84(2)(b) allows the seller to recover the
price at which the buyer resold contract goods even if the seller was not in a position
to resell them for that price. For example, assume that Buyer contracts with Seller
for goods at a price of $100, which Seller delivers. Payment is due a month after
delivery. Two weeks later Buyer resells the goods for $175 at no additional cost to
itself. Seller could not have sold the goods for more than $100. When Buyer later
refuses to pay the purchase price, Seller avoids the contract. On these facts, Seller's
damages under Article 74 are $100; it suffers no other loss from Buyer's breach.
Buyer's $175 resale price represents a "benefit derived from the goods." In addition,
the resale makes restitution of the contract goods impossible. Thus, under Article 84
(2)(b) Seller is entitled to $175 in restitution from Buyer. This gives Seller $75 more
than it would have received had Buyer performed the contract. On similar facts, a
German court allowed a seller to recover the resale price from its breaching
buyer.[160]

Calculating the "benefits derived from the goods" is easy in the previous example,
because the example assumes that Buyer incurs no additional costs in reselling the
contract goods. Buyer's benefit from the goods is the resale price it receives from its

---

[158] Cf. Court of Appeals Oldenburg (Germany), 1 February 1995, available at http://cisgw3.law
.pace.edu/cases/950201g1.html (buyer received no benefit from subsale when furniture sold was
defective and seller unsuccessfully repaired it).

[159] See Court of Appeals (Finland), 31 May 2004, available at http://cisgw3.law.pace.edu/cases/
040531f5.html.

[160] See Court of Appeals Karlsruhe (Germany), 14 February 2004, available at http://cisgw3.law
.pace.edu/cases/080214g1.html.

buyer. The buyer's use of the goods before they are returned to the seller is a relatively easy case too. The benefits the buyer derived from the goods are the use value to the buyer between delivery and their return. The rental price for similar goods for this period might reliably measure this value. In more realistic cases in which the buyer incurs costs in reselling the goods, establishing the "benefits derived from the goods" is harder. The resale price incorporates both the cost of the goods and the buyer's other variable costs in reselling them. The part of the price attributed to other variable costs is a benefit that derives from the buyer's resources other than the goods. To calculate the benefit from the goods, these costs must be deducted from the price. This deduction from the resale price allows the seller restitution of the resale price in the amount of the net benefit derived from the goods, as one court has found.[161] It is not much of a stretch to read "benefits" in Article 84(2) as referring to the buyer's net benefits from the goods.

III. REMEDY STIPULATIONS, REMEDY LIMITATIONS, AND DAMAGE EXCLUSIONS

The CISG's remedies are default terms only. This is because Article 6 allows the contracting parties to opt out of them by agreement. Under Article 6 the parties may derogate from most of the CISG's provisions, including its damages measures and other remedies. One way in which they can do so is to fix the amount of damages recoverable in the event of breach. Another way is to limit available remedies, restricting the non-breaching party's remedy on breach to repair or replacement of the goods or recovery of the contract price or stated portion of it, as applicable. Finally, the recovery of certain sorts of damages can be excluded. Article 74 allows the recovery of lost profits and consequential damages. The parties' contract can provide that these damages are not recoverable in the event of breach. Whether the agreement fixes damages, limits remedies, or excludes certain sorts of damages is a matter of contract interpretation.

The CISG does not regulate contractually stipulated damages, remedy limitations, and damage exclusions. It instead leaves their regulation to applicable domestic law. Article 6 merely allows the parties to make inapplicable to their contract the allocation of risk of liability and damages made by the CISG's provisions. However, the CISG does not address the enforceability of the parties' own allocation of the risk through stipulations of damages, remedy limitations or damage exclusions. As ordinarily understood, the enforceability of contractual provisions allocating these risks is a matter of their "validity." These provisions have no legal effect if they are invalid. Article 4(a) excludes from the CISG's scope issues of "validity" (unless expressly provided for), leaving them to applicable domestic law. Thus, the question is whether the CISG tracks the ordinary understanding of the term "validity."

---

[161] See id.

Although the CISG does not define the term,[162] case law and commentary overwhelmingly considers the regulation of damage stipulations, remedy limitations and damage exclusions to be issues of validity under Article 4(a).[163] The Secretariat Commentary to the CISG supports this view, describing the issue of the enforceability of penalty clauses as one of "validity."[164] Applicable domestic law, not the CISG, therefore regulates damage stipulations, remedy limitations, and damage exclusions.

The decision of the CISG's drafters to leave the enforceability of these provisions to domestic law reflects their inability to reach consensus on a uniform rule regulating the provisions. Their failure is understandable given the difficulty of determining the optimal regulation of damage stipulations, remedy limitations, and damage exclusions. Consider the enforceability of damage stipulations. Penalty clauses affect the choice of contracting partner, investment in the contract's performance, and the decision to breach. This makes it difficult to evaluate the aggregate impact of enforcing or refusing to enforce them. When parties have limited information about the quality of their contracting partners, a party that agrees to a penalty clause risks having to pay the penalty if breaches the contract. For this reason, agreeing to the clause signals to the counterparty a willingness and ability to perform.

On the other hand, a penalty clause may or may not induce inefficient performance. It can induce efficient breach when the parties more accurately measure loss from breach than courts or arbitrators. In this case the damages stipulated are fully compensatory on an expectancy basis and not a "penalty." However, where courts or arbitrators forecast loss from breach more accurately than the parties, a penalty clause can induce inefficient performance. This is because the party subject to the penalty will perform when the penalty sum is greater than its performance cost, even when the non-breaching party's loss from breach is less than that sum.

Finally, a penalty clause can encourage efficient investment in the contract's performance. To see this, recognize that default remedies such as expectation damages induce the aggrieved party to make inefficiently high investments in the contract. This is because the aggrieved party recovers its investment whether or not the contract is performed. If the contract is breached, expectation damages give the aggrieved party the return on its investment had the contract been performed. If the contract is performed, the aggrieved party will get the value from its performance. Because the aggrieved party recovers its investment whether or not the contract is breached, it does not discount the value of its investment by the probability of breach. Thus, it will make an inefficiently high investment in its performance of the contract. A penalty clause decouples investment and damages by fixing damages without regard to investment. This makes the aggrieved party take into account the

---

[162] See Chapter 2.V.B.
[163] See, e.g., Foreign Trade Court of Arbitration attached to the Serbian Chamber of Commerce, Serbia, 15 July 2008, available at http://cisgw3.law.pace.edu/cases/080715sb.html.
[164] See Secretariat Commentary to the 1978 Draft, in Documentary History, supra note 23, at 428 (para. 10) (discussing then-Article 42).

likelihood of breach, because a dollar invested in the contract reduces its net recovery on breach by a dollar. The aggrieved party therefore is forced to calibrate the investment's cost with the discounted value of the investment. As a result, the victim will efficiently invest in its performance of the contract. The trouble is that the conditions required for penalties to assure efficient investment are demanding.[165] For example, in the simple case where only one of the contracting parties can invest in the contract's performance, the contract price must be set below the investing party's marginal cost of performance. Otherwise, the non-investing party might breach and the investing party will not be guaranteed the value of its investment. At the same time, to induce the investing party to enter into the contract, the non-investing party must pay or guarantee a large, non-recoverable payment (the penalty) to the investing party. This payment assures that the contract is profitable for the investing party. If the non-investing party can recover the payment or cancel the payment obligation by convincing a court that it is an unenforceable penalty, the design of the contract is infeasible. It is hard to guarantee that a court ex post will not find that the payment or payment obligation is an unenforceable penalty.

For the penalty to assure efficient investment, the investment also must have a particular feature. It must not benefit only the non-investing party by increasing the contract's value to it while leaving the investing party's cost of contractual perform-ance unaffected. Otherwise, the investing party receives the same return whether or not it invests. As a result, it will not invest in the contract when doing so benefits only the non-investing party. The assumption that investment does not benefit only the non-investing party limits the use of penalties to assure efficient investment in the contract. More generally, it is hard to gauge the efficiency of stipulated damages when its effects on the choice of contracting partner, investment and decision to breach are taken into account. Legal systems can reach different conclusions about the matter and the drafters of a uniform sales law are unlikely to agree on a uniform rule to regulate damage stipulations. It probably is not therefore surprising that Article 4(a) leaves the enforceability of damage stipulations to applicable domestic law.

Accordingly, a court or arbitral tribunal considering a contract containing damage stipulations, remedy limitations or damage exclusions must engage in a two-step inquiry. First, the forum must determine, based on its conflict of law rules, the country whose law regulates the provisions. Second, it must determine whether that country's applicable law enforces them in the circumstances of the contract and its performance.

The regulation of damage stipulations can illustrate the second step. Suppose a contract governed by the CISG contains a penalty clause that is not "manifestly excessive" but still super-compensatory. Legal systems take one of three approaches

---

[165] See Steven Walt, *Penalty Clauses and Liquidated Damages*, in Contract Law and Economics 178, 187–92 (Gerrit De Geest ed., 2011); Aaron S. Edlin & Alan Schwartz, *Optimal Penalties in Contracts*, 78 Chi.-Kent L. Rev. 33 (2003).

to penalty clauses. A few civil law systems enforce stipulations of damages even if they are penalties.[166] Other civil law systems enforce penalties for breach if they are not "manifestly excessive" in relation to the actual loss from breach. A court can reduce the penalty sum so that it is no longer excessive.[167] Some countries put an upper limit on the enforceable penalty sum, determined by the value of the principle obligation or a percentage of the contract price.[168] Common law systems adopt a third approach, enforcing damage stipulations only when the stipulated sum does not exceed the actual or reasonably anticipated loss from breach.[169] Penalty clauses are unenforceable. If the forum's conflicts rules select the law of a country that adopts either the first or second approach, the penalty clause in the contract is enforceable. The penalty clause is unenforceable if the country's law selected adopts the third approach. There is no reason to believe that the analysis would be different if the enforceability of a remedy limitation or damage exclusion were at issue.

Case law has been consistent in making the enforceability of damage stipulations turn on applicable domestic law. In an early case, *ICC Case 7197*,[170] the arbitral tribunal had to determine whether a penalty clause in a sales contract governed by the CISG was enforceable. The penalty clause limited damages to x percent of the contract price. The buyer breached and argued that its liability was limited to this amount. For its part, the seller argued that it was entitled to recover damages under Article 74 notwithstanding the limit fixed by the penalty clause. Thus, the question was whether the contract's penalty clause was enforceable. Finding that the CISG does not regulate penalty clauses, the court concluded that Article 7(2) left their enforceability to applicable domestic law.[171] The tribunal determined that Austrian law, the applicable law, would not enforce the penalty clause in the contract. Thus, the clause did not displace the damages available under Article 74 and the tribunal awarded the seller damages according to that Article.

ICC Case 9978[172] adopts follows the same reasoning, making explicit that the enforceability of a penalty clause is a matter of validity. The contract in dispute governed by the CISG contained a penalty clause, referred to by the court as a "penalty/liquidated damages (PLD) clause." The PLD clause limited damages to 2 percent of the contract price. When the seller breached, the buyer argued that it had a right to recover damages under Article 74. In response the seller maintained

---

[166] See, e.g., Polgari Torvenykonyv [PTK] [Civil Code] art. 346 (Hung.).

[167] See Code civil [C.civ.] art. 1152 (Fr.); Burgerliches Gesetzbuch [BGB] [Civil Code] § 343(1) (Ger.); Schwenzer, Hachem & Kee, supra note 32, at 639 n.579 (listing legal system allowing reduction; cf. The Principles of European Contract Law 9.509 (at 453) (1999).

[168] See, e.g., Codigo Civil para el Distrito Federal [C.C.D.F.] art. 1843 (Mex.); Codigo Civil [C.C.] art. 412 (Braz.); Codigo Civil [C.C.] art. 935 (Port.).

[169] See, e.g., U.C.C. § 2–718(1).

[170] 1 UNILEX D.1992–3 (Michael J. Bonell ed., 2008).

[171] Accord Court of Appeals Arnhem (Netherlands), (*Diepeveen-Drison B.V. v. Nieuenhoven Vichandel GmbH*), 22 August 1995, available at http://cisgw3.law.pace.edu/cases/950822n1 .html.

[172] 4 UNILEX E.1999–6.1 (Michael J. Bonell ed., 2008) (full text).

that its liability for breach was exempted under Article 79. The tribunal rejected both the buyer and the seller's respective arguments. While finding that the seller's nonperformance was not exempt under Article 79, it noted that the PLD clause, if enforceable, applied even if the seller were exempt. Article 79(5) insulates the exempted party only from "damages," and the PLD clause is not damages. The clause, if enforceable, instead displaces damages otherwise available under Articles 74–76. Against the buyer, the tribunal noted that the enforceability of the PLD clause is a matter of validity under Article 4(a) and therefore not governed by the CISG. Finding that the clause was valid under applicable domestic law (German law), the tribunal limited the buyer's recovery to 2 percent of the contract price. Courts and arbitrators in more recent cases involving penalty clauses analyze the issue of their enforceability in the same way.[173]

Several commentators argue that the CISG continues to govern the enforceability of stipulated damages even though Article 4(a) delegates their validity to applicable domestic law.[174] They reason that Article 7(2) makes applicable to damage stipulations in the contract the "general principles" underlying the CISG. These principles, they conclude, regulate damages stipulations whose validity is governed by applicable domestic law. We find this reasoning unpersuasive. Once the parties have opted out of the CISG damage provisions with a damage stipulation in the contract, the CISG no longer governs the enforceability of the stipulation. Domestic law alone regulates its validity.

To illustrate this position, assume that a clause in a contract governed by the CISG expressly bars the injured party from any remedy in the event of breach. The clause underestimates damages, giving the injured party nothing, without regard to the seriousness of the counterparty's breach. Article 4(a) considers the enforceability of the clause a matter of validity not addressed by the CISG. Thus, according to the last phrase in Article 7(2) ("in conformity with ..."), applicable domestic law determines the clause's validity. Applicable domestic law likely deems a clause depriving the injured party of any remedy to be invalid: Either the agreement containing it is not a contract at all[175] or the clause, while part of a contract, is unconscionable.[176] However, the argument just described maintains that under Article 7(2)'s first clause the general principles underlying the CISG continue to

---

[173] See, e.g., Foreign Court of Arbitration (Serbia), 15 July 2008, available at http://cisgw3.law.pace .edu/cases/080715sb.html; *American Mint LLC* v. *Gosoftware*, 2006 U.S. Dist. LEXIS 1569, at *19 (M.D. Pa. January 6, 2006); cf. ICC Case No. 12173 (2004), available at http://cisgw3.law .pace.edu/cases/041217311.html (interpreting a liquidated damages clause in accordance with Swiss law).

[174] See Ingeborg Schwenzer & Pascal Hashem, *Article 4*, in Schlechtriem & Schwenzer, supra note 6, at 93; Pascal Hashem, *Fixed Sums in CISG Contracts*, 13 Vindobona J. Int'l Comm. L. & Arb. 217 (2009); Ingeborg Schwenzer & Pascal Hashem, *CISG — Successes and Pitfalls*, 57 Am. J. Comp. L. 457, 474 (2009).

[175] Cf. Restatement (Second) of Contracts § 1 (1981) ("A contract is a promise or set of promises for the breach of which the law gives a remedy ...").

[176] See U.C.C. § 2–302.

apply. Those general principles in turn can invalidate the "no remedy" clause, even if applicable domestic law were to declare it valid.

One problem with this argument is that it relies heavily on general principles underlying the CISG. As we have argued throughout this text, identifying among these principles the standards that continue to regulate damage stipulations or other legal doctrines is problematic. Commentators taking the line described offer a principle to the effect that a damage stipulation must preserve some adequate remedy.[177] The CISG's damages provisions supposedly evince the principle. We are not so sure. The CISG's damage provisions could evince the more limited principle to the effect that parties have adequate remedies when their contract does not make these provisions inapplicable to it. After all, the CISG's remedial provisions are default rules only. This more limited principle does not apply when the parties' agreement displaces the CISG's damage provisions. Even if the relevant principle requires adequate remedies for parties, it conflicts with another underlying principle: freedom of contract. Article 6 reflects the principle that favors the parties' agreement over the CISG's provisions.[178] This pro-contract principle supports enforcement of damage stipulations that do not provide the protection given by the CISG's remedial provisions.

The more serious problem with the argument is that it badly misreads Article 7 (2)'s first clause. This clause in relevant part makes general principles underlying the CISG applicable only to "matters governed by this Convention which are not expressly settled in it." Article 6 allows parties to derogate from most of the CISG's provisions, including its remedial provisions. If the parties have effectively made inapplicable to their contract the CISG's remedies through an appropriately drafted damage stipulation, the CISG no longer governs the parties' remedies on breach. In Article 7(2)'s terms, "the matter" is no longer governed by "this Convention." The damage stipulation instead controls. Thus, Article 7(2)'s general principles underlying the CISG also no longer apply. How parties displace the CISG's remedial provisions is a matter governed by the CISG.[179] But the substance of the provision that supplants the CISG's remedies is regulated by applicable domestic law, not the CISG.

---

[177] See Ingeborg Schwenzer & Pascal Hachem, *The CISG—Successes and Pitfalls*, 57 Am. J. Comp. L. 457, 474 (2009).

[178] See Magnus, supra note 30, at 42; UNCITRAL Digest 45 (para. 31) (2012); cf. Supreme Court (Austria), 23 May 2005, available at http://cisgw3.law.pace.edu/cases/050523a3.html; Supreme Court (Austria), 7 September 2000, available at http://cisgw3.law.pace.edu/cases/000907a3 .html (parties generally free to modify rights provided by the CISG).

[179] See Chapter 2.IV.A.

The United Nations Convention on Contracts for the International Sale of Goods

The States Parties to this Convention,

Bearing in mind the broad objectives in the resolutions adopted by the sixth special session of the General Assembly of the United Nations on the establishment of a New International Economic Order,

Considering that the development of international trade on the basis of equality and mutual benefit is an important element in promoting friendly relations among States,

Being of the opinion that the adoption of uniform rules which govern contracts for the international sale of goods and take into account the different social, economic and legal systems would contribute to the removal of legal barriers in international trade and promote the development of international trade,

Have agreed as follows:

PART I. SPHERE OF APPLICATION AND GENERAL PROVISIONS

Chapter I. *Sphere of Application*

Article 1

(1) This Convention applies to contracts of sale of goods between parties whose places of business are in different States:
   (a) when the States are Contracting States; or
   (b) when the rules of private international law lead to the application of the law of a Contracting State.
(2) The fact that the parties have their places of business in different States is to be disregarded whenever this fact does not appear either from the contract or from any dealings between, or from information disclosed by, the parties at any time before or at the conclusion of the contract.

(3) Neither the nationality of the parties nor the civil or commercial character of the parties or of the contract is to be taken into consideration in determining the application of this Convention.

Article 2

This Convention does not apply to sales:

(a) of goods bought for personal, family or household use, unless the seller, at any time before or at the conclusion of the contract, neither knew nor ought to have known that the goods were bought for any such use;

(b) by auction;

(c) on execution or otherwise by authority of law;

(d) of stocks, shares, investment securities, negotiable instruments or money;

(e) of ships, vessels, hovercraft or aircraft;

(f) of electricity.

Article 3(1)

Contracts for the supply of goods to be manufactured or produced are to be considered sales unless the party who orders the goods undertakes to supply a substantial part of the materials necessary for such manufacture or production.

(2) This Convention does not apply to contracts in which the preponderant part of the obligations of the party who furnishes the goods consists in the supply of labour or other services.

Article 4

This Convention governs only the formation of the contract of sale and the rights and obligations of the seller and the buyer arising from such a contract. In particular, except as otherwise expressly provided in this Convention, it is not concerned with:

(a) the validity of the contract or of any of its provisions or of any usage;

(b) the effect which the contract may have on the property in the goods sold.

Article 5

This Convention does not apply to the liability of the seller for death or personal injury caused by the goods to any person.

Article 6

The parties may exclude the application of this Convention or, subject to article 12, derogate from or vary the effect of any of its provisions.

Chapter II. *General Provisions*

Article 7

(1) In the interpretation of this Convention, regard is to be had to its international character and to the need to promote uniformity in its application and the observance of good faith in international trade.

(2) Questions concerning matters governed by this Convention which are not expressly settled in it are to be settled in conformity with the general principles on which it is based or, in the absence of such principles, in conformity with the law applicable by virtue of the rules of private international law.

Article 8

(1) For the purposes of this Convention statements made by and other conduct of a party are to be interpreted according to his intent where the other party knew or could not have been unaware what that intent was.

(2) If the preceding paragraph is not applicable, statements made by and other conduct of a party are to be interpreted according to the understanding that a reasonable person of the same kind as the other party would have had in the same circumstances.

(3) In determining the intent of a party or the understanding a reasonable person would have had, due consideration is to be given to all relevant circumstances of the case including the negotiations, any practices which the parties have established between themselves, usages and any subsequent conduct of the parties.

Article 9

(1) The parties are bound by any usage to which they have agreed and by any practices which they have established between themselves.

(2) The parties are considered, unless otherwise agreed, to have impliedly made applicable to their contract or its formation a usage of which the parties knew or ought to have known and which in international trade is widely known to, and regularly observed by, parties to contracts of the type involved in the particular trade concerned.

Article 10

For the purposes of this Convention:

(a) if a party has more than one place of business, the place of business is that which has the closest relationship to the contract and its performance, having regard to the circumstances known to or contemplated by the parties at any time before or at the conclusion of the contract;

(b) if a party does not have a place of business, reference is to be made to his habitual residence.

Article 11
A contract of sale need not be concluded in or evidenced by writing and is not subject to any other requirement as to form. It may be proved by any means, including witnesses.

Article 12
Any provision of article 11, article 29 or Part II of this Convention that allows a contract of sale or its modification or termination by agreement or any offer, acceptance or other indication of intention to be made in any form other than in writing does not apply where any party has his place of business in a Contracting State which has made a declaration under article 96 of this Convention. The parties may not derogate from or vary the effect of this article.

Article 13
For the purposes of this Convention "writing" includes telegram and telex.

PART II. FORMATION OF THE CONTRACT

Article 14

(1) A proposal for concluding a contract addressed to one or more specific persons constitutes an offer if it is sufficiently definite and indicates the intention of the offeror to be bound in case of acceptance. A proposal is sufficiently definite if it indicates the goods and expressly or implicitly fixes or makes provision for determining the quantity and the price.

(2) A proposal other than one addressed to one or more specific persons is to be considered merely as an invitation to make offers, unless the contrary is clearly indicated by the person making the proposal.

Article 15

(1) An offer becomes effective when it reaches the offeree.

(2) An offer, even if it is irrevocable, may be withdrawn if the withdrawal reaches the offeree before or at the same time as the offer.

Article 16

(1) Until a contract is concluded an offer may be revoked if the revocation reaches the offeree before he has dispatched an acceptance.

(2) However, an offer cannot be revoked:

    (a) if it indicates, whether by stating a fixed time for acceptance or otherwise, that it is irrevocable; or

    (b) if it was reasonable for the offeree to rely on the offer as being irrevocable and the offeree has acted in reliance on the offer.

Article 17

An offer, even if it is irrevocable, is terminated when a rejection reaches the offeror.

Article 18

(1) A statement made by or other conduct of the offeree indicating assent to an offer is an acceptance. Silence or inactivity does not in itself amount to acceptance.

(2) An acceptance of an offer becomes effective at the moment the indication of assent reaches the offeror. An acceptance is not effective if the indication of assent does not reach the offeror within the time he has fixed or, if no time is fixed, within a reasonable time, due account being taken of the circumstances of the transaction, including the rapidity of the means of communication employed by the offeror. An oral offer must be accepted immediately unless the circumstances indicate otherwise.

(3) However, if, by virtue of the offer or as a result of practices which the parties have established between themselves or of usage, the offeree may indicate assent by performing an act, such as one relating to the dispatch of the goods or payment of the price, without notice to the offeror, the acceptance is effective at the moment the act is performed, provided that the act is performed within the period of time laid down in the preceding paragraph.

Article 19

(1) A reply to an offer which purports to be an acceptance but contains additions, limitations or other modifications is a rejection of the offer and constitutes a counter-offer.

(2) However, a reply to an offer which purports to be an acceptance but contains additional or different terms which do not materially alter the terms of the offer constitutes an acceptance, unless the offeror, without undue delay, objects orally to the discrepancy or dispatches a notice to

that effect. If he does not so object, the terms of the contract are the terms of the offer with the modifications contained in the acceptance.

(3) Additional or different terms relating, among other things, to the price, payment, quality and quantity of the goods, place and time of delivery, extent of one party's liability to the other or the settlement of disputes are considered to alter the terms of the offer materially.

Article 20

(1) A period of time for acceptance fixed by the offeror in a telegram or a letter begins to run from the moment the telegram is handed in for dispatch or from the date shown on the letter or, if no such date is shown, from the date shown on the envelope. A period of time for acceptance fixed by the offeror by telephone, telex or other means of instantaneous communication, begins to run from the moment that the offer reaches the offeree.

(2) Official holidays or non-business days occurring during the period for acceptance are included in calculating the period. However, if a notice of acceptance cannot be delivered at the address of the offeror on the last day of the period because that day falls on an official holiday or a non-business day at the place of business of the offeror, the period is extended until the first business day which follows.

Article 21

(1) A late acceptance is nevertheless effective as an acceptance if without delay the offeror orally so informs the offeree or dispatches a notice to that effect.

(2) If a letter or other writing containing a late acceptance shows that it has been sent in such circumstances that if its transmission had been normal it would have reached the offeror in due time, the late acceptance is effective as an acceptance unless, without delay, the offeror orally informs the offeree that he considers his offer as having lapsed or dispatches a notice to that effect.

Article 22

An acceptance may be withdrawn if the withdrawal reaches the offeror before or at the same time as the acceptance would have become effective.

Article 23

A contract is concluded at the moment when an acceptance of an offer becomes effective in accordance with the provisions of this Convention.

Article 24

For the purposes of this Part of the Convention, an offer, declaration of acceptance or any other indication of intention "reaches" the addressee when it is made orally to him or delivered by any other means to him personally, to his place of business or mailing address or, if he does not have a place of business or mailing address, to his habitual residence.

PART III. SALE OF GOODS

Chapter I. *General Provisions*

Article 25

A breach of contract committed by one of the parties is fundamental if it results in such detriment to the other party as substantially to deprive him of what he is entitled to expect under the contract, unless the party in breach did not foresee and a reasonable person of the same kind in the same circumstances would not have foreseen such a result.

Article 26

A declaration of avoidance of the contract is effective only if made by notice to the other party.

Article 27

Unless otherwise expressly provided in this Part of the Convention, if any notice, request or other communication is given or made by a party in accordance with this Part and by means appropriate in the circumstances, a delay or error in the transmission of the communication or its failure to arrive does not deprive that party of the right to rely on the communication.

Article 28

If, in accordance with the provisions of this Convention, one party is entitled to require performance of any obligation by the other party, a court is not bound to enter a judgement for specific performance unless the court would do so under its own law in respect of similar contracts of sale not governed by this Convention.

Article 29

(1) A contract may be modified or terminated by the mere agreement of the parties.

(2) A contract in writing which contains a provision requiring any modification or termination by agreement to be in writing may not be

otherwise modified or terminated by agreement. However, a party may be precluded by his conduct from asserting such a provision to the extent that the other party has relied on that conduct.

Chapter II. *Obligations of the Seller*

Article 30
The seller must deliver the goods, hand over any documents relating to them and transfer the property in the goods, as required by the contract and this Convention.

Section I. *Delivery of the goods and handing over of documents*

Article 31
If the seller is not bound to deliver the goods at any other particular place, his obligation to deliver consists:

(a) if the contract of sale involves carriage of the goods—in handing the goods over to the first carrier for transmission to the buyer;

(b) if, in cases not within the preceding subparagraph, the contract relates to specific goods, or unidentified goods to be drawn from a specific stock or to be manufactured or produced, and at the time of the conclusion of the contract the parties knew that the goods were at, or were to be manufactured or produced at, a particular place—in placing the goods at the buyer's disposal at that place;

(c) in other cases—in placing the goods at the buyer's disposal at the place where the seller had his place of business at the time of the conclusion of the contract.

Article 32

(1) If the seller, in accordance with the contract or this Convention, hands the goods over to a carrier and if the goods are not clearly identified to the contract by markings on the goods, by shipping documents or otherwise, the seller must give the buyer notice of the consignment specifying the goods.

(2) If the seller is bound to arrange for carriage of the goods, he must make such contracts as are necessary for carriage to the place fixed by means of transportation appropriate in the circumstances and according to the usual terms for such transportation.

(3) If the seller is not bound to effect insurance in respect of the carriage of the goods, he must, at the buyer's request, provide him with all available information necessary to enable him to effect such insurance.

Article 33

The seller must deliver the goods:

(a) if a date is fixed by or determinable from the contract, on that date;

(b) if a period of time is fixed by or determinable from the contract, at any time within that period unless circumstances indicate that the buyer is to choose a date; or

(c) in any other case, within a reasonable time after the conclusion of the contract.

Article 34

If the seller is bound to hand over documents relating to the goods, he must hand them over at the time and place and in the form required by the contract. If the seller has handed over documents before that time, he may, up to that time, cure any lack of conformity in the documents, if the exercise of this right does not cause the buyer unreasonable inconvenience or unreasonable expense. However, the buyer retains any right to claim damages as provided for in this Convention.

Section II. *Conformity of the goods and third party claims*

Article 35

(1) The seller must deliver goods which are of the quantity, quality and description required by the contract and which are contained or packaged in the manner required by the contract.

(2) Except where the parties have agreed otherwise, the goods do not conform with the contract unless they:

(a) are fit for the purposes for which goods of the same description would ordinarily be used;

(b) are fit for any particular purpose expressly or impliedly made known to the seller at the time of the conclusion of the contract, except where the circumstances show that the buyer did not rely, or that it was unreasonable for him to rely, on the seller's skill and judgement;

(c) possess the qualities of goods which the seller has held out to the buyer as a sample or model;

(d) are contained or packaged in the manner usual for such goods or, where there is no such manner, in a manner adequate to preserve and protect the goods.

(3) The seller is not liable under subparagraphs (a) to (d) of the preceding paragraph for any lack of conformity of the goods if at the time of the conclusion of the contract the buyer knew or could not have been unaware of such lack of conformity.

Article 36

(1) The seller is liable in accordance with the contract and this Convention for any lack of conformity which exists at the time when the risk passes to the buyer, even though the lack of conformity becomes apparent only after that time.

(2) The seller is also liable for any lack of conformity which occurs after the time indicated in the preceding paragraph and which is due to a breach of any of his obligations, including a breach of any guarantee that for a period of time the goods will remain fit for their ordinary purpose or for some particular purpose or will retain specified qualities or characteristics.

Article 37

If the seller has delivered goods before the date for delivery, he may, up to that date, deliver any missing part or make up any deficiency in the quantity of the goods delivered, or deliver goods in replacement of any non-conforming goods delivered or remedy any lack of conformity in the goods delivered, provided that the exercise of this right does not cause the buyer unreasonable inconvenience or unreasonable expense. However, the buyer retains any right to claim damages as provided for in this Convention.

Article 38

(1) The buyer must examine the goods, or cause them to be examined, within as short a period as is practicable in the circumstances.

(2) If the contract involves carriage of the goods, examination may be deferred until after the goods have arrived at their destination.

(3) If the goods are redirected in transit or redispatched by the buyer without a reasonable opportunity for examination by him and at the time of the conclusion of the contract the seller knew or ought to have known of the possibility of such redirection or redispatch, examination may be deferred until after the goods have arrived at the new destination.

Article 39

(1) The buyer loses the right to rely on a lack of conformity of the goods if he does not give notice to the seller specifying the nature of the lack of conformity within a reasonable time after he has discovered it or ought to have discovered it.

(2) In any event, the buyer loses the right to rely on a lack of conformity of the goods if he does not give the seller notice thereof at the latest within

a period of two years from the date on which the goods were actually handed over to the buyer, unless this time-limit is inconsistent with a contractual period of guarantee.

Article 40

The seller is not entitled to rely on the provisions of articles 38 and 39 if the lack of conformity relates to facts of which he knew or could not have been unaware and which he did not disclose to the buyer.

Article 41

The seller must deliver goods which are free from any right or claim of a third party, unless the buyer agreed to take the goods subject to that right or claim. However, if such right or claim is based on industrial property or other intellectual property, the seller's obligation is governed by article 42.

Article 42

(1) The seller must deliver goods which are free from any right or claim of a third party based on industrial property or other intellectual property, of which at the time of the conclusion of the contract the seller knew or could not have been unaware, provided that the right or claim is based on industrial property or other intellectual property:

    (a) under the law of the State where the goods will be resold or otherwise used, if it was contemplated by the parties at the time of the conclusion of the contract that the goods would be resold or otherwise used in that State; or

    (b) in any other case, under the law of the State where the buyer has his place of business.

(2) The obligation of the seller under the preceding paragraph does not extend to cases where:

    (a) at the time of the conclusion of the contract the buyer knew or could not have been unaware of the right or claim; or

    (b) the right or claim results from the seller's compliance with technical draw ings, designs, formulae or other such specifications furnished by the buyer.

Article 43

(1) The buyer loses the right to rely on the provisions of article 41 or article 42 if he does not give notice to the seller specifying the nature of the right or claim of the third party within a reasonable time after he has become aware or ought to have become aware of the right or claim.

(2) The seller is not entitled to rely on the provisions of the preceding paragraph if he knew of the right or claim of the third party and the nature of it.

Article 44

Notwithstanding the provisions of paragraph (1) of article 39 and paragraph (1) of article 43, the buyer may reduce the price in accordance with article 50 or claim damages, except for loss of profit, if he has a reasonable excuse for his failure to give the required notice.

Section III. *Remedies for breach of contract by the seller*

Article 45

(1) If the seller fails to perform any of his obligations under the contract or this Convention, the buyer may:
   (a) exercise the rights provided in articles 46 to 52;
   (b) claim damages as provided in articles 74 to 77.
(2) The buyer is not deprived of any right he may have to claim damages by exercising his right to other remedies.
(3) No period of grace may be granted to the seller by a court or arbitral tribunal when the buyer resorts to a remedy for breach of contract.

Article 46

(1) The buyer may require performance by the seller of his obligations unless the buyer has resorted to a remedy which is inconsistent with this requirement.
(2) If the goods do not conform with the contract, the buyer may require delivery of substitute goods only if the lack of conformity constitutes a fundamental breach of contract and a request for substitute goods is made either in conjunction with notice given under article 39 or within a reasonable time thereafter.
(3) If the goods do not conform with the contract, the buyer may require the seller to remedy the lack of conformity by repair, unless this is unreasonable having regard to all the circumstances. A request for repair must be made either in conjunction with notice given under article 39 or within a reasonable time thereafter.

Article 47

(1) The buyer may fix an additional period of time of reasonable length for performance by the seller of his obligations.

(2) Unless the buyer has received notice from the seller that he will not perform within the period so fixed, the buyer may not, during that period, resort to any remedy for breach of contract. However, the buyer is not deprived thereby of any right he may have to claim damages for delay in performance.

Article 48

(1) Subject to article 49, the seller may, even after the date for delivery, remedy at his own expense any failure to perform his obligations, if he can do so without unreasonable delay and without causing the buyer unreasonable inconvenience or uncertainty of reimbursement by the seller of expenses advanced by the buyer. However, the buyer retains any right to claim damages as provided for in this Convention.

(2) If the seller requests the buyer to make known whether he will accept performance and the buyer does not comply with the request within a reasonable time, the seller may perform within the time indicated in his request. The buyer may not, during that period of time, resort to any remedy which is inconsistent with performance by the seller.

(3) A notice by the seller that he will perform within a specified period of time is assumed to include a request, under the preceding paragraph, that the buyer make known his decision.

(4) A request or notice by the seller under paragraph (2) or (3) of this article is not effective unless received by the buyer.

Article 49

(1) The buyer may declare the contract avoided:
  (a) if the failure by the seller to perform any of his obligations under the contract or this Convention amounts to a fundamental breach of contract; or
  (b) in case of non-delivery, if the seller does not deliver the goods within the additional period of time fixed by the buyer in accordance with paragraph (1) of article 47 or declares that he will not deliver within the period so fixed.

(2) However, in cases where the seller has delivered the goods, the buyer loses the right to declare the contract avoided unless he does so:
  (a) in respect of late delivery, within a reasonable time after he has become aware that delivery has been made;
  (b) in respect of any breach other than late delivery, within a reasonable time:
    (i) after he knew or ought to have known of the breach;

    (ii) after the expiration of any additional period of time fixed by the buyer in accordance with paragraph (1) of article 47, or after the seller has declared that he will not perform his obligations within such an additional period; or

    (iii) after the expiration of any additional period of time indicated by the seller in accordance with paragraph (2) of article 48, or after the buyer has declared that he will not accept performance.

Article 50

If the goods do not conform with the contract and whether or not the price has already been paid, the buyer may reduce the price in the same proportion as the value that the goods actually delivered had at the time of the delivery bears to the value that conforming goods would have had at that time. However, if the seller remedies any failure to perform his obligations in accordance with article 37 or article 48 or if the buyer refuses to accept performance by the seller in accordance with those articles, the buyer may not reduce the price.

Article 51

(1) If the seller delivers only a part of the goods or if only a part of the goods delivered is in conformity with the contract, articles 46 to 50 apply in respect of the part which is missing or which does not conform.

(2) The buyer may declare the contract avoided in its entirety only if the failure to make delivery completely or in conformity with the contract amounts to a fundamental breach of the contract.

Article 52

(1) If the seller delivers the goods before the date fixed, the buyer may take delivery or refuse to take delivery.

(2) If the seller delivers a quantity of goods greater than that provided for in the contract, the buyer may take delivery or refuse to take delivery of the excess quantity. If the buyer takes delivery of all or part of the excess quantity, he must pay for it at the contract rate.

Chapter III. *Obligations of the Buyer*

Article 53

The buyer must pay the price for the goods and take delivery of them as required by the contract and this Convention.

Section I. *Payment of the price*

Article 54
The buyer's obligation to pay the price includes taking such steps and complying with such formalities as may be required under the contract or any laws and regulations to enable payment to be made.

Article 55
Where a contract has been validly concluded but does not expressly or implicitly fix or make provision for determining the price, the parties are considered, in the absence of any indication to the contrary, to have impliedly made reference to the price generally charged at the time of the conclusion of the contract for such goods sold under comparable circumstances in the trade concerned.

Article 56
If the price is fixed according to the weight of the goods, in case of doubt it is to be determined by the net weight.

Article 57

(1) If the buyer is not bound to pay the price at any other particular place, he must pay it to the seller:
   (a) at the seller's place of business; or
   (b) if the payment is to be made against the handing over of the goods or of documents, at the place where the handing over takes place.
(2) The seller must bear any increase in the expenses incidental to payment which is caused by a change in his place of business subsequent to the conclusion of the contract.

Article 58

(1) If the buyer is not bound to pay the price at any other specific time, he must pay it when the seller places either the goods or documents controlling their disposition at the buyer's disposal in accordance with the contract and this Convention. The seller may make such payment a condition for handing over the goods or documents.
(2) If the contract involves carriage of the goods, the seller may dispatch the goods on terms whereby the goods, or documents controlling their disposition, will not be handed over to the buyer except against payment of the price.
(3) The buyer is not bound to pay the price until he has had an opportunity to examine the goods, unless the procedures for delivery or payment agreed upon by the parties are inconsistent with his having such an opportunity.

Article 59
The buyer must pay the price on the date fixed by or determinable from the contract and this Convention without the need for any request or compliance with any formality on the part of the seller.

Section II. *Taking delivery*

Article 60
The buyer's obligation to take delivery consists:

   (a) in doing all the acts which could reasonably be expected of him in order to enable the seller to make delivery; and
   (b) in taking over the goods.

Section III. *Remedies for breach of contract by the buyer*

Article 61

   (1) If the buyer fails to perform any of his obligations under the contract or this Convention, the seller may:
   (a) exercise the rights provided in articles 62 to 65;
   (b) claim damages as provided in articles 74 to 77.
   (2) The seller is not deprived of any right he may have to claim damages by exercising his right to other remedies.
   (3) No period of grace may be granted to the buyer by a court or arbitral tribunal when the seller resorts to a remedy for breach of contract.

Article 62
The seller may require the buyer to pay the price, take delivery or perform his other obligations, unless the seller has resorted to a remedy which is inconsistent with this requirement.

Article 63

   (1) The seller may fix an additional period of time of reasonable length for performance by the buyer of his obligations.
   (2) Unless the seller has received notice from the buyer that he will not perform within the period so fixed, the seller may not, during that period, resort to any remedy for breach of contract. However, the seller is not deprived thereby of any right he may have to claim damages for delay in performance.

Article 64

(1) The seller may declare the contract avoided:
- (a) if the failure by the buyer to perform any of his obligations under the contract or this Convention amounts to a fundamental breach of contract; or
- (b) if the buyer does not, within the additional period of time fixed by the seller in accordance with paragraph (1) of article 63, perform his obligation to pay the price or take delivery of the goods, or if he declares that he will not do so within the period so fixed.
(2) However, in cases where the buyer has paid the price, the seller loses the right to declare the contract avoided unless he does so:
- (a) in respect of late performance by the buyer, before the seller has become aware that performance has been rendered; or
- (b) in respect of any breach other than late performance by the buyer, within a reasonable time:
  - (i) after the seller knew or ought to have known of the breach; or
  - (ii) after the expiration of any additional period of time fixed by the seller in accordance with paragraph (1) of article 63, or after the buyer has declared that he will not perform his obligations within such an additional period.

Article 65

(1) If under the contract the buyer is to specify the form, measurement or other features of the goods and he fails to make such specification either on the date agreed upon or within a reasonable time after receipt of a request from the seller, the seller may, without prejudice to any other rights he may have, make the specification himself in accordance with the requirements of the buyer that may be known to him.
(2) If the seller makes the specification himself, he must inform the buyer of the details thereof and must fix a reasonable time within which the buyer may make a different specification. If, after receipt of such a communication, the buyer fails to do so within the time so fixed, the specification made by the seller is binding.

Chapter IV. *Passing of Risk*

Article 66

Loss of or damage to the goods after the risk has passed to the buyer does not discharge him from his obligation to pay the price, unless the loss or damage is due to an act or omission of the seller.

Article 67

(1) If the contract of sale involves carriage of the goods and the seller is not bound to hand them over at a particular place, the risk passes to the buyer when the goods are handed over to the first carrier for transmission to the buyer in accordance with the contract of sale. If the seller is bound to hand the goods over to a carrier at a particular place, the risk does not pass to the buyer until the goods are handed over to the carrier at that place. The fact that the seller is authorized to retain documents controlling the disposition of the goods does not affect the passage of the risk.

(2) Nevertheless, the risk does not pass to the buyer until the goods are clearly identified to the contract, whether by markings on the goods, by shipping documents, by notice given to the buyer or otherwise.

Article 68

The risk in respect of goods sold in transit passes to the buyer from the time of the conclusion of the contract. However, if the circumstances so indicate, the risk is assumed by the buyer from the time the goods were handed over to the carrier who issued the documents embodying the contract of carriage. Nevertheless, if at the time of the conclusion of the contract of sale the seller knew or ought to have known that the goods had been lost or damaged and did not disclose this to the buyer, the loss or damage is at the risk of the seller.

Article 69

(1) In cases not within articles 67 and 68, the risk passes to the buyer when he takes over the goods or, if he does not do so in due time, from the time when the goods are placed at his disposal and he commits a breach of contract by failing to take delivery.

(2) However, if the buyer is bound to take over the goods at a place other than a place of business of the seller, the risk passes when delivery is due and the buyer is aware of the fact that the goods are placed at his disposal at that place.

(3) If the contract relates to goods not then identified, the goods are considered not to be placed at the disposal of the buyer until they are clearly identified to the contract.

Article 70

If the seller has committed a fundamental breach of contract, articles 67, 68 and 69 do not impair the remedies available to the buyer on account of the breach.

Chapter V. *Provisions Common to the Obligations of the Seller and of the Buyer*

Section I. *Anticipatory breach and instalment contracts*

Article 71

(1) A party may suspend the performance of his obligations if, after the conclusion of the contract, it becomes apparent that the other party will not perform a substantial part of his obligations as a result of:

(a) a serious deficiency in his ability to perform or in his creditworthiness; or

(b) his conduct in preparing to perform or in performing the contract.

(2) If the seller has already dispatched the goods before the grounds described in the preceding paragraph become evident, he may prevent the handing over of the goods to the buyer even though the buyer holds a document which entitles him to obtain them. The present paragraph relates only to the rights in the goods as between the buyer and the seller.

(3) A party suspending performance, whether before or after dispatch of the goods, must immediately give notice of the suspension to the other party and must continue with performance if the other party provides adequate assurance of his performance.

Article 72

(1) If prior to the date for performance of the contract it is clear that one of the parties will commit a fundamental breach of contract, the other party may declare the contract avoided.

(2) If time allows, the party intending to declare the contract avoided must give reasonable notice to the other party in order to permit him to provide adequate assurance of his performance.

(3) The requirements of the preceding paragraph do not apply if the other party has declared that he will not perform his obligations.

Article 73

(1) In the case of a contract for delivery of goods by instalments, if the failure of one party to perform any of his obligations in respect of any instalment constitutes a fundamental breach of contract with respect to that instalment, the other party may declare the contract avoided with respect to that instalment.

(2) If one party's failure to perform any of his obligations in respect of any instalment gives the other party good grounds to conclude that a fundamental breach of contract will occur with respect to future instalments, he may declare the contract avoided for the future, provided that he does so within a reasonable time.

(3) A buyer who declares the contract avoided in respect of any delivery may, at the same time, declare it avoided in respect of deliveries already made or of future deliveries if, by reason of their interdependence, those deliveries could not be used for the purpose contemplated by the parties at the time of the conclusion of the contract.

Section II. *Damages*

Article 74
Damages for breach of contract by one party consist of a sum equal to the loss, including loss of profit, suffered by the other party as a consequence of the breach. Such damages may not exceed the loss which the party in breach foresaw or ought to have foreseen at the time of the conclusion of the contract, in the light of the facts and matters of which he then knew or ought to have known, as a possible consequence of the breach of contract.

Article 75
If the contract is avoided and if, in a reasonable manner and within a reasonable time after avoidance, the buyer has bought goods in replacement or the seller has resold the goods, the party claiming damages may recover the difference between the contract price and the price in the substitute transaction as well as any further damages recoverable under article 74.

Article 76
(1) If the contract is avoided and there is a current price for the goods, the party claiming damages may, if he has not made a purchase or resale under article 75, recover the difference between the price fixed by the contract and the current price at the time of avoidance as well as any further damages recoverable under article 74. If, however, the party claiming damages has avoided the contract after taking over the goods, the current price at the time of such taking over shall be applied instead of the current price at the time of avoidance.

(2) For the purposes of the preceding paragraph, the current price is the price prevailing at the place where delivery of the goods should have been made or, if there is no current price at that place, the price at such other place as serves as a reasonable substitute, making due allowance for differences in the cost of transporting the goods.

Article 77

A party who relies on a breach of contract must take such measures as are reasonable in the circumstances to mitigate the loss, including loss of profit, resulting from the breach. If he fails to take such measures, the party in breach may claim a reduction in the damages in the amount by which the loss should have been mitigated.

Section III. *Interest*

Article 78

If a party fails to pay the price or any other sum that is in arrears, the other party is entitled to interest on it, without prejudice to any claim for damages recoverable under article 74.

Section IV. *Exemptions*

Article 79

(1) A party is not liable for a failure to perform any of his obligations if he proves that the failure was due to an impediment beyond his control and that he could not reasonably be expected to have taken the impediment into account at the time of the conclusion of the contract or to have avoided or overcome it or its consequences.

(2) If the party's failure is due to the failure by a third person whom he has engaged to perform the whole or a part of the contract, that party is exempt from liability only if:

    (a) he is exempt under the preceding paragraph; and

    (b) the person whom he has so engaged would be so exempt if the provisions of that paragraph were applied to him.

(3) The exemption provided by this article has effect for the period during which the impediment exists.

(4) The party who fails to perform must give notice to the other party of the impediment and its effect on his ability to perform. If the notice is not received by the other party within a reasonable time after the party who fails to perform knew or ought to have known of the impediment, he is liable for damages resulting from such non-receipt.

(5) Nothing in this article prevents either party from exercising any right other than to claim damages under this Convention.

Article 80

A party may not rely on a failure of the other party to perform, to the extent that such failure was caused by the first party's act or omission.

Section V. *Effects of avoidance*

Article 81

(1) Avoidance of the contract releases both parties from their obligations under it, subject to any damages which may be due. Avoidance does not affect any provision of the contract for the settlement of disputes or any other provision of the contract governing the rights and obligations of the parties consequent upon the avoidance of the contract.

(2) A party who has performed the contract either wholly or in part may claim restitution from the other party of whatever the first party has supplied or paid under the contract. If both parties are bound to make restitution, they must do so concurrently.

Article 82

(1) The buyer loses the right to declare the contract avoided or to require the seller to deliver substitute goods if it is impossible for him to make restitution of the goods substantially in the condition in which he received them.

(2) The preceding paragraph does not apply:

  (a) if the impossibility of making restitution of the goods or of making restitution of the goods substantially in the condition in which the buyer received them is not due to his act or omission;

  (b) if the goods or part of the goods have perished or deteriorated as a result of the examination provided for in article 38; or

  (c) if the goods or part of the goods have been sold in the normal course of business or have been consumed or transformed by the buyer in the course of normal use before he discovered or ought to have discovered the lack of conformity.

Article 83

A buyer who has lost the right to declare the contract avoided or to require the seller to deliver substitute goods in accordance with article 82 retains all other remedies under the contract and this Convention.

Article 84

(1) If the seller is bound to refund the price, he must also pay interest on it, from the date on which the price was paid.

(2) The buyer must account to the seller for all benefits which he has derived from the goods or part of them:

(a) if he must make restitution of the goods or part of them; or

(b) if it is impossible for him to make restitution of all or part of the goods or to make restitution of all or part of the goods substantially in the condition in which he received them, but he has nevertheless declared the contract avoided or required the seller to deliver substitute goods.

Section VI. *Preservation of the goods*

Article 85

If the buyer is in delay in taking delivery of the goods or, where payment of the price and delivery of the goods are to be made concurrently, if he fails to pay the price, and the seller is either in possession of the goods or otherwise able to control their disposition, the seller must take such steps as are reasonable in the circumstances to preserve them. He is entitled to retain them until he has been reimbursed his reasonable expenses by the buyer.

Article 86

(1) If the buyer has received the goods and intends to exercise any right under the contract or this Convention to reject them, he must take such steps to preserve them as are reasonable in the circumstances. He is entitled to retain them until he has been reimbursed his reasonable expenses by the seller.

(2) If goods dispatched to the buyer have been placed at his disposal at their destination and he exercises the right to reject them, he must take possession of them on behalf of the seller, provided that this can be done without payment of the price and without unreasonable inconvenience or unreasonable expense. This provision does not apply if the seller or a person authorized to take charge of the goods on his behalf is present at the destination. If the buyer takes possession of the goods under this paragraph, his rights and obligations are governed by the preceding paragraph.

Article 87

A party who is bound to take steps to preserve the goods may deposit them in a warehouse of a third person at the expense of the other party provided that the expense incurred is not unreasonable.

Article 88

(1) A party who is bound to preserve the goods in accordance with article 85 or 86 may sell them by any appropriate means if there has been an unreasonable delay by the other party in taking possession of the goods

or in taking them back or in paying the price or the cost of preservation, provided that reasonable notice of the intention to sell has been given to the other party.

(2) If the goods are subject to rapid deterioration or their preservation would involve unreasonable expense, a party who is bound to preserve the goods in accordance with article 85 or 86 must take reasonable measures to sell them. To the extent possible he must give notice to the other party of his intention to sell.

(3) A party selling the goods has the right to retain out of the proceeds of sale an amount equal to the reasonable expenses of preserving the goods and of selling them. He must account to the other party for the balance.

PART IV. FINAL PROVISIONS

Article 89

The Secretary-General of the United Nations is hereby designated as the depositary for this Convention.

Article 90

This Convention does not prevail over any international agreement which has already been or may be entered into and which contains provisions concerning the matters governed by this Convention, provided that the parties have their places of business in States parties to such agreement.

Article 91

(1) This Convention is open for signature at the concluding meeting of the United Nations Conference on Contracts for the International Sale of Goods and will remain open for signature by all States at the Headquarters of the United Nations, New York until 30 September 1981.

(2) This Convention is subject to ratification, acceptance or approval by the signatory States.

(3) This Convention is open for accession by all States which are not signatory States as from the date it is open for signature.

(4) Instruments of ratification, acceptance, approval and accession are to be deposited with the Secretary-General of the United Nations.

Article 92

(1) A Contracting State may declare at the time of signature, ratification, acceptance, approval or accession that it will not be bound by Part II of

this Convention or that it will not be bound by Part III of this Convention.

(2) A Contracting State which makes a declaration in accordance with the preceding paragraph in respect of Part II or Part III of this Convention is not to be considered a Contracting State within paragraph (1) of article 1 of this Convention in respect of matters governed by the Part to which the declaration applies.

Article 93

(1) If a Contracting State has two or more territorial units in which, according to its constitution, different systems of law are applicable in relation to the matters dealt with in this Convention, it may, at the time of signature, ratification, acceptance, approval or accession, declare that this Convention is to extend to all its territorial units or only to one or more of them, and may amend its declaration by submitting another declaration at any time.

(2) These declarations are to be notified to the depositary and are to state expressly the territorial units to which the Convention extends.

(3) If, by virtue of a declaration under this article, this Convention extends to one or more but not all of the territorial units of a Contracting State, and if the place of business of a party is located in that State, this place of business, for the purposes of this Convention, is considered not to be in a Contracting State, unless it is in a territorial unit to which the Convention extends.

(4) If a Contracting State makes no declaration under paragraph (1) of this article, the Convention is to extend to all territorial units of that State.

Article 94

(1) Two or more Contracting States which have the same or closely related legal rules on matters governed by this Convention may at any time declare that the Convention is not to apply to contracts of sale or to their formation where the parties have their places of business in those States. Such declarations may be made jointly or by reciprocal unilateral declarations.

(2) A Contracting State which has the same or closely related legal rules on matters governed by this Convention as one or more non-Contracting States may at any time declare that the Convention is not to apply to contracts of sale or to their formation where the parties have their places of business in those States.

(3) If a State which is the object of a declaration under the preceding paragraph subsequently becomes a Contracting State, the declaration

made will, as from the date on which the Convention enters into force in respect of the new Contracting State, have the effect of a declaration made under paragraph (1), provided that the new Contracting State joins in such declaration or makes a reciprocal unilateral declaration.

Article 95

Any State may declare at the time of the deposit of its instrument of ratification, acceptance, approval or accession that it will not be bound by subparagraph (1)(b) of article 1 of this Convention.

Article 96

A Contracting State whose legislation requires contracts of sale to be concluded in or evidenced by writing may at any time make a declaration in accordance with article 12 that any provision of article 11, article 29, or Part II of this Convention, that allows a contract of sale or its modification or termination by agreement or any offer, acceptance, or other indication of intention to be made in any form other than in writing, does not apply where any party has his place of business in that State.

Article 97

(1) Declarations made under this Convention at the time of signature are subject to confirmation upon ratification, acceptance or approval.

(2) Declarations and confirmations of declarations are to be in writing and be formally notified to the depositary.

(3) A declaration takes effect simultaneously with the entry into force of this Convention in respect of the State concerned. However, a declaration of which the depositary receives formal notification after such entry into force takes effect on the first day of the month following the expiration of six months after the date of its receipt by the depositary. Reciprocal unilateral declarations under article 94 take effect on the first day of the month following the expiration of six months after the receipt of the latest declaration by the depositary.

(4) Any State which makes a declaration under this Convention may withdraw it at any time by a formal notification in writing addressed to the depositary. Such withdrawal is to take effect on the first day of the month following the expiration of six months after the date of the receipt of the notification by the depositary.

(5) A withdrawal of a declaration made under article 94 renders inoperative, as from the date on which the withdrawal takes effect, any reciprocal declaration made by another State under that article.

Article 98
No reservations are permitted except those expressly authorized in this Convention.

Article 99

(1) This Convention enters into force, subject to the provisions of paragraph (6) of this article, on the first day of the month following the expiration of twelve months after the date of deposit of the tenth instrument of ratification, acceptance, approval or accession, including an instrument which contains a declaration made under article 92.

(2) When a State ratifies, accepts, approves or accedes to this Convention after the deposit of the tenth instrument of ratification, acceptance, approval or accession, this Convention, with the exception of the Part excluded, enters into force in respect of that State, subject to the provisions of paragraph (6) of this article, on the first day of the month following the expiration of twelve months after the date of the deposit of its instrument of ratification, acceptance, approval or accession.

(3) A State which ratifies, accepts, approves or accedes to this Convention and is a party to either or both the Convention relating to a Uniform Law on the Formation of Contracts for the International Sale of Goods done at The Hague on 1 July 1964 (1964 Hague Formation Convention) and the Convention relating to a Uniform Law on the International Sale of Goods done at The Hague on 1 July 1964 (1964 Hague Sales Convention) shall at the same time denounce, as the case may be, either or both the 1964 Hague Sales Convention and the 1964 Hague Formation Convention by notifying the Government of the Netherlands to that effect.

(4) A State party to the 1964 Hague Sales Convention which ratifies, accepts, approves or accedes to the present Convention and declares or has declared under article 92 that it will not be bound by Part II of this Convention shall at the time of ratification, acceptance, approval or accession denounce the 1964 Hague Sales Convention by notifying the Government of the Netherlands to that effect.

(5) A State party to the 1964 Hague Formation Convention which ratifies, accepts, approves or accedes to the present Convention and declares or has declared under article 92 that it will not be bound by Part III of this Convention shall at the time of ratification, acceptance, approval or accession denounce the 1964 Hague Formation Convention by notifying the Government of the Netherlands to that effect.

(6) For the purpose of this article, ratifications, acceptances, approvals and accessions in respect of this Convention by States parties to the 1964 Hague Formation Convention or to the 1964 Hague Sales

Convention shall not be effective until such denunciations as may be required on the part of those States in respect of the latter two Conventions have themselves become effective. The depositary of this Convention shall consult with the Government of the Netherlands, as the depositary of the 1964 Conventions, so as to ensure necessary co-ordination in this respect.

Article 100

(1) This Convention applies to the formation of a contract only when the proposal for concluding the contract is made on or after the date when the Convention enters into force in respect of the Contracting States referred to in subparagraph (1)(a) or the Contracting State referred to in subparagraph (1)(b) of article 1.

(2) This Convention applies only to contracts concluded on or after the date when the Convention enters into force in respect of the Contracting States referred to in subparagraph (1)(a) or the Contracting State referred to in subparagraph (1)(b) of article 1.

Article 101

(1) A Contracting State may denounce this Convention, or Part II or Part III of the Convention, by a formal notification in writing addressed to the depositary.

(2) The denunciation takes effect on the first day of the month following the expiration of twelve months after the notification is received by the depositary. Where a longer period for the denunciation to take effect is specified in the notification, the denunciation takes effect upon the expiration of such longer period after the notification is received by the depositary.

DONE at Vienna, this day of eleventh day of April, one thousand nine hundred and eighty, in a single original, of which the Arabic, Chinese, English, French, Russian and Spanish texts are equally authentic.

IN WITNESS WHEREOF the undersigned plenipotentiaries, being duly authorized by their respective Governments, have signed this Convention.

CISG status table

State	Entry into force
Albania	June 1, 2010
Argentina[a]	January 1, 1988
Armenia[a,b]	January 1, 2010
Australia	April 1, 1989
Austria	January 1, 1989
Bahrain	January 10, 2014
Belarus[a]	November 1, 1990
Belgium	November 1, 1997
Benin	August 1, 2012
Bosnia and Herzegovina	March 6, 1992
Brazil	April 1, 2014
Bulgaria	August 1, 1991
Burundi	October 1, 1999
Canada	May 1, 1992
Chile[a]	March 1, 1991
China[b]	January 1, 1988
Colombia	August 1, 2002
Congo	July 1, 2015
Croatia	October 8, 1991
Cuba	December 1, 1995
Cyprus	April 1, 2006
Czech Republic[b]	January 1, 1993
Denmark[c]	March 1, 1990
Dominican Republic	July 1, 2011
Ecuador	February 1, 1993
Egypt	January 1, 1988
El Salvador	December 1, 2007
Estonia	October 1, 1994

(continued)

(*continued*)

State	Entry into force
Finland[c]	January 1, 1989
France	January 1, 1988
Gabon	January 1, 2006
Georgia	September 1, 1995
Germany	January 1, 1991
Greece	February 1, 1999
Guinea	February 1, 1992
Guyana	October 1, 2015
Honduras	November 1, 2003
Hungary	January 1, 1988
Iceland[c]	June 1, 2002
Iraq	April 1, 1991
Israel	February 1, 2003
Italy	January 1, 1988
Japan	August 1, 2009
Kyrgyzstan	June 1, 2000
Latvia	August 1, 1998
Lebanon	December 1, 2009
Lesotho	January 1, 1988
Liberia	October 1, 2006
Lithuania	February 1, 1996
Luxembourg	February 1, 1998
Mauritania	September 1, 2000
Madagascar	October 1, 2015
Macedonia	December 1, 1991
Mexico	January 1, 1989
Moldova	January 22, 1998
Mongolia	January 1, 1999
Montenegro	June 3, 2006
Netherlands	January 1, 1992
New Zealand	October 1, 1995
Norway[c]	August 1, 1989
Paraguay[a]	February 1, 2007
Peru	April 1, 2000
Poland	June 1, 1996
Republic of Korea	March 1, 2005
Republic of Moldova	November 1, 1995
Romania	June 1, 1992
Russian Federation[a]	September 1, 1991
Saint Vincent and the Grenadines[b]	October 1, 2001
San Marino	March 1, 2013
Serbia	April 27, 1992
Singapore[b]	March 1, 1996
Slovakia[b]	January 1, 1993
Slovenia	June 25, 1991

State	Entry into force
Spain	August 1, 1991
Sweden[c]	January 1, 1989
Switzerland	March 1, 1991
Syrian Arab Republic	January 1, 1988
The former Yugoslav Republic of Macedonia	November 17, 1991
Turkey	August 1, 2011
Uganda	March 1, 1993
Ukraine[a]	February 1, 1991
United States of America[b]	January 1, 1988
Uruguay	February 1, 2000
Uzbekistan	December 1, 1997
Zambia	January 1, 1988

[a] This State declared, in accordance with Articles 12 and 96 of the Convention, that any provision of Article 11, Article 29, or Part II of the Convention that allowed a contract of sale or its modification or termination by agreement or any offer, acceptance or other indication of intention to be made in any form other than in writing, would not apply where any party had his place of business in its territory.

[b] This State declared, in accordance with Article 95 of the Convention, that it would not be bound by subparagraph (1) (b) of Article 1.

[c] Denmark, Finland, Iceland, Norway, and Sweden declared, in accordance with Article 94 of the Convention, that the Convention would not apply to contracts of sale or to their formation where the parties have their places of business in Denmark, Finland, Iceland, Norway, or Sweden.

Table of cases

BELGIUM

BULGARIA

CANADA

ICC

Index